CONS	connection-oriented network service	**EOT**	end of transmission
COTS	connection-oriented transport service	**FCC**	Federal Communications Commission
CRC	cyclic redundancy check	**FCS**	frame check sequence
CS	convergence sublayer	**FDDI**	fiber distributed data interface
CSMA	carrier sense multiple access	**FDM**	frequency-division multiplexing
CSMA/CD	carrier sense multiple access with collision detection	**FECN**	forward explicit congestion notification
CSU	channel service unit	**FM**	frequency modulation
CTD	cell transfer delay	**FRAD**	Frame Relay assembler/disassembler
CVDT	cell variation delay tolerance	**FSK**	frequency shift keying
DAC	dual attachment concentrator	**FTAM**	file transfer, access, and management
DAS	dual attachment station	**FTP**	file transfer protocol
DC	direct current	**FTTC**	fiber to the curb
DCE	data circuit–terminating equipment	**GFI**	general format identifier
DDS	digital data service	**HDB3**	high-density bipolar 3
DES	data encryption standard	**HDLC**	high-level data link control
DHCP	dynamic host configuration protocol	**HDSL**	high bit rate digital subscriber line
DIB	directory information base	**HF**	high frequency
DLCI	data link connection identifier	**HTML**	HyperText Markup Language
DMT	discrete multitone technique	**HTTP**	HyperText Transfer Protocol
DNS	Domain Name System	**ICMP**	internet control message protocol
DPSK	differential phase shift keying	**IDN**	integrated digital network
DQDB	distributed queue dual bus	**IEEE**	Institute of Electrical and Electronics Engineers
DS	directory service		
DSA	directory system agent	**IGMP**	internet group message protocol
DSL	digital subscriber line	**IP**	Internetworking Protocol
DSU	digital service unit	**IPCP**	Internetwork Protocol Control Protocol
DSU/CSU	digital service unit/channel service unit		
		IPng	IP next generation
DTE	data terminal equipment	**ISDN**	integrated services digital network
DUA	directory user agent	**ISO**	International Standards Organization
EHF	extremely high frequency	**ISOC**	Internet Society
EIA	Electronics Industries Association	**ITU–T**	International Telecommunications Union–Telecommunication Standardization Sector
EMI	electromagnetic interference		
ENQ/ACK	enquiry/acknowledgment		

DATA COMMUNICATIONS
AND
NETWORKING

Second Edition

DATA COMMUNICATIONS
AND
NETWORKING

Second Edition

Behrouz A. Forouzan

DeAnza College

with

Catherine Coombs   and   Sophia Chung Fegan

Boston Burr Ridge, IL Dubuque, IA Madison, WI New York San Francisco St. Louis
Bangkok Bogotá Caracas Lisbon London Madrid
Mexico City Milan New Delhi Seoul Singapore Sydney Taipei Toronto

McGraw-Hill Higher Education

*A Division of The **McGraw-Hill** Companies*

DATA COMMUNICATIONS AND NETWORKING

Published by McGraw-Hill, an imprint of the McGraw-Hill Companies, Inc. 1221 Avenue of the Americas, New York, NY, 10020. Copyright © 2001, 1998 by The McGraw-Hill Companies, Inc. All rights reserved. No part of this publication may be reproduced or distributed in any form or by any means, or stored in a database or retrieval system, without the prior written consent of The McGraw-Hill Companies, Inc., including, but not limited to, in any network or other electronic storage or transmission, or broadcast for distance learning.

Some ancillaries, including electronic and print components, may not be available to customers outside the United States.

This book is printed on acid-free paper.

1 2 3 4 5 6 7 8 9 0 DOC/DOC 0 9 8 7 6 5 4 3 2 1 0

ISBN 0-07-232204-7

Publisher: *Thomas Casson*
Executive editor: *Elizabeth A. Jones*
Developmental editor: *Emily J. Gray*
Senior marketing manager: *John T. Wannemacher*
Senior project manager: *Amy Hill*
Senior production supervisor: *Heather D. Burbridge*
Freelance design coordinator: *Gino Cieslik*
Supplement coordinator: *Mark Sienicki*
New media: *Judi David*
Cover design: *Joanne Schopler*
Cover illustration: *Tony Stone*
Compositor: *Interactive Composition Corporation*
Typeface: *10/12 Times Roman*
Printer: *R. R. Donnelley & Sons Company*

Library of Congress Cataloging-in Publication Data

Forouzan, Behrouz A.
    Data communications and networking / Behrouz Forouzan.
        p. cm.
    Includes index.
        ISBN 0-07-232204-7 (alk. paper)
        1. Data transmission systems. 2. Computer networks. I. Title.

    TK5105 .F6617 2001
    004.6--dc21   00-025675
www.mhhe.com

To Faezeh with love.

BRIEF CONTENTS

TABLE OF CONTENTS

Website and On-Line Learning Center for Data Communications and Networking, Second Edition

On-Line Learning Center

The on-line learning center provides additional resources for both instructor and student.

For the instructor:

PowerPoint Slides. A full set of color PowerPoints for every chapter provides excellent supplemental lecture materials.

Solutions are available (password-protected).

PageOut. This McGraw-Hill product offers instant course website development. An interactive course syllabus allows you to post content to coincide with your lectures. When students visit your PageOut website, your syllabus will direct them to components of Forouzan's On-line Learning Center, or specific material of your own.

For the student:

Approximately 80 automated quiz questions per chapter. This resource allows you to test your knowledge of concepts on-line. An immediate response will let you know how you are doing.

Animated figures from the book. Flash animations of selected figures from the book help networking concepts come to life. You can watch as the diagrams actively demonstrate their concepts.

Preface

Data communications and networking may be the fastest growing technologies in our culture today. One of the ramifications of that growth is a dramatic increase in the number of professions where an understanding of these technologies is essential for success—and a proportionate increase in the number and types of students taking courses to learn about them. Today, students wanting to understand the concepts and mechanisms underlying telecommunications and networking come from a variety of academic and professional backgrounds. To be useful, a textbook on data communications and networking must be accessible to students without technical backgrounds while still providing substance comprehensive enough to challenge more experienced readers. This text is written with this new mix of students in mind.

Features of the Book

Several features of this text are designed to make it particularly easy for students to understand data communications and networking.

Structure

We have used the seven-layer OSI model as the framework for the text not only because a thorough understanding of the model is essential to understanding most current networking theory but also because it is based on a structure of interdependencies: Each layer builds upon the layer beneath it and supports the layer above it. In the same way, each concept introduced in our text builds upon the concepts examined in the previous sections.

The OSI model was chosen because it is a model, not a protocol. The model is independent of any protocol such as TCP/IP, IPX/SPX (Novell), or AppleTalk. We believe that in an introductory course, the model should be understood before the actual protocols are discussed. The OSI model shows the layered architecture necessary for the design of network systems.

This text is designed for students with little or no background in telecommunication or data communication. For this reason, we use a bottom-up approach. In this approach, students can learn first about telecommunications (lower layers) before learning about data communications (upper layers). For example, students can learn about signaling, encoding, modulating, and error detection before learning about data transfer across the Internet. This eliminates the need for two courses: one for telecommunications and one for data communications.

The first nine chapters emphasize the physical layer, which is essential for understanding the rest of the layers. These chapters are particularly needed for students with no background in networking and telecommunications.

Chapters 10 through 12 describe all issues related to local area networks. Chapter 13 discusses metropolitan area networks. Chapter 14 describes switching techniques as background preparation for wide area networks.

Chapters 15 to 20 discuss topics associated with wide area networks. Chapter 21 discusses the network layer functions and the topic of internetworking local and wide area networks together. Chapters 22 and 23 focus on upper layer protocols (transport, session, presentation, and application layers).

Chapters 24 and 25 are dedicated to the TCP/IP protocol suite. These two chapters give a brief introduction and prepare the students for a course on the TCP/IP protocol suite.

Visual Approach

The book presents highly technical subject matter without complex formulas by using a balance of text and figures. The approximately 700 figures accompanying the text provide a visual and intuitive opportunity for understanding the material. Figures are particularly important in explaining networking concepts, which are based on connections and transmission. These are both often more easily grasped visually than verbally.

For example, Figure 3.8 shows the encapsulation of a network-layer packet in a data-link-layer frame. The figure also shows how network-layer addresses are unchanged compared to the data-link-layer addresses that change from station to station. Another figure, Figure 5.36, shows how an 8-QAM signal can carry three bits in each baud. Figure 8.4 clearly shows how FDM combines three modulated signals into one composite signal. Figures 25.3, 25.4, 25.5, and 25.6 show how the domain name system is divided into three domains: country, generic, and inverse domains.

Highlighted Points

We have repeated important concepts in boxes for quick reference and immediate attention.

Examples and Applications

Whenever appropriate, we have included examples that illustrate the concept introduced in the text. They also help students do the exercises at the end of each chapter.

Also, we have added real-life applications throughout each chapter. For example, in Chapter 8, after a discussion of FDM, we give an application, the analog hierarchy of the telephone system. Similarly, after discussion of TDM, we give an application, the DS hierarchy of the telephone system.

Summary

Each chapter ends with a summary of the material covered in that chapter. The summary is a brief overview of all the important points in the chapter.

Key Terms

Each chapter includes a list of key terms used throughout the chapter for a quick reference.

Practice Set

Each chapter includes a practice set designed to reinforce salient concepts and encourage students to apply them. It consists of three parts: review questions, multiple choice questions, and exercises. Review questions are intended to test students for their first-level understanding of the material presented in the chapter. Multiple choice questions test students' grasp of basic concepts and terminology. Exercises require deeper understanding of the material.

Appendixes

The appendixes are intended to provide quick reference material or a review of materials needed to understand the concepts discussed in the book.

Glossary and Acronyms

The book contains an extensive glossary. A list of acronyms appears on the endpapers.

Changes in the Second Edition

In this edition, material on the newer technologies has been added, the contents of the chapters have been revised, and the end materials have been augmented and improved.

New Material

We have added the following new material:

- 56K modems and cable modems (Chapter 6).
- Transmission impairment and transmission media performance (Chapter 7).
- Digital subscriber line (DSL) technology and fiber to the curb (FTTC) (Chapter 8).
- Switched and Gigabit Ethernet (Chapter 12).
- Point-to-Point Protocol (PPP) (Chapter 15).
- Traffic control (Chapter 18).
- Switching fabrics and ATM LANs (Chapter 19).
- Additional encryption methods (Chapter 23).
- Lempel-Ziv-Welch compression method (Appendix G).
- Spanning Tree algorithm (Appendix I).

Revision

All chapters have been revised, particularly Chapters 4, 9, 18, and 19 and Appendix H.

End Material Augmentation and Improvement

- Several examples are added to many chapters to clarify the materials.
- Key terms are added at the end of each chapter.

- Review questions are added at the end of each chapter.
- The quality and quantity of the multiple choice questions have been improved.
- The quality and quantity of the exercises have been improved. Most of the old exercises have been revised and many exercises have been added.

Online Supplementary Material at www.mhhe.com/forouzan

Online Learning Center

The McGraw-Hill Online Learning Center is a "digital cartridge" that contains the book's pedagogy and supplements. As students read through *Data Communications and Networking,* they can go online to take self-grading quizzes. They also get appropriate access to lecture materials such as PowerPoint slides and animated figures from the book. Solutions are also available over the Web. The solutions to odd-numbered problems are provided to students, and instructors can use a password to access the complete set of solutions.

Additionally, McGraw-Hill makes it easy to create a website for your networking course with an exclusive McGraw-Hill product called PageOut. It requires no prior knowledge of HTML, no long hours, and no design skills on your part. Instead, Page-Out offers a series of templates. Simply fill them with your course information and click on one of 16 designs. The process takes under an hour and leaves you with a professionally designed website.

Although PageOut offers "instant" development, the finished website offers powerful features. An interactive course syllabus allows you to post content to coincide with your lectures, so when students visit your PageOut website, your syllabus will direct them to components of Forouzan's Online Learning Center, or specific material of your own.

How to Use the Book

This book is written for both an academic and a professional audience. The book can be used as a self-study guide for interested professionals. As a textbook, it can be used for a one-semester or one-quarter course. The chapters are organized to provide a great deal of flexibility. The following are some guidelines:

- Chapters 1 through 12 are fundamental.
- Chapter 13 is optional.
- Chapters 14 through 18 can be covered in detail for a semester course or briefly for a quarter course.
- Chapters 19 through 25 are fundamental.

Acknowledgments

It is obvious that the development of a book of this scope needs the support of many people. We must thank the De Anza students and staff; their encouragement and support enabled the project to materialize and contributed to its success. We especially thank Claudia Gohler and Anastasia Mazharina for their tremendous assistance in preparing solutions to the end materials.

The most important contribution to the development of a book such as this comes from peer reviews. We cannot express our gratitude in words to the many reviewers who spent numerous hours reading the manuscript and providing us with helpful comments and ideas. We would especially like to acknowledge the contributions of the following reviewers for the first and second editions of this book.

First edition reviewers:

Russell J. Clark, *University of Dayton*
Charles K. Davis, *University of Houston*
James M. Frazier, *University of North Carolina at Charlotte*
John W. Gray, *University of Massachusetts at Dartmouth*
Thomas F. Hain, *University of South Alabama*
Paul N. Higbee, *University of North Florida*
Seung Bae Im, *California State University at Chico*
Rose M. Laird, *Northern Virginia Community College*
Jorg Liebeherr, *University of Virginia*
Wallace C. Liu, *California State University at Fresno*
Peter Maggiacomo, *Sinclair Community College*
Larry D. Owens, *California State University at Fresno*
Michael Peterson, *Iowa Western Community College*
Satya Prakash Saraswat, *Bentley College*
T. Radhakrishnan, *Concordia University*
Heidi Schmidt, *San Francisco State University*
Gordon Springer, *University of Missouri at Columbia*

Second edition reviewers:

Jay Benson, *Anne Arundel Community College*
John Besci, *Clayton College and State University*
David L. Doss, *Illinois State University*
Timothy W. Price, *Indiana University–Purdue University Indianapolis*
Xiaojun Shen, *University of Missouri, Kansas City*
Zixiang (Alex) Tan, *Syracuse University*

Special thanks go to the staff of McGraw-Hill. Betsy Jones, our executive editor, proved how a proficient editor can make the impossible possible. Emily Gray, the developmental editor, gave us help whenever we needed it. Amy Hill, our project manager, guided us through the production process with enormous enthusiasm. We also thank Heather Burbridge in production, Gino Cieslik in design, and Betsy Blumenthal, the copy editor.

Trademark Notices

Throughout the text we have used several trademarks. Rather than insert a trademark symbol with each mention of the trademarked name, we acknowledge the trademarks here and state that they are used with no intention of infringing upon them. Other product names, trademarks, and registered trademarks are the property of their respective owners.

- Apple, AppleTalk, EtherTalk, LocalTalk, TokenTalk, and Macintosh are registered trademarks of Apple Computer, Inc.
- Bell and StarLan are registered trademarks of AT&T.
- DEC, DECnet, VAX, and DNA are trademarks of Digital Equipment Corp.
- IBM, SDLC, SNA, and IBM PC are registered trademarks of International Business Machines Corp.
- Novell, Netware, IPX, and SPX are registered trademarks of Novell, Inc.
- Network File System and NFS are registered trademarks of Sun Microsystems, Inc.
- PostScript is a registered trademark of Adobe Systems, Inc.
- UNIX is a registered trademark of UNIX System Laboratories, Inc., a wholly owned subsidiary of Novell, Inc.
- Xerox is a trademark and Ethernet is a registered trademark of Xerox Corp.

CHAPTER 1

Introduction

In this chapter, we introduce the need for studying data communications and networking and we discuss those concepts. We define protocols and standards, which are terms used throughout the book.

1.1 WHY STUDY DATA COMMUNICATIONS

When cartoonists and disk jockeys are giving out their e-mail addresses to fans, it is a sign of the increasing interconnectivity that defines the way we communicate with the people and institutions of interest to us. The Internet and the World Wide Web are pointing to the real possibility of collaboration on a global scale. Through a computer and modem, a musician in Minneapolis can gain direct access to the facilities of the Institute pour le Recherche et Coordination Acoustique Musique in Paris. A cancer researcher at Stanford University can compare research findings with colleagues at the National Institutes of Health in Washington. An accounting manager in Dallas can get cost-of-manufacturing data from a subsidiary in Singapore in time to present slides at an important meeting.

Networks are changing the way we do business and the way we live. Business decisions have to be made ever more quickly, and the decision makers require immediate access to accurate information. But before we ask how quickly we can get hooked up, we need to know how networks operate, what types of technology are available, and which design best fills which set of needs. When a company adds a new division, the technology has to be flexible enough to reflect changing configurations. Is a particular design robust enough to handle the growth? Understanding what it does and when to use each type of technology is essential to providing the right system in today's dynamically changing information environment.

The development of the personal computer brought about tremendous changes for business, industry, science, and education. Information processing technology, once the domain of highly trained technicians, became friendly enough for nontechnical workers to use. Soon salespeople, accountants, professors, researchers, secretaries, and managers began designing their own spreadsheets, presentations, and databases. Corporations and universities began buying microcomputers to facilitate the management of information. As these microcomputers were installed, the traditional terminals that had provided passive connections to mainframes were removed. Terminal emulation through a PC now provided a new smart link to a central server.

Even with all this new processing power, people had no efficient way to share data. Except for those with computers connected directly to a mainframe, anyone wanting to get or send information had to do it manually. In the 1970s, a Toronto company that handled data processing for a local bank would generate material, write it to tape, and then hire an armored car to transport it three blocks to the bank's computer—every week. (A courier carrying a tape on an airplane was considered the ultimate bandwidth for data communication.) In the newer PC and workstation world, data could be either copied onto a floppy disk and physically reloaded onto another PC—even one as close as the next desk—or printed out; mailed, faxed, or couriered to its destination; then rekeyed into a remote computer. This not only was time-consuming but also created other inconveniences. Retyping data could compound human errors, and the problems associated with floppy disk transfer were sometimes worse. In addition to the size limitations, which often required multiple, carefully sequenced disks to carry one transmission, floppies turned out to be a terrific way for a virus to hop from computer to computer.

And standards of productivity were changing. Why wait a week for that report from Germany to arrive by mail when, if computers could talk to each other, it could appear almost instantaneously? The time had come for connecting personal computers into a computer network.

A similar revolution is occurring in telecommunications networks. Technological advances are making it possible for communications links to carry more and faster signals. As a result, services are evolving to allow use of the expanded capacity, including extensions to established telephone services such as conference calling, call waiting, voice mail, and caller ID; new digital services include video conferences and information retrieval.

Developing the right hardware has been one of the challenges facing network designers but by no means the only one. Designing connections between personal computers, workstations, and other digital devices requires an understanding of the needs of the users. How does information flow? Who is sharing data and what kind is being shared? How much physical distance does the information have to travel? Is data sharing limited to several PCs within one office, or do the data also need to be shared with local field offices, or with an unpredictable number of subscribers all over the world? In fact, to manage their business effectively, many institutions today must have more than one type of network.

1.2   DATA COMMUNICATION

When we communicate, we are sharing information. This sharing can be local or remote. Between individuals, local communication usually occurs face to face, while remote communication takes place over distance. The term **telecommunication,** which includes telephony, telegraphy, and television, means communication at a distance (*tele* is Greek for far).

The word *data* refers to facts, concepts, and instructions presented in whatever form is agreed upon by the parties creating and using the data. In the context of computer information systems, data are represented by binary information units (or bits) produced and consumed in the form of 0s and 1s.

> In computer information systems, data are represented by binary information units (or bits) produced and consumed in the form of 0s and 1s.

Data communication is the exchange of data (in the form of 0s and 1s) between two devices via some form of transmission medium (such as a wire cable). Data communication is considered local if the communicating devices are in the same building or a similarly restricted geographical area, and is considered remote if the devices are farther apart.

For data communication to occur, the communicating devices must be part of a communication system made up of a combination of hardware and software. The effectiveness of a data communication system depends on three fundamental characteristics:

1. **Delivery.** The system must deliver data to the correct destination. Data must be received by the intended device or user and only by that device or user.

2. **Accuracy.** The system must deliver data accurately. Data that have been altered in transmission and left uncorrected are unusable.

3. **Timeliness.** The system must deliver data in a timely manner. Data delivered late are useless. In the case of video, audio, and voice data, timely delivery means delivering data as they are produced, in the same order that they are produced, and without significant delay. This kind of delivery is called real-time transmission.

Components

A data communication system is made up of five components (see Figure 1.1).

Figure 1.1   *Data communication system components*

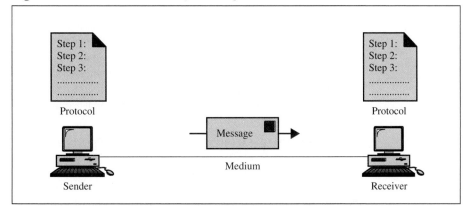

1. **Message.** The **message** is the information (data) to be communicated. It can consist of text, numbers, pictures, sound, or video—or any combination of these.

2. **Sender.** The **sender** is the device that sends the data message. It can be a computer, workstation, telephone handset, video camera, and so on.

3. **Receiver.** The **receiver** is the device that receives the message. It can be a computer, workstation, telephone handset, television, and so on.

4. **Medium.** The transmission **medium** is the physical path by which a message travels from sender to receiver. It can consist of twisted pair wire, coaxial cable, fiber-optic cable, laser, or radio waves (terrestrial or satellite microwave).

5. **Protocol.** A **protocol** is a set of rules that govern data communication. It represents an agreement between the communicating devices. Without a protocol, two devices may be connected but not communicating, just as a person speaking French cannot be understood by a person who speaks only Japanese.

1.3   NETWORKS

A **network** is a set of devices (often referred to as nodes) connected by media links. A node can be a computer, printer, or any other device capable of sending and/or receiving data generated by other nodes on the network. The links connecting the devices are often called communication channels.

Distributed Processing

Networks use **distributed processing,** in which a task is divided among multiple computers. Instead of a single large machine being responsible for all aspects of a process, each separate computer (usually a personal computer or workstation) handles a subset.

Advantages of distributed processing include the following:

- **Security/encapsulation.** A system designer can limit the kinds of interactions that a given user can have with the entire system. For example, a bank can allow users access to their own accounts through an automated teller machine (ATM) without allowing them access to the bank's entire database.

- **Distributed databases.** No one system needs to provide storage capacity for the entire database. For example, the World Wide Web gives users access to information that may be actually stored and manipulated anywhere on the Internet.

- **Faster problem solving.** Multiple computers working on parts of a problem concurrently often can solve the problem faster than a single machine working alone. For example, networks of PCs have broken encryption codes that were presumed to be unbreakable because of the amount of time it would take a single computer to crack them.

- **Security through redundancy.** Multiple computers running the same program at the same time can provide security through redundancy. For example, in the space shuttle, three computers run the same program so that if one has a hardware error, the other two can override it.

- **Collaborative processing.** Both multiple computers and multiple users may interact on a task. For example, in multiuser network games the actions of each player are visible to and affect all the others.

Network Criteria

To be considered effective and efficient, a network must meet a number of criteria. The most important of these are performance, reliability, and security (see Figure 1.2).

Figure 1.2   *Network criteria*

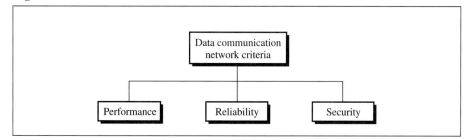

Performance

Performance can be measured in many ways, including transit time and response time. Transit time is the amount of time required for a message to travel from one device to another. Response time is the elapsed time between an inquiry and a response.

The performance of a network depends on a number of factors, including the number of users, the type of transmission medium, the capabilities of the connected hardware, and the efficiency of the software.

- **Number of users.** Having a large number of concurrent users can slow response time in a network not designed to coordinate heavy traffic loads. The design of a given network is based on an assessment of the average number of users that will be communicating at any one time. In peak load periods, however, the actual number of users can exceed the average and thereby decrease performance. How a network responds to loading is a measure of its performance.

- **Type of transmission medium.** The medium defines the speed at which data can travel through a connection (the data rate). Today's networks are moving to faster and faster transmission media, such as fiber-optic cabling. A medium that can carry data at 100 megabits per second is 10 times more powerful than a medium that can carry data at only 10 megabits per second. However, the speed of light imposes an upper bound on the data rate.

- **Hardware.** The types of hardware included in a network affect both the speed and capacity of transmission. A higher-speed computer with greater storage capacity provides better performance.

- **Software.** The software used to process data at the sender, receiver, and intermediate nodes also affects network performance. Moving a message from node to node through a network requires processing to transform the raw data into transmittable signals, to route these signals to the proper destination, to ensure error-free delivery, and to recast the signals into a form the receiver can use. The software that provides these services affects both the speed and the reliability of a network link. Well-designed software can speed the process and make transmission more effective and efficient.

Reliability

In addition to accuracy of delivery, network reliability is measured by frequency of failure, the time it takes a link to recover from a failure, and the network's robustness in a catastrophe.

- **Frequency of failure.** All networks fail occasionally. A network that fails often, however, is of little value to a user.
- **Recovery time of a network after a failure.** How long does it take to restore service? A network that recovers quickly is more useful than one that does not.
- **Catastrophe.** Networks must be protected from catastrophic events such as fire, earthquake, or theft. One protection against unforeseen damage is a reliable system to back up network software.

Security

Network **security** issues include protecting data from unauthorized access and viruses.

- **Unauthorized access.** For a network to be useful, sensitive data must be protected from unauthorized access. Protection can be accomplished at a number of levels. At the lowest level are user identification codes and passwords. At a higher level are encryption techniques. In these mechanisms, data are systematically altered in such a way that if they are intercepted by an unauthorized user, they will be unintelligible.
- **Viruses.** Because a network is accessible from many points, it can be susceptible to computer viruses. A virus is an illicitly introduced code that damages the system. A good network is protected from viruses by hardware and software designed specifically for that purpose.

Applications

In the short time they have been around, data communication networks have become an indispensable part of business, industry, and entertainment. Some of the network applications in different fields are the following:

- **Marketing and sales.** Computer networks are used extensively in both marketing and sales organizations. Marketing professionals use them to collect, exchange, and analyze data relating to customer needs and product development cycles. Sales applications include teleshopping, which uses order-entry computers or telephones connected to an order-processing network, and on-line reservation services for hotels, airlines, and so on.
- **Financial services.** Today's financial services are totally dependent on computer networks. Applications include credit history searches, foreign exchange and investment services, and electronic funds transfer (EFT), which allows a user to transfer money without going into a bank (an automated teller machine is a kind of electronic funds transfer; automatic paycheck deposit is another).
- **Manufacturing.** Computer networks are used today in many aspects of manufacturing, including the manufacturing process itself. Two applications that use networks to provide essential services are computer-assisted design (CAD) and

computer-assisted manufacturing (CAM), both of which allow multiple users to work on a project simultaneously.

- **Electronic messaging.** Probably the most widely used network application is electronic mail (e-mail).

- **Directory services.** Directory services allow lists of files to be stored in a central location to speed worldwide search operations.

- **Information services.** Network information services include bulletin boards and data banks. A World Wide Web site offering the technical specifications for a new product is an information service.

- **Electronic data interchange (EDI).** EDI allows business information (including documents such as purchase orders and invoices) to be transferred without using paper.

- **Teleconferencing.** Teleconferencing allows conferences to occur without the participants being in the same place. Applications include simple text conferencing (where participants communicate through their keyboards and computer monitors), voice conferencing (where participants at a number of locations communicate simultaneously over the phone), and video conferencing (where participants can see as well as talk to one another).

- **Cellular telephone.** In the past, two parties wishing to use the services of the telephone company had to be linked by a fixed physical connection. Today's cellular networks make it possible to maintain wireless phone connections even while traveling over large distances.

- **Cable television.** Future services provided by cable television networks may include video on request, as well as the same information, financial, and communications services currently provided by the telephone companies and computer networks.

1.4   PROTOCOLS AND STANDARDS

Protocols

In computer networks, communication occurs between entities in different systems. An entity is anything capable of sending or receiving information. Examples include application programs, file transfer packages, browsers, database management systems, and electronic mail software. A system is a physical object that contains one or more entities. Examples include computers and terminals.

But two entities cannot just send bit streams to each other and expect to be understood. For communication to occur, the entities must agree on a protocol. As defined on page 4, a protocol is a set of rules that govern data communication. A protocol defines what is communicated, how it is communicated, and when it is communicated. The key elements of a protocol are syntax, semantics, and timing.

Syntax

Syntax refers to the structure or format of the data, meaning the order in which they are presented. For example, a simple protocol might expect the first eight bits of data to be the address of the sender, the second eight bits to be the address of the receiver, and the rest of the stream to be the message itself.

Semantics

Semantics refers to the meaning of each section of bits. How is a particular pattern to be interpreted, and what action is to be taken based on that interpretation? For example, does an address identify the route to be taken or the final destination of the message?

Timing

Timing refers to two characteristics: when data should be sent and how fast they can be sent. For example, if a sender produces data at 100 Mbps but the receiver can process data at only 1 Mbps, the transmission will overload the receiver and data will be largely lost.

> In data communication, a protocol is a set of rules (conventions) that govern all aspects of information communication.

Standards

With so many factors to synchronize, a great deal of coordination across the nodes of a network is necessary if communication is to occur at all, let alone accurately or efficiently. A single manufacturer can build all of its products to work well together, but what if some of the best components for your needs are not made by the same company? What good is a television that can pick up only one set of signals if local stations are broadcasting another? Where there are no standards, difficulties arise. Automobiles are an example of nonstandardized products. A steering wheel from one make or model of car will not fit into another model without modification. A **standard** provides a model for development that makes it possible for a product to work regardless of the individual manufacturer.

Standards are essential in creating and maintaining an open and competitive market for equipment manufacturers and in guaranteeing national and international interoperability of data and telecommunications technology and processes. They provide guidelines to manufacturers, vendors, government agencies, and other service providers to ensure the kind of interconnectivity necessary in today's marketplace and in international communications.

Badly thought-out standards can slow development by forcing adherence to early, possibly inflexible, designs. But today pragmatism and consumer pressure have forced the industry to recognize the need for general models, and there is growing agreement as to what those models are. The intelligence and foresight of designers seem to be such that the standards now being adopted will encourage rather than hinder technical advancement.

Data communication standards fall into two categories: *de facto (*meaning "by fact" or "by convention") and *de jure (*meaning "by law" or "by regulation"). See Figure 1.3.

Figure 1.3 *Categories of standards*

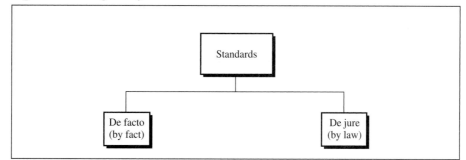

De jure standards are those that have been legislated by an officially recognized body. Standards that have not been approved by an organized body but have been adopted as standards through widespread use are de facto standards. De facto standards are often established originally by manufacturers seeking to define the functionality of a new product or technology.

De facto standards can be further subdivided into two classes: *proprietary* and *nonproprietary.* Proprietary standards are those originally invented by a commercial organization as a basis for the operation of its products. They are called proprietary because they are wholly owned by the company that invented them. These standards are also called *closed* standards because they close off communications between systems produced by different vendors. Nonproprietary standards are those originally developed by groups or committees that have passed them into the public domain; they are also called *open* standards because they open communications between different systems.

1.5 STANDARDS ORGANIZATIONS

Standards are developed by cooperation among **standards creation committees, forums,** and government **regulatory agencies.**

Standards Creation Committees

While many organizations are dedicated to the establishment of standards, data and telecommunications in North America rely primarily on those published by the following:

- The International Standards Organization (ISO).
- The International Telecommunications Union–Telecommunication Standards Sector (ITU-T, formerly the CCITT).
- The American National Standards Institute (ANSI).
- The Institute of Electrical and Electronics Engineers (IEEE).

- The Electronic Industries Association (EIA).
- Telcordia.

ISO

The **International Standards Organization (ISO;** also referred to as the International Organization for Standardization) is a multinational body whose membership is drawn mainly from the standards creation committees of various governments throughout the world. Created in 1947, the ISO is an entirely voluntary organization dedicated to worldwide agreement on international standards. With a membership that currently includes representative bodies from 82 industrialized nations, it aims to facilitate the international exchange of goods and services by providing models for compatibility, improved quality, increased productivity, and decreased prices. The ISO is active in developing cooperation in the realms of scientific, technological, and economic activity. Of primary concern to this book are the ISO's efforts in the field of information technology, which have resulted in the creation of the Open Systems Interconnection (OSI) model for network communications. The United States is represented in the ISO by ANSI.

> The ISO is an organization dedicated to worldwide agreement on international standards in a variety of fields.

ITU-T

By the early 1970s a number of countries were defining national standards for telecommunications, but there was still little international compatibility. The United Nations responded by forming, as part of its International Telecommunications Union (ITU), a committee, the Consultative Committee for International Telegraphy and Telephony (CCITT). This committee was devoted to the research and establishment of standards for telecommunications in general and phone and data systems in particular. On March 1, 1993, the name of this committee was changed to the **International Telecommunications Union–Telecommunication Standards Sector (ITU-T).**

The ITU-T is divided into study groups, each devoted to a different aspect of the industry. National committees (such as ANSI in the United States and the CEPT in Europe) submit proposals to these study groups. If the study group agrees, the proposal is ratified and becomes part of the ITU-T standard, issued every four years.

The best-known ITU-T standards are the V series (V.32, V.33, V.42), which define data transmission over phone lines; the X series (X.25, X.400, X.500), which define transmission over public digital networks; e-mail and directory services; and the Integrated Services Digital Network (ISDN), which includes parts of the other series and defines the emerging international digital network. Current projects include an extension of ISDN called Broadband ISDN, popularly known as the Information Superhighway.

> ITU-T is an international standards organization related to the United Nations that develops standards for telecommunications. Two popular standards developed by ITU-T are the V series and the X series.

ANSI

Despite its name, the **American National Standards Institute (ANSI)** is a completely private nonprofit corporation not affiliated with the U.S. federal government. However, all ANSI activities are undertaken with the welfare of the United States and its citizens occupying primary importance. ANSI's expressed aims include serving as the national coordinating institution for voluntary standardization in the United States, furthering the adoption of standards as a way of advancing the U.S. economy, and ensuring the participation and protection of the public interests. ANSI members include professional societies, industry associations, governmental and regulatory bodies, and consumer groups. Current areas of discussion include internetwork planning and engineering; ISDN services, signaling, and architecture; and optical hierarchy (SONET).

ANSI submits proposals to the ITU-T and is the designated voting member from the United States to the ISO. Similar services are provided in the European Community by the Committee of European Post, Telegraph, and Telephone (CEPT) and the European Telecommunications Standards Institute (ETSI).

ANSI, a nonprofit organization, is the U.S. voting representative to both the ISO and the ITU-T.

IEEE

The **Institute of Electrical and Electronics Engineers (IEEE)** is the largest professional engineering society in the world. International in scope, it aims to advance theory, creativity, and product quality in the fields of electrical engineering, electronics, and radio as well as in all related branches of engineering. As one of its goals, the IEEE oversees the development and adoption of international standards for computing and communication. The IEEE has a special committee for local area networks (LANs), out of which has come Project 802 (e.g., the 802.3, 802.4, and 802.5 standards).

The IEEE is the largest national professional group involved in developing standards for computing, communication, electrical engineering, and electronics. It sponsored an important standard for local area networks called Project 802.

EIA

Aligned with ANSI, the **Electronic Industries Association (EIA)** is a nonprofit organization devoted to the promotion of electronics manufacturing concerns. Its activities include public awareness education and lobbying efforts in addition to standards development. In the field of information technology, the EIA has made significant contributions by defining physical connection interfaces and electronic signaling specifications for data communication. In particular, EIA-232-D, EIA-449, and EIA-530 define serial transmission between two digital devices (e.g., computer to modem).

EIA is an association of electronics manufacturers in the United States. It is responsible for developing the EIA-232-D and EIA-530 standards.

Telcordia

Telcordia, formerly called Bellcore, is an outgrowth of the Bell Labs. Telcordia provides research and development resources for the advancement of telecommunications technology. It is an important source of draft standards to ANSI.

Forums

Telecommunications technology development is moving faster than the ability of standards committees to ratify standards. Standards committees are procedural bodies and by nature slow moving. To accommodate the need for working models and agreements and to facilitate the standardization process, many special interest groups have developed forums made up of representatives from interested corporations. The forums work with universities and users to test, evaluate, and standardize new technologies. By concentrating their efforts on a particular technology, the forums are able to speed acceptance and use of those technologies in the telecommunications community. The forums present their conclusions to the standards bodies.

Some important forums for the telecommunications industry include the following.

Frame Relay Forum

The Frame Relay Forum was formed by DEC, Northern Telecom, Cisco, and Strata-Com to promote the acceptance and implementation of Frame Relay. Today, it has around 40 members representing North America, Europe, and the Pacific Rim. Issues under review include flow control, encapsulation, translation, and multicasting. Results are submitted to the ISO.

ATM Forum and ATM Consortium

The ATM Forum and the ATM Consortium exist to promote the acceptance and use of Asynchronous Transfer Mode (ATM) technology. The ATM Forum is made up of customer premises equipment (e.g., PBX systems) vendors and central office (e.g., telephone exchange) providers. It is concerned with the standardization of services to ensure interoperability. The ATM Consortium is made up of vendors of hardware and software that support ATM.

Internet Society (ISOC) and Internet Engineering Task Force (IETF)

The Internet Society and the Internet Engineering Task Force (IETF) are concerned with speeding the growth and evolution of Internet communications. The **Internet Society (ISOC)** concentrates on user issues, including enhancements to the TCP/IP protocol suite. The IETF is the standards body for the Internet itself. It reviews Internet software and hardware. Important contributions include the development of Simple Network Management Protocol (SNMP) and the review of performance standards for bridges, routers, and router protocols.

Regulatory Agencies

All communications technology is subject to regulation by government agencies such as the **Federal Communications Commission (FCC)** in the United States. The purpose of these agencies is to protect the public interest by regulating radio, television, and wire/cable communications.

FCC

The FCC has authority over interstate and international commerce as it relates to communications. Every piece of communications technology must have FCC approval before it may be marketed (check the bottom of your telephone for an FCC approval code). Specific FCC responsibilities include the following:

■ To review rate and service-charge applications made by telegraph and telephone providers.

■ To review the technical specifications of communications hardware.

■ To establish reasonable common carrier rates of return.

■ To divide and allocate radio frequencies.

■ To assign carrier frequencies for radio and television broadcasts.

1.6 STRUCTURE OF THE BOOK

The OSI model, introduced in Chapter 3, forms a framework for the topics covered in this text. The lowest level of the model, the physical layer, relates directly to Chapters 4 through 9. The next four chapters, 10 through 13, describe issues concerning the data link layer. These include a discussion of both local and metropolitan area networks. Switching is covered in Chapter 14.

Chapters 15 through 20 discuss the emerging wide area networks such as PPP, ISDN, X.25, Frame Relay, ATM, and SONET. Chapter 21 then shows how to connect networks using networking and internetworking devices.

The upper OSI model layers—transport, session, presentation, and application layers—are discussed in Chapters 22 and 23.

Chapters 24 and 25 are devoted to TCP/IP and the Internet protocols.

1.7 KEY TERMS AND CONCEPTS

American National Standards Institute (ANSI)

data communication

de facto standards

de jure standards

distributed processing

Electronic Industries Association (EIA)

Federal Communications Commission (FCC)

forum

Institute of Electrical and Electronics Engineers (IEEE)

International Standards Organization (ISO)

International Telecommunications Union–Telecommunication Standards Sector (ITU-T)

Internet Society (ISOC)

medium

message

network

protocol

receiver

regulatory agency

security

semantics

sender

standard

standards creation committees

syntax

Telcordia

telecommunication

timing

1.8   SUMMARY

- Data communication is the transfer of data from one device to another via some form of transmission medium.
- A data communication system must transmit data to the correct destination in an accurate and timely manner.
- The five basic components of a data communication system are the message, the sender, the receiver, the medium, and the protocol.
- Networks allow shared access to information devices.
- Networks use distributed processing, in which a task is divided among multiple computers.
- Networks are judged by their performance, reliability, and security.
- A protocol is a set of rules that govern data communication; the key elements of a protocol are syntax, semantics, and timing.
- Standards are necessary to ensure that products from different manufacturers can work together as expected.
- The ISO, ITU-T, ANSI, IEEE, EIA, and Telcordia (Bellcore) are some of the organizations involved in standards creation.

- Forums consist of representatives from corporations that test, evaluate, and standardize new technologies.
- Some important forums are the Frame Relay Forum, the ATM Forum, the Internet Society, and the Internet Engineering Task Force.
- The FCC is a regulatory agency that regulates radio, television, and wire/cable communications.

1.9   PRACTICE SET

Review Questions

1. Identify the five components of a data communication system.
2. What are the advantages of distributed processing?
3. What are the three criteria necessary for an effective and efficient network?
4. What is the relationship between telecommunications and data communications? Is one a subset of the other? Give reasons for your answers.
5. Explain the differences between a standards creation committee, a forum, and a regulatory agency.
6. What three fundamental characteristics determine the effectiveness of a data communications system?
7. Name the factors that affect the performance of a network.
8. Name the factors that affect the reliability of a network.
9. Name the factors that affect the security of a network.
10. How are networks used in marketing and sales?
11. How are networks used in financial services?
12. How are networks used in manufacturing?
13. How are networks used in teleconferencing?
14. How do telephone companies use networks?
15. Why are protocols needed?
16. Why are standards needed?
17. What are the key elements of a protocol?
18. What is the difference between a de facto standard and a de jure standard?
19. What is the purpose of the ITU-T?
20. What is the purpose of ANSI?
21. What is the difference between IEEE and EIA?
22. Name three forums and their purposes.
23. What does the FCC have to do with communications?

Multiple Choice Questions

24. _____ are rules that govern a communication exchange.
    a. Media
    b. Criteria
    c. Protocols
    d. all of the above

25. The _____ is the physical path over which a message travels.
    a. protocol
    b. medium
    c. signal
    d. all of the above

26. Frequency of failure and network recovery time after a failure are measures of the _____ of a network.
    a. performance
    b. reliability
    c. security
    d. feasibility

27. The performance of a data communications network depends on _____.
    a. the number of users
    b. the transmission media
    c. the hardware and software
    d. all of the above

28. Viruses are a network _____ issue.
    a. performance
    b. reliability
    c. security
    d. all of the above

29. Protection of data from a natural disaster such as a tornado is a network _____ issue.
    a. performance
    b. reliability
    c. security
    d. management

30. Which agency is the U.S. voting member to the ISO?
    a. USO
    b. IEEE
    c. NATO
    d. ANSI

31. Which agency created standards for telephone communications (V series) and for network interfaces and public networks (X series)?

    a. ATT

    b. ITU-T

    c. ANSI

    d. ISO

32. Which organization has authority over interstate and international commerce in the communications field?

    a. ITU-T

    b. IEEE

    c. FCC

    d. Internet Society

33. _____ are special-interest groups that quickly test, evaluate, and standardize new technologies.

    a. Forums

    b. Regulatory agencies

    c. Standards organizations

    d. all of the above

34. Which agency developed standards for electrical connections and the physical transfer of data between devices?

    a. EIA

    b. ITU-T

    c. ANSI

    d. ISO

35. Which organization consists of computer scientists and engineers and is known for its development of LAN standards?

    a. EIA

    b. ITU-T

    c. ANSI

    d. IEEE

36. The information to be communicated in a data communication system is the _____.

    a. medium

    b. protocol

    c. message

    d. transmission

37. _____ is the division of one task among multiple computers.

    a. Distributed processing

    b. Distributed messaging

    c. Distributed telephony

    d. Electronic messaging

38. Which international agency is concerned with standards in science and technology?
    a. ISO
    b. OSI
    c. EIA
    d. ANSI

39. If a protocol specifies that data should be sent at 100 Mbps, this is a _____ issue.
    a. syntax
    b. semantics
    c. timing
    d. none of the above

40. When a protocol specifies that the address of the sender must occupy the first four bytes of a message, this is a _____ issue.
    a. syntax
    b. semantics
    c. timing
    d. none of the above

41. When a protocol specifies that the address of the sender means the most recent sender and not the original source, this is a _____ issue.
    a. syntax
    b. semantics
    c. timing
    d. none of the above

42. What is the main difference between a de facto standard and a de jure standard?
    a. A de facto standard has been legislated by an officially recognized body; a de jure standard has not.
    b. A de jure standard has been legislated by an officially recognized body; a de facto standard has not.
    c. The inventing company can wholly own a de jure standard and not a de facto standard.
    d. A de jure standard is proprietary; a de facto standard is not.

Exercises

43. Give two examples of a product that uses nonstandardized parts. Give two examples of a product that uses standardized parts.

44. Give five instances of how networks are a part of your life today.

45. How can networks be used to make a building secure?

46. Find at least three standards defined by ISO.

47. Find at least three standards defined by ITU-T.

48. Find at least three standards defined by ANSI.

49. Find at least three standards defined by IEEE.

50. Find at least three standards defined by EIA.

51. Find at least two standards organizations that are not mentioned in the chapter.

52. Give your own example of how the number of users can affect the performance of a network.

53. Give your own example of how the type of transmission medium can affect the performance of a network.

54. Give your own example of how the hardware can affect the performance of a network.

55. Give your own example of how the software can affect the performance of a network.

56. Define criteria for network reliability other than those defined in the chapter.

57. Define criteria for network security other than those defined in the chapter.

58. Define the syntax and semantics in the following sentence: "The dog drove the car safely to the destination." Is the syntax correct? Are the semantics right?

59. Define the syntax and semantics in the following sentence: "The man drove the car safely to the destination." Is the syntax correct? Are the semantics right?

CHAPTER 2

Basic Concepts

Before examining the specifics of how data are transmitted from one device to another, it is important to understand the relationship between the communicating devices. Five general concepts provide the basis for this relationship:

■ Line configuration.

■ Topology.

■ Transmission mode.

■ Categories of networks.

■ Internetworks.

2.1 LINE CONFIGURATION

Line configuration refers to the way two or more communication devices attach to a *link*. A **link** is the physical communication pathway that transfers data from one device to another. For the purposes of visualization, it is simplest to imagine any link as a line drawn between two points. For communication to occur, two devices must be connected in some way to the same link at the same time. There are two possible line configurations: point-to-point and multipoint (see Figure 2.1).

> Line configuration defines the attachment of communication devices to a link.

Point-to-Point

A **point-to-point line configuration** provides a dedicated link between two devices. The entire capacity of the channel is reserved for transmission between those two devices. Most point-to-point line configurations use an actual length of wire or cable to connect the two ends, but other options, such as microwave or satellite links, are also possible (see Figure 2.2). When you change television channels by infrared remote control, you are establishing a point-to-point line configuration between the remote control and the television's control system.

Figure 2.1 *Two categories of line configuration*

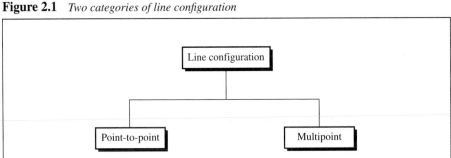

Figure 2.2 *Point-to-point line configuration*

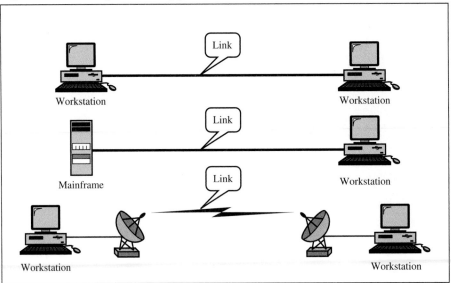

Multipoint

A **multipoint** (also called **multidrop**) **line configuration** is one in which more than two specific devices share a single link (see Figure 2.3).

In a multipoint environment, the capacity of the channel is shared, either spatially or temporally. If several devices can use the link simultaneously, it is a *spatially shared* line configuration. If users must take turns, it is a *time-shared* line configuration.

2.2 TOPOLOGY

The term **topology** refers to the way a network is laid out, either physically or logically. Two or more devices connect to a link; two or more links form a topology. The topology of a network is the geometric representation of the relationship of all the links and linking devices (usually called **nodes**) to each other. There are five basic topologies possible: mesh, star, tree, bus, and ring (see Figure 2.4).

Figure 2.3   *Multipoint line configuration*

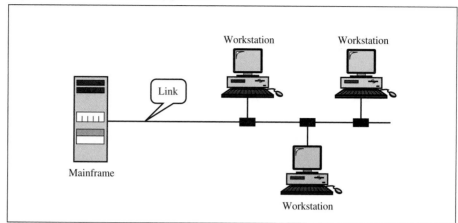

Figure 2.4   *Categories of topology*

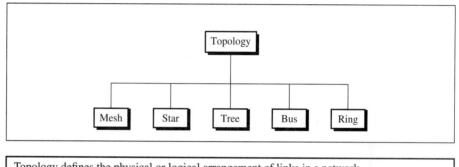

Topology defines the physical or logical arrangement of links in a network.

These five labels describe how the devices in a network are interconnected rather than their physical arrangement. For example, having a star topology does not mean that all of the computers in the network must be placed physically around a hub in a star shape. A consideration when choosing a topology is the relative status of the devices to be linked. Two relationships are possible: **peer-to-peer,** where the devices share the link equally, and **primary–secondary,** where one device controls traffic and the others must transmit through it. Ring and mesh topologies are more convenient for peer-to-peer transmission, while star and tree are more convenient for primary–secondary. A bus topology is equally convenient for either.

Mesh

In a **mesh topology,** every device has a dedicated point-to-point link to every other device. The term *dedicated* means that the link carries traffic only between the two devices it connects. A fully connected mesh network therefore has $n(n - 1)/2$ physical channels to link n devices. To accommodate that many links, every device on the network must have $n - 1$ input/output (I/O) ports (see Figure 2.5).

Figure 2.5   *Fully connected mesh topology (for five devices)*

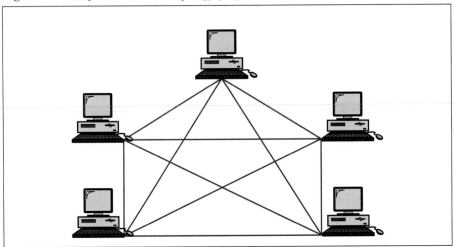

A mesh offers several advantages over other network topologies. First, the use of dedicated links guarantees that each connection can carry its own data load, thus eliminating the traffic problems that can occur when links must be shared by multiple devices.

Second, a mesh topology is robust. If one link becomes unusable, it does not incapacitate the entire system.

Another advantage is privacy or security. When every message sent travels along a dedicated line, only the intended recipient sees it. Physical boundaries prevent other users from gaining access to messages.

Finally, point-to-point links make fault identification and fault isolation easy. Traffic can be routed to avoid links with suspected problems. This facility enables the network manager to discover the precise location of the fault and aids in finding its cause and solution.

The main disadvantages of a mesh are related to the amount of cabling and the number of I/O ports required. First, because every device must be connected to every other device, installation and reconfiguration are difficult. Second, the sheer bulk of the wiring can be greater than the available space (in walls, ceilings, or floors) can accommodate. And, finally, the hardware required to connect each link (I/O ports and cable) can be prohibitively expensive. For these reasons a mesh topology is usually implemented in a limited fashion—for example, as a backbone connecting the main computers of a hybrid network that can include several other topologies.

Example 2.1

The Lucky Ducky Corporation has a fully connected mesh network consisting of eight devices. Calculate the total number of cable links needed and the number of ports for each device.

Solution

The formula for the number of links for a fully connected mesh is $n(n-1)/2$, where n is the number of devices.

$$\text{Number of links} = n(n-1)/2 = 8(8-1)/2 = 28$$

$$\text{Number of ports per device} = n - 1 = 8 - 1 = 7$$

Star

In a **star topology,** each device has a dedicated point-to-point link only to a central controller, usually called a **hub.** The devices are not directly linked to each other. Unlike a mesh topology, a star topology does not allow direct traffic between devices. The controller acts as an exchange: If one device wants to send data to another, it sends the data to the controller, which then relays the data to the other connected device (see Figure 2.6).

Figure 2.6   *Star topology*

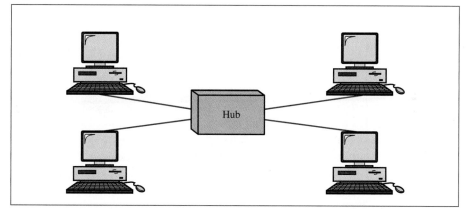

A star topology is less expensive than a mesh topology. In a star, each device needs only one link and one I/O port to connect it to any number of others. This factor also makes it easy to install and reconfigure. Far less cabling needs to be housed, and additions, moves, and deletions involve only one connection: between that device and the hub.

Other advantages include robustness. If one link fails, only that link is affected. All other links remain active. This factor also lends itself to easy fault identification and fault isolation. As long as the hub is working, it can be used to monitor link problems and bypass defective links.

However, although a star requires far less cable than a mesh, each node must be linked to a central hub. For this reason more cabling is required in a star than in some other topologies (such as tree, ring, or bus).

Tree

A **tree topology** is a variation of a star. As in a star, nodes in a tree are linked to a central hub that controls the traffic to the network. However, not every device plugs directly into the central hub. The majority of devices connect to a secondary hub that in turn is connected to the central hub (see Figure 2.7).

The central hub in the tree is an active hub. An **active hub** contains a repeater, which is a hardware device that regenerates the received bit patterns before sending them out (repeaters are discussed at length in Chapter 21). Repeating strengthens transmissions and increases the distance a signal can travel.

Figure 2.7 *Tree topology*

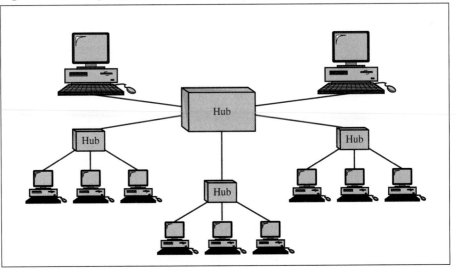

The secondary hubs may be active or passive hubs. A **passive hub** provides a simple physical connection between the attached devices.

The advantages and disadvantages of a tree topology are generally the same as those of a star. The addition of secondary hubs, however, brings two further advantages. First, it allows more devices to be attached to a single central hub and can therefore increase the distance a signal can travel between devices. Second, it allows the network to isolate and prioritize communications from different computers. For example, the computers attached to one secondary hub can be given priority over computers attached to another secondary hub. In this way, the network designers and operator can guarantee that time-sensitive data will not have to wait for access to the network.

A good example of tree topology can be seen in cable TV technology where the main cable from the main office is divided into main branches and each branch is divided into smaller branches and so on. The hubs are used when a cable is divided.

Bus

The preceding examples all describe point-to-point configurations. A **bus topology,** on the other hand, is multipoint. One long cable acts as a **backbone** to link all the devices in the network (see Figure 2.8).

Nodes are connected to the bus cable by drop lines and taps. A drop line is a connection running between the device and the main cable. A tap is a connector that either splices into the main cable or punctures the sheathing of a cable to create a contact with the metallic core. As a signal travels along the backbone, some of its energy is transformed into heat. Therefore, it becomes weaker and weaker the farther it has to travel. For this reason there is a limit on the number of taps a bus can support and on the distance between those taps.

Advantages of a bus topology include ease of installation. Backbone cable can be laid along the most efficient path, then connected to the nodes by drop lines of various lengths. In this way, a bus uses less cabling than mesh, star, or tree topologies. In a star,

Figure 2.8 *Bus topology*

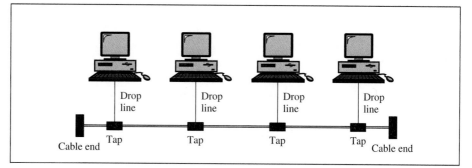

for example, four network devices in the same room require four lengths of cable reaching all the way to the hub. In a bus, this redundancy is eliminated. Only the backbone cable stretches through the entire facility. Each drop line has to reach only as far as the nearest point on the backbone.

Disadvantages include difficult reconfiguration and fault isolation. A bus is usually designed to be optimally efficient at installation. It can therefore be difficult to add new devices. As mentioned above, signal reflection at the taps can cause degradation in quality. This degradation can be controlled by limiting the number and spacing of devices connected to a given length of cable. Adding new devices may therefore require modification or replacement of the backbone.

In addition, a fault or break in the bus cable stops all transmission, even between devices on the same side of the problem. The damaged area reflects signals back in the direction of origin, creating noise in both directions.

Ring

In a **ring topology,** each device has a dedicated point-to-point line configuration only with the two devices on either side of it. A signal is passed along the ring in one direction, from device to device, until it reaches its destination. Each device in the ring incorporates a repeater. When a device receives a signal intended for another device, its repeater regenerates the bits and passes them along (see Figure 2.9).

A ring is relatively easy to install and reconfigure. Each device is linked only to its immediate neighbors (either physically or logically). To add or delete a device requires moving only two connections. The only constraints are media and traffic considerations (maximum ring length and number of devices). In addition, fault isolation is simplified. Generally in a ring, a signal is circulating at all times. If one device does not receive a signal within a specified period, it can issue an alarm. The alarm alerts the network operator to the problem and its location.

However, unidirectional traffic can be a disadvantage. In a simple ring, a break in the ring (such as a disabled station) can disable the entire network. This weakness can be solved by using a dual ring or a switch capable of closing off the break.

Example 2.2

If the devices in Example 2.1 are configured as a ring instead of a mesh, how many cable links are required?

Figure 2.9   *Ring topology*

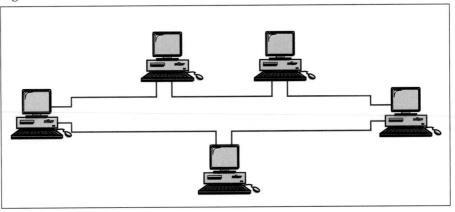

Solution

To connect *n* devices in a ring topology, we need *n* cable links. An eight-device ring needs eight cable links.

Hybrid Topologies

Often a network combines several topologies as subnetworks linked together in a larger topology. For instance, one department of a business may have decided to use a bus topology while another department has a ring. The two can be connected to each other via a central controller in a star topology (see Figure 2.10).

Figure 2.10   *Hybrid topology*

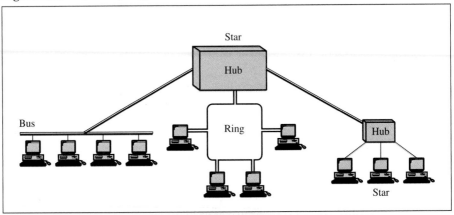

2.3   TRANSMISSION MODE

The term *transmission mode* is used to define the direction of signal flow between two linked devices. There are three types of transmission modes: *simplex*, *half-duplex*, and *full-duplex* (see Figure 2.11).

Figure 2.11   *Transmission modes*

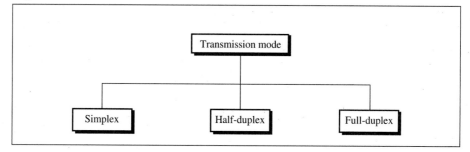

Simplex

In **simplex mode,** the communication is unidirectional, as on a one-way street. Only one of the two stations on a link can transmit; the other can only receive (see Figure 2.12).

Figure 2.12   *Simplex*

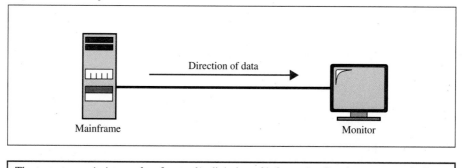

The term *transmission mode* refers to the direction of information flow between two devices.

Keyboards and traditional monitors are both examples of simplex devices. The keyboard can only introduce input; the monitor can only accept output.

Half-Duplex

In **half-duplex mode,** each station can both transmit and receive, but not at the same time. When one device is sending, the other can only receive, and vice versa (see Figure 2.13).

The half-duplex mode is like a one-lane road with two-directional traffic. While cars are traveling one direction, cars going the other way must wait. In a half-duplex transmission, the entire capacity of a channel is taken over by whichever of the two devices is transmitting at the time. Walkie-talkies and CB (citizen's band) radios are both half-duplex systems.

Full-Duplex

In **full-duplex mode** (also called **duplex**), both stations can transmit and receive simultaneously (see Figure 2.14).

Figure 2.13   *Half-duplex*

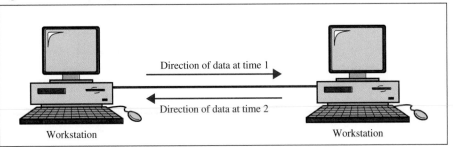

Figure 2.14   *Full-duplex*

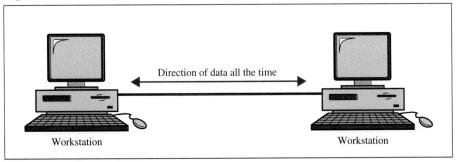

The full-duplex mode is like a two-way street with traffic flowing in both directions at the same time. In full-duplex mode, signals going in either direction share the capacity of the link. This sharing can occur in two ways: either the link must contain two physically separate transmission paths, one for sending and the other for receiving, or the capacity of the channel is divided between signals traveling in opposite directions.

One common example of full-duplex communication is the telephone network. When two people are communicating by a telephone line, both can talk and listen at the same time.

2.4   CATEGORIES OF NETWORKS

Today when we speak of networks, we are generally referring to three primary categories: local area networks, metropolitan area networks, and wide area networks. Into which category a network falls is determined by its size, its ownership, the distance it covers, and its physical architecture (see Figure 2.15).

Local Area Network (LAN)

A **local area network (LAN)** is usually privately owned and links the devices in a single office, building, or campus (see Figure 2.16). Depending on the needs of an organization and the type of technology used, a LAN can be as simple as two PCs and a

Figure 2.15   *Categories of networks*

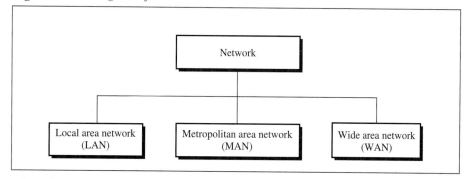

printer in someone's home office, or it can extend throughout a company and include voice, sound, and video peripherals. Currently, LAN size is limited to a few kilometers.

Figure 2.16   *LAN*

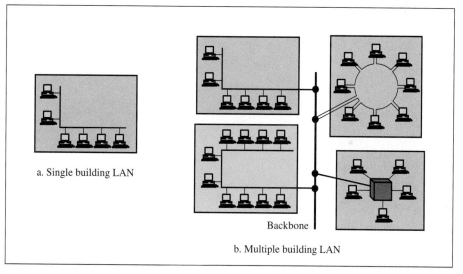

LANs are designed to allow resources to be shared between personal computers or workstations. The resources to be shared can include hardware (e.g., a printer), software (e.g., an application program), or data. A common example of a LAN, found in many business environments, links a work group of task-related computers, for example, engineering workstations or accounting PCs. One of the computers may be given a large-capacity disk drive and become a server to the other clients. Software can be stored on this central server and used as needed by the whole group. In this example, the size of the LAN may be determined by licensing restrictions on the number of users per copy of software, or by restrictions on the number of users licensed to access the operating system.

In addition to size, LANs are distinguished from other types of networks by their transmission media and topology. In general, a given LAN will use only one type of transmission medium. The most common LAN topologies are bus, ring, and star.

Traditionally, LANs have data rates in the 4 to 16 Mbps range. Today, however, speeds are increasing and can reach 100 Mbps with gigabit systems in development. LANs are discussed at length in Chapter 12.

Metropolitan Area Network (MAN)

A **metropolitan area network (MAN)** is designed to extend over an entire city. It may be a single network such as a cable television network, or it may be a means of connecting a number of LANs into a larger network so that resources may be shared LAN-to-LAN as well as device-to-device. For example, a company can use a MAN to connect the LANs in all of its offices throughout a city (see Figure 2.17).

Figure 2.17   *MAN*

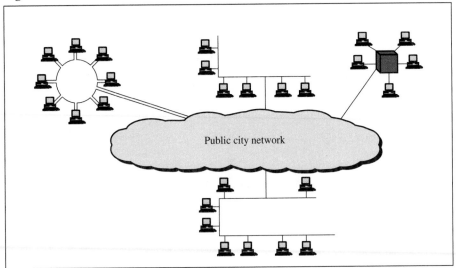

A MAN may be wholly owned and operated by a private company, or it may be a service provided by a public company, such as a local telephone company. Many telephone companies provide a popular MAN service called Switched Multi-megabit Data Services (SMDS), which is discussed in Chapter 13.

Wide Area Network (WAN)

A **wide area network (WAN)** provides long-distance transmission of data, voice, image, and video information over large geographical areas that may comprise a country, a continent, or even the whole world (see Figure 2.18).

In contrast to LANs (which depend on their own hardware for transmission), WANs may utilize public, leased, or private communication devices, usually in combinations, and can therefore span an unlimited number of miles.

Figure 2.18   *WAN*

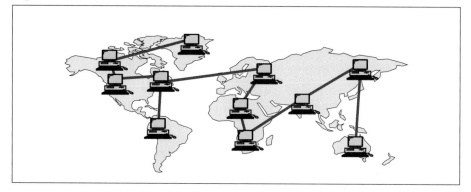

A WAN that is wholly owned and used by a single company is often referred to as an enterprise network.

2.5   INTERNETWORKS

When two or more networks are connected, they become an **internetwork,** or **internet** (see Figure 2.19; in the figure, the boxes labeled R represent routers). Individual networks are joined into internetworks by the use of internetworking devices. These devices, which include routers and gateways, are discussed in Chapter 21. The term *internet* (lowercase *i*) should not be confused with the **Internet** (uppercase *I*). The first is a generic term used to mean an interconnection of networks. The second is the name of a specific worldwide network.

Figure 2.19   *Internetwork (internet)*

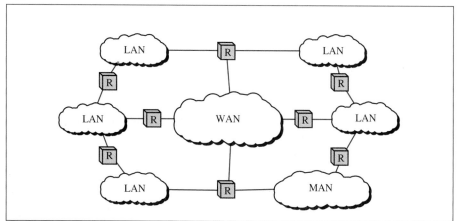

2.6   KEY TERMS AND CONCEPTS

active hub

backbone

bus topology

duplex mode

full-duplex mode

half-duplex mode

hub

hybrid topology

internet

Internet

internetwork

line configuration

link

local area network (LAN)

mesh topology

metropolitan area network (MAN)

multidrop line configuration

multipoint line configuration

node

passive hub

peer-to-peer relationship

point-to-point line configuration

primary–secondary relationship

ring topology

simplex mode

star topology

topology

tree topology

wide area network (WAN)

2.7   SUMMARY

■   A line configuration defines the relationship of communication devices to a communications pathway.

■   In a point-to-point line configuration, two and only two devices are connected by a dedicated link.

■   In a multipoint line configuration, three or more devices share a link.

■   Topology refers to the physical or logical arrangement of a network. Devices may be arranged in a mesh, star, tree, bus, ring, or hybrid topology.

■   Communication between two devices can occur in one of three transmission modes: simplex, half-duplex, or full-duplex.

- Simplex transmission means that data flows in one direction only.
- Half-duplex transmission allows data to flow in both directions, but not at the same time.
- Full-duplex transmission allows data to flow in both directions at the same time.
- A network can be categorized as a local area network (LAN), a metropolitan area network (MAN), or a wide area network (WAN).
- A LAN is a data communication system within a building, plant, or campus, or between nearby buildings.
- A MAN is a data communication system covering an area the size of a town or city.
- A WAN is a data communication system spanning states, countries, or the whole world.
- An internet is a network of networks.

2.8   PRACTICE SET

Review Questions

1. How is topology related to line configuration?
2. Define the three transmission modes.
3. Give an advantage for each type of network topology.
4. What are the advantages of a multipoint connection over a point-to-point connection?
5. What are some of the factors that determine whether a communication system is a LAN, MAN, or WAN?
6. What are the two types of line configuration?
7. Name the five basic network topologies.
8. Distinguish between a peer-to-peer relationship and a primary–secondary relationship.
9. Give a disadvantage for each type of network topology.
10. Give the formula that finds the number of cable links necessary for a mesh network topology.
11. Categorize the five basic topologies in terms of line configuration.
12. For n devices in a network, what is the number of cable links required for a mesh, ring, bus, and star topology?
13. What is the difference between a central and a secondary hub? What is the difference between a passive and an active hub? How do these categories interrelate?
14. What is the limiting factor in the size of a bus network topology? Include a discussion of taps in your answer.
15. For each type of network topology, discuss the implication of a single cable fault.
16. What is an internet? What is the Internet?

Multiple Choice Questions

17. Which topology requires a central controller or hub?
    a. mesh
    b. star
    c. bus
    d. ring

18. Which topology requires a multipoint connection?
    a. mesh
    b. star
    c. bus
    d. ring

19. Communication between a computer and a keyboard involves _____ transmission.
    a. simplex
    b. half-duplex
    c. full-duplex
    d. automatic

20. In a network with 25 computers, which topology would require the most extensive cabling?
    a. mesh
    b. star
    c. bus
    d. ring

21. A tree topology is a variation of a _____ topology.
    a. mesh
    b. star
    c. bus
    d. ring

22. A television broadcast is an example of _____ transmission.
    a. simplex
    b. half-duplex
    c. full-duplex
    d. automatic

23. In a _____ topology, if there are n devices in a network, each device has $n - 1$ ports for cables.
    a. mesh
    b. star
    c. bus
    d. ring

24. A _____ connection provides a dedicated link between two devices.
   a. point-to-point
   b. multipoint
   c. primary
   d. secondary

25. In a _____ connection, more than two devices can share a single link.
   a. point-to-point
   b. multipoint
   c. primary
   d. secondary

26. In _____ transmission, the channel capacity is shared by both communicating devices at all times.
   a. simplex
   b. half-duplex
   c. full-duplex
   d. half-simplex

27. MacKenzie Publishing, with headquarters in London and branch offices throughout Asia, Europe, and South America, is probably connected by a _____.
   a. LAN
   b. MAN
   c. WAN
   d. none of the above

28. BAF Plumbing has a network consisting of two workstations and one printer. This is most probably a _____.
   a. LAN
   b. MAN
   c. WAN
   d. none of the above

29. Which topology features a point-to-point line configuration?
   a. mesh
   b. ring
   c. star
   d. all of the above

30. In a _____ link, the only traffic is between the two connected devices.
   a. secondary
   b. primary
   c. dedicated
   d. none of the above

31. In a mesh topology, the relationship between one device and another is _____.
    a. primary-to-peer
    b. peer-to-primary
    c. primary-to-secondary
    d. peer-to-peer
32. A cable break in a _____ topology stops all transmission.
    a. mesh
    b. bus
    c. star
    d. primary
33. A network that contains multiple hubs is most likely configured in a _____ topology.
    a. mesh
    b. tree
    c. bus
    d. star
34. Security and privacy are less of an issue for devices in a _____ topology.
    a. mesh
    b. tree
    c. bus
    d. star

Exercises

35. Assume six devices are arranged in a mesh topology. How many cables are needed? How many ports are needed for each device?
36. Define the type of topology in Figure 2.20.

Figure 2.20 *Exercise 36*

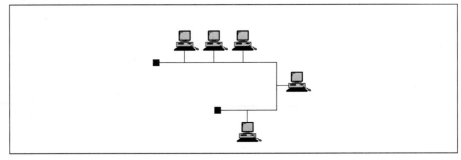

37. Define the type of topology in Figure 2.21.

Figure 2.21   *Exercise 37*

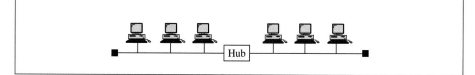

38. Define the type of topology in Figure 2.22.

Figure 2.22   *Exercise 38*

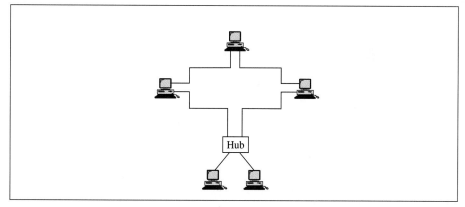

39. Define the type of topology in Figure 2.23.

Figure 2.23   *Exercise 39*

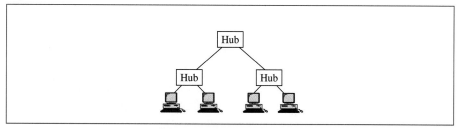

40. Define the type of topology in Figure 2.24.
41. Which of the networks in Figure 2.25 is a ring topology?
42. For each of the following four networks, discuss the consequences if a connection fails:
    a. Five devices arranged in a mesh topology.
    b. Five devices arranged in a star topology (not counting the hub).
    c. Five devices arranged in a bus topology.
    d. Five devices arranged in a ring topology.

Figure 2.24   *Exercise 40*

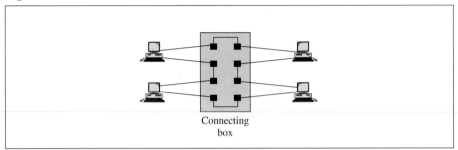

Connecting
box

Figure 2.25   *Exercise 41*

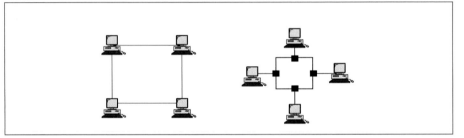

43. Draw a hybrid topology with a star backbone and three ring networks

44. Draw a hybrid topology with a ring backbone and two bus networks.

45. Draw a hybrid topology with a bus backbone connecting two ring backbones. Each ring backbone connects three star networks.

46. Draw a hybrid topology with a star backbone connecting two bus backbones. Each bus backbone connects three ring networks.

47. A network contains four computers. If there are only four lengths of cable in this network, which topology is used?

48. Match the following to a topology type (each can apply to more than one topology):

    a. New devices can be added easily.

    b. Control is through a central device.

    c. Transmission time is spent relaying data through nondestination nodes.

49. Suppose you add two new devices to an existing five-device network. If you have a fully connected mesh topology, how many new cable lines are needed? If, however, the devices are arranged in a ring, how many new cable lines are needed?

50. Five computers are connected to a common cable in a multipoint configuration. The cable can transfer only 100,000 bits per second. If all computers have data to send, what is the average data rate for each computer?

51. When a party makes a local telephone call to another party, is this a point-to-point or multipoint line configuration? Explain your answer.

52. Which transmission mode (simplex, half-duplex, or full-duplex) can be compared to the following? Justify your answer.

    a. A heated argument between Lucy and Desi.

    b. A computer-to-monitor connection.

    c. A polite conversation between Aunt Gertrude and Aunt Rowena.

    d. A television broadcast.

    e. A reversible commuter lane.

    f. A turnstile.

CHAPTER 3

The OSI Model

Established in 1947, the International Standards Organization (ISO) is a multinational body dedicated to worldwide agreement on international standards. An ISO standard that covers all aspects of network communications is the **Open Systems Interconnection (OSI)** model. An **open system** is a model that allows any two different systems to communicate regardless of their underlying architecture. Vendor-specific protocols close off communication between unrelated systems. The purpose of the OSI model is to open communication between different systems without requiring changes to the logic of the underlying hardware and software. The OSI model is not a protocol; it is a model for understanding and designing a network architecture that is flexible, robust, and interoperable.

> ISO is the organization. OSI is the model.

3.1 THE MODEL

The Open Systems Interconnection model is a layered framework for the design of network systems that allows for communication across all types of computer systems. It consists of seven separate but related layers, each of which defines a segment of the process of moving information across a network (see Figure 3.1). Understanding the fundamentals of the OSI model provides a solid basis for exploration of data communication.

Layered Architecture

The OSI model is built of seven ordered layers: physical (layer 1), data link (layer 2), network (layer 3), transport (layer 4), session (layer 5), presentation (layer 6), and application (layer 7). Figure 3.2 shows the layers involved when a message is sent from device A to device B. As the message travels from A to B, it may pass through many intermediate nodes. These intermediate nodes usually involve only the first three layers of the OSI model. In developing the model, the designers distilled the process of transmitting data down to its most fundamental elements. They identified which networking

43

Figure 3.1   *The OSI model*

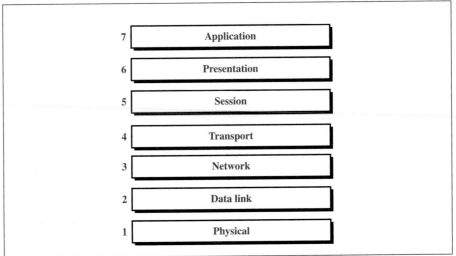

7	**Application**
6	**Presentation**
5	**Session**
4	**Transport**
3	**Network**
2	**Data link**
1	**Physical**

Figure 3.2   *OSI layers*

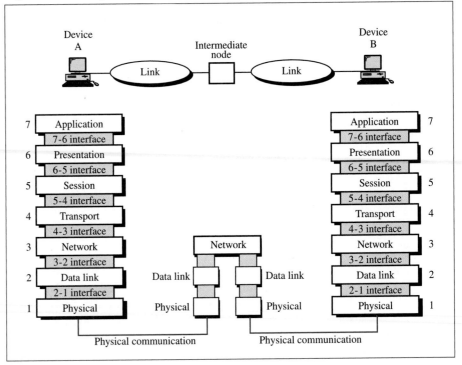

functions had related uses and collected those functions into discrete groups that became the layers. Each layer defines a family of functions distinct from those of the other layers. By defining and localizing functionality in this fashion, the designers created an architecture that is both comprehensive and flexible. Most important, the OSI model allows complete transparency between otherwise incompatible systems.

A mnemonic for remembering the layers of the OSI model is: **Please Do Not Touch Steve's Pet Alligator** (**P**hysical, **D**ata Link, **N**etwork, **T**ransport, **S**ession, **P**resentation, **A**pplication).

Peer-to-Peer Processes

Within a single machine, each layer calls upon the services of the layer just below it. Layer 3, for example, uses the services provided by layer 2 and provides services for layer 4. Between machines, layer x on one machine communicates with layer x on another machine. This communication is governed by an agreed-upon series of rules and conventions called protocols. The processes on each machine that communicate at a given layer are called **peer-to-peer processes.** Communication between machines is therefore a peer-to-peer process using the protocols appropriate to a given layer.

At the physical layer, communication is direct: Machine A sends a stream of bits to machine B. At the higher layers, however, communication must move down through the layers on machine A, over to machine B, and then back up through the layers. Each layer in the sending machine adds its own information to the message it receives from the layer just above it and passes the whole package to the layer just below it. This information is added in the form of **headers** or **trailers** (control data added to the beginning or end of a data parcel). Headers are added to the message at layers 6, 5, 4, 3, and 2. A trailer is added at layer 2.

Headers are added to the data at layers 6, 5, 4, 3, and 2. Trailers are usually added only at layer 2.

At layer 1 the entire package is converted to a form that can be transferred to the receiving machine. At the receiving machine, the message is unwrapped layer by layer, with each process receiving and removing the data meant for it. For example, layer 2 removes the data meant for it, then passes the rest to layer 3. Layer 3 removes the data meant for it and passes the rest to layer 4, and so on.

Interfaces between Layers

The passing of the data and network information down through the layers of the sending machine and back up through the layers of the receiving machine is made possible by an **interface** between each pair of adjacent layers. Each interface defines what information and services a layer must provide for the layer above it. Well-defined interfaces and layer functions provide modularity to a network. As long as a layer still provides the expected services to the layer above it, the specific implementation of its functions can be modified or replaced without requiring changes to the surrounding layers.

Organization of the Layers

The seven layers can be thought of as belonging to three subgroups. Layers 1, 2, and 3—physical, data link, and network—are the network support layers; they deal with the physical aspects of moving data from one device to another (such as electrical specifications, physical connections, physical addressing, and transport timing and reliability). Layers 5, 6, and 7—session, presentation, and application—can be thought of as the user support layers; they allow interoperability among unrelated software systems. Layer 4, the transport layer, ensures end-to-end reliable data transmission while layer 2 ensures reliable transmission on a single link. The upper OSI layers are almost always implemented in software; lower layers are a combination of hardware and software, except for the physical layer, which is mostly hardware.

In Figure 3.3, which gives an overall view of the OSI layers, L7 data means the data unit at layer 7, L6 data means the data unit at layer 6, and so on.The process starts out at layer 7 (the application layer), then moves from layer to layer in descending sequential order. At each layer (except layers 7 and 1), a header is added to the data unit. At layer 2, a trailer is added as well. When the formatted data unit passes through the physical layer (layer 1), it is changed into an electromagnetic signal and transported along a physical link.

Figure 3.3   *An exchange using the OSI model*

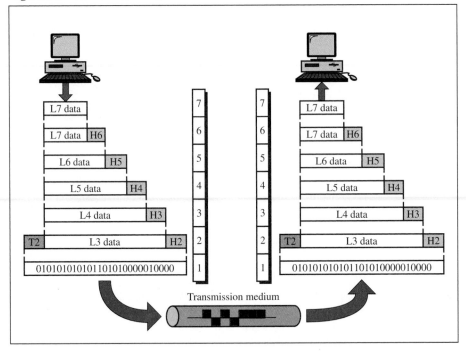

Upon reaching its destination, the signal passes into layer 1 and is transformed back into bits. The data units then move back up through the OSI layers. As each block of data reaches the next higher layer, the headers and trailers attached to it at the corresponding sending layer are removed, and actions appropriate to that layer are taken. By the time it reaches layer 7, the message is again in a form appropriate to the application and is made available to the recipient.

3.2   FUNCTIONS OF THE LAYERS

In this section we briefly describe the functions of each layer in the OSI model.

Physical Layer

The **physical layer** coordinates the functions required to transmit a bit stream over a physical medium. It deals with the mechanical and electrical specifications of the interface and transmission medium. It also defines the procedures and functions that physical devices and interfaces have to perform for transmission to occur. Figure 3.4 shows the position of the physical layer with respect to the transmission medium and the data link layer.

Figure 3.4   *Physical layer*

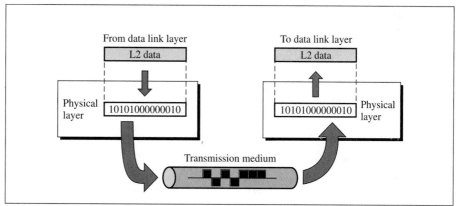

The physical layer is concerned with the following:

- **Physical characteristics of interfaces and media.** The physical layer defines the characteristics of the interface between the devices and the transmission medium. It also defines the type of transmission medium (see Chapter 7).

- **Representation of bits.** The physical layer data consist of a stream of **bits** (sequence of 0s and 1s) without any interpretation. To be transmitted, bits must be encoded into signals—electrical or optical. The physical layer defines the type of **encoding** (how 0s and 1s are changed to signals).

- **Data rate.** The **transmission rate**—the number of bits sent each second—is also defined by the physical layer. In other words, the physical layer defines the duration of a bit, which is how long it lasts.

- **Synchronization of bits.** The sender and receiver must be synchronized at the bit level. In other words, the sender and the receiver clocks must be synchronized.

- **Line configuration.** The physical layer is concerned with the connection of devices to the medium. In a *point-to-point configuration,* two devices are connected together through a dedicated link. In a *multipoint configuration,* a link is shared between several devices.

- **Physical topology.** The physical topology defines how devices are connected to make a network. Devices can be connected using a *mesh topology* (every device connected to every other device), a *star topology* (devices are connected through a central device), a *ring topology* (every device is connected to the next, forming a ring), or a *bus topology* (every device on a common link).

- **Transmission mode.** The physical layer also defines the direction of transmission between two devices: simplex, half-duplex, or full-duplex. In the *simplex mode,* only one device can send; the other can only receive. The simplex mode is a one-way communication. In the *half-duplex mode,* two devices can send and receive, but not at the same time. In a *full-duplex* (or simply duplex) *mode,* two devices can send and receive at the same time.

Data Link Layer

The **data link layer** transforms the physical layer, a raw transmission facility, to a reliable link and is responsible for **node-to-node** delivery. It makes the physical layer appear error free to the upper layer (network layer). Figure 3.5 shows the relationship of the data link layer to the network and physical layers.

Figure 3.5 *Data link layer*

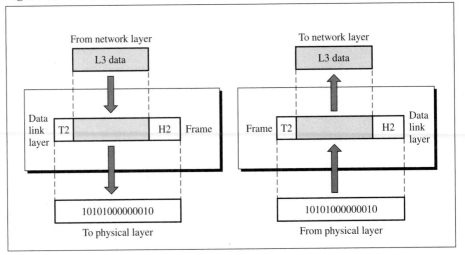

Specific responsibilities of the data link layer include the following:

- **Framing.** The data link layer divides the stream of bits received from the network layer into manageable data units called **frames.**

- **Physical addressing.** If frames are to be distributed to different systems on the network, the data link layer adds a header to the frame to define the **physical address** of the sender **(source address)** and/or receiver **(destination address)** of the frame. If the frame is intended for a system outside the sender's network, the receiver address is the address of the device that connects one network to the next.

■ **Flow control.** If the rate at which the data are absorbed by the receiver is less than the rate produced in the sender, the data link layer imposes a flow control mechanism to prevent overwhelming the receiver.

■ **Error control.** The data link layer adds reliability to the physical layer by adding mechanisms to detect and retransmit damaged or lost frames. It also uses a mechanism to prevent duplication of frames. Error control is normally achieved through a trailer added to the end of the frame.

■ **Access control.** When two or more devices are connected to the same link, data link layer protocols are necessary to determine which device has control over the link at any given time.

Example 3.1

In Figure 3.6 a node with physical address 10 sends a frame to a node with physical address 87. The two nodes are connected by a link. At the data link level this frame contains physical (link) addresses in the header. These are the only addresses needed. The rest of the header contains other information needed at this level. The trailer usually contains extra bits needed for error detection.

Figure 3.6   *Data link layer (Example 3.1)*

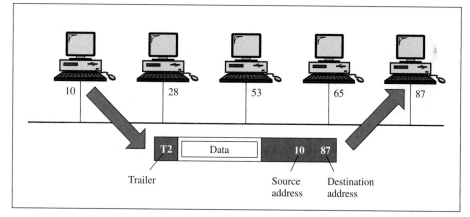

Trailer   Source   Destination
                 address   address

Network Layer

The **network layer** is responsible for the source-to-destination delivery of a packet possibly across multiple networks (links). Whereas the data link layer oversees the delivery of the packet between two systems on the same network (links), the network layer ensures that each packet gets from its point of origin to its final destination.

If two systems are connected to the same link, there is usually no need for a network layer. However, if the two systems are attached to different networks (links) with connecting devices between the networks (links), there is often a need for the network layer to accomplish source-to-destination delivery. Figure 3.7 shows the relationship of the network layer to the data link and transport layers.

Figure 3.7   *Network layer*

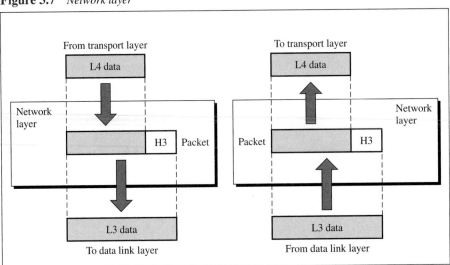

Specific responsibilities of the network layer include the following:

■ **Logical addressing.** The physical addressing implemented by the data link layer handles the addressing problem locally. If a packet passes the network boundary, we need another addressing system to help distinguish the source and destination systems. The network layer adds a header to the packet coming from the upper layer that, among other things, includes the **logical addresses** of the sender and receiver.

■ **Routing.** When independent networks or links are connected together to create an *internetwork* (a network of networks) or a large network, the connecting devices (called *routers* or *gateways*) route the packets to their final destination. One of the functions of the network layer is to provide this mechanism.

Example 3.2

Now imagine that in Figure 3.8 we want to send data from a node with network address A and physical address 10, located on one local area network, to a node with a network address P and physical address 95, located on another local area network. Because the two devices are located on different networks, we cannot use physical addresses only; the physical addresses have only local jurisdiction. What we need here are universal addresses that can pass through the boundaries of local area networks. The network (logical) addresses have this characteristic. The packet at the network layer contains the logical addresses, which remain the same from the original source to the final destination (A and P, respectively, in the figure). They will not change when we go from network to network. However, the physical addresses will change when the packet moves from one network to another. The box with the R is a router (internetwork device), which we will discuss in Chapter 21.

Transport Layer

The **transport layer** is responsible for **source-to-destination** (end-to-end) **delivery** of the entire message. Whereas the network layer oversees end-to-end delivery of individ-

Figure 3.8   *Network layer (Example 3.2)*

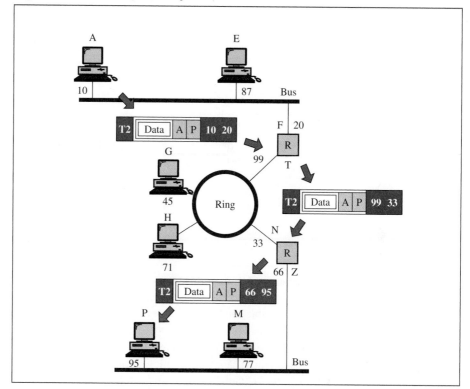

ual packets, it does not recognize any relationship between those packets. It treats each one independently, as though each piece belonged to a separate message, whether or not it does. The transport layer, on the other hand, ensures that the whole message arrives intact and in order, overseeing both error control and flow control at the source-to-destination level. Figure 3.9 shows the relationship of the transport layer to the network and session layers.

For added security, the transport layer may create a *connection* between the two end ports. A connection is a single logical path between the source and destination that is associated with all packets in a message. Creating a connection involves three steps: connection establishment, data transfer, and connection release. By confining transmission of all packets to a single pathway, the transport layer has more control over sequencing, flow, and error detection and correction.

Specific responsibilities of the transport layer include the following:

- **Service-point addressing.** Computers often run several programs at the same time. For this reason, source-to-destination delivery means delivery not only from one computer to the next but also from a specific process (running program) on one computer to a specific process (running program) on the other. The transport layer header therefore must include a type of address called a *service-point address* (or **port address**). The network layer gets each packet to the correct computer; the transport layer gets the entire message to the correct process on that computer.

Figure 3.9   *Transport layer*

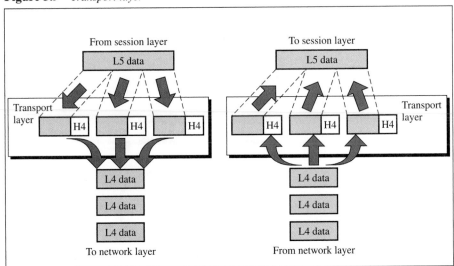

■ **Segmentation and reassembly.** A message is divided into transmittable segments, each segment containing a sequence number. These numbers enable the transport layer to reassemble the message correctly upon arriving at the destination and to identify and replace packets that were lost in the transmission.

■ **Connection control.** The transport layer can be either connectionless or connection-oriented. A connectionless transport layer treats each segment as an independent packet and delivers it to the transport layer at the destination machine. A connection-oriented transport layer makes a connection with the transport layer at the destination machine first before delivering the packets. After all the data are transferred, the connection is terminated.

■ **Flow control.** Like the data link layer, the transport layer is responsible for flow control. However, flow control at this layer is performed end to end rather than across a single link.

■ **Error control.** Like the data link layer, the transport layer is responsible for error control. However, error control at this layer is performed end to end rather than across a single link. The sending transport layer makes sure that the entire message arrives at the receiving transport layer without **error** (damage, loss, or duplication). Error correction is usually achieved through retransmission.

Example 3.3

Figure 3.10 shows an example of a transport layer. Data coming from the upper layers have service-point (port) addresses j and k (j is the address of the sending application and k is the address of the receiving application). Since the data size is larger than the network layer can handle, the data are split into two packets, each packet retaining the service-point addresses (j and k). Then in the network layer, network addresses (A and P) are added to each packet. The packets may travel on different paths and arrive at the destination either in order or out of order. The two packets are delivered to the destination network layer, which is responsible for removing the network layer headers. The two packets are now passed to the transport layer, where they are combined for delivery to the upper layers.

Figure 3.10   *Transport layer (Example 3)*

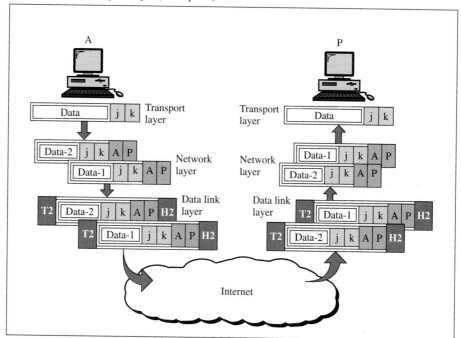

Session Layer

The services provided by the first three layers (physical, data link, and network) are not sufficient for some processes. The **session layer** is the network *dialog controller*. It establishes, maintains, and synchronizes the interaction between communicating systems.

Specific responsibilities of the session layer include the following:

- **Dialog control.** The session layer allows two systems to enter into a dialog. It allows the communication between two processes to take place either in half-duplex (one way at a time) or full-duplex (two ways at a time). For example, the dialog between a terminal connected to a mainframe can be half-duplex.

- **Synchronization.** The session layer allows a process to add checkpoints (synchronization points) into a stream of data. For example, if a system is sending a file of 2000 pages, it is advisable to insert checkpoints after every 100 pages to ensure that each 100-page unit is received and acknowledged independently. In this case, if a crash happens during the transmission of page 523, retransmission begins at page 501: pages 1 to 500 need not be retransmitted. Figure 3.11 illustrates the relationship of the session layer to the transport and presentation layers.

Figure 3.11   *Session layer*

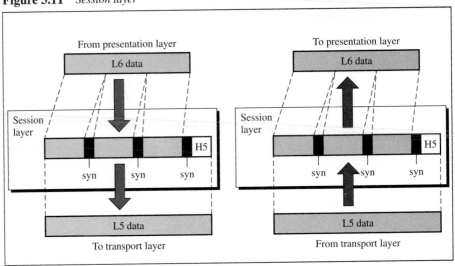

Presentation Layer

The **presentation layer** is concerned with the syntax and semantics of the information exchanged between two systems. Figure 3.12 shows the relationship between the presentation layer and the application and session layers.

Figure 3.12   *Presentation layer*

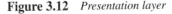

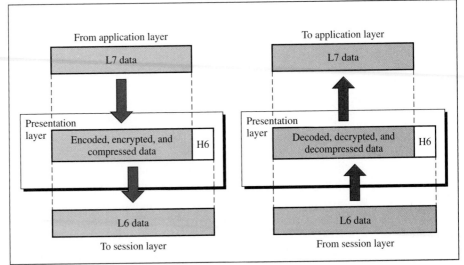

Specific responsibilities of the presentation layer include the following:

■   **Translation.** The processes (running programs) in two systems are usually exchanging information in the form of character strings, numbers, and so on. The information should be changed to bit streams before being transmitted. Because different computers use different encoding systems, the presentation layer is responsible for interoperability between these different encoding methods. The presentation layer at the sender changes the information from its sender-dependent format into a common format. The presentation layer at the receiving machine changes the common format into its receiver-dependent format.

■ **Encryption.** To carry sensitive information, a system must be able to assure privacy. Encryption means that the sender transforms the original information to another form and sends the resulting message out over the network. Decryption reverses the original process to transform the message back to its original form.

■ **Compression.** Data compression reduces the number of bits to be transmitted. Data compression becomes particularly important in the transmission of multimedia such as text, audio, and video.

Application Layer

The **application layer** enables the user, whether human or software, to access the network. It provides user interfaces and support for services such as electronic mail, remote file access and transfer, shared database management, and other types of distributed information services.

Figure 3.13 shows the relationship of the application layer to the user and the presentation layer. Of the many application services available, the figure shows only three: X.400 (message-handling services); X.500 (directory services); and file transfer, access, and management (FTAM). The user in this example uses X.400 to send an e-mail message. Note that no headers or trailers are added at this layer.

Figure 3.13 *Application layer*

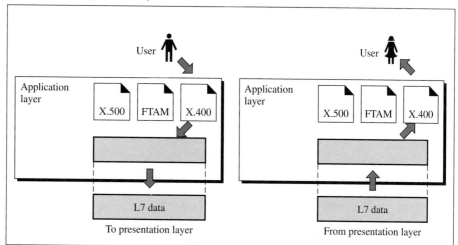

Specific services provided by the application layer include the following:

■ **Network virtual terminal.** A network virtual terminal is a software version of a physical terminal and allows a user to log on to a remote host. To do so, the application creates a software emulation of a terminal at the remote host. The user's computer talks to the software terminal, which, in turn, talks to the host, and vice versa. The remote host believes it is communicating with one of its own terminals and allows you to log on.

■ **File transfer, access, and management (FTAM).** This application allows a user to access files in a remote computer (to make changes or read data), to retrieve files from a remote computer; and to manage or control files in a remote computer.

■ **Mail services.** This application provides the basis for e-mail forwarding and storage.

■ **Directory services.** This application provides distributed database sources and access for global information about various objects and services.

Summary of Layer Functions

The functions of the seven layers are summarized in Figure 3.14.

Figure 3.14   *Summary of layer functions*

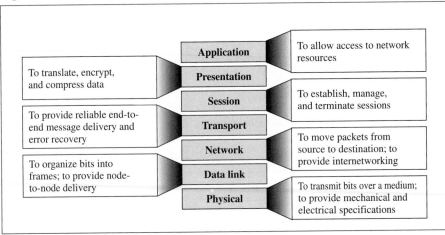

3.3   TCP/IP PROTOCOL SUITE

The TCP/IP protocol suite, used in the Internet, was developed prior to the OSI model. Therefore, the layers in the **Transmission Control Protocol/Internetworking Protocol (TCP/IP)** protocol suite do not match exactly with those in the OSI model. The TCP/IP protocol suite is made of five layers: physical, data link, network, transport, and application. The first four layers provide physical standards, network interface, internetworking, and transport functions that correspond to the first four layers of the OSI model. The three topmost layers in the OSI model, however, are represented in TCP/IP by a single layer called the *application layer* (see Figure 3.15).

TCP/IP is a hierarchical protocol made up of interactive modules, each of which provides a specific functionality, but they are not necessarily interdependent. Whereas the OSI model specifies which functions belong to each of its layers, the layers of the

Figure 3.15   *TCP/IP and the OSI model*

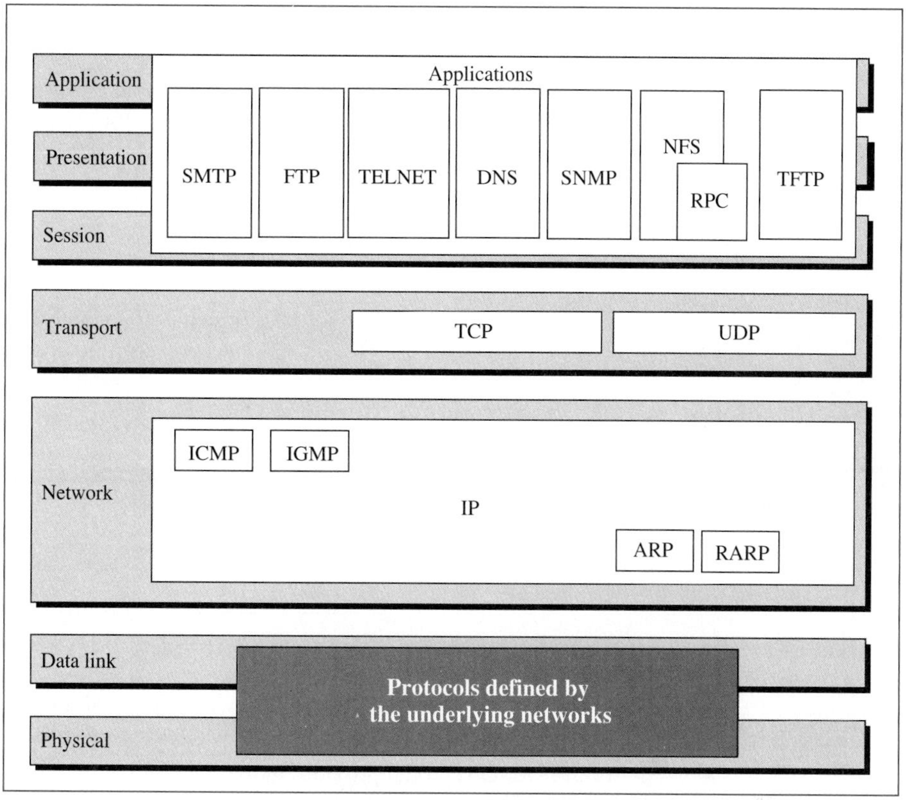

TCP/IP protocol suite contain relatively independent protocols that can be mixed and matched depending on the needs of the system. The term *hierarchical* means that each upper-level protocol is supported by one or more lower-level protocols.

At the transport layer, TCP/IP defines two protocols: Transmission Control Protocol (TCP) and User Datagram Protocol (UDP). At the network layer, the main protocol defined by TCP/IP is Internetworking Protocol (IP), although there are some other protocols that support data movement in this layer. See Chapters 24 and 25 for a discussion of TCP/IP protocols.

3.4   KEY TERMS AND CONCEPTS

application layer	error
bit	frame
data link layer	header
destination address	interface

logical address	presentation layer
network layer	session layer
node-to-node delivery	source address
open system	source-to-destination delivery
Open Systems Interconnection (OSI)	trailer
peer-to-peer process	Transmission Control Protocol/Internet-working Protocol (TCP/IP)
physical address	
physical layer	transmission rate
port address	transport layer

3.5   SUMMARY

- The International Standards Organization (ISO) created a model called the Open Systems Interconnection (OSI), which allows diverse systems to communicate.
- The seven-layer OSI model provides guidelines for the development of universally compatible architecture, hardware, and software.
- The physical, data link, and network layers are the network support layers.
- The session, presentation, and application layers are the user support layers.
- The transport layer links the network support layers and the user support layers.
- The physical layer coordinates the functions required to transmit a bit stream over a physical medium.
- The data link layer is responsible for delivering data units from one station to the next without errors.
- The network layer is responsible for the source-to-destination delivery of a packet across multiple network links.
- The transport layer is responsible for the source-to-destination delivery of the entire message.
- The session layer establishes, maintains, and synchronizes the interactions between communicating devices.
- The presentation layer ensures interoperability between communicating devices through transformation of data into a mutually agreed-upon format.

- The application layer enables the users to access the network.
- TCP/IP, a five-layer hierarchical protocol suite developed before the OSI model, is the protocol suite used in the Internet.

3.6 PRACTICE SET

Review Questions

1. Which OSI layers are the network support layers?
2. Which OSI layers are the user support layers?
3. What is the difference between network layer delivery and transport layer delivery?
4. How are OSI and ISO related to each other?
5. List the layers of the OSI model.
6. What is a peer-to-peer process?
7. How does information get passed from one OSI layer to the next?
8. What are headers and trailers and how do they get added and removed?
9. Group the OSI layers by function.
10. What are the concerns of the physical layer?
11. What are the responsibilities of the data link layer?
12. What are the responsibilities of the network layer?
13. What are the responsibilities of the transport layer?
14. The transport layer creates a connection between the source and destination. What are the three events involved in a connection?
15. What is the difference between a service-point address, a logical address, and a physical address?
16. What are the responsibilities of the session layer?
17. What is the purpose of the dialog controller?
18. What are the responsibilities of the presentation layer?
19. What is the purpose of translation by the presentation layer?
20. Name some services provided by the application layer.
21. How do the layers of the TCP/IP protocol suite correlate to the layers of the OSI model?

Multiple Choice Questions

22. The _____ model shows how the network functions of a computer ought to be organized.
    a. ITU-T

    b. OSI

    c. ISO

    d. ANSI

23. The OSI model consists of _____ layers.

    a. three

    b. five

    c. seven

    d. eight

24. The _____ layer decides the location of synchronization points.

    a. transport

    b. session

    c. presentation

    d. application

25. The end-to-end delivery of the entire message is the responsibility of the _____ layer.

    a. network

    b. transport

    c. session

    d. presentation

26. The _____ layer is the layer closest to the transmission medium.

    a. physical

    b. data link

    c. network

    d. transport

27. In the _____ layer, the data unit is called a frame.

    a. physical

    b. data link

    c. network

    d. transport

28. Decryption and encryption of data are the responsibility of the _____ layer.

    a. physical

    b. data link

    c. presentation

    d. session

29. Dialog control is a function of the _____ layer.

    a. transport

    b. session

   c. presentation

   d. application

30. Mail services and directory services are available to network users through the
_____ layer.

   a. data link

   b. session

   c. transport

   d. application

31. Node-to-node delivery of the data unit is the responsibility of the _____ layer.

   a. physical

   b. data link

   c. transport

   d. network

32. As the data packet moves from the lower to the upper layers, headers are _____.

   a. added

   b. subtracted

   c. rearranged

   d. modified

33. As the data packet moves from the upper to the lower layers, headers are _____.

   a. added

   b. removed

   c. rearranged

   d. modified

34. The _____ layer lies between the network layer and the session layer.

   a. physical

   b. data link

   c. transport

   d. presentation

35. Layer 2 lies between the physical layer and the _____ layer.

   a. network

   b. data link

   c. transport

   d. presentation

36. When data are transmitted from device A to device B, the header from A's layer 5
is read by B's _____ layer.

   a. physical

   b. transport

   c. session

   d. presentation

37. In the _____ layer, translations from one character code to another occur.
    a. transport
    b. session
    c. presentation
    d. application

38. The _____ layer changes bits into electromagnetic signals.
    a. physical
    b. data link
    c. transport
    d. presentation

39. The _____ layer can use the trailer of the frame for error detection.
    a. physical
    b. data link
    c. transport
    d. presentation

40. Why was the OSI model developed?
    a. Manufacturers disliked the TCP/IP protocol suite.
    b. The rate of data transfer was increasing exponentially.
    c. Standards were needed to allow any two systems to communicate.
    d. none of the above

41. The physical layer is concerned with the transmission of _____ over the physical medium.
    a. programs
    b. dialogs
    c. protocols
    d. bits

42. Which layer functions as a liaison between user support layers and network support layers?
    a. network layer
    b. physical layer
    c. transport layer
    d. session layer

43. What is the main function of the transport layer?
    a. node-to-node delivery
    b. end-to-end message delivery
    c. synchronization
    d. updating and maintenance of routing tables

44. Session layer checkpoints _____.
    a. allow just a portion of a file to be resent

    b. detect and recover errors

    c. control the addition of headers

    d. are involved in dialog control

45. Which of the following is an application layer service?

    a. network virtual terminal

    b. file transfer, access, and management

    c. mail service

    d. all of the above

Exercises

46. Match the following to one of the seven OSI layers:

    a. Route determination.

    b. Flow control.

    c. Interface to outside world.

    d. Access to the network provided for the end user.

    e. ASCII changed to EBCDIC.

    f. Packet switching.

47. Match the following to one of the seven OSI layers:

    a. Reliable end-to-end data transmission.

    b. Network selection.

    c. Frames defined.

    d. User services such as e-mail and file transfer provided.

    e. Transmission of bit stream across physical medium.

48. Match the following to one of the seven OSI layers:

    a. Direct communication with the user's application program.

    b. Error correction and retransmission.

    c. Mechanical, electrical, and functional interface.

    d. Responsibility for information between adjacent nodes.

    e. Reassembly of data packets.

49. Match the following to one of the seven OSI layers:

    a. Provides format and code conversion services.

    b. Establishes, manages, and terminates sessions.

    c. Ensures reliable transmission of data.

    d. Provides log-in and log-out procedures.

    e. Provides independence from differences in data representation.

    f. Synchronizes users.

CHAPTER 4

Signals

A major concern of the physical layer is moving information in the form of electromagnetic signals across a transmission medium. Whether you are collecting numerical statistics from another computer, sending animated pictures from a design workstation, or causing a bell to ring in a distant control center, you are working with the transmission of *information* across network connections. Information can be voice, image, numeric data, characters, or **code**—any message that is readable by and has meaning to the destination user, whether human or machine.

> Information can be in the form of data, voice, picture, and so on.

Generally, the information usable to a person or application is not in a form that can be transmitted over a network. For example, you cannot roll up a photograph, insert it into a wire, and transmit it across town. You can transmit, however, an encoded description of the photograph. Instead of sending the actual photograph, you can use an encoder to create a stream of 1s and 0s that tells the receiving device how to reconstruct the image of the photograph. (Encoding is the subject of Chapter 5.)

But even 1s and 0s cannot be sent as such across network links. They must be further converted into a form that transmission media can accept. Transmission media work by conducting energy along a physical path. So a data stream of 1s and 0s must be turned into energy in the form of electromagnetic signals.

> To be transmitted, information must be transformed into electromagnetic signals.

4.1 ANALOG AND DIGITAL

Both data and the signals that represent them can take either *analog* or *digital* form. **Analog** refers to something that is continuous—a set of specific points of data and all possible points between. **Digital** refers to something that is discrete—a set of specific points of data with no other points in between.

Analog and Digital Data

Data can be analog or digital. An example of **analog data** is the human voice. When somebody speaks, a continuous wave is created in the air. This can be captured by a microphone and converted to an analog signal.

An example of **digital data** is data stored in the memory of a computer in the form of 0s and 1s. It is usually converted to a digital signal when it is transferred from one position to another inside or outside the computer.

Analog and Digital Signals

Like the information they represent, **signals** can be either analog or digital. An **analog signal** is a continuous wave form that changes smoothly over time. As the wave moves from value A to value B, it passes through and includes an infinite number of values along its path. A **digital signal,** on the other hand, is discrete. It can have only a limited number of defined values, often as simple as 1 and 0. The transition of a digital signal from value to value is instantaneous, like a light being switched on and off.

We usually illustrate signals by plotting them on a pair of perpendicular axes. The vertical axis represents the value or strength of a signal. The horizontal axis represents the passage of time. Figure 4.1 illustrates an analog and a digital signal. The curve representing the analog signal is smooth and continuous, passing through an infinite number of points. The vertical lines of the digital signal, however, demonstrate the sudden jump the signal makes from value to value; its flat highs and lows indicate that those values are fixed. Another way to express the difference is that the analog signal changes continuously with respect to time, while the digital signal changes instantaneously.

> Signals can be analog or digital. Analog signals can have any value in a range; digital signals can have only a limited number of values.

Figure 4.1   *Comparison of analog and digital signals*

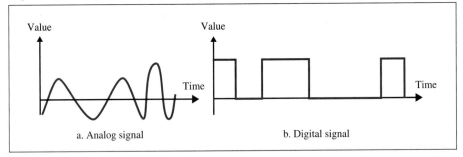

a. Analog signal   b. Digital signal

4.2   PERIODIC AND APERIODIC SIGNALS

Both analog and digital signals can be of two forms: *periodic* and *aperiodic* (nonperiodic).

Periodic Signals

A signal is a **periodic signal** if it completes a pattern within a measurable time frame, called a **period,** and repeats that pattern over identical subsequent periods. The completion of one full pattern is called a **cycle.** A period is defined as the amount of time (expressed in seconds) required to complete one full cycle. The duration of a period, represented by T, may be different for each signal, but it is constant for any given periodic signal. Figure 4.2 illustrates hypothetical periodic signals.

> A periodic signal consists of a continuously repeated pattern. The period of a signal (T) is expressed in seconds.

Figure 4.2   *Examples of periodic signals*

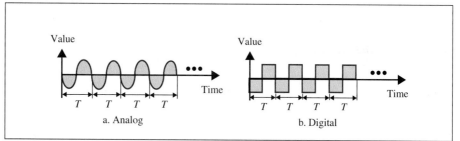

Aperiodic Signals

An **aperiodic,** or nonperiodic, **signal** changes constantly without exhibiting a pattern or cycle that repeats over time. Figure 4.3 shows examples of aperiodic signals.

> An aperiodic, or nonperiodic, signal has no repetitive pattern.

Figure 4.3   *Examples of aperiodic signals*

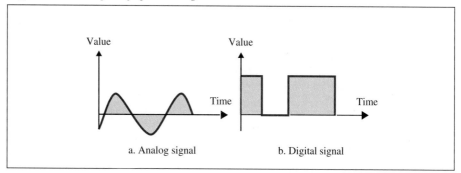

It has been proved, however, by a technique called a **Fourier transform** (see **Appendix D**), that any aperiodic signal can be decomposed into an infinite number of periodic signals. Understanding the characteristics of periodic signals, therefore, provides insight into aperiodic signals as well.

> An aperiodic signal can be decomposed into an infinite number of periodic signals. A sine wave is the simplest periodic signal.

4.3   ANALOG SIGNALS

Analog signals can be classified as simple or composite. A simple analog signal, or a **sine wave**, cannot be decomposed into simpler signals. A composite analog signal is composed of multiple sine waves.

Simple Analog Signals

The sine wave is the most fundamental form of a periodic analog signal. Visualized as a simple oscillating curve, its change over the course of a cycle is smooth and consistent, a continuous, rolling flow. Figure 4.4 shows a sine wave. Each cycle consists of a single arc above the time axis followed by a single arc below it. Sine waves can be fully described by three characteristics: *amplitude, period* or *frequency,* and *phase.*

Figure 4.4   *A sine wave*

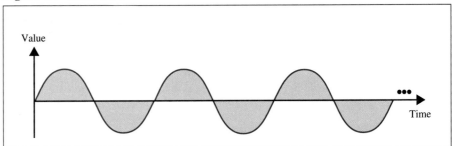

Amplitude

On a graph, the **amplitude** of a signal is the value of the signal at any point on the wave. It is equal to the vertical distance from a given point on the wave form to the horizontal axis. The maximum amplitude of a sine wave is equal to the highest value it reaches on the vertical axis (see Figure 4.5).

Amplitude is measured in either *volts, amperes,* or *watts,* depending on the type of signal. Volts refer to voltage; amperes refer to current; and watts refer to power.

> Amplitude refers to the height of the signal. The unit for amplitude depends on the type of the signal. For electrical signals, the unit is normally volts, amperes, or watts.

Period and Frequency

Period refers to the amount of time, in seconds, a signal needs to complete one cycle. **Frequency** refers to the number of periods in one second. The frequency of a signal is its number of cycles per second. Figure 4.6 shows the concept of period and frequency.

Figure 4.5   *Amplitude*

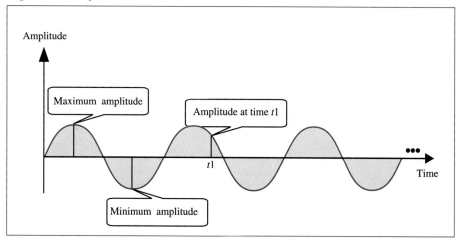

Figure 4.6   *Period and frequency*

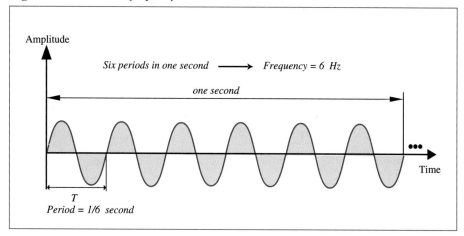

Unit of Period   Period is expressed in seconds. The communications industry uses five units to measure period: second (s), **millisecond** (ms = 10^{-3} s), **microsecond** (μs = 10^{-6} s), **nanosecond** (ns = 10^{-9} s), and **picosecond** (ps = 10^{-12} s). See Table 4.1.

Table 4.1   *Units of periods*

Unit	Equivalent
Seconds	1 s
Milliseconds (ms)	10^{-3} s
Microseconds (μs)	10^{-6} s
Nanoseconds (ns)	10^{-9} s
Picoseconds (ps)	10^{-12} s

Example 4.1

Show 100 milliseconds in seconds, microseconds, nanoseconds, and picoseconds.

Solution

We manipulate the powers of 10 to find the appropriate unit. We replace 10^{-3} seconds with milliseconds, 10^{-6} seconds with microseconds, 10^{-9} seconds with nanoseconds, and 10^{-12} seconds with picoseconds.

$$100 \text{ milliseconds} = 100 \times 10^{-3} \text{ seconds} = 0.1 \text{ second}$$

$$100 \text{ milliseconds} = 100 \times 10^{-3} \text{ seconds} = 100 \times 10^{3} \times 10^{-6} \text{ seconds} = 10^{5} \text{ } \mu s$$

$$100 \text{ milliseconds} = 100 \times 10^{-3} \text{ seconds} = 100 \times 10^{6} \times 10^{-9} \text{ seconds} = 10^{8} \text{ ns}$$

$$100 \text{ milliseconds} = 100 \times 10^{-3} \text{ seconds} = 100 \times 10^{9} \times 10^{-12} \text{ seconds} = 10^{11} \text{ ps}$$

Unit of Frequency   Frequency is expressed in **hertz (Hz),** after the German physicist Heinrich Rudolf Hertz. The communications industry uses five units to measure frequency: hertz (Hz), **kilohertz** (KHz = 10^{3} Hz), **megahertz** (MHz = 10^{6} Hz), **gigahertz** (GHz = 10^{9} Hz), and **terahertz** (THz = 10^{12} Hz). See Table 4.2.

Table 4.2   *Units of frequency*

Unit	Equivalent
Hertz (Hz)	1 Hz
Kilohertz (KHz)	10^{3} Hz
Megahertz (MHz)	10^{6} Hz
Gigahertz (GHz)	10^{9} Hz
Terahertz (THz)	10^{12} Hz

Example 4.2

Show 14 MHz in Hz, KHz, GHz, and THz.

Solution

We manipulate the powers of 10 to find the appropriate unit. We replace 10^{3} Hz with KHz, 10^{6} Hz with MHz, 10^{9} Hz with GHz, and 10^{12} Hz with THz.

$$14 \text{ MHz} = 14 \times 10^{6} \text{ Hz}$$

$$14 \text{ MHz} = 14 \times 10^{6} \text{ Hz} = 14 \times 10^{3} \times 10^{3} \text{ Hz} = 14 \times 10^{3} \text{ KHz}$$

$$14 \text{ MHz} = 14 \times 10^{6} \text{ Hz} = 14 \times 10^{-3} \times 10^{9} \text{ Hz} = 14 \times 10^{-3} \text{ GHz}$$

$$14 \text{ MHz} = 14 \times 10^{6} \text{ Hz} = 14 \times 10^{-6} \times 10^{12} \text{ Hz} = 14 \times 10^{-6} \text{ THz}$$

Converting Frequency to Period and Vice Versa   Mathematically, the relationship between frequency and period is that they are the multiplicative inverse of each other; if one is given, the other can be derived.

$$\text{Frequency} = 1/\text{Period} \qquad \text{Period} = 1/\text{Frequency}$$

> Period is the amount of time it takes a signal to complete one cycle; frequency is the number of cycles per second. Frequency and period are inverses of each other: $f = 1/T$ and $T = 1/f$.

Example 4.3

A sine wave has a frequency of 6 Hz. What is its period?

Solution

Let T be the period and f be the frequency. Then,

$$T = 1/f = 1/6 = 0.17 \text{ second}$$

Example 4.4

A sine wave has a frequency of 8 KHz. What is its period?

Solution

Let T be the period and f be the frequency. Then,

$$T = 1/f = 1/8000 = 0.000125 \text{ second} = 125 \times 10^{-6} \text{ seconds} = 125 \, \mu s$$

Example 4.5

A sine wave completes one cycle in 4 seconds. What is its frequency?

Solution

Let T be the period and f be the frequency. Then,

$$f = 1/T = 1/4 = 0.25 \text{ Hz}$$

Example 4.6

A sine wave completes one cycle in 25 μs. What is its frequency?

Solution

Let T be the period and f be the frequency. Then,

$$f = 1/T = 1/(25 \times 10^{-6}) = 40,000 \text{ Hz} = 40 \times 10^3 \text{ Hz} = 40 \text{ KHz}$$

More about Frequency

We know already that frequency is the relationship of a signal to time and that the frequency of a wave form is the number of cycles it completes per second. But another way to look at frequency is as a measurement of the rate of change. Electromagnetic signals are oscillating wave forms; that is, they fluctuate continuously and predictably above and below a mean energy level. The rate at which a sine wave moves from its lowest to its highest level is its frequency. A 40 Hz signal has half the frequency of an 80 Hz signal; it completes one cycle in twice the time of the 80 Hz signal, so each cycle also takes twice as long to change from its lowest to its highest voltage levels. Frequency, therefore, though described in cycles per second (Hz), is a general measurement of the rate of change of a signal with respect to time.

> Frequency is rate of change with respect to time. Change in a short span of time means high frequency. Change in a long span of time means low frequency.

If the value of a signal changes over a very short span of time, its frequency is high. If it changes over a long span of time, its frequency is low.

Two Extremes   What if a signal does not change at all? What if it maintains a constant voltage level the entire time it is active? In such a case, its frequency is zero. Conceptually, this idea is a simple one. If a signal does not change at all, it never completes a cycle, so its frequency is 0 Hz.

But what if a signal changes instantaneously? What if it jumps from one level to another in no time? Then its frequency is infinite. In other words, when a signal changes instantaneously, its period is zero; since frequency is the inverse of period, then, in this case, the frequency is 1/0, or infinity.

> If a signal does not change at all, its frequency is zero. If a signal changes instantaneously, its frequency is infinity.

Phase

The term **phase** describes the position of the waveform relative to time zero. If we think of the wave as something that can be shifted backward or forward along the time axis, phase describes the amount of that shift. It indicates the status of the first cycle.

> Phase describes the position of the waveform relative to time zero.

Phase is measured in degrees or radians (360 degrees is 2π radians). A phase shift of 360 degrees corresponds to a shift of a complete period; a phase shift of 180 degrees corresponds to a shift of half a period; and a phase shift of 90 degrees corresponds to a shift of a quarter of a period (see Figure 4.7).

Figure 4.7   *Relationship between different phases*

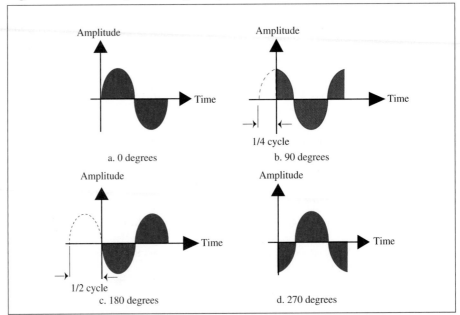

a. 0 degrees

b. 90 degrees

1/4 cycle

c. 180 degrees

1/2 cycle

d. 270 degrees

Example 4.7

A sine wave is offset 1/6 of a cycle with respect to time zero. What is its phase?

Solution

We know that one complete cycle is 360 degrees. Therefore, 1/6 of a cycle is

$$1/6 \times 360 = 60 \text{ degrees}$$

A visual comparison of amplitude, frequency, and phase provides a reference useful for understanding their functions. Changes in all three attributes can be introduced into a signal and controlled electronically. Such control provides the basis for all telecommunications and will be discussed in Chapter 5 (see Figures 4.8, 4.9, and 4.10).

Figure 4.8 *Amplitude change*

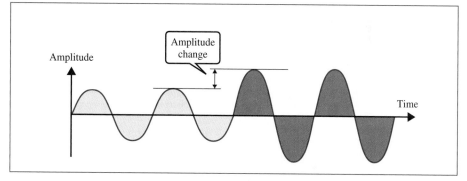

Figure 4.9 *Frequency change*

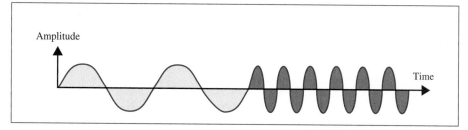

4.4 TIME AND FREQUENCY DOMAINS

A sine wave is comprehensively defined by its amplitude, frequency, and phase. We have been showing a sine wave using what is called a **time-domain plot.** The time-domain plot shows changes in signal amplitude with respect to time (it is an amplitude versus time plot). Phase and frequency are not explicitly measured on a time-domain plot.

Figure 4.10   *Phase change*

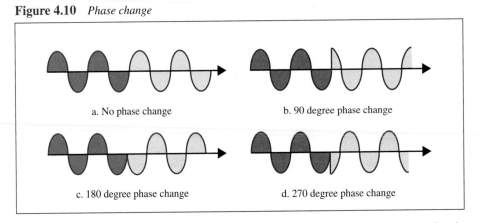

a. No phase change

b. 90 degree phase change

c. 180 degree phase change

d. 270 degree phase change

To show the relationship between amplitude and frequency, we can use what is called a **frequency-domain plot.** Figure 4.11 compares the time domain (instantaneous amplitude with respect to time) and the frequency domain (maximum amplitude with respect to frequency).

Figure 4.11   *Time and frequency domains*

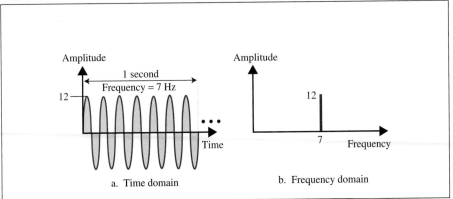

a. Time domain

b. Frequency domain

Figure 4.12 gives examples of both the time-domain and frequency-domain plots of three signals with varying frequencies and amplitudes. Compare the models within each pair to see which sort of information each is best suited to convey.

A low-frequency signal in the frequency domain corresponds to a signal with a long period in the time domain and vice versa. A signal that changes rapidly in the time domain corresponds to high frequencies in the frequency domain.

Figure 4.12   *Time and frequency domains for different signals*

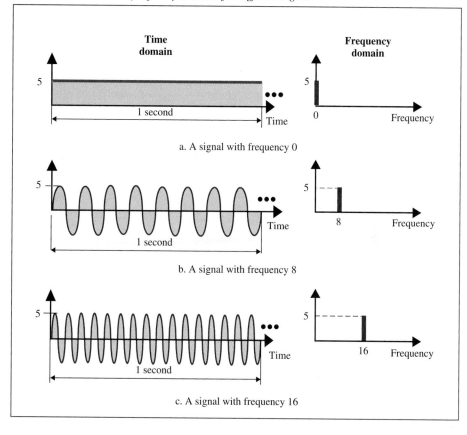

a. A signal with frequency 0

b. A signal with frequency 8

c. A signal with frequency 16

4.5   COMPOSITE SIGNALS

So far, we have focused attention on simple periodic signals (sine waves). But what about periodic signals that are not sine waves? Many useful wave forms do not change in a single smooth curve between a minimum and a maximum amplitude; they jump, slide, wobble, spike, and dip. But as long as any irregularities are consistent, cycle after cycle, a signal is still periodic and logically must be describable in the same terms used for sine waves. In fact, it can be shown that any periodic signal, no matter how complex, can be decomposed into a collection of sine waves, each having a measurable amplitude, frequency, and phase.

To decompose a **composite signal** into its components, **Fourier analysis** (discussed in Appendix D) is needed. However, the concept of decomposition can be seen with a simple example. Figure 4.13 shows a periodic signal decomposed into two sine waves. The first sine wave (middle plot) has a frequency of 6 while the second sine wave has a frequency of 0. Adding these two point by point results in the top graph. Notice that the original signal looks like a sine wave that has had its time axis shifted downward. The average amplitude of this signal is nonzero. This factor indicates the presence of a zero-frequency component, a **direct current (DC)** component. This DC component is responsible for the 10-unit upward shift of the sine wave.

Figure 4.13   *A signal with a DC component*

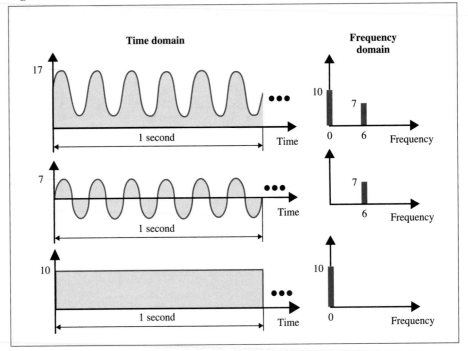

In contrast to the time-domain graph, which illustrates a composite signal as a single entity, a frequency-domain graph shows the composite signal as a series of component frequencies. Instead of showing the impact of each component on the others, it shows the signal as a set of independent frequencies.

Although the time-domain graph is more useful for understanding the impact of the two signals on each other, the vertical bars of the frequency-domain graph give a more concise view of the relative frequencies and amplitudes of the composite sine waves.

Figure 4.14 shows a composite signal decomposed into four components. This signal is close to a digital signal. For an exact digital signal, we need an infinite number of odd harmonic signals (*f, 3f, 5f, 7f, 9f, …*), each with a different amplitude. The frequency-domain graphs are also shown.

Frequency Spectrum and Bandwidth

Two terms need mentioning here: *spectrum* and *bandwidth*. The frequency **spectrum** of a signal is the collection of all the component frequencies it contains and is shown

Figure 4.14 *Composite waveform*

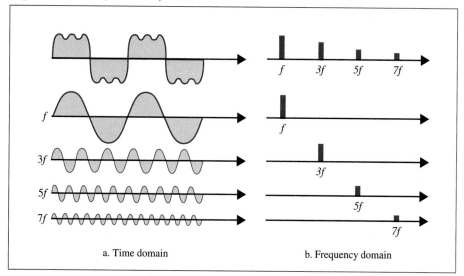

a. Time domain   b. Frequency domain

using a frequency-domain graph. The **bandwidth** of a signal is the width of the frequency spectrum (see Figure 4.15). In other words, bandwidth refers to the range of component frequencies, and frequency spectrum refers to the elements within that range. To calculate the bandwidth, subtract the lowest frequency from the highest frequency of the range.

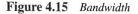

> The frequency spectrum of a signal is the combination of all sine wave signals that make up that signal.

Figure 4.15 *Bandwidth*

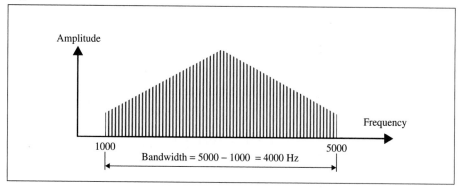

Example 4.8

If a periodic signal is decomposed into five sine waves with frequencies of 100, 300, 500, 700, and 900 Hz, what is the bandwidth? Draw the spectrum, assuming all components have a maximum amplitude of 10 volts.

Solution

Let f_h be the highest frequency, f_l be the lowest frequency, and B be the bandwidth. Then,

$$B = f_h - f_l = 900 - 100 = 800 \text{ Hz}$$

The spectrum has only five bars, at 100, 300, 500, 700 and 900 (see Figure 4.16).

Figure 4.16   *Example 4.8*

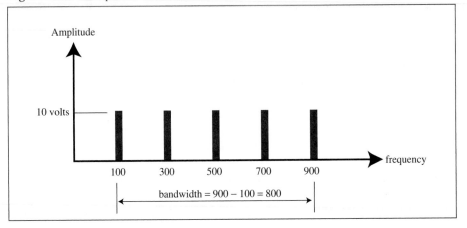

Example 4.9

A signal has a bandwidth of 20 Hz. The highest frequency is 60 Hz. What is the lowest frequency? Draw the spectrum if the signal contains all integral frequencies of the same amplitude.

Solution

Let f_h be the highest frequency, f_l be the lowest frequency, and B be the bandwidth. Then,

$$B = f_h - f_l \quad \Rightarrow \quad 20 = 60 - f_l \quad \Rightarrow \quad f_l = 60 - 20 = 40 \text{ Hz}$$

The spectrum contains all integral frequencies. We show this by a series of bars (see Figure 4.17).

Figure 4.17   *Example 4.9*

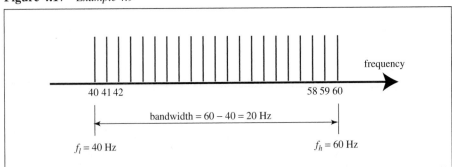

4.6   DIGITAL SIGNALS

In addition to being represented by an analog signal, data also can be represented by a digital signal. For example, a 1 can be encoded as a positive voltage and a 0 as zero voltage (see Figure 4.18).

Figure 4.18   *A digital signal*

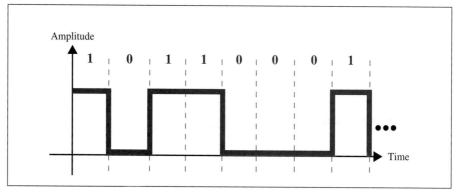

Bit Interval and Bit Rate

Most digital signals are aperiodic and, thus, period or frequency is not appropriate. Two new terms, *bit interval* (instead of period) and *bit rate* (instead of frequency) are used to describe digital signals. The **bit interval** is the time required to send one single bit. The **bit rate** is the number of bit intervals per second. This means that the bit rate is the number of bits sent in one second, usually expressed in **bits per second (bps).** See Figure 4.19.

Figure 4.19   *Bit rate and bit interval*

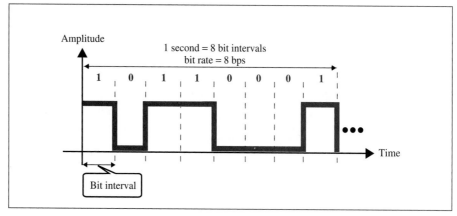

Example 4.10

A digital signal has a bit rate of 2000 bps. What is the duration of each bit (bit interval)?

Solution

The bit interval is the inverse of the bit rate.

bit interval = 1/(bit rate) = 1/2000 = 0.000500 second = 500 $\times$ 10^{-6} seconds = 500 μs

Example 4.11

A digital signal has a bit interval of 40 microseconds. What is the bit rate?

Solution

The bit rate is the inverse of the bit interval.

$$\text{bit rate} = 1/(\text{bit interval}) = 1/(40 \times 10^{-6}) = 25{,}000 \text{ bits per second}$$
$$= 25 \times 10^3 \text{ bits per second} = 25 \text{ Kbps}$$

Decomposition of a Digital Signal

A digital signal can be decomposed into an infinite number of simple sine waves called **harmonics,** each with a different amplitude, frequency, and phase (see Figure 4.20). This means that when we send a digital signal along a transmission medium, we are sending an infinite number of simple signals. To receive an exact replica of the digital signal, all of the frequency components must be faithfully transferred through the transmission medium. If some of the components are not passed through the medium, corruption of the signal at the receiver is the result. Since no practical medium (such as a cable) is capable of transferring the entire range of frequencies, we always have corruption.

Figure 4.20   *Harmonics of a digital signal*

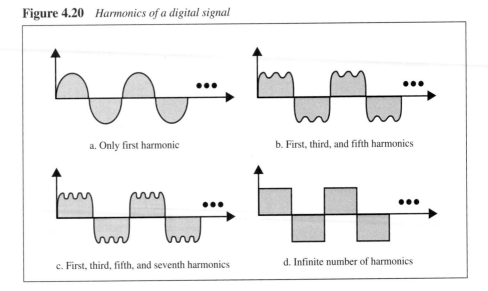

a. Only first harmonic

b. First, third, and fifth harmonics

c. First, third, fifth, and seventh harmonics

d. Infinite number of harmonics

Although the frequency spectrum of a digital signal contains an infinite number of frequencies with different amplitudes, if we send only those components whose amplitudes are significant (above an acceptable threshold), we can still recreate the digital signal with reasonable accuracy at the receiver (minimum distortion). We call this part of the infinite spectrum the significant spectrum, and its bandwidth the significant bandwidth (see Figure 4.21).

Figure 4.21   *Exact and significant spectrums*

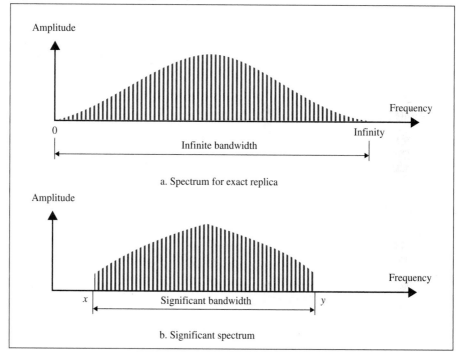

a. Spectrum for exact replica

b. Significant spectrum

4.7   KEY TERMS AND CONCEPTS

amplitude	bandwidth
analog	bit interval
analog data	bit rate
analog signal	bits per second (bps)
aperiodic signal	code

composite signal	megahertz (MHz)
cycle	microsecond
digital	millisecond
digital data	nanosecond
digital signal	period
direct current (DC)	periodic signal
Fourier analysis	phase
Fourier transform	picosecond
frequency	signal
frequency-domain plot	sine wave
gigahertz (GHz)	spectrum
harmonics	terahertz (THz)
hertz (Hz)	time-domain plot
kilohertz (KHz)	

4.8 SUMMARY

■ Information must be transformed into electromagnetic signals prior to transmission across a network.

■ Information and signals can be either analog (continuous values) or digital (discrete values).

■ A signal is periodic if it consists of a continuously repeating pattern.

■ A periodic signal can be decomposed into a set of sine waves.

■ Each sine wave can be characterized by its

   a. Amplitude—the instantaneous height of the wave.

   b. Frequency—the number of cycles per second.

   c. Phase—the shift of the wave along the time axis.

■ Frequency and period are inverses of each other.

■ A time-domain graph plots amplitude as a function of time.

■ A frequency-domain graph plots each sine wave's peak amplitude against its frequency.

- The bandwidth of a signal is the range of frequencies the signal occupies. Bandwidth is determined by finding the difference between the highest and lowest frequency components.

- The spectrum of a signal consists of the sine waves that make up the signal.

- Bit rate (number of bits per second) and bit interval (duration of one bit) are terms used to describe digital signals.

- A digital signal can be decomposed into an infinite number of sine waves (harmonics).

- The significant spectrum of a digital signal is the portion of the signal's spectrum that can adequately reproduce the original signal.

4.9   PRACTICE SET

Review Questions

1. Describe the three characteristics of a sine wave.
2. What is the spectrum of a signal?
3. What is the difference between information and signals?
4. Give two examples of analog information.
5. Give two examples of digital information.
6. Contrast an analog signal with a digital signal.
7. Contrast a periodic signal with an aperiodic signal.
8. What is the difference between digital data and analog data?
9. A signal has been received that only has values of −1, 0, and 1. Is this an analog or a digital signal?
10. What is the relationship between period and frequency?
11. What are the units of period?
12. What are the units of frequency?
13. Compare a high-frequency signal with a low-frequency signal.
14. What does the amplitude of a signal measure?
15. What does the frequency of a signal measure?
16. What does the phase of a signal measure?
17. Compare the axes of a time-domain plot with the axes of a frequency-domain plot.
18. What is the difference between a simple periodic signal and a composite periodic signal?
19. Which type of plot shows the components of a composite signal?
20. Which type of plot shows the amplitude of a signal at a given time?
21. Which type of plot shows the phase of a signal at a given time?
22. How is the bandwidth of a signal related to its spectrum?

23. How can a composite signal be decomposed into its individual frequencies?

24. What is a bit interval and what is its counterpart in an analog signal?

25. What is bit rate and what is its counterpart in an analog signal?

Multiple Choice Questions

26. Before information can be transmitted, it must be transformed into _____.
    a. periodic signals
    b. electromagnetic signals
    c. aperiodic signals
    d. low-frequency sine waves

27. A periodic signal completes one cycle in 0.001 second. What is the frequency?
    a. 1 Hz
    b. 100 Hz
    c. 1 KHz
    d. 1 MHz

28. Which of the following can be determined from a frequency-domain graph of a signal?
    a. frequency
    b. phase
    c. power
    d. all of the above

29. Which of the following can be determined from a frequency-domain graph of a signal?
    a. bandwidth
    b. phase
    c. power
    d. all of the above

30. In a frequency-domain plot, the vertical axis measures the _____.
    a. peak amplitude
    b. frequency
    c. phase
    d. slope

31. In a frequency-domain plot, the horizontal axis measures the _____.
    a. peak amplitude
    b. frequency
    c. phase
    d. slope

32. In a time-domain plot, the vertical axis is a measure of _____.
    a. amplitude
    b. frequency
    c. phase
    d. time

33. In a time-domain plot, the horizontal axis is a measure of _____.
    a. signal amplitude
    b. frequency
    c. phase
    d. time

34. If the bandwidth of a signal is 5 KHz and the lowest frequency is 52 KHz, what is the highest frequency?
    a. 5 KHz
    b. 10 KHz
    c. 47 KHz
    d. 57 KHz

35. What is the bandwidth of a signal that ranges from 40 KHz to 4 MHz?
    a. 36 MHz
    b. 360 KHz
    c. 3.96 MHz
    d. 396 KHz

36. When one of the components of a signal has a frequency of zero, the average amplitude of the signal _____.
    a. is greater than zero
    b. is less than zero
    c. is zero
    d. a or b

37. A periodic signal can always be decomposed into _____.
    a. exactly an odd number of sine waves
    b. a set of sine waves
    c. a set of sine waves, one of which must have a phase of zero degrees
    d. none of the above

38. As frequency increases, the period _____.
    a. decreases
    b. increases
    c. remains the same
    d. doubles

39. Given two sine waves A and B, if the frequency of A is twice that of B, then the period of B is _____ that of A.
    a. one-half
    b. twice
    c. the same as
    d. indeterminate from

40. In Figure 4.2, part a, how many values along the vertical axis are represented?
    a. 1
    b. 2
    c. 3
    d. an infinite number of values

41. In Figure 4.2, part b, how many values along the vertical axis are represented?
    a. 1
    b. 2
    c. 3
    d. an infinite number of values

42. A sine wave is _____.
    a. periodic and continuous
    b. aperiodic and continuous
    c. periodic and discrete
    d. aperiodic and discrete

43. If the maximum amplitude of a sine wave is 2 volts, the minimum amplitude is _____ volts.
    a. 2
    b. 1
    c. –2
    d. between –2 and 2

44. A sine wave completes 1000 cycles in one second. What is its period?
    a. 1 ms
    b. 10 ms
    c. 100 ms
    d. 1000 ms

45. In Figure 4.7, part b, if the maximum amplitude is A, and the period is P seconds, what is the amplitude at $P/2$ seconds?
    a. A
    b. $-A$
    c. 0
    d. any value between A and $-A$

Exercises

46. How many KHz are
    a. in one Hz?
    b. in one MHz?
    c. in one GHz?
    d. in one THz?

47. Rewrite the following:
    a. 10,000 Hz in KHz.
    b. 25,340 KHz in MHz.
    c. 108 GHz in KHz.
    d. 2,456,764 Hz in MHz.

48. Rewrite the following:
    a. 0.005 second in milliseconds.
    b. 0.1231 millisecond in microseconds.
    c. 0.0000234 second in picoseconds.
    d. 0.003451 second in nanoseconds.

49. Given the frequencies listed below, calculate the corresponding periods. Express the result in seconds, milliseconds, microseconds, nanoseconds, and picoseconds.
    a. 24 Hz
    b. 8 MHz
    c. 140 KHz
    d. 12 THz

50. Given the following periods, calculate the corresponding frequencies. Express the frequencies in Hz, KHz, MHz, GHz, and THz.
    a. 5 s
    b. 12 μs
    c. 220 ns
    d. 81 ps

51. What is the phase shift for the following?
    a. A sine wave with the maximum amplitude at time zero.
    b. A sine wave with maximum amplitude after 1/4 cycle.
    c. A sine wave with zero amplitude after 3/4 cycle and increasing.
    d. A sine wave with minimum amplitude after 1/4 cycle.

52. Show the phase shift in degrees corresponding to each of the following delays in cycles:
    a. 1 cycle
    b. 1/2 cycle
    c. 3/4 cycle
    d. 1/3 cycle

53. Show the delay in cycles corresponding to each of the following degrees:

   a. 45

   b. 90

   c. 60

   d. 360

54. Draw the time-domain plot of a sine wave (for only 1 second) with a maximum amplitude of 15 volts, a frequency of 5, and a phase of 270 degrees.

55. Draw two sine waves on the same time-domain plot. The characteristics of each signal are given below:

   Signal A: amplitude 40, frequency 9, phase 0.

   Signal B: amplitude 10, frequency 9, phase 90.

56. Draw two periods of a sine wave with a phase shift of 90 degrees. On the same diagram, draw a sine wave with the same amplitude and frequency but with a 90-degree phase shift from the first.

57. What is the bandwidth of a signal that can be decomposed into four sine waves with frequencies at 0 Hz, 20 Hz, 50 Hz, and 200 Hz? All maximum amplitudes are the same. Draw the frequency spectrum.

58. A periodic composite signal with a bandwidth of 2000 Hz is composed of two sine waves. The first one has a frequency of 100 Hz with a maximum amplitude of 20 volts; the second one has a maximum amplitude of 5 volts. Draw the frequency spectrum.

59. Show how a sine wave can change its phase by drawing two periods of an arbitrary sine wave with phase shift of 0 degrees followed by the two periods of the *same signal* with a phase shift of 90 degrees.

60. Imagine we have a sine wave called *A*. Show the negative of *A*. In other words, show the signal −*A*. Can we relate the negation of a signal to the phase shift? How many degrees?

61. Which signal has a higher bandwidth: A signal that changes 100 times per second or a signal that changes 200 times per second?

62. What is the bit rate for each of the following signals?

   a. A signal in which a bit lasts 0.001 second.

   b. A signal in which a bit lasts 2 milliseconds.

   c. A signal in which 10 bits last 20 microseconds.

   d. A signal in which 1000 bits last 250 picoseconds.

63. What is the duration of a bit for each of the following signals?

   a. A signal with a bit rate of 100 bps.

   b. A signal with a bit rate of 200 Kbps.

   c. A signal with a bit rate of 5 Mbps.

   d. A signal with a bit rate of 1 Gbps.

64. A device is sending out data at the rate of 1000 bps.
    a. How long does it take to send out 10 bits?
    b. How long does it take to send out a single character (8 bits)?
    c. How long does it take to send a file of 100,000 characters?
65. What is the bit rate for the signal in Figure 4.22?

Figure 4.22   *Exercise 65*

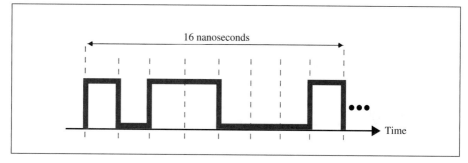

66. What is the frequency of the signal in Figure 4.23?

Figure 4.23   *Exercise 66*

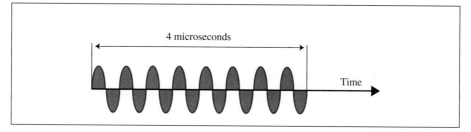

67. Draw the time-domain representation (for the first 1/100 second) of the signal shown in Figure 4.24.

Figure 4.24   *Exercise 67*

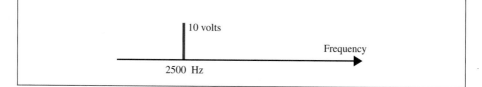

68. Draw the frequency domain representation of the signal shown in Figure 4.25.
69. What is the bandwidth of the composite signal shown in Figure 4.26?
70. What is the bandwidth of the signal shown in Figure 4.27?

Figure 4.25   *Exercise 68*

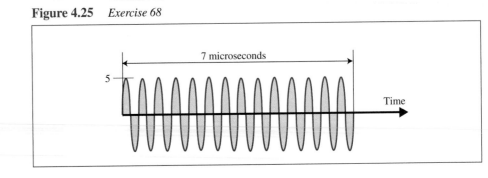

Figure 4.26   *Exercise 69*

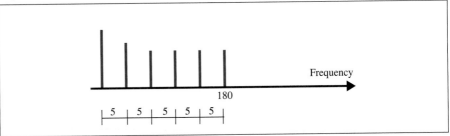

Figure 4.27   *Exercise 70*

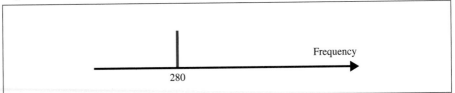

71. A composite signal contains frequencies from 10 KHz to 30 KHz, each with an amplitude of 10 volts. Draw the frequency spectrum.

72. A composite signal contains frequencies from 10 KHz to 30 KHz. The amplitude is zero for the lowest and the highest signals and 30 volts for the 20-KHz signal. Assuming that the amplitudes change gradually from the minimum to the maximum, draw the frequency spectrum.

73. Two signals have the same frequencies. However, whenever the first signal is at its maximum amplitude, the second signal has an amplitude of zero. What is the phase shift between the two signals?

CHAPTER 5

Encoding and Modulating

As we discussed in Chapter 4, information must be transformed into signals before it can be transported across communication media.

> We must transform data into signals to send them from one place to another.

How information is transformed depends on its original format and on the format used by the communication hardware. If you want to send a love letter by smoke signal, you need to know which smoke patterns match which words in your message before you actually build your fire. Words are information and puffs of smoke are a representation of that information.

A simple signal by itself does not carry information any more than a straight line conveys words. The signal must be manipulated so that it contains identifiable changes that are recognizable to the sender and receiver as representing the information intended. First the information must be translated into agreed-upon patterns of 0s and 1s, for example, using American Standard Code for Information Interchange (ASCII) tabulated in Appendix A.

Data stored in a computer are in the form of 0s and 1s. To be carried from one place to another (inside or outside the computer), data are usually converted to digital signals. This is called *digital-to-digital conversion* or *encoding digital data into a digital signal*.

Sometimes, we need to convert an analog signal (such as voice in a telephone conversation) into a digital signal for several reasons, such as to decrease the effect of noise. This is called *analog-to-digital conversion* or *digitizing an analog signal*.

At other times, we want to send a digital signal coming out of a computer through a medium designed for an analog signal. For example, to send data from one place to another using the public telephone line, the digital signal produced by the computer should be converted to an analog signal. This is called *digital-to-analog conversion* or *modulating a digital signal*.

Often an analog signal is sent over long distances using analog media. For example, voice or music from a radio station, which is naturally an analog signal, is transmitted through the air. However, the frequency of the voice or music is not appropriate for this kind of transmission; the signal should be carried by a higher-frequency signal. This is called *analog-to-analog conversion* or *modulating an analog signal.*

Figure 5.1 shows these four different conversion methods.

Figure 5.1   *Different conversion schemes*

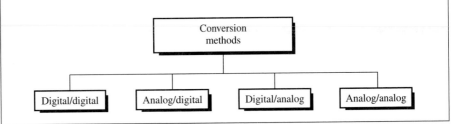

5.1   DIGITAL-TO-DIGITAL CONVERSION

Digital-to-digital encoding or conversion is the representation of digital information by a digital signal. For example, when you transmit data from your computer to your printer, both the original data and the transmitted data are digital. In this type of **encoding,** the binary 1s and 0s generated by a computer are translated into a sequence of voltage pulses that can be propagated over a wire. Figure 5.2 shows the relationship between the digital information, the digital-to-digital encoding hardware, and the resultant digital signal.

Figure 5.2   *Digital-to-digital encoding*

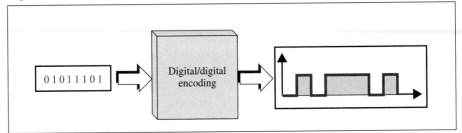

Of the many mechanisms for digital-to-digital encoding, we will discuss only those most useful for data communication. These fall into three broad categories: *unipolar, polar,* and *bipolar* (see Figure 5.3).

Unipolar encoding is simple, with only one technique in use. **Polar encoding** has three subcategories, NRZ, RZ, and biphase, two of which have multiple variations of their own. The third option, **bipolar encoding,** has three variations: AMI, B8ZS, and HDB3.

Unipolar

Unipolar encoding is very simple and very primitive. Although it is almost obsolete today, its simplicity provides an easy introduction to the concepts developed with the

Figure 5.3 *Types of digital-to-digital encoding*

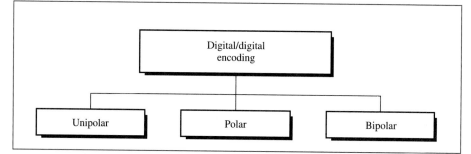

more complex encoding systems and allows us to examine the kinds of problems that any digital transmission system must overcome.

Digital transmission systems work by sending voltage pulses along a medium link, usually a wire or cable. In most types of encoding, one voltage level stands for binary 0 and another level stands for binary 1. The polarity of a pulse refers to whether it is positive or negative. Unipolar encoding is so named because it uses only one polarity. This polarity is assigned to one of the two binary states, usually the 1. The other state, usually the 0, is represented by zero voltage.

Unipolar encoding uses only one level of value.

Figure 5.4 shows the idea of unipolar encoding. In this example, the 1s are encoded as a positive value and the 0s are encoded as the zero value. In addition to being straightforward, unipolar encoding is inexpensive to implement.

Figure 5.4 *Unipolar encoding*

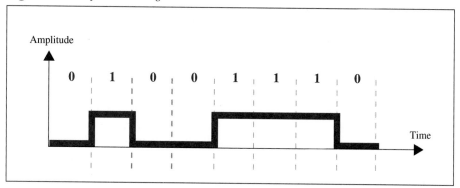

However, unipolar encoding has at least two problems that make it less desirable: a DC component and synchronization.

DC Component

The average amplitude of a unipolar encoded signal is nonzero. This creates what is called a direct current (DC) component (a component with zero frequency). When a signal contains a DC component, it cannot travel through media that cannot handle DC components.

Synchronization

When a signal is unvarying, the receiver cannot determine the beginning and ending of each bit. Therefore, a synchronization problem in unipolar encoding can occur whenever the data stream includes a long uninterrupted series of 1s or 0s. Digital encoding schemes use changes in voltage level to indicate changes in bit type. A signal change also indicates that one bit has ended and a new bit has begun. In unipolar encoding, however, a series of one kind of bit, say seven 1s, occurs with no voltage changes, just an unbroken positive voltage that lasts seven times as long as a single 1 bit. Whenever there is no signal change to indicate the start of the next bit in a sequence, the receiver has to rely on a timer. Given an expected bit rate of 1000 bps, if the receiver detects a positive voltage lasting 0.005 second, it reads one 1 per 0.001 second, or five 1s.

Unfortunately, lack of synchronization between the sender's and the receiver's clocks distorts the timing of the signal so that, for example, five 1s can be stretched to 0.006 second, causing an extra 1 bit to be read by the receiver. That one extra bit in the data stream causes everything after it to be decoded erroneously. A solution developed to control the synchronization of unipolar transmission is to use a separate, parallel line that carries a clock pulse and allows the receiving device to resynchronize its timer to that of the signal. But doubling the number of lines used for transmission increases the cost and so proves uneconomical.

Polar

Polar encoding uses two voltage levels: one positive and one negative. By using both levels, in most polar encoding methods the average voltage level on the line is reduced and the DC component problem of unipolar encoding is alleviated. In **Manchester** and **differential Manchester encoding** (see page 97), each bit consists of both positive and negative voltages, so the DC component is totally eliminated.

> Polar encoding uses two levels (positive and negative) of amplitude.

Of the many existing variations of polar encoding, we will examine only the three most popular: **nonreturn to zero (NRZ), return to zero (RZ),** and **biphase.** NRZ encoding includes two methods: **nonreturn to zero, level (NRZ-L),** and **nonreturn to zero, invert (NRZ-I).** Biphase also refers to two methods. The first, Manchester, is the method used by ethernet LANs. The second, Differential Manchester, is the method used by Token Ring LANs (see Figure 5.5).

Nonreturn to Zero (NRZ)

In NRZ encoding, the level of the signal is always either positive or negative. The two most popular methods of NRZ transmission are discussed below.

Figure 5.5 *Types of polar encoding*

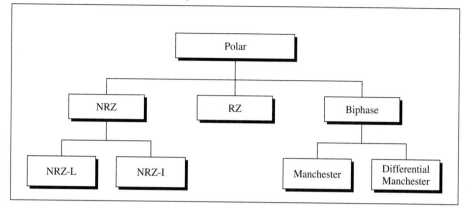

NRZ-L   In NRZ-L encoding, the level of the signal depends on the type of bit it represents. A positive voltage usually means the bit is a 0, and a negative voltage means the bit is a 1 (or vice versa); thus, the level of the signal is dependent upon the state of the bit.

> In NRZ-L the level of the signal is dependent upon the state of the bit.

A problem can arise when there is a long stream of 0s or 1s in the data. The receiver receives a continuous voltage and should determine how many bits are sent by relying on its clock, which may or may not be synchronized with the sender clock.

NRZ-I   In NRZ-I, an inversion of the voltage level represents a 1 bit. It is the transition between a positive and a negative voltage, not the voltages themselves, that represents a 1 bit. A 0 bit is represented by no change. NRZ-I is superior to NRZ-L due to the synchronization provided by the signal change each time a 1 bit is encountered. The existence of 1s in the data stream allows the receiver to resynchronize its timer to the actual arrival of the transmission. A string of 0s can still cause problems, but because 0s are not as likely, they are less of a problem.

> In NRZ-I the signal is inverted if a 1 is encountered.

Figure 5.6 shows the NRZ-L and NRZ-I representations of the same series of bits. In the NRZ-L sequence, positive and negative voltages have specific meanings: positive for 0 and negative for 1. In the NRZ-I sequence, the voltages per se are meaningless. Instead, the receiver looks for changes from one level to another as its basis for recognition of 1s.

Return to Zero (RZ)

As you can see, anytime the original data contain strings of consecutive 1s or 0s, the receiver can lose its place. As we mentioned in our discussion of unipolar encoding, one

Figure 5.6 *NRZ-L and NRZ-I encoding*

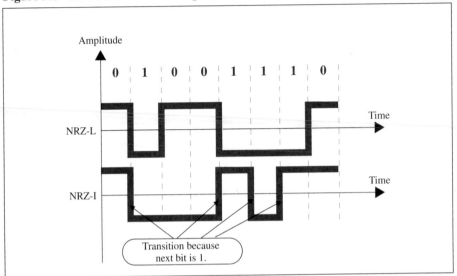

way to assure synchronization is to send a separate timing signal on a separate channel. However, this solution is both expensive and prone to errors of its own. A better solution is to somehow include synchronization in the encoded signal, something like the solution provided by NRZ-I, but one capable of handling strings of 0s as well as 1s.

To assure synchronization, there must be a signal change for each bit. The receiver can use these changes to build up, update, and synchronize its clock. As we saw above, NRZ-I accomplishes this for sequences of 1s. But to change with every bit, we need more than just two values. One solution is return to zero (RZ) encoding, which uses three values: positive, negative, and zero. In RZ, the signal changes not between bits but during each bit. Like NRZ-L, a positive voltage means 1 and a negative voltage means 0. But, unlike NRZ-L, halfway through each bit interval, the signal returns to zero. A 1 bit is actually represented by positive-to-zero and a 0 bit by negative-to-zero, rather than by positive and negative alone. Figure 5.7 illustrates the concept.

The main disadvantage of RZ encoding is that it requires two signal changes to encode one bit and therefore occupies more bandwidth. But of the three alternatives we have examined so far, it is the most effective.

A good encoded digital signal must contain a provision for synchronization.

Biphase

Probably the best existing solution to the problem of synchronization is biphase encoding. In this method, the signal changes at the middle of the bit interval but does not return to zero. Instead, it continues to the opposite pole. As in RZ, these midinterval transitions allow for synchronization.

As mentioned earlier, there are two types of biphase encoding in use on networks today: Manchester and differential Manchester.

Figure 5.7 *RZ encoding*

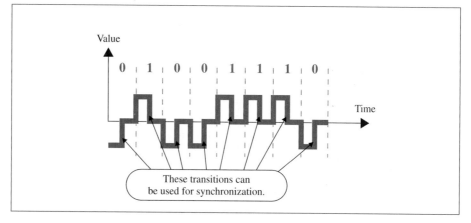

Biphase encoding is implemented in two different ways: Manchester and differential Manchester.

Manchester   Manchester encoding uses the inversion at the middle of each bit interval for both synchronization and bit representation. A negative-to-positive transition represents binary 1 and a positive-to-negative transition represents binary 0. By using a single transition for a dual purpose, Manchester encoding achieves the same level of synchronization as RZ but with only two levels of amplitude.

In Manchester encoding, the transition at the middle of the bit is used for both synchronization and bit representation.

Differential Manchester   In differential Manchester, the inversion at the middle of the bit interval is used for synchronization, but the presence or absence of an additional transition at the beginning of the interval is used to identify the bit. A transition means binary 0 and no transition means binary 1. Differential Manchester requires two signal changes to represent binary 0 but only one to represent binary 1.

In differential Manchester encoding, the transition at the middle of the bit is used only for synchronization. The bit representation is shown by the inversion or noninversion at the beginning of the bit.

Figure 5.8 shows the Manchester and differential Manchester signals for the same bit pattern.

Bipolar

Bipolar encoding, like RZ, uses three voltage levels: positive, negative, and zero. Unlike RZ, however, the zero level in bipolar encoding is used to represent binary 0.

Figure 5.8   *Manchester and differential Manchester encoding*

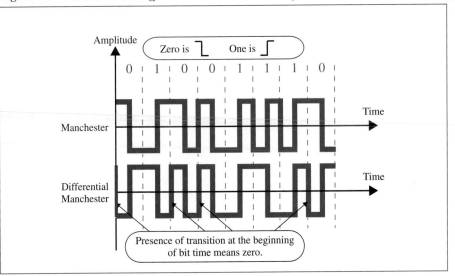

The 1s are represented by alternating positive and negative voltages. If the first 1 bit is represented by the positive amplitude, the second will be represented by the negative amplitude, the third by the positive amplitude, and so on. This alternation occurs even when the 1 bits are not consecutive.

In bipolar encoding, we use three levels: positive, zero, and negative.

Three types of bipolar encoding are in popular use by the data communications industry: AMI, B8ZS, and HDB3 (see Figure 5.9).

Figure 5.9   *Types of bipolar encoding*

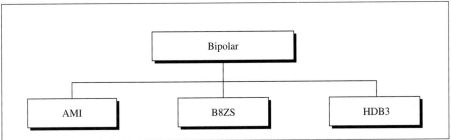

Bipolar Alternate Mark Inversion (AMI)

Bipolar **alternate mark inversion (AMI)** is the simplest type of bipolar encoding. In the name *alternate mark inversion,* the word *mark* comes from telegraphy and means 1. So AMI means alternate 1 inversion. A neutral, zero voltage represents binary 0. Binary

1s are represented by alternating positive and negative voltages. Figure 5.10 gives an example.

Figure 5.10 *Bipolar AMI encoding*

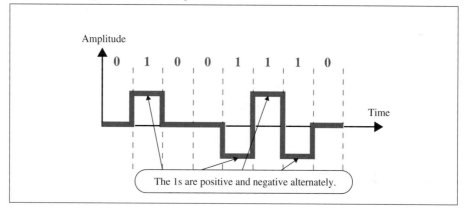

The 1s are positive and negative alternately.

A variation of bipolar AMI is called **pseudoternary,** in which binary 0 alternates between positive and negative voltages.

By inverting on each occurrence of a 1, bipolar AMI accomplishes two things: first, the DC component is zero, and second, a long sequence of 1s stays synchronized. There is no mechanism to ensure the synchronization of a long string of 0s.

Two variations of bipolar AMI have been developed to solve the problem of synchronizing sequential 0s, especially for long-distance transmission. The first, used in North America, is called **bipolar 8-zero substitution (B8ZS).** The second, used in Europe and Japan, is called **high-density bipolar 3 (HDB3).** Both are adaptations of bipolar AMI that modify the original pattern only in the case of multiple consecutive 0s.

Bipolar 8-Zero Substitution (B8ZS)

B8ZS is the convention adopted in North America to provide synchronization of long strings of 0s. In most situations, B8ZS functions identically to bipolar AMI. Bipolar AMI changes poles with every 1 it encounters. These changes provide the synchronization needed by the receiver. But the signal does not change during a string of 0s, so synchronization is often lost.

The difference between B8ZS and bipolar AMI occurs whenever eight or more consecutive 0s are encountered in the data stream. The solution provided by B8ZS is to force artificial signal changes, called violations, within the 0 string. Anytime eight 0s occur in succession, B8ZS introduces changes in the pattern based on the polarity of the previous 1 (the 1 occurring just before the 0s). See Figure 5.11.

If the previous 1 bit was positive, the eight 0s will be encoded as zero, zero, zero, positive, negative, zero, negative, positive. Remember that the receiver is looking for alternating polarities to identify 1s. When it finds two consecutive positive charges surrounding three 0s, it recognizes the pattern as a deliberately introduced violation and not an error. It then looks for the second pair of the expected violations. When it finds them, the receiver translates all eight bits to 0s and reverts back to normal bipolar AMI mode.

If the polarity of the previous 1 is negative, the pattern of violations is the same but with inverted polarities. Both positive and negative patterns are shown in Figure 5.11.

Figure 5.11   *B8ZS encoding*

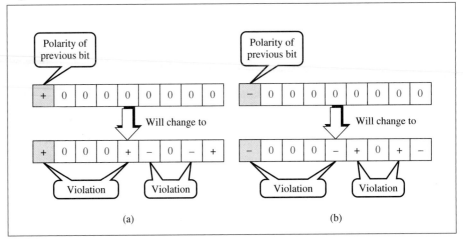

(a)   (b)

In B8ZS if eight 0s come one after another, we change the pattern in one of two ways based on the polarity of the previous 1.

High-Density Bipolar 3 (HDB3)

The problem of synchronizing strings of consecutive 0s is solved differently in Europe and Japan than in the United States. This convention, called HDB3, introduces changes into the bipolar AMI pattern every time four consecutive 0s are encountered instead of waiting for the eight expected by B8ZS in North America. Although the name is HDB3, the pattern changes whenever there are four 0s in succession (see Figure 5.12).

Figure 5.12   *HDB3 encoding*

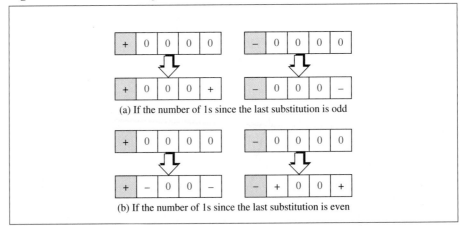

> In HDB3 if four 0s come one after another, we change the pattern in one of four ways based on the polarity of the previous 1 and the number of 1s since the last substitution.

As in B8ZS, the pattern of violations in HDB3 is based on the polarity of the previous 1 bit. But unlike B8ZS, HDB3 also looks at the number of 1s that have occurred in the bit stream since the last substitution. Whenever the number of 1s since the last substitution is odd, B8ZS puts a violation in the place of the fourth consecutive 0. If the polarity of the previous bit was positive, the violation is positive. If the polarity of the previous bit was negative, the violation is negative.

Whenever the number of 1s since the last substitution is even, B8ZS puts violations in the places of both the first and the fourth consecutive 0s. If the polarity of the previous bit was positive, both violations are negative. If the polarity of the previous bit was negative, both violations are positive. All four patterns are shown in Figure 5.12.

As you can see, the point is to violate the standard pattern in ways that a machine can recognize as deliberate, and to use those violations to synchronize the system.

Example 5.1

Using B8ZS, encode the bit stream 10000000000100. Assume that the polarity of the first 1 is positive.

Solution
See Figure 5.13.

Figure 5.13   *Solution to Example 5.1*

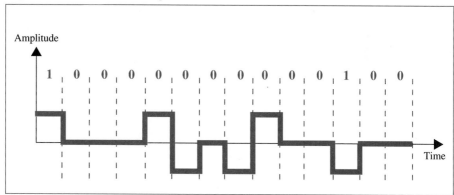

Example 5.2

Using HDB3, encode the bit stream 10000000000100. Assume that the number of 1s so far is odd and the first 1 is positive.

Solution
See Figure 5.14.

Figure 5.14   *Solution to Example 5.2*

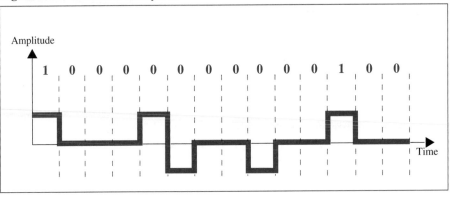

5.2   ANALOG-TO-DIGITAL CONVERSION

We sometimes need to digitize an analog signal. For example, to send human voice over a long distance, we need to digitize it since digital signals are less prone to noise. This is called an **analog-to-digital conversion** or digitizing an analog signal. This requires a reduction of the potentially infinite number of values in an analog message so that they can be represented as a digital stream with a minimum loss of information. Several methods for analog-to-digital conversion will be discussed later in this chapter. Figure 5.15 shows the analog-to-digital converter, called a codec (coder-decoder).

Figure 5.15   *Analog-to-digital conversion*

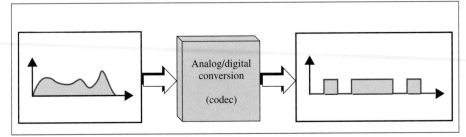

In analog-to-digital conversion, we are representing the information contained in a continuous wave form as a series of digital pulses (1s or 0s).

Analog-to-digital conversion can make use of any of the digital signals discussed in Section 5.1. The structure of the transporting signal is not the problem. Instead, the problem is how to translate information from an infinite number of values to a discrete number of values without sacrificing sense or quality.

Pulse Amplitude Modulation (PAM)

The first step in analog-to-digital conversion is called **pulse amplitude modulation (PAM).** This technique takes an analog signal, samples it, and generates a series of pulses based on the results of the sampling. The term **sampling** means measuring the amplitude of the signal at equal intervals.

The method of sampling used in PAM is more useful to other areas of engineering than it is to data communication. However, PAM is the foundation of an important analog-to-digital conversion method called **pulse code modulation (PCM).**

In PAM, the original signal is sampled at equal intervals as shown in Figure 5.16. PAM uses a technique called sample and hold. At a given moment, the signal level is

Figure 5.16   *PAM*

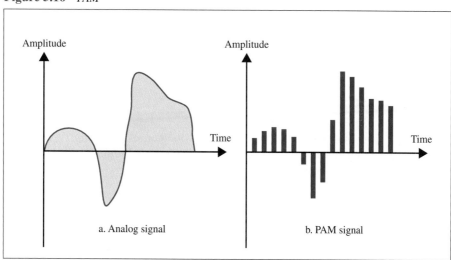

a. Analog signal

b. PAM signal

read, then held briefly. The sampled value occurs only instantaneously in the actual wave form, but is generalized over a still short but measurable period in the PAM result.

The reason PAM is not useful to data communications is that, although it translates the original wave form to a series of pulses, these pulses are still of any amplitude (still an analog signal, not digital). To make them digital, we must modify them by using pulse code modulation (PCM).

> Pulse amplitude modulation (PAM) has some applications, but it is not used by itself in data communication. However, it is the first step in another very popular conversion method called pulse code modulation (PCM).

Pulse Code Modulation (PCM)

PCM modifies the pulses created by PAM to create a completely digital signal. To do so, PCM first quantizes the PAM pulses. Quantization is a method of assigning integral values in a specific range to sampled instances. The result of quantization is presented in Figure 5.17.

Figure 5.17   *Quantized PAM signal*

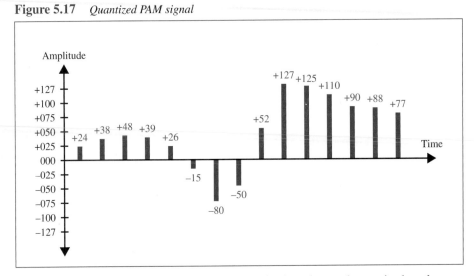

Figure 5.18 shows a simple method of assigning sign and magnitude values to quantized samples. Each value is translated into its seven-bit binary equivalent. The eighth bit indicates the sign.

Figure 5.18   *Quantizing using sign and magnitude*

+024	00011000	−015	10001111	+125	01111101
+038	00100110	−080	11010000	+110	01101110
+048	00110000	−050	10110010	+090	01011010
+039	00100111	+052	00110110	+088	01011000
+026	00011010	+127	01111111	+077	01001101

Sign bit
+ is 0 − is 1

The binary digits are then transformed into a digital signal using one of the digital-to-digital encoding techniques. Figure 5.19 shows the result of the pulse code modulation of the original signal encoded finally into a unipolar signal. Only the first three sampled values are shown.

PCM is actually made up of four separate processes: PAM, quantization, binary encoding, and digital-to-digital encoding. Figure 5.20 shows the entire process in graphic form. PCM is the sampling method used to digitize voice in T-line transmission in the North American telecommunication system (see Chapter 8).

Sampling Rate

As you can tell from the preceding figures, the accuracy of any digital reproduction of an analog signal depends on the number of samples taken. Using PAM and PCM, we

Figure 5.19 *PCM*

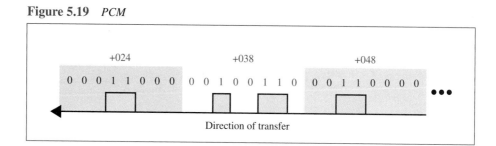

Figure 5.20 *From analog signal to PCM digital code*

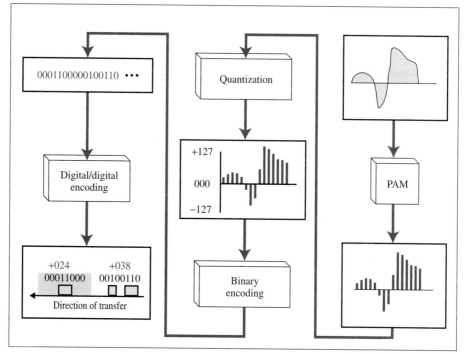

can reproduce the wave form exactly by taking infinite samples, or we can reproduce the barest generalization of its direction of change by taking three samples. Obviously, we prefer to find a number somewhere between these two extremes. So the question is, How many samples are sufficient?

Actually, it requires remarkably little information for the receiving device to reconstruct an analog signal. According to the **Nyquist theorem,** to ensure the accurate reproduction of an original analog signal using PAM, the **sampling rate** must be at least twice the highest frequency of the original signal. So if we want to sample telephone voice with maximum frequency 4000 Hz, we need a sampling rate of 8000 samples per second.

According to the Nyquist theorem, the sampling rate must be at least two times the highest frequency.

A sampling rate of twice the frequency of *x* Hz means that the signal must be sampled every 1/2 *x* seconds. Using the voice-over-phone-lines example above, that means one sample every 1/8000 second. Figure 5.21 illustrates the concept.

Figure 5.21   *Nyquist theorem*

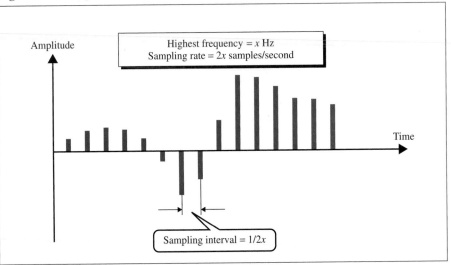

Example 5.3

What sampling rate is needed for a signal with a bandwidth of 10,000 Hz (1,000 to 11,000 Hz)?

Solution

The sampling rate must be twice the highest frequency in the signal:

$$\text{Sampling rate} = 2(11,000) = 22,000 \text{ samples/second}$$

How Many Bits per Sample?

After we have found the sampling rate, we need to determine the number of bits to be transmitted for each sample. This depends on the level of precision needed. The number of bits are chosen such that the original signal can be reproduced with the desired precision in amplitude.

Example 5.4

A signal is sampled. Each sample requires at least 12 levels of precision (+0 to +5 and –0 to –5). How many bits should be sent for each sample?

Solution

We need four bits; one bit for the sign and three bits for the value. A three-bit value can represent $2^3 = 8$ levels (000 to 111), which is more than what we need. A two-bit value is not enough since $2^2 = 4$. A four-bit value is too much because $2^4 = 16$.

Bit Rate

After finding the number of bits per sample, we can calculate the bit rate using the following formula:

$$\text{Bit rate} = \text{Sampling rate} \times \text{Number of bits per sample}$$

Example 5.5

We want to digitize the human voice. What is the bit rate assuming eight bits per sample?

Solution

The human voice normally contains frequencies from 0 to 4000 Hz. So the sampling rate is:

$$\text{Sampling rate} = 4000 \times 2 = 8000 \text{ samples/second}$$

The bit rate can be calculated as:

$$\text{Bit rate} = \text{Sampling rate} \times \text{Number of bits per sample} = 8000 \times 8 = 64{,}000 \text{ bits/s} = 64 \text{ Kbps}$$

5.3   DIGITAL-TO-ANALOG CONVERSION

Digital-to-analog conversion or **digital-to-analog modulation** is the process of changing one of the characteristics of an analog signal based on the information in a digital signal (0s and 1s). When you transmit data from one computer to another across a public access phone line, for example, the original data are digital, but because telephone wires carry analog signals, the data must be converted. The digital data must be modulated on an analog signal that has been manipulated to look like two distinct values corresponding to binary 1 and binary 0. Figure 5.22 shows the relationship between the digital information, the digital-to-analog modulating hardware, and the resultant analog signal.

Figure 5.22   *Digital-to-analog modulation*

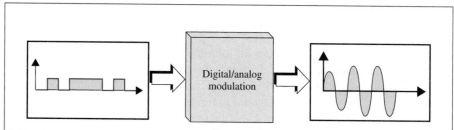

Of the many mechanisms for digital-to-analog modulation, we will discuss only those most useful for data communications.

As discussed in Chapter 4, a sine wave is defined by three characteristics: **amplitude, frequency,** and **phase.** When we vary any one of these characteristics, we create a second version of that wave. If we then say that the original wave represents binary 1, the variation can represent binary 0, or vice versa. So, by changing one aspect of a simple electrical signal back and forth, we can use it to represent digital data. Any of the three characteristics listed above can be altered in this way, giving us at least three mechanisms for modulating digital data into an analog signal: *amplitude shift keying (ASK), frequency shift keying (FSK),* and *phase shift keying (PSK).* In addition, there is a fourth (and better) mechanism that combines changes in both amplitude and phase called *quadrature amplitude modulation (QAM).* QAM is the most efficient of these options and is the mechanism used in all modern modems (see Figure 5.23).

Figure 5.23   *Types of digital-to-analog modulation*

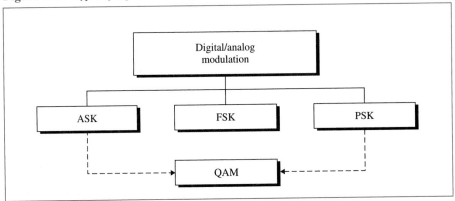

Aspects of Digital-to-Analog Conversion

Before we discuss specific methods of digital-to-analog modulation, two basic issues must be defined: bit/baud rate and carrier signal.

Bit Rate and Baud Rate

Two terms used frequently in data communication are *bit rate* and *baud rate.* Bit rate is the number of bits transmitted during one second. **Baud rate** refers to the number of signal units per second that are required to represent those bits. In discussions of computer efficiency, the bit rate is the more important—we want to know how long it takes to process each piece of information. In data transmission, however, we are more concerned with how efficiently we can move those data from place to place, whether in pieces or blocks. The fewer signal units required, the more efficient the system and the less bandwidth required to transmit more bits; so we are more concerned with baud rate. The baud rate determines the bandwidth required to send the signal.

Bit rate equals the baud rate times the number of bits represented by each signal unit. The baud rate equals the bit rate divided by the number of bits represented by each signal shift. Bit rate is always greater than or equal to the baud rate.

> Bit rate is the number of bits per second. Baud rate is the number of signal units per second. Baud rate is less than or equal to the bit rate.

An analogy can clarify the concept of bauds and bits. In transportation, a baud is analogous to a car, a bit is analogous to a passenger. A car can carry one or more passengers. If 1000 cars go from one point to another carrying only one passenger (the driver), then 1000 passengers are transported. However, if each car carries four passengers (carpooling), then 4000 passengers are transported. Note that the number of cars, not the number of passengers, determines the traffic and, therefore, the need for wider highways. Similarly, the number of bauds determines the required bandwidth, not the number of bits.

Example 5.6

An analog signal carries four bits in each signal element. If 1000 signal elements are sent per second, find the baud rate and the bit rate.

Solution

$$\text{Baud rate} = \text{Number of signal elements} = 1000 \text{ bauds per second}$$

$$\text{Bit rate} = \text{Baud rate} \times \text{Number of bits per signal element} = 1000 \times 4 = 4000 \text{ bps}$$

Example 5.7

The bit rate of a signal is 3000. If each signal element carries six bits, what is the baud rate?

Solution

$$\text{Baud rate} = \text{Bit rate} / \text{Number of bits per signal element} = 3000 / 6 = 500 \text{ baud per second}$$

Carrier Signal

In analog transmission, the sending device produces a high-frequency signal that acts as a basis for the information signal. This base signal is called the **carrier signal** or carrier frequency. The receiving device is tuned to the frequency of the carrier signal that it expects from the sender. Digital information is then modulated on the carrier signal by modifying one or more of its characteristics (amplitude, frequency, phase). This kind of modification is called modulation (or shift keying) and the information signal is called a modulating signal.

Amplitude Shift Keying (ASK)

In **amplitude shift keying (ASK),** the strength of the carrier signal is varied to represent binary 1 or 0. Both frequency and phase remain constant while the amplitude changes. Which voltage represents 1 and which represents 0 is left to the system designers. A bit duration is the period of time that defines one bit. The peak amplitude of the signal during each bit duration is constant and its value depends on the bit (0 or 1). The speed of transmission using ASK is limited by the physical characteristics of the transmission medium. Figure 5.24 gives a conceptual view of ASK.

Unfortunately, ASK transmission is highly susceptible to noise interference. The term *noise* refers to unintentional voltages introduced onto a line by various phenomena such as heat or electromagnetic induction created by other sources. These unintentional voltages combine with the signal to change the amplitude. A 0 can be changed to 1, and a 1 to 0. You can see how noise would be especially problematic for ASK, which relies solely on amplitude for recognition. Noise usually affects the amplitude; therefore, ASK is the modulating method most affected by noise.

Figure 5.24   *ASK*

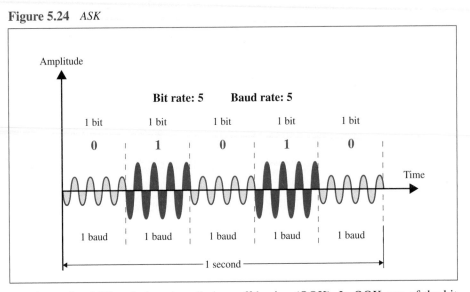

A popular ASK technique is called on-off-keying (OOK). In OOK one of the bit values is represented by no voltage. The advantage is a reduction in the amount of energy required to transmit information.

Bandwidth for ASK

As you will recall from Chapter 4, the bandwidth of a signal is the total range of frequencies occupied by that signal. When we decompose an ASK-modulated signal, we get a spectrum of many simple frequencies. However, the most significant ones are those between $f_c - N_{baud}/2$ and $f_c + N_{baud}/2$ with the carrier frequency, f_c, at the middle. (see Figure 5.25).

Figure 5.25   *Relationship between baud rate and bandwidth in ASK*

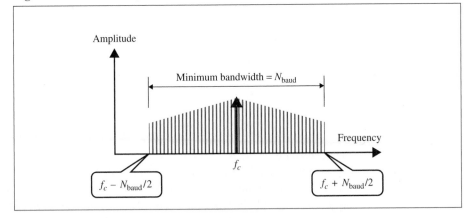

Bandwidth requirements for ASK are calculated using the formula

$$BW = (1 + d) \times N_{baud}$$

where
BW is the bandwidth
N_{baud} is the baud rate
d is a factor related to the condition of the line (with a minimum value of 0)

As you can see, the minimum bandwidth required for transmission is equal to the baud rate.

Although there is only one carrier frequency, the process of modulation produces a complex signal that is a combination of many simple signals, each with a different frequency.

Example 5.8

Find the minimum bandwidth for an ASK signal transmitting at 2000 bps. The transmission mode is half-duplex.

Solution

In ASK the baud rate and bit rate are the same. The baud rate is therefore 2000. An ASK signal requires a minimum bandwidth equal to its baud rate. Therefore, the minimum bandwidth is 2000 Hz.

Example 5.9

Given a bandwidth of 5000 Hz for an ASK signal, what are the baud rate and bit rate?

Solution

In ASK the baud rate is the same as the bandwidth, which means the baud rate is 5000. But because the baud rate and the bit rate are also the same for ASK, the bit rate is 5000 bps.

Example 5.10

Given a bandwidth of 10,000 Hz (1000 to 11,000 Hz), draw the full-duplex ASK diagram of the system. Find the carriers and the bandwidths in each direction. Assume there is no gap between the bands in two directions.

Solution

For full-duplex ASK, the bandwidth for each direction is

$$BW = 10,000/2 = 5000 \text{ Hz}$$

The carrier frequencies can be chosen at the middle of each band (see Figure 5.26).

$$f_{c(forward)} = 1000 + 5000/2 = 3500 \text{ Hz}$$

$$f_{c(backward)} = 11,000 - 5000/2 = 8500 \text{ Hz}$$

Frequency Shift Keying (FSK)

In **frequency shift keying (FSK),** the frequency of the carrier signal is varied to represent binary 1 or 0. The frequency of the signal during each bit duration is constant and

Figure 5.26   *Solution to Example 5.10*

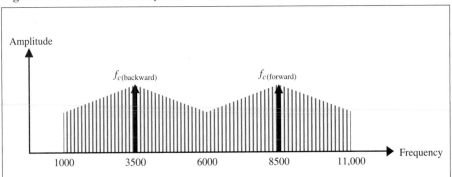

its value depends on the bit (0 or 1): both peak amplitude and phase remain constant. Figure 5.27 gives the conceptual view of FSK.

FSK avoids most of the noise problems of ASK. Because the receiving device is looking for specific frequency changes over a given number of periods, it can ignore voltage spikes. The limiting factors of FSK are the physical capabilities of the carrier.

Figure 5.27   *FSK*

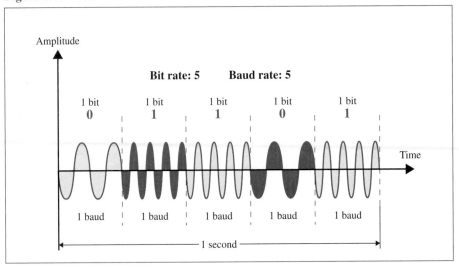

Bandwidth for FSK

Although FSK shifts between two carrier frequencies, it is easier to analyze as two coexisting frequencies. We can say that the FSK spectrum is the combination of two ASK spectra centered around f_{c0} and f_{c1}. The bandwidth required for FSK transmission is equal to the baud rate of the signal plus the frequency shift (difference between the two carrier frequencies): $BW = (f_{c1} - f_{c0}) + N_{baud}$. See Figure 5.28.

Although there are only two carrier frequencies, the process of modulation produces a composite signal that is a combination of many simple signals, each with a different frequency.

Figure 5.28   *Relationship between baud rate and bandwidth in FSK*

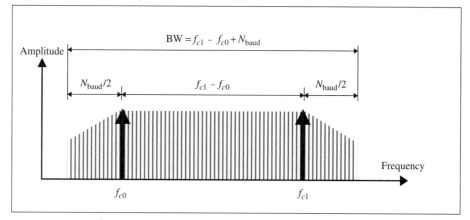

Example 5.11

Find the minimum bandwidth for an FSK signal transmitting at 2000 bps. Transmission is in half-duplex mode and the carriers must be separated by 3000 Hz.

Solution

For FSK, if f_{c1} and f_{c0} are the carrier frequencies, then

$$BW = \text{Baud rate} + (f_{c1} - f_{c0})$$

However, the baud rate here is the same as the bit rate. Therefore,

$$BW = \text{Bit rate} + (f_{c1} - f_{c0}) = 2000 + 3000 = 5000 \text{ Hz}$$

Example 5.12

Find the maximum bit rates for an FSK signal if the bandwidth of the medium is 12,000 Hz and the difference between the two carriers must be at least 2000 Hz. Transmission is in full-duplex mode.

Solution

Because the transmission is full duplex, only 6000 Hz is allocated for each direction. For FSK, if f_{c1} and f_{c0} are the carrier frequencies,

$$BW = \text{Baud rate} + (f_{c1} - f_{c0})$$

$$\text{Baud rate} = BW - (f_{c1} - f_{c0}) = 6000 - 2000 = 4000$$

But because the baud rate is the same as the bit rate, the bit rate is 4000 bps.

Phase Shift Keying (PSK)

In **phase shift keying (PSK),** the phase of the carrier is varied to represent binary 1 or 0. Both peak amplitude and frequency remain constant as the phase changes. For example, if we start with a phase of 0 degrees to represent binary 0, then we can change the phase to 180 degrees to send binary 1. The phase of the signal during each bit duration is constant and its value depends on the bit (0 or 1). Figure 5.29 gives a conceptual view of PSK.

Figure 5.29   *PSK*

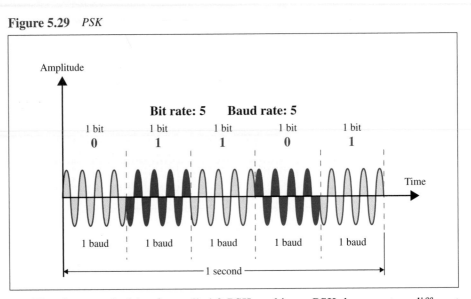

The above method is often called 2-PSK, or binary PSK, because two different phases (0 and 180 degrees) are used. Figure 5.30 makes this point clearer by showing the relationship of phase to bit value. A second diagram, called a **constellation** or phase-state diagram, shows the same relationship by illustrating only the phases.

Figure 5.30   *PSK constellation*

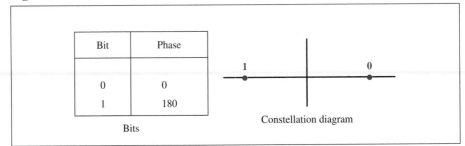

PSK is not susceptible to the noise degradation that affects ASK, nor to the bandwidth limitations of FSK. This means that smaller variations in the signal can be detected reliably by the receiver. Therefore, instead of utilizing only two variations of a signal, each representing one bit, we can use four variations and let each **phase shift** represent two bits (see Figure 5.31).

The constellation diagram for the signal in Figure 5.31 is given in Figure 5.32. A phase of 0 degrees now represents 00; 90 degrees represents 01; 180 degrees represents 10; and 270 degrees represents 11. This technique is called 4-PSK or Q-PSK. The pair of bits represented by each phase is called a **dibit.** We can transmit data two times as fast using 4-PSK as we can using 2-PSK.

We can extend this idea to 8-PSK. Instead of 90 degrees, we now vary the signal by shifts of 45 degrees. With eight different phases, each shift can represent three bits (one **tribit**) at a time. (As you can see, the relationship of number of bits per shift to number

Figure 5.31   *4-PSK*

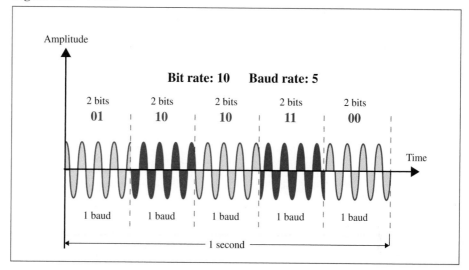

Figure 5.32   *4-PSK characteristics*

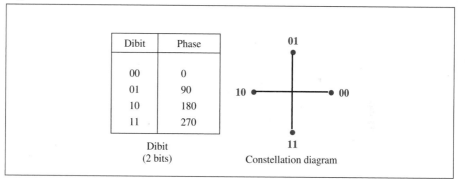

of phases is a power of two. When we have four possible phases, we can send two bits at a time—2^2 equals 4. When we have eight possible phases, we can send three bits at a time—2^3 equals 8). Figure 5.33 shows the relationships between the phase shifts and the tribits each one represents: 8-PSK is three times faster than 2-PSK.

Bandwidth for PSK

The minimum bandwidth required for PSK transmission is the same as that required for ASK transmission—and for the same reasons. As we have seen, the maximum bit rate in PSK transmission, however, is potentially much greater than that of ASK. So while the maximum baud rates of ASK and PSK are the same for a given bandwidth, PSK bit rates using the same bandwidth can be two or more times greater (see Figure 5.34).

Example 5.13

Find the bandwidth for a 4-PSK signal transmitting at 2000 bps. Transmission is in half-duplex mode.

Figure 5.33 *8-PSK characteristics*

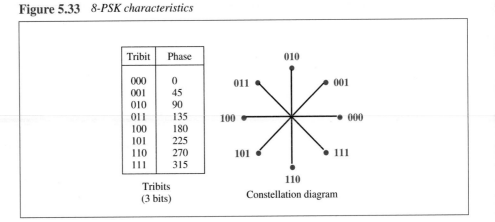

Figure 5.34 *Relationship between baud rate and bandwidth in PSK*

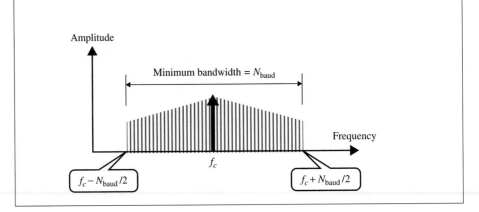

Solution

For 4-PSK the baud rate is half of the bit rate. The baud rate is therefore 1000. A PSK signal requires a bandwidth equal to its baud rate. Therefore, the bandwidth is 1000 Hz.

Example 5.14

Given a bandwidth of 5000 Hz for an 8-PSK signal, what are the baud rate and bit rate?

Solution

For PSK the baud rate is the same as the bandwidth, which means the baud rate is 5000. But in 8-PSK the bit rate is three times the baud rate, so the bit rate is 15,000 bps.

Quadrature Amplitude Modulation (QAM)

PSK is limited by the ability of the equipment to distinguish small differences in phase. This factor limits its potential bit rate.

So far, we have been altering only one of the three characteristics of a sine wave at a time, but what if we alter two? Bandwidth limitations make combinations of FSK with other changes practically useless. But why not combine ASK and PSK? Then we could have *x* variations in phase and *y* variations in amplitude, giving us *x* times *y* possible variations and the corresponding number of bits per variation. **Quadrature amplitude modulation (QAM)** does just that. The term *quadrature* is derived from the restrictions required for minimum performance and is related to trigonometry.

> Quadrature amplitude modulation (QAM) means combining ASK and PSK in such a way that we have maximum contrast between each bit, dibit, tribit, quadbit, and so on.

Possible variations of QAM are numerous. Theoretically, any measurable number of changes in amplitude can be combined with any measurable number of changes in phase. Figure 5.35 shows two possible configurations, 4-QAM and 8-QAM. In both cases, the number of amplitude shifts is fewer than the number of phase shifts. Because amplitude changes are susceptible to noise and require greater shift differences than do phase changes, the number of phase shifts used by a QAM system is always larger than the number of amplitude shifts. The time-domain plot corresponding to the 8-QAM signal in Figure 5.35 is shown in Figure 5.36.

Figure 5.35   *4-QAM and 8-QAM constellations*

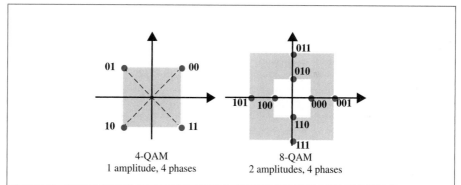

Other geometric relationships are also possible. Three popular 16-QAM configurations are shown in Figure 5.37. The first example, three amplitudes and 12 phases, handles noise best because of a greater ratio of phase shift to amplitude. It is the ITU-T recommendation. The second example, four amplitudes and eight phases, is the OSI recommendation. If you examine the graph carefully, you will notice that although it is based on concentric circles, not every intersection of phase and amplitude is utilized. In fact, 4 times 8 should allow for 32 possible variations. But by using only half of those possibilities, the measurable differences between shifts are increased and greater signal readability is ensured. In addition, several QAM designs link specific amplitudes with specific phases. This means that even with the noise problems associated with amplitude shifting, the meaning of a shift can be recovered from phase information. In general, therefore, a second advantage of QAM over ASK is its lower susceptibility to noise.

Figure 5.36   *Time domain for an 8-QAM signal*

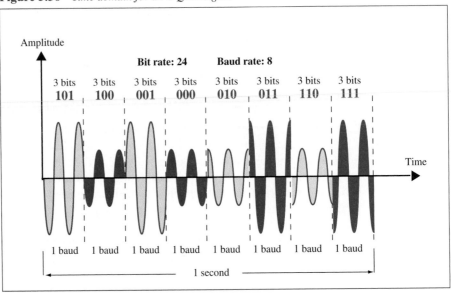

Figure 5.37   *16-QAM constellations*

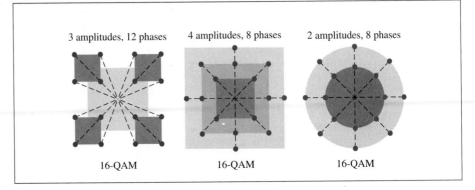

Bandwidth for QAM

The minimum bandwidth required for QAM transmission is the same as that required for ASK and PSK transmission. QAM has the same advantages as PSK over ASK.

Bit/Baud Comparison

Assuming that an FSK signal over voice-grade phone lines can send 1200 bits per second, the bit rate is 1200 bps. Each frequency shift represents a single bit; so it requires 1200 signal elements to send 1200 bits. Its baud rate, therefore, is also 1200 bps. Each signal variation in an 8-QAM system, however, represents three bits. So a bit rate of 1200 bps, using 8-QAM, has a baud rate of only 400. As Figure 5.38 shows, a dibit system has a baud rate of one-half the bit rate, a tribit system has a baud rate of one-third the bit rate, and a **quadbit** system has a baud rate of one-fourth the bit rate.

Figure 5.38 *Bit and baud*

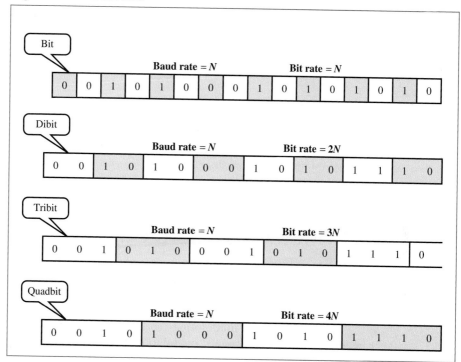

Table 5.1 shows the comparative bit and baud rates for the various methods of digital-to-analog modulation.

Table 5.1 *Bit and baud rate comparison*

Modulation	Units	Bits/Baud	Baud Rate	Bit Rate
ASK, FSK, 2-PSK	Bit	1	N	N
4-PSK, 4-QAM	Dibit	2	N	2N
8-PSK, 8-QAM	Tribit	3	N	3N
16-QAM	Quadbit	4	N	4N
32-QAM	Pentabit	5	N	5N
64-QAM	Hexabit	6	N	6N
128-QAM	Septabit	7	N	7N
256-QAM	Octabit	8	N	8N

Example 5.15

A constellation diagram consists of eight equally spaced points on a circle. If the bit rate is 4800 bps, what is the baud rate?

Solution

The constellation indicates 8-PSK with the points 45 degrees apart. Since $2^3 = 8$, three bits are transmitted with each signal element. Therefore, the baud rate is

$$4800/3 = 1600 \text{ baud}$$

Example 5.16

Compute the bit rate for a 1000-baud 16-QAM signal.

Solution

A 16-QAM signal means that there are four bits per signal element since $2^4 = 16$. Thus,

$$(1000)(4) = 4000 \text{ bps}$$

Example 5.17

Compute the baud rate for a 72,000-bps 64-QAM signal.

Solution

A 64-QAM signal means that there are six bits per signal element since $2^6 = 64$. Thus,

$$72,000/6 = 12,000 \text{ baud}$$

5.4 ANALOG-TO-ANALOG CONVERSION

Analog-to-analog conversion is the representation of analog information by an analog signal. Radio, that familiar utility, is an example of an analog-to-analog communication. Figure 5.39 shows the relationship between the analog information, the analog-to-analog conversion hardware, and the resultant analog signal.

Analog-to-analog modulation can be accomplished in three ways: **amplitude modulation (AM), frequency modulation (FM),** and **phase modulation (PM).** See Figure 5.40.

Figure 5.39 *Analog-to-analog modulation*

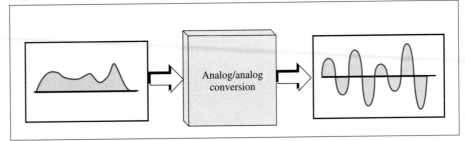

Figure 5.40 *Types of analog-to-analog modulation*

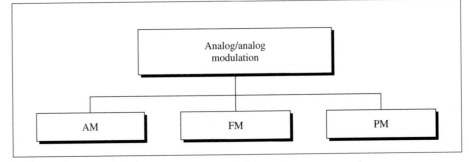

Amplitude Modulation (AM)

In AM transmission, the carrier signal is modulated so that its amplitude varies with the changing amplitudes of the modulating signal. The frequency and phase of the carrier remain the same; only the amplitude changes to follow variations in the information. Figure 5.41 shows how this concept works. The modulating signal becomes an envelope to the carrier.

Figure 5.41   *Amplitude modulation*

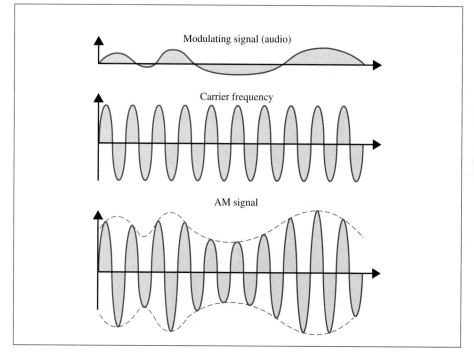

AM Bandwidth

The bandwidth of an AM signal is equal to twice the bandwidth of the modulating signal and covers a range centered around the carrier frequency (see Figure 5.42). The shaded portion of the graph is the frequency spectrum of the signal.

The bandwidth of an audio signal (speech and music) is usually 5 KHz. Therefore, an AM radio station needs a minimum bandwidth of 10 KHz. In fact, the Federal Communications Commission (FCC) allows 10 KHz for each AM station.

AM stations are allowed carrier frequencies anywhere between 530 and 1700 KHz (1.7 MHz). However, each station's carrier frequency must be separated from those on either side of it by at least 10 KHz (one AM bandwidth) to avoid interference. If one station uses a carrier frequency of 1100 KHz, the next station's carrier frequency cannot be lower than 1110 KHz (see Figure 5.43).

> The total bandwidth required for AM can be determined from the bandwidth of the audio signal: $BW_t = 2 \times BW_m$.

Figure 5.42   *AM bandwidth*

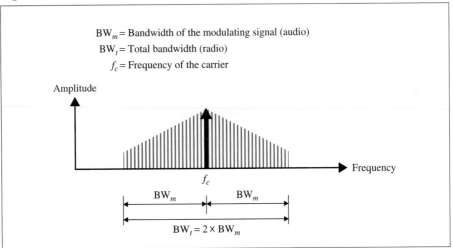

Figure 5.43   *AM band allocation*

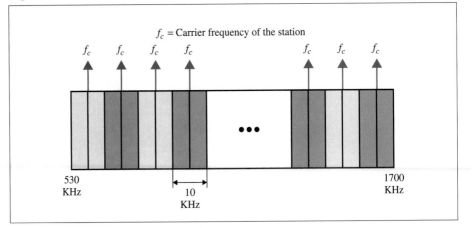

Example 5.18

We have an audio signal with a bandwidth of 4 KHz. What is the bandwidth needed if we modulate the signal using AM? Ignore FCC regulations, for now.

Solution

An AM signal requires twice the bandwidth of the original signal:

$$BW = 2 \times 4 \text{ KHz} = 8 \text{ KHz}$$

Frequency Modulation (FM)

In FM transmission, the frequency of the carrier signal is modulated to follow the changing voltage level (amplitude) of the modulating signal. The peak amplitude and phase of the carrier signal remain constant, but as the amplitude of the information signal changes, the frequency of the carrier changes correspondingly. Figure 5.44 shows the relationships of the modulating signal, the carrier signal, and the resultant FM signal.

Figure 5.44   *Frequency modulation*

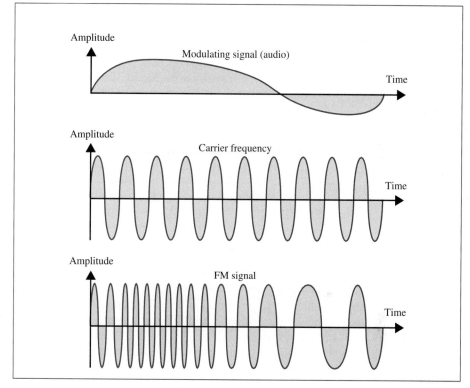

FM Bandwidth

The bandwidth of an FM signal is equal to 10 times the bandwidth of the modulating signal and, like AM bandwidths, covers a range centered around the carrier frequency. Figure 5.45 shows both the bandwidth, and, in the shaded portion, the frequency spectrum of an FM signal.

> The total bandwidth required for FM can be determined from the bandwidth of the audio signal: $BW_t = 10 \times BW_m$.

The bandwidth of an audio signal (speech and music) broadcast in stereo is almost 15 KHz. Each FM radio station, therefore, needs a minimum bandwidth of 150 KHz. The FCC allows 200 KHz (0.2 MHz) for each station to provide some room for guard bands.

The bandwidth of a stereo audio signal is usually 15 KHz. Therefore, an FM station needs at least a bandwidth of 150 KHz. The FCC requires the minimum bandwidth to be at least 200 KHz (0.2 MHz).

Figure 5.45   *FM bandwidth*

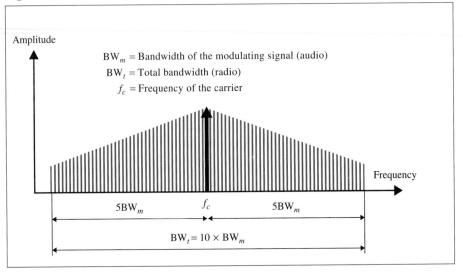
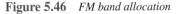

FM stations are allowed carrier frequencies anywhere between 88 and 108 MHz. Stations must be separated by at least 200 KHz to keep their bandwidths from overlapping. To create even more privacy, the FCC requires that in a given area, only alternate bandwidth allocations may be used. The others remain unused to prevent any possibility of two stations interfering with each other. Given 88 to 108 MHz as a range, there are 100 potential FM bandwidths in an area, of which 50 can operate at any one time. Figure 5.46 illustrates this concept.

Figure 5.46   *FM band allocation*

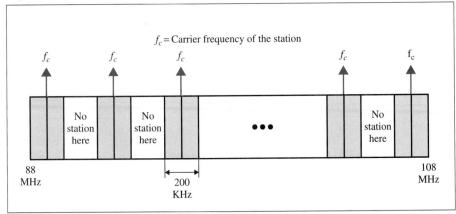

Example 5.19

We have an audio signal with a bandwidth of 4 MHz. What is the bandwidth needed if we modulate the signal using FM? Ignore FCC regulations.

Solution

An FM signal requires 10 times the bandwidth of the original signal:

$$BW = 10 \times 4 \text{ MHz} = 40 \text{ MHz}$$

Phase Modulation (PM)

Due to simpler hardware requirements, phase modulation (PM) is used in some systems as an alternative to frequency modulation. In PM transmission, the phase of the carrier signal is modulated to follow the changing voltage level (amplitude) of the modulating signal. The peak amplitude and frequency of the carrier signal remain constant, but as the amplitude of the information signal changes, the phase of the carrier changes correspondingly. The analysis and the final result (modulated signal) are similar to those of frequency modulation.

5.5   KEY TERMS AND CONCEPTS

alternate mark inversion (AMI)

amplitude

amplitude modulation (AM)

amplitude shift keying (ASK)

analog-to-analog modulation

analog-to-digital conversion

baud rate

biphase (encoding)

bipolar 8-zero substitution (B8ZS)

bipolar encoding

carrier signal

constellation

dibit

differential Manchester encoding

digital-to-analog modulation

digital-to-digital encoding

encoding

frequency

frequency modulation (FM)

frequency shift keying (FSK)

high-density bipolar 3 (HDB3)

Manchester encoding

nonreturn to zero (NRZ)

nonreturn to zero, invert (NRZ-I)

nonreturn to zero, level (NRZ-L)

Nyquist theorem

phase	quadbit
phase modulation (PM)	quadrature amplitude modulation (QAM)
phase shift	
phase shift keying (PSK)	return to zero (RZ)
polar encoding	sampling
pseudoternary	sampling rate
pulse amplitude modulation (PAM)	tribit
pulse code modulation (PCM)	unipolar encoding

5.6 SUMMARY

- There are four types of conversion:
  - a. Digital-to-digital.
  - b. Analog-to-digital.
  - c. Digital-to-analog.
  - d. Analog-to-analog.
- Categories of digital-to-digital encoding include the following:
  - a. Unipolar—one voltage level is used.
  - b. Polar—two voltage levels are used. Variations of polar encoding include the following:
    NRZ (non-return to zero)
    NRZ-L (non-return to zero, level)
    NRZ-I (non-return to zero, invert)
    RZ (return to zero)
    Biphase: Manchester and differential Manchester
  - c. Bipolar—ones are represented by alternating positive and negative voltages:
    AMI (alternate mark inversion)
    B8ZS (bipolar 8-zero substitution)
    HDB3 (high-density bipolar 3)
- Analog-to-digital conversion relies on PCM (pulse code modulation).
- PCM involves sampling, quantizing each sample to a set number of bits, and then assigning voltage levels to the bits.
- The Nyquist theorem says that the sampling rate must be at least twice the highest frequency component in the original signal.
- Digital-to-analog modulation can be accomplished using the following:
  - a. Amplitude shift keying (ASK)—the amplitude of the carrier signal varies.
  - b. Frequency shift keying (FSK)—the frequency of the carrier signal varies.

c. Phase shift keying (PSK)—the phase of the carrier signal varies.

d. Quadrature amplitude modulation (QAM)—both the phase and amplitude of the carrier signal vary.

■ QAM enables a higher data transmission rate than other digital-to-analog methods.

■ Baud rate and bit rate are not synonymous. Bit rate is the number of bits transmitted per second. Baud rate is the number of signal units transmitted per second. One signal unit can represent one or more bits.

■ The minimum required bandwidth for ASK and PSK is the baud rate.

■ The minimum required bandwidth (BW) for FSK modulation is $BW = f_{c1} - f_{c0} + N_{baud}$, where f_{c1} is the frequency representing a 1 bit, f_{c0} is the frequency representing a 0 bit, and N_{baud} is the baud rate.

■ Analog-to-analog modulation can be implemented using the following:

a. Amplitude modulation (AM).

b. Frequency modulation (FM).

c. Phase modulation (PM).

■ In AM the amplitude of the carrier wave varies with the amplitude of the modulating wave.

■ In FM the frequency of the carrier wave varies with the amplitude of the modulating wave.

■ In AM radio, the bandwidth of the modulated signal must be twice the bandwidth of the modulating signal.

■ In FM radio, the bandwidth of the modulated signal must be 10 times the bandwidth of the modulating signal.

■ In PM the phase of the carrier signal varies with the amplitude of the modulating signal.

5.7   PRACTICE SET

Review Questions

1. What is the difference between encoding and modulation?
2. What is digital-to-digital encoding?
3. What is analog-to-digital conversion?
4. What is digital-to-analog conversion?
5. What is analog-to-analog conversion?
6. Why is frequency modulation superior to amplitude modulation?
7. What is the advantage of QAM over ASK or PSK?
8. How do the three categories of digital-to-digital encoding differ?
9. What is the DC component?
10. Why is synchronization a problem in data communications?

11. How does NRZ-L differ from NRZ-I?

12. Discuss the two types of biphase encoding in use on networks.

13. What is the major disadvantage in using NRZ encoding? How do RZ encoding and biphase encoding attempt to solve the problem?

14. Compare and contrast RZ and bipolar AMI.

15. What are the three types of bipolar encoding?

16. Compare and contrast B8ZS and HDB3 encoding.

17. List the steps that take an analog signal to PCM digital code.

18. How does the sampling rate affect the transmitted digital signal?

19. How does the number of bits allotted for each sample affect the transmitted digital signal?

20. What are the four methods that convert a digital signal to an analog signal?

21. What is the difference between bit rate and baud rate? Give an example where both are the same. Give an example where they are different.

22. What is modulation?

23. What is the purpose of a carrier signal in modulation?

24. How is baud rate related to transmission bandwidth in ASK?

25. How is baud rate related to transmission bandwidth in FSK?

26. How is baud rate related to transmission bandwidth in PSK?

27. What kind of information can be obtained from a constellation diagram?

28. How is baud rate related to transmission bandwidth in QAM?

29. How is QAM related to ASK and PSK?

30. What is the major factor that makes PSK superior to ASK?

31. How does AM differ from ASK?

32. How does FM differ from FSK?

33. Compare the FM bandwidth with the AM bandwidth in terms of the modulating signal.

Multiple Choice Questions

34. ASK, PSK, FSK, and QAM are examples of _____ modulation.
    a. digital-to-digital
    b. digital-to-analog
    c. analog-to-analog
    d. analog-to-digital

35. Unipolar, bipolar, and polar encoding are types of _____ encoding.
    a. digital-to-digital
    b. digital-to-analog
    c. analog-to-analog
    d. analog-to-digital

36. PCM is an example of _____ conversion.
    a. digital-to-digital
    b. digital-to-analog
    c. analog-to-analog
    d. analog-to-digital

37. AM and FM are examples of _____ modulation.
    a. digital-to-digital
    b. digital-to-analog
    c. analog-to-analog
    d. analog-to-digital

38. In QAM, both phase and _____ of a carrier frequency are varied.
    a. amplitude
    b. frequency
    c. bit rate
    d. baud rate

39. Which of the following is most affected by noise?
    a. PSK
    b. ASK
    c. FSK
    d. QAM

40. If the frequency spectrum of a signal has a bandwidth of 500 Hz with the highest frequency at 600 Hz, what should be the sampling rate according to the Nyquist theorem?
    a. 200 samples/sec
    b. 500 samples/sec
    c. 1000 samples/sec
    d. 1200 samples/sec

41. If the baud rate is 400 for a 4-PSK signal, the bit rate is _____ bps.
    a. 100
    b. 400
    c. 800
    d. 1600

42. If the bit rate for an ASK signal is 1200 bps, the baud rate is _____.
    a. 300
    b. 400
    c. 600
    d. 1200

43. If the bit rate for an FSK signal is 1200 bps, the baud rate is _____.
    a. 300
    b. 400

c. 600

d. 1200

44. If the bit rate for a QAM signal is 3000 bps and a signal element is represented by a tribit, what is the baud rate?

a. 300

b. 400

c. 1000

d. 1200

45. If the baud rate for a QAM signal is 3000 and a signal element is represented by a tribit, what is the bit rate?

a. 300

b. 400

c. 1000

d. 9000

46. If the baud rate for a QAM signal is 1800 and the bit rate is 9000, how many bits are there per signal element?

a. 3

b. 4

c. 5

d. 6

47. In 16-QAM, there are 16 _____.

a. combinations of phase and amplitude

b. amplitudes

c. phases

d. bits per second

48. Which modulation technique involves tribits, eight different phase shifts, and one amplitude?

a. FSK

b. 8-PSK

c. ASK

d. 4-PSK

49. The Nyquist theorem specifies the minimum sampling rate to be_____.

a. equal to the lowest frequency of a signal

b. equal to the highest frequency of a signal

c. twice the bandwidth of a signal

d. twice the highest frequency of a signal

50. Given an AM radio signal with a bandwidth of 10 KHz and the highest frequency component at 705 KHz, what is the frequency of the carrier signal?

a. 700 KHz

b. 705 KHz

c. 710 KHz

d. cannot be determined from given information

51. One factor in the accuracy of a reconstructed PCM signal is the _____.

    a. signal bandwidth

    b. carrier frequency

    c. number of bits used for quantization

    d. baud rate

52. Which encoding type always has a nonzero average amplitude?

    a. unipolar

    b. polar

    c. bipolar

    d. all of the above

53. Which of the following encoding methods does not provide for synchronization?

    a. NRZ-L

    b. RZ

    c. B8ZS

    d. HDB3

54. Which encoding method uses alternating positive and negative values for 1s?

    a. NRZ-I

    b. RZ

    c. Manchester

    d. AMI

55. Deliberate violations of alternate mark inversion are used in which type of digital-to-digital encoding?

    a. AMI

    b. B8ZS

    c. RZ

    d. Manchester

56. A modulated signal is formed by _____.

    a. changing the modulating signal by the carrier wave

    b. changing the carrier wave by the modulating signal

    c. quantization of the source data

    d. sampling at the Nyquist frequency

57. If FCC regulations are followed, the carrier frequencies of adjacent AM radio stations are _____ apart.

    a. 5 KHz

    b. 10 KHz

    c. 200 KHz

    d. 530 KHz

58. If FCC regulations are followed, _____ potential FM stations are theoretically possible in a given area.
    a. 50
    b. 100
    c. 133
    d. 150

59. In PCM, an analog-to- _____ conversion occurs.
    a. analog
    b. digital
    c. QAM
    d. differential

60. If the maximum value of a PCM signal is 31 and the minimum value is −31, how many bits were used for coding?
    a. 4
    b. 5
    c. 6
    d. 7

61. When an ASK signal is decomposed, the result is _____.
    a. always one sine wave
    b. always two sine waves
    c. an infinite number of sine waves
    d. none of the above

62. RZ encoding involves _____ level(s) of signal amplitude.
    a. 1
    b. 3
    c. 4
    d. 5

63. Which quantization level results in a more faithful reproduction of the signal?
    a. 2
    b. 8
    c. 16
    d. 32

64. Which encoding technique attempts to solve the loss of synchronization due to long strings of 0s?
    a. B8ZS
    b. HDB3
    c. AMI
    d. a and b

65. Which conversion type involves modulation of a signal?

    a. digital-to-digital conversion

    b. analog-to-digital conversion

    c. digital-to-analog conversion

    d. all of the above

66. Which conversion type needs sampling of a signal?

    a. digital-to-digital conversion

    b. analog-to-digital conversion

    c. digital-to-analog conversion

    d. all of the above

67. The bandwidth of an FM signal requires 10 times the bandwidth of the _____ signal.

    a. carrier

    b. modulating

    c. bipolar

    d. sampling

68. Modulation of an analog signal can be accomplished through modulation of the _____ of the carrier signal.

    a. amplitude

    b. frequency

    c. phase

    d. any of the above

69. Modulation of a digital signal can be accomplished through modulation of the _____ of the carrier signal.

    a. amplitude

    b. frequency

    c. phase

    d. any of the above

Exercises

70. If the bit rate of a signal is 1000 bits/seconds, how many bits can be sent in 5 seconds? How many bits in 1/5 second? How many bits in 100 milliseconds?

71. Assume a data stream is made of ten 0s. Encode this stream using the following encoding schemes. How many changes (vertical line) can you find for each scheme?

    a. unipolar

    b. polar NRZ-L

    c. polar NRZ-I

d. RZ

e. Manchester

f. Differential Manchester

g. AMI

h. pseudoternary

i. B8ZS

j. HDB3

72. Repeat Exercise 71 for a data stream of ten 1s.

73. Repeat Exercise 71 for a data stream of ten alternating 0s and 1s.

74. Repeat Exercise 71 for a data stream of three 0s followed by two 1s followed by two 0s and another three 1s.

75. Figure 5.47 is the unipolar encoding of a data stream. What is the data stream?

Figure 5.47 *Exercise 75*

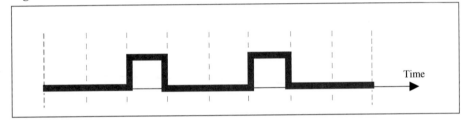

76. Figure 5.48 is the NRZ-L encoding of a data stream. What is the data stream?

Figure 5.48 *Exercises 76 and 77*

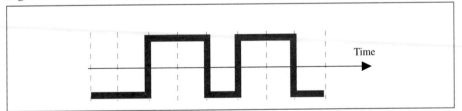

77. Repeat Exercise 76 if the figure is the NRZ-I encoding of a data stream.

78. Figure 5.49 is the RZ encoding of a data stream. What is the data stream?

Figure 5.49 *Exercise 78*

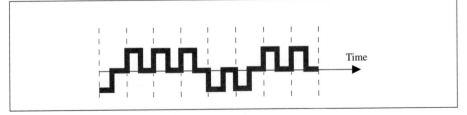

79. Figure 5.50 is the Manchester encoding of a data stream. What is the data stream?

Figure 5.50 *Exercises 79 and 80*

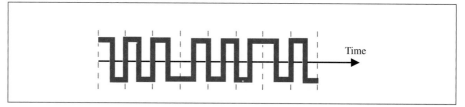

80. Repeat Exercise 79 if the figure is the differential Manchester encoding of a data stream?
81. Figure 5.51 is the AMI encoding of a data stream. What is the data stream?

Figure 5.51 *Exercises 81 and 82*

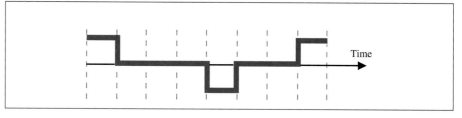

82. Repeat Exercise 81 if the figure is the pseudoternary encoding of a data stream.
83. Figure 5.52 is the B8ZS encoding of a data stream. What is the data stream?

Figure 5.52 *Exercise 83*

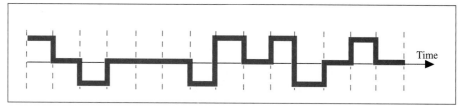

84. Figure 5.53 is the HDB3 encoding of a data stream. What is the data stream?

Figure 5.53 *Exercise 84*

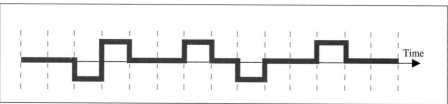

85. How many amplitude levels are there for each of the following methods?
    a. Unipolar
    b. NRZ-L
    c. NRZ-I
    d. RZ
    e. Manchester
    f. Differential Manchester

86. What is the sampling rate for PCM if the frequency ranges from 1000 to 4000 Hz?

87. Using the Nyquist theorem, calculate the sampling rate for the following analog signals:
    a. An analog signal with bandwidth of 2000 Hz.
    b. An analog signal with frequencies from 2000 to 6000 Hz.
    c. A signal with a horizontal line in the time-domain representation.
    d. A signal with a vertical line in the time-domain representation.

88. If a signal is sampled 8000 times per second, what is the interval between each sample?

89. If the interval between two samples in a digitized signal is 125 microseconds, what is the sampling rate?

90. A signal is sampled. Each sample represents one of four levels. How many bits are needed to represent each sample? If the sampling rate is 8000 samples per second, what is the bit rate?

91. Calculate the baud rate for the given bit rate and type of modulation:
    a. 2000 bps, FSK
    b. 4000 bps, ASK
    c. 6000 bps, 2-PSK
    d. 6000 bps, 4-PSK
    e. 6000 bps, 8-PSK
    f. 4000 bps, 4-QAM
    g. 6000 bps, 16-QAM
    h. 36,000 bps, 64-QAM

92. Calculate the baud rate for the given bit rate and bit combination:
    a. 2000 bps, dibit
    b. 6000 bps, tribit
    c. 6000 bps, quadbit
    d. 6000 bps, bit

93. Calculate the bit rate for the given baud rate and type of modulation.
    a. 1000 baud, FSK
    b. 1000 baud, ASK
    c. 1000 baud, 8-PSK
    d. 1000 baud, 16-QAM

94. Draw the constellation diagram for the following:
    a. ASK, amplitudes of 1 and 3.
    b. 2-PSK, amplitude of 1 at 0 and 180 degrees.
95. Data from a source ranges in value between -1.0 and 1.0. To what do the data points 0.91, -0.25, 0.56, and 0.71 transform if eight-bit quantization is used?
96. The data points of a constellation are at $(4, 0)$ and $(6, 0)$. Draw the constellation. Show the amplitude and phase for each point. Is the modulation ASK, PSK, or QAM? How many bits per baud can one send with this constellation?
97. Repeat Exercise 96 if the data points are at $(4, 5)$ and $(8, 10)$.
98. Repeat Exercise 96 if the data points are at $(4, 0)$ and $(-4, 0)$.
99. Repeat Exercise 96 if the data points are at $(4, 4)$ and $(-4, 4)$.
100. Repeat Exercise 96 if the data points are at $(4, 0)$, $(4, 4)$, $(-4, 0)$, and $(-4, -4)$.
101. Does the constellation in Figure 5.54 represent ASK, FSK, PSK, or QAM?

Figure 5.54   *Exercise 101*

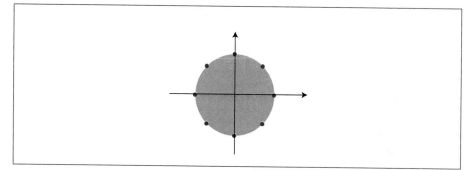

102. Does the constellation in Figure 5.55 represent ASK, FSK, PSK, or QAM?

Figure 5.55   *Exercise 102*

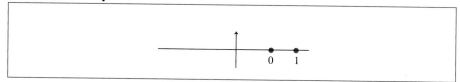

103. Does the constellation in Figure 5.56 represent ASK, FSK, PSK, or QAM?
104. Does the constellation in Figure 5.57 represent ASK, FSK, PSK, or QAM?
105. Can a constellation have 12 points? Why or why not?
106. Can a constellation have 18 points? Why or why not?
107. Can you define a general rule for the number of points in a constellation?
108. If the number of points in a constellation is eight, how many bits can we send per baud?

Figure 5.56 Exercise 103

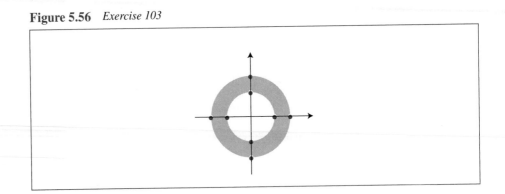

Figure 5.57 Exercise 104

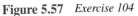

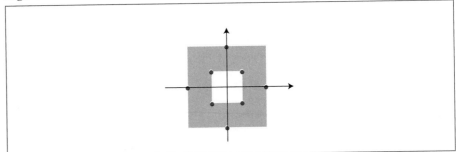

109. Calculate the bandwidth required for each of the following AM stations. Disregard FCC rules.
    a. Modulating signal with a bandwidth of 4 KHz.
    b. Modulating signal with a bandwidth of 8 KHz.
    c. Modulating signal with frequencies of 2000 to 3000 Hz.
110. Calculate the bandwidth required for each of the following FM stations. Disregard FCC rules.
    a. Modulating signal with a bandwidth of 12 KHz.
    b. Modulating signal with a bandwidth of 8 KHz.
    c. Modulating signal with frequencies of 2000 to 3000 Hz.

CHAPTER 6

Transmission of Digital Data: Interfaces and Modems

Once we have encoded our information into a format that can be transmitted, the next step is to investigate the transmission process itself. Information-processing equipment generates encoded signals but ordinarily requires assistance to transmit those signals over a communication link. For example, a PC generates a digital signal but needs an additional device to modulate a carrier frequency before it is sent over a telephone line. How do we relay encoded data from the generating device to the next device in the process? The answer is a bundle of wires, a sort of minicommunication link, called an **interface.**

Because an interface links two devices not necessarily made by the same manufacturer, its characteristics must be defined and standards must be established. Characteristics of an interface include its mechanical specifications (how many wires are used to transport the signal), its electrical specifications (the frequency, amplitude, and phase of the expected signal), and its functional specifications (if multiple wires are used, what does each one do?). These characteristics are all described by several popular standards and are incorporated in the physical layer of the OSI model.

6.1 DIGITAL DATA TRANSMISSION

Of primary concern when considering the transmission of data from one device to another is the wiring, and of primary concern when considering the wiring is the data stream. Do we send one bit at a time, or do we group bits into larger groups and, if so, how? The transmission of binary data across a link can be accomplished either in parallel mode or serial mode. In parallel mode, multiple bits are sent with each clock pulse. In serial mode, one bit is sent with each clock pulse. While there is only one way to send parallel data, there are two subclasses of serial transmission: synchronous and asynchronous (see Figure 6.1).

Figure 6.1 *Data transmission*

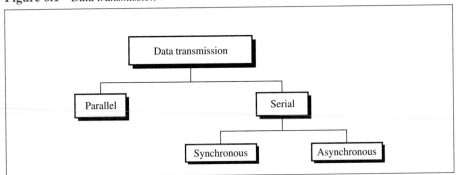

Parallel Transmission

Binary data, consisting of 1s and 0s, may be organized into groups of n bits each. Computers produce and consume data in groups of bits much as we conceive of and use spoken language in the form of words rather than letters. By grouping, we can send data n bits at a time instead of one. This is called **parallel transmission.**

The mechanism for parallel transmission is a conceptually simple one: use n wires to send n bits at one time. That way each bit has its own wire, and all n bits of one group can be transmitted with each clock pulse from one device to another. Figure 6.2 shows how parallel transmission works for $n = 8$. Typically, the eight wires are bundled in a cable with a connector at each end.

Figure 6.2 *Parallel transmission*

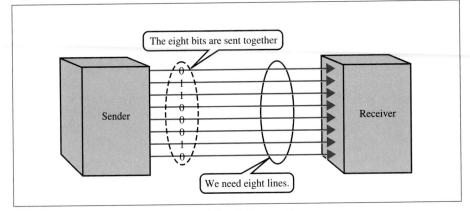

The advantage of parallel transmission is speed. All else being equal, parallel transmission can increase the transfer speed by a factor of n over serial transmission. But there is a significant disadvantage: cost. Parallel transmission requires n communication lines (wires in the example) just to transmit the data stream. Because this is expensive, parallel transmission is usually limited to short distances.

Serial Transmission

In **serial transmission** one bit follows another, so we need only one communication channel rather than *n* to transmit data between two communicating devices (see Figure 6.3).

Figure 6.3   *Serial transmission*

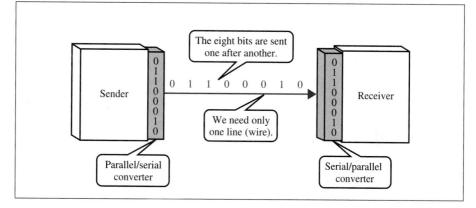

The advantage of serial over parallel transmission is that with only one communication channel, serial transmission reduces the cost of transmission over parallel by roughly a factor of *n*.

Since communication within devices is parallel, conversion devices are required at the interface between the sender and the line (parallel-to-serial) and between the line and the receiver (serial-to-parallel).

Serial transmission occurs in one of two ways: asynchronous or synchronous.

Asynchronous Transmission

Asynchronous transmission is so named because the timing of a signal is unimportant. Instead, information is received and translated by agreed-upon patterns. As long as those patterns are followed, the receiving device can retrieve the information without regard to the rhythm in which it is sent. Patterns are based on grouping the bit stream into bytes. Each group, usually eight bits, is sent along the link as a unit. The sending system handles each group independently, relaying it to the link whenever ready, without regard to a timer.

Without a synchronizing pulse, the receiver cannot use timing to predict when the next group will arrive. To alert the receiver to the arrival of a new group, therefore, an extra bit is added to the beginning of each byte. This bit, usually a 0, is called the **start bit.** To let the receiver know that the byte is finished, one or more additional bits are appended to the end of the byte. These bits, usually 1s, are called **stop bits.** By this method, each byte is increased in size to at least 10 bits, of which 8 are information and 2 or more are signals to the receiver. In addition, the transmission of each byte may then be followed by a gap of varying duration. This gap can be represented either by an idle channel or by a stream of additional stop bits.

> In asynchronous transmission, we send one start bit (0) at the beginning and one or more stop bits (1s) at the end of each byte. There may be a gap between each byte.

The start and stop bits and the gap alert the receiver to the beginning and end of each byte and allow it to synchronize with the data stream. This mechanism is called asynchronous because, at the byte level, sender and receiver do not have to be synchronized. But within each byte, the receiver must still be synchronized with the incoming bit stream. That is, some synchronization is required, but only for the duration of a single byte. The receiving device resynchronizes at the onset of each new byte. When the receiver detects a start bit, it sets a timer and begins counting bits as they come in. After *n* bits, the receiver looks for a stop bit. As soon as it detects the stop bit, it ignores any received pulses until it detects the next start bit.

> Asynchronous here means "asynchronous at the byte level," but the bits are still synchronized; their durations are the same.

Figure 6.4 is a schematic illustration of asynchronous transmission. In this example, the start bits are 0s, the stop bits are 1s, and the gap is represented by an idle line rather than by additional stop bits.

Figure 6.4 *Asynchronous transmission*

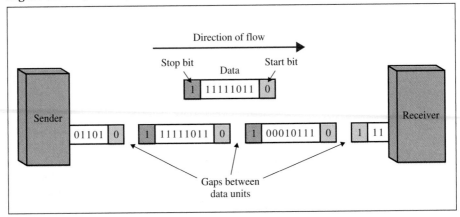

The addition of stop and start bits and the insertion of gaps into the bit stream make asynchronous transmission slower than forms of transmission that can operate without the addition of control information. But it is cheap and effective, two advantages that make it an attractive choice for situations like low-speed communication. For example, the connection of a terminal to a computer is a natural application for asynchronous transmission. A user types only one character at a time, types extremely slowly in data processing terms, and leaves unpredictable gaps of time between each character.

Synchronous Transmission

In **synchronous transmission,** the bit stream is combined into longer "frames," which may contain multiple bytes. Each byte, however, is introduced onto the transmission link without a gap between it and the next one. It is left to the receiver to separate the bit stream into bytes for decoding purposes. In other words, data are transmitted as an unbroken string of 1s and 0s, and the receiver separates that string into the bytes, or characters, it needs to reconstruct the information.

> In synchronous transmission, we send bits one after another without start/stop bits or gaps. It is the responsibility of the receiver to group the bits.

Figure 6.5 gives a schematic illustration of synchronous transmission. We have drawn in the divisions between bytes. In reality, those divisions do not exist; the sender puts its data onto the line as one long string. If the sender wishes to send data in separate bursts, the gaps between bursts must be filled with a special sequence of 0s and 1s that means *idle*. The receiver counts the bits as they arrive and groups them in eight-bit units.

Figure 6.5   *Synchronous transmission*

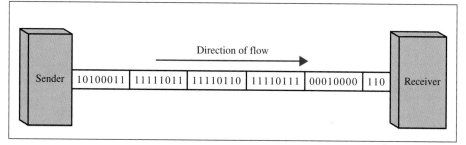

Without gaps and start/stop bits, there is no built-in mechanism to help the receiving device adjust its bit synchronization in midstream. Timing becomes very important, therefore, because the accuracy of the received information is completely dependent on the ability of the receiving device to keep an accurate count of the bits as they come in.

The advantage of synchronous transmission is speed. With no extra bits or gaps to introduce at the sending end and remove at the receiving end and, by extension, with fewer bits to move across the link, synchronous transmission is faster than asynchronous transmission. For this reason, it is more useful for high-speed applications like the transmission of data from one computer to another. Byte synchronization is accomplished in the data link layer.

6.2   DTE-DCE INTERFACE

At this point we must clarify two terms important to computer networking: **data terminal equipment (DTE)** and **data circuit–terminating equipment (DCE).** There are usually four basic functional units involved in the communication of data: a DTE and DCE on one end and a DCE and DTE on the other end, as shown in Figure 6.6. The DTE generates the data and passes them, along with any necessary control characters, to a DCE. The DCE converts the signal to a format appropriate to the transmission medium and introduces it onto the network link. When the signal arrives at the receiving end, this process is reversed.

Figure 6.6   *DTEs and DCEs*

Data Terminal Equipment (DTE)

Data terminal equipment (DTE) includes any unit that functions either as a source of or as a destination for binary digital data. At the physical layer, it can be a terminal, microcomputer, computer, printer, fax machine, or any other device that generates or consumes digital data. DTEs do not often communicate directly with one another; they generate and consume information but need an intermediary to be able to communicate. Think of a DTE as operating the way your brain does when you talk. Let's say you have an idea that you want to communicate to a friend. Your brain creates the idea but cannot transmit that idea to your friend's brain by itself. Unfortunately or fortunately, we are not a species of mind readers. Instead, your brain passes the idea to your vocal chords and mouth, which convert it to sound waves that can travel through the air or over a telephone line to your friend's ear and from there to his or her brain, where it is converted back into information. In this model, your brain and your friend's brain are DTEs. Your vocal chords and mouth are your DCE. His or her ear is also a DCE. The air or telephone wire is your transmission medium.

> A DTE is any device that is a source of or destination for binary digital data.

Data Circuit–Terminating Equipment (DCE)

Data circuit–terminating equipment (DCE) includes any functional unit that transmits or receives data in the form of an analog or digital signal through a network. At the physical layer, a DCE takes data generated by a DTE, converts them to an appropriate signal, and then introduces the signal onto the telecommunication link. Commonly used DCEs at this layer include modems (modulator/demodulators, discussed in Section 6.4). In any network, a DTE generates digital data and passes them to a DCE; the DCE converts the data to a form acceptable to the transmission medium and sends the converted signal to another DCE on the network. The second DCE takes the signal off the line, converts it to a form usable by its DTE, and delivers it. To make this communication possible, both the sending and receiving DCEs must use the same modulating method (e.g., FSK), much the way that if you want to communicate to someone who understands only Japanese, you must speak Japanese. The two DTEs do not need to be coordinated with each other, but each must be coordinated with its own DCE and the DCEs must be coordinated so that data translation occurs without loss of integrity.

> A DCE is any device that transmits or receives data in the form of an analog or digital signal through a network.

Standards

Over the years, many standards have been developed to define the connection between a DTE and a DCE (see Figure 6.7). Though their solutions differ, each standard provides a model for the mechanical, electrical, and functional characteristics of the connection.

Figure 6.7   *DTE-DCE interface*

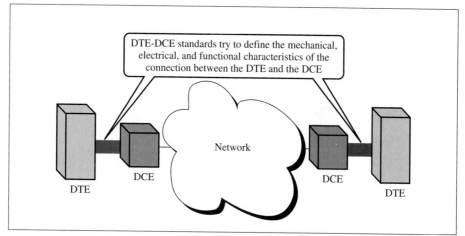

Of the organizations involved in DTE-DCE interface standards, the most active are the Electronic Industries Association (EIA) and the International Telecommunication Union–Telecommunication Standards Committee (ITU-T). The EIA standards are called, appropriately enough, EIA-232, EIA-442, EIA-449, and so on. The ITU-T standards are called the **V series** and the X series.

> The EIA and the ITU-T have been involved in developing DTE-DCE interface standards. The EIA standards are called EIA-232, EIA-442, EIA-449, and so on. The ITU-T standards are called the V series and the X series.

EIA-232 Interface

One important interface standard developed by the EIA is the **EIA-232,** which defines the mechanical, electrical, and functional characteristics of the interface between a

DTE and a DCE. Originally issued in 1962 as the RS-232 standard (recommended standard), the EIA-232 has been revised several times. The most recent version, EIA-232-D, defines not only the type of connectors to be used but also the specific cable and plugs and the functionality of each pin.

> EIA-232 (previously called RS-232) defines the mechanical, electrical, and functional characteristics of the interface between a DTE and a DCE.

Mechanical Specification

The mechanical specification of the EIA-232 standard defines the interface as a 25-wire cable with a male and a female DB-25 pin connector attached to either end. The length of the cable may not exceed 15 meters (about 50 feet).

A **DB-25** connector is a plug with 25 pins or receptacles, each of which is attached to a single wire with a specific function. With this design, the EIA has created the possibility of 25 separate interactions between a DTE and a DCE. Fewer are actually used in current practice, but the standard allows for future inclusion of functionality.

The EIA-232 calls for a 25-wire cable terminated at one end by a male connector and at the other end by a female connector. The term *male connector* refers to a plug with each wire in the cable connecting to a pin. The term *female connector* refers to a receptacle with each wire in the cable connecting to a metal tube, or sheath. In the DB-25 connector, these pins and tubes are arranged in two rows, with 13 on the top and 12 on the bottom.

As we will see in the next section, another implementation of EIA-232 uses a 9-wire cable with a male and a female DB-9 pin connector attached to either end.

Electrical Specification

The electrical specification of the standard defines the voltage levels and the type of signal to be transmitted in either direction between the DTE and the DCE.

Sending the Data   The electrical specification for sending data is shown in Figure 6.8. EIA-232 states that all data must be transmitted as logical 1s and 0s (called mark and space) using NRZ-L encoding, with 0 defined as a positive voltage and 1 defined as a negative voltage. However, rather than defining a single range bounded by highest and lowest amplitudes, EIA-232 defines two distinct ranges, one for positive voltages and one for negative. A receiver recognizes and accepts as an intentional signal any voltage that falls within these ranges, but no voltages that fall outside the ranges. To be recognized as data, the amplitude of a signal must fall between 3 and 15 volts or between −3 and −15 volts. By allowing valid signals to fall within two 12-volt ranges, EIA-232 makes it unlikely that degradation of a signal by noise will affect its recognizability. In other words, as long as a pulse falls within one of the acceptable ranges, the precision of that pulse is unimportant.

Figure 6.8 shows a square wave degraded by noise into a curve. The amplitude of the fourth bit is lower than intended (compared to that of the second bit), and rather than staying at one single voltage, it covers a range of many voltages. If the receiver were looking only for a fixed voltage, the degradation of this pulse would have made it unrecoverable. The bit also would have been unrecoverable if the receiver were looking only for pulses that held a single voltage for their entire duration.

Figure 6.8 *Electrical specification for sending data in EIA-232*

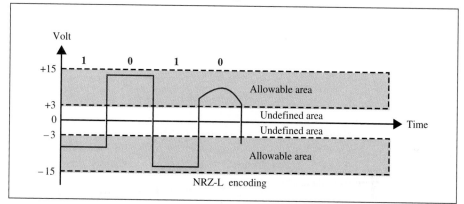

Control and Timing

Only 4 wires out of the 25 available in an EIA-232 interface are used for data functions. The remaining 21 are reserved for functions like control, timing, grounding, and testing. The electrical specifications for these other wires are similar to those governing data transmission, but simpler. Any of the other functions is considered ON if it transmits a voltage of at least +3 and OFF if it transmits a voltage with a value less than −3 volts.

> The electrical specification of EIA-232 defines that signals other than data must be sent using
> OFF ⇨ less than −3 volts and ON ⇨ greater than +3 volts

Figure 6.9 shows one of these signals. The specification for control signals is conceptually reversed from that for data transmission. A positive voltage means ON and a negative voltage means OFF. Also note that OFF is still signified by the transmission of a specific voltage range. An absence of voltage on one of these wires while the system is running means that something is not working properly, and not that the line is turned off.

A final important function of the electrical specification is the definition of bit rate. EIA-232 allows for a maximum bit rate of 20 Kbps, although in practice this often is exceeded.

Functional Specification

Two different implementations of EIA-232 are available: DB-25 and DB-9.

DB-25 Implementation   EIA-232 defines the functions assigned to each of the 25 pins in the DB-25 connector. Figure 6.10 shows the ordering and functionality of each pin of a male connector. Remember that a female connector will be the mirror image of the male, so that pin 1 in the plug matches tube 1 in the receptacle, and so on.

Figure 6.9   *Electrical specification for control signals in EIA-232*

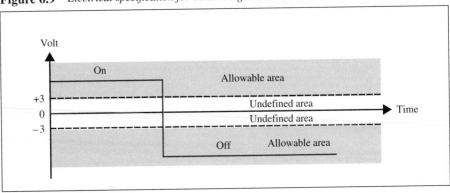

Each communications function has a mirror or answering function for traffic in the opposite direction, to allow for full-duplex operation. For example, pin 2 is for transmitting data, while pin 3 is for receiving data. In this way, both parties can transmit data at the same time. As you can see from Figure 6.10, not every pin is functional. Pins 9 and 10 are reserved for future use. Pin 11 is as yet unassigned.

Figure 6.10   *Functions of pins in EIA-232, DB-25*

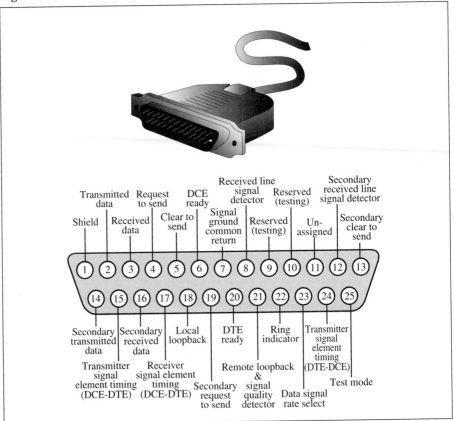

DB-9 Implementation Many of the pins on the DB-25 implementation are not necessary in a single asynchronous connection. A simpler 9-pin version of EIA-232 known as **DB-9** and shown in Figure 6.11 was developed. Note that there is no pin-to-pin relationship in the two implementations.

Figure 6.11 *Functions of pins in EIA-232, DB-9*

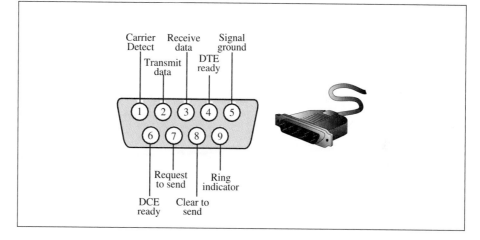

An Example

This example, Figure 6.12, demonstrates the functioning of EIA-232 in synchronous full-duplex mode over a leased line using only the primary channel. The DCEs here are modems, and the DTEs are computers. There are five distinct steps, from preparation to clearing. This is a full-duplex model, so both computer/modem systems can transmit data concurrently. In terms of the EIA model, however, one system is still classified as the initiator and the other as the responder.

Step 1 shows the preparation of the interfaces for transmission. The two grounding circuits, 1 (shield) and 7 (signal ground), are active between both the sending computer/modem combination (left) and the receiving computer/modem combination (right).

Step 2 ensures that all four devices are ready for transmission. First the sending DTE activates pin 20 and sends a DTE ready message to its DCE. The DCE answers by activating pin 6 and returning a DCE ready message. This same sequence is performed by the remote computer and modem.

Step 3 sets up the physical connection between the sending and receiving modems. This step can be thought of as the *on* switch for transmission. It is the first step that involves the network. First, the sending DTE activates pin 4 and sends its DCE a request-to-send message. The DCE transmits a carrier signal to the idle receiving modem. When the receiving modem detects the carrier signal, it activates pin 8, the received line signal detector, telling its computer that a transmission is about to begin. After transmitting the carrier signal, the sending DCE activates pin 5, sending its DTE a clear-to-send message. The remote computer and modem perform the same step.

Figure 6.12 *Synchronous full-duplex transmission*

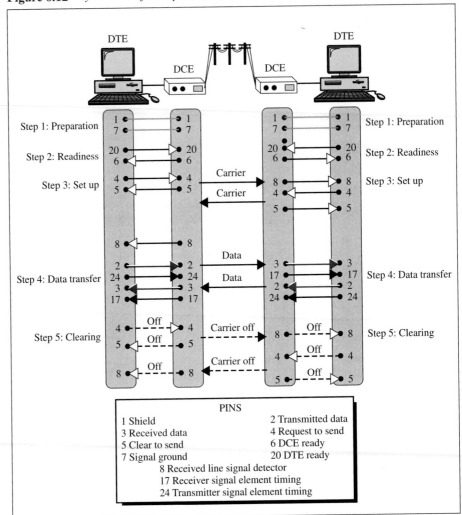

Step 4 is the data transfer procedure. The initiating computer transfers its data stream to its modem over circuit 2, accompanied by the timing pulse of circuit 24. The modem converts the digital data to an analog signal and sends it out over the network. The responding modem retrieves the signal, converts it back into digital data and passes the data along to its computer via circuit 3, accompanied by the timing pulse of circuit 17.

Likewise, the responding computer follows the same procedure in sending data to the initializing computer.

Once both sides have completed their transmissions, both computers deactivate their request-to-send circuits; the modems turn off their carrier signals, their received line signal detectors (there is no longer any signal to detect), and their clear-to-send circuits (Step 5).

Null Modem

Suppose you need to connect two DTEs in the same building, for example, two workstations or a terminal to a workstation. Modems are not needed to connect two compatible digital devices directly; the transmission never needs to cross analog lines, such as telephone lines, and therefore does not need to be modulated. But you do need an interface to handle the exchange (readiness establishment, data transfer, receipt, etc.), just as an EIA-232 DTE-DCE cable does.

The solution, provided by the EIA standard, is called a **null modem.** A null modem provides the DTE-DTE interface without the DCEs. But why use a null modem? If all you need is the interface, why not just use a standard EIA-232 cable? To understand the problem, examine Figure 6.13. Part *a* shows a connection using a telephone network. The two DTEs are exchanging information through DCEs. Each DTE sends its data through pin 2 and the DCE receives it on pin 2; and each DTE receives data through pin 3 that has been forwarded by the DCE using its own pin 3. As you can see, the EIA-232 cable connects DTE pin 2 to DCE pin 2 and DCE pin 3 to DTE pin 3. Traffic using pin 2 is always outgoing from the DTEs. Traffic using pin 3 is always incoming to the DTEs. A DCE recognizes the direction of a signal and passes it along to the appropriate circuit.

Figure 6.13 *Using regular data pin connections with and without DCEs*

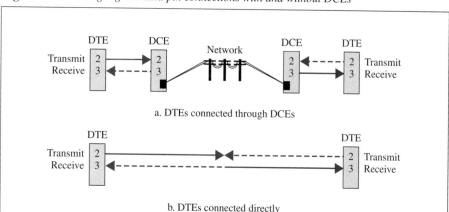

a. DTEs connected through DCEs

b. DTEs connected directly

Part *b* of the figure shows what happens when we use the same connections between two DTEs. Without DCEs to switch the signals to or from the appropriate pins, both DTEs are attempting to transmit over the same pin 2 wire—and to receive over the same pin 3 wire. The DTEs are transmitting to each other's transmit pins, not to their receive pins. The receive circuit (3) is void because it has been isolated completely from the transmission. The transmit circuit (2) therefore ends up full of collision noise and signals that can never be received by either DTE. No data can get through from one device to another.

Crossing Connections For transmission to occur, the wires must be crossed so that pin 2 of the first DTE connects to pin 3 of the second DTE and pin 2 of the second DTE connects to pin 3 of the first. These two pins are the most important. Several other pins, however, have similar problems and also need rewiring (see Figure 6.14).

Figure 6.14   *Null modem pin connections*

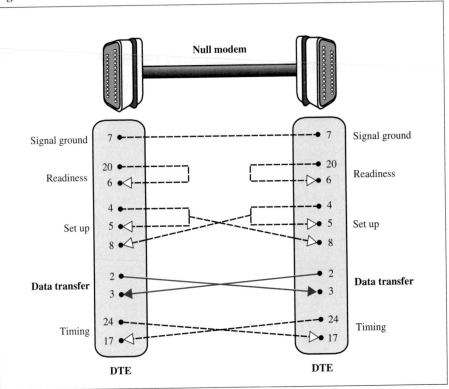

A null modem is an EIA-232 interface that completes the necessary circuits to fool the DTEs at either end into believing that they have DCEs and a network between them. Because its purpose is to make connections, a null modem can be either a length of cable or a device, or you can make one yourself using a standard EIA-232 cable and a break-out box that allows you to cross-connect wires in any way you desire. Of these options, the cable is the most commonly used and the most convenient (see Figure 6.14).

Other Differences   Whereas an EIA-232 DTE-DCE interface cable has a female connector at the DTE end and a male connector at the DCE end, a null modem has female connectors at both ends to allow it to connect to the EIA-232 DTE ports, which are male.

6.3   OTHER INTERFACE STANDARDS

Both data rate and cable length (signal distance capability) are restricted by EIA-232: data rate to 20 Kbps and cable length to 50 feet (15 meters). To meet the needs of users who require more speed and/or distance, the EIA and the ITU-T have introduced additional interface standards: EIA-449, EIA-530, and X.21.

EIA-449

The mechanical specifications of **EIA-449** define a combination of two connectors: one with 37 pins (**DB-37**) and one with 9 pins (**DB-9**), for a combined 46 pins (see Figure 6.15).

Figure 6.15   *EIA-449 DBs*

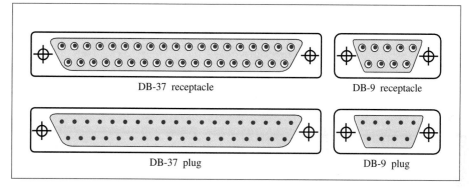

DB-37 receptacle   DB-9 receptacle

DB-37 plug   DB-9 plug

The functional specifications of the EIA-449 give the DB-37 pins properties similar to those of the DB-25. The major functional difference between the 25- and 37-pin connectors is that all functions relating to the secondary channel have been removed from DB-37. Because the secondary channel is seldom used, EIA-449 separates those functions out and puts them in the second, 9-pin connector (DB-9). In this way, a second channel is available to systems that need it.

DB-37 Pin Functions

To maintain compatibility with EIA-232, EIA-449 defines two categories of pins to be used in exchanging data, control, and timing information (see Table 6.1).

Table 6.1   *DB-37 pins*

Pin	Function	Category	Pin	Function	Category
1	Shield		20	Receive Common	II
2	Signal rate indicator		21	Unassigned	I
3	Unassigned		22	Send data	I
4	Send data	I	23	Send timing	I
5	Send timing	I	24	Receive data	I
6	Receive data	I	25	Request to send	I
7	Request to send	I	26	Receive timing	I
8	Receive timing	I	27	Clear to send	I
9	Clear to send	I	28	Terminal in service	II

Table 6.1 (*continued*)   *DB-37 pins*

Pin	Function	Category	Pin	Function	Category
10	Local loopback	II	29	Data mode	I
11	Data mode	I	30	Terminal ready	I
12	Terminal ready	I	31	Receive ready	I
13	Receive ready	I	32	Select standby	II
14	Remote loopback	II	33	Signal quality	
15	Incoming call		34	New signal	II
16	Select frequency	II	35	Terminal timing	I
17	Terminal timing	I	36	Standby indicator	II
18	Test mode	II	37	Send common	II
19	Signal ground				

Category I Pins

Category I includes those pins whose functions are compatible with those of EIA-232 (although most have been renamed). For each Category I pin, EIA-449 defines two pins, one in the first column and one in the second column. For example, both pins 4 and 22 are called send data. These two pins have the equivalent functionality of pin 2 in EIA-232. Both pins 5 and 23 are called send timing, and both pins 6 and 24 are called receive data. Even more interesting, these pairs of pins are vertically adjacent to one another in the connector, with the pin from the second column occupying the position essentially below its counterpart from the first column. (Number the DB-37 connector based on the numbering of the DB-25 connector to see these relationships.) This structure is what gives EIA-449 its power. How the pins relate will become clear later in this section, when we discuss the two alternate methods of signaling defined in the electrical specifications.

Category II Pins

Category II pins are those that have no equivalent in EIA-232 or have been redefined. The numbers and functions of these new pins are as follows:

- **Local loopback.** Pin 10 is used for local loopback testing.
- **Remote loopback.** Pin 14 is used for remote loopback testing.
- **Select frequency.** Pin 16 is used to choose between two different frequency rates.
- **Test mode.** Pin 18 is used to do testing at different levels.
- **Receive common.** Pin 20 provides a common signal return line for unbalanced circuits from the DCE to the DTE.
- **Terminal in service.** Pin 28 indicates to the DCE whether or not the DTE is operational.

- **Select standby.** Pin 32 allows the DTE to request the use of standby equipment in the event of failure.

- **New signal.** Pin 34 is available for multiple-point applications where a primary DTE controls several secondary DTEs. When activated, pin 34 indicates that one DTE has finished its data exchange and a new one is about to start.

- **Standby indicator.** Pin 36 provides the confirmation signal from the DCE in response to select standby (pin 32).

- **Send common.** Pin 37 provides a common signal return line for unbalanced circuits from the DTE to the DCE.

DB-9 Pin Functions

Table 6.2 lists the pin functions of the DB-9 connector. Note that the DB-9 connector here is different from the one discussed in EIA-232.

Table 6.2 *DB-9 pins*

Pin	Function
1	Shield
2	Secondary receive ready
3	Secondary send data
4	Secondary receive data
5	Signal ground
6	Receive common
7	Secondary request to send
8	Secondary clear to send
9	Send common

Electrical Specifications: RS-423 and RS-422

EIA-449 uses two standards to define its electrical specifications: RS-423 (for unbalanced circuits) and RS-422 (for balanced circuits).

RS-423: Unbalanced Mode

RS-423 is an unbalanced circuit specification, meaning that it defines only one line for propagating a signal. All signals in this standard use a common return (or ground) to complete the circuit. Figure 6.16 gives a conceptual view of this type of circuit as well as the specifications for the standard. In unbalanced-circuit mode, EIA-449 calls for the use of only the first pin of each pair of Category I pins and all Category II pins.

Figure 6.16   *RS-423: Unbalanced mode*

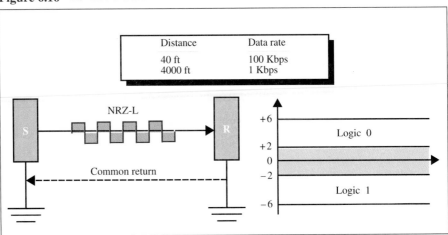

RS-422: Balanced Mode

RS-422 is a balanced circuit specification, meaning that it defines two lines for the propagation of each signal. Signals again use a common return (or ground) for the return of the signal. Figure 6.17 gives a conceptual view of and the specifications for this standard. In balanced mode, EIA-449 utilizes all pairs of pins in Category I but does not use the Category II pins. As you can see from the electrical specifications for this standard, the ratio of data rate to distance is much higher than that of the unbalanced standard or of EIA-232: 10 Mbps for transmissions of 40 feet.

Figure 6.17   *RS-422: Balanced mode*

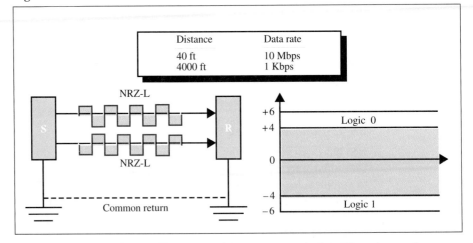

In balanced mode, two lines carry the same transmission. They do not, however, carry identical signals. The signal on one line is the complement of the signal on the other. When plotted, the complement looks like a mirror image of the original signal (see Figure 6.17). Instead of listening to either actual signal, the receiver detects the differences between the two. This mechanism makes a balanced circuit less susceptible to noise than an unbalanced circuit and improves performance.

As the complementary signals arrive at the receiver, they are put through a subtracter (a differential amplifier). This mechanism subtracts the second signal from the first before interpretation. Because the two signals complement each other, the result of this subtraction is a doubling of the value of the first signal. For example, if at a given moment the first signal has a voltage of 5, the second signal will have a voltage of −5. The result of subtraction, therefore, is 5 − (−5), which equals 10.

If noise is added to the transmission, it impacts both signals in the same way (positive noise affects both signals positively; negative noise affects both negatively). As a result, the noise is eliminated during the subtraction process (see Figure 6.18). For example, say that two volts of noise are introduced at the point where the first signal is at 5 volts and its complement is at −5 volts. The addition distorts the first signal to 7 volts, and the second to −3 volts. 7 − (−3) still equals 10. It is this ability to neutralize the effects of noise that allows the superior data rates of balanced transmission.

Figure 6.18   *Canceling of noise in the balanced mode*

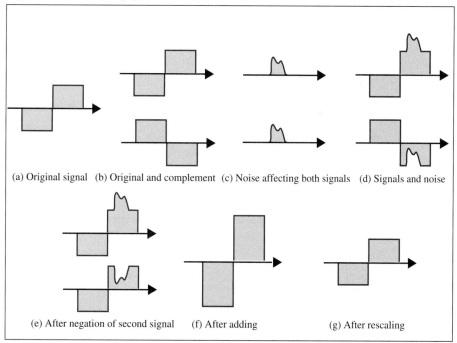

(a) Original signal   (b) Original and complement   (c) Noise affecting both signals   (d) Signals and noise

(e) After negation of second signal   (f) After adding   (g) After rescaling

EIA-530

EIA-449 provides much better functionality than EIA-232. However, it requires a DB-37 connector that the industry has been reluctant to embrace because of the amount of investment already put into the DB-25. To encourage acceptance of the new standard, therefore, the EIA developed a version of EIA-449 that uses DB-25 pins: **EIA-530.**

The pin functions of EIA-530 are essentially those of EIA-449 Category I plus three pins from Category II (the loopback circuits). Of the EIA-232 pins, some have been omitted, including ring indicator, signal quality detector, and data signal rate selector. EIA-530 does not support a secondary circuit.

X.21

X.21 is an interface standard designed by the ITU-T to address many of the problems existing in the EIA interfaces and, at the same time, pave the way for all-digital communication.

Using Data Circuits for Control

A large proportion of the circuits in the EIA interfaces are used for control. These circuits are necessary because the standards implement control functions as separate signals. With a separate line, control information is represented only by positive and negative voltages. But, if control signals are encoded using meaningful control characters from a system such as ASCII, they can be transmitted over data lines.

For this reason, X.21 eliminates most of the control circuits of the EIA standards and instead directs their traffic over the data circuits. To make this consolidation of functionality possible, both the DTE and the DCE must have added circuit logic that enables them to transform the control codes into bit streams that can be sent over the data line. Both also need additional logic to discriminate between control information and data upon receipt.

This design allows X.21 not only to use fewer pins but also to be used in digital telecommunications where control information is sent from device to device over a network rather than just between a DTE and a DCE. As digital technology emerges, more and more control information must be handled, including dialing, redialing, hold, and so on. X.21 is useful both as an interface to connect digital computers to analog devices such as modems and as a connector between digital computers and digital interfaces such as ISDN and X.25, described in Chapters 16 and 17.

X.21 is designed to work with balanced circuits at 64 Kbps, a rate that is becoming the industry standard.

Pin Functions

Figure 6.19 shows the connector specified by X.21, the **DB-15.** As the name indicates, the DB-15 is a 15-pin connector.

Figure 6.19   *DB-15 connector*

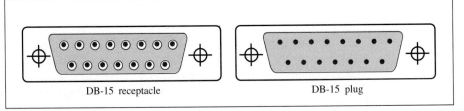

| DB-15 receptacle | DB-15 plug |

- **Byte timing.** Another advantage offered by X.21 is that of timing lines to control byte synchronization in addition to the bit synchronization provided by the EIA standards. By adding a byte timing pulse (pins 7 and 14), X.21 improves the overall synchronization of transmissions.
- **Control and initiation.** Pins 3 and 5 of the DB-15 connector are used for the initial handshake, or agreement to begin transmitting. Pin 3 is the equivalent of request to send. Pin 5 is the equivalent of clear to send. Table 6.3 lists the functions for each pin.

Table 6.3 *DB-15 pins*

Pin	*Function*	*Pin*	*Function*
1	Shield	9	Transmit data or control
2	Transmit data or control	10	Control
3	Control	11	Receive data or control
4	Receive data or control	12	Indication
5	Indication	13	Signal element timing
6	Signal element timing	14	Byte timing
7	Byte timing	15	Reserved
8	Signal ground		

6.4 MODEMS

The most familiar type of DCE is a **modem.** Anyone who has surfed the Internet, logged on to an office computer from home, or filed a news story from a word processor over a phone line has used a modem. The external or internal modem associated with your personal computer is what converts the digital signal generated by the computer into an analog signal to be carried by a public access phone line. It is also the device that converts the analog signals received over a phone line into digital signals usable by your computer.

The term *modem* is a composite word that refers to the two functional entities that make up the device: a signal *mod*ulator and a signal *dem*odulator. The relationship of the two parts is shown in Figure 6.20.

Modem stands for modulator/demodulator.

A **modulator** converts a digital signal into an analog signal using ASK, FSK, PSK, or QAM. A **demodulator** converts an analog signal into a digital signal. While a demodulator resembles an analog-to-digital converter, it is not in fact a converter of any kind. It does not sample a signal to create a digital facsimile; it merely reverses the process of **modulation**—that is, it performs **demodulation.**

> A modulator converts a digital signal to an analog signal. A demodulator converts an analog signal to a digital signal.

Figure 6.20   *Modem concept*

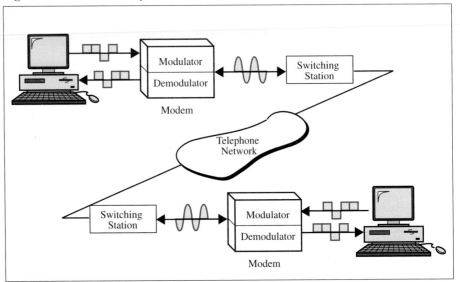

Figure 6.20 shows the relationship of modems to a communication link. The two PCs at the ends are the DTEs; the modems are the DCEs. The DTE creates a digital signal and relays it to the modem via an interface (like the EIA-232, as discussed before). The modulated signal is received by the demodulation function of the second modem. The demodulator takes the ASK, FSK, PSK, or QAM signal and decodes it into whatever format its computer can accept. It then relays the resulting digital signal to the receiving computer via an interface. Each DCE must be compatible with both its own DTE and with other DCEs.

Transmission Rate

You may have heard modems described as high-speed or low-speed to indicate how many bits per second a specific device is capable of transmitting or receiving. But before talking about different commercial modems and their data rates, we need to examine the limitations on the transmission rate of the medium itself.

Bandwidth

We defined the concept of bandwidth at the end of Chapter 4. Now we can apply that concept to physical media to see its effect on transmission. The data rate of a link depends on the type of encoding used and the bandwidth of the medium. The **medium bandwidth** is related to the inherent limitation of the physical property of the medium; every line has a range of frequencies it can pass. If the frequency of a signal is too low, it cannot overcome the capacitance of the line. If it is too high, it can be impeded by the inductance of the line. So we can say that every line has an upper limit and a lower limit on the frequencies of the signals it can carry. This limited range is called the bandwidth.

> Every line has an upper limit and a lower limit on the frequencies of the signals it can carry. This limited range is called the bandwidth.

Traditional telephone lines can carry frequencies between 300 Hz and 3300 Hz, giving them a bandwidth of 3000 Hz. All of this range is used for transmitting voice, where a great deal of interference and distortion can be accepted without loss of intelligibility. As we have seen, however, data signals require a higher degree of accuracy to ensure integrity. For safety's sake, therefore, the edges of this range are not used for data communication. In general, we can say that the signal bandwidth must be smaller than the cable bandwidth. The effective bandwidth of a telephone line being used for data transmission is 2400 Hz, covering the range from 600 Hz to 3000 Hz. Note that today some telephone lines are capable of handling more bandwidth than traditional lines. However, modem design is still based on traditional capability (see Figure 6.21).

> A telephone line has a bandwidth of almost 3000 Hz.

Figure 6.21 *Telephone line bandwidth*

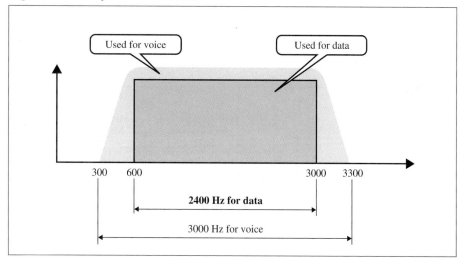

Modem Speed

As we have seen, each type of analog conversion manipulates the signal in a different way: ASK manipulates amplitude, FSK manipulates frequency, PSK manipulates phase, and QAM manipulates both phase and amplitude.

ASK As you will recall from Chapter 5, the bandwidth required for ASK transmission is equal to the baud rate of the signal. Assuming that the entire link is being used by one signal, as it would be for simplex or half-duplex transmission, the maximum baud rate for ASK modulating is equal to the entire bandwidth of the transmission medium. Because the effective bandwidth of a telephone line is 2400 Hz, the maximum baud rate is also 2400. And because the baud rate and the bit rate are the same in ASK modulation, the maximum bit rate is also 2400 (see Figure 6.22).

Figure 6.22   *Baud rate in half-duplex ASK*

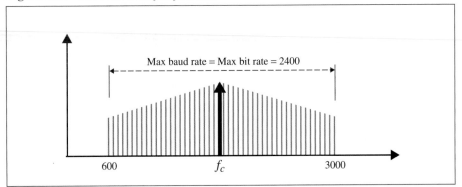

For full-duplex transmission, only half of the total bandwidth can be used in either direction. Therefore, the maximum speed for ASK transmission in full-duplex mode is 1200 bps. Figure 6.23 shows this relationship. The total available bandwidth is 2400 Hz; each direction therefore has an available 1200 Hz centered around its own carrier frequency. (Note: Some modem specifications indicate half-duplex by the abbreviation *HDX* and full-duplex by the abbreviation *FDX.*)

Figure 6.23   *Baud rate in full-duplex ASK*

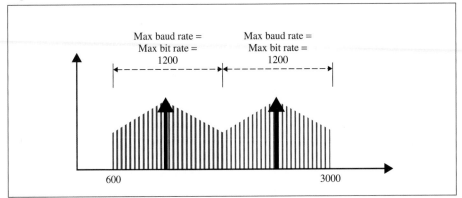

Although ASK's bit rate equals that of more popular types of modulation, its noise problems make it impractical for use in a modem.

Although ASK has a good bit rate, it is not used today because of noise.

FSK   As you will recall from Chapter 5, the bandwidth required for FSK transmission is equal to the baud rate of the signal plus the frequency shift. Assuming that the entire link is being used by one signal, as it would for simplex or half-duplex transmission, the maximum baud rate for FSK modulation is equal to the entire bandwidth of the transmission medium minus the frequency shift. Because the effective bandwidth of a telephone line is 2400 Hz, the maximum baud rate is therefore 2400 minus the frequency shift. And because the baud rate and the bit rate are the same in FSK modulation, the maximum bit rate is also 2400 minus the frequency shift (see Figure 6.24).

Figure 6.24 *Baud rate in half-duplex FSK*

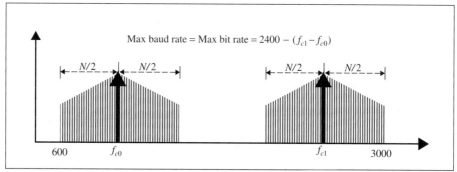

For full-duplex transmission, only half of the total bandwidth of the link can be used for either direction. Therefore, the maximum theoretical rate for FSK in full-duplex mode is half of the total bandwidth minus half the frequency shift. Full-duplex FSK partitions are shown in Figure 6.25.

Figure 6.25 *Baud rate in full-duplex FSK*

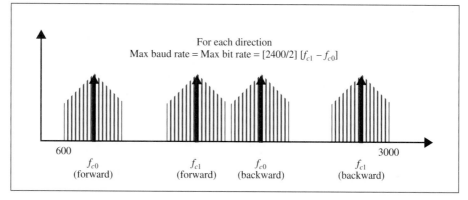

PSK and QAM As you recall, the minimum bandwidth required for PSK or QAM transmission is the same as that required for ASK transmission but the bit rate can be greater depending on the number of bits that can be represented by each signal unit.

Comparison Table 6.4 summarizes the maximum bit rate over standard twisted-wire telephone lines for each of the modulation mechanisms examined above. These figures assume a traditional two-wire line. If four-wire lines are used, the data rates for full-duplex transmission can be doubled. In that case, two wires can be used for sending and two for receiving the data, thereby doubling the available bandwidth. However, these numbers are theoretical and cannot always be achieved with available technology.

Table 6.4   *Theoretical bit rates for modems*

Modulation	Half-Duplex	Full-Duplex
ASK	2400	1200
FSK	< 2400	< 1200
2-PSK	2400	1200
4-PSK, 4-QAM	4800	2400
8-PSK, 8-QAM	7200	3600
16-QAM	9600	4800
32-QAM	12,000	6000
64-QAM	14,400	7200
128-QAM	16,800	8400
256-QAM	19,200	9,600

Modem Standards

In this section we will introduce two modem standards: **Bell modems** and ITU-T modems.

Bell Modems

The first commercial modems were produced by the Bell Telephone Company in the early 1970s. As the first and, for a long time, lone manufacturer in the marketplace, Bell defined the development of the technology and provided a de facto standard upon which subsequent manufacturers have built. Today there are dozens of companies producing hundreds of different types of modems worldwide.

As complex and powerful as many models have become, they all evolved from the original and relatively simple first models from Bell. Examining those first modems provides us with an understanding of the basic characteristics of modems. Figure 6.26 shows the specifications of the major Bell modems.

103/113 Series   One of the earliest commercially available modem series was the Bell 103/113. The Bell 103/113 series modems operate in full-duplex mode over two-wire switched telephone lines. Transmission is asynchronous, using FSK modulation. Session originator frequencies are 1070 Hz = 0 and 1270 Hz = 1. Answerer frequencies are 2025 Hz = 0 and 2225 Hz = 1. The data rate is 300 bps. The 113 series is a variation of the 103 series with additional testing features.

202 Series   The Bell 202 series modems operate in half-duplex mode over two-wire switched telephone lines. Transmission is asynchronous, using FSK modulation. Because the 202 series is half-duplex, only one pair of transmission frequencies is used: 1200 Hz = 0, and 2400 Hz = 1.

Figure 6.26   *Bell modems*

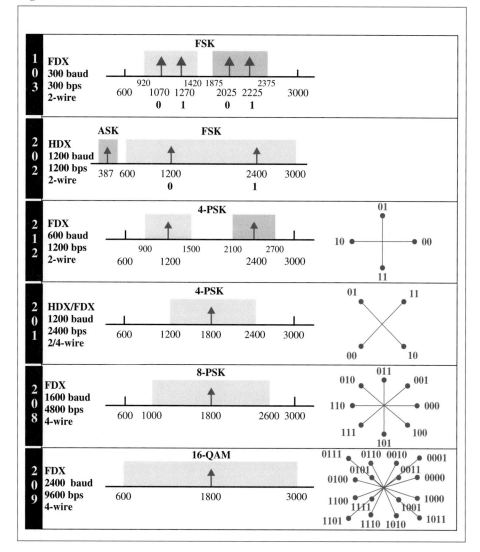

Note that the 202 series includes a secondary transmission frequency operating in either direction at 387 Hz, using ASK modulation, with a data rate of only 5 bps. This channel is used by the receiving device to tell the sender that it is connected and to send interruption messages calling for a halt to transmission (flow control) or asking for data to be resent (error control).

212 Series   The Bell 212 series modems have two speeds. The option of a second speed allows for compatibility with a wider number of systems. Both speeds operate in full-duplex mode over switched telephone lines. The slower speed, 300 bps, uses FSK modulation for asynchronous transmission, just like the 103/113 series. The higher speed, 1200 bps, can operate in either asynchronous or synchronous mode and uses 4-PSK modulation. While the 1200 bps is the same data rate as that achieved by the 202 series, the 212 series achieves that rate in full-duplex rather than half-duplex mode.

Note that by moving from FSK to PSK modulation, the designers have dramatically increased the efficiency of transmission.

In series 202, two frequencies are used to send different bits in one direction. In series 212, two frequencies represent two different directions of transmission. The modulation is done by varying the phase on either frequency, with each of four phase shifts representing two bits.

201 Series   The 201 series modems operate in either half-duplex mode over two-wire switched lines or full-duplex mode over four-wire leased lines. The entire bandwidth of a two-wire line is dedicated to a single direction of transmission. Four-wire lines allow for two completely separate channels, one in each direction, to be processed through a single modem on each end.

Transmission is synchronous, using 4-PSK modulation, which means that only one frequency is needed for transmission over each pair of wires. Splitting the two directions of transmission into two physically separate lines allows each direction to use the entire bandwidth of the line. This means that with essentially the same technology, the data rate is doubled to 2400 bps (or 1200 baud) in both half and full-duplex modes (2400 bps is still half the theoretical maximum data rate for 4-PSK modulation over two-wire phone lines).

208 Series   The 208 series modems operate in full-duplex mode over four-wire leased lines. Transmission is synchronous, using 8-PSK modulation. Like the 201 series, the 208 series modems achieve full-duplex status by doubling the number of wires used and dedicating the equivalent of an entire line to each direction of transmission. The difference here is that the modulation/demodulation technology is now able to distinguish between eight different phase shifts. This modem has a baud rate of 1600. At three bits per baud (8-PSK creates tribits), that rate translates to a bit rate of 4800 bps.

209 series   The 209 series modems operate in full-duplex mode over four-wire leased lines. Transmission is synchronous, using 16-QAM modulation. These modems achieve full-duplex status by doubling the number of wires so that each direction of transmission has a channel to itself. This series, however, allows for use of the entire bandwidth of each channel. And because each shift represents a quadbit, with 16-QAM, the data rate is 9600 bps.

ITU-T Modem Standards

Today, many of the most popular modems available are based on standards published by the ITU-T. For our purposes, these modems can be divided into two groups: those that are essentially equivalent to Bell series modems—for example, **V.21** is similar to

Bell modem 103—and those that are not. Those ITU-T modems that are Bell series compatible are listed in Table 6.5 with their Bell equivalents.

Table 6.5 *ITU-T/Bell compatibility*

ITU-T	*Bell*	*Baud Rate*	*Bit Rate*	*Modulation*
V.21	103	300	300	FSK
V.22	212	600	1200	4-PSK
V.23	202	1200	1200	FSK
V.26	201	1200	2400	4-PSK
V.27	208	1600	4800	8-PSK
V.29	209	2400	9600	16-QAM

The ITU-T modems that do not have equivalents in the Bell series are described below. Their characteristics are given in Figure 6.27.

V.22bis The term *bis* indicates that this modem is the second generation of the **V.22** series (*bis* is Latin for twice). The **V.22bis** is a two-speed modem, meaning that it can operate at either 1200 or 2400 bps. Which speed is used depends on the speed of the DCE at the other end of the exchange. When a V.22bis receives data from a 2400 bps modem, it operates in 2400 bps mode for compatibility.

In 1200 bps mode, the V.22bis uses 4-DPSK (dibit) modulation at a transmission rate of 600 baud. **DPSK** stands for **differential phase shift keying,** which means that the bit pattern defines the phase change, not the current phase. The rules for representing each of the four bit patterns are as follows:

00 ⇨	90 degree phase change
01 ⇨	0 degree phase change
10 ⇨	180 degree phase change
11 ⇨	270 degree phase change

In 2400 bps mode, the V.22bis uses 16-QAM (quadbit). The two least significant digits in each quadbit are modulated using the same differential scheme described above for 1200 bps transmission. The two most significant digits are modulated based on the constellation diagram shown in Figure 6.28.

V.32 The **V.32** is an enhanced version of the V.29 (see Table 6.5) that uses a combined modulation and encoding technique called **trellis-coded modulation.** Trellis is essentially QAM plus a redundant bit. The data stream is divided into four-bit sections. Instead of a quadbit, however, a quintbit (five-bit pattern) is transmitted. The value of the extra bit is calculated from the values of the data bits.

In any QAM system, the receiver compares each received signal point to all valid points in the constellation and selects the point closest as the intended bit value. A signal distorted by transmission noise can arrive closer in value to an adjacent point

Figure 6.27   *ITU-T modem standards*

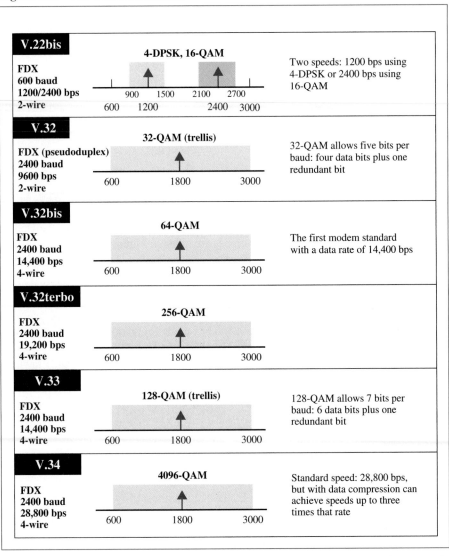

than to the intended point, resulting in a misidentification of the point and an error in the received data. The closer the points are in the constellation, the more likely that transmission noise can result in a signal's being misidentified. By adding a redundant bit to each quadbit, trellis-coded modulation increases the amount of information used to identify each bit pattern and thereby reduces the number of possible matches. For this reason, a trellis-encoded signal is much less likely than a plain QAM signal to be misread when distorted by noise. Some manufacturers of V.32-compliant modems use the trellis facility to provide functions such as error detection or error correction.

Figure 6.28 *V.22bis 16-QAM constellation*

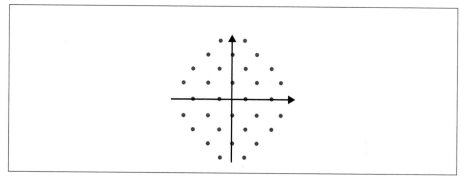

V.32 calls for 32-QAM with a baud rate of 2400. Because only four bits of each quintbit represent data, the resulting speed is 4 × 2400 = 9600 bps. The constellation diagram is shown in Figure 6.29.

Figure 6.29 *V.32 constellation*

V.32 modems can be used with a two-wire switched line in what is called pseudo-duplex mode. Pseudo-duplex is based on a technique called echo cancellation.

V.32bis   The **V.32bis** modem was the first of the ITU-T standards to support 14,400 bps transmission. The V.32bis uses 64-QAM transmission (six bits per baud) at a rate of 2400 baud (2400 × 6 = 14,400 bps).

An additional enhancement provided by the V.32bis is the inclusion of an automatic fall-back and fall-forward feature that enables the modem to adjust its speed upward or downward depending on the quality of the line or signal.

V.32terbo   The V.32terbo is an enhanced version of the V.32bis (*terbo* is a pun on the word *ter* which is Latin for third). It uses 256-QAM to provide a bit rate of 19,200 bps.

V.33   The V.33 is also based on the V.32. This modem, however, uses trellis-coded modulation based on 128-QAM at 2400 baud. Each signal change represents a pattern of seven bits: six data bits and one redundant bit. Six bits of data per change (baud) give it a speed of 6 × 2400 = 14,400 bps. The constellation diagram for this scheme is shown in Figure 6.30.

Figure 6.30 *V.33 constellation*

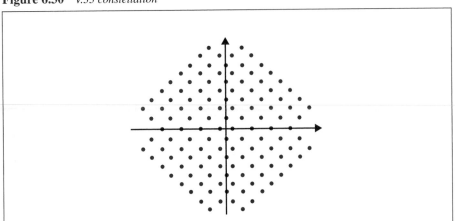

V.34 The **V.34** modem, sometimes called V.fast, provides a bit rate of 28,800 or 33,600 bps. In addition, the V.34 provides data compression, which allows data rates as fast as two to three times its normal speed.

V.42 The **V.42** standard, adopted by ITU-T, uses a protocol called **link access procedure for modems (LAPM).** LAPM is a version of a data link protocol called HDLC, which we will study in Chapter 11. The standard uses a second protocol called error correction procedure for DCEs that allows the modem to correct errors.

V.42bis After V.42, ITU-T adopted **V.42bis.** This standard includes all of the features of V.42 but also adds the Lempel-Ziv-Welch compression method (discussed in Appendix G). Modems using this standard can achieve a compression ratio of 3:1 to 4:1. Note that the data rate of the modem is not increased; the compression allows the user to send more bits in a predefined period of time.

Intelligent Modems

The purpose of a modem is to modulate and demodulate a signal. Many of today's modems, however, do more. In particular, a class of modems called **intelligent modems** contain software to support a number of additional functions, such as automatic answering and dialing.

Intelligent modems were first introduced by Hayes Microcomputer Products, Inc. More recently, other manufacturers have come out with what are referred to as **Hayes-compatible modems.**

Instructions in the Hayes and Hayes-compatible modems are called AT commands (AT is short for attention). The AT command format is:

AT command [parameter] command [parameter]...

Each command starts with the letters AT followed by one or more commands, each of which can take one or more parameters. For example, to have the modem dial (408) 864-8902, the command is **TD4088648902**.

A few sample commands are given in Table 6.6. This list represents only a small subset of the available commands.

Table 6.6 *AT commands*

Command	Meaning	Parameters
A	Put modem in answer mode	
B	Use V.22bis at 1200 bps	
D	Dial the number	The number to dial
E	Enable/disable echo printing	0 or 1
H	Put modem on/off hook	0 or 1
L	Adjust speaker volume	n
P	Use pulse dialing	
T	Use tone dialing	

6.5 56K MODEMS

Traditional modems have a limitation on the data rate (maximum of 33.6 Kbps), as determined by the Shannon formula (see Chapter 7). However, new modems, with a bit rate of 56,000 bps, called **56K modems,** are now on the market. These modems may be used only if one party is using digital signaling (such as through an Internet provider). They are asymmetrical in that the downloading (flow of data from the Internet provider to the PC) is a maximum of 56 Kbps, while the uploading (flow of data from the PC to the Internet provider) can be a maximum of 33.6 Kbps. Do these modems violate the Shannon capacity principle? No, the approach is different. Let us compare the two approaches.

Traditional Modems

Let us see what happens when we use traditional modems to send data from a computer at site A to another computer at site B and vice versa. See Figure 6.31.

From Site A to Site B

Transmission of data from site A to site B follows these steps:

1. Digital data are modulated by the modem at site A.
2. Analog data are sent from the modem to the switching station at site A using the local loop.
3. At the switching station, analog data are converted to digital using PCM.
4. Digital data travel through the digital network of the telephone company and arrive at the switching station of site B.
5. At the switching station, digital data are converted to analog using inverse PCM.

Figure 6.31   *Traditional modems*

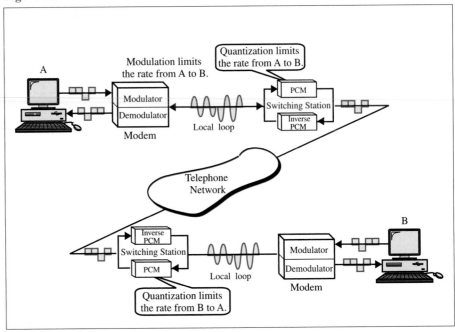

6. Analog data are sent from the switching station at site B to the modem using the local loop.

7. Analog data are demodulated by the modem at site B.

The limiting factor is step 3. Here, the analog signal is quantized to create the digital signal. The quantization noise resulting from this process limits the data rate to 33.6 Kbps.

From Site B to Site A

Transmission of data from site B to site A follows the same steps. Again the limiting factor is the quantization step using PCM.

Result

The maximum data rate in each direction is limited to 33.6 Kbps.

56K Modems

If one side is an Internet provider and the signal does not have to pass through a PCM converter, quantization is eliminated in one direction and the data rate can be increased to 56 Kbps (see Figure 6.32).

Uploading

Transmission of data from the subscriber to the Internet provider (**uploading**) follows these steps:

1. Digital data are modulated by the modem at site A.

Figure 6.32   *56K modems*

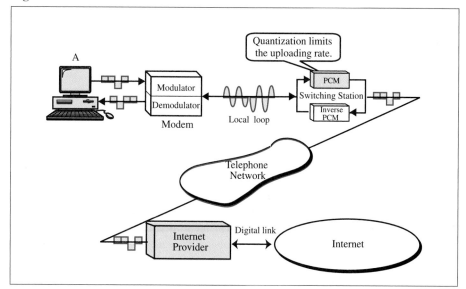

2. Analog data are sent from the modem to the switching station at site A on the local loop.

3. At the switching station, data are converted to digital using PCM.

4. Digital data travel through the digital network of the telephone company and are received by the Internet provider computer.

The limiting factor in these steps is again step 3. This means there is no improvement here. However, the user does not need such a high data rate since, in this direction, only small blocks of data (such as an e-mail or a small file) are sent.

Downloading

Transmission of data from the Internet provider to the modem at site A (**downloading**) follows these steps:

1. Digital data are sent by the computer of the Internet provider through the digital telephone network.

2. At the switching station, digital data are converted to analog using inverse PCM.

3. Analog data are sent from the switching station at site A to the modem on the local loop.

4. Analog data are demodulated by the modem at site A.

Note that, in this direction, there is no quantization of data using PCM. The limitation when uploading is not an issue here; data can be sent at 56 Kbps. This is what the user is looking for, since large files are typically downloaded from the Internet.

Result

The maximum data rate in the uploading direction is still 33.6 Kbps, but the data rate in the downloading direction is now 56 Kbps.

Why Only 56 Kbps?

Since these modems are not limited by the Shannon capacity formula in downloading, why 56 Kbps? Why not more? The answer is in the way the telephone companies digitize voice. Switching stations use PCM and inverse PCM, sampling at 8000 samples per second with 128 different levels (7 bits per sample). This results in a 56 Kbps (8000 × 7 = 56,000) data rate at the switching station.

6.6 CABLE MODEM

The data rate limitation of traditional modems is mostly due to the narrow bandwidth of the local loop telephone line (up to 4 KHz). If higher bandwidths are available, one can design a modem that can handle much higher data rates.

Fortunately, cable TV provides residential premises with a coaxial cable that has a bandwidth up to 750 MHz and sometimes even more. This bandwidth is normally divided into 6 MHz bands using frequency division multiplexing (see Chapter 8). Each band provides a TV channel. Two bands can be set aside to allow a user to download and upload information from the Internet.

Figure 6.33 shows the **cable modem** concept. Instead of the traditional cable box, we show a splitter. The splitter directs the TV bands to the TV set and the Internet access bands to the PC.

Figure 6.33   *Cable modem*

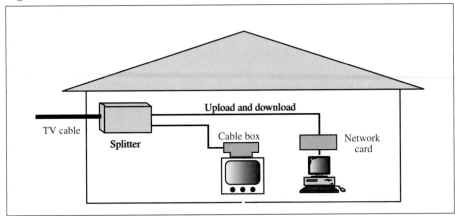

Downloading

Downloading usually requires a 6 MHz bandwidth in a range above 40 MHz. The demodulation technique used is 64-QAM (6 bits at a time). This means that a user can download information at a rate of

$$6 \text{ MHz} \times 6 = 36 \text{ Mbps}$$

However, PCs are not yet capable of receiving data at this rate. Presently, the rate is something between 3 and 10 Mbps.

Uploading

Uploading requires a 6 MHz bandwidth in a range below 40 MHz. At this low frequency, home appliances can create a noisy environment that affects modulation. The modulation technique that is normally used is QPSK (4 bits at a time). This means that a user can upload information at a rate of

$$6\,\text{MHz} \times 2 = 12 \ \text{Mbps}$$

Presently, the uploading rate is between 500 Kbps and 1 Mbps.

6.7   KEY TERMS AND CONCEPTS

56K modem	Hayes-compatible modem
asynchronous transmission	intelligent modem
Bell modems	interface
cable modem	link access procedure for modems (LAPM)
data circuit–terminating equipment (DCE)	medium bandwidth
data terminal equipment (DTE)	modem
DB-9	modulation
DB-15	modulator
DB-25	null modem
DB-37	parallel transmission
demodulation	RS-422 standard
demodulator	RS-423 standard
differential phase shift keying (DPSK)	serial transmission
downloading	start bit
EIA-232	stop bit
EIA-449	synchronous transmission
EIA-530	trellis-coded modulation

uploading	V.32bis
V series	V.34
V.21	V.42
V.22	V.42bis
V.22bis	X.21
V.32	

6.8   SUMMARY

■ Digital transmission can be either parallel or serial in mode.

■ In parallel transmission, a group of bits is sent simultaneously, with each bit on a separate line.

■ In serial transmission, there is only one line and the bits are sent sequentially.

■ Serial transmission can be either synchronous or asynchronous.

■ In asynchronous serial transmission, each byte (group of eight bits) is framed with a start bit and a stop bit. There may be a variable-length gap between each byte.

■ In synchronous serial transmission, bits are sent in a continuous stream without start and stop bits and without gaps between bytes. Regrouping the bits into meaningful bytes is the responsibility of the receiver.

■ A DTE (data terminal equipment) is a source or destination for binary digital data.

■ A DCE (data circuit-terminating equipment) receives data from a DTE and changes it into a form appropriate for network transmission. It can also perform the reverse transformation.

■ A DTE-DCE interface is defined by its mechanical, electrical, and functional characteristics.

■ The EIA-232 standard defines a widely used DTE-DCE interface that consists of a 25-pin connector (DB-25), each pin having a specific function. The functions can be categorized as ground, data, control, timing, reserved, and unassigned.

■ The EIA-449 standard provides better data rate and distance capability than the EIA-232 standard.

■ EIA-449 specifies a 37-pin connector (DB-37) used by the primary channel; the secondary channel has its own 9-pin connector.

■ DB-37 pins are divided into Category I (pins compatible with EIA-232) and Category II (new pins not compatible with EIA-232).

- The electrical specifications of EIA-449 are defined by standards RS-423 and RS-422.
- RS-422 is a balanced circuit with two lines for signal propagation. Signal degradation from noise is less a problem with RS-422 than with RS-423.
- X.21 eliminates many of the control pins of interfaces by sending control information over data pins.
- A null modem connects two close, compatible DTEs that do not require networks or modulation.
- A modem is a DCE that modulates and demodulates signals.
- A modem changes digital signals to analog signals using ASK, FSK, PSK, or QAM modulation.
- The physical properties of a transmission line limit the frequencies of signals it can transmit.
- A regular telephone line uses frequencies between 600 Hz and 3000 Hz for data communication. This requires a bandwidth of 2400 Hz.
- ASK modulation is especially susceptible to noise.
- Because it uses two carrier frequencies, FSK modulation requires more bandwidth than ASK and PSK.
- PSK and QAM modulation have two advantages over ASK:
  a. They are not as susceptible to noise.
  b. Each signal change can represent more than one bit.
- The most popular modems today have surpassed the capabilities of the older Bell modems and are based on standards (the V series) defined by the ITU-T.
- Trellis coding is a technique that uses redundancy to provide a lower error rate.
- An intelligent modem contains software to perform functions in addition to modulation and demodulation.
- 56K modems are asymmetrical; they download at a rate of 56 Kbps and send data at 33.6 Kbps.
- The coaxial cable used for cable TV can provide customers with a high bandwidth (and therefore high data rate) medium for data communication.

6.9   PRACTICE SET

Review Questions

1. Explain the two modes for transmitting binary data across a link.
2. What are the advantages and disadvantages of parallel transmission?
3. Compare the two methods of serial transmission. Discuss the advantages and disadvantages of each.

4. What are the functions of a DTE? What are the functions of a DCE? Give an example of each.

5. What standards organizations are involved in DTE-DCE interface standards?

6. Name some popular DTE-DCE standards.

7. What implementations of EIA-232 are availabie? How are they different?

8. What is the purpose of a null modem?

9. Describe the data pins of a null modem.

10. Compare RS-423 with RS-422.

11. How is X.21 able to eliminate most of the control circuits of the EIA standards?

12. What does the term *modem* stand for?

13. What is the function of a modulator? What is the function of a demodulator?

14. What factors affect the data rate of a link?

15. Define the bandwidth of a line. What is the bandwidth of a traditional telephone line?

16. What is an intelligent modem?

17. Explain the asymmetry of 56K modems.

18. How does a cable modem achieve such a high data rate?

19. What is the difference between a primary and a secondary channel in a modem?

20. Why are there pairs of send data, send timing, and receive data pins in the DB-37 connector?

21. What is the difference between a balanced circuit and an unbalanced circuit?

22. What is the relationship between the data rate and the distance that the data can reliably travel on an EIA interface?

23. The transmission of characters from the terminal to the host computer is asynchronous. Explain why.

24. What does the mechanical specification of EIA-232 describe?

25. What does the electrical specification of EIA-232 describe?

26. What does the functional specification of EIA-232 describe?

27. According to the EIA-449 standard, what is the difference between Category I and Category II pins?

28. Why are modems needed for telephone communications?

29. In a two-wire telephone line, why does full-duplex transmission have half the bit rate of half-duplex transmission?

30. FSK is a good choice for low-speed modems. Explain why it is not suitable for high-speed modems.

31. Explain the difference in transmission capacity when a four-wire line is used instead of a two-wire line.

32. The minimum bandwidth of an ASK signal could be equal to the bit rate. Explain why this is impossible for FSK.

Multiple Choice Questions

33. In _____ transmission, bits are transmitted simultaneously, each across its own wire.
    a. asynchronous serial
    b. synchronous serial
    c. parallel
    d. a and b

34. In _____ transmission, bits are transmitted over a single wire, one at a time.
    a. asynchronous serial
    b. synchronous serial
    c. parallel
    d. a and b

35. In _____ transmission, a start bit and a stop bit frame a character byte.
    a. asynchronous serial
    b. synchronous serial
    c. parallel
    d. a and b

36. In asynchronous transmission, the gap time between bytes is _____.
    a. fixed
    b. variable
    c. a function of the data rate
    d. zero

37. Synchronous transmission does not have _____.
    a. a start bit
    b. a stop bit
    c. gaps between bytes
    d. all of the above

38. A _____ is a device that is a source of or destination for binary digital data.
    a. data terminal equipment
    b. data transmission equipment
    c. digital terminal encoder
    d. digital transmission equipment

39. A _____ is a device that transmits or receives data in the form of an analog or digital signal through a network.
    a. digital connecting equipment
    b. data circuit–terminating equipment
    c. data converting equipment
    d. digital communication equipment

40. EIA-232 defines _____ characteristics of the DTE-DCE interface.
    a. mechanical
    b. electrical
    c. functional
    d. all of the above

41. The encoding method specified in the EIA-232 standard is _____.
    a. NRZ-I
    b. NRZ-L
    c. Manchester
    d. differential Manchester

42. The EIA-232 standard specifies that 0 must be _____ volts.
    a. greater than −15
    b. less than −15
    c. between −3 and −15
    d. between 3 and 15

43. The EIA-232 interface has _____ pins.
    a. 20
    b. 24
    c. 25
    d. 30

44. Data are sent over pin _____ of the EIA-232 interface.
    a. 2
    b. 3
    c. 4
    d. all of the above

45. The majority (13) of the pins of the EIA-232 interface are used for _____ purposes.
    a. control
    b. timing
    c. data
    d. testing

46. In the EIA-232 standard, what does −12 V on a data pin represent?
    a. 1
    b. 0
    c. undefined
    d. either a 1 or 0 depending on the coding scheme

47. Which of the following pins are needed prior to data transmission?
    a. request to send (4) and clear to send (5)
    b. received line signal detector (8)

   c. DTE ready (20) and DCE ready (6)

   d. all of the above

48. Which pin is needed for local loopback testing?

   a. local loopback (18)

   b. remote loopback and signal quality detector (21)

   c. test mode (25)

   d. a and c

49. Which pin is needed for remote loopback testing?

   a. remote loopback and signal quality detector (21)

   b. local loopback (18)

   c. test mode (25)

   d. a and c

50. Which pin is currently not in use?

   a. 9

   b. 10

   c. 11

   d. all of the above

51. Which pin is used by the secondary channel?

   a. 12

   b. 13

   c. 19

   d. all of the above

52. A maximum cable length of 50 feet is specified in standard _____.

   a. EIA-449

   b. EIA-232

   c. RS-423

   d. RS-422

53. A cable range of 40 feet to _____ feet is possible according to the EIA-449 standard.

   a. 50

   b. 500

   c. 4000

   d. 5000

54. The maximum data rate for RS-422 is _____ times that of the maximum RS-423 data rate.

   a. 0.1

   b. 10

   c. 100

   d. 500

55. In the RS-422 circuit, if noise changes a voltage from 10 V to 12 V, its complement would have a value of _____ V.
    a. −2
    b. −8
    c. −10
    d. −12

56. If 0.5 V of noise corrupts a bit on an RS-422 circuit, _____ volts will be added to the complementary bit.
    a. −1.0
    b. −0.5
    c. 0.5
    d. 1.0

57. X.21 eliminates many of the _____ pins found in EIA standards.
    a. data
    b. timing
    c. control
    d. ground

58. X.21 uses a _____ connector.
    a. DB-15
    b. DB-25
    c. DB-37
    d. DB-9

59. Control information (other than handshaking) in X.21 is mostly sent through the _____ pins.
    a. data
    b. timing
    c. control
    d. ground

60. A null modem connects the data transmit pin (2) of one DTE to the _____.
    a. data receive pin (3) of the same DTE
    b. data receive pin (3) of the other DTE
    c. data transmit pin (2) of the other DTE
    d. signal ground of the other DTE

61. If you have two close, compatible DTEs that can communicate data that do not need to be modulated, a good interface would be _____.
    a. a null modem
    b. an EIA-232 cable
    c. a DB-45 connector
    d. a transceiver

62. Given a transmission line with H as the highest frequency and L as the lowest frequency, the bandwidth of the line is _____.

    a. H

    b. L

    c. $H - L$

    d. $L - H$

63. For a telephone line, the bandwidth for voice is usually _____ the bandwidth for data.

    a. equivalent to

    b. less than

    c. greater than

    d. twice

64. For a given bit rate, the minimum bandwidth for ASK is _____ the minimum bandwidth for FSK.

    a. equivalent to

    b. less than

    c. greater than

    d. twice

65. As the bit rate of an FSK signal increases, the bandwidth _____.

    a. decreases

    b. increases

    c. remains the same

    d. doubles

66. For FSK, as the difference between the two carrier frequencies increases, the bandwidth _____.

    a. decreases

    b. increases

    c. remains the same

    d. halves

67. Which of the following modulation techniques are used by modems?

    a. 16-QAM

    b. FSK

    c. 8-PSK

    d. all of the above

68. 2-PSK usually requires _____ FSK for the same data rate.

    a. more bandwidth than

    b. less bandwidth than

    c. the same bandwidth as

    d. an order of magnitude more bandwidth than

69. Which of the following modems uses FSK modulation?
    a. Bell 103
    b. Bell 201
    c. Bell 212
    d. all of the above

70. Which ITU-T modem standard uses trellis coding?
    a. V.32
    b. V.33
    c. V.34
    d. a and b

71. In trellis coding the number of data bits is _____ the number of transmitted bits.
    a. equal to
    b. less than
    c. more than
    d. double that of

72. For the V.22bis standard, at its lower speed, if we are currently in the third quadrant and the next dibit is 11, there is a _____ -degree phase change.
    a. 0
    b. 90
    c. 180
    d. 270

73. What is the object of trellis coding?
    a. to narrow the bandwidth
    b. to simplify modulation
    c. to increase the data rate
    d. to reduce the error rate

74. In _____ modulation, the phase change is a function of the current bit pattern as well as the phase of the previous bit pattern.
    a. FSK
    b. PSK
    c. DPSK
    d. ASK

75. The bit rate always equals the baud rate in which type of signal?
    a. FSK
    b. QAM
    c. 4-PSK
    d. all of the above

76. A modulator converts a(n)_____ signal to a(n) _____ signal.
    a. digital; analog
    b. analog; digital
    c. PSK; FSK
    d. FSK; PSK

77. The DB-9 implementation of EIA-232 is used in a _____ connection.
    a. single asynchronous
    b. single synchronous
    c. simplex
    d. any of the above

78. The _____ standard uses the LAPM protocol.
    a. V.32
    b. V.32bis
    c. V.34
    d. V.42

79. The _____ standard uses the Lempel-Ziv-Welch compression method.
    a. V.32
    b. V.32bis
    c. V.42
    d. V.42bis

80. A 56K modem can download at a rate of _____Kbps and upload at a rate of _____ Kbps.
    a. 33.6; 33.6
    b. 33.6; 56.6
    c. 56.6; 33.6
    d. 56.6; 56.6

81. Users connected to the Internet via a cable TV provider enjoy a high data rate due to _____.
    a. modulation at the switching station
    b. modulation at the premise site
    c. AMI modulation
    d. high bandwidth of the coaxial cable

Exercises

82. If we want to transmit 1000 ASCII (see Appendix A) characters asynchronously, what is the minimum number of extra bits needed? What is the efficiency in percentage?

83. The ASCII (see Appendix A) letter *A* is sent using EIA-232 interface standards and synchronous transmission. Draw a plot of the transmission (amplitude versus time), assuming a bit rate of 10 bps.

84. Draw the time-domain graph for the bit pattern 10110110 as it would appear on an RS-422 circuit. Assume a 1 is 5 volts and a 0 is −5 volts. Draw the complement also.

85. Using the data in the preceding problem, assume that the first and last bits are corrupted by 1 volt of noise. Draw both lines and draw the difference of the complement from the signal.

86. Create a two-column table. In the first column, list the pins in a DB-9 implementation of EIA-232. In the second column, list the corresponding pins in the DB-25 implementation of EIA-232.

87. An imaginary cable modem has a 6 MHz channel for a cable TV channel. It uses 128-QAM for downloading and 8-PSK for uploading. What is the bit rate in each direction? Note that the same band is used for uploading and downloading.

88. Write a Hayes command to dial the number 864-8902 and adjust the speaker volume to level 10.

89. Write a Hayes command to dial the number (408)864-8902 and enable echo printing.

90. Repeat Exercise 89, but disable echo printing.

91. How many pins are needed if we use DB-25 in asynchronous mode with only one channel?

92. How many pins are needed if we use DB-25 in synchronous mode with only one channel?

93. How many pins are needed for the secondary channel in DB-25?

94. Redo the example of Figure 6.12 in the text using asynchronous transmission.

95. Redo the example of Figure 6.12 using a DB-9 connector.

96. Using RS-423 (unbalanced mode), what is the data rate if the distance between DTE and DCE is 1000 feet?

97. Using RS-422 (balanced mode), what is the data rate if the distance between DTE and DCE is 1000 feet?

98. How much improvement in data rate can be achieved over 1000 feet if we move from RS-423 to RS-422?

99. Show the bit pattern in an asynchronous transmission with one start and one stop bit if the data to be sent is "Hello". Use ASCII code (Appendix A).

100. Some modems send 4 bits per character (instead of 8) if the data are purely numeric (digits 0 to 9). Show how this can be done using the ASCII table in Appendix A.

101. The *local loopback test* tests the operation of the local DCE (modem). A signal is sent from the local DTE to the local DCE and returned to the local DTE. Draw a figure and show which EIA-232 pins are used for this test.

102. The *remote loopback test* tests the operation of the remote DCE (modem). A signal is sent from the local DTE to the local DCE, from the local DCE to the remote DCE (through the telephone network) and then returned. Draw a figure to show which EIA-232 pins are used for this test.

CHAPTER 7

Transmission Media

As discussed in Chapter 4, computers and other telecommunication devices use signals to represent data. These signals are transmitted from one device to another in the form of electromagnetic energy. Electromagnetic signals can travel through a vacuum, air, or other transmission media.

Electromagnetic energy, a combination of electrical and magnetic fields vibrating in relation to each other, includes power, voice, radio waves, **infrared light,** visible light, ultraviolet light, and X, gamma, and cosmic rays. Each of these constitutes a portion of the **electromagnetic spectrum** (see Figure 7.1). Not all portions of the spectrum are currently usable for telecommunications, however, and media to harness those that are usable are limited to a few types. Voice-band frequencies are generally transmitted as current over metal cables, such as twisted-pair or coaxial cable. Radio frequencies can travel through air or space but require specific transmitting and receiving mechanisms. Visible light, the third type of electromagnetic energy currently used for communications, is harnessed using fiber-optic cable.

Figure 7.1 *Electromagnetic spectrum*

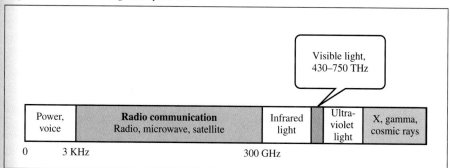

Transmission media can be divided into two broad categories: guided and unguided (see Figure 7.2).

Figure 7.2 *Classes of transmission media*

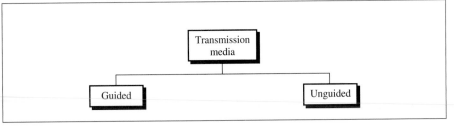

7.1 GUIDED MEDIA

Guided media, which are those that provide a conduit from one device to another, include **twisted-pair cable, coaxial cable,** and fiber-optic cable (see Figure 7.3). A signal traveling along any of these media is directed and contained by the physical limits of the medium. Twisted-pair and coaxial cable use metallic (copper) conductors that accept and transport signals in the form of electrical current. **Optical fiber** is a glass or plastic cable that accepts and transports signals in the form of light.

Figure 7.3 *Categories of guided media*

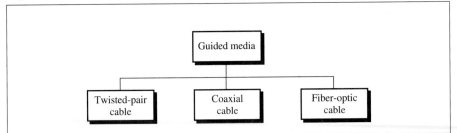

Twisted-Pair Cable

Twisted-pair cable comes in two forms: unshielded and shielded.

Unshielded Twisted-Pair (UTP) Cable

Unshielded twisted-pair (UTP) cable is the most common type of telecommunication medium in use today. Although most familiar from its use in telephone systems, its frequency range is suitable for transmitting both data and voice (see Figure 7.4). A twisted pair consists of two conductors (usually copper), each with its own colored plastic insulation. The plastic insulation is color-banded for identification (see Figure 7.5). Colors are used both to identify the specific conductors in a cable and to indicate which wires belong in pairs and how they relate to other pairs in a larger bundle.

A twisted pair consists of two conductors each surrounded by an insulating material.

Figure 7.4   *Frequency range for twisted-pair cable*

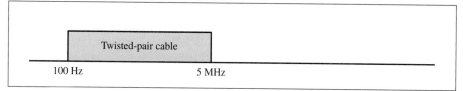

Figure 7.5   *Twisted-pair cable*

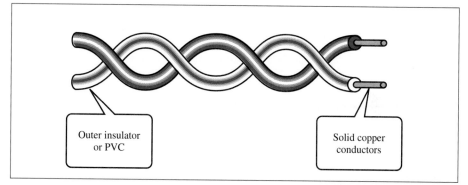

In the past, two parallel flat wires were used for communication. However, electromagnetic interference from devices such as a motor can create noise over those wires. If the two wires are parallel, the wire closest to the source of the noise gets more interference and ends up with a higher voltage level than the wire farther away, which results in an uneven load and a damaged signal (see Figure 7.6).

Figure 7.6   *Effect of noise on parallel lines*

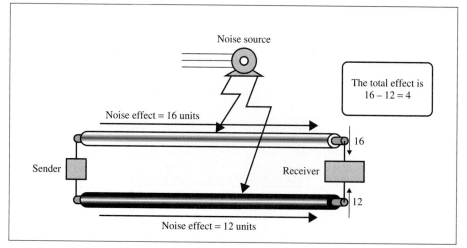

If, however, the two wires are twisted around each other at regular intervals (between 2 and 12 twists per foot), each wire is closer to the noise source for half the time and farther away for the other half. With twisting, therefore, the cumulative effect of the interference is equal on both wires (examine Figure 7.7). Each section of wire has a "load" of 4 when it is on the top of the twist and 3 when it is on the bottom. The total effect of the noise at the receiver is therefore 0 (14 − 14). Twisting does not always eliminate the impact of noise, but it does significantly reduce it.

Figure 7.7   *Effect of noise on twisted-pair lines*

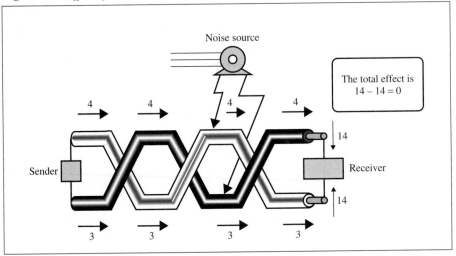

Advantages of UTP are its cost and ease of use. UTP is cheap, flexible, and easy to install. Higher grades of UTP are used in many LAN technologies, including Ethernet and Token Ring. Figure 7.8 shows a cable containing five unshielded twisted pairs.

Figure 7.8   *Cable with five unshielded twisted pairs of wires*

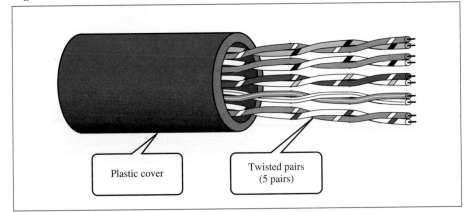

The Electronic Industries Association (EIA) has developed standards to grade UTP cables by quality. Categories are determined by cable quality, with 1 as the lowest and 5 as the highest. Each EIA category is suitable for certain uses and not for others:

- **Category 1.** The basic twisted-pair cabling used in telephone systems. This level of quality is fine for voice but inadequate for all but low-speed data communication.
- **Category 2.** The next higher grade, suitable for voice and for data transmission of up to 4 Mbps.
- **Category 3.** Required to have at least three twists per foot and can be used for data transmission of up to 10 Mbps. It is now the standard cable for most telephone systems.
- **Category 4.** Must also have at least three twists per foot as well as other conditions to bring the possible transmission rate to 16 Mbps.
- **Category 5.** Used for data transmission up to 100 Mbps.

UTP Connectors   UTP is most commonly connected to network devices via a type of snap-in plug like that used with telephone jacks. Connectors are either male (the plug) or female (the receptacle). Male connectors snap into female connectors and have a repressible tab (called a key) that locks them in place. Each wire in a cable is attached to one conductor (or pin) in the connector. The most frequently used of these plugs is an RJ45 connector with eight conductors, one for each wire of four twisted pairs (see Figure 7.9).

Figure 7.9   *UTP connection*

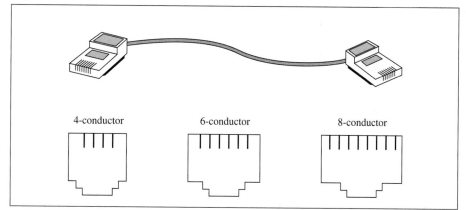

Shielded Twisted-Pair (STP) Cable

Shielded twisted-pair (STP) cable has a metal foil or braided-mesh covering that encases each pair of insulated conductors (see Figure 7.10). The metal casing prevents the penetration of electromagnetic noise. It also can eliminate a phenomenon called **crosstalk,** which is the undesired effect of one circuit (or channel) on another circuit (or channel). It occurs when one line (acting as a kind of receiving antenna) picks up some of the signals traveling down another line (acting as a kind of sending antenna). This effect can be experienced during telephone conversations when one can hear other conversations in the background. Shielding each pair of a twisted-pair cable can eliminate most crosstalk.

Figure 7.10   *Shielded twisted-pair cable*

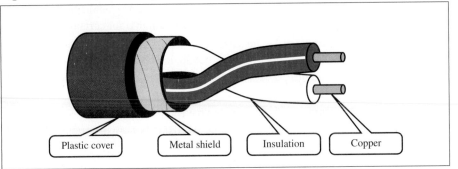

| Plastic cover | Metal shield | Insulation | Copper |

STP has the same quality considerations and uses the same connectors as UTP, but the shield must be connected to a ground. Materials and manufacturing requirements make STP more expensive than UTP but less susceptible to noise.

Coaxial Cable

Coaxial cable (or *coax*) carries signals of higher frequency ranges than twisted-pair cable (see Figure 7.11), in part because the two media are constructed quite differently. Instead of having two wires, coax has a central core conductor of solid or stranded wire (usually copper) enclosed in an insulating sheath, which is, in turn, encased in an outer conductor of metal foil, braid, or a combination of the two (also usually copper). The outer metallic wrapping serves both as a shield against noise and as the second conductor, which completes the circuit. This outer conductor is also enclosed in an insulating sheath, and the whole cable is protected by a plastic cover (see Figure 7.12).

Figure 7.11   *Frequency range of coaxial cable*

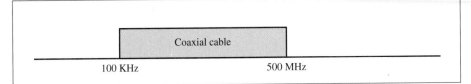

Coaxial cable

100 KHz   500 MHz

Coaxial Cable Standards

Different coaxial cable designs are categorized by their radio government (RG) ratings. Each RG number denotes a unique set of physical specifications, including the wire gauge of the inner conductor, the thickness and type of the inner insulator, the construction of the shield, and the size and type of the outer casing.

Each cable defined by RG ratings is adapted for a specialized function. The following are a few of the common ones:

- **RG-8.** Used in thick Ethernet.
- **RG-9.** Used in thick Ethernet.
- **RG-11.** Used in thick Ethernet.

Figure 7.12   *Coaxial cable*

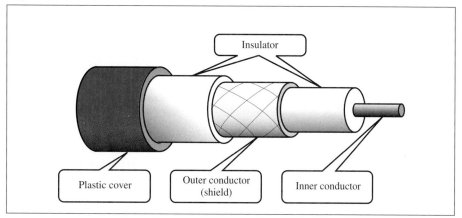

- **RG-58.** Used in thin Ethernet.
- **RG-59.** Used for TV.

Coaxial Cable Connectors

Over the years, a number of connectors have been designed for use with coaxial cable, usually by manufacturers seeking specific solutions to specific product requirements. A few of the most widely used connector designs have become standardized. The most common of these is called a barrel connector because of its shape. Of the barrel connectors, the most popular is the bayonet network connector (BNC), which pushes on and locks into place with a half turn. Other types of barrel connectors either screw together, and thus require more effort to install, or push on without locking, which is less secure. Generally, a cable terminates in a male connector that plugs or screws onto a corresponding female connector attached to the device. All coaxial connectors have a single pin protruding from the center of the male connector that slides into a ferrule in the female connector. Coaxial connectors are familiar from cable TV and VCR hookups, which employ both threaded and slip-on styles.

Two other commonly used types of connectors are T-connectors and terminators. A T-connector (used in thin Ethernet) allows a secondary cable or cables to branch off from a main line. A cable running from a computer, for example, can branch to connect several terminals. **Terminators** are required for bus topologies where one main cable acts as a backbone with branches to several devices but does not itself terminate in a device. If the main cable is left unterminated, any signal transmitted over the line echoes back and interferes with the original signal. A terminator absorbs the wave at the end and eliminates echo-back.

Optical Fiber

Up until this point, we have discussed conductive (metal) cables that transmit signals in the form of current. Optical fiber, on the other hand, is made of glass or plastic and transmits signals in the form of light. To understand optical fiber, we first need to explore several aspects of the nature of light.

The Nature of Light

Light is a form of electromagnetic energy. It travels at its fastest in a vacuum: 300,000 kilometers/second (approximately 186,000 miles/second). The speed of light depends on the density of the medium through which it is traveling (the higher the density, the slower the speed).

> Light, a form of electromagnetic energy, travels at 300,000 kilometers/second, or approximately 186,000 miles/second, in a vacuum. This speed decreases as the medium through which the light travels becomes denser.

Refraction   Light travels in a straight line as long as it is moving through a single uniform substance. If a ray of light traveling through one substance suddenly enters another (more or less dense) substance, its speed changes abruptly, causing the ray to change direction. This change is called **refraction.** A straw sticking out of a glass of water appears bent, or even broken, because the light by which we see it changes direction as it moves from the air to the water.

The direction in which a light ray is refracted depends on the change in density encountered. A beam of light moving from a less dense into a more dense medium is bent toward the vertical axis (examine Figure 7.13). The two angles made by the beam of light in relation to the vertical axis are called I, for incident, and R, for refracted. In Figure 7.13a, the beam travels from a less dense medium into a more dense medium. In this case, angle R is smaller than angle I. In Figure 7.13b, however, the beam travels from a more dense medium into a less dense medium. In this case, the value of I is smaller than the value of R. In other words, when light travels into a more dense medium, the **angle of incidence** is greater than the **angle of refraction;** and when light travels into a less dense medium, the angle of incidence is less than the angle of refraction.

Figure 7.13   *Refraction*

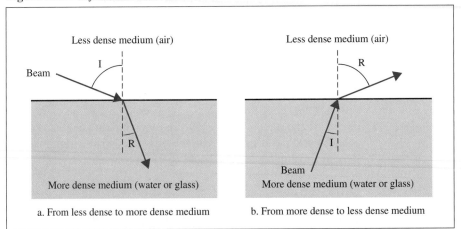

a. From less dense to more dense medium

b. From more dense to less dense medium

Fiber-optic technology takes advantage of the properties shown in Figure 7.13b to control the propagation of light through the fiber channel.

Critical Angle   Now examine Figure 7.14. Once again we have a beam of light moving from a more dense into a less dense medium. In this example, however, we gradually increase the angle of incidence measured from the vertical. As the angle of incidence increases, so does the angle of refraction. It, too, moves away from the vertical and closer and closer to the horizontal.

Figure 7.14   *Critical angle*

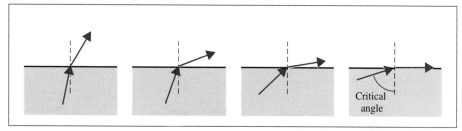

At some point in this process, the change in the incident angle results in a refracted angle of 90 degrees, with the refracted beam now lying along the horizontal. The incident angle at this point is known as the **critical angle.**

Reflection   When the angle of incidence becomes greater than the critical angle, a new phenomenon occurs called **reflection** (or, more accurately, complete reflection, because some aspects of reflection always coexist with refraction). Light no longer passes into the less dense medium at all. In this case, the angle of incidence is always equal to the **angle of reflection** (see Figure 7.15).

Figure 7.15   *Reflection*

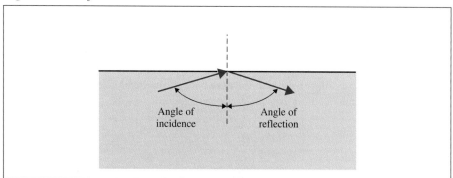

Optical fibers use reflection to guide light through a channel. A glass or plastic core is surrounded by a cladding of less dense glass or plastic. The difference in density of the two materials must be such that a beam of light moving through the core is reflected off the cladding instead of being refracted into it. Information is encoded onto a beam of light as a series of on-off flashes that represent 1 and 0 bits.

Propagation Modes

Current technology supports two modes for propagating light along optical channels, each requiring fiber with different physical characteristics: multimode and single mode. Multimode, in turn, can be implemented in two forms: step-index or graded-index (see Figure 7.16).

Figure 7.16   *Propagation modes*

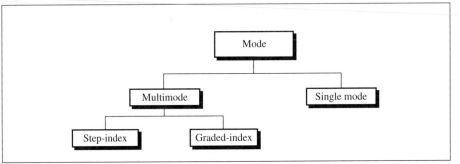

Multimode   Multimode is so named because multiple beams from a light source move through the core in different paths. How these beams move within the cable depends on the structure of the core.

In **multimode step-index fiber,** the density of the core remains constant from the center to the edges. A beam of light moves through this constant density in a straight line until it reaches the interface of the core and the **cladding.** At the interface, there is an abrupt change to a lower density that alters the angle of the beam's motion. The term *step-index* refers to the suddenness of this change.

Figure 7.17 shows various beams (or rays) traveling through a step-index fiber. Some beams in the middle travel in straight lines through the core and reach the destination without reflecting or refracting. Some beams strike the interface of the core and cladding at an angle smaller than the critical angle; these beams penetrate the cladding and are lost. Still others hit the edge of the core at angles greater than the critical angle and reflect back into the core and off the other side, bouncing back and forth down the channel until they reach the destination.

Figure 7.17   *Multimode step-index fiber*

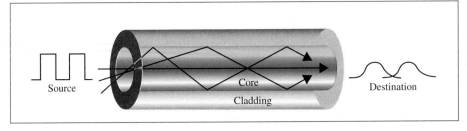

Every beam reflects off the interface at an angle equal to its angle of incidence. The greater the angle of incidence, the wider the angle of reflection. A beam with a smaller angle of incidence will require more bounces to travel the same distance than a beam with a larger angle of incidence. Consequently, the beam with the smaller incident angle must travel farther to reach the destination. This difference in path length means that different beams arrive at the destination at different times. As these different beams are recombined at the receiver, they result in a signal that is no longer an exact replica of the signal that was transmitted. Such a signal has been distorted by propagation delays. This distortion limits the available data rate and makes multimode step-index cable inadequate for certain precise applications.

A second type of fiber, called **multimode graded-index fiber,** decreases this distortion of the signal through the cable. The word *index* here refers to the index of refraction. As we saw above, index of refraction is related to density. A graded-index fiber, therefore, is one with varying densities. Density is highest at the center of the core and decreases gradually to its lowest at the edge. Figure 7.18 shows the impact of this variable density on the propagation of light beams.

Figure 7.18 *Multimode graded-index fiber*

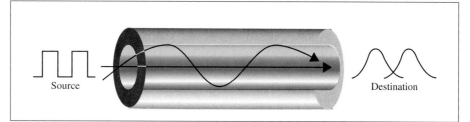

The signal is introduced at the center of the core. From this point, only the horizontal beam moves in a straight line through the constant density at the center. Beams at other angles move through a series of constantly changing densities. Each density difference causes each beam to refract into a curve. In addition, varying the refraction varies the distance each beam travels in a given period of time, resulting in different beams intersecting at regular intervals. Careful placement of the receiver at one of these intersections allows the signal to be reconstructed with far greater precision.

Single Mode   Single mode uses step-index fiber and a highly focused source of light that limits beams to a small range of angles, all close to the horizontal. The **single-mode fiber** itself is manufactured with a much smaller diameter than that of multimode fibers, and with substantially lower density (index of refraction). The decrease in density results in a critical angle that is close enough to 90 degrees to make the propagation of beams almost horizontal. In this case, propagation of different beams is almost identical and delays are negligible. All of the beams arrive at the destination "together" and can be recombined without distortion to the signal (see Figure 7.19).

Figure 7.19   *Single-mode fiber*

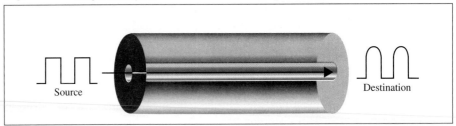

Source   Destination

Fiber Sizes

Optical fibers are defined by the ratio of the diameter of their core to the diameter of their cladding, both expressed in microns (micrometers). The common sizes are shown in Table 7.1. The last size listed is used only for single mode.

Table 7.1   *Fiber types*

Fiber Type	Core (microns)	Cladding (microns)
62.5/125	62.5	125
50/125	50.0	125
100/140	100.0	140
8.3/125	8.3	125

Cable Composition

Figure 7.20 shows the composition of a typical fiber-optic cable. A core is surrounded by cladding, forming the fiber. In most cases, the fiber is covered by a buffer layer that protects it from moisture. Finally, the entire cable is encased in an outer jacket.

Figure 7.20   *Fiber construction*

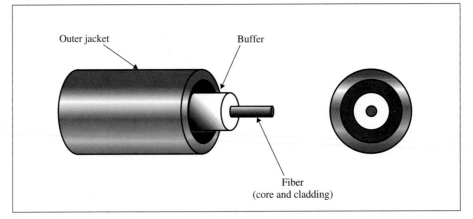

Outer jacket   Buffer

Fiber
(core and cladding)

Both core and cladding can be made of either glass or plastic but must be of different densities. In addition, the inner core must be ultrapure and completely regular in size and shape. Chemical differences in material, and even small variations in the size or shape of the channel, alter the angle of reflection and distort the signal. Some applications can handle a certain amount of distortion and their cables can be made more cheaply, but others depend on complete uniformity.

The outer jacket (or sheath) can be made of several materials, including Teflon coating, plastic coating, fibrous plastic, metal tubing, and metal mesh. Each of these jacketing materials has its own purpose. Plastics are lightweight and inexpensive but do not provide structural strength and can emit fumes when burned. Metal tubing provides strength but raises cost. Teflon is lightweight and can be used in open air, but it is expensive and does not increase cable strength. The choice of the material depends on where the cable is to be installed.

Light Sources for Optical Cable

As we have seen, the purpose of fiber-optic cable is to contain and direct a beam of light from source to target. For transmission to occur, the sending device must be equipped with a light source and the receiving device with a photosensitive cell (called a photodiode) capable of translating the received light into current usable by a computer. The light source can be either a **light-emitting diode (LED)** or an injection laser diode (ILD). LEDs are the cheaper source, but they provide unfocused light that strikes the boundaries of the channel at uncontrollable angles and diffuses over distance. For this reason, LEDs are limited to short-distance use.

Lasers, on the other hand, can be focused to a very narrow range, allowing control over the angle of incidence. Laser signals preserve the character of the signal over considerable distances.

Fiber-Optic Connectors

Connectors for fiber-optic cable must be as precise as the cable itself. With metallic media, connections are not required to be exact as long as both conductors are in physical contact. With optical fiber, on the other hand, any misalignment of one segment of core either with another segment or with a photodiode results in the signal reflecting back toward the sender, and any difference in the size of two connected channels results in a change in the angle of the signal. In addition, the connection must be complete yet not overly tight. A gap between two cores results in a dissipated signal; an overly tight connection can compress the two cores and alter the angle of reflection.

Given these constraints, manufacturers have developed several connectors that are both precise and easy to use. All of the popular connectors are barrel shaped and come in male and female versions. The cable is equipped with a male connector that locks or threads into a female connector attached to the device to be connected.

Advantages of Optical Fiber

The major advantages offered by fiber-optic cable over twisted-pair and coaxial cable are noise resistance, less signal attenuation, and higher bandwidth.

- **Noise resistance.** Because fiber-optic transmission uses light rather than electricity, noise is not a factor. External light, the only possible interference, is blocked from the channel by the outer jacket.

■ **Less signal attenuation.** Fiber-optic transmission distance is significantly greater than that of other guided media. A signal can run for miles without requiring regeneration.

■ **Higher bandwidth.** Fiber-optic cable can support dramatically higher bandwidths (and hence data rates) than either twisted-pair or coaxial cable. Currently, data rates and bandwidth utilization over fiber-optic cable are limited not by the medium but by the signal generation and reception technology available.

Disadvantages of Optical Fiber

The main disadvantages of fiber optics are cost, installation/maintenance, and fragility.

■ **Cost.** Fiber-optic cable is expensive. Because any impurities or imperfections in the core can throw off the signal, manufacturing must be painstakingly precise. Also, a laser light source can cost thousands of dollars, compared to hundreds of dollars for electrical signal generators.

■ **Installation/maintenance.** Any roughness or cracking in the core of an optical cable diffuses light and alters the signal. All splices must be polished and precisely fused. All connections must be perfectly aligned and matched for core size and must provide a completely light-tight seal. Metallic media connections, on the other hand, can be made by cutting and crimping using relatively unsophisticated tools.

■ **Fragility.** Glass fiber is more easily broken than wire, making it less useful for applications where hardware portability is required.

As manufacturing techniques have improved and costs have come down, high data rates and immunity to noise have made fiber optics increasingly popular.

7.2   UNGUIDED MEDIA

Unguided media, or **wireless communication,** transport electromagnetic waves without using a physical conductor. Instead, signals are broadcast through air (or, in a few cases, water), and thus are available to anyone who has a device capable of receiving them.

Radio Frequency Allocation

The section of the electromagnetic spectrum defined as radio communication is divided into eight ranges, called bands, each regulated by government authorities. These bands are rated from very low frequency (VLF) to extremely high frequency (EHF). Figure 7.21 shows all eight bands and their acronyms.

Propagation of Radio Waves

Types of Propagation

Radio wave transmission utilizes five different types of propagation: surface, tropospheric, ionospheric, line-of-sight, and space (see Figure 7.22).

Figure 7.21   *Radio communication band*

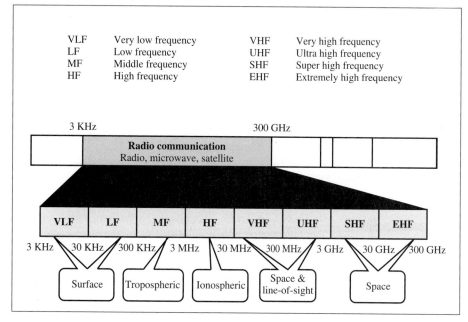

Figure 7.22   *Types of propagation*

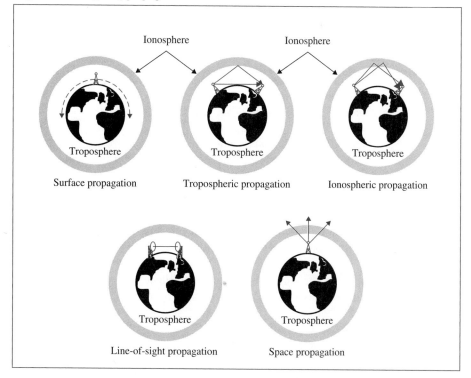

Radio technology considers the earth as surrounded by two layers of atmosphere: the troposphere and the ionosphere. The **troposphere** is the portion of the atmosphere extending outward approximately 30 miles from the earth's surface (in radio terminology, the troposphere includes the high-altitude layer called the stratosphere) and contains what we generally think of as air. Clouds, wind, temperature variations, and weather in general occur in the troposphere, as does jet plane travel. The **ionosphere** is the layer of atmosphere above the troposphere but below space. It is beyond what we think of as atmosphere and contains free electrically charged particles (hence the name).

Surface Propagation   In surface propagation, radio waves travel through the lowest portion of the atmosphere, hugging the earth. At the lowest frequencies, signals emanate in all directions from the transmitting antenna and follow the curvature of the planet. Distance depends on the amount of power in the signal: the greater the power, the greater the distance. Surface propagation can also take place in seawater.

Tropospheric Propagation   **Tropospheric propagation** can work two ways. Either a signal can be directed in a straight line from antenna to antenna (line-of-sight), or it can be broadcast at an angle into the upper layers of the troposphere where it is reflected back down to the earth's surface. The first method requires that the placement of the receiver and the transmitter be within line-of-sight distances, limited by the curvature of the earth in relation to the height of the antennas. The second method allows greater distances to be covered.

Ionospheric Propagation   In **ionospheric propagation,** higher-frequency radio waves radiate upward into the ionosphere where they are reflected back to earth. The density difference between the troposphere and the ionosphere causes each radio wave to speed up and change direction, bending back to earth. This type of transmission allows for greater distances to be covered with lower power output.

Line-of-Sight Propagation   In **line-of-sight propagation,** very high frequency signals are transmitted in straight lines directly from antenna to antenna. Antennas must be directional, facing each other, and either tall enough or close enough together not to be affected by the curvature of the earth. Line-of-sight propagation is tricky because radio transmissions cannot be completely focused. Waves emanate upward and downward as well as forward and can reflect off the surface of the earth or parts of the atmosphere. Reflected waves that arrive at the receiving antenna later than the direct portion of the transmission can corrupt the received signal.

Space Propagation   **Space propagation** utilizes satellite relays in place of atmospheric refraction. A broadcast signal is received by an orbiting satellite, which rebroadcasts the signal to the intended receiver back on the earth. Satellite transmission is basically line-of-sight with an intermediary (the satellite). The distance of the satellite from the earth makes it the equivalent of a super-high-gain antenna and dramatically increases the distance coverable by a signal.

Propagation of Specific Signals

The type of propagation used in radio transmission depends on the frequency (speed) of the signal. Each frequency is suited for a specific layer of the atmosphere and is most efficiently transmitted and received by technologies adapted to that layer.

VLF   Very low frequency (VLF) waves are propagated as surface waves, usually through air but sometimes through seawater. VLF waves do not suffer much attenuation in transmission but are susceptible to the high levels of atmospheric noise (heat and electricity) active at low altitudes. VLF waves are used mostly for long-range radio navigation and for submarine communication (see Figure 7.23).

Figure 7.23   *Frequency range for VLF*

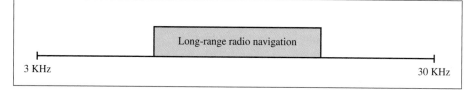

LF   Similar to VLF, **low frequency (LF)** waves are also propagated as surface waves. LF waves are used for long-range radio navigation and for radio beacons or navigational locators (see Figure 7.24). Attenuation is greater during the daytime, when absorption of waves by natural obstacles increases.

Figure 7.24   *Frequency range for LF*

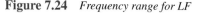
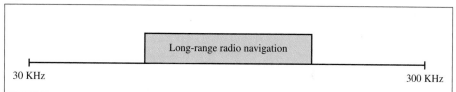

MF   Middle frequency (MF) signals are propagated in the troposphere. These frequencies are absorbed by the ionosphere. The distance they can cover is therefore limited by the angle needed to reflect the signal within the troposphere without entering the ionosphere. Absorption increases during the daytime, but most MF transmissions rely on line-of-sight antennas to increase control and avoid the absorption problem altogether. Uses for MF transmissions include AM radio, maritime radio, radio direction finding (RDF), and emergency frequencies (see Figure 7.25).

Figure 7.25   *Frequency range for MF*

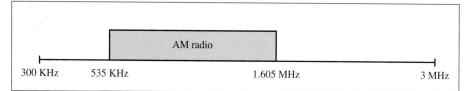

HF   High frequency (HF) signals use ionospheric propagation. These frequencies move into the ionosphere, where the density difference reflects them back to earth. Uses for HF signals include amateur radio (ham radio), citizen's band (CB) radio, international broadcasting, military communication, long-distance aircraft and ship communication, telephone, telegraph, and facsimile (see Figure 7.26).

Figure 7.26   *Frequency range for HF*

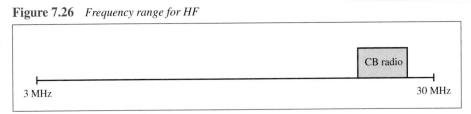

VHF   Most **very high frequency (VHF)** waves use line-of-sight propagation. Uses for VHF include VHF television, FM radio, aircraft AM radio, and aircraft navigational aid (see Figure 7.27).

Figure 7.27   *Frequency range for VHF*

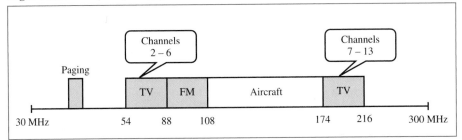

UHF   **Ultrahigh frequency (UHF)** waves always use line-of-sight propagation. Uses for UHF include UHF television, mobile telephone, cellular radio, paging, and microwave links (see Figure 7.28). Note that microwave communication begins at 1 GHz in the UHF band and continues into the SHF and EHF bands.

Figure 7.28   *Frequency range for UHF*

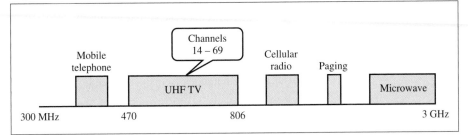

SHF   **Superhigh frequency (SHF)** waves are transmitted using mostly line-of-sight and some space propagation. Uses for SHF include terrestrial and satellite microwave and radar communication (see Figure 7.29).

Figure 7.29   *Frequency range for SHF*

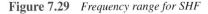
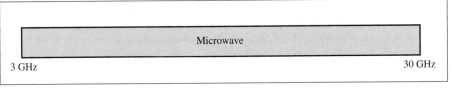

EHF   Extremely high frequency (EHF) waves use space propagation. Uses for EHF are predominantly scientific and include radar, satellite, and experimental communications (see Figure 7.30).

Figure 7.30   *Frequency range for EHF*

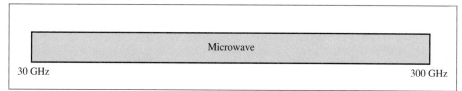

Terrestrial Microwave

Microwaves do not follow the curvature of the earth and therefore require line-of-sight transmission and reception equipment. The distance coverable by a line-of-sight signal depends to a large extent on the height of the antenna: the taller the antennas, the longer the sight distance. Height allows the signal to travel farther without being stopped by the curvature of the planet and raises the signal above many surface obstacles, such as low hills and tall buildings that would otherwise block transmission. Typically, antennas are mounted on towers that are in turn often mounted on hills or mountains.

Microwave signals propagate in one direction at a time, which means that two frequencies are necessary for two-way communication such as a telephone conversation. One frequency is reserved for **microwave transmission** in one direction and the other for transmission in the other. Each frequency requires its own transmitter and receiver. Today, both pieces of equipment usually are combined in a single piece of equipment called a transceiver, which allows a single antenna to serve both frequencies and functions.

Repeaters

To increase the distance served by **terrestrial microwave,** a system of repeaters can be installed with each antenna. A signal received by one antenna can be converted back into transmittable form and relayed to the next antenna (see Figure 7.31). The distance required between repeaters varies with the frequency of the signal and the environment in which the antennas are found. A repeater may broadcast the regenerated signal either at the original frequency or at a new frequency, depending on the system.

Terrestrial microwave with repeaters provides the basis for most contemporary telephone systems worldwide.

Antennas

Two types of antennas are used for terrestrial microwave communications: parabolic dish and horn.

A **parabolic dish antenna** is based on the geometry of a parabola: every line parallel to the line of symmetry (line of sight) reflects off the curve at angles such that they

Figure 7.31 *Terrestrial microwave*

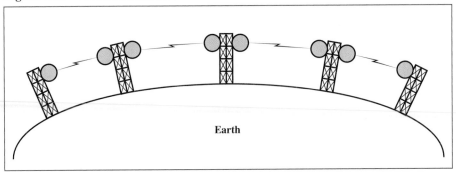

intersect in a common point called the focus (see Figure 7.32). The parabolic dish works like a funnel, catching a wide range of waves and directing them to a common point. In this way, more of the signal is recovered than would be possible with a single-point receiver.

Figure 7.32 *Parabolic dish antenna*

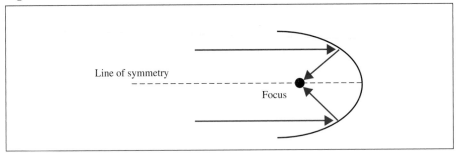

Outgoing transmissions are broadcast through a horn aimed at the dish. The microwaves hit the dish and are deflected outward in a reversal of the receipt path.

A **horn antenna** looks like a gigantic scoop. Outgoing transmissions are broadcast up a stem (resembling a handle) and deflected outward in a series of narrow parallel beams by the curved head (see Figure 7.33). Received transmissions are collected by the scooped shape of the horn, in a manner similar to the parabolic dish, and are deflected down into the stem.

Satellite Communication

Satellite transmission is much like line-of-sight microwave transmission in which one of the stations is a satellite orbiting the earth. The principle is the same as terrestrial microwave, with a satellite acting as a supertall antenna and repeater (see Figure 7.34). Although in satellite transmission signals must still travel in straight lines, the limitations imposed on distance by the curvature of the earth are reduced. In this way, satellite relays allow microwave signals to span continents and oceans with a single bounce.

Figure 7.33   *Horn antenna*

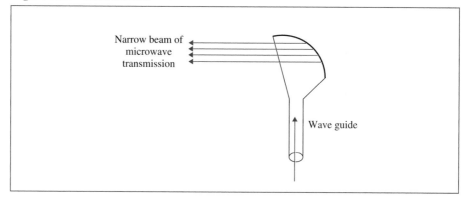

Figure 7.34   *Satellite communication*

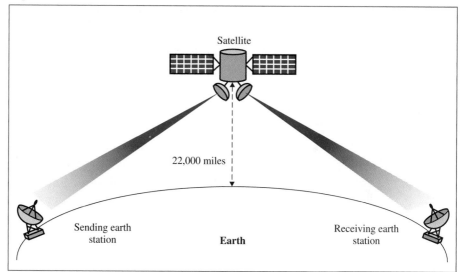

Satellite microwave can provide transmission capability to and from any location on earth, no matter how remote. This advantage makes high-quality communication available to undeveloped parts of the world without requiring a huge investment in ground-based infrastructure. Satellites themselves are extremely expensive, of course, but leasing time or frequencies on one can be relatively cheap.

Geosynchronous Satellites

Line-of-sight propagation requires that the sending and receiving antennas be locked onto each other's location at all times (one antenna must have the other in sight). For this reason, a satellite that moves faster or slower than the earth's rotation is useful only for short periods of time (just as a stopped clock is accurate twice a day). To ensure constant communication, the satellite must move at the same speed as the earth so that it seems to remain fixed above a certain spot. Such satellites are called geosynchronous.

Because orbital speed is based on distance from the planet, only one orbit can be geosynchronous. This orbit occurs at the equatorial plane and is approximately 22,000 miles from the surface of the earth.

But one geosynchronous satellite cannot cover the whole earth. One satellite in orbit has line-of-sight contact with a vast number of stations, but the curvature of the earth still keeps much of the planet out of sight. It takes a minimum of three satellites equidistant from each other in **geosynchronous orbit** to provide full global transmission. Figure 7.35 shows three satellites, each 120 degrees from another in geosynchronous orbit around the equator. The view is from the North Pole.

Figure 7.35 *Satellites in geosynchronous orbit*

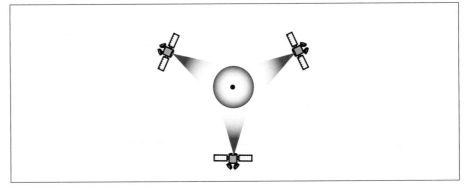

Frequency Bands for Satellite Communication

The frequencies reserved for satellite microwave communication are in the gigahertz (GHz) range. Each satellite sends and receives over two different bands. Transmission from the earth to the satellite is called **uplink.** Transmission from the satellite to the earth is called **downlink.** Table 7.2 gives the band names and frequencies for each range.

Table 7.2 *Satellite frequency bands*

Band	Downlink	Uplink
C	3.7 to 4.2 GHz	5.925 to 6.425 GHz
Ku	11.7 to 12.2 GHz	14 to 14.5 GHz
Ka	17.7 to 21 GHz	27.5 to 31 GHz

Cellular Telephony

Cellular telephony is designed to provide stable communications connections between two moving devices or between one mobile unit and one stationary (land) unit. A service provider must be able to locate and track a caller, assign a channel to the call, and transfer the signal from channel to channel as the caller moves out of the range of one channel and into the range of another.

To make this tracking possible, each cellular service area is divided into small regions called cells. Each cell contains an antenna and is controlled by a small office, called the cell office. Each cell office, in turn, is controlled by a switching office called a **mobile telephone switching office (MTSO).** The MTSO coordinates communication between all of the cell offices and the telephone central office. It is a computerized center that is responsible for connecting calls as well as recording call information and billing (see Figure 7.36).

Figure 7.36   *Cellular system*

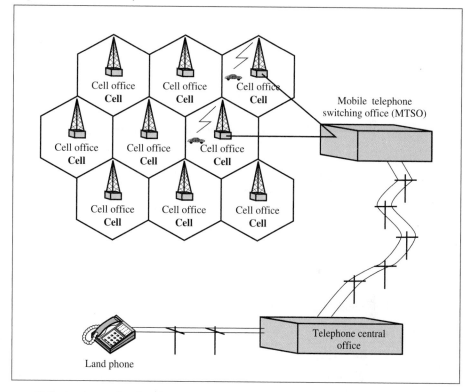

Cell size is not fixed and can be increased or decreased depending on the population of the area. The typical radius of a cell is 1 to 12 miles. High-density areas require more, geographically smaller cells to meet traffic demands than do lower density areas. Once determined, cell size is optimized to prevent the interference of adjacent cell signals. The transmission power of each cell is kept low to prevent its signal from interfering with those of other cells.

Cellular Bands

Traditional cellular transmission is analog. To minimize noise, frequency modulation (FM) is used for communication between the mobile telephone itself and the cell office. The FCC has assigned two bands for cellular use (see Figure 7.37). The band between 824 and 849 MHz carries those communications that initiate from mobile phones. The band between 869 and 894 MHz carries those communications that initiate from land phones. Carrier frequencies are spaced every 30 KHz, allowing each band to support up to 833 carriers. However, two carriers are required for full-duplex communication, which doubles the required width of each channel to 60 KHz and leaves only 416 channels available for each band.

Figure 7.37 *Cellular bands*

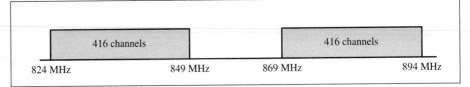

Each band, therefore, is divided into 416 FM channels (for a total of 832 channels). Of these, some are reserved for control and setup data rather than voice communication. In addition, to prevent interference, channels are distributed among the cells in such a way that adjacent cells do not use the same channels. This restriction means that each cell normally has access to only 40 channels.

Transmitting

To place a call from a mobile phone, the caller enters a code of 7 or 10 digits (a phone number) and presses the send button. The mobile phone then scans the band, seeking a setup channel with a strong signal, and sends the data (phone number) to the closest cell office using that channel. The cell office relays the data to the MTSO. The MTSO sends the data on to the telephone central office. If the called party is available, a connection is made and the result is relayed back to the MTSO. At this point, the MTSO assigns an unused voice channel to the call and a connection is established. The mobile phone automatically adjusts its tuning to the new channel and voice communication can begin.

Receiving

When a land phone places a call to a mobile phone, the telephone central office sends the number to the MTSO. The MTSO searches for the location of the mobile phone by sending query signals to each cell in a process called paging. Once the mobile phone is found, the MTSO transmits a ringing signal and, when the mobile phone is answered, assigns a voice channel to the call, allowing voice communication to begin.

Handoff

It may happen that, during a conversation, the mobile phone moves from one cell to another. When it does, the signal may become weak. To solve this problem, the MTSO monitors the level of the signal every few seconds. If the strength of the signal diminishes, the MTSO seeks a new cell that can accommodate the communication better. The MTSO then changes the channel carrying the call (hands the signal off from the old channel to a new one). Handoffs are performed so smoothly that most of the time they are transparent to the users.

Digital

Analog (FM) cellular services are based on a standard called analog circuit switched cellular (ACSC). To transmit digital data using an ACSC service requires a modem with a maximum speed of 9600 to 19,200 bps.

Since 1993, however, several service providers have been moving to a cellular data standard called cellular digital packet data (CDPD). CDPD provides low-speed digital service over the existing cellular network. It is based on the OSI model.

To use the existing digital services, such as 56K switched service, CDPD uses what is called a trisector. A trisector is a combination of three cells each using 19.2 Kbps, for a total of 57.6 Kbps (which can be accommodated on a 56K switched line by eliminating some overhead). Under this scheme, the United States is divided into 12,000 trisectors. For every 60 trisectors, there is one router.

Integration with Satellites and PCs

Cellular telephony is moving fast toward integrating the existing system with satellite communication. This integration will make it possible to have mobile communication between any two points on the globe. Another goal is to combine cellular telephony and personal computer communication under a scheme called mobile personal communication to enable people to use small, mobile personal computers to send and receive data, voice, image, and video.

7.3   TRANSMISSION IMPAIRMENT

Transmission media are not perfect. The imperfections cause impairment in the signal sent through the medium. This means that the signal at the beginning and end of the medium are not the same. What is sent is not what is received. Three types of impairment usually occur: attenuation, distortion, and noise (see Figure 7.38).

Figure 7.38 *Impairment types*

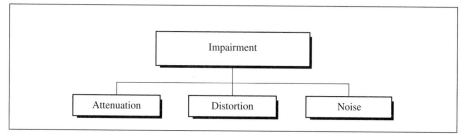

Attenuation

Attenuation means loss of energy. When a signal, simple or complex, travels through a medium, it loses some of its energy so that it can overcome the resistance of the medium. That is why a wire carrying electrical signals gets warm, if not hot, after a while. Some of the electrical energy in the signal is converted to heat. To compensate for this loss, amplifiers are used to amplify the signal. Figure 7.39 shows the effect of attenuation and amplification.

Figure 7.39 *Attenuation*

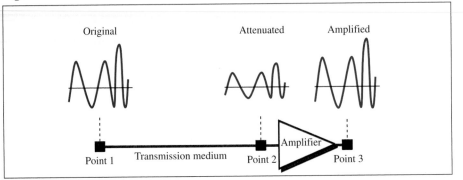

Decibel

To show that a signal has lost or gained strength, engineers use the concept of decibel. The **decibel (dB)** measures the relative strengths of two signals or a signal at two different points. Note that the dB is negative if a signal is attenuated and positive if a signal is amplified.

$$\text{dB} = 10 \log_{10} (P_2/P_1)$$

where P_1 and P_2 are the power of a signal at points 1 and 2.

Example 7.1

Imagine a signal travels through a transmission medium and its power is reduced to half. This means that $P_2 = (1/2)P_1$. In this case, the attenuation (loss of power) can be calculated as

$$10 \log_{10} (P_2/P_1) = 10 \log_{10} (0.5 \, P_1/P_1) = 10 \log_{10} (0.5) = 10 \, (-0.3) = -3 \text{ dB}$$

Engineers know that −3 dB, or a loss of 3 dB, is equivalent to losing half the power.

Example 7.2

Imagine a signal travels through an amplifier and its power is increased 10 times. This means that $P_2 = 10 \times P_1$. In this case the amplification (gain of power) can be calculated as

$$10 \log_{10} (P_2/P_1) = 10 \log_{10} (10 \, P_1/P_1) = 10 \log_{10} (10) = 10 \, (1) = 10 \text{ dB}$$

Example 7.3

One of the reasons that engineers use the decibel to measure the changes in the strength of a signal is that decibel numbers can be added (or subtracted) when we are talking about several points instead of just two (cascading). In Figure 7.40 a signal travels a long distance from point 1 to point 4. The signal is attenuated by the time it reaches point 2. Between points 2 and 3, the signal is amplified. Again, between points 3 and 4, the signal is attenuated. We can find the resultant dB for the signal just by adding the dB measurements between each set of points.

Figure 7.40 *Example 7.3*

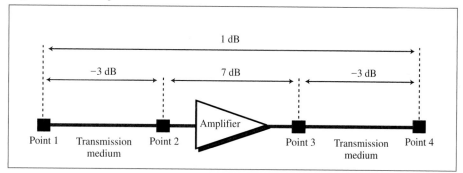

In this case, the decibel can be calculated as

$$dB = -3 + 7 - 3 = +1$$

which means that the signal has gained power.

Distortion

Distortion means that the signal changes its form or shape. Distortion occurs in a composite signal, made of different frequencies. Each signal component has its own propagation speed (see the next section) through a medium and, therefore, its own delay in arriving at the final destination. Figure 7.41 shows the effect of distortion on a composite signal.

Figure 7.41 *Distortion*

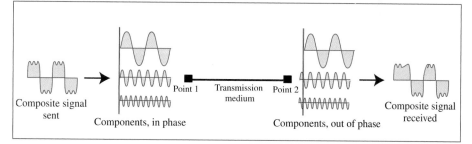

Noise

Noise is another problem. Several types of noise such as thermal noise, induced noise, crosstalk, and impulse noise may corrupt the signal. Thermal noise is the random motion of electrons in a wire that creates an extra signal not originally sent by the transmitter. Induced noise comes from sources such as motors and appliances. These devices act as a sending antenna and the transmission medium acts as the receiving antenna. Crosstalk is the effect of one wire on the other. One wire acts as a sending antenna and the other as the receiving antenna. Impulse noise is a spike (a signal with high energy in a very short period of time) that comes from power lines, lightning, and so on. Figure 7.42 shows the effect of noise on a signal.

Figure 7.42 *Noise*

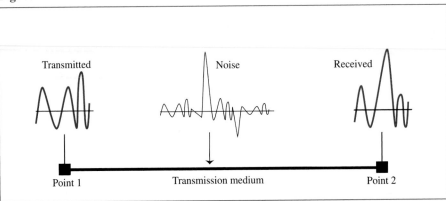

7.4 PERFORMANCE

Transmission media are roads on which data travel. To measure the performance of transmission media, we can use three concepts: throughput, propagation speed, and propagation time.

Throughput

The **throughput** is the measurement of how fast data can pass through a point. In other words, if we consider any point in the transmission medium as a wall through which bits pass, throughput is the number of bits that can pass this wall in one second. Figure 7.43 shows the concept.

Figure 7.43 *Throughput*

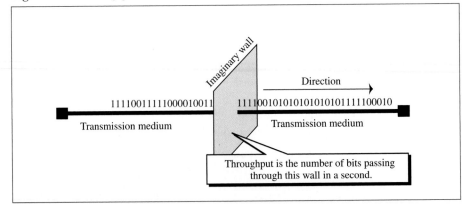

Propagation Speed

Propagation speed measures the distance a signal or a bit can travel through a medium in one second. The propagation speed of electromagnetic signals depends on the medium and the frequency of the signal. For example, in a vacuum, light is propagated with a speed of 3×10^8 m/s. It is almost the same in a twisted-pair cable. However, in coaxial and fiber optic cables, the speed is 2×10^8 m/s for frequencies in the MHz to GHz range.

Propagation Time

Propagation time measures the time required for a signal (or a bit) to travel from one point of the transmission medium to another. The propagation time is calculated by dividing the distance by the propagation speed.

Propagation time = Distance/Propagation speed

Figure 7.44 shows the concept.

Figure 7.44   *Propagation time*

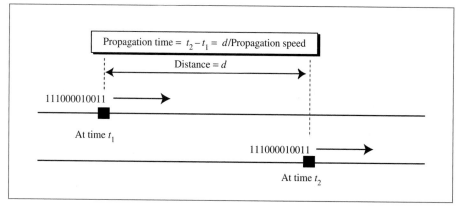

Propagation times are usually normalized to kilometers. For example, the propagation time for a twisted pair normalized to kilometers is

Propagation time $= 1000$ m$/(3 \times 10^8$ m/s$) = 3.33 \times 10^{-6}$ s/m $= 3.33$ μs/km

For coaxial or fiber optic cable, it is usually

Propagation time $= 1000$ m$/(2 \times 10^8$ m/s$) = 5 \times 10^{-6}$ s/m $= 5$ μs/km

7.5   WAVELENGTH

Wavelength is another characteristic of a signal traveling through a transmission medium. Wavelength binds the period or the frequency of a simple sine wave to the propagation speed of the medium. In other words, while the frequency of a signal is independent of the medium, the wavelength depends on both the frequency and the medium. Although wavelength can be associated with electrical signals, it is customary to use wavelengths when talking about the transmission of light in an optical fiber. The wavelength is the distance a simple signal can travel in one period (see Figure 7.45).

Figure 7.45   *Wavelength*

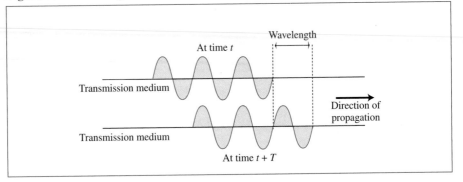

Wavelength can be calculated given the propagation speed and the period of the signal

$$\text{Wavelength} = \text{Propagation speed} \times \text{Period}$$

However, since period and frequency are related to each other, we can also say

$$\text{Wavelength} = \text{Propagation speed} \times (1/\text{Frequency}) = \text{Propagation speed/Frequency}$$

If we represent wavelength by λ, propagation speed by c, and frequency by f, we get

$$\lambda = c/f$$

The wavelength is normally measured in micrometers (microns) instead of meters. For example, the wavelength of red light (frequency = 4×10^{14}) in air is

$$\lambda = c/f = (3 \times 10^8)/(4 \times 10^{14}) = 0.75 \times 10^{-6} \text{ m} = 0.75 \text{ }\mu\text{m}$$

In a coaxial or fiber-optic cable, however, the wavelength is lower ($0.5 \text{ }\mu\text{m}$) because the propagation speed in the cable is less than in the air.

7.6   SHANNON CAPACITY

Engineers are often interested in the maximum data rate of a channel. In 1944, Claude Shannon introduced a formula to determine the theoretical highest data rate for a channel:

$$C = B \log_2 (1 + S/N)$$

In this formula, B is the bandwidth of the channel, S/N is the signal to noise ratio, and C is the capacity (called the **Shannon capacity**) of the channel in bps.

Example 7.4

Consider an extremely noisy channel in which the value of the signal-to-noise ratio is almost zero. In other words, the noise is so strong that the signal is faint. For this channel, the capacity is calculated as

$$C = B \log_2 (1 + S/N) = B \log_2 (1 + 0) = B \log_2 (1) = B \times 0 = 0$$

This means that the capacity of this channel is zero regardless of the bandwidth. In other words, we cannot send any data through this channel.

Example 7.5

We can calculate the theoretical highest bit rate of a regular telephone line. A telephone line normally has a bandwidth of 3000 Hz (300 Hz to 3300 Hz). The signal-to-noise ratio is usually 3162 (35 dB). For this channel, the capacity is calculated as

$$C = B \log_2 (1 + S/N) = 3000 \log_2 (1 + 3162) = 3000 \log_2 (3163)$$
$$= 3000 \times 11.62 = 34,860 \text{ bps}$$

This means that the highest bit rate for a telephone line is 34.860 Kbps. If we want to send data faster than this, we should either increase the bandwidth of the line or improve the signal-to-noise ratio.

7.7   MEDIA COMPARISON

When evaluating the suitability of a particular medium to a specific application, five factors should be kept in mind: cost, speed, attenuation, electromagnetic interference, and security.

- **Cost.** This is the cost of the materials, plus installation.

- **Speed.** The speed is the maximum number of bits per second that a medium can transmit reliably. Among other factors, speed varies with frequency (higher frequencies can transport more bits per second), with the physical size of the medium and/or transmission equipment, and with the conditioning of the conductor.

- **Attenuation.** As discussed earlier, attenuation is the tendency of an electromagnetic signal to become weak or distorted over distance. During transmission, the signal's energy can become absorbed or dissipated by the medium itself. For example, a wire's resistance can leach energy from a signal and emit it in the form of heat.

- **Electromagnetic interference (EMI). Electromagnetic interference (EMI)** is the susceptibility of the medium to external electromagnetic energy inadvertently introduced onto a link that interferes with the intelligibility of a signal. Familiar effects of EMI are static (audio) and snow (visual).

- **Security.** This is protection against eavesdropping. How easy is it for an unauthorized device to listen in on the link? Some media, like broadcast radio and unshielded twisted-pair cable, are easily intercepted. Others, like fiber-optic cable, are more secure.

Table 7.3 compares the various media based on the qualities listed above.

Table 7.3   *Transmission media performance*

Medium	Cost	Speed	Attenuation	EMI	Security
UTP	Low	1–100 Mbps	High	High	Low
STP	Moderate	1–150 Mbps	High	Moderate	Low
Coax	Moderate	1 Mbps–1 Gbps	Moderate	Moderate	Low
Optical fiber	High	10 Mbps–2 Gbps	Low	Low	High
Radio	Moderate	1–10 Mbps	Low–high	High	Low
Microwave	High	1 Mbps–10 Gbps	Variable	High	Moderate
Satellite	High	1 Mbps–10 Gbps	Variable	High	Moderate
Cellular	High	9.6–19.2 Kbps	Low	Moderate	Low

7.8   KEY TERMS AND CONCEPTS

angle of incidence

angle of reflection

angle of refraction

attenuation

cellular telephony

cladding

coaxial cable

critical angle

crosstalk

decibel (dB)

distortion

downlink

electromagnetic interference (EMI)

electromagnetic spectrum

extremely high frequency (EHF)

geosynchronous orbit

guided media

high frequency (HF)

horn antenna

infrared light

ionosphere

ionospheric propagation

laser

light-emitting diode (LED)

line-of-sight propagation

low frequency (LF)

microwave

microwave transmission

middle frequency (MF)

mobile telephone switching office (MTSO)

multimode graded-index fiber

multimode step-index fiber

noise

optical fiber

parabolic dish antenna

propagation speed

propagation time

radio wave

reflection

refraction

Shannon capacity

shielded twisted-pair (STP)

single-mode fiber

space propagation

superhigh frequency (SHF)

terminator

terrestrial microwave

throughput

transmission medium

troposphere

tropospheric propagation

twisted-pair cable

ultrahigh frequency (UHF)

unguided medium

unshielded twisted-pair (UTP)

uplink

very high frequency (VHF)

very low frequency (VLF)

wavelength

wireless communication

7.9   SUMMARY

■ Signals travel from transmitter to receiver via a path. This path, called the medium, can be guided or unguided.

■ A guided medium is contained within physical boundaries, while an unguided medium is boundless.

■ The most popular types of guided media are the following:

   a. Twisted-pair cable (metallic).

   b. Coaxial cable (metallic).

   c. Optical fiber (glass or plastic).

■ Twisted-pair cable consists of two insulated copper wires twisted together. Twisting allows each wire to have approximately the same noise environment.

■ Shielded twisted-pair cable consists of insulated twisted pairs encased in a metal foil or braided-mesh covering.

■ Coaxial cable consists of the following layers (starting from the center):

   a. A metallic rod-shaped inner conductor.

   b. An insulator covering the rod.

   c. A metallic outer conductor (shield).

   d. An insulator covering the shield.

   e. A plastic cover.

■ Both twisted-pair cable and coaxial cable transmit data in the form of an electric current.

■ Fiber-optic cables are composed of a glass or plastic inner core surrounded by cladding, all encased in an outside jacket.

■ Fiber-optic cables carry data signals in the form of light. The signal is propagated along the inner core by reflection.

■ Fiber-optic transmission is becoming increasingly popular due to its noise resistance, low attenuation, and high bandwidth capabilities.

■ In fiber optics, signal propagation can be multimode (multiple beams from a light source) or single mode (essentially one beam from a light source).

■ In multimode step-index propagation, the core density is constant and the light beam changes direction suddenly at the interface between the core and the cladding.

■ In multimode graded-index propagation, the core density decreases with distance from the center. This causes a curving of the light beams.

■ Radio waves can be used to transmit data. These waves use unguided media and are usually propagated through the air.

■ Regulatory authorities have divided up and defined the uses for the electromagnetic spectrum dealing with radio communication.

■ Radio wave propagation is dependent on frequency. There are five propagation types:

   a. Surface propagation.

   b. Tropospheric propagation.

    c. Ionospheric propagation.

    d. Line-of-sight propagation.

    e. Space propagation.

■ VLF and LF waves use surface propagation. These waves follow the contour of the earth.

■ MF waves are propagated in the troposphere, either through direct line-of-sight propagation from transmitter to receiver or through reflection, with the ionosphere as the upper bound.

■ HF waves travel to the ionosphere, where they are reflected back to a receiver in the troposphere.

■ VHF and UHF waves use line-of-sight propagation; the transmitter and receiver must have a clear path between them; no tall buildings or hills are allowed in the line of sight.

■ VHF, UHF, SHF, and EHF waves can be propagated into space and received by satellites.

■ Terrestrial microwaves use line-of-sight propagation for data transmission.

■ Repeaters are used to increase the distance a microwave can travel.

■ The parabolic dish antenna and the horn antenna are used for transmission and reception of microwaves.

■ Satellite communication uses a satellite in geosynchronous orbit to relay signals. A system of three correctly spaced satellites can cover most of the earth.

■ Geosynchronous orbit occurs at the equatorial plane and approximately 22,000 miles above the earth.

■ Cellular telephony provides mobile communication.

■ The cellular system consists of mobile phones, cells, MTSOs, and the telephone central office.

■ Attenuation, distortion, and noise can impair a signal.

■ Attenuation is the loss of a signal's energy due to the resistance of the medium.

■ The decibel measures the relative strength of two signals or a signal at two different points.

■ Distortion is the alteration of a signal due to the differing propagation speeds of each of the frequencies that make up a signal.

■ Noise is the external energy that corrupts a signal.

■ We can evaluate transmission media by throughput, propagation speed, and propagation time.

■ The wavelength of a frequency is defined as the propagation speed divided by the frequency.

■ The Shannon capacity is a formula to determine the theoretical maximum data rate for a channel.

■ Five factors to consider when evaluating the suitability of a medium are cost, throughput, attenuation, EMI, and security.

7.10   PRACTICE SET

Review Questions

1. Which parts of the electromagnetic spectrum are used for communication?
2. Name the two major categories of transmission media.
3. How do guided media differ from unguided media?
4. What are the three major classes of guided media?
5. What is the major advantage of shielded twisted pair over unshielded twisted pair?
6. Why is coaxial cable superior to twisted-pair cable?
7. What happens to a beam of light as it travels to a less dense medium? What happens if it travels to a denser medium?
8. A light beam travels to a less dense medium. What happens to the beam in each of the following cases:
   a. The incident angle is less than the critical angle.
   b. The incident angle is equal to the critical angle.
   c. The incident angle is greater than the critical angle.
9. What is reflection?
10. Discuss the modes for propagating light along optical channels.
11. What is the purpose of cladding in an optical fiber? Discuss its density relative to the core.
12. Name the advantages of optical fiber over twisted-pair and coaxial cable.
13. What are the disadvantages of optical fiber as a transmission medium?
14. What is the frequency range for radio communication?
15. What are the methods used to propagate radio waves?
16. How are terrestrial microwaves relayed from source to destination?
17. Why are communication satellites in geosynchronous orbit?
18. What is a handoff in cellular telephony?
19. Name three types of transmission impairment.
20. What does a decibel measure?
21. What are the three criteria used to evaluate transmission media?
22. What is the relationship between propagation speed and propagation time?
23. What is the wavelength of a signal and how is it calculated?
24. What does the Shannon capacity have to do with communications?
25. Explain what crosstalk is and what is needed to reduce it.
26. Describe the components of a fiber-optic cable. Draw a picture.
27. Why should the light ray be reflective rather than refractive in fiber optics?
28. Describe the layers of the atmosphere. What types of radio communication utilize each?

29. How does ionospheric propagation work? What are the uses for this type of propagation?

30. Why is there a distance limit for terrestrial microwave? What factors do you need to calculate this limit?

31. In a fiber-optic cable, does the light energy from the source equal the light energy recovered at the destination? Discuss this in terms of the propagation mode.

Multiple Choice Questions

32. Transmission media are usually categorized as _____.
    a. fixed or unfixed
    b. guided or unguided
    c. determinate or indeterminate
    d. metallic or nonmetallic

33. _____ cable consists of an inner copper core and a second conducting outer sheath.
    a. Twisted-pair
    b. Coaxial
    c. Fiber-optic
    d. Shielded twisted-pair

34. In fiber optics, the signal source is _____ waves.
    a. light
    b. radio
    c. infrared
    d. very low frequency

35. At the lower end of the electromagnetic spectrum we have _____.
    a. radio waves
    b. power and voice
    c. ultraviolet light
    d. infrared light

36. _____ are the highest frequency electromagnetic waves in use for data communications.
    a. Visible light waves
    b. Cosmic rays
    c. Radio waves
    d. Gamma rays

37. Smoke signals are an example of communication through _____.
    a. a guided medium
    b. an unguided medium
    c. a refractive medium
    d. a small or large medium

38. Which of the following primarily uses guided media?
    a. cellular telephone system
    b. local telephone system
    c. satellite communications
    d. radio broadcasting

39. Which of the following is not a guided medium?
    a. twisted-pair cable
    b. coaxial cable
    c. fiber-optic cable
    d. atmosphere

40. In an environment with many high-voltage devices, the best transmission medium would be _____.
    a. twisted-pair cable
    b. coaxial cable
    c. optical fiber
    d. the atmosphere

41. What is the major factor that makes coaxial cable less susceptible to noise than twisted-pair cable?
    a. inner conductor
    b. diameter of cable
    c. outer conductor
    d. insulating material

42. The RG number gives us information about _____.
    a. twisted pairs
    b. coaxial cables
    c. optical fibers
    d. all of the above

43. In an optical fiber, the inner core is _____ the cladding.
    a. more dense than
    b. less dense than
    c. the same density as
    d. another name for

44. The inner core of an optical fiber is _____ in composition.
    a. glass or plastic
    b. copper
    c. bimetallic
    d. liquid

45. When making connections in fiber optics, which of the following could contribute to signal distortion?
    a. inner cores of connecting fibers angularly or laterally misaligned
    b. a gap between connecting inner cores

   c. roughness of connecting fiber faces

   d. all of the above

46. Radio communication frequencies range from _____.

   a. 3 KHz to 300 KHz

   b. 300 KHz to 3 GHz

   c. 3 KHz to 300 GHz

   d. 3 KHz to 3000 GHz

47. The radio communication spectrum is divided into bands based on _____.

   a. amplitude

   b. frequency

   c. cost and hardware

   d. transmission medium

48. In _____ propagation, low-frequency radio waves hug the earth.

   a. surface

   b. tropospheric

   c. ionospheric

   d. space

49. The type of propagation used in radio communication is highly dependent on the _____ of the signal.

   a. data rate

   b. frequency

   c. baud rate

   d. power

50. VLF propagation occurs in _____.

   a. the troposphere

   b. the ionosphere

   c. space

   d. all of the above

51. If a satellite is in geosynchronous orbit, it completes one orbit in _____.

   a. one hour

   b. 24 hours

   c. one month

   d. one year

52. If a satellite is in geosynchronous orbit, its distance from the sending station _____.

   a. is constant

   b. varies according to the time of day

   c. varies according to the radius of the orbit

   d. none of the above

53. When a beam of light travels through media of two different densities, if the angle of incidence is greater than the critical angle, _____ occurs.
    a. reflection
    b. refraction
    c. incidence
    d. criticism

54. When the angle of refraction is _____ the angle of incidence, the light beam is moving from a more dense to a less dense medium.
    a. more than
    b. less than
    c. equal to
    d. none of the above

55. If the critical angle is 50 degrees and the angle of incidence is 60 degrees, the angle of reflection is _____ degrees.
    a. 10
    b. 50
    c. 60
    d. 110

56. If the angle of refraction is 90 degrees and the angle of incidence is 48 degrees, the critical angle is _____ degrees.
    a. 42
    b. 48
    c. 90
    d. 138

57. If the angle of refraction is 70 degrees and the angle of incidence is 50 degrees, the critical angle must be greater than _____ degrees.
    a. 50
    b. 60
    c. 70
    d. 120

58. In _____ propagation, the beam of propagated light is almost horizontal and the low-density core has a small diameter compared to the cores of the other propagation modes.
    a. multimode step-index
    b. multimode graded-index
    c. multimode single-index
    d. single mode

59. _____ is the propagation method subject to the most distortion.
    a. Multimode step-index
    b. Multimode graded-index

   c. Multimode single-index

   d. Single mode

60. In _____ propagation, the core is of varying densities.

   a. multimode step-index

   b. multimode graded-index

   c. multimode single-index

   d. single mode

61. When we talk about unguided media, usually we are referring to _____.

   a. metallic wires

   b. nonmetallic wires

   c. the atmosphere

   d. none of the above

62. Optical fibers, unlike wire media, are highly resistant to _____.

   a. high-frequency transmission

   b. low-frequency transmission

   c. electromagnetic interference

   d. refraction

63. In cellular telephony, a service area is divided into small regions called _____.

   a. cells

   b. cell offices

   c. MTSOs

   d. relay sites

64. What determines the size of a cell?

   a. the area terrain

   b. the area population

   c. the number of MTSOs

   d. all of the above

65. The MTSO is responsible for _____.

   a. connecting the cell with the telephone central office

   b. assigning channels for transmission

   c. billing functions

   d. all of the above

66. The MTSO searches for the location of a mobile phone. This is called _____.

   a. handoff

   b. handon

   c. paging

   d. receiving

67. A signal is measured at two different points. The power is P_1 at the first point and P_2 at the second point. The dB is 0. This means _____.

   a. P_2 is zero

b. P_2 equals P_1

c. P_2 is much larger than P_1

d. P_2 is much smaller than P_1

68. _____ is a type of transmission impairment in which the signal loses strength due to the resistance of the transmission medium.

a. Attenuation

b. Distortion

c. Noise

d. Decibel

69. _____ is a type of transmission impairment in which the signal loses strength due to the different propagation speed of each frequency that makes up the signal.

a. Attenuation

b. Distortion

c. Noise

d. Decibel

70. _____ is a type of transmission impairment in which an outside source such as crosstalk corrupts a signal.

a. Attenuation

b. Distortion

c. Noise

d. Decibel

71. The performance of transmission media can be measured by _____.

a. throughput

b. propagation speed

c. propagation time

d. all of the above

72. The _____ has units of meters/second or kilometers/second.

a. throughput

b. propagation speed

c. propagation time

d. b or c

73. _____ has units of bits/second.

a. Throughput

b. Propagation speed

c. Propagation time

d. b or c

74. The _____ has units of seconds.

a. throughput

b. propagation speed

   c. propagation time

   d. b or c

75. When propagation speed is multiplied by propagation time, we get the _____.

   a. throughput

   b. wavelength of the signal

   c. distortion factor

   d. distance a signal or bit has traveled

76. Propagation time is _____ proportional to distance and _____ proportional to propagation speed.

   a. inversely; directly

   b. directly; inversely

   c. inversely; inversely

   d. directly; directly

77. Wavelength is _____ proportional to propagation speed and _____ proportional to period.

   a. inversely; directly

   b. directly; inversely

   c. inversely; inversely

   d. directly; directly

78. The wavelength of a signal depends on the _____.

   a. frequencies of the signal

   b. medium

   c. phase of the signal

   d. a and b

79. The wavelength of green light in air is _____ the wavelength of green light in fiber-optic cable.

   a. less than

   b. greater than

   c. equal to

   d. none of the above

80. Using the Shannon formula to calculate the data rate for a given channel, if $C = B$, then _____.

   a. the signal is less than the noise

   b. the signal is greater than the noise

   c. the signal is equal to the noise

   d. not enough information is given to answer the question

Exercises

81. Given that the speed of light is 186,000 miles/second and a satellite is at geosynchronous orbit, how long would it take for a signal to go from the earth station to the satellite (minimum time)?

82. A beam of light moves from one medium to another, less dense medium. The critical angle is 60 degrees. Draw the path of the light through both media when the angle of incidence is

    a. 40 degrees.

    b. 50 degrees.

    c. 60 degrees.

    d. 70 degrees.

    e. 80 degrees.

83. A signal travels from point A to point B. At point A, the signal power is 100 watts. At point B, the power is 90 watts. What is the attenuation in dB?

84. The attenuation of a signal is –10 dB. What is the final signal power if it was originally 5 watts?

85. A signal has passed through three cascaded amplifiers, each with a 4 dB gain. What is the total gain? How much is the signal amplified?

86. Data pass through a point at a rate of 100 kilobits every five seconds. What is the throughput?

87. If the throughput at the connection between a device and the transmission medium is 5 Kbps, how long does it take to send 100,000 bits out of this device?

88. The distance between the earth and the moon is approximately 400,000 kilometers. How long does it take for the light from the moon to reach the earth?

89. The light of the sun takes approximately eight minutes to reach the earth. What is the distance between the sun and the earth?

90. What is the wavelength of infrared light in a vacuum? Is it longer or shorter than the wavelength of red light?

91. A signal has a wavelength of 1 μm in air. How far can the front of the wave travel during five periods?

92. The wavelength of red light in a fiber is 0.5 μm. How long does it take the front of the wave to reach the end of the fiber if the length of the fiber is 2000 Km?

93. A line has a signal-to-noise ratio of 1000 and a bandwidth of 4000 KHz. What is the maximum data rate supported by this line?

94. We measure the performance of a telephone line (4 KHz of bandwidth). When the signal is 10 volts, the noise is 5 millivolts. What is the maximum data rate supported by this telephone line?

CHAPTER 8

Multiplexing

Whenever the transmission capacity of a medium linking two devices is greater than the transmission needs of the devices, the link can be shared, much as a large water pipe can carry water to several separate houses at once. **Multiplexing** is the set of techniques that allows the simultaneous transmission of multiple signals across a single data link.

As data- and telecommunications usage increases, so does traffic. We can accommodate this increase by continuing to add individual lines each time a new channel is needed, or we can install higher capacity links and use each to carry multiple signals. As described in Chapter 7, today's technology includes high-bandwidth media such as coaxial cable, optical fiber, and terrestrial and satellite microwaves. Each of these has a carrying capacity far in excess of that needed for the average transmission signal. If the transmission capacity of a link is greater than the transmission needs of the devices connected to it, the excess capacity is wasted. An efficient system maximizes the utilization of all facilities. In addition, the expensive technology involved often becomes cost-effective only when links are shared.

Figure 8.1 shows two possible ways of linking four pairs of devices. In Figure 8.1*a*, each pair has its own link. If the full capacity of each link is not being utilized, a portion of that capacity is being wasted. In Figure 8.1*b*, transmissions between the pairs are multiplexed; the same four pairs share the capacity of a single link.

8.1 MANY TO ONE/ONE TO MANY

In a multiplexed system, *n* devices share the capacity of one link. Figure 8.1*b* shows the basic format of a multiplexed system. The four devices on the left direct their transmission streams to a **multiplexer (MUX),** which combines them into a single stream (many to one). At the receiving end, that stream is fed into a **demultiplexer (DEMUX),** which separates the stream back into its component transmissions (one to many) and directs them to their intended receiving devices.

In Figure 8.1*b* the word **path** refers to the physical link. The word **channel** refers to a portion of a path that carries a transmission between a given pair of devices. One path can have many (*n*) channels.

Figure 8.1   *Multiplexing versus no multiplexing*

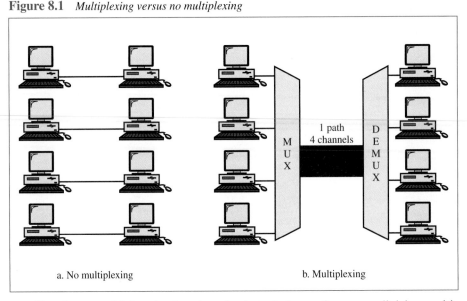

a. No multiplexing   b. Multiplexing

Signals are multiplexed using three basic techniques: frequency-division multiplexing (FDM), time-division multiplexing (TDM), and wave-division multiplexing (WDM). TDM is further subdivided into synchronous TDM (usually just called TDM) and asynchronous TDM, also called statistical TDM or concentrator (see Figure 8.2).

Figure 8.2   *Categories of multiplexing*

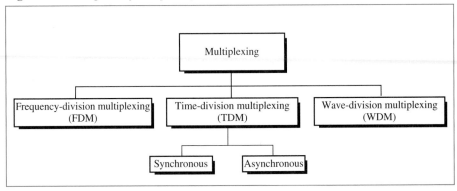

8.2   FREQUENCY-DIVISION MULTIPLEXING (FDM)

Frequency-division multiplexing (FDM) is an analog technique that can be applied when the **bandwidth** of a link is greater than the combined bandwidths of the signals to be transmitted. In FDM, signals generated by each sending device modulate different carrier frequencies. These modulated signals are then combined into a single composite signal that can be transported by the link. Carrier frequencies are separated by enough bandwidth to accommodate the modulated signal. These bandwidth ranges are the channels through which the various signals travel. Channels must be separated by strips of unused bandwidth (**guard bands**) to prevent signals from overlapping. In addition, carrier frequencies must not interfere with the original data frequencies. Failure to adhere to either condition can result in unrecoverability of the original signals.

Figure 8.3 gives a conceptual view of FDM. In this illustration, the transmission path is divided into three parts, each representing a channel to carry one transmission. As an analogy, imagine a point where three narrow streets merge to form a three-lane highway. Each of the three streets corresponds to a lane of the highway. Each car merging onto the highway from one of the streets still has its own lane and can travel without interfering with cars in other lanes.

Figure 8.3   *FDM*

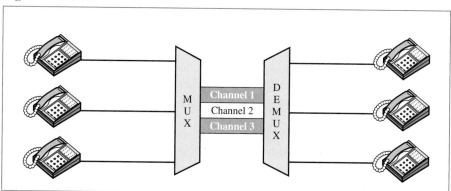

Keep in mind that although Figure 8.3 shows the path as divided spatially into separate channels, actual channel divisions are achieved by frequency rather than by space.

The FDM Process

Figure 8.4 is a conceptual time-domain illustration of the multiplexing process. FDM is an analog process and we show it here using telephones as the input and output devices. Each telephone generates a signal of a similar frequency range. Inside the multiplexer, these similar signals are modulated onto different carrier frequencies ($f_1, f_2,$ and f_3). The resulting modulated signals are then combined into a single composite signal that is sent out over a media link that has enough bandwidth to accommodate it.

Figure 8.5 is the frequency-domain illustration for the same concept. (Note that the horizontal axis of this figure denotes frequency, not time. All three carrier frequencies exist at the same time within the bandwidth.) In FDM, signals are modulated onto separate carrier frequencies ($f_1, f_2,$ and f_3) using either AM or FM modulation. As you recall from Chapter 5, modulating one signal onto another results in a bandwidth of at

Figure 8.4   *FDM multiplexing process, time domain*

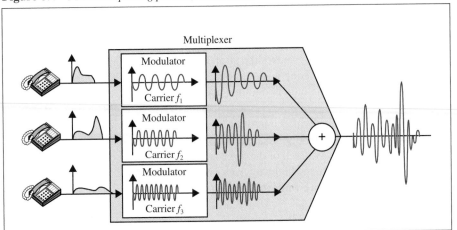

least twice the original. To allow more efficient use of the path, the actual bandwidth can be lowered by suppressing half the band, using techniques that are beyond the scope of this book. In this illustration, the bandwidth of the resulting composite signal is more than three times the bandwidth of each input signal: three times the bandwidth to accommodate the necessary channels, plus extra bandwidth to allow for the necessary guard bands.

Figure 8.5   *FDM multiplexing process, frequency domain*

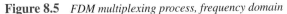
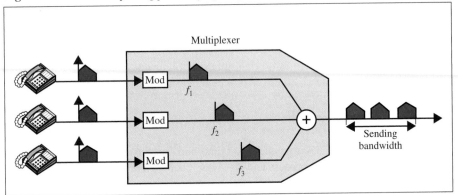

Demultiplexing

The demultiplexer uses a series of filters to decompose the multiplexed signal into its constituent component signals. The individual signals are then passed to a demodulator that separates them from their carriers and passes them to the waiting receivers. Figure 8.6 is a time-domain illustration of FDM multiplexing, again using three telephones as the communication devices. The frequency domain of the same example is shown in Figure 8.7.

Figure 8.6   *FDM demultiplexing process, time domain*

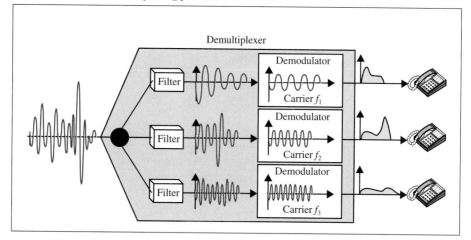

Figure 8.7   *FDM demultiplexing, frequency domain*

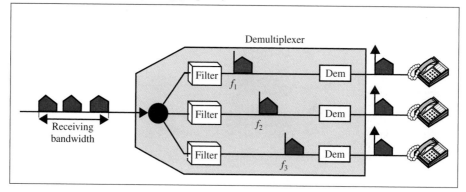

8.3   WAVE-DIVISION MULTIPLEXING (WDM)

Wave-division multiplexing (WDM) is conceptually the same as FDM, except that the multiplexing and demultiplexing involve light signals transmitted through fiber-optic channels. The idea is the same: we are combining different signals of different frequencies. However, the difference is that the frequencies are very high.

Figure 8.8 gives a conceptual view of a WDM multiplexer and demultiplexer. Very narrow bands of light from different sources are combined to make a wider band of light. At the receiver, the signals are separated by the demultiplexer.

One may wonder about the mechanism of a WDM. Although the technology is very complex, the idea is very simple. We want to combine multiple light sources into one single light at the multiplexer and do the reverse at the demultiplexer. Combining and splitting of light sources are easily handled by a prism. Recall from basic physics

Figure 8.8   *WDM*

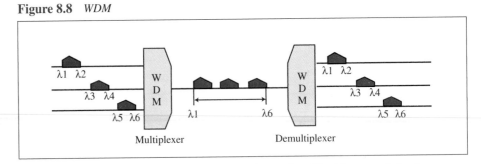

that a prism bends a beam of light based on the angle of incidence and the frequency. Using this technique, a multiplexer can be made to combine several input beams of light, each containing a narrow band of frequencies, into one output beam of a wider band of frequencies. A demultiplexer can also be made to reverse the process. Figure 8.9 shows the concept.

Figure 8.9   *Prisms in WDM multiplexing and demultiplexing*

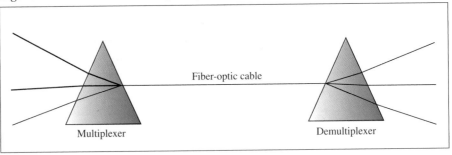

8.4   TIME-DIVISION MULTIPLEXING (TDM)

Time-division multiplexing (TDM) is a digital process that can be applied when the data rate capacity of the transmission medium is greater than the data rate required by the sending and receiving devices. In such a case, multiple transmissions can occupy a single link by subdividing them and interleaving the portions.

Figure 8.10 gives a conceptual view of TDM. Note that the same link is used as in FDM; here, however, the link is shown sectioned by time rather than frequency.

In the TDM figure, portions of signals 1, 2, 3, and 4 occupy the link sequentially. As an analogy, imagine a ski lift that serves several runs. Each run has its own line and the skiers in each line take turns getting on the lift. As each chair reaches the top of the mountain, the skier riding it gets off and skis down the run for which he or she waited in line.

TDM can be implemented in two ways: synchronous TDM and asynchronous TDM.

Figure 8.10   *TDM*

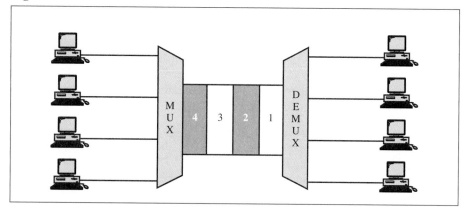

Synchronous TDM

In **synchronous time-division multiplexing,** the term *synchronous* has a different meaning from that used in other areas of telecommunications. Here synchronous means that the multiplexer allocates exactly the same time slot to each device at all times, whether or not a device has anything to transmit. Time slot A, for example, is assigned to device A alone and cannot be used by any other device. Each time its allocated time slot comes up, a device has the opportunity to send a portion of its data. If a device is unable to transmit or does not have data to send, its time slot remains empty.

Frames   Time slots are grouped into frames. A frame consists of one complete cycle of time slots, including one or more slots dedicated to each sending device (see Figure 8.11). In a system with *n* input lines, each frame has at least *n* slots, with each slot allocated to carrying data from a specific input line. If all the input devices

Figure 8.11   *Synchronous TDM*

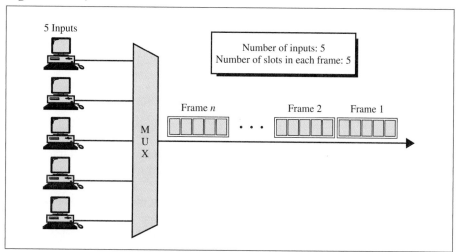

sharing a link are transmitting at the same data rate, each device has one time slot per frame. However, it is possible to accommodate varying data rates. A transmission with two slots per frame will arrive twice as quickly as one with one slot per frame. The time slots dedicated to a given device occupy the same location in each frame and constitute that device's channel. In Figure 8.11, we show five input lines multiplexed onto a single path using synchronous TDM. In this example, all of the inputs have the same data rate, so the number of time slots in each frame is equal to the number of input lines.

Interleaving   Synchronous TDM can be compared to a very fast rotating switch. As the switch opens in front of a device, that device has the opportunity to send a specified amount (x bits) of data onto the path. The switch moves from device to device at a constant rate and in a fixed order. This process is called **interleaving.**

Interleaving can be done by bit, by byte, or by any other data unit. In other words, the multiplexer can take one byte from each device, then another byte from each device, and so on. In a given system, the interleaved units will always be of the same size.

Figure 8.12 shows interleaving and frame building. In the example, we interleave the various transmissions by character (equal to one byte each), but the concept is the same for data units of any length. As you can see, each device is sending a different message. The multiplexer interleaves the different messages and forms them into frames before putting them onto the link.

Figure 8.12   *Synchronous TDM, multiplexing process*

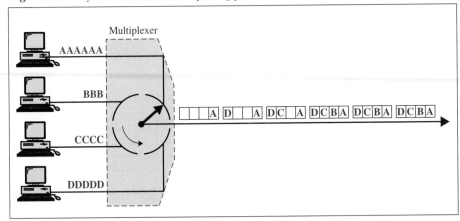

At the receiver, the demultiplexer decomposes each frame by extracting each character in turn. As a character is removed from a frame, it is passed to the appropriate receiving device (see Figure 8.13).

Figures 8.12 and 8.13 also point out the major weakness of synchronous TDM. By assigning each time slot to a specific input line, we end up with empty slots whenever not all the lines are active. In Figure 8.12, only the first three frames are completely filled. The last three frames have a collective six empty slots. Having 6 empty slots out of 24 means that a quarter of the capacity of the link is being wasted.

Figure 8.13   *Synchronous TDM, demultiplexing process*

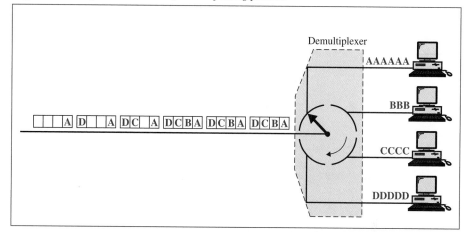

Framing Bits   Because the time slot order in a synchronous TDM system does not vary from frame to frame, very little overhead information needs to be included in each frame. The order of receipt tells the demultiplexer where to direct each time slot, so no addressing is necessary. Various factors, however, can cause timing inconsistencies. For this reason, one or more synchronization bits are usually added to the beginning of each frame. These bits, called **framing bits,** follow a pattern, frame to frame, that allows the demultiplexer to synchronize with the incoming stream so that it can separate the time slots accurately. In most cases, this synchronization information consists of one bit per frame, alternating between 0 and 1 (01010101010), as shown in Figure 8.14.

Figure 8.14   *Framing bits*

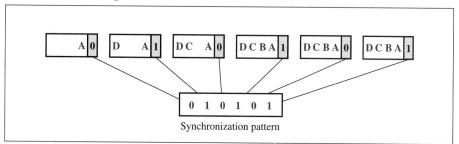

Synchronous TDM Example   Imagine that we have four input sources on a synchronous TDM link, where transmissions are interleaved by character. If each source is creating 250 characters per second, and each frame is carrying 1 character from each source, the transmission path must be able to carry 250 frames per second (see Figure 8.15).

If we assume that each character consists of eight bits, then each frame is 33 bits long: 32 bits for the four characters plus 1 framing bit. Looking at the bit relationships, we see that each device is creating 2000 bps (250 characters with 8 bits per character), but the line is carrying 8250 bps (250 frames with 33 bits per frame): 8000 bits of data and 250 bits of overhead.

Figure 8.15   *Data rate calculation for frames*

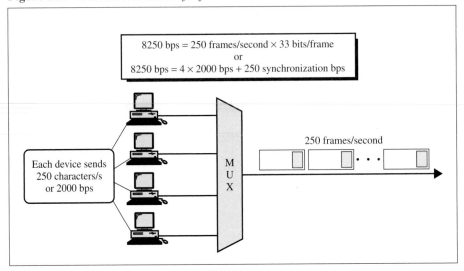

Bit Stuffing   As noted previously, it is possible to connect devices of different data rates to a synchronous TDM. For example, device A uses one time slot, while the faster device B uses two. The number of slots in a frame and the input lines to which they are assigned remain fixed throughout a given system, but devices of different data rates may control different numbers of those slots. Remember: the time-slot length is fixed. For this technique to work, therefore, the different data rates must be integer multiples of each other. For example, we can accommodate a device that is five times faster than the other devices by giving it five slots to one for each of the other devices. We, however, cannot accommodate a device that is five and a half times faster by this method, because we cannot introduce half a time slot into a frame.

When the speeds are not integer multiples of each other, they can be made to behave as if they were, by a technique called **bit stuffing.** In bit stuffing, the multiplexer adds extra bits to a device's source stream to force the speed relationships among the various devices into integer multiples of each other. For example, if we have one device with a bit rate of 2.75 times that of the other devices, we can add enough bits to raise the rate to 3 times that of the others. The extra bits are then discarded by the demultiplexer.

Asynchronous TDM

As we saw in the previous section, synchronous TDM does not guarantee that the full capacity of a link is used. In fact, it is more likely that only a portion of the time slots is in use at a given instant. Because the time slots are preassigned and fixed, whenever a connected device is not transmitting, the corresponding slot is empty and that much of the path is wasted. For example, imagine that we have multiplexed the output of 20 identical computers onto a single line. Using synchronous TDM, the speed of that line must be at least 20 times the speed of each input line. But what if only 10 computers are in use at a time? Half of the capacity of the line is wasted.

Asynchronous time-division multiplexing, or **statistical time-division multiplexing,** is designed to avoid this type of waste. As with the term *synchronous,* the term *asynchronous* means something different in multiplexing than it means in other areas of data communications. Here it means flexible or not fixed.

Like synchronous TDM, asynchronous TDM allows a number of lower-speed input lines to be multiplexed to a single higher-speed line. Unlike synchronous TDM, however, in asynchronous TDM the total speed of the input lines can be greater than the capacity of the path. In a synchronous system, if we have n input lines, the frame contains a fixed number of at least n time slots. In an asynchronous system, if we have n input lines, the frame contains no more than m slots, with m less than n (see Figure 8.16). In this way, asynchronous TDM supports the same number of input lines as synchronous TDM with a lower capacity link. Or, given the same link, asynchronous TDM can support more devices than synchronous TDM.

Figure 8.16   *Asynchronous TDM*

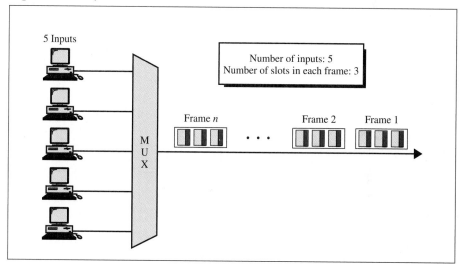

The number of time slots in an asynchronous TDM frame (m) is based on a statistical analysis of the number of input lines that are likely to be transmitting at any given time. Rather than being preassigned, each slot is available to any of the attached input lines that has data to send. The multiplexer scans the input lines, accepts portions of data until a frame is filled, and then sends the frame across the link. If there are not enough data to fill all the slots in a frame, the frame is transmitted only partially filled; thus full-link capacity may not be used 100 percent of the time. But the ability to allocate time slots dynamically, coupled with the lower ratio of time slots to input lines, greatly reduces the likelihood and degree of waste.

Figure 8.17 shows a system where five computers are sharing a data link using asynchronous TDM. In this example, the frame size is three slots. The figure shows how the multiplexer handles three levels of traffic. In the first case, only three of the five

Figure 8.17   *Examples of asynchronous TDM frames*

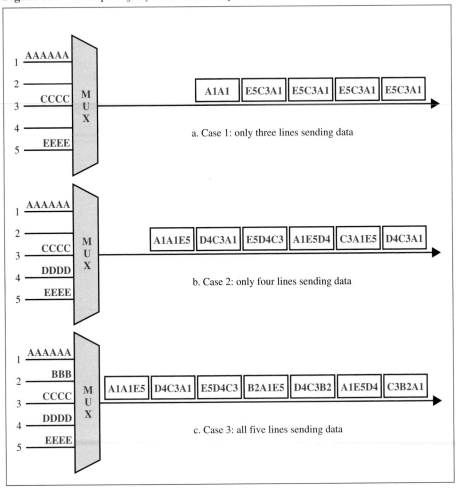

a. Case 1: only three lines sending data

b. Case 2: only four lines sending data

c. Case 3: all five lines sending data

computers have data to send (the average scenario for this system, as indicated by the fact that a frame size of three slots was chosen). In the second case, four lines are sending data, one more than the number of slots per frame. In the third case (statistically rare), all lines are sending data. In each case, the multiplexer scans the devices in order, from 1 to 5, filling time slots as it encounters data to be sent.

In the first case, the three active input lines correspond to the three slots in each frame. For the first four frames, the input is symmetrically distributed among all the communicating devices. By the fifth frame, however, devices 3 and 5 have completed their transmissions, but device 1 still has two characters to go. The multiplexer picks up the A from device 1, scans down the line without finding another transmission, and returns to device 1 to pick up the last A. There being no data to fill the final slot, the multiplexer then transmits the fifth frame with only two slots filled. In a synchronous TDM system, six frames of five time slots each would have been required to transmit all of the data—a total of 30 time slots. But only 14 of those slots would have been filled, leaving the line unused for more than half the elapsed time. With the asynchronous system shown here, only one frame is transmitted partially empty. During the rest of the transmission time, the entire capacity of the link is active.

In the second case, there is one more active input line than there are slots in each frame. This time, as the multiplexer scans from 1 to 5, it fills up a frame before all of the lines have been checked. The first frame, therefore, carries data from devices 1, 3, and 4, but not 5. The multiplexer continues its scan where it left off, putting the first portion of device 5's transmission into the first slot of the next frame, then moving back to the top of the line and putting the second portion of device 1's data into the second slot, and so on. As you can see, when the number of active senders does not equal the number of slots in a frame, the time slots are not filled symmetrically. Device 1, in this example, occupies the first slot in the first frame, the second slot in the second frame, and so on.

In the third case, the frames are filled as above, but here all five input lines are active. In this example, device 1 occupies the first slot in the first frame, the third slot in the second frame, and no slots at all in the third frame.

In cases 2 and 3, if the speed of the line is equal to three of the input lines, then the data to be transmitted will arrive faster than the multiplexer can put it on the link. In that case, a buffer is needed to store data until the multiplexer is ready for it.

Addressing and Overhead   Cases 2 and 3 in the above example illustrate a major weakness of asynchronous TDM: How does the demultiplexer know which slot belongs to which output line? In synchronous TDM, the device to which the data in a time slot belong is indicated by the position of the time slot in the frame. But in asynchronous TDM, data from a given device might be in the first slot of one frame and in the third of the next. In the absence of fixed positional relationships, each time slot must carry an address telling the demultiplexer how to direct the data. This address, for local use only, is attached by the multiplexer and discarded by the demultiplexer once it has been read. In Figure 8.17, the address is specified by a digit.

Adding address bits to each time slot increases the overhead of an asynchronous system and somewhat limits its potential efficiency. To limit their impact, addresses usually consist of only a small number of bits and can be made even shorter by appending a full address only to the first portion of a transmission, with abbreviated versions to identify subsequent portions.

The need for addressing makes asynchronous TDM inefficient for bit or byte interleaving. Imagine bit interleaving with each bit carrying an address: one bit of data plus, say, three bits of address. All of a sudden it takes four bits to transport one bit of data. Even if the link is kept full, only a quarter of the capacity is used to transport data; the rest is **overhead.** For this reason, asynchronous TDM is efficient only when the size of the time slots is kept relatively large.

Variable-Length Time Slots   Asynchronous TDM can accommodate traffic of varying data rates by varying the length of the time slots. Stations transmitting at a faster data rate can be given a longer slot. Managing variable-length fields requires that control bits be appended to the beginning of each time slot to indicate the length of the coming data portion. These extra bits also increase the overhead of the system and, again, are efficient only with larger time slots.

Inverse Multiplexing

As its name implies, **inverse multiplexing** is the opposite of multiplexing. Inverse multiplexing takes the data stream from one high-speed line and breaks it into portions that can be sent across several lower-speed lines simultaneously, with no loss in the collective data rate (see Figure 8.18).

Figure 8.18 *Multiplexing and inverse multiplexing*

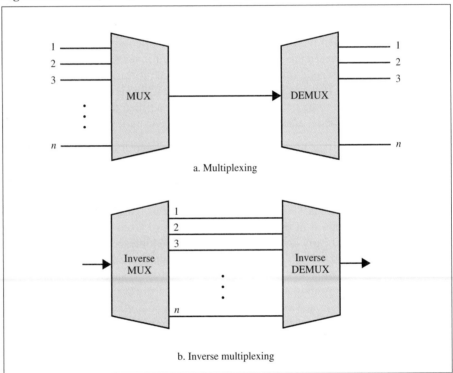

Why do we need inverse multiplexing? Think of an organization that wants to send data, voice, and video, each of which requires a different data rate. To send voice, it may need a 64 Kbps link. To send data, it may need a 128 Kbps link. And to send video, it may need a 1.544 Mbps link. To accommodate all of these needs, the organization has two options. It can lease a 1.544 Mbps channel from a common carrier (the telephone company) and use the full capacity only sometimes, which is not an efficient use of the facility. Or it can lease several separate channels of lower data rates. Using an agreement called **bandwidth on demand,** the organization can use any of these channels whenever and however it needs them. Voice transmissions can be sent intact over any of the channels. Data or video signals can be broken up and sent over two or more lines. In other words, the data and video signals can be inversely multiplexed over multiple lines.

8.5   MULTIPLEXING APPLICATION: THE TELEPHONE SYSTEM

Multiplexing has long been an essential tool of the telephone industry. A look at some telephone company basics can help us understand the application of both FDM and TDM in the field. Of course, different parts of the world use different systems. We will concentrate only on the system used in North America.

The North American telephone system includes many **common carriers** that offer local and long-distance services to subscribers. These carriers include local companies such as Pacific Bell and long-distance providers such as AT&T, MCI, and Sprint.

For the purposes of this discussion, we will think of these various carriers as a single entity called the telephone network, and the line connecting a subscriber to that network as a *service line* (see Figure 8.19).

Figure 8.19   *Telephone network*

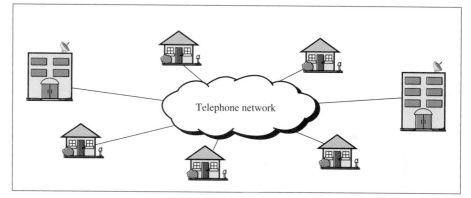

Common Carrier Services and Hierarchies

Telephone companies began by providing their subscribers with **analog services** that used analog networks. Later technology allowed the introduction of digital services and networks. Today, North American providers are in the process of changing even their service lines from analog to digital. It is anticipated that soon the entire network will be digital. For now, however, both types of services are available and both FDM and TDM are in use (see Figure 8.20).

Figure 8.20   *Categories of telephone services*

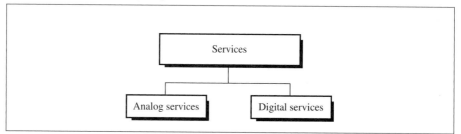

Analog Services

Of the many analog services available to subscribers, two are particularly relevant to our discussion here: switched services and leased services (see Figure 8.21).

Figure 8.21   *Categories of analog services*

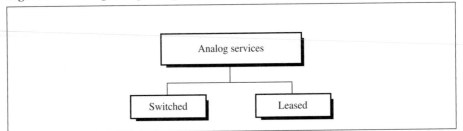

Analog Switched Service

Analog switched service is the familiar dial-up service most often encountered when using a home telephone. It uses two-wire (or, for specialized uses, four-wire) twisted-pair cable to connect the subscriber's handset to the network via an exchange. This connection is called the **local loop.** The network it joins is sometimes referred to as a public switched telephone network (PSTN).

The signal on a local loop is analog, and the bandwidth is usually between 0 and 4000 Hz. (For more information on telephone bandwidth, refer back to Chapter 7.)

With switched lines, when the caller dials a number, the call is conveyed to a switch, or series of switches, at the exchange. The appropriate switches are then activated to link the caller's line to that of the person being called. The switch connects the two lines for the duration of the call (see Figure 8.22).

Figure 8.22   *Analog switched service*

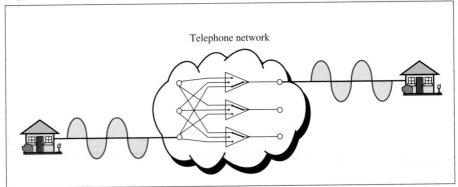

Analog Leased Service

An **analog leased service** offers customers the opportunity to lease a line, sometimes called a dedicated line, that is permanently connected to another customer. Although the connection still passes through the switches in the telephone network, subscribers experience it as a single line because the switch is always closed; no dialing is needed (see Figure 8.23).

Figure 8.23   *Analog leased service*

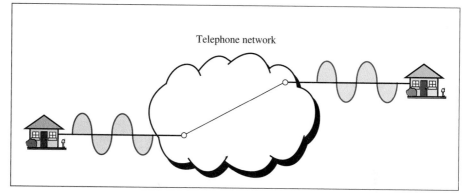

Conditioned Lines   Telephone carriers also offer a service called conditioning. **Conditioning** means improving the quality of a line by lessening attenuation, signal distortion, or delay distortion. Conditioned lines are analog, but their quality makes them usable for digital data communication if they are connected to modems.

The Analog Hierarchy

To maximize the efficiency of their infrastructure, telephone companies have traditionally multiplexed signals from lower bandwidth lines onto higher bandwidth lines. In this way, many switched or leased lines can be combined into fewer but bigger channels. For analog lines, FDM is used.

One of these hierarchical systems used by AT&T is made up of groups, supergroups, master groups, and jumbo groups (see Figure 8.24).

In this **analog hierarchy,** 12 voice channels are multiplexed onto a higher bandwidth line to create a **group.** (To conserve bandwidth, AT&T uses modulation techniques that suppress the carrier and the lower sidebands of each signal, and recover them upon demultiplexing.) A group has 48 KHz of bandwidth and supports 12 voice channels.

At the next level, up to five groups can be multiplexed to create a composite signal called a **supergroup.** A supergroup has a bandwidth of 240 KHz and supports up to 60 voice channels. Supergroups can be made up of either five groups or 60 independent voice channels.

At the next level, 10 supergroups are multiplexed to create a **master group.** A master group must have 2.40 MHz of bandwidth, but the need for guard bands between the channels increases the necessary bandwidth to 2.52 MHz. Master groups support up to 600 voice channels.

Finally, six master groups can be combined into a **jumbo group.** A jumbo group must have 15.12 MHz (6×2.52 MHz) but is augmented to 16.984 MHz to allow for guard bands between the master groups.

Figure 8.24   *Analog hierarchy*

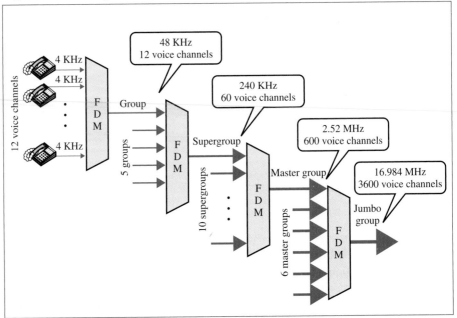

There are many variations of this hierarchy in the telecommunications industry (the ITU-T has approved a different system for use in Europe). However, because this analog hierarchy will be replaced by digital services in the near future, we will limit our discussion to the system above.

Digital Services

Recently telephone companies began offering digital services to their subscribers. One advantage is that digital services are less sensitive than analog services to noise and other forms of interference. A telephone line acts like an antenna and will pick up noise during both analog and digital transmission. In analog transmissions, both signal and noise are analog and cannot be easily separated. In digital transmission, on the other hand, the signal is digital but the interference is still analog. The signal therefore can be distinguished and separated easily. Another advantage to digital transmission is its lower cost. Because it needs to differentiate between only two or three levels of voltage instead of a continuous range of values, digital transmission equipment uses less expensive electronics than does the corresponding analog equipment.

We will examine three different types of digital services: switched/56, DDS, and DS (see Figure 8.25).

Switched/56 Service

Switched/56 is the digital version of an analog switched line. It is a switched digital service that allows data rates of up to 56 Kbps. To communicate through this service, both parties must subscribe. A caller with normal telephone service cannot connect to a telephone or computer with switched/56 even if using a modem. On the whole,

Figure 8.25   *Categories of digital services*

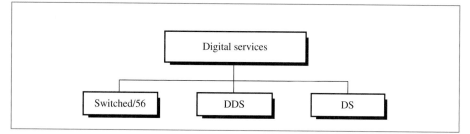

digital and analog services represent two completely different domains for the telephone companies.

Because the line in a switched/56 service is already digital, subscribers do not need modems to transmit digital data. However, they do need another device called a **digital service unit (DSU).** This device changes the rate of the digital data created by the subscriber's device to 56 Kbps and encodes it in the format used by the service provider (see Figure 8.26). The DSU is often included in the dialing process (DSU with dial pad).

Figure 8.26   *Switched/56 service*

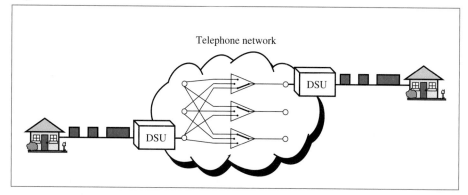

Ironically, a DSU is more expensive than a modem. So why would a subscriber elect to pay for the switched/56 service and DSU? Because the digital line has better speed, better quality, and less susceptibility to noise than an equivalent analog line.

Bandwidth on Demand   Switched/56 supports bandwidth on demand, allowing subscribers to obtain higher speeds by using more than one line (see the section on inverse multiplexing, above). This option allows switched/56 to support video conferencing, fast facsimile, multimedia, and fast data transfer, among other features.

Digital Data Service (DDS)

Digital data service (DDS) is the digital version of an analog leased line; it is a digital leased line with a maximum data rate of 64 Kbps.

Like switched/56, DDS requires the use of a DSU. The DSU for this service is cheaper than that required for switched/56, however, because it does not need a dial pad (see Figure 8.27).

Figure 8.27   *DDS service*

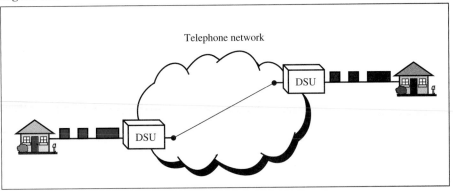

Digital Signal (DS) Service

After offering switched/56 and DDS services, the telephone companies saw a need to develop a hierarchy of digital services much like that used for analog services. The next step was **digital signal (DS) service.** DS is a hierarchy of digital signals. Figure 8.28 shows the data rates supported by each level.

Figure 8.28   *DS hierarchy*

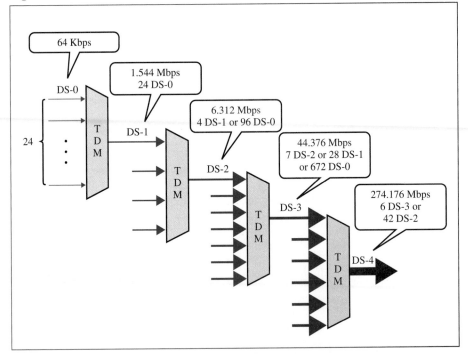

- A DS-0 service resembles DDS. It is a single digital channel of 64 Kbps.
- DS-1 is a 1.544-Mbps service; 1.544 Mbps is 24 times 64 Kbps plus 8 Kbps of overhead. It can be used as a single service for 1.544-Mbps transmissions, or it can

be used to multiplex 24 DS-0 channels or to carry any other combination desired by the user that can fit within its 1.544-Mbps capacity.

- DS-2 is a 6.312-Mbps service; 6.312 Mbps is 96 times 64 Kbps plus 168 Kbps of overhead. It can be used as a single service for 6.312-Mbps transmissions, or it can be used to multiplex 4 DS-1 channels, 96 DS-0 channels, or a combination of these service types.

- DS-3 is a 44.376-Mbps service; 44.376 Mbps is 672 times 64 Kbps plus 1.368 Mbps of overhead. It can be used as a single service for 44.376-Mbps transmissions, or it can be used to multiplex 7 DS-2 channels, 28 DS-1 channels, 672 DS-0 channels, or a combination of these service types.

- DS-4 is a 274.176-Mbps service; 274.176 is 4032 times 64 Kbps plus 16.128 Mbps of overhead. It can be used to multiplex 6 DS-3 channels, 42 DS-2 channels, 168 DS-1 channels, 4032 DS-0 channels, or a combination of these service types.

T Lines

DS-0, DS-1, and so on are the names of services. To implement those services, the telephone companies use **T lines** (T-1 to T-4). These are lines with capacities precisely matched to the data rates of the DS-1 to DS-4 services (see Table 8.1).

Table 8.1   *DS and T line rates*

Service	Line	Rate (Mbps)	Voice Channels
DS-1	**T-1**	1.544	24
DS-2	**T-2**	6.312	96
DS-3	**T-3**	44.736	672
DS-4	**T-4**	274.176	4032

T-1 is used to implement DS-1, T-2 is used to implement DS-2, and so on. As you can see from Table 8.1, DS-0 is not actually offered as a service, but it has been defined as a basis for reference purposes. Telephone companies believe that customers needing the level of service that would be found in DS-0 can substitute DDS.

T Lines for Analog Transmission   T lines are digital lines designed for the transmission of digital data, voice, or audio signals. However, they also can be used for analog transmission (regular telephone connections), provided the analog signals are sampled first, then time-division multiplexed.

The possibility of using T lines as analog carriers opened up a new generation of services for the telephone companies. Earlier, when an organization wanted 24 separate telephone lines, it needed to run 24 twisted-pair cables from the company to the central exchange. (Remember those old movies showing a busy executive with 10 telephones lined up on his desk? Or the old office telephones with a big fat cable running from them? Those cables contained a bundle of separate lines.) Today, that same organization can combine the 24 lines into one T-1 line and run only the T-1 line to the exchange. Figure 8.29 shows how 24 voice channels can be multiplexed onto one T-1 line. (Refer back to Chapter 5 for PCM encoding.)

Figure 8.29   *T-1 line for multiplexing telephone lines*

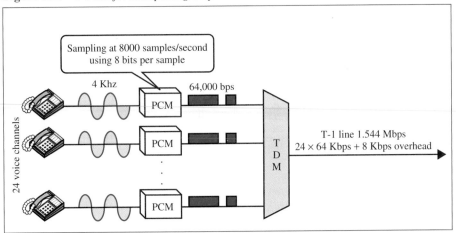

The T-1 Frame   As noted above, DS-1 requires 8 Kbps of overhead. To understand how this overhead is calculated, we must examine the format of a 24-voice-channel frame.

The frame used on a T-1 line is usually 193 bits divided into 24 slots of 8 bits each plus 1 extra bit for synchronization ($24 \times 8 + 1 = 193$); see Figure 8.30. In other words, each slot contains 1 signal segment from each channel; 24 segments are interleaved in one frame. If a T-1 line carries 8000 frames, the data rate is 1.544 Mbps ($193 \times 8000 = 1.544$ Mbps)—the capacity of the line.

Figure 8.30   *T-1 frame structure*

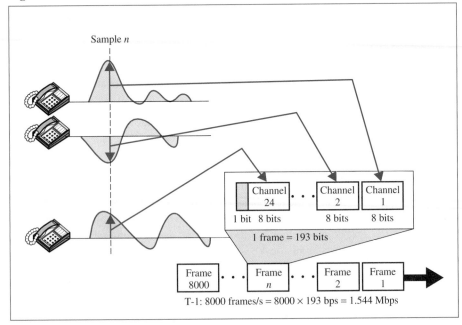

Fractional T Lines   Many subscribers may not need the entire capacity of a T line. To accommodate these customers, the telephone companies have developed **fractional T line** services, which allow several subscribers to share one line by multiplexing their transmissions.

For example, a small business may need only one-fourth of the capacity of a T-1 line. If four businesses that size have offices in the same building, they can share a T-1 line. To do so, they direct their transmissions through a device called a **digital service unit/channel service unit (DSU/CSU).** This device lets them divide the capacity of the line into four interleaved channels (see Figure 8.31).

Figure 8.31   *Fractional T-1 line*

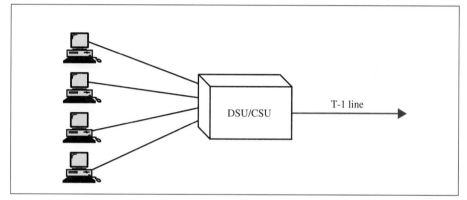

E Lines

Europeans use a version of T lines called **E lines.** The two systems are conceptually identical, but their capacities differ. Table 8.2 shows the E lines and their capacities.

Table 8.2   *E line rates*

Line	Rate (Mbps)	Voice Channels
E-1	2.048	30
E-2	8.448	120
E-3	34.368	480
E-4	139.264	1920

Other Multiplexing Services

We have discussed multiplexing over physical cable, but multiplexing is equally vital to the efficient use of both terrestrial and satellite microwave transmission. Today telephone service providers are introducing other powerful services, such as ISDN, SONET, and ATM, which also depend on multiplexing. These services will be discussed in Chapters 16 through 20.

8.6   DIGITAL SUBSCRIBER LINE (DSL)

One example of multiplexing, demultiplexing, and modulation is a technology called the DSL family. The **digital subscriber line (DSL)** is a newer technology that uses the existing telecommunication networks such as the local loop telephone line to accomplish high-speed delivery of data, voice, video, and multimedia.

DSL is a family of technologies; five of them will be discussed here: ADSL, RADSL, HDSL, VDSL, and SDSL.

ADSL

Telephone companies have installed high-speed digital wide area networks to handle communication between their central offices. The link between the user (subscriber) and the network, however, is still an analog line (local loop). The challenge is to make these links digital—a digital subscriber line—without changing the existing local loops. The local loop is a twisted-pair cable with a potential bandwidth of 1 MHz or more.

Asymmetric digital subscriber line (ADSL) is asymmetrical, which means it provides higher bit rates in the downstream direction (from the telephone central office to the subscriber's site) than the upstream direction (from the subscriber site to the telephone central office). This is what subscribers usually want. They want to receive high-volume files quickly from the Internet, but they usually have small files, such as a short e-mail message, to send.

ADSL divides the bandwidth of a twisted-pair cable (one megahertz) into three bands. The first band, normally between 0 and 25 KHz, is used for regular telephone service (known as plain old telephone service or POTS). This service uses only 4 KHz of this band; the rest is used as the guard band to separate the voice channel from the data channels. The second band, usually between 25 and 200 KHz, is used for upstream communication. The third band, usually 250 KHz to 1 MHz, is used for downstream communication. Some implementations overlap the downstream and upstream band to provide more bandwidth in the downstream direction. Figure 8.32 shows the bands.

Figure 8.32   *Bands for ADSL*

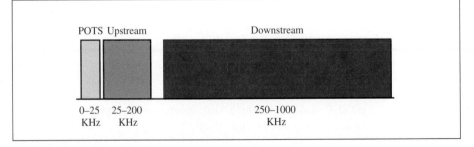

Modulation Techniques

Most implementations of ADSL originally used a modulation technique called carrier-less amplitude/phase (CAP). Later, another modulation technique, known as discrete multitone (DMT) was standardized by ANSI.

CAP   Carrierless amplitude/phase (CAP) is a modulation technique that is similar to QAM, but with one important difference: the carrier signal is eliminated. The technique, however, is more complex than QAM and is not standardized.

DMT   The discrete multitone technique (DMT) combines QAM and FDM. The available bandwidth for each direction is divided into 4-KHz channels, each having its own carrier frequency.

Figure 8.33 shows the concept of DMT with N channels. The bits created by the source are passed through a serial-to-parallel converter, where a block of N bits is divided into N parallel paths, each consisting of one bit. The QAM signals created from each path are frequency multiplexed together and the result is sent to the line.

Figure 8.33   *DMT*

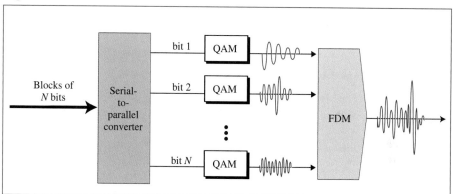

The ANSI standard defines a rate of 60 Kbps for each 4-KHz channel, which means a QAM modulation with 15 bits per baud.

- The upstream channel usually occupies 25 channels, which means a bit rate of 25 × 60 Kbps, or 1.5 Mbps. Normally, however, the bit rate in this direction ranges from 64 Kbps to 1 Mbps due to noise.

- The downstream channel usually occupies 200 channels, which means a bit rate of 200 × 60 Kbps, or 12 Mbps. Normally, however, the bit rate in this direction ranges from 500 Kbps to 8 Mbps due to noise.

Figure 8.34 shows the ADSL and the bit rates in each direction.

RADSL

The **rate adaptive asymmetrical digital subscriber line (RADSL)** is a technology based on ADSL. It allows different data rates depending on the type of communication:

Figure 8.34   *ADSL modem*

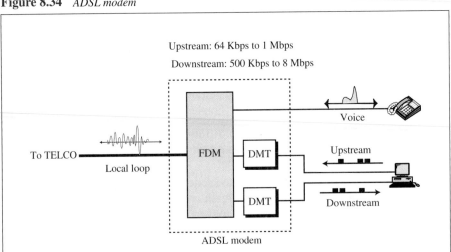

voice, data, multimedia, and so on. Differing rates may also be assigned to subscribers based on their demand of the bandwidth. RADSL is beneficial to the customer because the cost is based on the data rate needed.

HDSL

The **high bit rate digital subscriber line (HDSL)** was designed by Bellcore (now Telcordia) as an alternative to the T-1 line (1.544 Mbps). The T-1 line uses AMI encoding, which is very susceptible to attenuation at high frequencies. This limits the length of a T-1 line to 1 Km. For longer distances, a repeater (amplifier) is necessary, which means increased costs.

HDSL uses 2B1Q encoding (see Chapter 16), which is less susceptible to attenuation. A data rate of almost 2 Mbps can be achieved without repeaters up to a distance of 3.6 Km. HDSL uses two twisted-pair wires to achieve full-duplex transmission.

SDSL

The **symmetric** (or single-line) **digital subscriber line (SDSL)** is the same as HDSL but uses one single twisted-pair cable, available to most residential subscribers, to achieve the same data rate as HDSL. A technique called *echo cancellation* is employed to create a full-duplex transmission.

VDSL

The **very high bit rate digital subscriber line (VDSL),** an alternative approach that is similar to ADSL, uses coaxial, fiber-optic, or twisted-pair cable for short distances (300 to 1800 meters). The modulating technique is DMT with a bit rate of 50 to 55 Mbps downstream and 1.5 to 2.5 Mbps upstream.

8.7   FTTC

Optical fiber has many advantages, among them noise resistance and high bandwidth capacity. However, compared to other types of cable, it is very expensive. Telephone and cable TV companies have devised a method, called **fiber to the curb (FTTC)** to employ optical fiber while keeping the expense down. Optical fiber is the medium from the central office of the telephone company or from the head office of a cable company to the curb. The medium from the curb to the subscriber premise is the less expensive twisted-pair or coaxial cable.

FTTC in the Telephone Network

The telephone system uses fiber-optic cables to connect and multiplex different voice channels. Copper twisted-pair cable coming from individual premises is multiplexed in the junction boxes and converted to optical signals. Optical signals at the switching station are multiplexed, using WDM, to create wider bandwidth optical signals (see Figure 8.35).

Figure 8.35   *FTTC in the telephone network*

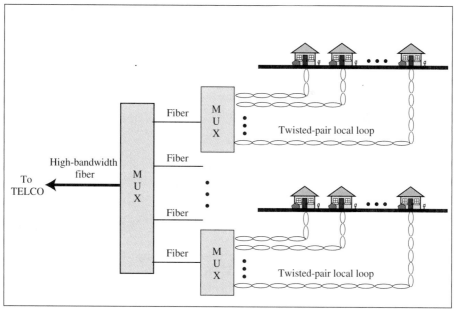

FTTC in the Cable TV Network

The cable TV system uses fiber-optic cables to connect and multiplex different cable channels. Coaxial cables coming from individual premises are multiplexed in the junction boxes and converted to optical signals. Optical signals at the switching station are multiplexed, using WDM, to create wider bandwidth optical signals (see Figure 8.36).

Figure 8.36 *FTTC in the cable TV network*

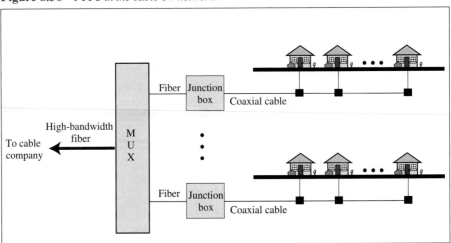

8.8   KEY TERMS AND CONCEPTS

analog hierarchy

analog leased service

analog service

analog switched service

asymmetric digital subscriber line
   (ADSL)

asynchronous time-division
   multiplexing

bandwidth

bandwidth on demand

bit stuffing

carrierless amplitude/phase (CAP)

channel

common carrier

conditioning

demultiplexer (DEMUX)

digital data service (DDS)

digital service unit (DSU)

digital service unit/channel service unit
   (DSU/CSU)

digital signal (DS) service

digital subscriber line (DSL)

discrete multitone technique (DMT)

E lines

fiber to the curb (FTTC)

fractional T line

framing bit

frequency-division multiplexing (FDM)

group

guard band

high bit rate digital subscriber line
   (HDSL)

interleaving

inverse multiplexing

jumbo group

local loop

master group

multiplexer (MUX)

multiplexing

overhead

path

rate adaptive asymmetrical digital subscriber line (RADSL)

statistical time-division multiplexing

supergroup

switched/56

symmetric digital subscriber line
   (SDSL)

synchronous time-division multiplexing

T lines

T-1 line

T-2 line

T-3 line

T-4 line

time-division multiplexing (TDM)

very high bit rate digital subscriber line
   (VDSL)

wave-division multiplexing (WDM)

8.9   SUMMARY

- Multiplexing is the simultaneous transmission of multiple signals across a single data link.
- Two types of multiplexing are frequency-division multiplexing (FDM) and time-division multiplexing (TDM).
- In FDM, each signal modulates a different carrier frequency. The modulated carriers are combined to form a new signal that is then sent across the link.
- In FDM, multiplexers modulate and combine signals while demultiplexers decompose and demodulate.
- In FDM, guard bands keep the modulated signals from overlapping and interfering with one another.

- In TDM, digital signals from *n* devices are interleaved with one another, forming a frame of data (bits, bytes, or any other data unit).

- TDM can be classified as either synchronous or asynchronous (statistical).

- In synchronous TDM, each frame contains at least one time slot dedicated to each device. The order in which each device sends its data to the frame is unvarying. If a device has no data to send, its time slot is sent empty.

- In synchronous TDM, a bit may be added to the beginning of each frame for synchronization.

- In asynchronous TDM, the time-slot order of a frame depends on which devices have data to send at that time.

- Asynchronous TDM adds device addresses to each time slot.

- Inverse multiplexing splits a data stream from one high-speed line onto multiple lower speed lines.

- Telephone services can be analog or digital.

- Analog switched service requires dialing, switching, and a temporary dedicated link.

- Analog leased service is a permanent dedicated link between two customers. No dialing is necessary.

- Telephone companies use multiplexing to combine voice channels into successively larger groups for more efficient transmission.

- Switched/56 service is the digital equivalent of an analog switched line. It requires a digital service unit (DSU) to ensure a 56-Kbps data rate.

- Digital data service (DDS) is the digital equivalent of an analog leased line. DDS also requires a DSU.

- Digital signal (DS) is a hierarchy of TDM signals.

- T lines (T-1 to T-4) are the implementation of DS services. A T-1 line consists of 24 voice channels.

- Fractional T line service allows several subscribers to share one line by multiplexing their signals.

- T lines are used in North America. The European standard defines a variation called E lines.

- Digital subscriber line (DSL) is a technology that uses existing telecommunication networks to accomplish the high-speed delivery of data, voice, video, and multimedia.

- The DSL family includes asymmetric digital subscriber line (ADSL), rate adaptive asymmetrical digital subscriber line (RADSL), high bit rate asymmetric digital subscriber line (HDSL), single digital subscriber line (SDSL), and very high bit rate digital subscriber line (VDSL).

- The downstream bandwidth in ADSL is about 4.5 times as wide as the upstream direction.

- ADSL uses either the carrierless amplitude/phase (CAP) or the discrete multitone modulation (DMT) technique.

- Wave division multiplexing (WDM) is similar in concept to FDM. The signals being multiplexed, however, are light waves.

- Cable TV and telephone networks use fiber to the curb (FTTC) to reduce the amount of optical fiber needed.

- The discrete multitone technique combines elements of QAM and FDM and results in a much wider bandwidth for the downstream direction.

8.10   PRACTICE SET

Review Questions

1. What are the three major multiplexing techniques?
2. How does FDM combine multiple signals into one?
3. What is the purpose of a guard band?
4. How is one FDM signal separated into its original components?
5. How is WDM similar to FDM? How are they different?
6. What are the two types of TDM?
7. How does TDM combine multiple signals into one?
8. What are the two types of TDM implementations and how do they differ from each other?
9. How is one TDM signal separated into its original components? Consider both implementations of TDM.
10. What is inverse multiplexing?
11. What is the difference between an analog switched service and an analog leased service?
12. Describe the analog hierarchy in which groups of signals are successively multiplexed onto higher bandwidth lines.
13. What are the three types of digital services available to telephone customers?
14. What is the function of a DSU in switched/56 service?
15. Describe the DS hierarchy.
16. How are T lines related to DS service?
17. How can T lines be used for analog transmission?
18. How does ADSL divide the bandwidth of a twisted-pair cable?
19. How does ADSL modulate a signal?
20. What is FTTC and who uses it?
21. Name two ways in which digital services are superior to analog services.
22. How does a DSU differ from a modem?

23. What is the relationship between the number of slots in a frame and the number of input lines for synchronous TDM? For asynchronous TDM?

24. A DS-0 signal has a data rate of 64 Kbps. Where does this number come from?

Multiple Choice Questions

25. The sharing of a medium and its path by two or more devices is called _____.
    a. modulation
    b. encoding
    c. line discipline
    d. multiplexing

26. Which multiplexing technique transmits analog signals?
    a. FDM
    b. synchronous TDM
    c. asynchronous TDM
    d. b and c

27. Which multiplexing technique transmits digital signals?
    a. FDM
    b. synchronous TDM
    c. asynchronous TDM
    d. b and c

28. Which multiplexing technique shifts each signal to a different carrier frequency?
    a. FDM
    b. synchronous TDM
    c. asynchronous TDM
    d. none of the above

29. Which of the following is necessary for multiplexing?
    a. high-capacity data links
    b. parallel transmission
    c. QAM
    d. modems

30. Multiplexing involves _____.
    a. one path and one channel
    b. one path and multiple channels
    c. multiple paths and one channel
    d. multiple paths and multiple channels

31. In synchronous TDM, for n signal sources, each frame contains at least _____ slots.
    a. n
    b. $n + 1$

c. $n - 1$

d. 0 to n

32. In asynchronous TDM, for n signal sources, each frame contains m slots, where m is usually _____ n.

a. less than

b. greater than

c. equal to

d. 1 less than

33. In asynchronous TDM, the transmission rate of the multiplexed path is usually _____ the sum of the transmission rates of the signal sources.

a. greater than

b. less than

c. equal to

d. 1 less than

34. Which type of multiplexing has multiple paths?

a. FDM

b. asynchronous TDM

c. synchronous TDM

d. inverse multiplexing

35. Which type of telephone service is least expensive?

a. analog switched line

b. analog leased line

c. switched/56 service

d. DDS service

36. Which type of analog telephone service requires dialing?

a. analog switched line

b. analog leased line

c. switched/56 service

d. DDS service

37. Which type of analog telephone service provides a dedicated line between two customers?

a. analog switched line

b. analog leased line

c. switched/56 service

d. all of the above

38. Switched service means that connections between subscribers must involve _____.

a. modems

b. dedicated lines

    c. dialing

    d. leased lines

39. Leased service means that connections between subscribers must involve _____.

    a. modems

    b. dedicated lines

    c. dialing

    d. phase shifts

40. To decrease attenuation and distortion of a signal, a line can be _____.

    a. multiplexed

    b. grounded

    c. extended

    d. conditioned

41. In switched/56 service, the 56 stands for _____.

    a. the number of dedicated lines possible per connection

    b. the data rate in Kbps

    c. the number of microseconds to make a connection

    d. the resistance of the line in ohms

42. A digital service unit (DSU) is needed in _____.

    a. DDS service

    b. switched/56 service

    c. analog leased service

    d. a and b

43. Which telephone service offers the subscriber a choice of transmission speeds?

    a. analog switched service

    b. analog leased service

    c. switched/56 service

    d. DS service

44. In AT&T's FDM hierarchy, the bandwidth of each group type can be found by multiplying _____ and adding extra bandwidth for guard bands.

    a. the number of voice channels by 4000 Hz

    b. the sampling rate by 4000 Hz

    c. the number of voice channels by 8 bits/sample

    d. the sampling rate by 8 bits/sample

45. DS-0 through DS-4 are _____ while T-1 through T-4 are _____.

    a. services, multiplexers

    b. services, signals

    c. services, lines

    d. multiplexers, signals

46. In a T-1 line, _____ interleaving occurs.
    a. bit
    b. byte
    c. DS-0
    d. switch

47. Guard bands increase the bandwidth for _____.
    a. FDM
    b. synchronous TDM
    c. asynchronous TDM
    d. all of the above

48. Which multiplexing technique involves signals composed of light beams?
    a. FDM
    b. synchronous TDM
    c. asynchronous TDM
    d. WDM

49. DSL is an example of _____.
    a. multiplexing
    b. demultiplexing
    c. modulation
    d. all of the above

50. In the DSL family, _____ uses 2B1Q encoding to lessen the effects of attenuation.
    a. ADSL
    b. RADSL
    c. HDSL
    d. VDSL

51. In the DSL family, for _____, the cost is dependent on the type of communication desired.
    a. ADSL
    b. RADSL
    c. HDSL
    d. VDSL

52. _____ is similar to HDSL but uses only one single twisted-pair cable.
    a. SDSL
    b. ADSL
    c. VDSL
    d. RDSL

53. If the distance from the subscriber to the telephone central office is 1800 meters or less, _____ is a good choice.
    a. SDSL

     b. ADSL

     c. VDSL

     d. RDSL

54. In ADSL the largest frequency band is used for _____.

     a. POTS

     b. upstream communication

     c. downstream communication

     d. all of the above

55. In ADSL the smallest frequency band is used for _____.

     a. POTS

     b. upstream communication

     c. downstream communication

     d. all of the above

56. _____ is a modulation technique that eliminates the use of a carrier signal.

     a. TDM

     b. FDM

     c. CAP

     d. DMT

57. _____ is a modulation technique that uses elements of both QAM and FDM.

     a. TDM

     b. CAP

     c. DMT

     d. FTTC

58. In FTTC _____ is the medium from the cable company office to the subscriber's curb.

     a. coaxial

     b. twisted-pair

     c. untwisted-pair

     d. optical fiber

Exercises

59. Given the following information, find the minimum bandwidth for the path:

     FDM multiplexing.

     Five devices, each requiring 4000 Hz.

     200-Hz guard band for each device.

60. Given the following information, find the maximum bandwidth for each signal source:

     FDM multiplexing.

Total available bandwidth = 7900 Hz.

Three signal sources.

A 200-Hz guard band for each device.

61. Four signals are multiplexed. We take one measurement n of the multiplexed signal. For FDM what does n represent? For TDM what does n represent?

62. Five signal sources are multiplexed using synchronous TDM. Each source produces 100 characters per second. Assume that there is byte interleaving and that each frame requires one bit for synchronization. What is the frame rate? What is the bit rate on the path?

63. In asynchronous TDM, how is the number of slots per frame derived?

64. Draw the synchronous TDM frames showing the character data given the following information:

Four signal sources.

Source 1 message: T E G

Source 2 message: A

Source 3 message:

Source 4 message: E F I L

65. Do the previous problem assuming asynchronous TDM and a frame size of three characters.

66. What is the time duration for a T-1 frame?

67. The T-2 line offers a 6.312-Mbps service. Why is this number not 4×1.544 Mbps?

68. Assume there is a small town of 500 households, each with one telephone. If every phone connection is point-to-point (a dedicated line), how many total lines are necessary? How can multiplexing help?

69. The bandwidth for analog switched service is usually between 0 and 4000 Hz. Why?

70. In Figure 8.29 the sampling rate is 8000 samples per second. Why?

71. If a single mode optical fiber can transmit at 2 Gbps, how many telephone channels can one cable carry?

72. Calculate the overhead (in bits) per voice channel for each T line. What is the percentage of overhead per voice channel?

73. Three voice-grade lines, each using 4 KHz, are frequency multiplexed together using AM and cancelling the lower modulated band. Draw the frequency-domain representation of the resulting signal if the carrier frequencies are at 4, 10, and 16 KHz respectively. What is the bandwidth of the resulting signal?

74. If we want to combine 20 voice-grade signals (each of 4 KHz) with a guard band of 1 KHz between them, how much bandwidth do we need?

75. Show the frequency-domain representation of the resulting signals in each stage in Figure 8.37. Assume no guard band. Choose appropriate carrier frequencies.

Figure 8.37   *Example 75*

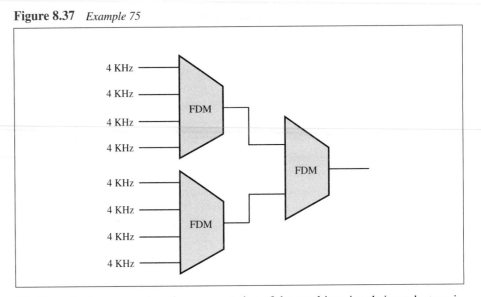

76. Show the frequency-domain representation of the resulting signals in each stage in Figure 8.38. Assume no guard band. Choose appropriate carrier frequencies.

Figure 8.38   *Exercise 76*

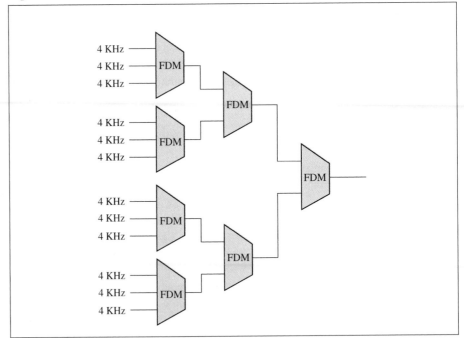

77. We have multiplexed 100 computers using synchronous TDM. If each computer sends data at the rate of 14.4 Kbps, what is the minimum bit rate of the line? Can a T-1 line handle this situation?

78. In Exercise 77, if only 70 computers are sending data at any time, how much of the bandwidth is wasted?

79. What is the minimum bit rate of each line in Figure 8.39 if we are using synchronous TDM? Ignore framing (synchronization) bits.

Figure 8.39 *Exercise 79*

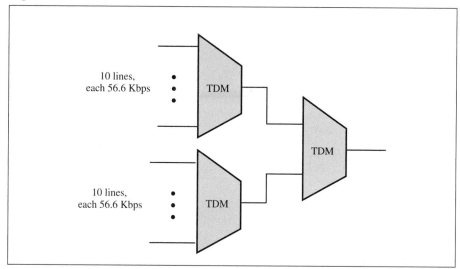

80. Figure 8.40 shows a multiplexer. If the slot is only 10 bits long (three bits taken from each input plus one framing bit), what is the output bit stream? What is the output bit rate? What is the duration of each bit in the output line? How many slots are sent per second? What is the duration of each slot?

Figure 8.40 *Exercise 80*

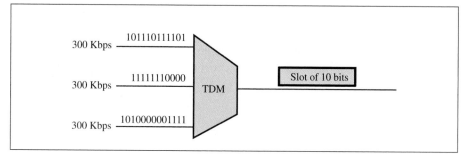

81. Figure 8.41 shows a demultiplexer. If the input slot is 12 bits long (ignore framing bits), what is the bit stream in each output? What is the bit rate for each output line?

Figure 8.41 *Exercise 81*

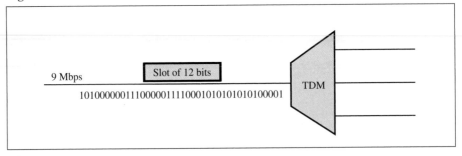

82. Figure 8.42 shows an inverse multiplexer. If the input data rate is 15 Mbps, what is the rate for each line? Can we use the service of T-1 lines for this purpose? Ignore the framing bits.

Figure 8.42 *Exercise 82*

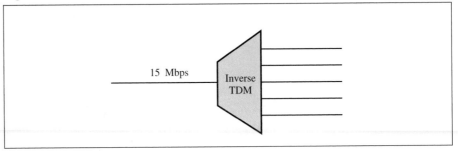

83. Figure 8.43 shows a statistical TDM multiplexer. How much is the data rate of each line reduced if all 10 lines are sending data? How many stations can send data at the same time with full capacity? Ignore extra bits needed for addressing.

84. Figure 8.44 shows a statistical TDM multiplexer. What is the output? Ignore extra bits for addressing.

85. What is the overhead (number of extra bits per second) in a T-1 line?

86. If we want to connect two Ethernet LANs with 10 Mbps data rates, how many T-1 lines do we need? Do we need multiplexers or inverse multiplexers? Show the configuration.

Figure 8.43 *Exercise 83*

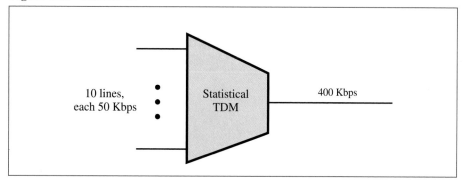

Figure 8.44 *Exercise 84*

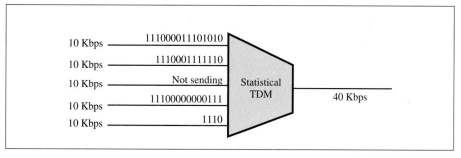

CHAPTER 9

Error Detection
and Correction

Networks must be able to transfer data from one device to another with complete accuracy. A system that cannot guarantee that the data received by one device are identical to the data transmitted by another device is essentially useless. Yet anytime data are transmitted from source to destination, they can become corrupted in passage. In fact, it is more likely that some part of a message will be altered in transit than that the entire contents will arrive intact. Many factors, including line noise, can alter or wipe out one or more bits of a given data unit. Reliable systems must have a mechanism for detecting and correcting such **errors.**

> Data can be corrupted during transmission. For reliable communication, errors must be detected and corrected.

Error detection and correction are implemented either at the data link layer or the transport layer of the OSI model.

9.1 TYPES OF ERRORS

Whenever an electromagnetic signal flows from one point to another, it is subject to unpredictable interference from heat, magnetism, and other forms of electricity. This interference can change the shape or timing of the signal. If the signal is carrying encoded binary data, such changes can alter the meaning of the data. In a single-bit error, a 0 is changed to a 1 or a 1 to a 0. In a burst error, multiple bits are changed. For example, a 0.01-second burst of impulse noise on a transmission with a data rate of 1200 bps might change all or some of 12 bits of information (see Figure 9.1).

Single-Bit Error

The term **single-bit error** means that only one bit of a given data unit (such as a byte, character, data unit, or packet) is changed from 1 to 0 or from 0 to 1.

Figure 9.1 *Types of errors*

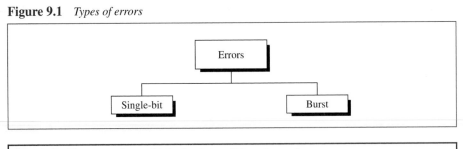

In a single-bit error, only one bit in the data unit has changed.

Figure 9.2 shows the effect of a single-bit error on a data unit. To understand the impact of the change, imagine that each group of eight bits is an ASCII character with a 0 bit added to the left. In the figure, 00000010 (ASCII *STX*) was sent, meaning *start of text,* but 00001010 (ASCII *LF*) was received, meaning *line feed.* (For more information about ASCII code, see Appendix A.)

Figure 9.2 *Single-bit error*

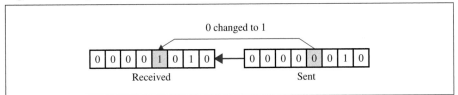

Single-bit errors are the least likely type of error in serial data transmission. To see why, imagine a sender sends data at 1Mbps. This means that each bit lasts only 1/1,000,000 second, or 1 μs. For a single-bit error to occur, the noise must have a duration of only 1 μs, which is very rare; noise normally lasts much longer than this.

However, a single-bit error can happen if we are sending data using parallel transmission. For example, if eight wires are used to send all of the eight bits of a byte at the same time and one of the wires is noisy, one bit can be corrupted in each byte. Think of parallel transmission inside a computer, between CPU and memory, for example.

Burst Error

The term **burst error** means that two or more bits in the data unit have changed from 1 to 0 or from 0 to 1.

A burst error means that two or more bits in the data unit have changed.

Figure 9.3 shows the effect of a burst error on a data unit. In this case, 0100010001000011 was sent, but 0101110101000011 was received. Note that a burst error does not necessarily mean that the errors occur in consecutive bits. The length of the burst is measured from the first corrupted bit to the last corrupted bit. Some bits in between may not have been corrupted.

Figure 9.3 *Burst error of length five*

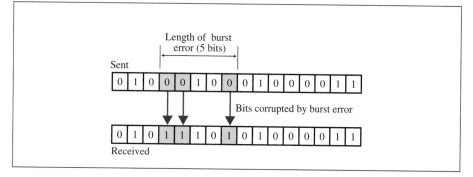

Burst error is most likely to happen in a serial transmission. The duration of noise is normally longer than the duration of a bit, which means that when noise affects data, it affects a set of bits. The number of bits affected depends on the data rate and duration of noise. For example, if we are sending data at 1 Kbps, a noise of 1/100 seconds can affect 10 bits; if we are sending data at 1 Mbps, the same noise can affect 10,000 bits.

9.2   DETECTION

Even if we know what types of errors can occur, will we recognize one when we see it? If we have a copy of the intended transmission for comparison, of course we will. But what if we don't have a copy of the original? Then we will have no way of knowing we have received an error until we have decoded the transmission and failed to make sense of it. For a machine to check for errors this way would be slow, costly, and of questionable value. We don't need a system where computers decode whatever comes in, then sit around trying to decide if the sender really meant to use the word *glbrshnif* in the middle of an array of weather statistics. What we need is a mechanism that is simple and completely objective.

Redundancy

One **error detection** mechanism that would satisfy these requirements would be to send every data unit twice. The receiving device would then be able to do a bit-for-bit comparison between the two versions of the data. Any discrepancy would indicate an error, and an appropriate correction mechanism could be set in place. This system would be completely accurate (the odds of errors being introduced onto exactly the same bits in both sets of data are infinitesimally small), but it would also be insupportably slow. Not only would the transmission time double, but the time it takes to compare every unit bit by bit must be added.

The concept of including extra information in the transmission solely for the purposes of comparison is a good one. But instead of repeating the entire data stream, a shorter group of bits may be appended to the end of each unit. This technique is called **redundancy** because the extra bits are redundant to the information; they are discarded as soon as the accuracy of the transmission has been determined.

> Error detection uses the concept of redundancy, which means adding extra bits for detecting errors at the destination.

Figure 9.4 shows the process of using redundant bits to check the accuracy of a data unit. Once the data stream has been generated, it passes through a device that analyzes it and adds on an appropriately coded redundancy check. The data unit, now enlarged by several bits (in this illustration, seven), travels over the link to the receiver. The receiver puts the entire stream through a checking function. If the received bit stream passes the checking criteria, the data portion of the data unit is accepted and the redundant bits are discarded.

Figure 9.4 *Redundancy*

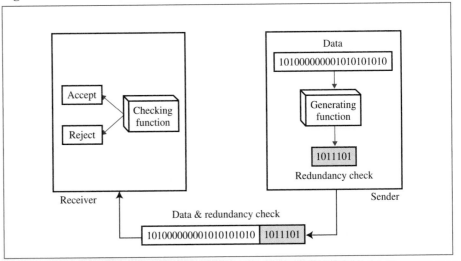

Figure 9.5 *Detection methods*

Four types of redundancy checks are used in data communications: vertical redundancy check (VRC) (also called parity check), longitudinal redundancy check (LRC), cyclical redundancy check (CRC), and checksum. The first three, VRC, LRC, and CRC, are normally implemented in the physical layer for use in the data link layer. The fourth, checksum, is used primarily by upper layers (see Figure 9.5).

Figure 9.5 *Detection methods*

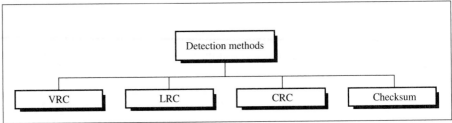

9.3 VERTICAL REDUNDANCY CHECK (VRC)

The most common and least expensive mechanism for error detection is the **vertical redundancy check (VRC),** often called a **parity check.** In this technique, a redundant bit, called a **parity bit,** is appended to every data unit so that the total number of 1s in the unit (including the parity bit) becomes even.

Suppose we want to transmit the binary data unit 1100001 [ASCII *a* (97)]; see Figure 9.6. Adding together the number of 1s gives us 3, an odd number. Before transmitting, we pass the data unit through a parity generator. The parity generator counts the 1s and appends the parity bit (a 1 in this case) to the end. The total number of 1s is now four, an even number. The system now transmits the entire expanded unit across the network link. When it reaches its destination, the receiver puts all eight bits through an **even-parity** checking function. If the receiver sees 11100001, it counts four 1s, an even number, and the data unit passes. But what if the data unit has been damaged in transit? What if, instead of 11100001, the receiver sees 11100101? Then, when the parity checker counts the 1s, it gets 5, an odd number. The receiver knows that an error has been introduced into the data somewhere and therefore rejects the whole unit.

> In vertical redundancy check (VRC), a parity bit is added to every data unit so that the total number of 1s becomes even.

Figure 9.6 *Even parity VRC concept*

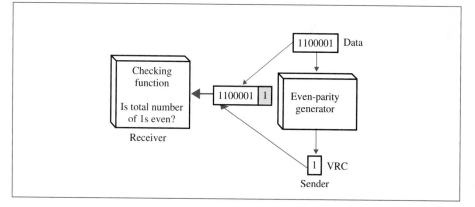

Note that for the sake of simplicity, we are discussing here even-parity checking, where the number of 1s should be an even number. Some systems may use **odd-parity** checking, where the number of 1s should be odd. The principle is the same; the calculation is different.

Example 9.1

Imagine the sender wants to send the word "world." In ASCII (see Appendix A), the five characters are coded as

    1110111 1101111 1110010 1101100 1100100
      w   o   r   l   d

Each of the first four characters has an even number of 1s, so the parity bit is a 0. The last character ("d"), however, has three 1s (an odd number), so the parity bit is a 1 to make the total number of 1s even. The following shows the actual bits sent (the parity bits are underlined).

    1110111<u>0</u>   1101111<u>0</u>   1110010<u>0</u>   1101100<u>0</u>   1100100<u>1</u>

Example 9.2

Now suppose the word "world," in the previous example, is received by the receiver without being corrupted in transmission.

    1110111<u>0</u>   1101111<u>0</u>   1110010<u>0</u>   1101100<u>0</u>   1100100<u>1</u>

The receiver counts the 1s in each character and comes up with even numbers (6, 6, 4, 4, 4). The data would be accepted.

Example 9.3

Now suppose the word "world," in Example 9.1, is received by the receiver but corrupted during transmission.

    111*1*111<u>0</u>   1101111<u>0</u>   1110*1*100   1101100<u>0</u>   1100100<u>1</u>

The receiver counts the 1s in each character and comes up with even and odd numbers (7, 6, 5, 4, 4). The receiver knows that the data are corrupted, discards them, and asks for retransmission.

Performance

VRC can detect all single-bit errors. It can also detect burst errors as long as the total number of bits changed is odd (1, 3, 5, etc.). Let's say we have an even-parity data unit where the total number of 1s, including the parity bit, is 6: 1000111011. If any three bits change value, the resulting parity will be odd and the error will be detected: 1*111*111011:9, 0*11*0111011:7, 1*1000*10011:5—all odd. The VRC checker would return a result of 1 and the data unit would be rejected. The same holds true for any odd number of errors.

Suppose, however, that two bits of the data unit are changed: 1*11*0111011:8, 1*1000*11011:6, 1000011010:4. In each case the number of 1s in the data unit is still even. The VRC checker will add them and return an even number although the data unit contains two errors. VRC cannot detect errors where the total number of bits changed is even. If any two bits change in transmission, the changes cancel each other and the data unit will pass a parity check even though the data unit is damaged. The same holds true for any even number of errors.

> VRC can detect all single-bit errors. It can detect burst errors only if the total number of errors in each data unit is odd.

9.4   LONGITUDINAL REDUNDANCY CHECK (LRC)

In **longitudinal redundancy check (LRC),** a block of bits is organized in a table (rows and columns). For example, instead of sending a block of 32 bits, we organize them in a table made of four rows and eight columns, as shown in Figure 9.7. We then calculate the parity bit for each column and create a new row of eight bits, which are the parity bits for the whole block. Note that the first parity bit in the fifth row is calculated based on all first bits. The second parity bit is calculated based on all second bits, and so on. We then attach the eight parity bits to the original data and send them to the receiver.

Figure 9.7   *LRC*

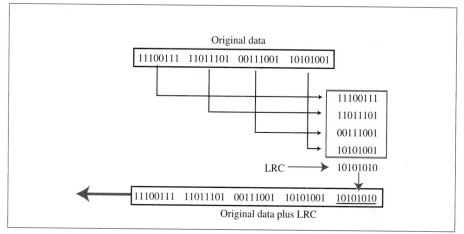

In longitudinal redundancy check (LRC), a block of bits is divided into rows and a redundant row of bits is added to the whole block.

Example 9.4

Suppose the following block is sent:

← 10101001 00111001 11011101 11100111   10101010
                                               (LRC)

However, it is hit by a burst noise of length eight and some bits are corrupted.

← 10100011   10001001   11011101 11100111 10101010
                                               (LRC)

When the receiver checks the LRC, some of the bits do not follow the even-parity rule and the whole block is discarded (the nonmatching bits are shown in bold).

← 10100011   10001001   11011101 11100111 **10101010**
                                               (LRC)

Performance

LRC increases the likelihood of detecting burst errors. As we showed in the previous example, an LRC of *n* bits can easily detect a burst error of *n* bits. A burst error of more than *n* bits is also detected by LRC with a very high probability. There is, however, one pattern of errors that remains elusive. If two bits in one data unit are damaged and two bits *in exactly the same positions* in another data unit are also damaged, the LRC checker will not detect an error. Consider, for example, two data units: 11110000 and 11000011. If the first and last bits in each of them are changed, making the data units read *0*111000*1* and *0*100001*0*, the errors cannot be detected by LRC.

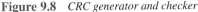

9.5   CYCLIC REDUNDANCY CHECK (CRC)

The third and most powerful of the redundancy checking techniques is the **cyclic redundancy check (CRC).** Unlike VRC and LRC, which are based on addition, CRC is based on binary division. In CRC, instead of adding bits together to achieve a desired parity, a sequence of redundant bits, called the CRC or the CRC remainder, is appended to the end of a data unit so that the resulting data unit becomes exactly divisible by a second, predetermined binary number. At its destination, the incoming data unit is divided by the same number. If at this step there is no remainder, the data unit is assumed to be intact and is therefore accepted. A remainder indicates that the data unit has been damaged in transit and therefore must be rejected.

The redundancy bits used by CRC are derived by dividing the data unit by a predetermined divisor; the remainder is the CRC. To be valid, a CRC must have two qualities: it must have exactly one less bit than the divisor, and appending it to the end of the data string must make the resulting bit sequence exactly divisible by the divisor.

Both the theory and the application of CRC error detection are straightforward. The only complexity is in deriving the CRC. In order to clarify this process, we will start with an overview and add complexity as we go. Figure 9.8 provides an outline of the three basic steps.

Figure 9.8   *CRC generator and checker*

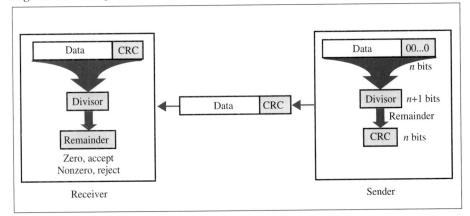

First, a string of n 0s is appended to the data unit. The number n is one less than the number of bits in the predetermined divisor, which is $n + 1$ bits.

Second, the newly elongated data unit is divided by the divisor using a process called binary division. The remainder resulting from this division is the CRC.

Third, the CRC of n bits derived in step 2 replaces the appended 0s at the end of the data unit. Note that the CRC may consist of all 0s.

The data unit arrives at the receiver data first, followed by the CRC. The receiver treats the whole string as a unit and divides it by the same divisor that was used to find the CRC remainder.

If the string arrives without error, the CRC checker yields a remainder of zero and the data unit passes. If the string has been changed in transit, the division yields a non-zero remainder and the data unit does not pass.

The CRC Generator

A CRC generator uses modulo-2 division. Figure 9.9 shows this process. In the first step, the four-bit divisor is subtracted from the first four bits of the dividend. Each bit of the divisor is subtracted from the corresponding bit of the dividend without disturbing the next higher bit. In our example, the divisor, 1101, is subtracted from the first four bits of the dividend, 1001, yielding 100 (the leading 0 of the remainder is dropped off).

Figure 9.9   *Binary division in a CRC generator*

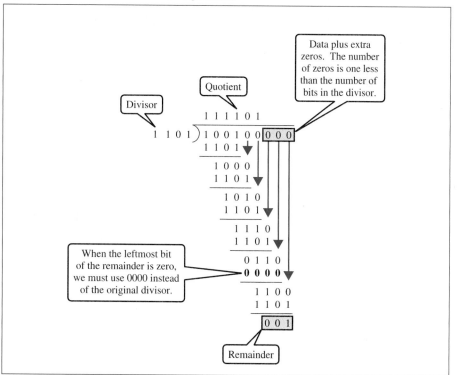

The next unused bit from the dividend is then pulled down to make the number of bits in the remainder equal to the number of bits in the divisor. The next step, therefore, is 1000 − 1101, which yields 101, and so on.

In this process, the divisor always begins with a 1; the divisor is subtracted from a portion of the previous dividend/remainder that is equal to it in length; the divisor can only be subtracted from a dividend/remainder whose leftmost bit is 1. Anytime the left-most bit of the dividend/remainder is 0, a string of 0s, of the same length as the divisor, replaces the divisor in that step of the process. For example, if the divisor is four bits long, it is replaced by four 0s. (Remember, we are dealing with bit patterns, not with quantitative values; 0000 is not the same as 0.) This restriction means that, at any step, the leftmost subtraction will be either 0 − 0 or 1 − 1, both of which equal 0. So, after subtraction, the leftmost bit of the remainder will always be a leading zero, which is dropped off, and the next unused bit of the dividend is pulled down to fill out the remainder. Note that only the first bit of the remainder is dropped—if the second bit is also 0, it is retained, and the dividend/remainder for the next step will begin with 0. This process repeats until the entire dividend has been used.

The CRC Checker

A CRC checker functions exactly like the generator. After receiving the data appended with the CRC, it does the same modulo-2 division. If the remainder is all 0s, the CRC is dropped and the data accepted; otherwise, the received stream of bits is discarded and data are resent. Figure 9.10 shows the same process of division in the receiver. We assume that there is no error. The remainder is therefore all 0s and the data are accepted.

Figure 9.10 *Binary division in CRC checker*

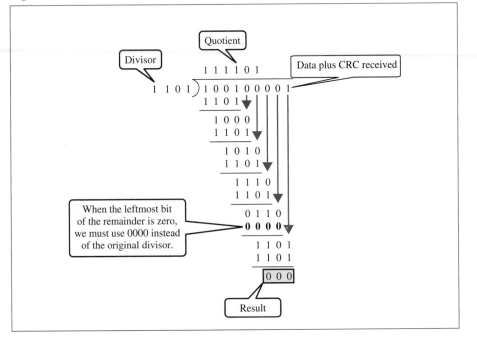

Polynomials

The CRC generator (the divisor) is most often represented not as a string of 1s and 0s, but as an algebraic polynomial (see Figure 9.11). The polynomial format is useful for two reasons: It is short, and it can be used to prove the concept mathematically (which is beyond the scope of this book).

Figure 9.11 *A polynomial*

$$x^7 + x^5 + x^2 + x + 1$$

The relationship of a polynomial to its corresponding binary representation is shown in Figure 9.12.

Figure 9.12 *A polynomial representing a divisor*

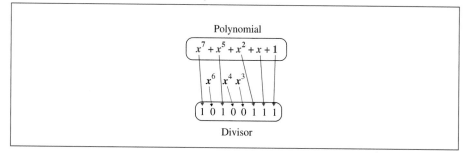

A polynomial should be selected to have at least the following properties:

■ It should not be divisible by x.

■ It should be divisible by $(x + 1)$.

The first condition guarantees that all burst errors of a length equal to the degree of the polynomial are detected. The second condition guarantees that all burst errors affecting an odd number of bits are detected (the proof is beyond the scope of this book).

Example 9.5

It is obvious that we cannot choose x (binary 10) or $x^2 + x$ (binary 110) as the polynomial because both are divisible by x. However, we can choose $x + 1$ (binary 11) because it is not divisible by x, but is divisible by $x + 1$. We can also choose $x^2 + 1$ (binary 101) because it is divisible by $x + 1$ (binary division).

The standard polynomials used by popular protocols for CRC generation are shown in Figure 9.13. The numbers 12, 16, and 32 refer to the size of the CRC remainder. The CRC divisors are 13, 17, and 33 bits, respectively.

Figure 9.13   *Standard polynomials*

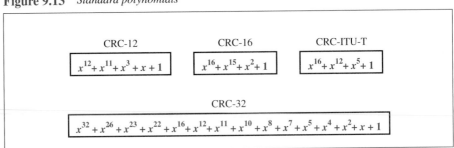

Performance

CRC is a very effective error detection method. If the divisor is chosen according to the previously mentioned rules,

a. CRC can detect all burst errors that affect an odd number of bits.

b. CRC can detect all burst errors of length less than or equal to the degree of the polynomial.

c. CRC can detect with a very high probability burst errors of length greater than the degree of the polynomial.

Example 9.6

The CRC-12 ($x^{12} + x^{11} + x^3 + x + 1$), which has a degree of 12, will detect all burst errors affecting an odd number of bits, will detect all burst errors with a length less than or equal to 12, and will detect 99.97 percent of the time burst errors with a length of 12 or more.

9.6   CHECKSUM

The error detection method used by the higher-layer protocols is called **checksum**. Like VRC, LRC, and CRC, checksum is based on the concept of redundancy.

Checksum Generator

In the sender, the checksum generator subdivides the data unit into equal segments of n bits (usually 16). These segments are added together using **one's complement** arithmetic (see Appendix C) in such a way that the total is also n bits long. That total (sum) is then complemented and appended to the end of the original data unit as redundancy bits, called the checksum field. The extended data unit is transmitted across the network. So if the sum of the data segment is T, the checksum will be $-T$ (see Figures 9.14 and 9.15).

Checksum Checker

The receiver subdivides the data unit as above and adds all segments together and complements the result. If the extended data unit is intact, the total value found by adding the data segments and the checksum field should be zero. If the result is not zero, the packet contains an error and the receiver rejects it (see Appendix C).

Figure 9.14   *Checksum*

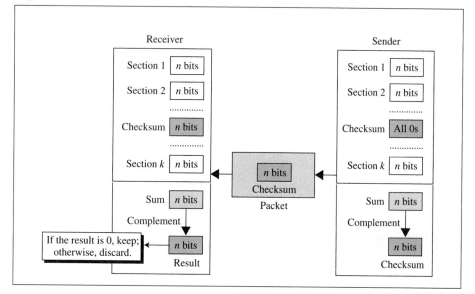

The sender follows these steps:

- The unit is divided into k sections, each of n bits.
- All sections are added together using one's complement to get the sum.
- The sum is complemented and becomes the checksum.
- The checksum is sent with the data.

Figure 9.15   *Data unit and checksum*

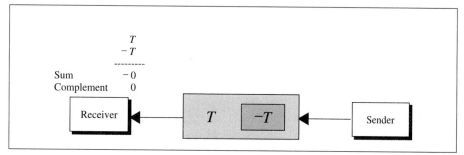

The receiver follows these steps:

- The unit is divided into k sections, each of n bits.
- All sections are added together using one's complement to get the sum.
- The sum is complemented.
- If the result is zero, the data are accepted: otherwise, they are rejected.

Example 9.7

Suppose the following block of 16 bits is to be sent using a checksum of 8 bits.

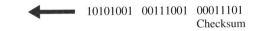 10101001 00111001

The numbers are added using one's complement arithmetic (see Appendix C).

```
                                    10101001
                                    00111001
                                 ----------------
                     Sum            11100010
                     Checksum       00011101
```

The pattern sent is:

10101001 00111001 00011101
Checksum

Example 9.8

Now suppose the receiver receives the pattern sent in Example 9.7 and there is no error.

10101001 00111001 00011101

When the receiver adds the three sections together, it will get all 1s, which, after complementing, is all 0s and shows that there is no error.

```
                          10101001
                          00111001
                          00011101
                       ------------------
              Sum         11111111
              Complement  00000000       means that the pattern is OK.
```

Example 9.9

Now suppose there is a burst error of length five that affects four bits.

10101*111* *11*111001 00011101

When the receiver adds the three sections together, it gets

```
                              10101111
                              11111001
                              00011101
                          ------------------------
              Result     1    11000101
              Carry                   1
                          ------------------------
              Sum             11000110
              Complement      00111001       means that the pattern is corrupted.
```

Performance

The checksum detects all errors involving an odd number of bits, as well as most errors involving an even number of bits. However, if one or more bits of a segment are damaged and the corresponding bit or bits of opposite value in a second segment are also damaged, the sums of those columns will not change and the receiver will not detect a problem. If the last digit of one segment is a 0 and it gets changed to a 1 in transit, then the last 1 in another segment must be changed to a 0 if the error is to go undetected. In LRC, two 0s could both change to 1s without altering the parity because carries were discarded. Checksum retains all carries; so, although two 0s becoming 1s would not alter the value of their own column, they would change the value of the next higher column. But anytime a bit inversion is balanced by an opposite bit inversion in the corresponding digit of another data segment, the error is invisible.

9.7 ERROR CORRECTION

The mechanisms that we have covered up to this point detect errors but do not correct them. **Error correction** can be handled in two ways. In one, when an error is discovered, the receiver can have the sender retransmit the entire data unit. In the other, a receiver can use an error-correcting code, which automatically corrects certain errors.

In theory, it is possible to correct any binary code errors automatically. Error-correcting codes, however, are more sophisticated than error-detection codes and require more redundancy bits. The number of bits required to correct a multiple-bit or burst error is so high that in most cases it is inefficient to do so. For this reason, most error correction is limited to one-, two-, or three-bit errors.

Single-Bit Error Correction

The concept underlying error correction can be most easily understood by examining the simplest case: single-bit errors.

As we saw earlier, single-bit errors can be detected by the addition of a redundant (parity) bit to the data unit (VRC). A single additional bit can detect single-bit errors in any sequence of bits because it must distinguish between only two conditions: error or no error. A bit has two states (0 and 1). These two states are sufficient for this level of detection.

But what if we want to correct as well as detect single-bit errors? Two states are enough to detect an error but not to correct it. An error occurs when the receiver reads a 1 bit as a 0 or a 0 bit as a 1. To correct the error, the receiver simply reverses the value of the altered bit. To do so, however, it must know which bit is in error. The secret of error correction, therefore, is to locate the invalid bit or bits.

For example, to correct a single-bit error in an ASCII character, the error correction code must determine which of the seven bits has changed. In this case, we have to distinguish between eight different states: no error, error in position 1, error in position 2, and so on, up to error in position 7. To do so requires enough redundancy bits to show all eight states.

At first glance, it looks like a three-bit redundancy code should be adequate because three bits can show eight different states (000 to 111) and can therefore indicate the locations of eight different possibilities. But what if an error occurs in the redundancy bits themselves? Seven bits of data (the ASCII character) plus three bits of redundancy equals 10 bits. Three bits, however, can identify only eight possibilities. Additional bits are necessary to cover all possible error locations.

Redundancy Bits

To calculate the number of redundancy bits (r) required to correct a given number of data bits (m), we must find a relationship between m and r. Figure 9.16 shows m bits of data with r bits of redundancy added to them. The length of the resulting code is $m + r$.

Figure 9.16 *Data and redundancy bits*

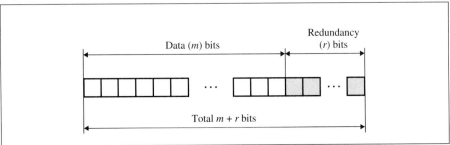

If the total number of bits in a transmittable unit is $m + r$, then r must be able to indicate at least $m + r + 1$ different states. Of these, one state means no error and $m + r$ states indicate the location of an error in each of the $m + r$ positions.

So, $m + r + 1$ states must be discoverable by r bits; and r bits can indicate 2^r different states. Therefore, 2^r must be equal to or greater than $m + r + 1$:

$$2^r \geq m + r + 1$$

The value of r can be determined by plugging in the value of m (the original length of the data unit to be transmitted). For example, if the value of m is 7 (as in a seven-bit ASCII code), the smallest r value that can satisfy this equation is 4:

$$2^4 \geq 7 + 4 + 1$$

Table 9.1 shows some possible m values and the corresponding r values.

Table 9.1 *Relationship between data and redundancy bits*

Number of Data Bits (m)	Number of Redundancy Bits (r)	Total Bits (m + r)
1	2	3
2	3	5
3	3	6
4	3	7
5	4	9
6	4	10
7	4	11

Hamming Code

So far, we have examined the number of bits required to cover all of the possible single-bit error states in a transmission. But how do we manipulate those bits to discover which state has occurred? A technique developed by R. W. Hamming provides a practical solution.

Positioning the Redundancy Bits

The **Hamming code** can be applied to data units of any length and uses the relationship between data and redundancy bits discussed above. For example, a seven-bit ASCII code requires four redundancy bits that can be added to the end of the data unit or interspersed with the original data bits. In Figure 9.17, these bits are placed in positions 1, 2, 4, and 8 (the positions in an 11-bit sequence that are powers of 2). For clarity in the examples below, we refer to these bits as r_1, r_2, r_4, and r_8.

Figure 9.17   *Positions of redundancy bits in Hamming code*

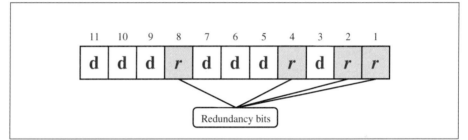

In the Hamming code, each r bit is the VRC bit for one combination of data bits: r_1 is the VRC bit for one combination of data bits, r_2 is the VRC bit for another combination of data bits, and so on. The combinations used to calculate each of the four r values for a seven-bit data sequence are as follows:

$$r_1: \text{bits } 1, 3, 5, 7, 9, 11$$

$$r_2: \text{bits } 2, 3, 6, 7, 10, 11$$

$$r_4: \text{bits } 4, 5, 6, 7$$

$$r_8: \text{bits } 8, 9, 10, 11$$

Each data bit may be included in more than one VRC calculation. In the sequences above, for example, each of the original data bits is included in at least two sets, while the r bits are included in only one.

To see the pattern behind this strategy, look at the binary representation of each bit position. The r_1 bit is calculated using all bit positions whose binary representation includes a 1 in the rightmost position. The r_2 bit is calculated using all bit positions with a 1 in the second position, and so on (see Figure 9.18).

Figure 9.18   *Redundancy bits calculation*

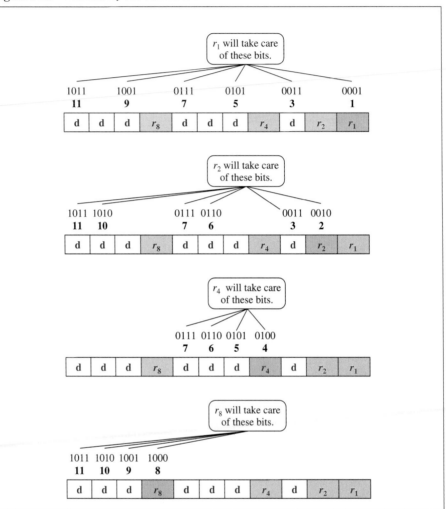

Calculating the *r* Values

Figure 9.19 shows a Hamming code implementation for an ASCII character. In the first step, we place each bit of the original character in its appropriate position in the 11-bit unit. In the subsequent steps, we calculate the even parities for the various bit combinations. The parity value for each combination is the value of the corresponding *r* bit. For example, the value of r_1 is calculated to provide even parity for a combination of bits 3, 5, 7, 9, and 11. The value of r_2 is calculated to provide even parity with bits 3, 6, 7, 10, and 11, and so on. The final 11-bit code is sent through the transmission line.

Error Detection and Correction

Now imagine that by the time the above transmission is received, the number 7 bit has been changed from 1 to 0 (see Figure 9.20).

Figure 9.19   *Example of redundancy bit calculation*

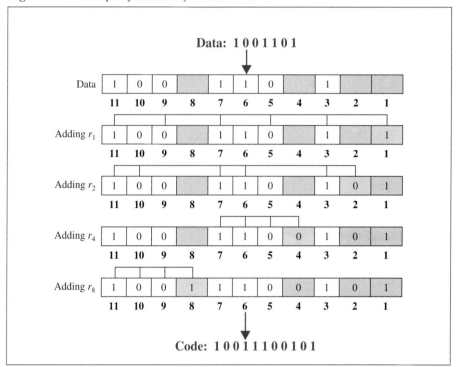

Figure 9.20   *Single-bit error*

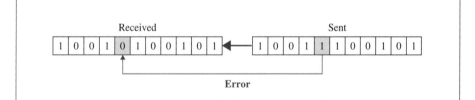

The receiver takes the transmission and recalculates four new VRCs using the same sets of bits used by the sender plus the relevant parity (r) bit for each set (see Figure 9.21). Then it assembles the new parity values into a binary number in order of r position (r_8, r_4, r_2, r_1). In our example, this step gives us the binary number 0111 (7 in decimal), which is the precise location of the bit in error.

Once the bit is identified, the receiver can reverse its value and correct the error.

Burst Error Correction

A Hamming code can be designed to correct burst errors of certain lengths. The number of redundancy bits required to make these corrections, however, is dramatically higher than that required for single-bit errors. To correct double-bit errors, for example, we must take into consideration that the two bits can be a combination of any two bits in

Figure 9.21   *Error detection using Hamming code*

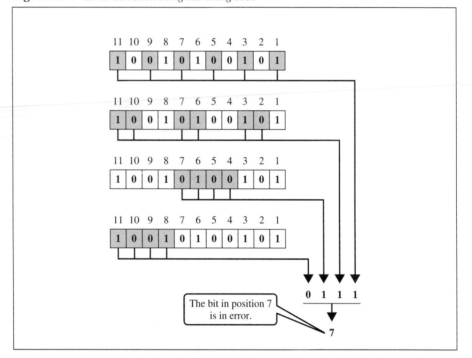

the entire sequence. Three-bit correction means any three bits in the entire sequence, and so on. So the simple strategy used by the Hamming code to correct single-bit errors must be redesigned to be applicable for multiple-bit correction. We leave the details of these more sophisticated schemes to advanced books on **error handling.**

9.8   KEY TERMS AND CONCEPTS

burst error	error handling
checksum	even parity
cyclic redundancy check (CRC)	Hamming code
error	longitudinal redundancy check (LRC)
error correction	odd parity
error detection	one's complement

parity bit   single-bit error

parity check   vertical redundancy check (VRC)

redundancy

9.9   SUMMARY

- Transmission errors are usually detected at the physical layer of the OSI model.
- Transmission errors are usually corrected at the data link layer of the OSI model.
- Errors can be categorized as follows:
  a. Single-bit: one bit error per data unit.
  b. Burst: two or more bit errors per data unit.
- Redundancy is the concept of sending extra bits for use in error detection.
- Four common methods of error detection are the following:
  a. Vertical redundancy check (VRC).
  b. Longitudinal redundancy check (LRC).
  c. Cyclic redundancy check (CRC).
  d. Checksum.
- In VRC an extra bit (parity bit) is added to the data unit.
- VRC can detect only an odd number of errors; it cannot detect an even number of errors.
- In LRC a redundant data unit follows n data units.
- CRC, the most powerful of the redundancy checking techniques, is based on binary division.
- Checksum is used by the higher-layer protocols (TCP/IP) for error detection.
- To calculate a checksum:
  a. Divide the data into sections.
  b. Add the sections together using one's complement arithmetic.
  c. Take the complement of the final sum; this is the checksum.
- At the receiver, when using the checksum method, the data and checksum should add up to zero if there are no errors present.
- The Hamming code is a single-bit error correction method using redundant bits. The number of bits is a function of the length of the data bits.
- In the Hamming code, for a data unit of m bits, use the formula $2r \geq m + r + 1$ to determine r, the number of redundant bits needed.

9.10   PRACTICE SET

Review Questions

1. How does a single-bit error differ from a burst error?
2. Discuss the concept of redundancy in error detection.
3. What are the four types of redundancy checks used in data communications?
4. How can the parity bit detect a damaged data unit?
5. What is the difference between even parity and odd parity?
6. Discuss VRC and the types of errors it can and cannot detect.
7. How is VRC related to LRC?
8. Discuss LRC and the types of errors it can and cannot detect.
9. What does the CRC generator append to the data unit?
10. What is the relationship between the size of the CRC remainder and the divisor?
11. How does the CRC checker know that the received data unit is undamaged?
12. What are the conditions for the polynomial used by the CRC generator?
13. How is CRC superior to LRC?
14. What is the error detection method used by the upper-layer protocols?
15. What kind of arithmetic is used to add segments in the checksum generator and checksum checker?
16. List the steps involved in creating a checksum.
17. How does the checksum checker know that the received data unit is undamaged?
18. What kind of error is undetectable by the checksum?
19. What is the formula to calculate the number of redundancy bits required to correct a bit error in a given number of data bits?
20. What is the purpose of the Hamming code?

Multiple Choice Questions

21. Error detection is usually done in the _____ layer of the OSI model.
    a. physical
    b. data link
    c. network
    d. any of the above
22. Which error detection method consists of a parity bit for each data unit as well as an entire data unit of parity bits?
    a. VRC
    b. LRC
    c. CRC
    d. checksum

23. Which error detection method uses one's complement arithmetic?
    a. VRC
    b. LRC
    c. CRC
    d. checksum

24. Which error detection method consists of just one redundant bit per data unit?
    a. VRC
    b. LRC
    c. CRC
    d. checksum

25. Which error detection method involves polynomials?
    a. VRC
    b. LRC
    c. CRC
    d. checksum

26. Which of the following best describes a single bit error?
    a. A single bit is inverted.
    b. A single bit is inverted per data unit.
    c. A single bit is inverted per transmission.
    d. any of the above

27. If the ASCII character G is sent and the character D is received, what type of error is this?
    a. single-bit
    b. multiple-bit
    c. burst
    d. recoverable

28. If the ASCII character H is sent and the character I is received, what type of error is this?
    a. single-bit
    b. multiple-bit
    c. burst
    d. recoverable

29. In cyclic redundancy checking, what is the CRC?
    a. the divisor
    b. the quotient
    c. the dividend
    d. the remainder

30. In cyclic redundancy checking, the divisor is _____ the CRC.
    a. the same size as
    b. one bit less than

    c. one bit more than

    d. two bits more than

31. If the data unit is 111111, the divisor 1010, and the remainder 110, what is the dividend at the receiver?

    a. 111111011

    b. 111111110

    c. 1010110

    d. 110111111

32. If the data unit is 111111 and the divisor 1010, what is the dividend at the transmitter?

    a. 111111000

    b. 1111110000

    c. 111111

    d. 1111111010

33. If odd parity is used for ASCII error detection, the number of 0s per eight-bit symbol is _____.

    a. even

    b. odd

    c. indeterminate

    d. 42

34. The sum of the checksum and data at the receiver is _____ if there are no errors.

    a. −0

    b. +0

    c. the complement of the checksum

    d. the complement of the data

35. The Hamming code is a method of _____.

    a. error detection

    b. error correction

    c. error encapsulation

    d. a and b

36. In CRC there is no error if the remainder at the receiver is _____.

    a. equal to the remainder at the sender

    b. zero

    c. nonzero

    d. the quotient at the sender

37. In CRC the quotient at the sender _____.

    a. becomes the dividend at the receiver

    b. becomes the divisor at the receiver

    c. is discarded

    d. is the remainder

38. Which error detection method involves the use of parity bits?
    a. VRC
    b. LRC
    c. CRC
    d. a and b

39. Which error detection method can detect a single-bit error?
    a. VRC
    b. LRC
    c. CRC
    d. all of the above

40. Which error detection method can detect a burst error?
    a. VRC
    b. LRC
    c. CRC
    d. b and c

41. For 10 groups, each of 8 bits, we calculate the LRC. How many bits make up the LRC?
    a. 10
    b. 8
    c. 18
    d. 80

42. At the CRC generator, _____ added to the data unit before the division process.
    a. 0s are
    b. 1s are
    c. a polynomial is
    d. a CRC remainder is

43. At the CRC generator, _____ added to the data unit after the division process.
    a. 0s are
    b. 1s are
    c. the polynomial is
    d. the CRC remainder is

44. At the CRC checker, _____ means that the data unit is damaged.
    a. a string of 0s
    b. a string of 1s
    c. a string of alternating 1s and 0s
    d. a nonzero remainder

Exercises

45. What is the maximum effect of a 2-ms burst of noise on data transmitted at
    a. 1500 bps?
    b. 12,000 bps?
    c. 96,000 bps?

46. Assuming even parity, find the parity bit for each of the following data units:
    a. 1001011
    b. 0001100
    c. 1000000
    d. 1110111

47. A receiver receives the bit pattern 01101011. If the system is using even parity VRC, is the pattern in error?

48. Find the LRC for the following block of data.

    10011001 01101111

49. Given a 10-bit sequence 1010011110 and a divisor of 1011, find the CRC. Check your answer.

50. Given a remainder of 111, a data unit of 10110011, and a divisor of 1001, is there an error in the data unit?

51. Find the checksum for the following bit sequence. Assume a 16-bit segment size.

    1001001110010011
    1001100001001101

52. Find the complement of 1110010001110011.

53. Add 11100011 and 00011100 in one's complement. Interpret the result.

54. For each data unit of the following sizes, find the minimum number of redundancy bits needed to correct one single-bit error:
    a. 12
    b. 16
    c. 24
    d. 64

55. Construct the Hamming code for the bit sequence 10011101.

56. Calculate the VRC and LRC for the following bit pattern using even parity:

    ← 0011101 1100111 1111111 0000000

57. A sender sends 01110001; the receiver receives 01000001. If only VRC is used, can the receiver detect the error?

58. The following block uses even-parity LRC. Which bits are in error?

    ← 10010101 01001111 11010000 11011011

59. A system uses LRC on a block of 8 bytes. How many redundant bits are sent per block? What is the ratio of useful bits to the total bits?

60. If a divisor is 101101, how many bits long is the CRC?

61. Find the binary equivalent of $x^8 + x^3 + x + 1$.

62. Find the polynomial equivalent of 100001110001.

63. A receiver receives the code 11001100111. When it uses the Hamming encoding algorithm, the result is 0101. Which bit is in error? What is the correct code?

64. In single-bit error correction, a code of three bits can be in one of four states: no error, first bit in error, second bit in error, and third bit in error. How many of these three bits should be redundant to correct this code? How many bits can be the actual data?

65. Using the logic in Exercise 64, find out how many redundant bits should be in a 10-bit code to detect an error.

66. The code 11110101101 was received. Using the Hamming encoding algorithm, what is the original code sent?

CHAPTER 10

Data Link Control

Up to this point, we have been examining the structure and transmission of signals across media links. But unless accurately received by a second device, a signal transmitted over a wire is just so much wasted electricity. With transmission alone we can put a signal onto a line, but we have no way of controlling which of several devices attached to that line will receive it, no way of knowing if the intended receiver is ready and able to receive it, and no way of keeping a second device on the line from transmitting at the same time and thereby destroying our signal. In the physical layer of the OSI model, we have transmission but we do not yet have communication.

Communication requires at least two devices working together, one to send and one to receive. Even such a basic arrangement requires a great deal of coordination for an intelligible exchange to occur. For example, in half-duplex transmission, it is essential that only one device transmit at a time. If both ends of the link put signals on the line simultaneously, they collide, leaving nothing on the line but noise. The coordination of half-duplex transmission is part of a procedure called **line discipline,** which is one of the functions included in the second layer of the OSI model, the data link layer.

In addition to line discipline, the most important functions in the data link layer are **flow control** and **error control** (see Figure 10.1). Collectively, these functions are known as data link control.

Figure 10.1   *Data link layer*

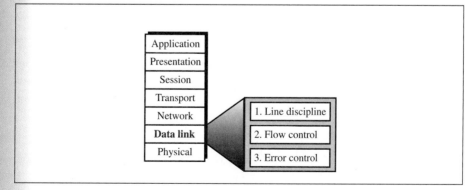

- Line discipline coordinates the link systems. It determines which device can send and when it can send.
- Flow control coordinates the amount of data that can be sent before receiving acknowledgment. It also provides the receiver's acknowledgment of frames received intact, and so is linked to error control.
- Error control means error detection and correction. It allows the receiver to inform the sender of any frames lost or damaged in transmission and coordinates the retransmission of those frames by the sender (see Figure 10.2).

Figure 10.2   *Data link layer functions*

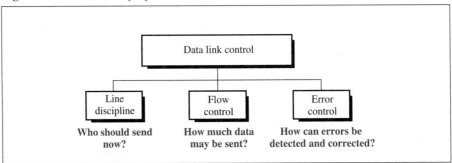

10.1   LINE DISCIPLINE

Whatever the system, no device in it should be allowed to transmit until that device has evidence that the intended receiver is able to receive and is prepared to accept the transmission. What if the receiving device does not expect a transmission, is busy, or is out of commission? With no way to determine the status of the intended receiver, the transmitting device may waste its time sending data to a nonfunctioning receiver or may interfere with signals already on the link. The line discipline functions of the data link layer oversee the establishment of links and the right of a particular device to transmit at a given time.

Line discipline answers the question, Who should send now?

Line discipline can be done in two ways: enquiry/acknowledgment (ENQ/ACK) and poll/select. The first method is used in peer-to-peer communication; the second method is used in primary–secondary communication (see Figure 10.3).

ENQ/ACK

Enquiry/acknowledgment (ENQ/ACK) is used primarily in systems where there is no question of the wrong receiver getting the transmission, that is, when there is a dedicated link between two devices so that the only device capable of receiving the transmission is the intended one.

Figure 10.3 *Line discipline categories*

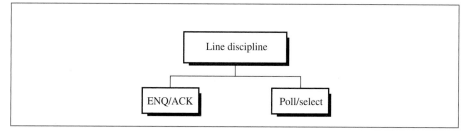

ENQ/ACK coordinates which device may start a transmission and whether or not the intended recipient is ready and enabled (see Figure 10.4). Using ENQ/ACK, a session can be initiated by either station on a link as long as both are of equal rank—a printer, for example, cannot initiate communication with a CPU.

Figure 10.4 *Line discipline concept: ENQ/ACK*

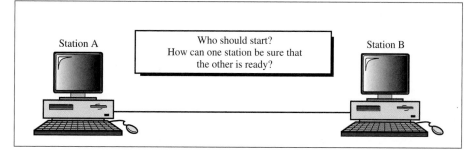

In both half-duplex and full-duplex transmission, the initiating device establishes the session. In half-duplex, the initiator then sends its data while the responder waits. The responder may take over the link when the initiator is finished or has requested a response. In full-duplex, both devices can transmit simultaneously once the session has been established.

How It Works   The initiator first transmits a frame called an enquiry (ENQ) asking if the receiver is available to receive data. The receiver must answer either with an **acknowledgement (ACK)** frame if it is ready to receive or with a **negative acknowledgement (NAK)** frame if it is not. By requiring a response even if the answer is negative, the initiator knows that its enquiry was in fact received even if the receiver is currently unable to accept a transmission. If neither an ACK nor a NAK is received within a specified time limit, the initiator assumes that the ENQ frame was lost in transit, disconnects, and sends a replacement. An initiating system ordinarily makes three such attempts to establish a link before giving up.

If the response to the ENQ is negative for three attempts, the initiator disconnects and begins the process again at another time. If the response is positive, the initiator is free to send its data. Once all of its data have been transmitted, the sending system finishes with an **end of transmission (EOT)** frame. This process is illustrated in Figure 10.5.

Figure 10.5 *ENQ/ACK line discipline*

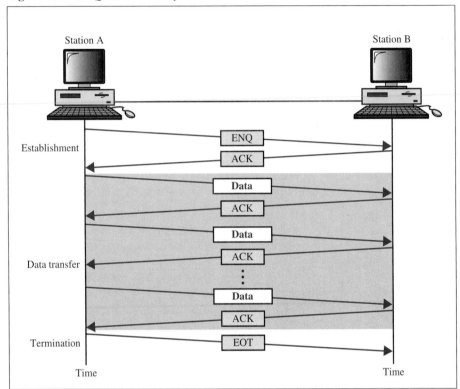

Poll/Select

The **poll/select** method of line discipline works with topologies where one device is designated as a **primary station** and the other devices are **secondary stations.** Multipoint systems must coordinate several nodes, not just two. The question to be determined in these cases, therefore, is more than just, Are you ready? It is also, Which of the several nodes has the right to use the channel?

How It Works   Whenever a multipoint link consists of a primary device and multiple secondary devices using a single transmission line, all exchanges must be made through the primary device even when the ultimate destination is a secondary device. (Although the illustrations that follow show a bus topology, the concepts are the same for any multipoint configuration.) The primary device controls the link; the secondary devices follow its instructions. It is up to the primary to determine which device is allowed to use the channel at a given time (see Figure 10.6). The primary, therefore, is always the initiator of a session. If the primary wants to receive data, it asks the secondaries if they have anything to send; this function is called *polling*. If the primary wants to send data, it tells the target secondary to get ready to receive; this function is called *selecting*.

Figure 10.6 *Poll/select discipline*

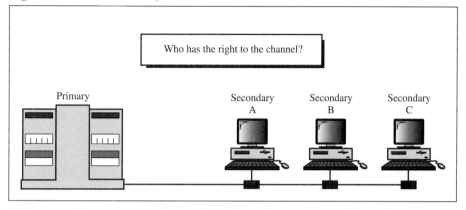

Addresses For point-to-point configurations, there is no need for addressing; any transmission put onto the link by one device can be intended only for the other. For the primary device in a multipoint topology to be able to identify and communicate with a specific secondary device, however, there must be an addressing convention. For this reason, every device on a link has an address that can be used for identification.

Poll/select protocols identify each frame as being either to or from a specific device on the link. Each secondary device has an address that differentiates it from the others. In any transmission, that address will appear in a specified portion of each frame, called an address field or header depending on the protocol. If the transmission comes from the primary device, the address indicates the recipient of the data. If the transmission comes from a secondary device, the address indicates the originator of the data. We will discuss addressing further when we discuss specific protocols in Chapter 12.

Select The **select** mode is used whenever the primary device has something to send. Remember that the primary controls the link. If the primary is not either sending or receiving data, it knows the link is available. If it has something to send, it sends it. What it does not know, however, is whether the target device is prepared to receive (usually, *prepared to receive* means *on*). So the primary must alert the secondary to the upcoming transmission and wait for an acknowledgment of the secondary's ready status. Before sending data, the primary creates and transmits a select (SEL) frame, one field of which includes the address of the intended secondary. Multipoint topologies use a single link for several devices, which means that any frame on the link is available to every device. As a frame makes its way down the link, each of the secondary devices checks the address field. Only when a device recognizes its own address does it open the frame and read the data. In the case of a SEL frame, the enclosed data consist of an alert that data are forthcoming.

If the secondary is awake and running, it returns an ACK frame to the primary. The primary then sends one or more data frames, each addressed to the intended secondary. Figure 10.7 illustrates this procedure.

Poll The polling function is used by the primary device to solicit transmissions from the secondary devices. As noted above, the secondaries are not allowed to transmit data unless asked (don't call us—we'll call you). By keeping all control with the primary,

Figure 10.7 *Select*

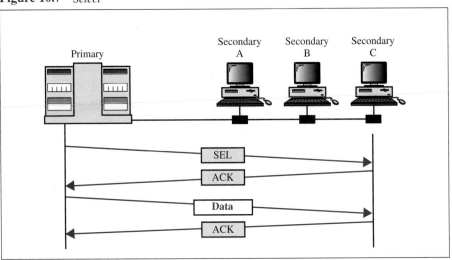

the multipoint system guarantees that only one transmission can occur at a time, thereby ensuring against signal collisions without requiring elaborate precedence protocols. When the primary is ready to receive data, it must ask **(poll)** each device in turn if it has anything to send. When the first secondary is approached, it responds either with a NAK frame if it has nothing to send or with data (in the form of a data frame) if it does.

If the response is negative (a NAK frame), the primary then polls the next secondary in the same way until it finds one with data to send. When the response is positive (a data frame), the primary reads the frame and returns an acknowledgment (ACK frame) verifying its receipt. The secondary may send several data frames one after the other, or it may be required to wait for an ACK before sending each one, depending on the protocol being used.

There are two possibilities for terminating the exchange: either the secondary sends all its data, finishing with an end of transmission (EOT) frame, or the primary says, "Time's up." Which of these occurs depends on the protocol and the length of the message. Once a secondary has finished transmitting, the primary can poll the remaining devices (see Figure 10.8).

10.2   FLOW CONTROL

The second aspect of data link control is flow control. In most protocols, flow control is a set of procedures that tells the sender how much data it can transmit before it must wait for an acknowledgment from the receiver. The flow of data must not be allowed to overwhelm the receiver. Any receiving device has a limited speed at which it can process incoming data and a limited amount of memory in which to store incoming data. The receiving device must be able to inform the sending device before those limits are reached and to request that the transmitting device send fewer frames or stop temporarily. Incoming data must be checked and processed before they can be used. The rate

Figure 10.8 *Poll*

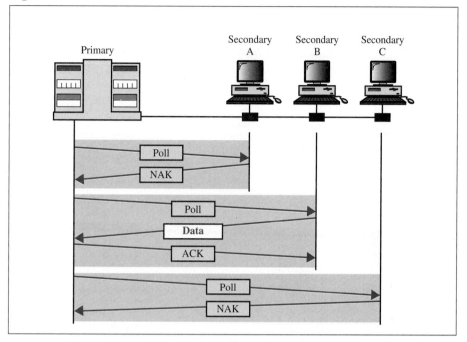

of such processing is often slower than the rate of transmission. For this reason, each receiving device has a block of memory, called a **buffer,** reserved for storing incoming data until they are processed. If the buffer begins to fill up, the receiver must be able to tell the sender to halt transmission until it is once again able to receive.

> Flow control refers to a set of procedures used to restrict the amount of data the sender can send before waiting for acknowledgment.

Two methods have been developed to control the flow of data across communications links: stop-and-wait and sliding window (see Figure 10.9).

Figure 10.9 *Categories of flow control*

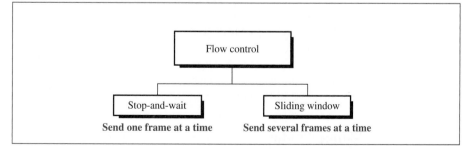

Stop-and-Wait

In a **stop-and-wait** method of flow control, the sender waits for an acknowledgment after every frame it sends (see Figure 10.10). Only when an acknowledgment has been received is the next frame sent. This process of alternately sending and waiting repeats until the sender transmits an end of transmission (EOT) frame. Stop-and-wait can be compared to a picky executive giving dictation: she says a word, her assistant says "OK," she says another word, her assistant says "OK," and so on.

> In the stop-and-wait method of flow control, the sender sends one frame and waits for an acknowledgment before sending the next frame.

Figure 10.10   *Stop-and-wait*

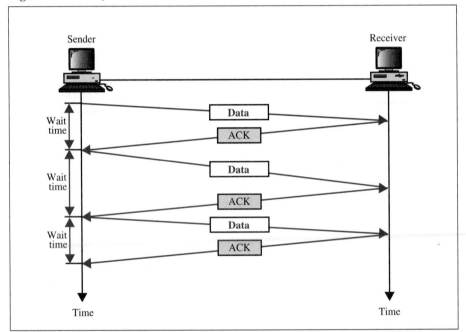

The advantage of stop-and-wait is simplicity: each frame is checked and acknowledged before the next frame is sent. The disadvantage is inefficiency: stop-and-wait is slow. Each frame must travel all the way to the receiver and an acknowledgment must travel all the way back before the next frame can be sent. In other words, each frame is alone on the line. Each frame sent and received uses the entire time needed to traverse the link. If the distance between devices is long, the time spent waiting for ACKs between each frame can add significantly to the total transmission time.

Sliding Window

In the **sliding window** method of flow control, the sender can transmit several frames before needing an acknowledgment. Frames can be sent one right after another, meaning that the link can carry several frames at once and its capacity can be used efficiently. The receiver acknowledges only some of the frames, using a single ACK to confirm the receipt of multiple data frames.

> In the sliding window method of flow control, several frames can be in transit at a time.

The *sliding window* refers to imaginary boxes at both the sender and the receiver. This window can hold frames at either end and provides the upper limit on the number of frames that can be transmitted before requiring an acknowledgment. Frames may be acknowledged at any point without waiting for the window to fill up and may be transmitted as long as the window is not yet full. To keep track of which frames have been transmitted and which received, sliding window introduces an identification scheme based on the size of the window. The frames are numbered modulo-*n*, which means they are numbered from 0 to *n* − 1. For example, if *n* = 8, the frames are numbered 0, 1, 2, 3, 4, 5, 6, 7, 0, 1, 2, 3, 4, 5, 6, 7, 0, 1, . . . The size of the window is *n* − 1 (in this case, 7). In other words, the window cannot cover the whole module (8 frames); it covers one frame less. The reason for this will be discussed at the end of this section.

When the receiver sends an ACK, it includes the number of the next frame it expects to receive. In other words, to acknowledge the receipt of a string of frames ending in frame 4, the receiver sends an ACK containing the number 5. When the sender sees an ACK with the number 5, it knows that all frames up through number 4 have been received.

The window can hold *n* − 1 frames at either end; therefore, a maximum of *n* − 1 frames may be sent before an acknowledgment is required. Figure 10.11 shows the relationship of a window to the main buffer.

Figure 10.11   *Sliding window*

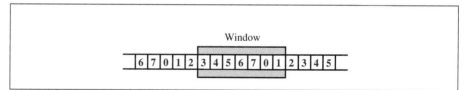

Sender Window

At the beginning of a transmission, the sender's window contains *n* − 1 frames. As frames are sent out, the left boundary of the window moves inward, shrinking the size of the window. Given a window of size *w*, if three frames have been transmitted since the last acknowledgment, then the number of frames left in the window is *w* − 3. Once an ACK arrives, the window expands to allow in a number of new frames equal to the number of frames acknowledged by that ACK. Figure 10.12 shows a sender sliding window of size 7.

Given a window of size 7, as shown in Figure 10.12, if frames 0 through 4 have been sent and no acknowledgment has been received, the sender's window contains two frames (numbers 5 and 6). Now, if an ACK numbered 4 is received, four frames (0 through 3) are known to have arrived undamaged and the sender's window expands

Figure 10.12 *Sender sliding window*

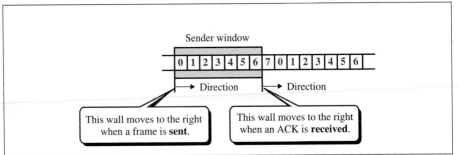

to include the next four frames in its buffer. At this point, the sender's window contains six frames (numbers 5, 6, 7, 0, 1, 2). If the received ACK had been numbered 2, the sender's window would have expanded by only two frames, to contain a total of four.

> Conceptually, the sliding window of the sender shrinks from the left when frames of data are sent. The sliding window of the sender expands to the right when acknowledgments are received.

Receiver Window

At the beginning of transmission, the receiver window contains not $n-1$ frames but $n-1$ spaces for frames. As new frames come in, the size of the receiver window shrinks. The receiver window therefore represents not the number of frames received but the number of frames that may still be received before an ACK must be sent. Given a window of size w, if three frames are received without an acknowledgment being returned, the number of spaces in the window is $w-3$. As soon as an acknowledgment is sent, the window expands to include places for a number of frames equal to the number of frames acknowledged. Figure 10.13 shows a receiving window of size 7. In the figure, the window contains spaces for seven frames, meaning that seven frames may be received before an ACK must be sent. With the arrival of the first frame, the receiving window shrinks, moving the boundary from space 0 to 1. The window has shrunk by one, so the receiver may now accept six frames before it is required to send an ACK. If frames 0 through 3 have arrived but have not been acknowledged, the window will contain three frame spaces.

Figure 10.13 *Receiver sliding window*

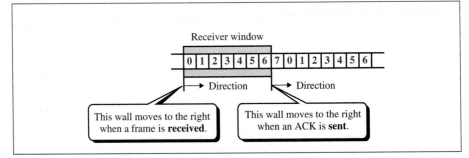

Conceptually, the sliding window of the receiver shrinks from the left when frames of data are received. The sliding window of the receiver expands to the right when acknowledgments are sent.

As each ACK is sent out, the receiving window expands to include as many new placeholders as newly acknowledged frames. The window expands to include a number of new frame spaces equal to the number of the most recently acknowledged frame minus the number of the previously acknowledged frame. In a seven-frame window, if the prior ACK was for frame 2 and the current ACK is for frame 5, the window expands by three (5 − 2). If the prior ACK was for frame 3 and the current ACK is for frame 1, the window expands by six (1 + 8 − 3).

An Example

Figure 10.14 shows a sample transmission that uses sliding window flow control with a window of seven frames. In this example, all frames arrive undamaged. As we will see in the next section, if errors are found in received frames, or if one or more frames are lost in transit, the process will become more complex.

Figure 10.14 *Example of sliding window*

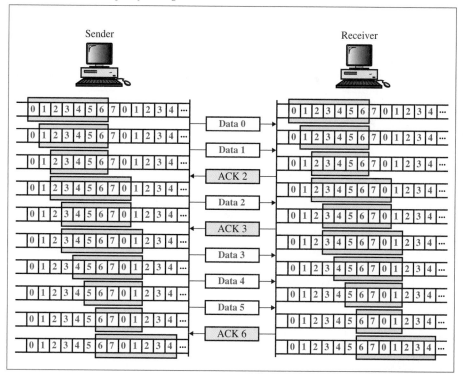

At the beginning of the transmission, both sender and receiver windows are fully expanded to include seven frames (seven transmittable frames in the sender window, seven placeholder frames in the receiver window). The frames within the windows are numbered 0 through 7 and are part of a larger data buffer, 13 of which are shown here.

More about Window Size

In the sliding window method of flow control, the size of the window is one less than the modulo range so that there is no ambiguity in the acknowledgment of the received frames. Assume that the frame sequence numbers are modulo-8 and the window size is also 8. Now imagine that frame 0 is sent and ACK 1 is received. The sender expands its window and sends frames 1, 2, 3, 4, 5, 6, 7, and 0. If it now receives an ACK 1 again, it is not sure if this is a duplicate of the previous ACK 1 (duplicated by the network) or a new ACK 1 confirming the most recently sent eight frames. But if the window size is 7 (instead of 8), this scenario could not happen.

10.3   ERROR CONTROL

In the data link layer, the term *error control* refers primarily to methods of error detection and retransmission.

Automatic Repeat Request (ARQ)

Error correction in the data link layer is implemented simply: anytime an error is detected in an exchange, a negative acknowledgment (NAK) is returned and the specified frames are retransmitted. This process is called **automatic repeat request (ARQ).**

> Error control in the data link layer is based on automatic repeat request (ARQ), which means retransmission of data in three cases: damaged frame, lost frame, and lost acknowledgment.

It sometimes happens that a frame is so damaged by noise during transmission that the receiver does not recognize it as a frame at all. In those cases, ARQ allows us to say that the frame has been lost. A second function of ARQ is the automatic retransmission of lost frames, including lost ACK and NAK frames (where the loss is detected by the sender instead of the receiver).

ARQ error control is implemented in the data link layer as an adjunct to flow control. In fact, stop-and-wait flow control is usually implemented as stop-and-wait ARQ and sliding window is usually implemented as one of two variants of sliding window ARQ, called go-back-*n* or selective-reject (see Figure 10.15).

Stop-and-Wait ARQ

Stop-and-wait ARQ is a form of stop-and-wait flow control extended to include retransmission of data in case of lost or damaged frames. For retransmission to work, four features are added to the basic flow control mechanism:

- ■ The sending device keeps a copy of the last frame transmitted until it receives an acknowledgment for that frame. Keeping a copy allows the sender to retransmit lost or damaged frames until they are received correctly.

Figure 10.15   *Categories of error control*

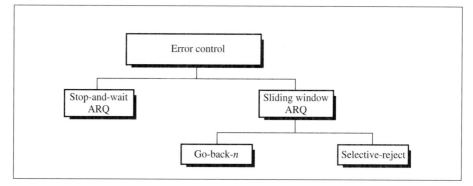

- For identification purposes, both data frames and ACK frames are numbered alternately 0 and 1. A data 0 frame is acknowledged by an ACK 1 frame, indicating that the receiver has gotten data 0 and is now expecting data 1. This numbering allows for identification of data frames in case of duplicate transmission (important in the case of lost acknowledgments, as we will see below).

- If an error is discovered in a data frame, indicating that it has been corrupted in transit, a NAK frame is returned. NAK frames, which are not numbered, tell the sender to retransmit the last frame sent. Stop-and-wait ARQ requires that the sender wait until it receives an acknowledgment for the last frame transmitted before it transmits the next one. When the sending device receives a NAK, it resends the frame transmitted after the last acknowledgment, regardless of number.

- The sending device is equipped with a timer. If an expected acknowledgment is not received within an allotted time period, the sender assumes that the last data frame was lost in transit and sends it again.

Damaged Frames

When a frame is discovered by the receiver to contain an error, it returns a NAK frame and the sender retransmits the last frame. For example, in Figure 10.16, the sender transmits a data frame: data 0. The receiver returns an ACK 1, indicating that data 0 arrived undamaged and it is now expecting data 1. The sender transmits its next frame: data 1. It arrives undamaged, and the receiver returns ACK 0. The sender transmits its next frame: data 0. The receiver discovers an error in data 0 and returns a NAK. The sender retransmits data 0. This time data 0 arrives intact, and the receiver returns ACK 1.

Lost Frame

Any of the three frame types can be lost in transit.

Lost Data Frame   Figure 10.17 shows how stop-and-wait ARQ handles the loss of a data frame. As noted above, the sender is equipped with a timer that starts every time a data frame is transmitted. If the frame never makes it to the receiver, the receiver can never acknowledge it, positively or negatively. The sending device waits for an ACK or NAK frame until its timer goes off, at which point it tries again. It retransmits the last data frame, restarts its timer, and waits for an acknowledgment.

Figure 10.16 *Stop-and-wait ARQ, damaged frame*

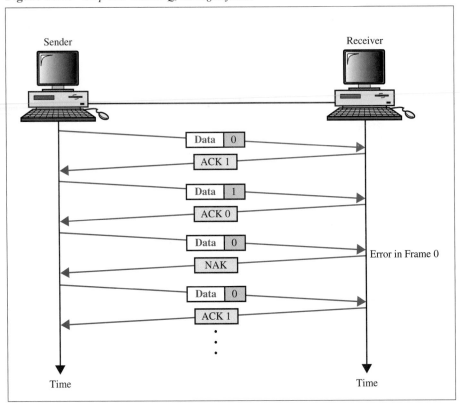

Figure 10.17 *Stop-and-wait ARQ, lost data frame*

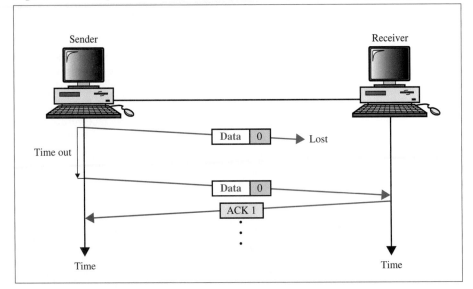

Lost Acknowledgment   In this case, the data frame has made it to the receiver and has been found to be either acceptable or not acceptable. But the ACK or NAK frame returned by the receiver is lost in transit. The sending device waits until its timer goes off, then retransmits the data frame. The receiver checks the number of the new data frame. If the lost frame was a NAK, the receiver accepts the new copy and returns the appropriate ACK (assuming the copy arrives undamaged). If the lost frame was an ACK, the receiver recognizes the new copy as a duplicate, acknowledges its receipt, then discards it and waits for the next frame (see Figure 10.18).

Figure 10.18   *Stop-and-wait ARQ, lost ACK frame*

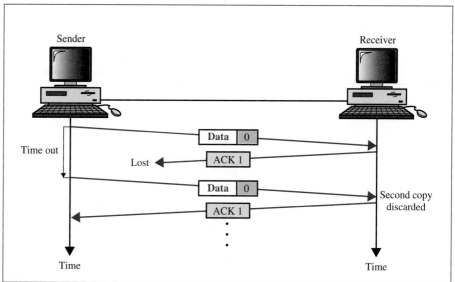

Sliding Window ARQ

Among the several popular mechanisms for continuous transmission error control, two protocols are the most popular: go-back-*n* ARQ and selective-reject ARQ, both based on sliding window flow control. To extend sliding window to cover retransmission of lost or damaged frames, three features are added to the basic flow control mechanism:

- The sending device keeps copies of all transmitted frames until they have been acknowledged. If frames 0 through 6 have been transmitted, and the last acknowledgment was for frame 2 (expecting 3), the sender keeps copies of frames 3 through 6 until it knows that they have been received undamaged.

- In addition to ACK frames, the receiver has the option of returning a NAK frame if the data have been received damaged. The NAK frame tells the sender to retransmit a damaged frame. Because sliding window is a continuous transmission mechanism (as opposed to stop-and-wait), both ACK and NAK frames must be numbered for identification. ACK frames, you will recall, carry the number of the next frame expected. NAK frames, on the other hand, carry the number of the damaged frame itself. In both cases, the message to the sender is the number of the frame that the receiver expects next. Note that data frames that are received without errors do not have to be acknowledged individually. If the last ACK was numbered 3, an ACK 6 acknowledges the receipt of frames 3 and 4 as well as frame 5. Every damaged frame, however, must be acknowledged. If data frames 4 and 5 are received damaged, both NAK 4 and NAK 5 must be returned. However, a NAK 4 tells the sender that all frames received before frame 4 have arrived intact.

■ Like stop-and-wait ARQ, the sending device in **sliding window ARQ** is equipped with a timer to enable it to handle lost acknowledgments. In sliding window ARQ, $n - 1$ frames (the size of the window) may be sent before an acknowledgment must be received. If $n - 1$ frames are awaiting acknowledgment, the sender starts a timer and waits before sending any more. If the allotted time has run out with no acknowledgment, the sender assumes that the frames were not received and retransmits one or all of the frames depending on the protocol. Note that as with stop-and-wait ARQ, the sender here has no way of knowing whether the lost frames are data, ACK, or NAK frames. By retransmitting the data frames, two possibilities are covered: lost data and lost NAK. If the lost frame was an ACK frame, the receiver can recognize the redundancy by the number on the frame and discard the redundant data.

Go-Back-*n* ARQ

In this sliding window **go-back-*n* ARQ** method, if one frame is lost or damaged, all frames sent since the last frame acknowledged are retransmitted.

Damaged Frame   What if frames 0, 1, 2, and 3 have been transmitted, but the first acknowledgment received is a NAK 3? Remember that a NAK means two things: (1) a positive acknowledgment of all frames received prior to the damaged frame and (2) a negative acknowledgment of the frame indicated. If the first acknowledgment is a NAK 3, it means that data frames 0, 1, and 2 were all received in good shape. Only frame 3 must be resent.

What if frames 0 through 4 have been transmitted before a NAK is received for frame 2? As soon as the receiver discovers an error, it stops accepting subsequent frames until the damaged frame has been replaced correctly. In the scenario above, data 2 arrives damaged and so is discarded, as are data 3 and data 4 whether or not they have arrived intact. Data 0 and data 1, which were received before the damaged frame, have already been accepted, a fact indicated to the sender by the NAK 2 frame. The retransmission therefore consists of frames 2, 3, and 4.

Figure 10.19 gives an example where six frames have been transmitted before an error is discovered in frame 3. In this case, an ACK 3 has been returned, telling the sender that frames 0, 1, and 2 have all been accepted. In the figure, the ACK 3 is sent before data 3 has arrived. Data 3 is discovered to be damaged, so a NAK 3 is sent immediately and frames 4 and 5 are discarded as they come in. The sending device retransmits all three frames (3, 4, and 5) sent since the last acknowledgment, and the process continues. The receiver discards frames 4 and 5 (as well as any subsequent frames) until it receives a good data 3.

Lost Data Frame   Sliding window protocols require that data frames be transmitted sequentially. If one or more frames are so noise corrupted that they become lost in

Figure 10.19   *Go-back-n, damaged data frame*

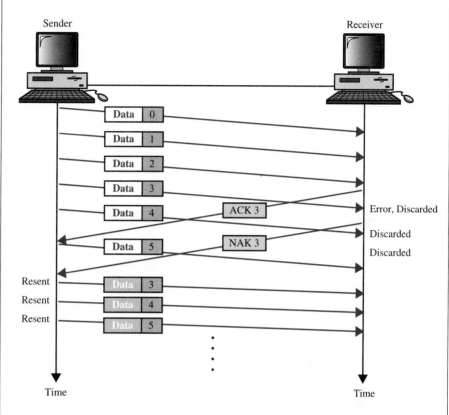

transit, the next frame to arrive at the receiver will be out of sequence. The receiver checks the identifying number on each frame, discovers that one or more have been skipped, and returns a NAK for the first missing frame. A NAK frame does not indicate whether the frame has been lost or damaged, just that it needs to be resent. The sending device then retransmits the frame indicated by the NAK, as well as any frames that it had transmitted after the lost one.

In Figure 10.20, data 0 and data 1 arrive intact but data 2 is lost. The next frame to arrive at the receiver is data 3. The receiver is expecting data 2 and so considers data 3 to be an error, discards it, and returns a NAK 2, indicating that 0 and 1 have been accepted but 2 is in error (in this case lost). In this example, because the sender has transmitted data 4 before receiving the NAK 2, data 4 arrives at the destination out of sequence and is therefore discarded. Once the sender receives the NAK 2, it retransmits all three pending frames (2, 3, and 4).

Lost Acknowledgment   The sender is not expecting to receive an ACK frame for every data frame it sends. It cannot use the absence of sequential ACK numbers to identify lost ACK or NAK frames. Instead, it uses a timer. The sending device can send as many frames as the window allows before waiting for an acknowledgment. Once that limit has been reached or the sender has no more frames to send, it must wait.

Figure 10.20 *Go-back-*n, *lost data frame*

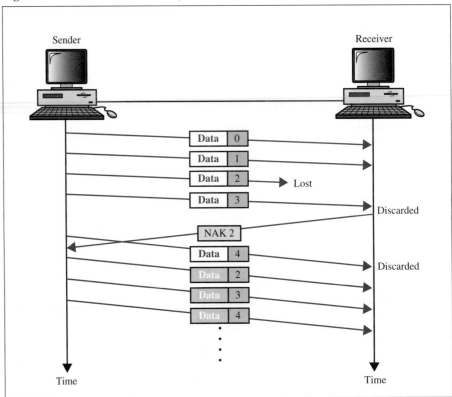

If the ACK (or, especially, if the NAK) sent by the receiver has been lost, the sender could wait forever. To avoid tying up both devices, the sender is equipped with a timer that begins counting whenever the window capacity is reached. If an acknowledgment has not been received within the time limit, the sender retransmits every frame transmitted since the last ACK.

Figure 10.21 shows a situation in which the sender has transmitted all of its frames and is waiting for an acknowledgment that has been lost along the way. The sender waits a predetermined amount of time, then retransmits the unacknowledged frames. The receiver recognizes that the new transmission is a repeat of an earlier one, sends another ACK, and discards the redundant data.

Selective-Reject ARQ

In **selective-reject ARQ,** only the specific damaged or lost frame is retransmitted. If a frame is corrupted in transit, a NAK is returned and the frame is resent out of sequence. The receiving device must be able to sort the frames it has and insert the retransmitted frame into its proper place in the sequence. To make such selectivity possible, a selective-reject ARQ system differs from a go-back-*n* ARQ system in the following ways:

- The receiving device must contain sorting logic to enable it to reorder frames received out of sequence. It must also be able to store frames received after a NAK has been sent until the damaged frame has been replaced.

Figure 10.21   *Go-back-*n, *lost ACK*

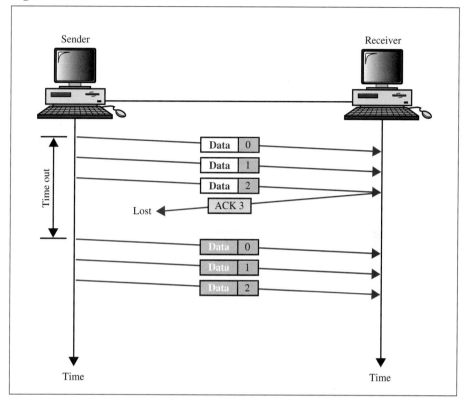

- The sending device must contain a searching mechanism that allows it to find and select only the requested frame for retransmission.
- A buffer in the receiver must keep all previously received frames on hold until all retransmissions have been sorted and any duplicate frames have been identified and discarded.
- To aid selectivity, ACK numbers, like NAK numbers, must refer to the frame received (or lost) instead of the next frame expected.
- This complexity requires a smaller window size than is needed by the go-back-*n* method if it is to work efficiently. It is recommended that the window size be less than or equal to $(n + 1)/2$, where $n - 1$ is the go-back-*n* window size.

Damaged Frames   Figure 10.22 shows a situation in which a damaged frame is received. As you can see, frames 0 and 1 are received but not acknowledged. Data 2 arrives and is found to contain an error, so a NAK 2 is returned. Like NAK frames in go-back-*n* error correction, a NAK here both acknowledges the intact receipt of any previously unacknowledged data frames and indicates an error in the current frame. In the figure, NAK 2 tells the sender that data 0 and data 1 have been accepted, but that data 2 must be resent. Unlike the receiver in a go-back-*n* system, however, the receiver in a selective-reject system continues to accept new frames while waiting for an error to be corrected. However, because an ACK implies the successful receipt not only of the

Figure 10.22   *Selective-reject, damaged data frame*

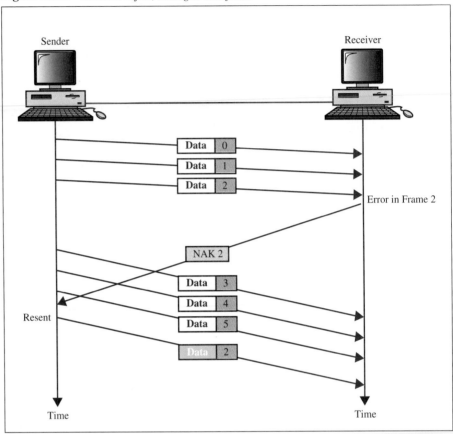

specific frame indicated but of all previous frames, frames received after the error frame cannot be acknowledged until the damaged frames have been retransmitted. In the figure, the receiver accepts data 3, 4, and 5 while waiting for a new copy of data 2. When the new data 2 arrives, an ACK 5 can be returned, acknowledging the new data 2 and the original frames 3, 4, and 5. Quite a bit of logic is required by the receiver to sort out-of-sequence retransmissions and to keep track of which frames are still missing and which have yet to be acknowledged.

Lost Frames   Although frames can be accepted out of sequence, they cannot be acknowledged out of sequence. If a frame is lost, the next frame will arrive out of sequence. When the receiver tries to reorder the existing frames to include it, it will discover the discrepancy and return a NAK. Of course, the receiver will recognize the omission only if other frames follow. If the lost frame was the last of the transmission, the receiver does nothing and the sender treats the silence like a lost acknowledgment.

Lost Acknowledgment   Lost ACK and NAK frames are treated by selective-reject ARQ just as they are by go-back-*n* ARQ. When the sending device reaches either the capacity of its window or the end of its transmission, it sets a timer. If no acknowledgment arrives in the time allotted, the sender retransmits all of the frames that remain unacknowledged. In most cases, the receiver will recognize any duplications and discard them.

Comparison between Go-Back-*n* and Selective-Reject

Although retransmitting only specific damaged or lost frames may seem more efficient than resending undamaged frames as well, it is in fact less so. Because of the complexity of the sorting and storage required by the receiver, and the extra logic needed by the sender to select specific frames for retransmission, selective-reject ARQ is expensive and not often used. In other words, selective-reject gives better performance, but in practice it is usually discarded in favor of go-back-*n* for simplicity of implementation.

> Note that the stop-and-wait protocol is a special case of the sliding-window protocol with a window size of 1.

10.4   KEY TERMS AND CONCEPTS

acknowledgment (ACK)	poll
automatic repeat request (ARQ)	poll/select
buffer	primary station
end of transmission (EOT)	secondary station
enquiry/acknowledgment (ENQ/ACK)	select
error control	selective-reject ARQ
flow control	sliding window
go-back-*n* ARQ	sliding window ARQ
line discipline	stop-and-wait
negative acknowledgment (NAK)	stop-and-wait ARQ

10.5   SUMMARY

■   The second layer in the OSI model, the data link layer, has three main functions: line discipline, flow control, and error control.

■   Line discipline establishes the status of a device (sender or receiver) on a link.

■   ENQ/ACK is a line discipline method used in point-to-point connections.

- The receiving device using ENQ/ACK line discipline responds with an acknowledgement (ACK) if it is ready to receive data or a negative acknowledgement (NAK) if it is not ready.
- Poll/select is a line discipline method. The primary device always initiates communication with either a poll or select (SEL) frame.
- A poll frame is sent to the secondary device by the primary to determine if the secondary has data to send. The secondary can respond by sending a NAK (no data to send) or a data frame.
- A SEL frame is sent from the primary device to the secondary device to tell the secondary to prepare to receive data. The secondary responds with an ACK or a NAK.
- Flow control is regulation of data transmission so that the receiver buffer does not become overwhelmed by data.
- There are two main methods of flow control:
  a. stop-and-wait
  b. sliding window
- In stop-and-wait flow control, each frame must be acknowledged by the receiver before the next frame can be sent.
- In sliding window flow control, the sending of data is constrained by an imaginary window that expands and contracts according to the acknowledgments received by the sender. Likewise, the receiving of data is constrained by an imaginary window that expands and contracts according to the data received.
- Error control, or how to handle lost or damaged data or acknowledgments, is simply the retransmission of data.
- Retransmission of data is initiated by automatic repeat request (ARQ).
- Three types of errors require ARQ: a damaged frame, a lost frame, and a lost acknowledgment.
- The method used to handle error control depends on the method used for flow control.
- For stop-and-wait flow control, stop-and-wait ARQ is used.
- For sliding window flow control, go-back-n or selective-reject ARQ is used.
- In stop-and-wait ARQ, the unacknowledged frame is retransmitted.
- In go-back-n ARQ, retransmission begins with the last unacknowledged frame even if subsequent frames have arrived correctly. Duplicate frames are discarded.
- In selective-reject ARQ, only the unacknowledged frame is retransmitted.

10.6   PRACTICE SET

Review Questions

1. Discuss the difference between communication and transmission.
2. What are the three main functions of the data link layer?

3. What is the purpose of line discipline?

4. What are the two main methods of line discipline? How does a system select which one to use?

5. What is the mechanism of ENQ/ACK?

6. What is the mechanism of poll/select?

7. Why are addresses needed in poll/select but not in ENQ/ACK?

8. What is the difference between polling and selecting?

9. Why is flow control needed?

10. Discuss the use of a buffer at the receiver in flow control.

11. What are the two methods that control the flow of data across communication links?

12. What is the mechanism of stop-and-wait flow control?

13. What is the mechanism of sliding window flow control?

14. What does the term *error control* mean in the data link layer?

15. What are the two main methods for error control?

16. In what situations does the sender retransmit a packet?

17. What is the mechanism of stop-and-wait ARQ error control?

18. What are the two types of sliding window ARQ error control? How do they differ from one another?

19. What are some of the parameters to be considered in flow control?

20. In stop-and-wait flow control, define and discuss the handling of
    a. A damaged frame.
    b. A lost frame.

21. In stop-and-wait ARQ, what happens if a NAK is lost in transit? Why is there no need for NAKs to be numbered?

22. Which sliding window ARQ is more popular? Why?

23. When are frames discarded in the three ARQ methods?

Multiple Choice Questions

24. The secondary device in a multipoint configuration sends data in response to

    _____.
    a. an ACK
    b. an ENQ
    c. a poll
    d. a SEL

25. In sliding window flow control, if the window size is 63, what is the range of sequence numbers?
    a. 0 to 63
    b. 0 to 64
    c. 1 to 63
    d. 1 to 64

26. In sliding window flow control, the frames to the left of the receiver window are frames _____.
   a. received but not acknowledged
   b. received and acknowledged
   c. not received
   d. not sent

27. Regulation of the rate of transmission of data frames is known as _____.
   a. line discipline
   b. flow control
   c. data rate control
   d. switch control

28. _____ decides the role (sender or receiver) of a device on a network.
   a. Line connection
   b. Link connection
   c. Line discipline
   d. Link decision

29. The retransmission of damaged or lost frames in the data link layer is known as _____.
   a. error control
   b. error conditioning
   c. line discipline
   d. flow control

30. When a primary device wants to send data to a secondary device, it needs to first send _____ frame.
   a. an ACK
   b. a poll
   c. a SEL
   d. an ENQ

31. When a secondary device is ready to send data, it must wait for _____ frame.
   a. an ACK
   b. a poll
   c. a SEL
   d. an ENQ

32. In a peer-to-peer system, when one device wants to send data to another device, it first sends _____ frame.
   a. an ACK
   b. a poll
   c. a SEL
   d. an ENQ

33. Flow control is needed to prevent _____.
   a. bit errors

b. overflow of the sender buffer

c. overflow of the receiver buffer

d. collision between sender and receiver

34. In go-back-n ARQ, if frames 4, 5, and 6 are received successfully, the receiver may send an ACK _____ to the sender.

   a. 5

   b. 6

   c. 7

   d. any of the above

35. For a sliding window of size $n - 1$ (n sequence numbers), there can be a maximum of _____ frames sent but unacknowledged.

   a. 0

   b. $n - 1$

   c. n

   d. $n + 1$

36. An ACK 3 in sliding window flow control (window size of 7) means that frame _____ is next expected by the receiver.

   a. 2

   b. 3

   c. 4

   d. 8

37. In stop-and-wait ARQ, if data 1 has an error, the receiver sends a _____ frame.

   a. NAK 0

   b. NAK 1

   c. NAK 2

   d. NAK

38. In _____ ARQ, when a NAK is received, all frames sent since the last frame acknowledged are retransmitted.

   a. stop-and-wait

   b. go-back-n

   c. selective-reject

   d. a and b

39. In _____ ARQ, if a NAK is received, only the specific damaged or lost frame is retransmitted.

   a. stop-and-wait

   b. go-back-n

   c. selective-reject

   d. a and b

40. ARQ stands for _____.

   a. automatic repeat quantization

b. automatic repeat request

c. automatic retransmission request

d. acknowledge repeat request

41. Which of the following is a data link layer function?

   a. line discipline

   b. flow control

   c. error control

   d. all of the above

42. In a _____ communication, the poll/select method is used to determine control of the line.

   a. peer-to-peer

   b. peer-to-primary

   c. primary-to-peer

   d. primary-to-secondary

43. A timer is set when _____ is sent out.

   a. a packet

   b. an ACK

   c. a NAK

   d. all of the above

44. Poll/select line discipline requires _____ to identify the packet recipient.

   a. a timer

   b. a buffer

   c. an address

   d. a dedicated line

45. For stop-and-wait flow control, for n data packets sent, _____ acknowledgments are needed.

   a. n

   b. $2n$

   c. $n - 1$

   d. $n + 1$

Exercises

46. Draw the sender and receiver windows for a system using go-back-n ARQ given the following:

   a. Frame 0 is sent; frame 0 is acknowledged.

   b. Frames 1 and 2 are sent; frames 1 and 2 are acknowledged.

   c. Frames 3, 4, and 5 are sent; NAK 4 is received.

   d. Frames 4, 5, 6, and 7 are sent; frames 4 through 7 are acknowledged.

47. Repeat Exercise 46 using selective-reject ARQ.

48. What can the receiver send in response to each of the following?

    a. A poll.

    b. A select.

49. What does the number on a NAK frame mean for

    a. Stop-and-wait ARQ?

    b. Go-back-*n* ARQ?

    c. Selective-reject ARQ?

50. What does the number on an ACK frame mean for

    a. Stop-and-wait ARQ?

    b. Go-back-*n* ARQ?

    c. Selective-reject ARQ?

51. ACK 7 has been received by the sender in a go-back-*n* sliding window system. Now frames 7, 0, 1, 2, and 3 are sent. For each of the following separate scenarios, discuss the significance of the receiving of

    a. An ACK 1.

    b. An ACK 4.

    c. An ACK 3.

    d. A NAK 1.

    e. A NAK 3.

    f. A NAK 7.

52. A sliding window protocol uses a window of size 15. How many bits are needed to define the sequence number?

53. A sliding window protocol is using seven bits to represent the sequence numbers. What is the size of the window?

54. A computer is using a sliding window of size 7. Complete the following sequence numbers for 20 packets:

    0, 1, 2, 3, 4, 5, 6,...

55. A computer is using the following sequence numbers. What is the size of the window?

    0, 1, 2, 3, 4, 5, 6, 7, 8, 9, 10, 11, 12, 13, 14, 15, 0, 1,..........................

56. We mentioned that the stop-and-wait protocol is actually the sliding window protocol with a window size of 1. Show the window operation for Figure 10.16

57. Repeat Exercise 56 for Figure 10.17.

58. Repeat Exercise 56 for Figure 10.18

59. Show the sender window operation for Figure 10.19. Show the exact locations of walls in each transmission. Assume a window size of 7.

60. Repeat Exercise 59 for Figure 10.20

61. Repeat Exercise 59 for Figure 10.21.

62. Computer A uses stop-and-wait ARQ protocol to send packets to computer B. If the distance between A and B is 4000 Km, how long does it take computer A to receive acknowledgment for a packet? Use the speed of light for propagation speed and assume the time between receiving and sending the acknowledgment is zero.

63. In Exercise 62, how long does it take for computer A to send out a packet of size 1000 bytes if the throughput is 100,000 Kbps?

64. Using the results of Exercises 62 and 63, how much time is computer A idle?

65. Repeat Exercise 64 for a system that uses a sliding window ARQ with a window size of 255.

66. In Figure 10.23, show the window after the sender has sent packets 0 to 11 and has received ACK8.

Figure 10.23   *Exercises 66, 67, 68, and 69*

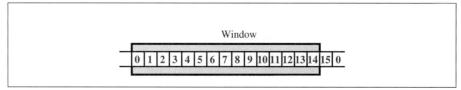

67. In Figure 10.23, show the window after the sender has sent packets 0 to 11 and has received NAK6.

68. In Figure 10.23, the sender has sent packets 0 to 14, no acknowledgment has been received, and timeout has expired. Show the sender window.

69. In Figure 10.23, the receiver has sent ACK6 and ACK9, but ACK6 is lost. Show the sender window.

CHAPTER 11

Data Link Protocols

In general, the word *protocol* refers to a set of rules or conventions for executing a particular task. In data communications, *protocol* is used in a narrower sense to mean the set of rules or specifications used to implement one or more layers of the OSI model. We have already encountered the EIA 232-D interface, which is a protocol used at the physical layer in the OSI model.

> A protocol in data communications is the set of rules or specifications used to implement one or more layers of the OSI model.

Data link protocols are sets of specifications used to implement the data link layer. To this end, they contain rules for line discipline, flow control, and error handling, among others.

> A data link protocol is a set of specifications used to implement the data link layer.

Data link protocols can be divided into two subgroups: asynchronous protocols and synchronous protocols (see Figure 11.1). Asynchronous protocols treat each character in a bit stream independently. Synchronous protocols take the whole bit stream and chop it into characters of equal size.

Figure 11.1 *Data link protocol categories*

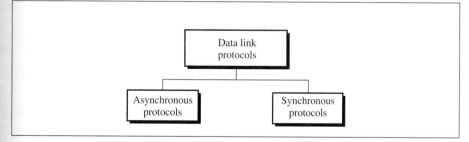

11.1 ASYNCHRONOUS PROTOCOLS

A number of **asynchronous** data link **protocols** have been developed over the last several decades, some of which are shown in Figure 11.2. Today, these protocols are employed mainly in modems. Due to its inherent slowness (stemming from the required additions of start and stop bits and extended spaces between **frames**), asynchronous transmission at this level is being replaced by higher-speed synchronous mechanisms.

Figure 11.2 *Asynchronous protocols*

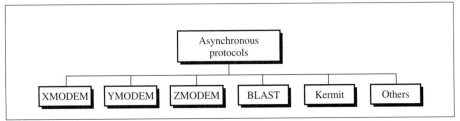

Asynchronous protocols are not complex and are inexpensive to implement. As discussed in Chapter 6, in asynchronous transmission a data unit is transmitted with no timing coordination between sender and receiver. A receiver does not need to know exactly when a data unit is sent; it only needs to recognize the beginning and the end of the unit. This is accomplished by using extra bits (start and stop bits) to frame the data unit.

> Asynchronous protocols, used primarily in modems, feature start and stop bits and variable-length gaps between characters.

A variety of asynchronous data link layer protocols have been developed; we will discuss only a few of them.

XMODEM

In 1979 Ward Christiansen designed a file transfer protocol for telephone-line communication between PCs. This protocol, now known as **XMODEM,** is a half-duplex stop-and-wait ARQ protocol. The frame with its fields is shown in Figure 11.3.

The first field is a one-byte start of header (SOH). The second field is a two-byte header. The first header byte, the sequence number, carries the frame number. The second header byte is used to check the validity of the sequence number. The fixed data field holds 128 bytes of data (binary, ASCII, Boolean, text, etc.). The last field, CRC, checks for errors in the data field only.

In this protocol, transmission begins with the sending of a NAK frame from the receiver to the sender. Each time the sender sends a frame, it must wait for an acknowledgment (ACK) before the next frame can be sent. If instead a NAK is received, the previously sent frame is sent again. A frame can also be resent if a response is not received by the sender after a specified amount of time. Besides a NAK or an ACK, the sender can receive a cancel signal (CAN), which aborts the transmission.

Figure 11.3   *XMODEM frame*

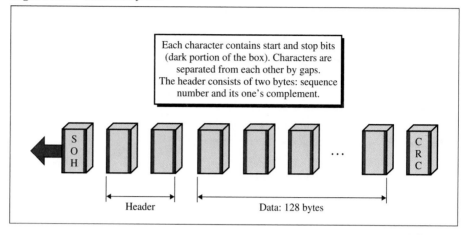

Each character contains start and stop bits
(dark portion of the box). Characters are
separated from each other by gaps.
The header consists of two bytes: sequence
number and its one's complement.

S O H

...

C R C

Header

Data: 128 bytes

YMODEM

YMODEM is a protocol similar to XMODEM, with the following major differences:

- The data unit is 1024 bytes.
- Two CANs are sent to abort a transmission.
- ITU-T CRC-16 is used for error checking.
- Multiple files can be sent simultaneously.

ZMODEM

ZMODEM is a newer protocol combining features of both XMODEM and YMODEM.

BLAST

Blocked asynchronous transmission (BLAST) is more powerful than XMODEM. It is full-duplex with sliding window flow control. It allows the transfer of data and binary files.

Kermit

Kermit, designed at Columbia University, is currently the most widely used asynchronous protocol. This file transfer protocol is similar in operation to XMODEM, with the sender waiting for a NAK before it starts transmission. Kermit allows the transmission of control characters as text using two steps. First, the control character, which is used as text, is transformed to a printable character by adding a fixed number to its ASCII code representation. Second, the # character is added to the front of the transformed character. In this way, a control character used as text is sent as two characters. When the receiver encounters a # character, it knows that this must be dropped and that the next character is a control character. If the sender wants to send a # character, it will send two of them. Note that Kermit is in fact a terminal emulation program as well as a file transfer protocol.

11.2   SYNCHRONOUS PROTOCOLS

The speed of synchronous transmission makes it the better choice, over asynchronous transmission, for LAN, MAN, and WAN technology. Protocols governing synchronous transmission can be divided into two classes: character-oriented protocols and bit-oriented protocols (see Figure 11.4).

Figure 11.4   *Synchronous protocols*

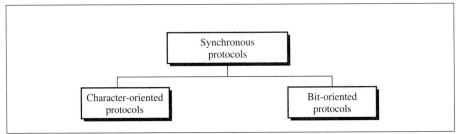

Character-oriented protocols (also called **byte-oriented protocols**) interpret a transmission frame or packet as a succession of characters, each usually composed of one byte (eight bits). All control information is in the form of an existing character encoding system (e.g., ASCII characters).

Bit-oriented protocols interpret a transmission frame or packet as a succession of individual bits, made meaningful by their placement in the frame and by their juxtaposition with other bits. Control information in a bit-oriented protocol can be one or multiple bits depending on the information embodied in the pattern.

> In a character-oriented protocol, the frame or packet is interpreted as a series of characters. In a bit-oriented protocol, the frame or packet is interpreted as a series of bits.

11.3   CHARACTER-ORIENTED PROTOCOLS

For reasons we will examine later in this section, character-oriented protocols are not as efficient as bit-oriented protocols and therefore are now seldom used. They are, however, easy to comprehend and employ the same logic and organization as the bit-oriented protocols. An understanding of character-oriented protocols provides an essential foundation for an examination of bit-oriented protocols.

In all data link protocols, control information is inserted into the data stream either as separate control frames or as additions to existing data frames. In character-oriented protocols, this information is in the form of code words taken from existing character sets such as ASCII or EBCDIC. These multibit characters carry information about line discipline, flow control, and error control. Of the several existing character-oriented protocols, the best known is IBM's binary synchronous communication (BSC).

Binary Synchronous Communication (BSC)

Binary synchronous communication (BSC) is a popular character-oriented data link protocol developed by IBM in 1964. Usable in both point-to-point and multipoint configurations, it supports half-duplex transmission using stop-and-wait ARQ flow control and error correction. BSC does not support full-duplex transmission or sliding window protocol.

> A popular character-oriented data link protocol is binary synchronous communication (BSC), which specifies half-duplex transmission with stop-and-wait ARQ. It was developed by IBM.

Control Characters

Table 11.1 is a list of standard **control characters** used in a BSC frame. Note that the character ACK is not used in this protocol. Remember that BSC uses stop-and-wait ARQ; acknowledgments must be either ACK 0 or ACK 1 to specify alternating data frames.

Table 11.1   *Control characters for BSC*

Character	ASCII Code	Function
ACK 0	DLE and 0	Good even frame received or ready to receive
ACK 1	DLE and 1	Good odd frame received
DLE	DLE	Data transparency marker
ENQ	ENQ	Request for a response
EOT	EOT	Sender terminating
ETB	ETB	End of transmission block; ACK required
ETX	ETX	End of text in a message
ITB	US	End of intermediate block in a multiblock transmission
NAK	NAK	Bad frame received or nothing to send
NUL	NULL	Filler character
RVI	DLE and <	Urgent message from receiver
SOH	SOH	Header information begins
STX	STX	Text begins
SYN	SYN	Alerts receiver to incoming frame
TTD	STX and ENQ	Sender is pausing but not relinquishing the line
WACK	DLE and ;	Good frame received but not ready to receive more

ASCII Codes

The characters in Table 11.1 are represented differently in different coding systems, and not all of them are available in every system. Whatever the system, not all control characters can be represented by a single character. Often they must be represented by two or three characters. The ASCII codes are also shown in Table 11.1. For a complete list of the ASCII code, see Appendix A.

BSC Frames

The BSC protocol divides a transmission into frames. If a frame is used strictly for control purposes, it is called a control frame. Control frames are used to exchange information between communicating devices, for example, to establish the initial connection, to control the flow of the transmission, to request error corrections, and to disconnect the devices at the close of a session. If a frame contains part or all of the message data itself, it is called a data frame. Data frames are used to transmit information, but may also contain control information applicable to that information (see Figure 11.5).

Figure 11.5 *BSC frames*

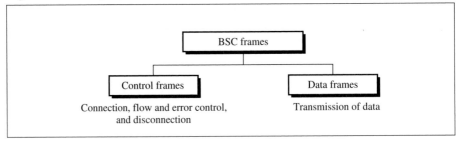

Data Frames

Figure 11.6 shows the format of a simple data frame. The arrow shows the direction of transmission. The frame begins with two or more synchronization (SYN) characters. These characters alert the receiver to the arrival of a new frame and provide a bit pattern

Figure 11.6 *A simple BSC data frame*

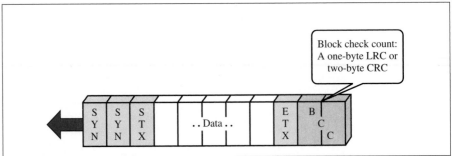

used by the receiving device to synchronize its timing with that of the sending device. From Appendix A, you will discover that the ASCII code for SYN is 0010110. The leading (eighth) bit of the **byte** is usually filled out by an additional 0. Two SYN characters together look like this: 0001011000010110.

After the two synchronization characters comes a start of text (STX) character. This character signals to the receiver that the control information is ending and the next byte will be data. Data or text can consist of varying numbers of characters. An end of text (ETX) character indicates the transition between text and more control characters.

Finally, one or two characters called the **block check count (BCC)** are included for error detection. A BCC field can be a one-character longitudinal redundancy check (LRC) or a two-character cyclic redundancy check (CRC).

Header Fields   A frame as simple as the one described above is seldom useful. Usually we need to include the address of the receiving device, the address of the sending device, and the identifying number of the frame (0 or 1) for stop-and-wait ARQ (see Figure 11.7). This information is included in a special field called a header, which begins with a start of header (SOH) character. The header comes after the SYNs and before the STX character; everything received after the SOH field but before the STX character is header information.

Figure 11.7   *A BSC frame with a header*

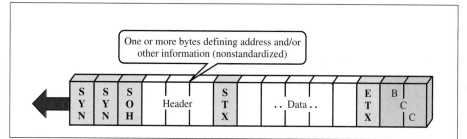

Multiblock Frames   The probability of an error in the block of text increases with the length of the frame. The more bits in a frame, the greater the likelihood that one of them will be corrupted in transit, and the greater the likelihood that changes in several bits will cancel each other out and make detection difficult. For this reason, text in a message is often divided between several blocks. Each block, except the last one, starts with an STX character and ends with an intermediate text block (ITB). The last block starts with an STX but ends with an ETX. Immediately after each ITB or ETX is a BCC field. In that way, the receiver can check each block separately for errors, thereby increasing the likelihood of detection. If any block contains an error, however, the entire frame must be retransmitted. After the ETX has been reached and the last BCC checked, the receiver sends a single acknowledgment for the entire frame. Figure 11.8 shows the structure of a multiblock frame; the example includes two blocks, but actual frames can have more than two.

Figure 11.8   *A multiblock frame*

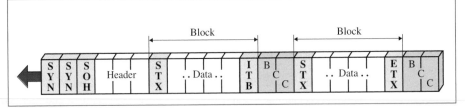

Multiframe Transmission   In the examples explored above, a single frame carries an entire message. After each frame, the message is complete and control of the line passes to the secondary device (half-duplex mode). Some messages, however, may be too long to fit into the format of a single frame. In such cases, the sender can split the message not only among blocks but among frames. Several frames can carry continuations of a single message. To let the receiver know that the end of the frame is not the end of the transmission, the ETX character in all frames but the last one is replaced by an end of transmission block (ETB). The receiver must acknowledge each frame separately but cannot take over control of the link until it sees the ETX in the last frame (see Figure 11.9).

Figure 11.9   *Multiframe transmission*

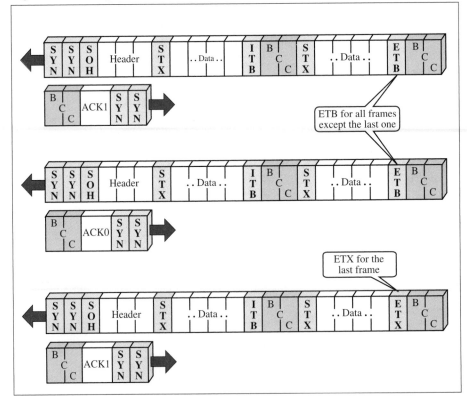

Control Frames

A control frame should not be confused with a control character. A control frame is used by one device to send commands to, or solicit information from, another device. A control frame contains control characters but no data; it carries information specific to the functioning of the data link layer itself. Figure 11.10 shows the basic format of a BSC control frame.

Figure 11.10   *BSC control frame*

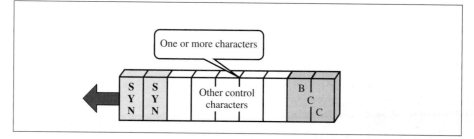

Control frames serve three purposes: establishing connections, maintaining flow and error control during data transmission, and terminating connections (see Figure 11.11).

Data Transparency

BSC was originally designed to transport only textual messages (words or figures composed of alphanumeric characters). Today, however, a user is just as likely to want to send binary sequences that contain nontextual information and commands, like programs and graphics. Unfortunately, messages of this sort can create problems for BSC transmission. If the text field of a transmission includes an eight-bit pattern that looks like a BSC control character, the receiver interprets it as one, destroying the sense of the message. For example, a receiver seeing the bit pattern 0000011 reads it as an ETX character. As we learned from the control frames above, whenever a receiver finds an ETX, it expects the next two bytes to be the BCC and begins an error check. But the pattern 0000011 here is intended as data and not as control information. Confusion between control information and data is called a lack of data **transparency.**

For a protocol to be useful, it must be transparent—it must be able to carry any combination of bits as data without their being confused with control information.

> Data transparency in data communication means we should be able to send any combination of bits as data.

Data transparency in BSC is achieved by a process called **byte stuffing.** It involves two activities: defining the transparent text region with the data link escape (DLE) characters and preceding any DLE character within the transparent region by an extra DLE character.

Figure 11.11   *Control frames*

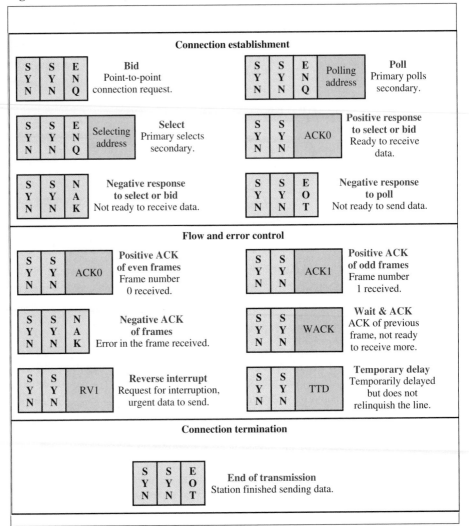

To define the transparent region, we insert one DLE character just before the STX character at the beginning of the text field and another just before the ETX (or ITB or ETB) character at the end of the text field. The first DLE tells the receiver that the text may contain control characters and to ignore them. The last DLE tells the receiver that the transparent region has ended.

Problems may still arise if the transparent region contains a DLE character as text. In that case, we insert an additional DLE just before each DLE within the text. Figure 11.12 shows an example of a transparent frame.

Figure 11.12 *Byte stuffing*

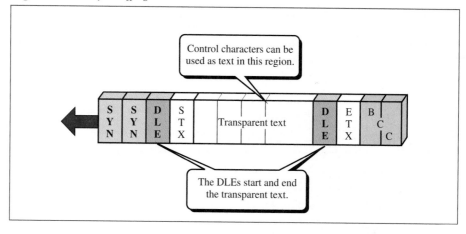

11.4   BIT-ORIENTED PROTOCOLS

In character-oriented protocols, bits are grouped into predefined patterns forming characters. By comparison, bit-oriented protocols can pack more information into shorter frames and avoid the transparency problems of character-oriented protocols.

Given the advantages of bit-oriented protocols and the lack of any preexisting coding system (like ASCII) to tie them to, it is no wonder that over the last two decades many different bit-oriented protocols have been developed, all vying to become the standard (see Figure 11.13). Most of these offerings have been proprietary, designed by manufacturers to support their own products. One of them, HDLC, is the design of the ISO and has become the basis for all bit-oriented protocols in use today.

Figure 11.13 *Bit-oriented protocols*

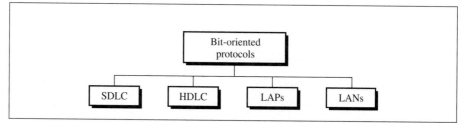

In 1975, IBM pioneered the development of bit-oriented protocols with **synchronous data link control (SDLC)** and lobbied the ISO to make SDLC the standard. In 1979, the ISO answered with **high-level data link control (HDLC),** which was based on SDLC. Adoption of HDLC by the ISO committees led to its adoption and extension by other organizations. The ITU-T was one of the first organizations to embrace

HDLC. Since 1981, ITU-T has developed a series of protocols called link access protocols (LAPs: LAPB, LAPD, LAPM, LAPX, etc.), all based on HDLC. Other protocols (such as Frame Relay, PPP, etc.) developed by both ITU-T and ANSI also derive from HDLC, as do most LANs' access control protocols. In short, all bit-oriented protocols in use today either derive from or are sources for HDLC. Through HDLC, therefore, we have a basis for understanding the others.

> All bit-oriented protocols are related to high-level data link control (HDLC), a bit-oriented protocol published by ISO. HDLC supports both half-duplex and full-duplex modes in point-to-point and multipoint configurations.

HDLC

HDLC is a bit-oriented data link protocol designed to support both half-duplex and full-duplex communication over point-to-point and multipoint links. Systems using HDLC can be characterized by their station types, their configurations, and their response modes.

Station Types

HDLC differentiates between three types of stations: primary, secondary, and combined.

A **primary station** in HDLC functions in the same way as the primary devices in the discussions of flow control in Chapter 10. The primary is the device in either a point-to-point or multipoint line configuration that has complete control of the link. The primary sends commands to the **secondary stations.** A primary issues commands; a secondary issues responses.

A **combined station** can both command and respond. A combined station is one of a set of connected peer devices programmed to behave either as a primary or as a secondary depending on the nature and direction of the transmission.

> Stations in HDLC are of three types: primary, secondary, and combined. A primary station sends commands. A secondary station sends responses. A combined station sends commands and responses.

Configurations

The word *configuration* refers to the relationship of hardware devices on a link. Primary, secondary, and combined stations can be configured in three ways: unbalanced, symmetrical, and balanced (see Figure 11.14). Any of these configurations can support both half-duplex and full-duplex transmission.

An **unbalanced configuration** (also called a master/slave configuration) is one in which one device is primary and the others are secondary. Unbalanced configurations can be point-to-point if only two devices are involved; more often they are multipoint, with one primary controlling several secondaries.

A **symmetrical configuration** is one in which each physical station on a link consists of two logical stations, one a primary and the other a secondary. Separate lines link the primary aspect of one physical station to the secondary aspect of another physical

Figure 11.14   *HDLC configurations*

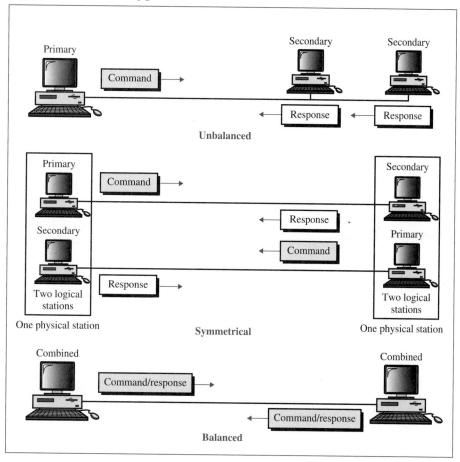

station. A symmetrical configuration behaves like an unbalanced configuration except that control of the link can shift between the two stations.

A **balanced configuration** is one in which both stations in a point-to-point topology are of the combined type. The stations are linked by a single line that can be controlled by either station.

HDLC does not support balanced multipoint. This necessitated the invention of media access protocols for LANs.

Modes of Communication

A mode in HDLC is the relationship between two devices involved in an exchange; the mode describes who controls the link. Exchanges over unbalanced configurations are always conducted in normal response mode. Exchanges over symmetrical or balanced configurations can be set to a specific mode using a frame designed to deliver the command (discussed in the section on U-frames). HDLC supports three modes of communication between stations: normal response mode (NRM), asynchronous response mode (ARM), and asynchronous balanced mode (ABM).

NRM **Normal response mode (NRM)** refers to the standard primary–secondary relationship. In this mode, a secondary device must have permission from the primary device before transmitting. Once permission has been granted, the secondary may initiate a response transmission of one or more frames containing data.

ARM In **asynchronous response mode (ARM),** a secondary may initiate a transmission without permission from the primary whenever the channel is idle. ARM does not alter the primary–secondary relationship in any other way. All transmissions from a secondary (even to another secondary on the same link) must still be made to the primary for relay to a final destination.

ABM In **asynchronous balanced mode (ABM),** all stations are equal and therefore only combined stations connected in point-to-point are used. Either combined station may initiate transmission with the other combined station without permission.

Figure 11.15 shows the relationships between these modes and station types.

Modes:

■ Normal response mode (NRM)
■ Asynchronous response mode (ARM)
■ Asynchronous balanced mode (ABM)

Figure 11.15 *HDLC modes*

	NRM	ARM	ABM
Station type	Primary & secondary	Primary & secondary	Combined
Initiator	Primary	Either	Any

Frames

To provide the flexibility necessary to support all of the options possible in the modes and configurations described above, HDLC defines three types of frames: **information frames (I-frames), supervisory frames (S-frames),** and **unnumbered frames (U-frames);** see Figure 11.16. Each type of frame works as an envelope for the transmission of a different type of message. I-frames are used to transport user data and control information relating to user data. S-frames are used only to transport control information, primarily data link layer flow and error controls. U-frames are reserved for system management. Information carried by U-frames is intended for managing the link itself.

Each frame in HDLC may contain up to six fields: a beginning flag field, an address field, a control field, an information field, a frame check sequence (FCS) field, and an ending flag field. In multiple frame transmissions, the ending **flag** of one frame can double as the beginning flag of the next frame.

Figure 11.16   *HDLC frame types*

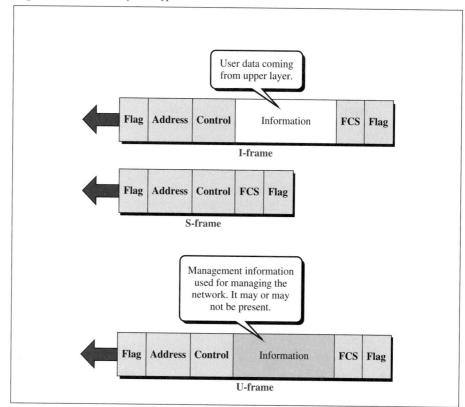

Flag Field

The flag field of an HDLC frame is an eight-bit sequence with a bit pattern 01111110 that identifies both the beginning and end of a frame and serves as a synchronization pattern for the receiver. Figure 11.17 shows the placement of the two flag fields in an I-frame.

Figure 11.17   *HDLC flag field*

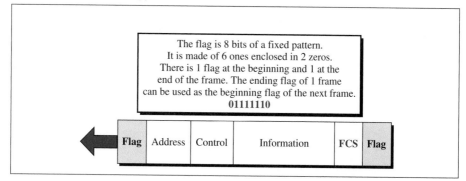

The flag field is the closest that HDLC comes to a control character that might be misread by a receiver. The flag field is also, therefore, HDLC's only potential cause of transparency problems. Once a station finds a flag on the line, determines that the frame is addressed to it, and begins reading the transmission, it is watching for the next flag that signifies the end of the frame. It is always possible that a bit sequence, whether control information or data, might contain the pattern 01111110. If that were to happen in the data, for example, the receiver would find it and assume that the end of the frame had been reached (with disastrous results).

To guarantee that a flag does not appear inadvertently anywhere else in the frame, HDLC uses a process called **bit stuffing.** Every time a sender wants to transmit a bit sequence having more than five consecutive 1s, it inserts (stuffs) one redundant 0 after the fifth 1. For example, the sequence 011111111000 becomes 0111110111000. This extra 0 is inserted regardless of whether the sixth bit is another 1 or not. Its presence tells the receiver that the current sequence is not a flag. Once the receiver has seen the stuffed 0, it is dropped from the data and the original bit stream is restored.

> Bit stuffing is the process of adding one extra 0 whenever there are five consecutive 1s in the data so that the receiver does not mistake the data for a flag.

Figure 11.18 shows bit stuffing at the sender and bit removal at the receiver. Note that even if we have a 0 after five 1s, we still stuff a 0. The 0 will be removed by the receiver.

Figure 11.18   *Bit stuffing and removal*

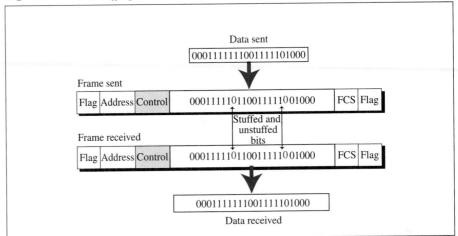

With three exceptions, bit stuffing is required whenever five 1s occur consecutively. The exceptions are when the bit sequence really is a flag, when the transmission is being aborted, and when the channel is being put into idle. The flowchart in Figure 11.19 shows the process the receiver follows to identify and discard a stuffed bit. As the receiver reads the incoming bits, it counts 1s. When it finds five consecutive 1s after a 0, it checks the next (seventh) bit. If the seventh bit is a 0, the receiver recognizes it as a stuffed bit, discards it, and resets its counter. If the seventh bit is a 1, the receiver checks the eighth bit. If the eighth bit is a 0, the sequence is recognized as a flag and treated accordingly. If the eighth bit is another 1, the receiver continues counting. A total of 7 to 14 consecutive 1s indicates an abort. A total of 15 or more 1s indicates an idle channel.

Figure 11.19 *Bit stuffing in HDLC*

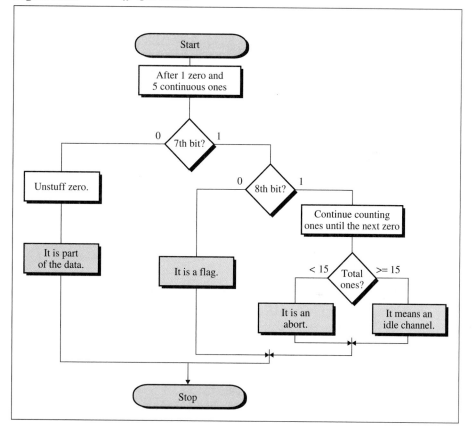

Address Field

The second field of an HDLC frame contains the address of the secondary station that is either the originator or destination of the frame (or the station acting as secondary in the case of combined stations). If a primary station creates a frame, it contains a *to* address. If a secondary creates the frame, it contains a *from* address. An **address field** can be one byte or several bytes long, depending on the needs of the network. One byte can identify up to 128 stations (because one bit is used for another purpose). Larger networks require multiple-byte address fields. Figure 11.20 shows the address field in relation to the rest of the frame.

If the address field is only one byte, the last bit is always a 1. If the address is more than one byte, all bytes but the last one will end with 0; only the last will end with 1.

Figure 11.20   *HDLC address field*

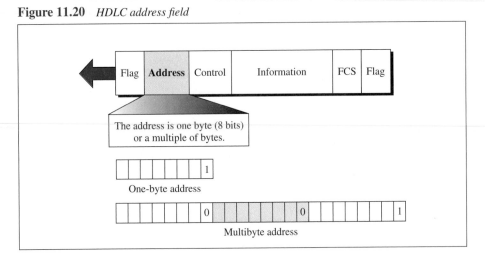

Ending each intermediate byte with 0 indicates to the receiver that there are more address bytes to come.

Control Field

The control field is a one- or two-byte segment of the frame used for flow management. We first discuss the one-byte case and then the two-byte case, called the extended mode.

Control fields differ depending on frame type. If the first bit of the control field is 0, the frame is an I-frame. If the first bit is a 1 and the second bit is 0, it is an S-frame. If both the first and second bits are 1s, it is a U-frame. The control fields of all three types of frames contain a bit called the **poll/final (P/F) bit** (discussed below).

An I-frame contains two 3-bit flow and error control sequences, called N(S) and N(R), flanking the P/F bit. N(S) specifies the number of the frame being sent (its own identifying number). N(R) indicates the number of the frame expected in return in a two-way exchange; thus N(R) is the acknowledgment field. If the last frame received was error-free, the N(R) number will be that of the next frame in the sequence. If the last frame was not received correctly, the N(R) number will be the number of the damaged frame, indicating the need for its retransmission.

The control field of an S-frame contains an N(R) field but not an N(S) field. S-frames are used to return N(R) when the receiver does not have data of its own to send. Otherwise the acknowledgment is contained in the control field of an I-frame (above). S-frames do not transmit data and so do not require N(S) fields to identify them. The two bits preceding the P/F bit in an S-frame are used to carry coded flow and error control information, which we will discuss later in this chapter.

U-frames have neither N(S) nor N(R) fields, and are not designed for user data exchange or acknowledgment. Instead, U-frames have two code fields, one two bits and the other three, flanking the P/F bit. These codes are used to identify the type of U-frame and its function (e.g., establishing the mode of an exchange). The control fields of all three types of frames are shown in Figure 11.21.

Figure 11.21 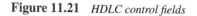 *HDLC control fields*

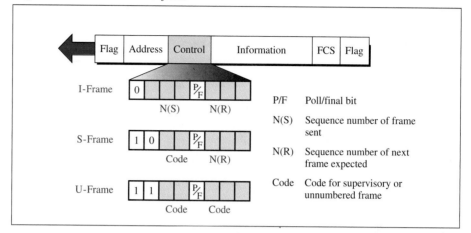

Figure 11.22 shows the control field in the extended mode. Note that in the extended mode, the control field in the I-frame and S-frame is two bytes long to allow seven bits for the sending and receiving sequence number (the sequence number is between 0 and 127). However, the control field in the U-frame is still one byte.

Figure 11.22 *HDLC control fields in the extended mode*

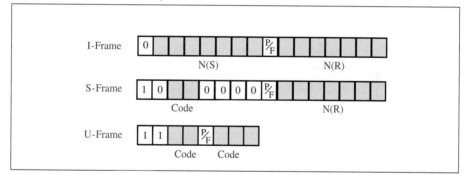

The P/F field is a single bit with a dual purpose. It has meaning only when it is set (bit = 1) and can mean poll or final. It means poll when the frame is sent by a primary station to a secondary (when the address field contains the address of the receiver). It means final when the frame is sent by a secondary to a primary (when the address field contains the address of the sender); see Figure 11.23.

Information Field

The information field contains the user's data in an I-frame, and network management information in a U-frame (see Figure 11.24). Its length can vary from one network to another but is always fixed within each network. An S-frame has no information field.

As we have seen in the several cases above, it is often possible to include flow, error, and other control information in an I-frame that also contains data. For example, in a two-way exchange of data (either half- or full-duplex), station 2 can acknowledge

Figure 11.23   *Poll/final field in HDLC*

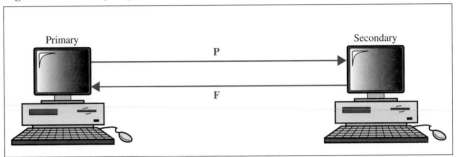

Figure 11.24   *Information field in HDLC*

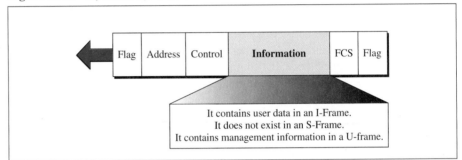

receipt of data from station 1 in the control field of its own data frame rather than sending a separate frame just for the acknowledgment. Combining data to be sent with control information this way is called **piggybacking.**

> Piggybacking means combining data to be sent and acknowledgment of the frame received in one single frame.

FCS Field

The **frame check sequence (FCS)** is HDLC's error detection field. It can contain either a two- or four-byte CRC (see Figure 11.25).

Figure 11.25   *Frame check sequence (FCS) field in HDLC*

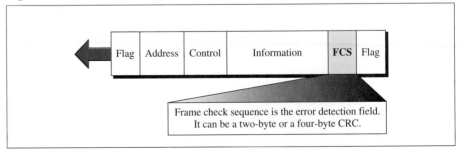

More about Frames

Of the three frames used by HDLC, the I-frame is the most straightforward. I-frames are designed for user information transport and piggybacked acknowledgments and nothing else. For this reason, the range of variation in I-frames is small—all differences relate either to the data (content and CRC), to the identifying number of the frame, or to the acknowledgment of received frames (ACK or NAK).

S-frames and U-frames, however, contain subfields within their control fields. As we saw in our discussion of control fields, these subfields carry codes that alter the meaning of the frame. For example, an S-frame coded for selective-reject (SREJ) cannot be used in the same context as an S-frame coded for receive ready (RR). In this section, we will examine the different types of and uses for S- and U-frames.

S-frames

Supervisory frames are used for acknowledgment, flow control, and error control whenever piggybacking that information onto an I-frame is either impossible or inappropriate (when the station either has no data of its own to send or needs to send a command or response other than an acknowledgment). S-frames do not have information fields, yet each one carries messages to the receiving station. These messages are based on the type of the S-frame and the context of the transmission. The type of each S-frame is determined by a two-bit code set into its control field just before the P/F bit. There are four types of S-frames: receive ready (RR), receive not ready (RNR), reject (REJ), and selective-reject (SREJ); see Figure 11.26.

Figure 11.26   *S-frame control field in HDLC*

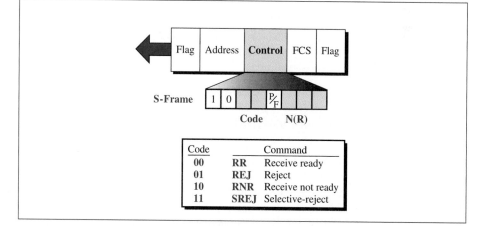

Receive Ready   An S-frame containing the code for RR (00) can be used in four possible ways, each having a different significance.

■   **ACK.** RR is used by a receiving station to return a positive acknowledgment of a received I-frame when the receiver has no data of its own to send (no I-frame on which to piggyback the acknowledgment). In this case, the N(R) field of the control frame contains the sequence number of the next frame expected by the receiver. In a one-byte control field, an N(R) field has three bits, allowing up to 8 frames to be acknowledged. In an extended mode control field, an N(R) field has 7 bits, allowing up to 128 frames to be acknowledged.

- **Poll.** When transmitted by the primary (or acting primary in a combined station) with the P/F bit (now functioning as the **poll** or **P bit**) set, RR asks the secondary if it has anything to send.

- **Negative response to poll.** When sent by a secondary with the P/F bit (now functioning as the **final** or **F bit**) set, RR tells the primary that the secondary has nothing to send. If the secondary does have data to transmit, it responds to the poll with an I-frame, not an S-frame.

- **Positive response to select.** When a secondary is able to receive a transmission from the primary, it returns an RR frame with the P/F (used as the F) bit set to 1. (For a description of selection, see RNR, below.)

Receive Not Ready   RNR frames can be used in three different ways:

- **ACK.** RNR returned by a receiver to a sending station acknowledges receipt of all frames up to, but not including, the one indicated in the N(R) field but requests that no more frames be sent until an RR frame is issued.

- **Select.** When a primary wishes to transmit data to a specific secondary, it alerts the secondary by sending an RNR frame with the P/F (used as the P) bit set. The RNR code tells the secondary not to send data of its own, that the frame is a select and not a poll.

- **Negative response to select.** When a selected secondary is unable to receive data, it returns an RNR frame with the P/F (used as the F) bit set.

Reject   A third type of S-frame is reject (REJ). REJ is the negative acknowledgment returned by a receiver in a go-back-*n* ARQ error correction system when the receiver has no data on which to piggyback the response. In an REJ frame, the N(R) field contains the number of the damaged frame to indicate that the frame and all that follow it need to be retransmitted.

Selective-Reject   A selective-reject (SREJ) frame is a negative acknowledgment in a selective-reject ARQ system. It is sent by the receiver to the sender to indicate that a specific frame (the number in the N(R) field) has been received damaged and must be resent. Figure 11.27 shows the use of the P/F bit in polling and selecting.

U-frames

Unnumbered frames are used to exchange session management and control information between connected devices. Unlike S-frames, U-frames contain an information field, but one used for system management information not user data. As with S-frames, however, much of the information carried by U-frames is contained in codes included in the control field. U-frame codes are divided into two sections: a two-bit prefix before the P/F bit and a three-bit suffix after the P/F bit. Together, these two segments (five bits) can be used to create up to 32 different types of U-frames. Some of the more common combinations are shown in Figure 11.28.

Figure 11.27   *Use of P/F bit in polling and selecting*

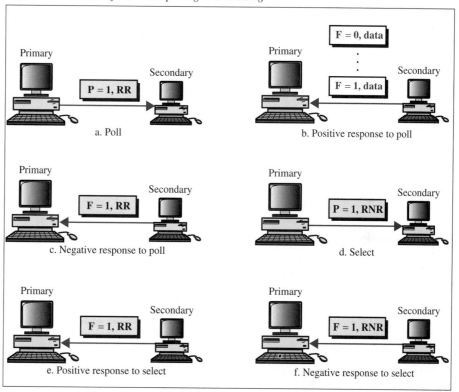

a. Poll

b. Positive response to poll

c. Negative response to poll

d. Select

e. Positive response to select

f. Negative response to select

The U-frame commands and responses listed in Table 11.2 can be divided into five basic functional categories: mode setting, unnumbered-exchange, disconnection, initialization, and miscellaneous.

Mode Setting   Mode-setting commands are sent by the primary station, or by a combined station wishing to control an exchange, to establish the mode of the session. A mode-setting U-frame tells the receiving station what format the transmission will take. For example, if a combined station wishes to establish a temporary primary-to-secondary relationship with another station, it sends a U-frame containing the code 00 001 (for set normal response mode). The addressed station understands that it is being selected to receive a transmission (as if from a primary) and adjusts itself accordingly (see Table 11.2).

Unnumbered-Exchange   Unnumbered-exchange codes are used to send or solicit specific pieces of data link information between devices. The unnumbered poll (UP) code (00 100) is transmitted by the primary station on a link (or the combined station acting as a primary) to establish the send/receive status of the addressed station in an unnumbered exchange. The unnumbered information (UI) code (00 000) is used for the transmission of specific pieces of information such as time/date for synchronization. UI frames can be sent either as commands (e.g., a list of parameters for the coming

Figure 11.28   *U-frame control field in HDLC*

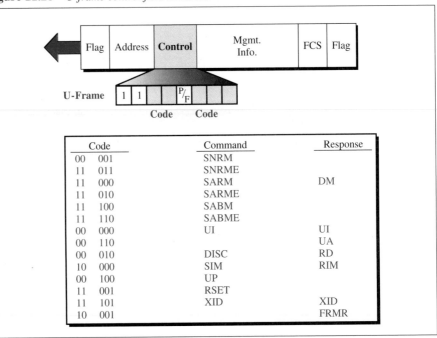

Table 11.2   *U-frame control command and response*

Command/Response	Meaning
SNRM	Set normal response mode
SNRME	Set normal response mode (extended)
SARM	Set asynchronous response mode
SARME	Set asynchronous response mode (extended)
SABM	Set asynchronous balanced mode
SABME	Set asynchronous balanced mode (extended)
UP	Unnumbered poll
UI	Unnumbered information
UA	Unnumbered acknowledgment
RD	Request disconnect
DISC	Disconnect
DM	Disconnect mode
RIM	Request information mode
SIM	Set initialization mode
RSET	Reset
XID	Exchange ID
FRMR	Frame reject

transmission) or as responses (e.g., a description of the capabilities of the addressed station to receive data). The unnumbered acknowledgment (UA) code (00 110) is returned by the addressed station in answer to an unnumbered poll, to acknowledge one of the unnumbered request frames (e.g., RD: request disconnect), or to accept a set-mode command (see Table 11.2).

Disconnection   There are three **disconnect** codes, one a command from the acting primary or combined station, the other two responses from the receiving station. The first of these, disconnect (DISC, 00 010), is sent by the first station to the second to terminate the connection. The second, request disconnect (RD, 00 010), is a request by the second station to the first that a DISC be issued. The third, disconnect mode (DM, 11 000), is transmitted by the addressed station to the initiating station as a negative response to a mode-setting command (see Table 11.2).

Initialization Mode   The code 10 000, used as a command (first system to second system), means set initialization mode (SIM). SIM prepares the addressed station to initialize its data link control functions. The SIM command is then followed by UI frames containing, for example, a new program or a new parameter set. The same code, 10 000, used as a response (second system to first system), means request initialization mode (RIM) and solicits a SIM command from the first station. It is used to respond to a mode-setting command when the second station cannot act upon the command without first receiving a SIM (see Table 11.2).

Miscellaneous   Of the final three commands, the first two—reset (RSET, 11 001) and exchange ID (XID, 11 101)—are commands from the initiating system to the addressed system. The third, frame reject (FRMR, 10 001) is a response sent from the addressed system to the initiating system.

RSET tells the second station the first station is resetting its send sequence numbering and instructs the second system to do likewise. It is usually issued in response to an FRMR.

XID requests an exchange of identifying data from the second station (What is your address?).

FRMR tells the first system that a U-frame received by the second system contains a syntax error (This doesn't look like an HDLC frame!). It is returned by the addressed system when, for example, a frame is identified as an S-frame but contains an information field (see Table 11.2).

Examples

This section shows some examples of communication using HDLC.

Example 11.1: Poll/Response

In Figure 11.29, the primary device (the mainframe) on a multipoint link polls the secondary device (A) with an S-frame containing the codes for poll. The flag field is first, followed by the address of the secondary being polled, in this case A. The third field, control, contains the code identifying the frame as an S-frame followed by the codes indicating the RR (receive ready) status of the sender, the P/F bit set to poll, and an

Figure 11.29   *Example of polling using HDLC*

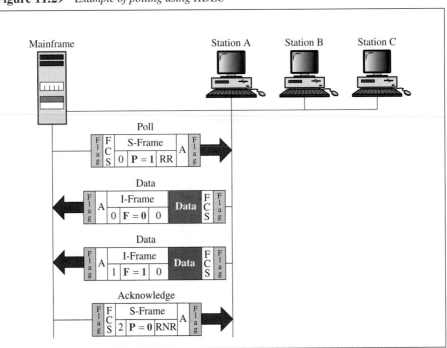

N(R) = 0 field. After the control field comes the error detection code (FCS) and the ending flag field.

Station A has data to send, so it responds with two I-frames numbered 0 and 1. The second of these has the P/F bit set for *final* to indicate the end of the data. The primary acknowledges both frames at once with an S-frame containing the number 2 in its N(R) field to tell station A that frames 0 and 1 have been received, and that if A sends additional frames, the primary expects number 2 to arrive next.

Example 11.2: Select/Response

This example uses the same multipoint configuration to show a primary device selecting a secondary device, station B, to receive a transmission (see Figure 11.30).

First, the primary sends out an S-frame addressed to station B that contains the codes for select. The select frame is identical to the poll frame in the previous example, except that the RR status in the control field has been changed to RNR, telling the secondary to be ready but not to send. Station B responds with another S-frame, addressed from B, that contains the code for RR as well as the final bit set, to indicate that the station is ready to receive and that this frame is the last.

The primary sends an I-frame containing its data. The frame is addressed to B, the N(S) field identifies it as frame number 0, the P bit is not set to indicate that the frame is not a poll, and the N(R) field indicates that if an I-frame is returned, it is expected also to be number 0. Station B responds with an RR frame with a dual purpose: the set

Figure 11.30 *Example of selecting using HDLC*

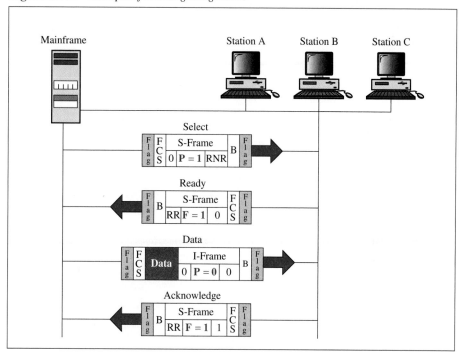

final bit tells the primary that B does not have anything to send, and the 1 in the N(R) field acknowledges the receipt of frame 0 and indicates that B next expects to receive frame 1.

Example 11.3: Peer Devices

The example in Figure 11.31 shows an exchange in asynchronous balanced mode (ABM) using piggybacked acknowledgments. The two stations are of equal status and are connected by a point-to-point link.

Station A issues a U-frame containing the code for SABM to establish a link in asynchronous balanced mode. The P bit is set to indicate that station A expects to control the session and to transmit first. Station B accepts the request by returning a U-frame containing the code for UA, with the F bit set. By agreeing to transmit in asynchronous balanced mode, both stations are now of combined type, rather than primary–secondary, so the P/F bit is no longer valid and can be ignored in the frames that follow.

Station A begins the exchange of information with an I-frame numbered 0 followed by another I-frame numbered 1. Station B piggybacks its acknowledgment of both frames onto an I-frame of its own. Station B's first I-frame is also numbered 0 (N(S) field) and contains a 2 in its N(R) field, acknowledging the receipt of A's frames 1 and 0 and indicating that it expects frame 2 to arrive next. Station B transmits its second and third I-frames (numbered 1 and 2) before accepting further frames from station A. Its

Figure 11.31 *Example of peer-to-peer communication using HDLC*

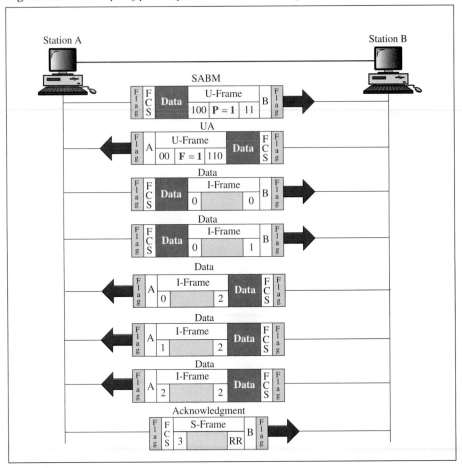

N(R) information, therefore, has not changed: B frames 1 and 2 indicate that station B is still expecting A frame 2 to arrive next.

Station A has sent all of its data. Therefore, it cannot piggyback an acknowledgment onto an I-frame and sends an S-frame instead. The RR code indicates that A is still ready to receive. The number 3 in the N(R) field tells B that frames 0, 1, and 2 have all been accepted and that A is now expecting frame number 3.

Example 11.4: Peer Communication with Error

In the previous example, suppose frame 1 sent from station B to A is in error. Station A, should inform station B to resend frames 1 and 2 (the system is using go-back-*n* protocol). Station A sends a reject supervisory frame to announce the error in frame 1. Figure 11.32 shows the situation.

Figure 11.32   *Example 11.4*

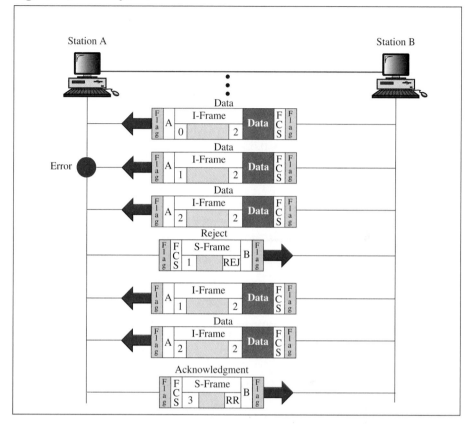

11.5   LINK ACCESS PROCEDURES

Several protocols under the general category **link access procedure (LAP)** have been developed. Each of these protocols is a subset of HDLC tailored for a specific purpose. LAPB, LAPD, and LAPM are the most common of these.

LAPB

Link access procedure, balanced (LAPB) is a simplified subset of HDLC used only for connecting a station to a network. It therefore provides only those basic control functions required for communication between a DTE and a DCE (e.g., it does not include poll and select characters).

LAPB is used only in balanced configurations of two devices, where both devices are of the combined type. Communication is always in asynchronous balanced mode. LAPB is used today in Integrated Services Digital Network (ISDN) on B channels. (See Chapter 16 for a discussion of ISDN.)

LAPD

Link access procedure for D channel (LAPD) is another simplified subset of HDLC used in Integrated Services Digital Network (ISDN). It is used for out-of-band (control) signaling. It uses asynchronous balanced mode (ABM).

LAPM

Link access procedure for modems (LAPM) is a simplified subset of HDLC for modems. It is designed to do asynchronous–synchronous conversion, error detection, and retransmission. It has been developed to apply HDLC features to modems.

11.6   KEY TERMS AND CONCEPTS

address field	control character
asynchronous balanced mode (ABM)	disconnect
asynchronous protocol	final bit (F bit)
asynchronous response mode (ARM)	flag
balanced configuration	frame
binary synchronous communication (BSC)	frame check sequence (FCS)
	high-level data link control (HDLC)
bit-oriented protocol	information frame (I-frame)
bit stuffing	Kermit
block check count (BCC)	link access procedure (LAP)
blocked asynchronous transmission (BLAST)	link access procedure, balanced (LAPB)
byte	link access procedure, for D channel (LAPD)
byte-oriented protocol	link access procedure, for modems (LAPM)
byte stuffing	
character-oriented protocol	normal response mode (NRM)
combined station	piggybacking

poll bit (P bit)	transparency
poll/final bit (P/F bit)	U-frame
primary station	unbalanced configuration
S-frame	
secondary station	unnumbered frame (U-frame)
supervisory frame (S-frame)	XMODEM
symmetrical configuration	YMODEM
synchronous data link control (SDLC)	ZMODEM

11.7 SUMMARY

- A protocol in data communication is a group of specifications used to implement one or more layers of the OSI model.
- Data link protocols can be classified as synchronous or asynchronous.
- Asynchronous protocols such as XMODEM, YMODEM, ZMODEM, BLAST, and Kermit are used in file transfer.
- Synchronous protocols can be classified into two groups:
  - a. Character-oriented protocols.
  - b. Bit-oriented protocols.
- In character-oriented protocols, the frame is interpreted as a series of characters.
- In bit-oriented protocols, each bit or group of bits can have meaning.
- Binary synchronous communication (BSC) is the most well-known character-oriented protocol.
- BSC operates in half-duplex mode using stop-and-wait ARQ in a point-to-point or multipoint link configuration.
- There are two types of BSC frames:
  - a. Control frames.
  - b. Data frames.
- Control frames perform these functions:
  - a. Make a connection.
  - b. Control flow and error.
  - c. Sever a connection.
- A bit pattern that resembles a BSC control character in the data field must not be recognized as a control character; it must be made transparent.
- Data transparency in BSC is achieved by a process called byte stuffing.

■ Byte stuffing involves

   a. Demarcation of the transparent region.

   b. Addition of DLE (in the transparent region) before every DLE character.

■ All bit-oriented protocols are related to high-level data link control (HDLC).

■ HDLC operates in half- or full-duplex mode in a point-to-point or multipoint link configuration.

■ HDLC stations are categorized as follows:

   a. Primary station—sends commands.

   b. Secondary station—sends responses.

   c. Combined station—sends commands and responses.

■ HDLC stations are configured as follows:

   a. Unbalanced—one primary, one or more secondaries.

   b. Symmetrical—two physical stations, each capable of switching from primary to secondary.

   c. Balanced—two combined stations, each of equal status.

■ HDLC stations communicate in one of three modes:

   a. Normal response mode (NRM)—the secondary station needs permission to transmit.

   b. Asynchronous response mode (ARM)—the secondary station does not need permission to transmit.

   c. Asynchronous balanced mode (ABM)—either combined station may initiate transmission.

■ HDLC protocol defines three types of frames:

   a. Information frame (I-frame)—for data transmission and control.

   b. Supervisory frame (S-frame)—for control.

   c. Unnumbered frame (U-frame)—for control and management.

■ HDLC handles data transparency by adding a 0 whenever there are five consecutive 1s following a 0. This is called bit stuffing.

11.8   PRACTICE SET

Review Questions

1. What is data transparency in BSC?
2. When would a DLE DLE pattern be seen in BSC?
3. What is the difference between the information fields in an HDLC I-frame and an HDLC U-frame?
4. Define the term **protocol** as it relates to data communications.
5. How are data link protocols divided into classes? What is the basis of the division?
6. How are asynchronous protocols primarily used?

7. Why are asynchronous protocols losing popularity?
8. How are synchronous protocols classified? What is the basis of the classification?
9. How do character-oriented protocols convey control information?
10. Describe the line configuration, transmission mode, and flow and error control methods used by BSC.
11. Describe the types of BSC frames.
12. Why should a long BSC message be divided into blocks?
13. How can a receiver distinguish between the end of a frame and the end of a message in a multiframe BSC transmission?
14. What are the uses of BSC control frames?
15. Describe the three HDLC station types.
16. For each of the HDLC configurations, discuss commands and responses.
17. How do the three HDLC frame types differ from one another?
18. In HDLC, what is bit stuffing and why is it needed?
19. Name and discuss briefly the bits in the HDLC control field.
20. What is piggybacking?
21. Name the four types of S-frames.
22. Name the five categories of U-frames.
23. How are LAPB, LAPD, and LAPM different from each other?

Multiple Choice Questions

24. BSC stands for _____.
    a. binary synchronous control
    b. binary synchronous communication
    c. bit-oriented synchronous communication
    d. byte-oriented synchronous communication
25. A negative response to a poll in BSC is _____.
    a. NAK
    b. EOT
    c. WACK
    d. b and c
26. A negative response to a select in BSC is _____.
    a. NAK
    b. EOT
    c. WACK
    d. b and c
27. In BSC, a receiver responds with _____ if the frame received is error-free and even-numbered.
    a. an ACK
    b. an ACK 0

   c. an ACK 1

   d. a or b

28. BSC protocol uses _____ mode for data transmission.

   a. simplex

   b. half-duplex

   c. full-duplex

   d. half-simplex

29. BSC frames can be categorized as either data frames or _____ frames.

   a. transmission

   b. control

   c. communication

   d. supervisory

30. In BSC protocol, after an ETB, ETX, or ITB, a _____ field follows.

   a. DLE

   b. EOT

   c. BCC

   d. SYN

31. In BSC protocol, _____ can terminate a transmission or be a negative response to a poll.

   a. DLE

   b. ETX

   c. EOT

   d. ETB

32. Which of the following are variable-length fields in BSC?

   a. data

   b. BCC

   c. header

   d. all of the above

33. HDLC is an acronym for _____.

   a. high-duplex line communication

   b. high-level data link control

   c. half-duplex digital link combination

   d. host double level circuit

34. The address field of a frame in HDLC protocol contains the address of the _____ station.

   a. primary

   b. secondary

   c. tertiary

   d. a and b

35. HDLC is a _____ protocol.
    a. character-oriented
    b. bit-oriented
    c. byte-oriented
    d. count-oriented

36. BSC is a _____ protocol.
    a. character-oriented
    b. bit-oriented
    c. byte-oriented
    d. count-oriented

37. The HDLC _____ field defines the beginning and end of a frame.
    a. flag
    b. address
    c. control
    d. FCS

38. What is present in all HDLC control fields?
    a. P/F bit
    b. N(R)
    c. N(S)
    d. code bits

39. Polling and selecting are functions of the _____ in HDLC protocol.
    a. I-frame
    b. S-frame
    c. U-frame
    d. a and b

40. In HDLC protocol, the poll/final bit's meaning in an I-frame is dependent on
    _____.
    a. the system configuration
    b. whether the frame is a command or a response
    c. the system mode
    d. none of the above

41. The shortest frame in HDLC protocol is usually the _____ frame.
    a. information
    b. supervisory
    c. management
    d. none of the above

42. When data and acknowledgment are sent on the same frame, this is called
   _____.
   a. piggybacking
   b. backpacking
   c. piggypacking
   d. a good idea

Exercises

43. What are the actual data in the frame shown in Figure 11.33?

Figure 11.33 *Exercise 43*

44. What are the actual data in the frame shown in Figure 11.34?

Figure 11.34 *Exercise 44*

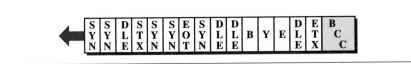

45. Show how a supervisory response frame in HDLC can simulate each of the following BSC frames.
   a. ACK 0
   b. ACK 1
   c. NAK
   d. WACK

46. Bit stuff the following data:

    000111111011111001110011111001

47. Bit stuff the following data:

   00011111111111111111111111111111110011111001

48. The HDLC frame in Figure 11.35 is sent from a primary to a secondary. Answer the following questions:
   a. What is the address of the secondary?
   b. What is the type of the frame?
   c. What is the sender sequence number (if present)?
   d. What is the acknowledgment number (if present)?

   e. Does the frame carry user data? If yes, what is the value of the data?
   f. Does the frame carry management data? If yes, what is the value of the data?
   g. What is the purpose of the frame?

Figure 11.35 *Exercises 48 and 49*

01111110 00001111 10001011 FCS 01111110

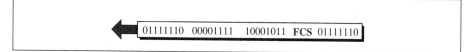

49. Repeat Exercise 48 with the frame sent from a secondary to a primary.
50. The HDLC frame in Figure 11.36 is sent from a primary to a secondary. Answer the following questions:
   a. What is the address of the secondary?
   b. What is the type of the frame?
   c. What is the sender sequence number (if present)?
   d. What is the acknowledgment number (if present)?
   e. Does the frame carry user data? If yes, what is the value of the data?
   f. Does the frame carry management data? If yes, what is the value of the data?
   g. What is the purpose of the frame?

Figure 11.36 *Exercises 50 and 51*

01111110 00000111 10101011 FCS 01111110

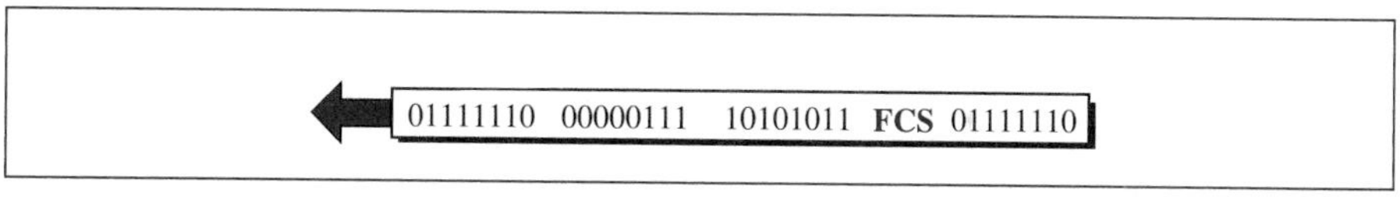

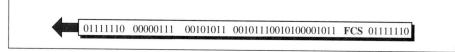

51. Repeat Exercise 50 with the frame sent from a secondary to a primary.
52. The frame in Figure 11.37 is sent from a primary to a secondary. Answer the following questions:
   a. What is the address of the secondary?
   b. What is the type of the frame?
   c. What is the sender sequence number (if present)?
   d. What is the acknowledgment number (if present)?
   e. Does the frame carry user data? If yes, what is the value of the data?
   f. Does the frame carry management data? If yes, what is the value of the data?

Figure 11.37 *Exercise 52*

01111110 00000111 00101011 00101110010100001011 FCS 01111110

53. The frame in Figure 11.38 is sent from a primary to a secondary. Answer the following questions:
   a. What is the address of the secondary?
   b. What is the type of the frame?

Figure 11.38   *Exercise 53*

01111110 00000111   00101011 001111100101111001010000l011 FCS 01111110

c. What is the sender sequence number (if present)?

d. What is the acknowledgment number (if present)?

e. Does the frame carry user data? If yes, what is the value of the data?

f. Does the frame carry management data? If yes, what is the value of the data?

54. The frame in Figure 11.39 is sent from a primary to a secondary. Answer the following questions:

   a. What is the address of the secondary?

   b. What is the type of the frame?

   c. What is the sender sequence number (if present)?

   d. What is the acknowledgment number (if present)?

   e. Does the frame carry user data? If yes, what is the value of the data?

   f. Does the frame carry management data? If yes, what is the value of the data?

Figure 11.39   *Exercise 54*

01111110 10000111   11001010 00101..........00001011 FCS 01111110

55. Using BSC, show the sequence of frames for the following scenario between two computers in a point-to-point configuration:

   a. Computer A asks permission from computer B to send data.

   b. Computer B responds positively.

   c. Computer A sends three frames, each consisting of 4 blocks of 100 bytes.

   d. Computer B acknowledges the receipt.

56. Using BSC, show the sequence of frames for the following scenario (computer A is the primary and computer B is the secondary):

   a. Computer A checks to see if computer B has data to send.

   b. Computer B sends a frame of 50 bytes.

   c. Computer A acknowledges the receipt.

57. Using Figure 11.29, show the exchange of frames if station A does not have data to send.

58. Using Figure 11.29, show the exchange of frames if frame 1 is lost.
59. Using Figure 11.30, show the exchange of frames if station B is not ready to receive data.
60. Using Figure 11.30, show the exchange of frames if the acknowledgment is lost.

CHAPTER 12

Local Area Networks

A **local area network (LAN)** is a data communication system that allows a number of independent devices to communicate directly with each other in a limited geographic area.

LANs are dominated by four architectures: Ethernet, Token Bus, Token Ring, and fiber distributed data interface (FDDI). Ethernet, Token Bus, and Token Ring are standards of the IEEE and are part of its Project 802; FDDI is an ANSI standard.

The data link control portion of the LAN protocols in use today are all based on HDLC. However, each protocol has adapted HDLC to fit the specific requirements of its own technology. (For example, ring technology has different needs than star technology, as we will see later in this chapter.) Differences in the protocols are necessary to handle the differing needs of the designs.

12.1   PROJECT 802

In 1985, the Computer Society of the IEEE started a project, called **Project 802,** to set standards to enable intercommunication between equipment from a variety of manufacturers. Project 802 does not seek to replace any part of the OSI model. Instead, it is a way of specifying functions of the physical layer, the data link layer, and, to a lesser extent, the network layer to allow for interconnectivity of major LAN protocols.

> In 1985, the Computer Society of the IEEE developed Project 802. It covers the first two layers of the OSI model and part of the third level.

The relationship of **IEEE Project 802** to the OSI model is shown in Figure 12.1. The IEEE has subdivided the data link layer into two sublayers: **logical link control (LLC)** and **medium access control (MAC).**

The LLC is non-architecture-specific; that is, it is the same for all IEEE-defined LANs. The MAC sublayer, on the other hand, contains a number of distinct modules; each carries proprietary information specific to the LAN product being used.

Figure 12.1 *LAN compared with the OSI model*

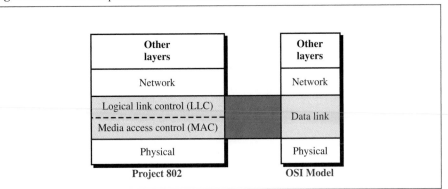

Project 802 has split the data link layer into two different sublayers: logical link control (LLC) and media access control (MAC).

In addition to the two sublayers, Project 802 contains a section governing **internetworking.** This section assures the compatibility of different LANs and MANs across protocols and allows data to be exchanged across otherwise incompatible networks.

The strength of Project 802 is modularity. By subdividing the functions necessary for LAN management, the designers were able to standardize those that can be generalized and to isolate those that must remain specific. Each subdivision is identified by a number: 802.1 (internetworking); 802.2 (LLC); and the MAC modules 802.3 (CSMA/CD), 802.4 (Token Bus), 802.5 (Token Ring), and others (see Figure 12.2).

Figure 12.2 *Project 802*

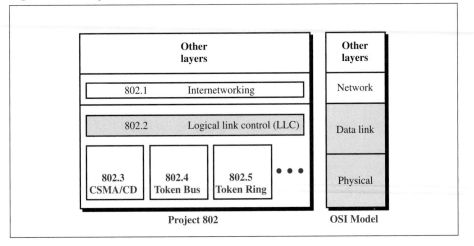

IEEE 802.1

IEEE 802.1 is the section of Project 802 devoted to internetworking issues in LANs and MANs. Although not yet complete, it seeks to resolve the incompatibilities between network architectures without requiring modifications in existing addressing, access, and error recovery mechanisms, among others. Some of these issues will be discussed in Chapter 21.

> IEEE 802.1 is an internetworking standard for LANs.

LLC

In general, the IEEE Project 802 model takes the structure of an HDLC frame and divides it into two sets of functions. One set contains the end-user portions of the frame: the logical addresses, control information, and data. These functions are handled by the **IEEE 802.2** logical link control (LLC) protocol. LLC is considered the upper layer of the IEEE 802 data link layer and is common to all LAN protocols.

> IEEE 802.2 logical link control (LLC) is the upper sublayer of the data link layer.

MAC

The second set of functions, the medium access control (MAC) sublayer, resolves the **contention** for the shared media. It contains the synchronization, flag, flow, and error control specifications necessary to move information from one place to another, as well as the physical address of the next station to receive and route a packet. MAC protocols are specific to the LAN using them (Ethernet, Token Ring, and Token Bus, etc.).

> Media access control (MAC) is the lower sublayer of the data link layer.

Protocol Data Unit (PDU)

The data unit in the LLC level is called the **protocol data unit (PDU).** The PDU contains four fields familiar from HDLC: a destination service access point (DSAP), a source service access point (SSAP), a control field, and an information field (see Figure 12.3).

DSAP and SSAP

The DSAP and SSAP are addresses used by the LLC to identify the protocol stacks on the receiving and sending machines that are generating and using the data. The first bit of the DSAP indicates whether the frame is intended for an individual or a group. The first bit of the SSAP indicates whether the communication is a command or response PDU (see Figure 12.3).

Control

The control field of the PDU is identical to the control field in HDLC. As in HDLC, PDU frames can be I-frames, S-frames, or U-frames and carry all of the codes and information that the corresponding HDLC frames carry (see Figure 12.4).

Figure 12.3 *PDU format*

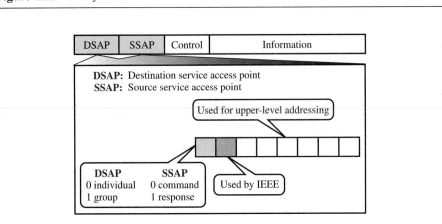

Figure 12.4 *Control field in a PDU*

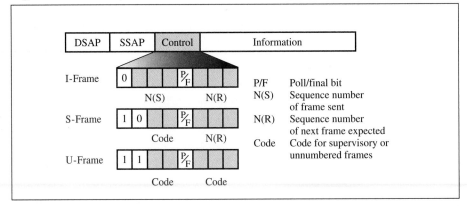

The PDU has no flag fields, no CRC, and no station address. These fields are added in the lower sublayer (the MAC layer).

12.2 ETHERNET

IEEE 802.3 supports a LAN standard originally developed by Xerox and later extended by a joint venture between Digital Equipment Corporation, Intel Corporation, and Xerox. This was called **Ethernet.**

IEEE 802.3 defines two categories: **baseband** and **broadband,** as shown in Figure 12.5. The word *base* specifies a digital signal (in this case, Manchester encoding). The word *broad* specifies an analog signal (in this case, PSK encoding). IEEE divides the baseband category into five different standards: **10Base5, 10Base2, 10Base-T, 1Base5,** and **100Base-T.** The first number (10, 1, or 100) indicates the data rate in Mbps. The last number or letter (5, 2, 1, or T) indicates the maximum cable length or the type of cable. IEEE defines only one specification for the broadband

Figure 12.5 *IEEE 802.3*

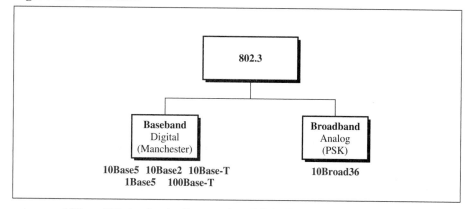

category: 10Broad36. Again, the first number (10) indicates the data rate. The last number defines the maximum cable length. However, the maximum cable length restriction can be changed using networking devices such as repeaters or bridges (see Chapter 21).

Access Method: CSMA/CD

Whenever multiple users have unregulated access to a single line, there is a danger of signals overlapping and destroying each other. Such overlaps, which turn the signals into unusable noise, are called **collisions.** As traffic increases on a multiple-access link, so do collisions. A LAN therefore needs a mechanism to coordinate traffic, minimize the number of collisions that occur, and maximize the number of frames that are delivered successfully. The access mechanism used in an Ethernet is called **carrier sense multiple access with collision detection (CSMA/CD,** standardized in IEEE 802.3).

CSMA/CD is the result of an evolution from **multiple access (MA)** to **carrier sense multiple access (CSMA),** and, finally, to carrier sense multiple access with collision detection (CSMA/CD). The original design was a multiple access method in which every workstation had equal access to a link. In MA, there was no provision for traffic coordination. Access to the line was open to any node at any time, with the assumption that the odds of two devices competing for access at the same time were small enough to be unimportant. Any station wishing to transmit did so, then relied on acknowledgments to verify that the transmitted frame had not been destroyed by other traffic on the line.

In a CSMA system, any workstation wishing to transmit must first listen for existing traffic on the line. A device listens by checking for a voltage. If no voltage is detected, the line is considered idle and the transmission is initiated. CSMA cuts down on the number of collisions but does not eliminate them. Collisions can still occur. If another station has transmitted too recently for its signal to have reached the listening station, the listener assumes the line is idle and introduces its own signal onto the line.

The final step is the addition of collision detection (CD). In CSMA/CD the station wishing to transmit first listens to make certain the link is free, then transmits its data, then listens again. During the data transmission, the station checks the line for the extremely high voltages that indicate a collision. If a collision is detected, the station quits the current transmission and waits a predetermined amount of time for the line to clear, then sends its data again (see Figure 12.6).

Figure 12.6   *Collision in CSMA/CD*

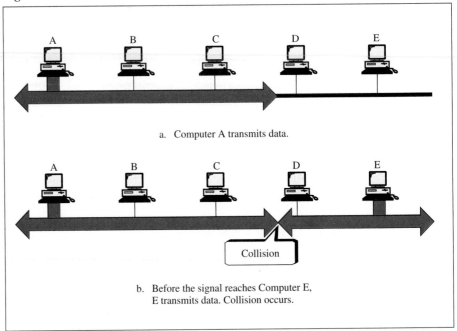

a. Computer A transmits data.

b. Before the signal reaches Computer E,
E transmits data. Collision occurs.

Addressing

Each station on an Ethernet network (such as a PC, workstation, or printer) has its own **network interface card (NIC).** The NIC usually fits inside the station and provides the station with a six-byte physical address. The number on the NIC is unique.

Electrical Specification

Signaling

The baseband systems use Manchester digital encoding (see Chapter 5). There is one broadband system, 10Broad36. It uses digital/analog conversion (differential PSK).

Data Rate

Ethernet LANs can support data rates between 1 and 100 Mbps.

Frame Format

IEEE 802.3 specifies one type of frame containing seven fields: preamble, SFD, DA, SA, length/type of PDU, 802.2 frame, and the CRC. Ethernet does not provide any mechanism for acknowledging received frames, making it what is known as an unreliable medium. Acknowledgments must be implemented at the higher layers. The format of the MAC frame in CSMA/CD is shown in Figure 12.7.

Figure 12.7 *802.3 MAC frame*

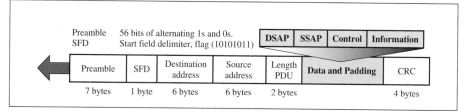

- **Preamble.** The first field of the 802.3 frame, the **preamble,** contains seven bytes (56 bits) of alternating 0s and 1s that alert the receiving system to the coming frame and enable it to synchronize its input timing. The pattern 1010101 provides only an alert and a timing pulse; it can be too easily aliased to be useful in indicating the beginning of the data stream. HDLC combined the alert, timing, and start synchronization into a single field: the flag. IEEE 802.3 divides these three functions between the preamble and the second field, the **start frame delimiter (SFD).**

- **Start frame delimiter (SFD).** The second field (one byte: 10101011) of the 802.3 frame signals the beginning of the frame. The SFD tells the receiver that everything that follows is data, starting with the addresses.

- **Destination address (DA).** The **destination address (DA)** field is allotted six bytes and contains the physical address of the packet's next destination. A system's physical address is a bit pattern encoded on its network interface card (NIC). Each NIC has a unique address that distinguishes it from any other NIC. If the packet must cross from one LAN to another to reach its destination, the DA field contains the physical address of the router connecting the current LAN to the next one. When the packet reaches the target network, the DA field contains the physical address of the destination device.

- **Source address (SA).** The **source address (SA)** field is also allotted six bytes and contains the physical address of the last device to forward the packet. That device can be the sending station or the most recent router to receive and forward the packet.

- **Length/type of PDU.** These next two bytes indicate the number of bytes in the coming PDU. If the length of the PDU is fixed, this field can be used to indicate type, or as a base for other protocols. For example, Novell and the Internet use it to identify the network layer protocol that is using the PDU.

- **802.2 frame (PDU).** This field of the 802.3 frame contains the entire 802.2 frame as a modular, removable unit. The PDU can be anywhere from 46 to 1500 bytes long, depending on the type of frame and the length of the information field. The PDU is generated by the upper (LLC) sublayer, then linked to the 802.3 frame.

- **CRC.** The last field in the 802.3 frame contains the error detection information, in this case a CRC-32.

Implementation

Although the bulk of the IEEE Project 802 standard focuses on the data link layer of the OSI model, the 802 model also defines some of the physical specifications for each of the protocols defined in the MAC layer. In the 802.3 standard, the IEEE defines the types of cable, connections, and signals that are to be used in each of five different Ethernet implementations. All Ethernet LANs are configured as logical buses, although they may be physically implemented in bus or star topologies. Each frame is transmitted to every station on the link but read only by the station to which it is addressed.

10BASE5: Thick Ethernet

The first of the physical standards defined in the IEEE 802.3 model is called 10Base5, **thick Ethernet,** or **Thicknet.** The nickname derives from the size of the cable, which is roughly the size of garden hose and too stiff to bend with your hands. 10Base5 is a bus topology LAN that uses baseband signaling and has a maximum segment length of 500 meters.

As we will see in Chapter 21, networking devices (such as repeaters and bridges) can be used to overcome the size limitation of local area networks. In thick Ethernet, a local area network can be divided into segments by connecting devices. In this case, the length of each segment is limited to 500 meters. However, to reduce collisions, the total length of the bus should not exceed 2500 meters (five segments). Also, the standard demands that each station be separated from each neighbor by 2.5 meters (200 stations per segment and 1000 stations total); see Figure 12.8.

Figure 12.8   *Ethernet segments*

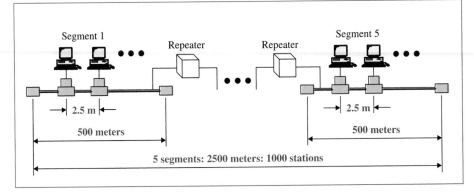

The physical connectors and cables utilized by 10Base5 include coaxial cable, network interface cards, transceivers, and attachment unit interface (AUI) cables. The interaction of these components is illustrated in Figure 12.9.

RG-8 Cable   RG-8 cable (RG stands for radio government) is a thick coaxial cable that provides the backbone of the IEEE 802.3 standard.

Transceiver   Each station is attached by an AUI cable to an intermediary device called a **medium attachment unit (MAU)** or, more commonly, a **transceiver** (short for transmitter-receiver). The transceiver performs the CSMA/CD function of checking for

Figure 12.9 *Topology of 10BASE5*

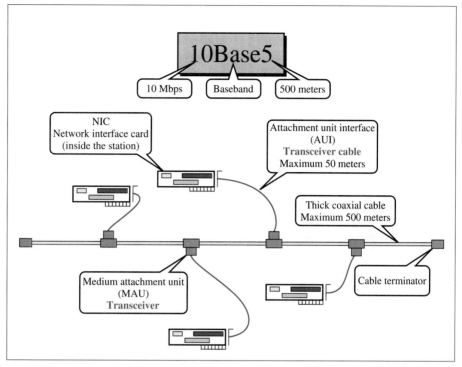

voltages and collisions on the line and may contain a small buffer. It also serves as the connector that attaches a station to the thick coaxial cable itself via a tap (see below).

AUI Cables Each station is linked to its corresponding transceiver by an **attachment unit interface (AUI),** also called a **transceiver cable.** An AUI is a 15-wire cable with plugs that performs the physical layer interface functions between the station and the transceiver. Each end of an AUI terminates in a DB-15 (15-pin) connector. One connector plugs into a port on the NIC, the other into a port on the transceiver. AUIs are restricted to a maximum length of 50 meters, allowing for some flexibility in placement of stations relative to the 10BASE5 backbone cable.

Transceiver Tap Each transceiver contains a connecting mechanism, called a tap because it allows the transceiver to tap into the line at any point. The tap is a thick cable-sized well with a metal spike in the center (see Figure 12.10). The spike is attached to wires inside the transceiver. When the cable is pressed into the well, the spike pierces the jacket and sheathing layers and makes an electrical connection between the transceiver and the cable. This kind of connector is often called a **vampire tap** because it bites the cable.

10BASE2: Thin Ethernet

The second Ethernet implementation defined by the IEEE 802 series is called 10Base2 or **thin Ethernet.**Thin Ethernet (also called **Thinnet, cheapnet, cheapernet,** and thin-wire Ethernet) provides an inexpensive alternative to 10Base5 Ethernet, with the same

Figure 12.10   *Transceiver connection in 10BASE5*

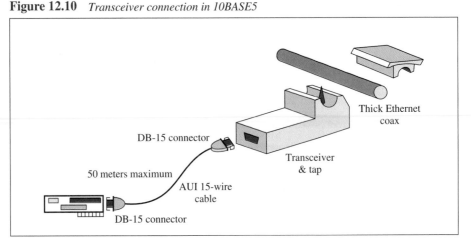

data rate. Like 10Base5, 10Base2 is a bus topology LAN. The advantages of thin Ethernet are reduced cost and ease of installation (the cable is lighter weight and more flexible than that used in thick Ethernet). The disadvantages are shorter range (185 meters as opposed to the 500 meters available with thick Ethernet) and smaller capacity (the thinner cable accommodates fewer stations). In many situations—such as a small number of users on a UNIX-based minicomputer or a network of personal computers and workstations—these disadvantages are irrelevant, and the cost savings make 10Base2 the better choice.

The physical layout of 10Base2 is illustrated in Figure 12.11. The connectors and cables utilized are: NICs, thin coaxial cable, and BNC-T connectors. In this technology,

Figure 12.11   *Topology of 10Base2*

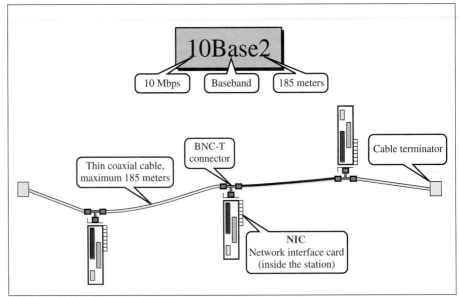

the transceiver circuitry has moved into the NIC, and the transceiver tap has been replaced by a connector that splices the station directly into the cable, eliminating the need for AUI cables.

NIC The NICs in a thin Ethernet system provide all of the same functionality as those in a thick Ethernet system, plus the functions of the transceivers. That means that a 10Base2 NIC not only provides the station with an address but also checks for voltages on the link.

Thin Coaxial Cable The cable required to implement the 10Base2 standard is RG-58. These cables are relatively easy to install and move around (especially inside existing buildings where cabling must be pulled through the walls and ceilings).

BNC-T The BNC-T connector is a T-shaped device with three ports: one for the NIC and one each for the input and output ends of the cable.

10BASE-T: Twisted-Pair Ethernet

The most popular standard defined in the IEEE 802.3 series is 10Base-T (also called **twisted-pair Ethernet**), a star-topology LAN using unshielded twisted pair (UTP) cable instead of coaxial cable. It supports a data rate of 10 Mbps and has a maximum length (hub to station) of 100 meters.

Instead of individual transceivers, 10Base-T Ethernet places all of its networking operations in an intelligent hub with a port for each station. Stations are linked into the hub by four-pair RJ-45 cable (eight-wire unshielded twisted-pair cable) terminating at each end in a male-type connector much like a telephone jack (see Figure 12.12). The hub fans out any transmitted frame to all of its connected stations. Logic in the NIC assures that the only station to open and read a given frame is the station to which that frame is addressed.

Figure 12.12 *10Base-T topology*

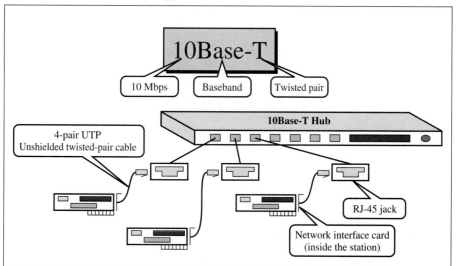

As Figure 12.12 shows, each station contains an NIC. A length of four-pair UTP of not more than 100 meters connects the NIC in the station to the appropriate port in the 10Base-T hub.

The weight and flexibility of the cable and the convenience of the RJ-45 jack and plug make 10Base-T the easiest of the 802.3 LANs to install and reinstall. When a station needs to be replaced, a new station can simply be plugged in.

1Base5: StarLAN

StarLAN is an AT&T product used infrequently today because of its slow speed. At only 1 Mbps, it is 10 times slower than the three standards discussed above.

What is interesting about StarLAN is its range, which can be increased by a mechanism called daisy chaining. Like 10Base-T, StarLAN uses twisted-pair cable to connect stations to a central intelligent hub. Unlike 10Base-T, which requires that each station have its own dedicated cable into the hub, StarLAN allows as many as 10 stations to be linked, each to the next, in a chain in which only the lead device connects to the hub (see Figure 12.13).

Figure 12.13   *1Base5*

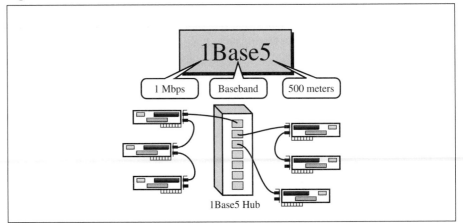

12.3   OTHER ETHERNET NETWORKS

During the last decade, there has been an evolution in Ethernet networks. Several new schemes have been devised to improve the performance and the speed of Ethernet LANs. We will discuss three of these efforts here: *Switched Ethernet, Fast Ethernet,* and *Gigabit Ethernet.*

Switched Ethernet

Switched Ethernet is an attempt to improve the performance of 10Base-T Ethernet. The 10Base-T Ethernet is a shared media network, which means that the entire media is involved in each transmission. This is because the topology, though physically a star, is logically a bus. When a station sends a frame to a hub, the frame is sent out from all ports (interfaces) and every station will receive it. In this situation, only one station can send a frame at any time. If two stations try to send frames simultaneously, there is a collision.

Figure 12.14 shows this situation. Station A is sending a frame to station E. The frame is received by the hub and is sent to every station. All of the cabling in the system is involved in this transmission. Another way to think about this is that one transmission uses the entire capacity of 10 Mbps; if one station uses it, no other station can.

Figure 12.14 *An Ethernet network using a hub*

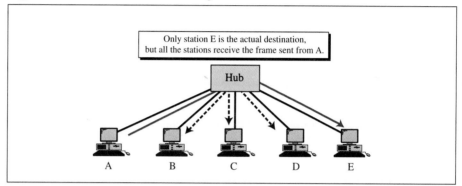

However, if we replace the hub with a switch, a device that can recognize the destination address and can route the frame to the port to which the destination station is connected, the rest of the media are not involved in the transmission process. This means that the switch can receive another frame from another station at the same time and can route this frame to its own final destination. In this way, theoretically, there is no collision.

Using a switch, instead of a hub, we can theoretically increase the capacity of a network with N devices to $N \times 10$ Mbps because 10Base-T uses two pairs of UTP for full-duplex communication.

Figure 12.15 shows a Switched Ethernet. When station A is sending a frame to station E, station B can also send a frame to station D without any collision.

Figure 12.15 *An Ethernet using a switch*

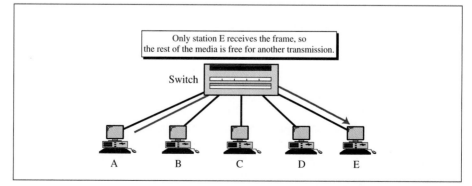

Fast Ethernet

With new applications such as computer-aided design (CAD), image processing, and real-time audio and video being implemented on LANs, there is a need for a LAN with a data rate higher than 10 Mbps. **Fast Ethernet** operates at 100 Mbps.

Fortunately, the way Ethernet was designed, it is easy to increase the speed if the collision domain (the maximum distance data travels between two stations) is decreased.

The collision domain of Ethernet is limited to 2500 meters. This limitation is needed to achieve the data rate of 10 Mbps using the CSMA/CD access method. For CSMA/CD to work, a station should be able to sense the collision before the whole frame is sent on the transmission media. If the whole frame is sent and collision is not detected, the station assumes that everything is fine and destroys the copy of the frame and starts sending the next one.

The minimum size of an Ethernet frame is 72 bytes or 576 bits. To send 576 bits at a data rate of 10 Mbps takes 57.6 microseconds (576 bits/10 Mbps = 57.6). Before the last bit is sent, the first bit must have reached the end of the domain, and, if there is a collision, it must be sensed by the sender. This implies that during the time that the sender transmits 576 bits, the collision must be detected. In other words, the collision must be detected during these 57.6 microseconds. This time is sufficient to allow a signal to make a round-trip of 5000 meters at a propagation speed in a typical transmission medium such as twisted-pair cable.

To increase the data rate without changing the minimum size of a frame, we decrease the round-trip time. With the speed of 100 Mbps, the round-trip time reduces to 5.76 microseconds (576 bits/100 Mbps). This means that the collision domain must be decreased 10 times, from 2500 meters to 250 meters. This decrease is not a problem because LANs today connect desktop computers that are not more than 50 to 100 meters away from the central hub. This means the collision domain is between 100 and 200 meters.

Fast Ethernet is a version of Ethernet with a 100 Mbps data rate. There is no change in the frame format. There is no change in the access method. The only two changes in the MAC layer are the data rate and the collision domain. The data rate is increased by a factor of 10; the collision domain is decreased by a factor of 10.

In the physical layer, the specification developed for Fast Ethernet is a star topology similar to 10Base-T; however, to match the physical layer to different resources available, IEEE has designed two categories of Fast Ethernet: 100Base-X and 100Base-T4. The first uses two cables between the station and the hub; the second uses four. 100Base-X itself is divided into two types: 100Base-TX and 100Base-FX (see Figure 12.16).

100Base-TX

The **100Base-TX** design uses two category 5 unshielded twisted-pair (UTP) or two shielded twisted-pair (STP) cables to connect a station to the hub. One pair is used to carry frames from the station to the hub and the other to carry frames from the hub to the station. The encoding is 4B/5B to handle the 100 Mbps; the signaling is NRZ-I. The

Figure 12.16   *Categories of Fast Ethernet implementations*

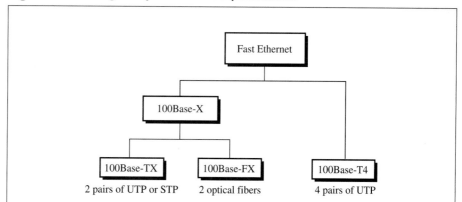
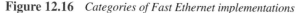

distance between the station and the hub (or switch) should be less than 100 meters (see Figure 12.17).

Figure 12.17   *100Base-TX implementation*

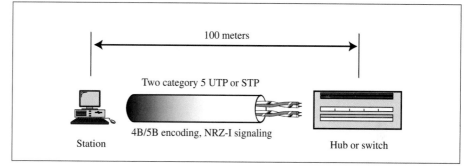

100Base-FX

The **100Base-FX** design uses two optical fibers, one to carry frames from the station to the hub and the other from the hub to the station. The encoding is 4B/5B and signaling is NRZ-I. The distance between the station and the hub (or switch) should be less than 2000 meters (see Figure 12.18).

100Base-T4

The **100Base-T4** scheme was designed in an effort to avoid rewiring. It requires four pairs of category 3 (voice grade) UTP that are already available for telephone service inside most buildings. Two of the four pairs are bidirectional; the other two are unidirectional. This means that in each direction, three pairs are used at the same time to carry data. Because a 100-Mbps data rate cannot be handled by a voice-grade UTP, the specification splits the 100-Mbps flow of data into three 33.66-Mbps flows. To reduce the baud rate of the transmission, a method called 8B/6T (eight binary/six ternary) is used in which each block of eight bits is transformed into six bauds of three voltage levels (positive, negative, and zero). Figure 12.19 shows the scheme and an encoding example.

Figure 12.18   *100Base-FX*

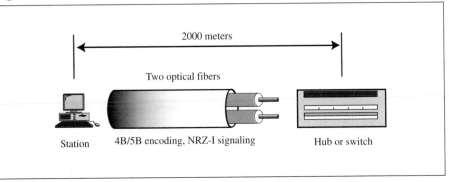

2000 meters

Two optical fibers

Station   4B/5B encoding, NRZ-I signaling   Hub or switch

Figure 12.19   *100Base-T4*

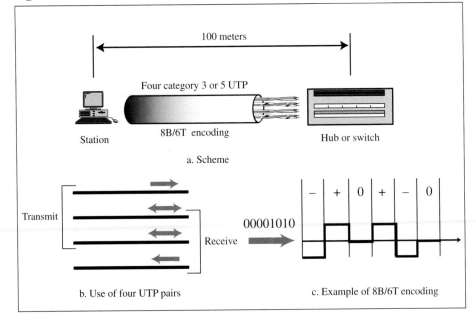

100 meters

Four category 3 or 5 UTP

Station   8B/6T encoding   Hub or switch

a. Scheme

Transmit

Receive

00001010

| − | + | 0 | + | − | 0 |

b. Use of four UTP pairs   c. Example of 8B/6T encoding

Gigabit Ethernet

The migration from 10 Mbps to 100 Mbps encouraged the IEEE 802.3 committee to design **Gigabit Ethernet,** which has a data rate of 1000 Mbps or 1 Gbps. The strategy is the same; the MAC layer and the access method remain the same, but the collision domain is reduced. The physical layer—the transmission media and the encoding system—however, changes. Gigabit Ethernet is mainly designed to use optical fiber, although the protocol does not eliminate the use of twisted pair cables. Gigabit Ethernet usually serves as a backbone to connect Fast Ethernet networks. An example is shown in Figure 12.20.

Figure 12.20 *Use of Gigabit Ethernet*

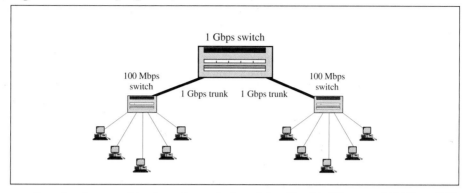

Four implementations have been designed for Gigabit Ethernet: 1000Base-LX, 1000Base-SX, 1000Base-CX, and 1000Base-T. The encoding is 8B/10B, which means a group of 8 binary bits are encoded into a group of 10 binary bits. Table 12.1 shows the features of the four implementations.

Table 12.1 *Comparison between the Gigabit Ethernet implementations*

Feature	1000Base-SX	1000Base-LX	1000Base-CX	1000Base-T
Medium	Optical fiber (multimode)	Optical fiber (multi- or single-mode)	STP	UTP
Signal	Short-wave laser	Long-wave laser	Electrical	Electrical
Max. distance	550 m	550 m (multimode) 5000 m (single mode)	25 m	25 m

12.4 TOKEN BUS

Local area networks have a direct application in factory automation and process control, where the nodes are computers controlling the manufacturing process. In this type of application, real-time processing with minimum delay is needed. Processing must occur at the same speed as the objects moving along the assembly line. Ethernet (IEEE 802.3) is not a suitable protocol for this purpose because the number of collisions is not predictable and the delay in sending data from the control center to the computers along the assembly line is not a fixed value. **Token Ring (IEEE 802.5;** see next section) is also not a suitable protocol because an assembly line resembles a bus topology and not a ring. **Token Bus (IEEE 802.4)** combines features of Ethernet and Token Ring. It combines the physical configuration of Ethernet (a bus topology) and the collision-free (predictable delay) feature of Token Ring. Token Bus is a physical bus that operates as a logical ring using **tokens.**

Stations are logically organized into a ring. A token is passed among stations. If a station wants to send data, it must wait and capture the token. However, like Ethernet, stations communicate via a common bus.

Token Bus is limited to factory automation and process control and has no commercial application in data communication. Also, the details of the operation are very involved. For these two reasons, we will not discuss this protocol further.

12.5   TOKEN RING

As mentioned previously, the network access mechanism used by Ethernet (CSMA/CD) is not infallible and may result in collisions. Stations may attempt to send data multiple times before a transmission makes it onto the link. This redundancy may create delays of indeterminable length if the traffic is heavy. There is no way to predict either the occurrence of collisions or the delays produced by multiple stations attempting to capture the link at the same time.

Token Ring resolves this uncertainty by requiring that stations take turns sending data. Each station may transmit only during its turn and may send only one frame during each turn. The mechanism that coordinates this rotation is called **token passing.** A token is a simple placeholder frame that is passed from station to station around the ring. A station may send data only when it has possession of the token.

Token Ring allows each station to send one frame per turn.

Access Method: Token Passing

Token passing is illustrated in Figure 12.21. Whenever the network is unoccupied, it circulates a simple three-byte token. This token is passed from NIC to NIC in sequence until it encounters a station with data to send. That station waits for the token to enter its network board. If the token is free, the station may then send a data frame. It keeps the token and sets a bit inside its NIC as a reminder that it has done so, then sends its one data frame.

This data frame proceeds around the ring, being regenerated by each station. Each intermediate station examines the destination address, finds that the frame is addressed to another station, and relays it to its neighbor. The intended recipient recognizes its own address, copies the message, checks for errors, and changes four bits in the last byte of the frame to indicate address recognized and frame copied. The full packet then continues around the ring until it returns to the station that sent it.

The sender receives the frame and recognizes itself in the source address field. It then examines the address-recognized bits. If they are set, it knows the frame was received. The sender then discards the used data frame and releases the token back to the ring.

Priority and Reservation

Generally, once a token has been released, the next station on the ring with data to send has the right to take charge of the ring. However, in the IEEE 802.5 model, another

Figure 12.21 *Token passing*

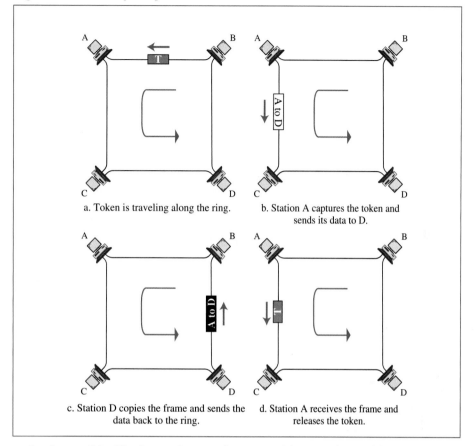

a. Token is traveling along the ring.

b. Station A captures the token and sends its data to D.

c. Station D copies the frame and sends the data back to the ring.

d. Station A receives the frame and releases the token.

option is possible. The busy token can be reserved by a station waiting to transmit, regardless of that station's location on the ring. Each station has a priority code. As a frame passes by, a station waiting to transmit may reserve the next open token by entering its priority code in the **access control (AC) field** of the token or data frame (discussed later in this section). A station with a higher priority may remove a lower priority reservation and replace it with its own. Among stations of equal priority, the process is first-come, first-served. Through this mechanism, the station holding the reservation gets the opportunity to transmit as soon as the token is free, whether or not it comes next physically on the ring.

Time Limits

To keep traffic moving, Token Ring imposes a time limit on any station wanting to use the ring. A starting delimiter (the first field of either a token or data frame) must reach each station within a specified interval (usually 10 milliseconds). In other words, each station expects to receive frames within regular time intervals (it receives a frame and expects to receive the next frame within a specified period).

Monitor Stations

Several problems may occur to disrupt the operation of a Token Ring network. In one scenario, a station may neglect to retransmit a token or a token may be destroyed by noise, in which case there is no token on the ring and no station may send data. In another scenario, a sending station may neglect to remove its used data frame from the ring or may not release the token once its turn has ended.

To handle these situations, one station on the ring is designated as a **monitor station.** The monitor sets a timer each time the token passes. If the token does not reappear in the allotted time, it is presumed to be lost and the monitor generates a new token and introduces it to the ring. The monitor guards against perpetually recirculating data frames by setting a bit in the AC field of each frame. As a frame passes, the monitor checks the status field. If the status bit has been set, it knows that the packet has already been around the ring and should have been discarded. The monitor then destroys the frame and puts a token onto the ring. If the monitor fails, a second station, designated as back-up, takes over.

Addressing

Token Ring uses a six-byte address, which is imprinted on the NIC card similar to Ethernet addresses.

Electrical Specification

Signaling

Token Ring uses differential Manchester encoding (see Chapter 5).

Data Rate

Token Ring supports data rates of up to 16 Mbps. (The original specification was 4 Mbps.)

Frame Formats

The Token Ring protocol specifies three types of frames: data/command, token, and **abort.** The token and abort frames are both truncated data/command frames (see Figure 12.22).

Data/Command Frame

In Token Ring, the data/command frame is the only one of the three types of frames that can carry a PDU and is the only one addressed to a specific destination rather than being available to the ring at large. This frame can carry either the user data or the management commands. The nine fields of the frame are start delimiter (SD), access control (AC), frame control (FC), destination address (DA), source address (SA), 802.2 PDU frame, CRC, end delimiter (ED), and frame status (FS).

Figure 12.22 *Token Ring frame*

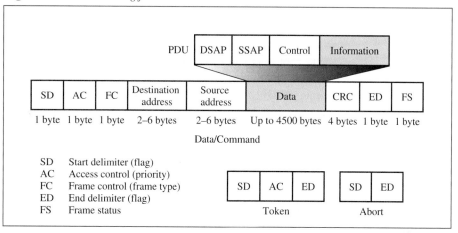

- **Start delimiter (SD).** The first field of the data/command frame, SD, is one byte long and is used to alert the receiving station to the arrival of a frame as well as to allow it to synchronize its retrieval timing. It is equivalent to the flag field in HDLC. Figure 12.23 shows the format of the SD. The J and K violations are created at the physical layer and are included in every start delimiter to ensure transparency in the data field. In this way, an SD bit pattern that appears in the data field cannot be taken for the start of a new frame. These violations are created by changing the encoding pattern for the duration of the bit. As you remember, in differential Manchester, each bit may have two transitions: one at the beginning and another at the middle. In the J violation, both transitions are canceled. In the K violation, the middle transition is canceled.

Figure 12.23 *Data frame fields*

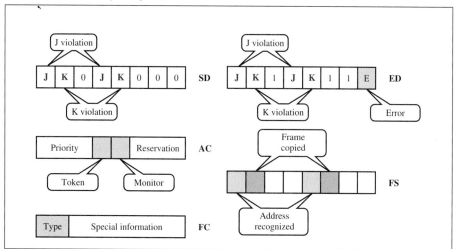

- **Access control (AC).** The AC field is one byte long and includes four subfields (see Figure 12.23). The first three bits are the priority field. The fourth bit is called the token bit and is set to indicate that the frame is a data/command frame rather than a token or an abort frame. The token bit is followed by a monitor bit. Finally, the last three bits are a reservation field that can be set by stations wishing to reserve access to the ring.
- **Frame control (FC).** The FC field is one byte long and contains two fields (see Figure 12.23). The first is a one-bit field used to indicate the type of information contained in the PDU (whether it is control information or data). The second uses the remaining seven bits of the byte and contains information used by the Token Ring logic (e.g., how to use the information in the AC field).
- **Destination address (DA).** The two- to six-byte DA field contains the physical address of the frame's next destination. If its ultimate destination is another network, the DA is the address of the router to the next LAN on its path. If its ultimate destination is on the current LAN, the DA is the physical address of the destination station.
- **Source address (SA).** The SA field is also two to six bytes long and contains the physical address of the sending station. If the ultimate destination of the packet is a station on the same network as the originating station, the SA is that of the originating station. If the packet has been routed from another LAN, the SA is the physical address of the most recent router.
- **Data.** The sixth field, data, is allotted 4500 bytes and contains the PDU. A Token Ring frame does not include a PDU length or type field.
- **CRC.** The CRC field is four bytes long and contains a CRC-32 error detection sequence.
- **End delimiter (ED).** The ED is a second flag field of one byte and indicates the end of the sender's data and control information. Like the SD, it is changed at the physical layer to include J and K violations. These violations are necessary to ensure that a bit sequence in the data field cannot be mistaken for an ED by the receiver (see Figure 12.23).
- **Frame status (FS).** The last byte of the frame is the FS field. It can be set by the receiver to indicate that the frame has been read, or by the monitor to indicate that the frame has already been around the ring. This field is not an acknowledgment, but it does tell the sender that the receiving station has copied the frame, which can now be discarded. Figure 12.23 shows the format of an FS field. As you can see, it contains two one-bit pieces of information: address recognized and frame copied. These bits come at the beginning of the field and are repeated in the fifth and sixth bits. This repetition is for the purpose of preventing errors and is necessary because the field contains information inserted after the frame leaves the sending station. It therefore cannot be included in the CRC and so has no error checking performed on it.

Token Frame

Because a token is really a placeholder and reservation frame, it includes only three fields: the SD, AC, and ED. The SD indicates that a frame is coming. The AC indicates that the frame is a token and includes the priority and reservation fields. The ED indicates the end of the frame.

Abort Frame

An abort frame carries no information at all—just starting and ending delimiters. It can be generated either by the sender to stop its own transmission (for whatever reason) or by the monitor to purge an old transmission from the line.

Implementation

Ring

The ring in a Token Ring consists of a series of 150-ohm, shielded twisted-pair sections linking each station to its immediate neighbors (see Figure 12.24). Each section connects an output port on one station to an input port on the next, creating a ring with unidirectional traffic flow. The output from the final station connects to the input of the first to complete the ring. A frame is passed to each station in sequence, where it is examined, regenerated, and then sent on to the next station.

> Each station in the Token Ring regenerates the frame.

Figure 12.24   *Token Ring*

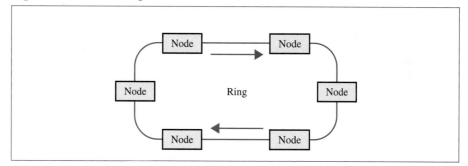

Switch

As Figure 12.24 shows, configuring the network as a ring introduces a potential problem: One disabled or disconnected node could stop the flow of traffic around the entire network. To solve this problem, each station is connected to an automatic switch. This switch can bypass an inactive station. While a station is disabled, the switch closes the ring without it. When the station comes on, a signal sent by the NIC moves the switch and brings the station into the ring (see Figure 12.25).

Each station's NIC has a pair of input and output ports combined in a nine-pin connector. A nine-wire cable connects the NIC to the switch. Of these wires, four are used for data and the remaining five are used to control the switch (to include or bypass a station).

Figure 12.25 *Token Ring switch*

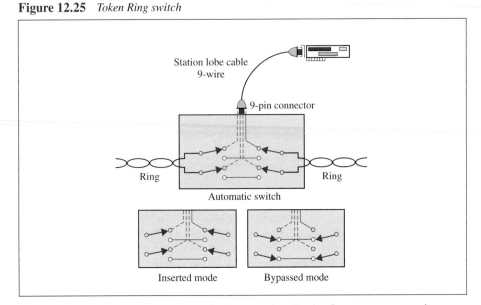

Figure 12.25 shows the two switching modes. In the first part, connections are completed to the station, thereby inserting it into the ring. In the second part, an alternate pair of connections is completed to bypass the station.

Multistation Access Unit (MAU)

For practical purposes, individual automatic switches are combined into a hub called a **multistation access unit (MAU);** see Figure 12.26. One MAU can support up to eight stations. Looked at from the outside, this system looks like a star with the MAU at the middle. But, as Figure 12.26 shows, it is in fact a ring.

Figure 12.26 *MAU*

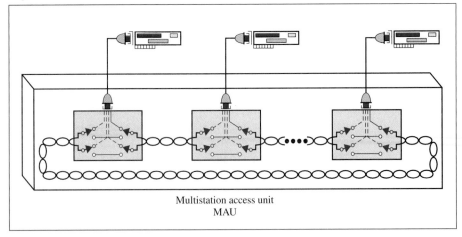

12.6   FDDI

Fiber distributed data interface (FDDI) is a local area network protocol standardized by ANSI and the ITU-T (ITU-T X.3). It supports data rates of 100 Mbps and provides a high-speed alternative to Ethernet and Token Ring. When FDDI was designed, speeds of 100 Mbps required fiber-optic cable. Today, however, comparable speeds are available using copper cable. The copper version of FDDI is known as CDDI.

Access Method: Token Passing

In FDDI, access is limited by time. A station may send as many frames as it can within its allotted access period, with the proviso that real-time data be sent first.

To implement this access mechanism, FDDI differentiates between two types of data frames: synchronous and asynchronous. *Synchronous* here refers to information that is real-time, while *asynchronous* refers to information that is not. These frames are usually called S-frames and A-frames.

Each station that captures the token is required to send S-frames first. In fact, it must send its S-frames whether or not its time allotment has run out (see below). Any remaining time may then be used to send A-frames. To understand how this mechanism ensures fair and timely link access, it is necessary to understand the FDDI time registers and timers.

Time Registers

FDDI defines three time registers to control circulation of the token and distribute link-access opportunities among the nodes equitably. Values are set when the ring is initialized and do not vary in the course of operation. The registers are called synchronous allocation (SA), target token rotation time (TTRT), and absolute maximum time (AMT).

Synchronous Allocation (SA)   The SA register indicates the length of time allowed each station for sending synchronous data. This value is different for each station and is negotiated during initialization of the ring.

Target Token Rotation Time (TTRT)   The TTRT register indicates the average time required for a token to circulate around the ring exactly once (the elapsed time between a token's arrival at a given station and its next arrival at the same station). Because it is an average, the actual time of any rotation may be greater or less than this value.

Absolute Maximum Time (AMT)   The AMT register holds a value equal to twice the TTRT. A token may not take longer than this time to make one rotation of the ring. If it does, some station or stations are monopolizing the network and the ring must be reinitialized.

Timers

Each station contains a set of timers that enable it to compare actual timings with the values contained in the registers. Timers can be set and reset, and their values decremented or incremented at a rate set by the system clock. The two timers used by FDDI are called the token rotation timer (TRT) and token holding timer (THT).

Token Rotation Timer (TRT)   The TRT runs continuously and measures the actual time taken by the token to complete a cycle. In our implementation, we use an incrementing TRT for simplicity, although some implementations may use a decrementing timer.

Token Holding Timer (THT)   The THT begins running as soon as the token is received. Its function is to show how much time remains for sending asynchronous frames once the synchronous frames have been sent. In our implementation, we use a decrementing THT for simplicity, although some implementations may use an incrementing one. In addition, we allow the value of THT to become negative (to make the concept easier to understand) although a real timer may stay at zero.

Station Procedure

When a token arrives, each station follows this procedure:

1. THT is set to the difference between TTRT and TRT (THT = TTRT – TRT).
2. TRT is reset to zero (TRT = 0).
3. The station sends its synchronous data.
4. The station sends asynchronous data as long as the value of THT is positive.

An Example

Figure 12.27 and Table 12.2 show how FDDI access works. We have simplified this example by showing only four stations and making the following assumptions: the TTRT is 30 time units; the time required for the token to go from one station to another is 1 time unit; each station is allowed to send two synchronous data units per turn; and each station has a lot of asynchronous data to send (waiting in buffers).

Figure 12.27   *FDDI operation*

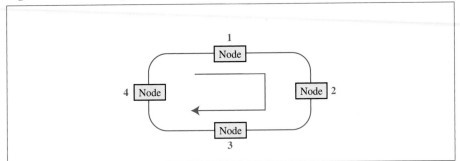

In round 0, the token travels from station to station; each station sets its TRT timer to 0. No data transfer occurs in this round.

In round 1, station 1 receives the token at time 4; its TRT is now 4 (in round 0, TRT was 0; it took 4 time units for the token to return). THT is set to 26 (THT = TTRT – TRT = 30 – 4). TRT is reset to 0. Now station 1 sends 2 data unit equivalents of synchronous data. THT is decremented to 24 (26 – 2), so station 1 can send 24 data unit equivalents of asynchronous data.

In the same round, station 2 follows the same procedure. The token arriving time is now 31 because the token arrived at station 1 at time 4, it was held 26 time units (2 for synchronous data and 24 for asynchronous data) and it took 1 time unit for the token to travel between stations $(4 + 26 + 1 = 31)$.

Note that the asynchronous allocation time is almost equally distributed between stations. In round 1, station 1 has the opportunity to send 24 time unit equivalents of asynchronous data, but the other stations did not have such an opportunity. However, in rounds 2, 3, and 4, station 1 was deprived of this privilege, but other stations (one in each round) had the opportunity to send. In round 2, station 2 sent 16; in round 3, station 3 sent 16; and in round 4, station 4 sent 16.

Table 12.2

Round	Station 1	Station 2	Station 3	Station 4
0	Arriving Time: 0 TRT = 0	Arriving Time: 1 TRT = 0	Arriving Time: 2 TRT = 0	Arriving Time: 3 TRT = 0
1	Arriving Time: 4 TRT is now 4 THT = 30 − 4 = 26 **TRT = 0** Syn Data: 2 THT is now 24 **Asyn Data: 24**	Arriving Time: 31 TRT is now 30 THT = 30 − 30 = 0 **TRT = 0** Syn Data: 2 THT is now −2 Asyn Data: 0	Arriving Time: 34 TRT is now 32 THT = 30 − 32 = −2 **TRT = 0** Syn Data: 2 THT is now −4 Asyn Data: 0	Arriving Time: 37 TRT is now 34 THT = 30 − 34 = −4 **TRT = 0** Syn Data: 2 THT is now −6 Asyn Data: 0
2	Arriving Time: 40 TRT is now 36 THT = 30 − 36 = −6 **TRT = 0** Syn Data: 2 THT is now −8 Asyn Data: 0	Arriving Time: 43 TRT is now 12 THT = 30 − 12 = 18 **TRT = 0** Syn Data: 2 THT is now 16 **Asyn Data: 16**	Arriving Time: 62 TRT is now 28 THT = 30 − 28 = 2 **TRT = 0** Syn Data: 2 THT is now 0 Asyn Data: 0	Arriving Time: 65 TRT is now 28 THT = 30 − 28 = 2 **TRT = 0** Syn Data: 2 THT is now 0 Asyn Data: 0
3	Arriving Time: 68 TRT is now 28 THT = 30 − 28 = 2 **TRT = 0** Syn Data: 2 THT is now 0 Asyn Data: 0	Arriving Time: 71 TRT is now 28 THT = 30 − 28 = 2 **TRT = 0** Syn Data: 2 THT is now 0 Asyn Data: 0	Arriving Time: 74 TRT is now 12 THT = 30 − 12 = 18 **TRT = 0** Syn Data: 2 THT is now 16 **Asyn Data: 16**	Arriving Time: 93 TRT is now 28 THT = 30 − 28 = 2 **TRT = 0** Syn Data: 2 THT is now 0 Asyn Data: 0
4	Arriving Time: 96 TRT is now 28 THT = 30 − 28 = 2 **TRT = 0** Syn Data: 2 THT is now 0 Asyn Data: 0	Arriving Time: 99 TRT is now 28 THT = 30 − 28 = 2 **TRT = 0** Syn Data: 2 THT is now 0 Asyn Data: 0	Arriving Time: 102 TRT is now 28 THT = 30 − 28 = 2 **TRT = 0** Syn Data: 2 THT is now 0 Asyn Data: 0	Arriving Time: 105 TRT is now 12 THT = 30 − 12 = 18 **TRT = 0** Syn Data: 2 THT is now 16 **Asyn Data: 16**

Addressing

FDDI uses a six-byte address, which is imprinted on the NIC card similar to Ethernet addresses.

Electrical Specification

Signaling (Physical Layer)

FDDI uses a special encoding mechanism called four bits/five bits (4B/5B). In this system, each four-bit segment of data is replaced by a five-bit code before being encoded in NRZ-I (refer back to Figure 5.6). The NRZ-I used here inverts on the 1 (see Figure 12.28).

Figure 12.28 *Encoding*

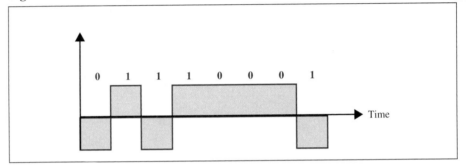

The reason for this extra encoding step is that, although NRZ-I provides adequate synchronization under average circumstances, sender and receiver may go out of synchronization anytime the data includes a long sequence of 0s. 4B/5B encoding transforms each four-bit data segment into a five-bit unit that contains no more than two consecutive 0s. Each of the 16 possible four-bit patterns is assigned a five-bit pattern to represent it. These five-bit patterns have been carefully selected so that even sequential data units cannot result in sequences of more than three 0s (none of the five-bit patterns start with more than one 0 or end with more than two 0s); see Table 12.3.

Table 12.3 *4B/5B encoding*

Data Sequence	Encoded Sequence	Data Sequence	Encoded Sequence
0000	11110	1000	10010
0001	01001	1001	10011
0010	10100	1010	10110
0011	10101	1011	10111
0100	01010	1100	11010
0101	01011	1101	11011
0110	01110	1110	11100
0111	01111	1111	11101

Five-bit codes that have not been assigned to represent a four-bit counterpart are used for control (see Table 12.4). The SD field contains the J and K codes, and the

ED field contains the symbols TT. To guarantee that these control codes do not endanger synchronization or transparency, the designers specify bit patterns that can never occur in the data field. In addition, their order is controlled to limit the number of sequential bit patterns possible. A K always follows a J, and an H is never followed by an R.

Table 12.4   *4B/5B control symbols*

Control Symbol	Encoded Sequence
Q (Quiet)	00000
I (Idle)	11111
H (Halt)	00100
J (Used in start delimiter)	11000
K (Used in start delimiter)	10001
T (Used in end delimiter)	01101
S (Set)	11001
R (Reset)	00111

Data Rate

FDDI supports data rates up to 100 Mbps.

Frame Format

The FDDI standard divides transmission functions into four protocols: physical medium dependent (PMD), physical (PHY), media access control (MAC), and logical link control (LLC). These protocols correspond to the physical and data link layers of the OSI model (see Figure 12.29). In addition, the standard specifies a fifth protocol (used for station management), details of which are beyond the scope of this book.

Figure 12.29   *FDDI layers*

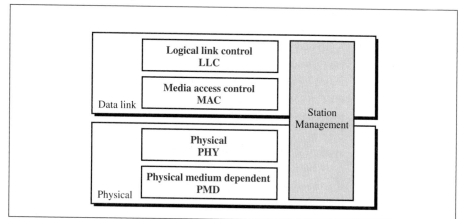

Logical Link Control

The LLC layer is similar to that defined in the IEEE 802.2 protocols.

Media Access Control

The FDDI MAC layer is almost identical to that defined for Token Ring. However, although the functions are similar, the FDDI MAC frame itself is different enough to warrant an independent discussion of each field (see Figure 12.30).

Figure 12.30 *FDDI frame types*

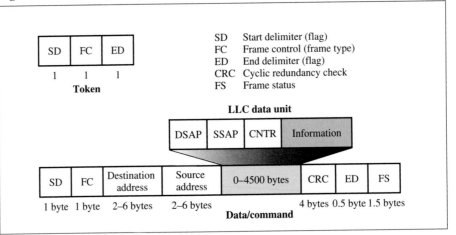

Each frame is preceded by 16 idle symbols (1111), for a total of 64 bits, to initialize clock synchronization with the receiver.

Frame Fields There are eight fields in the FDDI frame:

- **Start delimiter (SD).** The first byte of the field is the frame's starting flag. As in Token Ring, these bits are replaced in the physical layer by the control codes (violations) J and K (the five-bit sequences used to represent J and K are shown in Table 12.4).
- **Frame control (FC).** The second byte of the frame identifies the frame type.
- **Addresses.** The next two fields are the destination and source addresses. Each address consists of two to six bytes.
- **Data.** Each data frame can carry up to 4500 bytes of data.
- **CRC.** FDDI uses the standard IEEE four-byte cyclic redundancy check.
- **End delimiter (ED).** This field consists of half a byte in the data frame or a full byte in the token frame. It is changed in the physical layer with one T violation symbol in the data/command frame or two T symbols in the token frame. (The code for the T symbol is shown Table 12.4.)
- **Frame status (FS).** The FDDI FS field is similar to that of Token Ring. It is included only in the data/command frame and consists of 1.5 bytes.

Implementation: Physical Medium Dependent (PMD) Layer

The physical medium dependent (PMD) layer defines the required connections and electronic components. Specifications for this layer depend on whether the transmission medium used is fiber-optic or copper cable.

Dual Ring

FDDI is implemented as a dual ring (see Figure 12.31). In most cases, data transmission is confined to the primary ring. The secondary ring is provided in case the primary fails.

Figure 12.31   *FDDI ring*

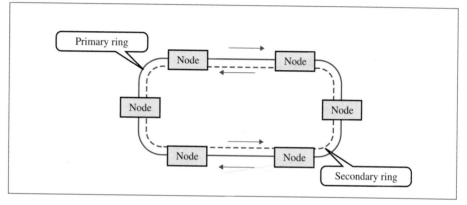

The secondary ring makes FDDI self-healing. Whenever a problem occurs on the primary ring, the secondary can be activated to complete data circuits and maintain service (see Figure 12.32).

Figure 12.32   *FDDI ring after a failure*

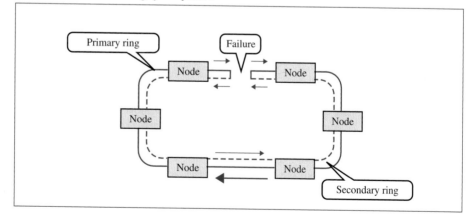

Nodes connect to one or both rings using a **media interface connector (MIC)** that can be either male or female depending on the requirements of the station.

Nodes

FDDI defines three types of nodes: dual attachment station (DAS), single attachment station (SAS), and dual attachment concentrator (DAC); see Figure 12.33.

Figure 12.33   *Node connections*

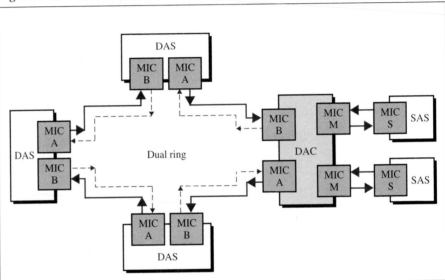

DAS   A **dual attachment station (DAS)** has two MICs (called MIC A and MIC B) and connects to both rings. To do so requires an expensive NIC with two inputs and two outputs. The connection to both rings gives it improved reliability and throughput. These improvements, however, are predicated on the stations remaining on. Faults are bypassed by a station's making a wrap connection from the primary ring to the secondary to switch signals from one input to another output. However, for DAS stations to make this switch, they must be active (turned on).

SAS   Most workstations, servers, and minicomputers attach to the ring in **single attachment station (SAS)** mode. An SAS has only one MIC (called MIC S) and therefore can connect only to one ring. Robustness is achieved by connecting SASs to intermediate nodes, called **dual attachment concentrators (DACs),** rather than to the FDDI ring directly. This configuration allows each workstation to operate through a simple NIC with only one input and one output. The concentrator (DAC) provides the connection to the dual ring. Faulty stations can be turned off and bypassed to keep the ring alive (see below).

DAC   As mentioned above, a dual attachment concentrator (DAC) connects an SAS to the dual ring. It provides wrapping (diverting traffic from one ring to the other to bypass a failure) as well as control functions. It uses MIC M to connect to an SAS.

12.7   COMPARISON

Table 12.5 compares the features of the three LANs discussed above. Ethernet is good for low-level loads but collapses as the load increases due to collisions and retransmissions. Token Ring and FDDI perform equally well at low- and high-level loads.

Table 12.5   *LAN comparison*

Network	Access Method	Signaling	Data Rate	Error Control
Ethernet	CSMA/CD	Manchester	1, 10 Mbps	No
Fast Ethernet	CSMA/CD	Several	100 Mbps	No
Gigabit Ethernet	CSMA/CD	Several	1 Gbps	No
Token Ring	Token passing	Differential Manchester	4, 16 Mbps	Yes
FDDI	Token passing	4B/5B, NRZ-I	100 Mbps	Yes

12.8   KEY TERMS AND CONCEPTS

1Base5

10Base-T

10Base2

10Base5

100Base-FX

100Base-T

100Base-T4

100Base-TX

abort

access control (AC) field

attachment unit interface (AUI)

baseband

broadband

carrier sense multiple access (CSMA)

carrier sense multiple access with collision detection (CSMA/CD)

cheapernet

cheapnet

collision

contention

destination address (DA)

dual attachment concentrator (DAC)

dual attachment station (DAS)

Ethernet

Fast Ethernet

fiber distributed data interface (FDDI)

Gigabit Ethernet

IEEE 802.1	protocol data unit (PDU)
IEEE 802.2	single attachment station (SAS)
IEEE 802.3	source address (SA)
IEEE 802.4	starLAN
IEEE 802.5	start frame delimiter (SFD)
IEEE Project 802	Switched Ethernet
internetworking	thick Ethernet
local area network (LAN)	Thicknet
logical link control (LLC)	thin Ethernet
media interface connector (MIC)	Thinnet
medium access control (MAC)	token
medium attachment unit (MAU)	Token Bus
monitor station	token passing
multiple access (MA)	Token Ring
multistation access unit (MAU)	transceiver
network interface card (NIC)	transceiver cable
preamble	twisted-pair Ethernet
Project 802	vampire tap

12.9   SUMMARY

- The purpose of the IEEE's Project 802 is to set up standards so that LAN equipment manufactured by different companies is compatible.
- Project 802 divides the data link layer into sublayers:
  a. Logical link control (LLC).
  b. Medium access control (MAC).

- The LLC is the upper sublayer and is the same for all LANs. Its functions include flow control and error detection. Logical addresses, control information, and data from the upper layers are packaged into a packet called the protocol data unit (PDU).

- The MAC sublayer coordinates the data link tasks within a specific LAN.

- The MAC sublayer is manufacturer-specific and dependent on the LAN type.

- Three LANs specified by Project 802 are the following:
  a. Ethernet (802.3).
  b. Token Bus (802.4).
  c. Token Ring (802.5).

- CSMA/CD operates as follows: Any station may listen to the line to determine if the line is clear. If clear, transmission can commence. If a collision occurs, transmission stops and the process is repeated.

- Switched Ethernet, Fast Ethernet, and Gigabit Ethernet are Ethernet implementations with improved performance and data rates.

- In Switched Ethernet, a switch that can direct a transmission to just the destination replaces the hub.

- In Fast Ethernet, the data rate is increased to 100 Mbps, but the collision domain is reduced to 250 meters.

- The four implementations of Fast Ethernet differ in media type, number of cables, collision domain, and encoding method.

- Gigabit Ethernet, with a 1-Gbps data rate, serves as a backbone to connecting Fast Ethernet networks.

- The four implementations of Gigabit Ethernet differ in signal source, media type, and collision domain.

- Token Bus (IEEE 802.4), used in factory automation and process control, combines features of Ethernet and Token Ring.

- Token Ring (IEEE 802.5) employs token passing as its method of transmission initiation.

- Switches in Token Ring can be encased in a multistation access unit (MAU).

- Capture of a frame called the token in Token Ring entitles a station to send one frame of data.

- In Token Ring, a frame travels from node to node, getting regenerated at each node, until the destination is reached.

- Fiber distributed data interface (FDDI) is a LAN protocol using optical fiber as a medium, with a 100-Mbps data rate.

- FDDI consists of a primary ring for data transmission and a secondary ring that assists in failure situations.

- A media interface connector (MIC) is a device that connects the dual FDDI ring to a node.

- A dual attachment station (DAS) is a node with 2 MICs.

- A single attachment station (SAS) is a node with one MIC. An SAS must attach to the FDDI rings via a dual attachment concentrator (DAC).

■ FDDI specifies protocols for the physical and data link layers.

■ The FDDI data link layer consists of an LLC sublayer and an MAC sublayer. The former is similar to that specified in IEEE Project 802.2. The latter is similar to that of the Token Ring protocol (802.5).

■ In the physical layer, FDDI uses 4B/5B encoding, a process that converts four bits to five bits.

■ 4B/5B encoding ensures that there cannot be a data sequence of more than three 0s transmitted across media in FDDI protocol. This takes care of the bit synchronization problems arising from long strings of 0s in NRZ-I encoding.

■ In FDDI protocol, token possession is controlled by three time values and two timers.

12.10   PRACTICE SET

Review Questions

1. Define and explain the data link layer in IEEE Project 802. Why is this layer divided into sublayers?
2. Explain CSMA/CD and its use. What part of the 802 project uses CSMA/CD?
3. Compare and contrast the SSAP and DSAP on the PDU with the source and destination address of the MAC frame.
4. Explain why there are no physical address, flag, or CRC fields in a PDU.
5. What does Project 802 have to do with the physical layer of the OSI model?
6. Contrast the IEEE Project 802.3 frame with the HDLC I-frame.
7. Contrast the IEEE Project 802.5 data/command frame with the HDLC I-frame.
8. What is the difference between baseband and broadband?
9. Discuss the placement of the transceiver in 10Base5, 10Base2, and 10Base-T standards.
10. What is a collision?
11. What are the advantages of FDDI over a basic Token Ring?
12. Why is there no AC field in the 802.3 frame?
13. Explain the mechanism whereby an SAS is able to access both the primary and secondary rings.
14. How does 4B/5B encoding guarantee that there will be no sequences of four or more 0s in the data field?
15. What types of transmission media are used in LANs?
16. How does a Token Ring LAN operate?
17. Suppose there is heavy traffic on both a CSMA/CD LAN and a Token Ring LAN. A station on which system is more likely to wait longer to send a frame? Why?
18. Why should there be fewer collisions on a Switched Ethernet network compared to a traditional Ethernet?

19. How is the collision domain related to the data rate in Ethernet networks?

20. Why is the maximum distance between the switch or hub and a station greater for 100Base-FX than for 100Base-TX?

21. Compare the data transmission rates for traditional Ethernet, Fast Ethernet, and Gigabit Ethernet.

Multiple Choice Questions

22. In CSMA/CD, the number of collisions is _____ that in MA.
    a. greater than
    b. less than
    c. equal to
    d. twice

23. In Ethernet, the source address field in the MAC frame is _____ address.
    a. the original sender's physical
    b. the previous station's physical
    c. the next destination's physical
    d. the original sender's service port

24. The counterpart to the 802.3 frame's preamble field is the _____ field on the 802.5 frame.
    a. SD
    b. AC
    c. FC
    d. FS

25. _____ uses a physical star topology.
    a. 10Base5
    b. 10Base2
    c. 10Base-T
    d. none of the above

26. 10Base2 uses _____ cable, while 10Base5 uses _____.
    a. thick coaxial, thin coaxial
    b. twisted-pair, thick coaxial
    c. thin coaxial, thick coaxial
    d. fiber-optic, thin coaxial

27. 10Base2 and 10Base5 have different _____.
    a. signal band types
    b. fields on the 802.3 frame
    c. maximum segment lengths
    d. maximum data rates

28. _____ specifies a star topology featuring a central hub and daisy chaining.
    a. 10Base5

   b. 10Base2

   c. 10Base-T

   d. 1Base5

29. The _____ is a product of the LLC sublayer.

   a. 802.3 frame

   b. 802.5 frame

   c. PDU

   d. preamble

30. The monitor station in the _____ standard ensures that one and only one token is circulating.

   a. 802.3

   b. 802.5

   c. FDDI

   d. all of the above

31. The _____ houses the switches in Token Ring.

   a. NIC

   b. MAU

   c. nine-pin connector

   d. transceiver

32. What can happen at a Token Ring station?

   a. examination of the destination address

   b. regeneration of the frame

   c. passing of the frame to the next station

   d. all of the above

33. In Token Ring, where is the token when a data frame is in circulation?

   a. at the receiving station

   b. at the sending station

   c. circulating in the ring

   d. none of the above

34. In Token Ring, when a frame reaches its destination station, which of the following occurs?

   a. The message is copied.

   b. Four bits in the packet are changed.

   c. The message is taken off the ring and replaced by the token.

   d. a and b

35. Which of the following is not a transceiver function?

   a. transmission and receipt of data

   b. checking of line voltages

   c. addition and subtraction of headers

   d. collision detection

36. Which of the following frame types is specified in the 802.5 standard?
    a. token
    b. abort
    c. data/command
    d. all of the above

37. Which Project 802 standard provides for a collision-free protocol?
    a. 802.2
    b. 802.3
    c. 802.5
    d. 802.6

38. Which LAN has the highest data rate?
    a. 10Base5
    b. 10Base-T
    c. twisted-pair Token Ring
    d. FDDI

39. Another term for CSMA/CD and the IEEE 802.3 standard is _____.
    a. Ethernet
    b. Token Ring
    c. FDDI
    d. Token Bus

40. IEEE Project 802 divides the data link layer into an upper _____ sublayer and a lower _____ sublayer.
    a. LLC, MAC
    b. MAC, LLC
    c. PDU, HDLC
    d. HDLC, PDU

41. FDDI is an acronym for _____.
    a. fast data delivery interface
    b. fiber distributed data interface
    c. fiber distributed digital interface
    d. fast distributed data interface

42. In FDDI, data normally travel on _____.
    a. the primary ring
    b. the secondary ring
    c. both rings
    d. neither ring

43. What is the main purpose of the secondary ring in FDDI protocol?
    a. If the primary ring fails, the secondary takes over.
    b. If the primary ring fails, the primary makes a wrap connection with the secondary to heal the ring.

    c. The secondary alternates with the primary in transmission of data.

    d. The secondary is used to send emergency messages when the primary is busy.

44. Which type of node has two MICs and is connected to both rings?

    a. SAS

    b. DAS

    c. DAC

    d. b and c

45. Which type of node has only one MIC and can therefore connect to only one ring?

    a. SAS

    b. DAS

    c. DAC

    d. a and b

46. In which OSI layers does the FDDI protocol operate?

    a. physical

    b. data link

    c. network

    d. a and b

47. Which fields in the MAC frame of FDDI are variable?

    a. preambles

    b. address fields

    c. data fields

    d. b and c

48. Which of the following is not a legitimate 4B/5B sequence?

    a. 11100 01010

    b. 10100 01111

    c. 11100 01001

    d. 11100 00111

49. In _____ a frame goes to just one destination instead of all stations.

    a. traditional Ethernet

    b. Switched Ethernet

    c. Token Ring

    d. a and b

50. In _____ a frame goes to all stations.

    a. traditional Ethernet

    b. Switched Ethernet

    c. Token Ring

    d. a and b

51. The collision domain is the _____ distance data travels between two stations.

    a. minimum

b. maximum

c. virtual

d. a and b

52. The collision domain of traditional Ethernet is _____ meters; the collision domain of Fast Ethernet is _____ meters.

   a. 250; 250

   b. 250; 2500

   c. 2500; 250

   d. 2500; 2500

53. In an Ethernet network, if the round-trip time _____, the collision domain _____.

   a. increases; decreases

   b. decreases; decreases

   c. decreases; increases

   d. none of the above

54. 100Base-X differs from 100Base-T4 in _____.

   a. the data transmission rate

   b. topology

   c. the frame format

   d. the number of cables between the station and the hub

55. The station-to-hub distance in _____ is 2000 meters.

   a. 100Base-TX

   b. 100Base-FX

   c. 100Base-T4

   d. 100Base-T1

56. _____ uses an 8B/6T encoding scheme.

   a. 100Base-TX

   b. 100Base-FX

   c. 100Base-T4

   d. 100Base-T1

57. Gigabit Ethernet has a _____ data rate than Fast Ethernet and a _____ collision domain.

   a. higher; higher

   b. higher; lower

   c. lower; lower

   d. lower; higher

Exercises

58. What is the smallest size of an Ethernet frame? What is the largest size of an Ethernet frame?

59. What is the smallest size of a Token Ring data frame? What is the largest size of a Token Ring data frame?

60. What is the ratio of useful data to the entire packet for the smallest Ethernet frame? What is the ratio for the largest frame? What is the average ratio?

61. What is the ratio of useful data to the entire packet for the smallest Token Ring frame? What is the ratio for the largest frame? What is the average ratio?

62. Why do you think that an Ethernet frame should have a minimum data size?

63. Imagine the length of a 10Base5 cable is 2500 meters. If the speed of propagation in a thick coaxial cable is 60 percent of the speed of light (300,000,000 meters/second), how long does it take for a bit to travel from the beginning to the end of the network? Ignore any propagation delay in the equipment.

64. Using the data in Exercise 63, find the maximum time it takes to sense a collision. The worst case occurs when data are sent from one end of the cable and the collision happens at the other end. Remember that the signal needs to make a round-trip.

65. The data rate of 10Base5 is 10 Mbps. How long does it take to create the smallest frame? Show your calculation.

66. Using the data in Exercises 64 and 65, find the minimum size of an Ethernet frame for collision detection to work properly.

67. Imagine the length of the ring in a Token Ring is 1000 meters. If the speed of propagation in a twisted-pair cable is 60 percent of the speed of light (300,000,000 meters/second), how long does it take for a bit to make a complete trip?

68. In a 16-Mbps Token Ring network, the length of the token is three bytes. How long does it take for a station to produce a token?

69. For a Token Ring to work properly, the first bit of data should not come back to the place where it was produced until the whole frame is produced. Since the token is three bytes long, what should be the minimum length of the ring for proper operation of the token-passing method? Use the result of Exercises 70 and 71.

70. Encode the following stream of bits using 4B/5B encoding:
    1101011011101111

71. What is the ratio of redundant bits in 4B/5B?

72. Using Table 12.6 as a guide, compare the Ethernet and Token Ring frames.

Table 12.6   Exercise 72.

Feature	Ethernet	Token Ring
Preamble		
SFD		
SD		
AC		
FC		
Destination address		
Source address		

Table 12.6   *Exercise 72. (Continued)*

Feature	Ethernet	Token Ring
Data size		
CRC		
ED		
FS		

CHAPTER 13

Metropolitan Area Networks

A **metropolitan area network (MAN)** is a network designed to extend over an entire city. When local area networks (LANs) in close proximity need to exchange data, they can be connected privately using cable and routers or gateways. When LANs of a single enterprise are distributed over a larger area (such as a city or large campus), however, privately owned connecting infrastructure is impractical. Most organizations find that even if they could get permits to lay cable on public land, a better alternative is to use the services of existing utilities, such as the telephone company.

One of these services is switched multimegabit data services (SMDS), which normally uses another protocol called distributed queue dual bus (DQDB). In this chapter, we first discuss DQDB and then concentrate on SMDS.

13.1   IEEE 802.6 (DQDB)

In addition to the protocols discussed in Chapter 12, another protocol in the IEEE Project 802 (**IEEE 802.6**) is **distributed queue dual bus (DQDB)**. Although DQDB resembles a LAN standard, it is designed to be used in MANs.

Access Method: Dual Bus

As its name implies, DQDB uses a **dual bus** configuration: Each device in the system connects to two backbone links. Access to these links is granted not by contention (as in 802.3) or token passing (as in 802.4 and 802.5) but by a mechanism called distributed queues.

Figure 13.1 shows a DQDB topology. In this illustration, the two unidirectional buses are labeled Bus A and Bus B. Five numbered stations connect to the buses as shown. Each bus connects to the stations directly through input and output ports; no drop lines are used.

Figure 13.1   *DQDB buses and nodes*

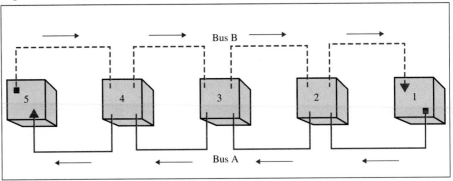

Directional Traffic

Each bus supports traffic in only one direction. The direction of traffic on one bus is the opposite of traffic on the other. In Figure 13.1, for example, where the beginning of each bus is represented by a square and the end by a triangle, Bus A traffic moves from right to left. The bus itself starts at station 1 and ends at station 5. Bus B traffic moves from left to right. The bus starts at station 5 and ends at station 1.

Upstream and Downstream Stations   The relationships of the stations on a DQDB network depend on the direction of traffic flow on a bus. As Bus A is configured, stations 1 and 2 are considered to be upstream with respect to station 3, and stations 4 and 5 are considered to be downstream with respect to station 3. In the example in Figure 13.1, station 1 has no upstream stations but has four downstream stations. For this reason, station 1 is regarded as the head of Bus A. Station 5 has no downstream stations but has four upstream stations; it is regarded as the end of Bus A.

As Bus B is configured, stations 1 and 2 are considered downstream with respect to station 3, and stations 4 and 5 are considered upstream with respect to station 3. In this case, station 5 has no upstream stations but has four downstream stations. It is therefore the head of Bus B. Station 1 has no downstream stations but has four upstream stations; it is the end of Bus B.

Transmission Slots

Data travel on each bus as a steady stream of 53-byte **slots.** These slots are not packets; they are merely continuous streams of bits. The head of Bus A (station 1 in Figure 13.1) generates empty slots for use on Bus A. The head of Bus B (station 5) generates empty slots for use on Bus B. The data rate is dependent on the number of slots generated per second. A number of different data rates are in use today.

An empty slot travels down its bus until a transmitting station drops data into it and the intended destination station reads the data. But which bus will the source station choose to carry data to a given destination station? The source station must choose the bus for which the destination station is considered downstream. This rule is intuitive. The slots in each bus travel from their head station to their end station. Within each bus, the slots are moving toward the next downstream station. If a station wants to send data, it must choose the bus whose traffic flows toward its destination.

> The source station must choose the bus for which the destination station is considered downstream.

Figure 13.2*a* shows station 2 sending data to station 4. Station 2 chooses a slot on Bus A because Bus A is flowing downstream from station 2 toward station 4. The transmission process is as follows: the head station in Bus A (station 1) creates an empty slot. Station 2 drops its data into the passing slot and addresses the slot to station 4. Station 3 reads the address and passes the slot along unread. Station 4 recognizes its address. It reads the data and changes the status of the slot to "read" before passing it along to station 5, where the slot is absorbed.

Figure 13.2   *Data transmission in DQDB*

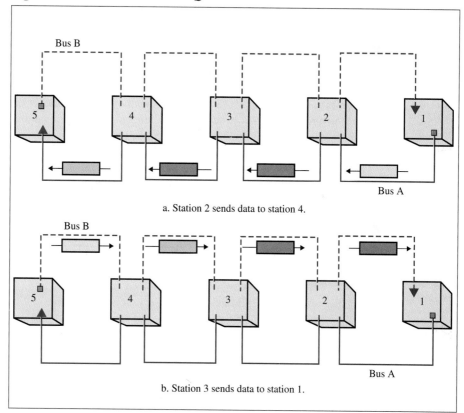

a. Station 2 sends data to station 4.

b. Station 3 sends data to station 1.

In Figure 13.2*b*, station 3 needs to send data to station 1. Station 1 is downstream from station 3 on Bus B, so Bus B is chosen to carry the data. The head of the bus (in this case, station 5) creates an empty slot and sends it down the bus. Station 4 ignores the slot (why it does so is discussed below) and passes it to station 3. Station 3 inserts its data into the slot and addresses the slot to station 1. Station 2 reads the address and relays the slot unread. Station 1 recognizes its address, reads the data, and discards the used slot. Note that because station 1 is the end of the bus, it does not set the read field, but just discards the frame once it has read the data.

Slot Reservation To send data downstream, a station must wait for the arrival of an unoccupied slot. But what is to stop an upstream station from monopolizing the bus and occupying all the slots? Should stations near the end of a bus suffer because the upstream stations have access to empty slots before they do? This imbalance can be more than an injustice; it can degrade quality of service—particularly if the system carries time-sensitive information such as voice or video.

The solution is to require stations to make reservations for the slots they want. But if you will look at Figure 13.2 again, you will notice a problem. A station makes a reservation to keep upstream stations from using slots on the bus. But how can station 2 make a reservation on Bus A? How can it communicate its reservation upstream to station 1? The solution, of course, is for station 2 to make its reservation for Bus A on Bus B, which is carrying traffic in the other direction. Station 2 sets a reservation bit in a slot on Bus B to tell each station it passes that a station is reserving a slot on Bus A. The slot passes every station downstream from station 2 on Bus B—the same stations that are upstream from it on Bus A.

These stations must respect the reservation of a downstream station and leave slots free for the downstream station's use. How this process works is described below. For now, just remember that to send data on one bus, a station must make a reservation on the other bus. Another important aspect of the reservation process is that no station may send data without first making a reservation, even if it sees slot after slot pass by empty. Empty slots may be reserved by downstream stations. In fact, even a station that has made a reservation cannot claim just any empty slot. It must wait for the arrival of the specific slot it reserved.

To send data on one bus, a station must use the other bus to make a reservation.

Distributed Queues

Making reservations and tracking the reservations of the other stations on a bus require that each station store two **queues**—one for each bus. Each station has one queue for Bus A, called queue A, and one queue for Bus B, called queue B.

A queue is a storage mechanism with first-in, first-out (FIFO) functionality. It is comparable to the waiting list at a restaurant. As patrons arrive, they sign the list. The first party on the list is seated first. Thus, a DQDB queue is essentially a waiting list for using empty slots. Figure 13.3 gives a conceptual view of a queue. Elements are inserted from the rear and removed from the front as the queue advances.

Remember, each station keeps two queues, queue A and queue B. Figure 13.4 shows these two queues for one station.

Using a Queue for Bus Access

For clarity, let's examine queue A by itself. Station X adds itself to queue A to reserve space on Bus A. To do so, it needs to know how many of its downstream neighbors have made slot requests on Bus A already. To track these reservations, it uses virtual

Figure 13.3   *Queues*

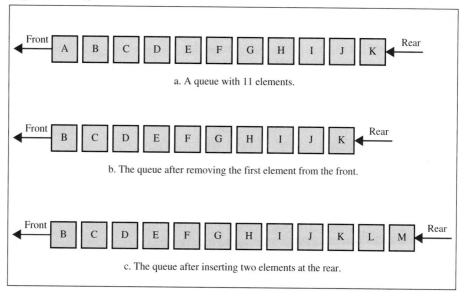

a. A queue with 11 elements.

b. The queue after removing the first element from the front.

c. The queue after inserting two elements at the rear.

Figure 13.4   *Distributed queues in a node*

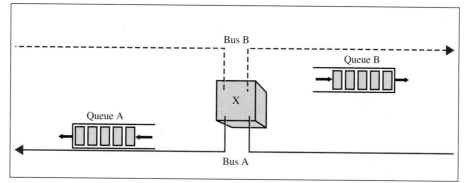

tokens. It adds a token at the rear of the queue each time a slot passes on Bus B with a reservation bit set. When the station needs to make a reservation for itself, it sets one of the reservation bits in a slot passing on Bus B (the slot can be occupied or not, provided a request bit is available). The station then inserts its own token into its queue A. This token, however, is of a different type from the others to indicate that it is the station's own reservation (see Figure 13.5).

Each time the station reads its queue A, it can tell how many downstream reservations have been made by counting how many tokens are in the queue. The station can also tell how many empty slots it must allow to pass before it can capture a slot for itself. The station watches the unoccupied slots passing in Bus A. For each empty slot that passes, it removes and discards one token from the front of the queue. When it sees an empty slot and finds its own token at the front of the queue, it discards the token but captures the empty slot and inserts its own data. The station knows it has satisfied the

Figure 13.5   *Reservation token in a queue*

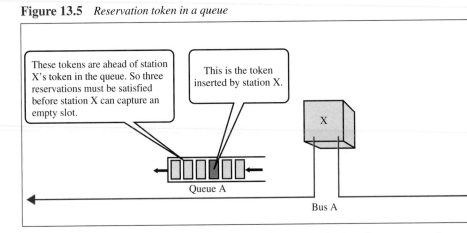

reservation requirements of the downstream stations by letting the same number of empty slots pass as there are tokens ahead of its own in its queue.

Now, referring back to Figure 13.2, let's examine the behavior of each of our original five stations with respect to Bus A.

Station 1 is responsible for slot creation. It creates empty slots continuously and releases them to Bus A. To use one of these slots to send its own data, however, it must take its place in its queue A just like any other station. If there are tokens in front of its own, station 1 releases empty slots for the downstream stations (stations 2, 3, 4, and 5) until its own token comes up. At that point, it inserts its own data into a slot and sets the slot's busy bit (to 1 for "on") before releasing the slot to the bus.

The behavior of stations 2, 3, and 4 is essentially the same as that of station 1 except that these stations do not create slots. Instead, they watch the empty slots as they pass. For each empty slot that passes, each station removes one token from its queue A until it removes its own token. At that point, it captures the next empty slot, loads data into it, sets the busy bit, and releases it back to the bus.

Station 5, on the other hand, cannot send data by Bus A (there is no station downstream from station 5 on Bus A). In fact, it does not even need a queue A, although it may contain a queue A for network compatibility in case a station is added downstream from it in the future.

The preceding description also applies to Bus B, with the difference that in Bus B station 5 creates and releases the slots and station 1 does not need a queue B.

Queue Structure

The DQDB standard states explicitly how logical queues A and B are to be used. However, the design of each queue is left to the implementors. Networks and stations can be made to simulate the operations of the queues as long as those simulations follow the stated rules.

Ring Configuration

DQDB can also be implemented as a ring. In this case, one station plays the roles of both header and end (see Figure 13.6). This topology has the advantage of being reconfigurable whenever a link or a station fails. Figure 13.6*b* shows the original ring reconfigured after a link failure.

Figure 13.6   *DQDB rings*

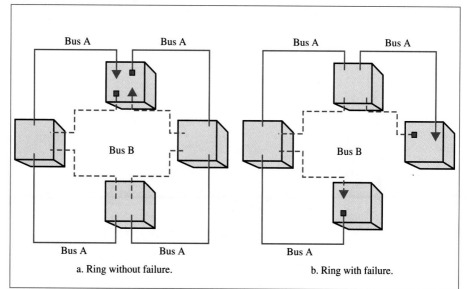

a. Ring without failure.   b. Ring with failure.

Operation: DQDB Layers

The IEEE defines both the medium access control (MAC) sublayer and the physical layer for DQDB. The specifics of the MAC layer functions are complex and fall beyond the scope of this book. In general, however, the MAC layer splits the data stream coming from the upper layers into 48-byte segments and adds a 5-byte header to each segment to create slots of 53 bytes each (see Figure 13.7). Having 53 bytes makes a DQDB slot compatible with the size of a cell in Asynchronous Transfer Mode (ATM); see Chapter 19.

The DQDB Header

The five bytes of the DQDB header are distributed among five major fields: access, address, type, priority, and CRC.

Access Field   The DQDB access field is an eight-bit field that controls access to the bus. It is subdivided into five subfields:

- **Busy (B).** The B bit indicates whether or not the slot is carrying data. When set, it means the slot is occupied.
- **Slot type (ST).** The ST bit can define two types of slots, one for packet transmissions and the other for isochronous transmission.
- **Reserved (R).** The R bit is reserved for future use.
- **Previous slot read (PSR).** The two-bit PSR field is set to 0 by the addressed station once it has read the contents of the slot.

Figure 13.7 *DQDB layers*

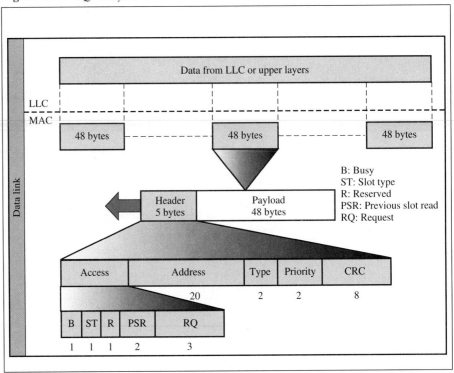

■ **Request (RQ).** The RQ field consists of three bits set by stations to make reservations for slots. The three bits can represent eight levels of priority in networks with different station levels. In networks with no priorities, the first bit is used.

Address Field   The address field holds a 20-bit virtual channel identifier (VCI) to be used for MAN and WAN transmission. When used in a LAN, this field contains all 1s and an additional header is added to carry the MAC physical address.

Type Field   The 2-bit type field identifies the payload as user data, management data, and so on.

Priority Field   The priority field identifies the priority of the slot in a network that uses priorities.

CRC Field   The CRC field carries an eight-bit cyclic redundancy check using $x^8 + x^2 + x + 1$ as the divisor that is used to detect single-bit or burst errors and to correct single-bit errors in the header.

Implementation

Physical layer specifications are left open. The DQDB standard defines the electronic devices used to access the dual bus. Access media can be either coaxial or fiber-optic cable with a variety of data rates.

13.2 SMDS

Switched multimegabit data services (SMDS) is a service for handling high-speed communications for metropolitan area networks. It was developed to support organizations that need to exchange data between LANs located in different parts of a city or large campus. Before the introduction of SMDS, making these exchanges was often difficult. One option was to subscribe to an existing telephone company service such as a leased T-1 line with the data rate of 1.544 Mbps, or to a DS-3 service with a leased T-3 line and data rate of 44.736 Mbps. These solutions, though adequate, were expensive. For example, consider an enterprise with four offices in four different parts of a city. To join their LANs into a MAN requires a mesh of six point-to-point connections, $n \times (n - 1)/2$; see Figure 13.8.

Figure 13.8 *Connecting LANs using T-1 or T-3 lines*

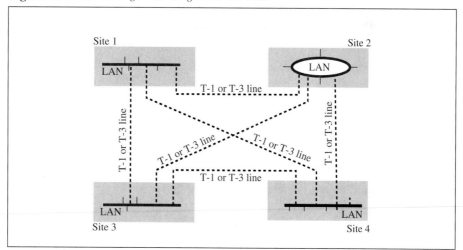

Of course, most companies' data traffic does not utilize a line 100 percent of the time. The lines would therefore be more affordable if they could be shared. Unfortunately, telephone companies do not offer switched-lease T lines. A subscriber must lease the line either all of the time or not at all.

SMDS provides the solution. It is a packet-switched datagram service for high-speed MAN traffic. SMDS is a switched service provided by common carriers; subscribers pay only for the time they use. Subscriber LANs link to an SMDS network through routers that are connected to switches using DQDB architecture (see Figure 13.9).

SMDS Architecture

Access to SMDS is coordinated through the **SMDS interface protocol (SIP).** The SIP protocol defines three levels, as shown in Figure 13.10.

Figure 13.9   *SMDS as a MAN: subscriber LANs linked to SMDS through routers*

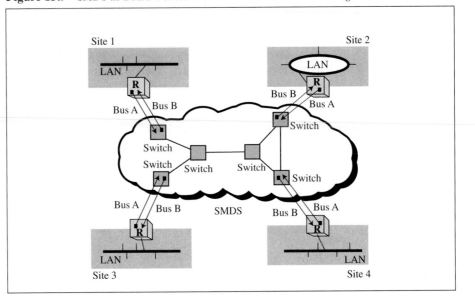

Figure 13.10   *SIP levels*

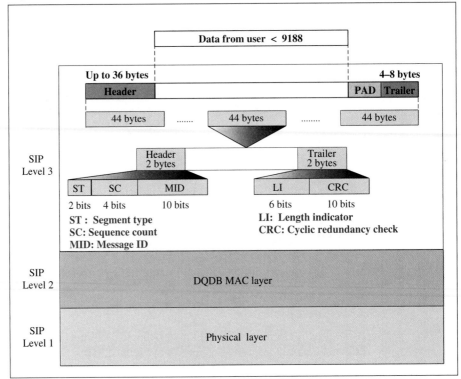

SIP Level 3

This level accepts the user data, which should be less than 9188 bytes, and adds a header and a trailer to it. The header and trailer contain management and control fields. The two most important fields of the header are the sender address and the receiver address. Each address is eight bytes long (64 bits). The first four bits define the type of the address, which is by default a telephone number. The next 60 bits are normally interpreted as 15 four-bit sections. Each section can define a digit between 0 and 9. Since fifteen digits can specify a telephone number consisting of a country code, area code, and local number, SMDS can even be used as a WAN. The address can define a telephone number in any country (see Figure 13.11).

Figure 13.11 *An address in SMDS*

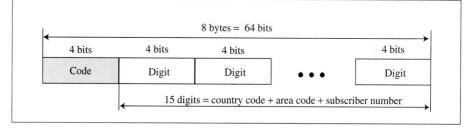

After the header and the trailer are added, the packet is divided into 44-byte sections. To each section, a two-byte header and a two-byte trailer are added, as shown in Figure 13.10. Each 48-byte section is passed to SIP level 2 for processing.

SIP Level 2

At this level DQDB comes into play. Level 2 receives the 48-byte sections and, as shown in Figure 13.7, a five-byte header is added. The 53-byte output from this layer is dropped in a slot and carried to its destination.

SIP Level 1

This is the physical level that defines the physical interface and the type of transmission medium and signaling system.

Features

We will briefly mention different features of SMDS:

■ SMDS can be thought of as a backbone network connecting different LANs of the same organization.

■ SMDS can be used to create a connection between LANs belonging to different organizations.

■ Although used mostly as a MAN, SMDS can also be used as a WAN.

■ SMDS is a switched-packet network; the same network is available to all users.

■ Subscribers pay only when they actually use the network.

- Since the user payload can be up to 9188 bytes, SMDS can receive and encapsulate frames from all LANs.
- The data rate ranges from 1.544 Mbps to 155 Mbps.
- Each user is assigned an average data rate.
- The instantaneous data rate can vary as long as the average is below the data rate assigned to a specific customer. This means that the transmission of data can be **bursty.**
- Since the addressing system is a telephone number, there is no need for a new addressing system to be assigned to each user.
- Multicasting is available; a user can send data that can be received by several users.

13.3 KEY TERMS AND CONCEPTS

bursty data

distributed queue dual bus (DQDB)

dual bus

IEEE 802.6

metropolitan area network (MAN)

queue

slot

SMDS interface protocol (SIP)

switched multimegabit data service (SMDS)

13.4 SUMMARY

- Distributed queue dual bus (DQDB) uses two unidirectional buses. The buses travel in opposite directions.
- Data transmission in DQDB occurs through capture of an empty slot and insertion of data into the slot.
- A station can transmit data only in the downstream direction. The reservation for a slot is made on the other bus.
- Through the use of first-in, first-out (FIFO) queues, each station has an equal opportunity to send its data.
- DQDB operates in the physical layer and the MAC sublayer.
- DQDB can also be implemented as a ring topology.
- In the MAC sublayer, a 5-byte header is added to a 48-byte payload.
- In the physical layer, the protocols define the electronic devices, media, and data rates.
- Switched multimegabit data services (SMDS) is a packet-switched datagram service used to handle high-speed communications in a MAN.

- SMDS is a good choice for users who
    a. Require a data rate greater than that of switched/56 or DDS.
    b. Do not need full-time use of a link.
- Access to SMDS is coordinated through SMDS interface protocol (SIP).
- SMDS uses DQDB for media access.

13.5   PRACTICE SET

Review Questions

1. Why are services such as DQDB and SMDS used in MANs?
2. Why are two buses needed in DQDB?
3. How are slots generated in DQDB?
4. Why is slot reservation needed in DQDB?
5. Describe the slot reservation method in DQDB.
6. Why are two queues needed at each station in DQDB?
7. Explain the FIFO queues in DQDB?
8. What is the advantage of implementing DQDB in a ring configuration?
9. Why was the slot size chosen to be 53 bytes in DQDB?
10. What is the purpose of the access field in the DQDB header?
11. Describe the physical layer of DQDB.
12. How is a LAN connected to SMDS?
13. What is the purpose of the SMDS interface protocol (SIP)?
14. Name the three SIP levels and their functions.
15. Why does the header added at level 3 contain a telephone number?
16. How is DQDB related to SMDS?

Multiple Choice Questions

17. DQDB is an acronym for _____.
    a. distributed queue data base
    b. differential queue data bus
    c. data queue dual bus
    d. distributed queue dual bus
18. A DQDB is composed of _____.
    a. 2 one-directional buses traveling in opposite directions
    b. 1 two-directional bus
    c. 2 two-directional buses traveling in opposite directions
    d. 1 one-directional bus

19. In a DQDB with bus A and bus B, if a source station sends data via bus B, the reservation is made on _____.
    a. the bus with the closest head
    b. the less busy bus
    c. bus B
    d. bus A

20. We have a six-element queue in the order A B C D E F, with A being the first in. If two elements are removed and element G and then H are inserted, which element is at the front of the queue?
    a. C
    b. D
    c. G
    d. H

21. DQDB operates in the _____ layer(s).
    a. physical
    b. data link
    c. physical and data link
    d. network

22. Which bit field in the DQDB access field byte is used for station reservations?
    a. B
    b. ST
    c. PSR
    d. RQ

23. Which bit field in the DQDB access field byte is set to 0 after the slot contents are read?
    a. B
    b. ST
    c. PSR
    d. RQ

24. Which field in the DQDB header identifies the type of payload?
    a. access
    b. address
    c. type
    d. priority

25. SMDS is an acronym for _____.
    a. switched multimegabit data services
    b. switched media data services
    c. synchronous multimegabit data services
    d. synchronous media data services

26. SMDS is a service designed to handle high-speed communications in _____.
    a. a LAN
    b. a MAN
    c. a WAN
    d. all of the above

27. The SMDS interface protocol (SIP) specifies the use of _____ as a medium access method between the router and SMDS.
    a. CSMA/CA
    b. CSMA/CD
    c. DQDB
    d. DBDQ

Exercises

28. There are 10 stations, numbered successively 1 through 10, connected in a DQDB. Station 1 generates the slots in Bus A; station 10 generates the slots in Bus B. Draw the system, labeling the heads, ends, buses, stations, and bus directions.

29. In Exercise 28, how many stations are upstream with respect to station 7? How many stations are downstream with respect to station 3?

30. Using Figure 13.1, match the following to stations 1, 2, 3, 4, and/or 5. There may be more than one match per problem.
    a. Generates empty slots.
    b. Doesn't need queue A.
    c. Doesn't need queue B.
    d. Needs both queues.

31. Explain how the address field in the DQDB header functions on a MAN and on a LAN.

32. The queues for a station are shown in Figure 13.12. How many empty slots in direction A should pass before the station can send a frame in this direction? How many empty slots in direction B should pass before the station can send a frame in this direction?

Figure 13.12 *Exercise 32*

33. The queues for a station are shown in Figure 13.13. The station observes the following events. Show the contents of the queues after each event (the events happen one after another):
    a. Three occupied slots pass bus A with their reservation bits set.
    b. Two empty slots pass bus B.

c. One empty slot passes bus B with the reservation bit set.

d. Two occupied slots pass bus B.

e. Two occupied slots pass bus B with the reservation bit set.

Figure 13.13 *Exercise 33*

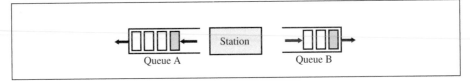

34. In Figure 13.14 all queues are originally empty. Show the contents of each queue after the following events (the events happen one after another):

    a. Station 2 makes a reservation to send a frame to station 5.

    b. Station 3 makes a reservation to send a frame to station 1.

    c. Station 2 transmits a frame to station 5.

    d. Station 4 makes a reservation to send a frame to station 1.

    e. Station 4 makes a reservation to send a frame to station 5.

    f. Station 3 transmits a frame to station 1.

    g. Station 1 makes a reservation to send data to station 4.

    h. Station 4 transmits a frame to station 1.

    i. Station 4 transmits a frame to station 5.

    j. Station 1 transmits a frame to station 4.

Figure 13.14 *Exercise 34*

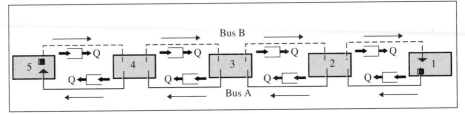

35. A user sends one 1000-byte packet to an SMDS network. Answer the following questions assuming a 36-byte header and a 4-byte trailer:

    a. Is there a need to add padding in SIP level 3? How many bytes?

    b. How many 48-byte sections are created in SIP level 3?

    c. How many 53-byte sections are created in SIP level 2?

36. Using Exercise 35, answer the following questions:

    a. How many overhead bytes are added to the user data in level 3?

    b. How many overhead bytes are added to the user data in level 2?

    c. What is the total number of bytes added to the user data?

    d. What is the percentage of the overhead to the user data?

37. Using Exercise 35, answer the following questions:
    a. If the network is sending the user data at 45 Mbps, how long does it take to send all the data?
    b. How long does it take to send one slot?

38. Show the telephone number (408)864-8902 (without parentheses or hyphen) in binary using four bits to represent a digit. How many bits do you need?

39. How can you use the result of Exercise 38 in the address field of SIP level 3?

CHAPTER 14

Switching

Whenever we have multiple devices, we have the problem of how to connect them to make one-on-one communication possible. One solution is to install a **point-to-point connection** between each pair of devices (a mesh topology) or between a central device and every other device (a star topology). These methods, however, are impractical and wasteful when applied to very large networks. The number and length of the links require too much infrastructure to be cost efficient, and the majority of those links would be idle most of the time. Imagine a network of six devices: A, B, C, D, E, and F. If device A has point-to-point links to devices B, C, D, E, and F, then whenever only A and B are connected, the links connecting A to each of the other devices are idle and wasted.

Other topologies employing multipoint connections, such as a bus, are ruled out because the distances between devices and the total number of devices increase beyond the capacities of the media and equipment.

A better solution is switching. A switched network consists of a series of interlinked nodes, called **switches.** Switches are hardware and/or software devices capable of creating temporary connections between two or more devices linked to the switch but not to each other. In a switched network, some of these nodes are connected to the communicating devices. Others are used only for routing.

Figure 14.1 shows a switched network. The communicating devices (in this example, computers) are labeled A, B, C, D, and so on, and the switches I, II, III, IV, and so on. Each switch is connected to multiple links and is used to complete the connections between them, two at a time.

Traditionally, three methods of switching have been important: circuit switching, packet switching, and message switching (see Figure 14.2). The first two are commonly used today. The third has been phased out in general communications but still has networking applications. New switching strategies are gaining prominence, among them cell relay (ATM) and Frame Relay. We will discuss these technologies in Chapters 18 and 19. Understanding the older methods provides a good basis for understanding the newer ones, so we will examine the older methods first.

Figure 14.1 *Switched network*

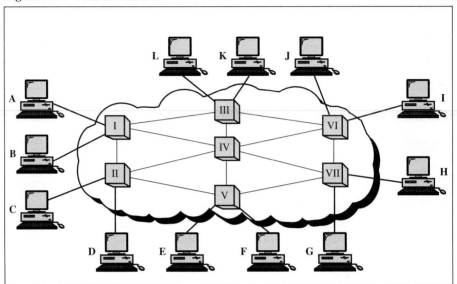

Figure 14.2 *Switching methods*

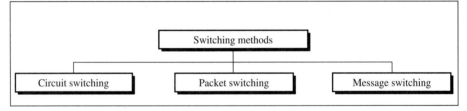

14.1 CIRCUIT SWITCHING

Circuit switching creates a direct physical connection between two devices such as phones or computers. For example, in Figure 14.3, instead of point-to-point connections between the three computers on the left (A, B, and C) to the four computers on the right (D, E, F, and G), requiring 12 links, we can use four switches to reduce the number and the total length of the links. In Figure 14.3, computer A is connected through switches I, II, and III to computer D. By moving the levers of the switches, any computer on the left can be connected to any computer on the right.

A circuit switch is a device with *n* inputs and *m* outputs that creates a temporary connection between an input link and an output link (see Figure 14.4). The number of inputs does not have to match the number of outputs.

An *n*-by-*n* folded switch can connect *n* lines in full-duplex mode. For example, it can connect *n* telephones in such a way that each phone can be connected to every other phone (see Figure 14.5).

Circuit switching today can use either of two technologies: space-division switches or time-division switches (see Figure 14.6).

Figure 14.3   *Circuit-switched network*

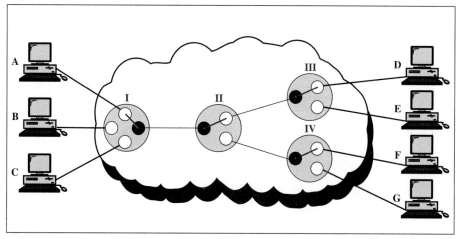

Figure 14.4   *A circuit switch*

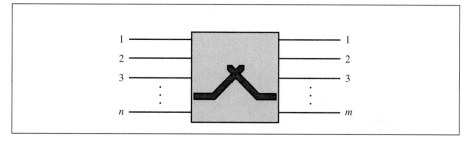

Figure 14.5   *A folded switch*

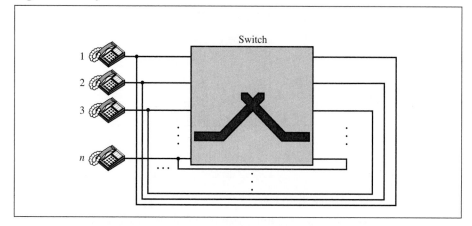

Figure 14.6 *Circuit switching*

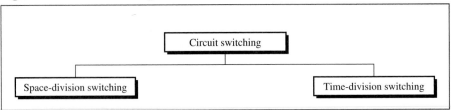

Space-Division Switches

In **space-division switching,** the paths in the circuit are separated from each other spatially. This technology was originally designed for use in analog networks but is used currently in both analog and digital networks. It has evolved through a long history of many designs.

Crossbar Switches

A **crossbar switch** connects n inputs to m outputs in a grid, using electronic microswitches (transistors) at each **crosspoint** (see Figure 14.7). The major limitation of this design is the number of crosspoints required. Connecting n inputs to m outputs using a crossbar switch requires $n \times m$ crosspoints. For example, to connect 1000 inputs to 1000 outputs requires a crossbar with 1,000,000 crosspoints. This factor makes the crossbar impractical because it makes the size of the crossbar huge. Such a switch is also inefficient because statistics show that, in practice, fewer than 25 percent of the crosspoints are in use at a given time. The rest are idle.

Figure 14.7 *Crossbar switch*

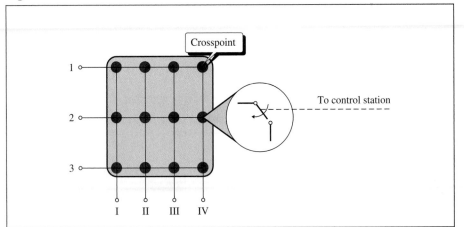

Multistage Switches

The solution to the limitations of the crossbar switch is to use **multistage switches,** which combine crossbar switches in several stages. In multistage switching, devices are linked to switches that, in turn, are linked to a hierarchy of other switches (see Figure 14.8).

Figure 14.8   *Multistage switch*

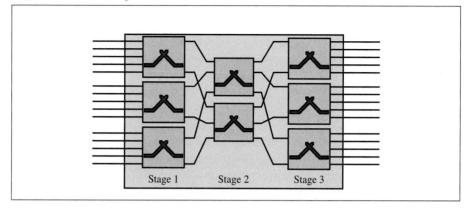

The design of a multistage switch depends on the number of stages and the number of switches required (or desired) in each stage. Normally, the middle stages have fewer switches than do the first and last stages. For example, imagine that we want a multistage switch as in Figure 14.8 to do the job of a single 15-by-15 crossbar switch. Assume that we have decided on a three-stage design that uses three switches in the first and final stages and two switches in the middle stage. Because there are three of them, each of the first-stage switches has inputs from one-third of the input devices, giving them five inputs each ($5 \times 3 = 15$).

Next, each of the first-stage switches must have an output to each of the intermediate switches. There are two intermediate switches; therefore, each first-stage switch has two outputs. Each third-stage switch must have inputs from each of the intermediate switches; two intermediate switches means two inputs. The intermediate switches must connect to all three first-stage switches and all three last-stage switches, and so must have three inputs and three outputs each.

Multiple Paths   Multistage switches provide several options for connecting each pair of linked devices. Figure 14.9 shows two ways traffic can move from an input to an output using the switch designed in the example above.

Figure 14.9   *Switching path*

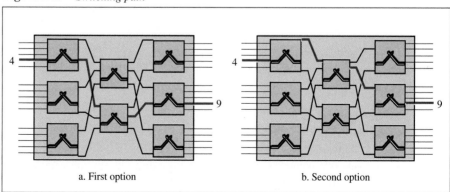

In Figure 14.9*a*, a pathway is established between input line 4 and output line 9. In this instance, the path uses the lower intermediate switch and that switch's center output line to reach the last-stage switch connected to line 9.

Figure 14.9*b* shows a pathway between the same input line 4 and the same output line 9 using the upper intermediate switch.

Let us compare the number of crosspoints in a 15-by-15 single-stage crossbar switch with the 15-by-15 multistage switch that we described above. In the single-stage switch, we need 225 crosspoints (15×15). In the multistage switch, we need

- Three first-stage switches, each with 10 crosspoints (5×2), for a total of 30 crosspoints at the first stage.
- Two second-stage switches, each with 9 crosspoints (3×3), for a total of 18 crosspoints at the second stage.
- Three third-stage switches, each with 10 crosspoints (5×2), for a total of 30 crosspoints at the last stage.

The total number of crosspoints required by our multistage switch is 78. In this example, the multistage switch requires only 35 percent as many crosspoints as the single-stage switch.

Blocking   This savings comes with a cost, however. The reduction in the number of crosspoints results in a phenomenon called **blocking** during periods of heavy traffic. Blocking refers to times when one input cannot be connected to an output because there is no path available between them—all of the possible intermediate switches are occupied.

In a single-stage switch, blocking does not occur. Because every combination of input and output has its own crosspoint, there is always a path. (Cases where two inputs are trying to contact the same output don't count. That path is not blocked; the output is merely busy.) In the multistage switch described in the example above, however, only two of the first five inputs can use the switch at a time, only two of the second five inputs can use the switch at a time, and so on. The small number of outputs at the middle stage further increases the restriction on the number of available links.

In large systems, such as those having 10,000 inputs and outputs, the number of stages can be increased to cut down the number of crosspoints required. As the number of stages increases, however, possible blocking increases as well. Many people have experienced blocking on public telephone systems in the wake of a natural disaster when calls being made to check on or reassure relatives far outnumber the ordinary load of the system. In those cases, it is often impossible to get a connection. Under normal circumstances, however, blocking is not usually a problem. In countries that can afford it, the number of switches between lines is calculated to make blocking unlikely. The formula for finding this number is based on statistical analysis, which is beyond the scope of this book.

Time-Division Switches

Time-division switching uses time-division multiplexing to achieve switching. There are two popular methods used in time-division multiplexing: the time-slot interchange and the TDM bus.

Time-Slot Interchange (TSI)

Figure 14.10 shows a system connecting four input lines to four output lines. Imagine that each input line wants to send data to an output line according to the following pattern:

$$1 \Rightarrow 3 \qquad 2 \Rightarrow 4 \qquad 3 \Rightarrow 1 \qquad 4 \Rightarrow 2$$

Figure 14.10a shows the results of ordinary time-division multiplexing. As you can see, the desired task is not accomplished. Data are output in the same order as they are input. Data from 1 go to 1, from 2 go to 2, from 3 go to 3, and from 4 go to 4.

In Figure 14.10b, however, we insert a device called a **time-slot interchange** **(TSI)** into the link. A TSI changes the ordering of the slots based on the desired connections. In this case, it changes the order of data from A, B, C, D to C, D, A, B. Now, when the demultiplexer separates the slots, it passes them to the proper outputs.

Figure 14.10 *Time-division multiplexing, without and with a time-slot interchange (TSI)*

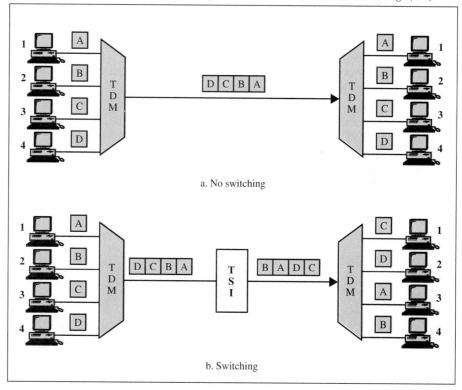

a. No switching

b. Switching

How a TSI works is shown in Figure 14.11. A TSI consists of random access memory (RAM) with several memory locations. The size of each location is the same as the size of a single time slot. The number of locations is the same as the number of inputs (in most cases, the number of inputs and outputs are equal). The RAM fills up with incoming data from time slots in the order received. Slots are then sent out in an order based on the decisions of a control unit.

Figure 14.11   *Time-slot interchange*

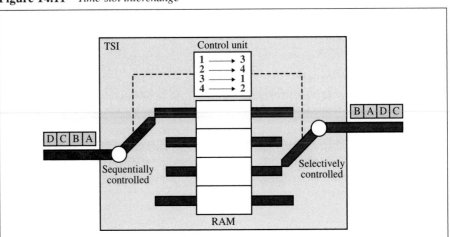

TDM Bus

Figure 14.12 shows a very simplified version of a **TDM bus.** The input and output lines are connected to a high-speed bus through input and output gates (microswitches). Each input gate is closed during one of the four time slots. During the same time slot, only one output gate is also closed. This pair of gates allows a burst of data to be transferred from one specific input line to one specific output line using the bus. The control unit opens and closes the gates according to switching need. For example, in the figure, at the first time slot the input gate 1 and output gate 3 will be closed; during the second time slot, input gate 2 and output gate 4 will be closed; and so on.

Figure 14.12   *TDM bus*

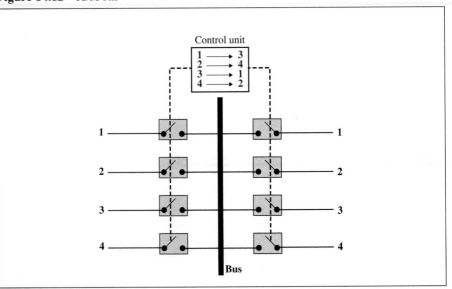

A folded TDM bus can be made with duplex lines (input and output) and dual gates.

Space- and Time-Division Switching Combinations

When we compare space-division and time-division switching, some interesting facts emerge. The advantage of space-division switching is that it is instantaneous. Its disadvantage is the number of crosspoints required to make space-division switching acceptable in terms of blocking.

The advantage of time-division switching is that it needs no crosspoints. Its disadvantage, in the case of TSI, is that processing each connection creates delays. Each time slot must be stored by the RAM, then retrieved and passed on.

In a third option, we combine space-division and time-division technology to take advantage of the best of both. Combining the two results in switches that are optimized both physically (the number of crosspoints) and temporally (the amount of delay). Multistage switches of this sort can be designed as time-space-time (TST), time-space-space-time (TSST), space-time-time-space (STTS), or other possible combinations.

Figure 14.13 shows a simple TST switch that consists of two time stages and one space stage and has 12 inputs and 12 outputs. Instead of one time-division switch, it divides the inputs into three groups (of four inputs each) and directs them to three time-slot interchanges. The result in this case is that the average delay is one-third of that which would result from using one time-slot interchange to handle all 12 inputs.

Figure 14.13   *TST switch*

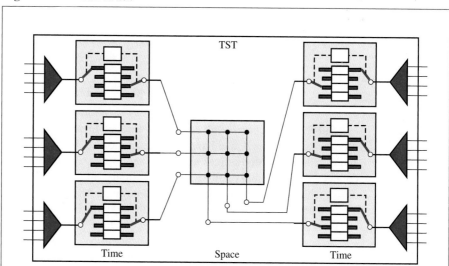

The last stage is a mirror image of the first stage. The middle stage is a space-division switch (crossbar) that connects the TSI groups together to allow connectivity between all possible input and output pairs (e.g., to connect input 3 of the first group to output 7 of the second group).

Public Switched Telephone Network (PSTN)

An example of a circuit-switched telephone network is the **Public Switched Telephone Network (PSTN)** in North America. The switching centers are organized into five classes: *regional offices* (class 1), *sectional offices* (class 2), *primary offices* (class 3), *toll offices* (class 4), and *end offices* (class 5). Figure 14.14 shows the hierarchical relationship between these offices.

Figure 14.14   *PSTN hierarchy*

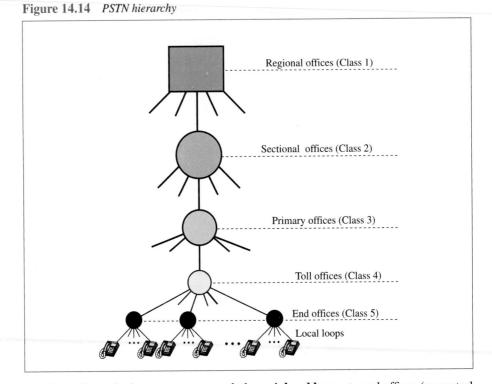

Subscriber telephones are connected, through **local loops,** to end offices (or central offices). A small town may have only one end office, but a large city will have several end offices. Many end offices are connected to one toll office. Several toll offices are connected to a primary office. Several primary offices are connected to a sectional office, which normally serves more than one state. And finally several sectional offices are connected to one regional office. All the regional offices are connected using mesh topology.

Accessing the switching station at the end offices is accomplished through dialing. In the past, telephones featured rotary or pulse dialing, in which a digital signal was sent to the end office for each number dialed. This type of dialing was prone to errors due to the inconsistency of humans during the dialing process.

Today, dialing is accomplished through the Touch-Tone technique. In this method, instead of sending a digital signal, the user sends two small bursts of analog signals, called *dual tone*. The frequency of the signals sent depends on the row and column of the pressed pad.

Figure 14.15 shows a 12-pad **Touch-Tone dialing** system. Note that there is also a variation with an extra column (16-pad Touch-Tone), which is used for special purposes.

Figure 14.15   *Touch-Tone dialing*

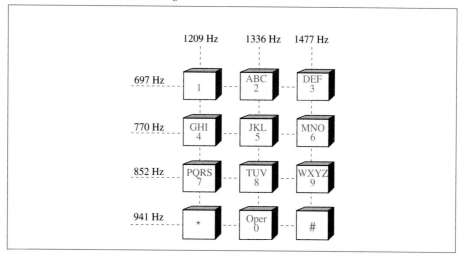

In Figure 14.15, when a user dials, for example, the number 8, two bursts of analog signals with frequencies 852 and 1336 Hz are sent to the end office.

14.2   PACKET SWITCHING

Circuit switching was designed for voice communication. In a telephone conversation, for example, once a circuit is established, it remains connected for the duration of the session. Circuit switching creates temporary (dialed) or permanent (leased) dedicated links that are well suited to this type of communication.

Circuit switching is less well suited to data and other nonvoice transmissions. Nonvoice transmissions tend to be bursty, meaning that data come in spurts with idle gaps between them. When circuit-switched links are used for data transmission, therefore, the line is often idle and its facilities wasted.

A second weakness of circuit-switched connections for data transmission is in its data rate. A circuit-switched link creates the equivalent of a single cable between two devices and thereby assumes a single data rate for both devices. This assumption limits the flexibility and usefulness of a circuit-switched connection for networks interconnecting a variety of digital devices.

Third, circuit switching is inflexible. Once a circuit has been established, that circuit is the path taken by all parts of the transmission whether or not it remains the most efficient or available.

Finally, circuit switching sees all transmissions as equal. Any request is granted to whatever link is available. But often with data transmission, we want to be able to prioritize: to say, for example, that transmission x can go anytime but transmission z is time dependent and must go immediately.

A better solution for data transmission is **packet switching. In a packet-switched network,** data are transmitted in discrete units of potentially variable length blocks called **packets.** The maximum length of the packet is established by the network. Longer transmissions are broken up into multiple packets. Each packet contains not only data but also a header with control information (such as priority codes and source and destination addresses). The packets are sent over the network node to node. At each node, the packet is stored briefly then routed according to the information in its header.

There are two popular approaches to packet switching: datagram and virtual circuit (see Figure 14.16).

Figure 14.16 *Packet-switching approaches*

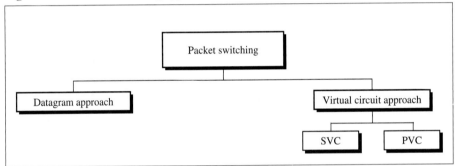

Datagram Approach

In the **datagram approach to packet switching,** each packet is treated independently from all others. Even when one packet represents just a piece of a multipacket transmission, the network (and network layer functions) treats it as though it existed alone. Packets in this technology are referred to as **datagrams.**

Figure 14.17 shows how the datagram approach can be used to deliver four packets from station A to station X. In this example, all four packets (or datagrams) belong to the same message but may go by different paths to reach their destination.

This approach can cause the datagrams of a transmission to arrive at their destination out of order. It is the responsibility of the transport layer in most protocols to reorder the datagrams before passing them on to the destination port.

The link joining each pair of nodes can contain multiple channels. Each of these channels is capable, in turn, of carrying datagrams either from several different sources or from one source. Multiplexing can be done using TDM or FDM (see Figure 14.18).

In Figure 14.18, devices A and B are sending datagrams to devices X and Y. Some paths use one channel while others use more than one. As you can see, the bottom link is carrying two packets from different sources in the same direction. The link on the right, however, is carrying datagrams in two directions.

Figure 14.17 *Datagram approach*

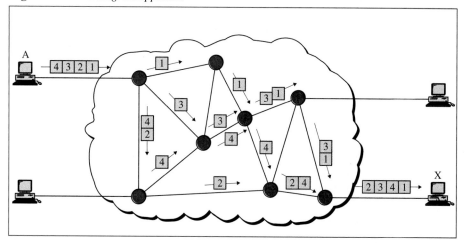

Figure 14.18 *Multiple channels in datagram approach*

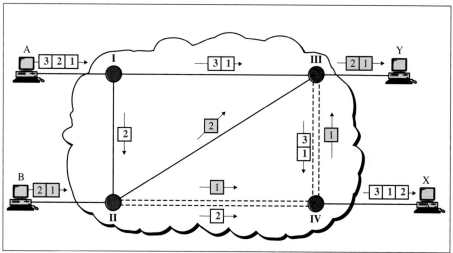

Virtual Circuit Approach

In the **virtual circuit approach to packet switching,** the relationship between all packets belonging to a message or session is preserved. A single route is chosen between sender and receiver at the beginning of the session. When the data are sent, all packets of the transmission travel one after another along that route.

Today, virtual circuit transmission is implemented in two formats: switched virtual circuit (SVC) and permanent virtual circuit (PVC).

SVC

The **switched virtual circuit (SVC)** format is comparable conceptually to dial-up lines in circuit switching. In this method, a **virtual circuit** is created whenever it is needed and exists only for the duration of the specific exchange. For example, imagine that station A wants to send four packets to station X. First, A requests the establishment of a connection to X. Once the connection is in place, the packets are sent one after another and in sequential order. When the last packet has been received and, if necessary, acknowledged, the connection is released and that virtual circuit ceases to exist (see Figure 14.19). Only one single route exists for the duration of transmission, although the network could pick an alternate route in response to failure or congestion.

Figure 14.19   *Switched virtual circuit (SVC)*

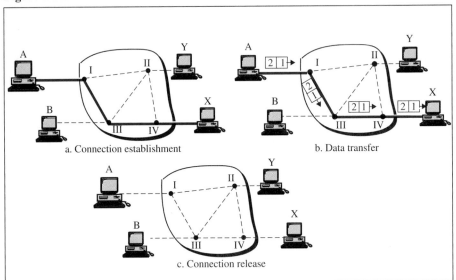

a. Connection establishment

b. Data transfer

c. Connection release

Each time that A wishes to communicate with X, a new route is established. The route may be the same each time, or it may differ in response to varying network conditions.

PVC

Permanent virtual circuits (PVC) are comparable to leased lines in circuit switching. In this method, the same virtual circuit is provided between two users on a continuous basis. The circuit is dedicated to the specific users. No one else can use it and, because it is always in place, it can be used without connection establishment and connection termination. Whereas two SVC users may get a different route every time they request a connection, two PVC users always get the same route (see Figure 14.20).

Circuit-Switched Connection versus Virtual-Circuit Connection

Although it seems that a circuit-switched connection and a virtual-circuit connection are the same, there are differences:

■ **Path versus route.** A circuit-switched connection creates a **path** between two points. The physical path is created by setting the switches for the duration of the dial (dial-up line) or the duration of the lease (leased line). A virtual-circuit

Figure 14.20 *Permanent virtual circuit (PVC)*

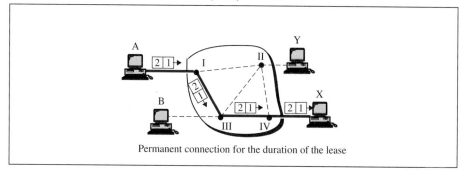

Permanent connection for the duration of the lease

connection creates a **route** between two points. This means each switch creates an entry in its routing table (see Chapter 21) for the duration of the session (SVC) or duration of the lease (PVC). Whenever, the switch receives a packet belonging to a virtual connection, it checks the table for the corresponding entry and routes the packet out of one of its interfaces. Figure 14.21 shows this difference.

Figure 14.21 *Path versus route*

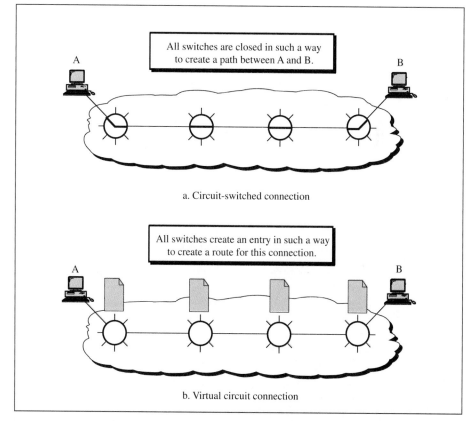

All switches are closed in such a way
to create a path between A and B.

a. Circuit-switched connection

All switches create an entry in such a way
to create a route for this connection.

b. Virtual circuit connection

■ **Dedicated versus sharing.** In a circuit-switched connection, the links that make a path are dedicated; they cannot be used by other connections. In a virtual circuit connection, the links that make a route can be shared by other connections. Figure 14.22 shows this difference.

Figure 14.22 *Dedicated versus shared*

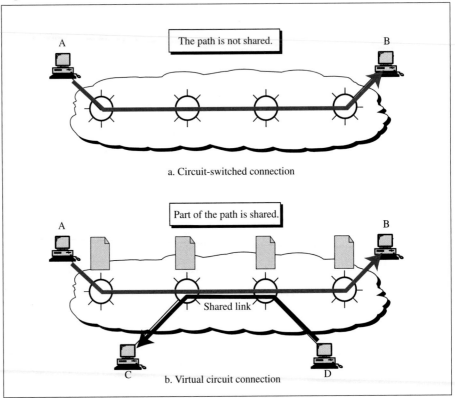

14.3 MESSAGE SWITCHING

Message switching is best known by the descriptive term **store and forward.** In this mechanism, a node (usually a special computer with a number of disks) receives a message, stores it until the appropriate route is free, then sends it along.

Store and forward is considered a switching technique because there is no direct link between the sender and receiver of a transmission. A message is delivered to the node along one path then rerouted along another to its destination.

Note that in message switching, the messages are stored and relayed from secondary storage (disk), while in packet switching the packets are stored and forwarded from primary storage (RAM).

Message switching was common in the 1960s and 1970s. The primary uses have been to provide high-level network services (e.g., delayed delivery, broadcast) for unintelligent devices. Since such devices have been replaced, this type of switch has virtually disappeared. Also, the delays inherent in the process, as well as the requirements for large-capacity storage media at each node, make it unpopular for direct communication (see Figure 14.23).

Figure 14.23   *Message switching*

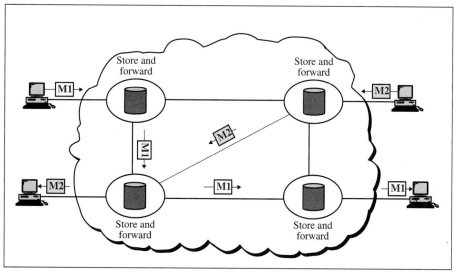

14.4   KEY TERMS AND CONCEPTS

blocking

circuit switching

crossbar switch

crosspoint

datagram

datagram approach to packet switching

local loop

message switching

multistage switch

packet

packet-switched network

packet switching

path

permanent virtual circuit (PVC)

point-to-point connection

Public Switched Telephone Network (PSTN)

route

space-division switching

store and forward

switch   Touch-Tone dialing

switched virtual circuit (SVC)   virtual circuit

TDM bus   virtual circuit approach to packet
                                                    switching
time-division switching

time-slot interchange (TSI)

14.5   SUMMARY

- Switching is a method in which multiple communication devices are connected to one another efficiently.
- A switch is intermediary hardware or software that links devices together temporarily.
- There are three fundamental switching methods: circuit switching, packet switching, and message switching
- In circuit switching, packets from a single device travel on dedicated links to the destination. Space-division and/or time-division switches may be used.
- In a space-division switch, the path from one device to another is spatially separate from other paths.
- A crossbar is the most common space-division switch. It connects n inputs to m outputs via $n \times m$ crosspoints.
- Multistage switches can reduce the number of crosspoints needed, but blocking may result.
- Blocking occurs when not every input has its own unique path to every output.
- In a time-division switch, the inputs are divided in time, using TDM. A control unit sends the input to the correct output device.
- The time-slot interchange and the TDM bus are two examples of a time-division switch.
- Space- and time-division switches may be combined.
- The PSTN is an example of a circuit-switched network.
- Packet switching is generally more efficient than circuit switching for nonvoice communication.
- There are two popular approaches to packet switching: the datagram approach and the virtual circuit approach.
- In the datagram approach, each packet (called a datagram) is treated independently from all other packets.
- In the virtual circuit approach, all packets of a message or session follow the exact same route. Virtual circuit packet switching is implemented in two forms: switched virtual circuit (SVC) and permanent virtual circuit (PVC).

■ In message switching (also known as store and forward), a node receives a message, stores it, and then sends it.

■ In circuit switching, the different segments of a message follow a dedicated path. In the virtual approach to packet switching, the segments follow a created route, the links of which may be shared by other connections.

14.6 PRACTICE SET

Review Questions

1. Which is more efficient, circuit switching or virtual circuit switching? Why?
2. Discuss the concept of switching as it relates to the problems involved in the connection of devices.
3. What are the three switching methods?
4. What are the two types of switches used in circuit switching?
5. What is a crosspoint in a crossbar switch?
6. What is the limiting factor in a crossbar switch? How does a multistage switch alleviate the problem?
7. How is blocking related to a crossbar switch?
8. How is blocking related to a multistage switch?
9. Compare the mechanism of a space-division switch to the mechanism of a time-division switch.
10. Name the two technologies used in a time-division switch.
11. Compare a TSI to a TDM bus.
12. What is the function of the control unit in a TSI and a TDM bus?
13. How is space-division switching superior to time-division switching?
14. How is time-division switching superior to space-division switching?
15. What are the five types of offices of the PSTN?
16. Why is circuit switching inefficient for the transmission of nonvoice data?
17. What is the fundamental difference between circuit switching and packet switching?
18. What are the two popular approaches to packet switching?
19. A message is broken up into three pieces. Discuss the transmission of the packets using the datagram approach to packet switching.
20. A message is broken up into three pieces. Discuss the transmission of the packets using a permanent virtual circuit.
21. A message is broken up into three pieces. Discuss the transmission of the packets using a switched virtual circuit.

22. Why has message switching been replaced by other switching methods?

Multiple Choice Questions

23. Which type of switching uses the entire capacity of a dedicated link?
    a. circuit switching
    b. datagram packet switching
    c. virtual circuit packet switching
    d. message switching

24. The _____ is a device that connects n inputs to m outputs.
    a. crosspoint
    b. crossbar
    c. modem
    d. RAM

25. In which type of switching do all the datagrams of a message follow the same channels of a path?
    a. circuit switching
    b. datagram packet switching
    c. virtual circuit packet switching
    d. message switching

26. How many crosspoints are needed in a single-stage switch with 40 inputs and 50 outputs?
    a. 40
    b. 50
    c. 90
    d. 2000

27. In a crossbar with 1000 crosspoints, how many statistically are in use at any time?
    a. 100
    b. 250
    c. 500
    d. 1000

28. The _____ of a TSI controls the order of delivery of slot values that are stored in RAM.
    a. crossbar
    b. crosspoint
    c. control unit
    d. transceiver

29. In _____ circuit switching, delivery of data is delayed because data must be stored and retrieved from RAM.

a. space-division

b. time-division

c. virtual

d. packet

30. In _____, each packet of a message need not follow the same path from sender to receiver.

    a. circuit switching

    b. message switching

    c. the virtual approach to packet switching

    d. the datagram approach to packet switching

31. In _____, each packet of a message follows the same path from sender to receiver.

    a. circuit switching

    b. message switching

    c. the virtual approach to packet switching

    d. the datagram approach to packet switching

32. A switched virtual circuit involves _____.

    a. connection establishment

    b. data transfer

    c. connection release

    d. all of the above

33. A permanent virtual circuit involves _____.

    a. connection establishment

    b. data transfer

    c. connection release

    d. all of the above

34. To create a _____, combine crossbar switches in stages.

    a. multistage switch

    b. crosspoint

    c. packet switch

    d. TSI

35. Which of the following is a time-division switch?

    a. TSI

    b. TDM bus

    c. crosspoint

    d. a and b

36. In a time-division switch, a _____ governs the destination of a packet stored in RAM.

    a. TDM bus

b. crosspoint

c. crossbar

d. control unit

37. The PSTN is an example of a _____ network.

a. packet-switched

b. circuit-switched

c. message-switched

d. none of the above

Exercises

38. How many crosspoints are needed if we use a crossbar switch to connect 1000 telephones in a small town?

39. In Figure 14.24, find the number of crosspoints needed.

Figure 14.24   *Exercises 39, 40, 42, and 43*

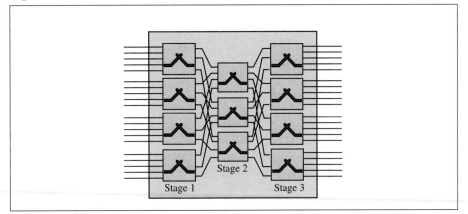

40. How many crosspoints are needed if we use only one crossbar switch in Figure 14.24?

41. Using Exercises 39 and 40, how much is the efficiency improved if we use three stages instead of one?

42. In Figure 14.24, how many users connected to each first-stage switch can access the system at the same time? How many total users can access the whole system? Is there any relationship between the first and the second answer? Can you say that the second answer can be obtained from the first answer?

43. In Figure 14.24, can we alleviate the blocking problem by adding more second-stage switches?

44. Which of the three-stage switches in Figure 14.25 has a better performance in terms of blocking? Justify your answer. Find the number of input/output connections for the middle switches.

Figure 14.25 *Exercise 44*

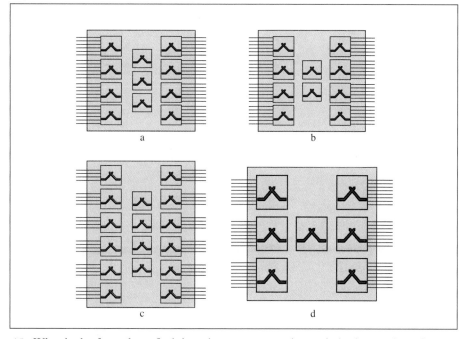

45. What is the formula to find, in a three-stage crossbar switch, the number of cross-points (n) in terms of the number of input/output lines (N), the number of first- and third-stage switches (K), and the number of second-stage switches (L)?

46. In Figure 14.12, what goes to the output lines if the input lines receive "A," "B," "C" and "D"?

47. Design a folded TDM bus with four lines.

48. Design a TSSST switch with 48 inputs and 48 outputs. The input multiplexers should be 4×1; the output multiplexers should be 1×4.

49. Design an STS switch with 10 inputs and 10 outputs. The first-stage switches should be 5×2 and the last-stage switches should be 2×5.

50. Show the sequence of signal frequencies sent when a user dials 864-8902 using a Touch-Tone phone.

51. Complete Table 14.1 to compare a circuit-switched network with a packet-switched network.

Table 14.1 *Exercise 51*

Issue	*Circuit-Switched*	*Packet-Switched*
Dedicated path		
Store and forward		
Need for connection establishment		
Routing table		
Delay		

52. Complete Table 14.2 to compare a datagram approach with a virtual circuit approach of a packet-switching network.

Table 14.2   *Exercise 52*

Issue	Datagram	Virtual Circuit
All packets follow the same route		
Table lookup		
Connection establishment		
Packet may arrive out of order		

53. Complete Table 14.3 to compare a PVC to an SVC connection.

Table 14.3   *Exercise 53*

Issue	PVC	SVC
Connection and disconnection		
Payment		
Table lookup		
Duration of an entry in a table		

CHAPTER 15

Point-to-Point Protocol (PPP)

Today, millions of Internet users need to connect their home computers to the computers of an Internet provider to access the Internet. There are also a lot of individuals who need to connect to a computer from home, but they do not want to go through the Internet. The majority of these users have either a dialup or leased telephone line. The telephone line provides a physical link, but to control and manage the transfer of data, there is a need for a point-to-point link protocol. Figure 15.1 shows a physical point-to-point connection.

Figure 15.1 *Point-to-point link*

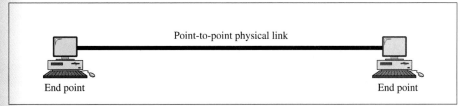

The first protocol devised for this purpose was **Serial Line Internet Protocol (SLIP).** However, SLIP has some deficiencies: it does not support protocols other than Internet Protocol (IP), it does not allow the IP addresses to be assigned dynamically, and it does not support authentication of the user. The **Point-to-Point Protocol (PPP)** is a protocol designed to respond to these deficiencies.

15.1 TRANSITION STATES

The different phases through which a PPP connection goes can be described using a **transition state** diagram as shown in Figure 15.2.

■ **Idle state.** The **idle state** means that the link is not being used. There is no active carrier and the line is quiet.

■ **Establishing state.** When one of the end points starts the communication, the connection goes into the **establishing state.** In this state, options are negotiated

Figure 15.2 *Transition states*

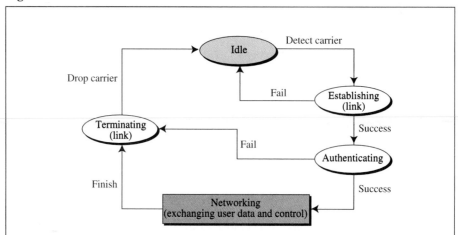

between the two parties. If the negotiation is successful, the system goes to the authenticating state (if authentication is required) or directly to the networking state. The LCP packets, discussed shortly, are used for this purpose. Several packets may be exchanged during this state.

- **Authenticating state.** The **authenticating state** is optional; the two end points may decide, during the establishing state, not to go through this state. However, if they decide to proceed with authentication, they send several authentication packets, discussed in a later section. If the result is successful, the connection goes to the networking state; otherwise, it goes to the terminating state.

- **Networking state.** The **networking state** is the heart of the transition states. When a connection reaches this state, the exchange of user control and data packets can be started. The connection remains in this state until one of the end points wants to terminate the connection.

- **Terminating state.** When the connection is in the **terminating state,** several packets are exchanged between the two ends for house cleaning and closing the link.

15.2 PPP LAYERS

Figure 15.3 shows the PPP layers. PPP has only physical and data link layers. This means that a protocol that wants to use the services of PPP should have other layers (network, transport, and so on).

> PPP operates only at the physical and data link layers.

Physical Layer

No specific protocol is defined for the physical layer in PPP. Instead, it is left to the implementer to use whatever is available. PPP supports any of the protocols recognized by ANSI.

Figure 15.3 *PPP layers*

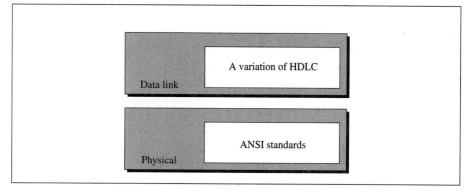

Data Link Layer

At the data link layer, PPP employs a version of HDLC. Figure 15.4 shows the format of a PPP frame.

Figure 15.4 *PPP frame*

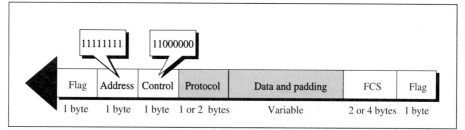

The descriptions of the fields are as follows:

- **Flag field.** The flag field, like the one in HDLC, identifies the boundaries of a PPP frame. Its value is 01111110.
- **Address field.** Because PPP is used for a point-to-point connection, it uses the broadcast address of HDLC, 11111111, to avoid a data link address in the protocol.
- **Control field.** The control field uses the format of the U-frame in HDLC. The value is 11000000 to show that the frame does not contain any sequence numbers and that there is no flow and error control.
- **Protocol field.** The protocol field defines what is being carried in the data field: user data or other information. We will discuss this field in detail shortly.
- **Data field.** This field carries either the user data or other information that we will discuss shortly.
- **FCS.** The frame check sequence field, as in HDLC, is simply a two-byte or four-byte CRC.

15.3   LINK CONTROL PROTOCOL (LCP)

The **Link Control Protocol (LCP)** is responsible for establishing, maintaining, configuring, and terminating links. It also provides negotiation mechanisms to set options between the two end points. Both end points of the link must reach an agreement about the options before the link can be established.

All LCP packets are carried in the payload field of the PPP frame. What defines the frame as one carrying an LCP packet is the value of the protocol field, which should be set to $C021_{16}$. Figure 15.5 shows the format of the LCP packet.

Figure 15.5   *LCP packet encapsulated in a frame*

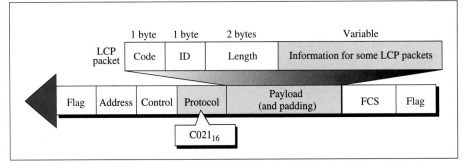

The descriptions of the fields are as follows:

- **Code.** This field defines the type of LCP packet. We will discuss these packets and their purpose in the next section.
- **ID.** This field holds a value used to match a request with the reply. One end point inserts a value in this field, which will be copied in the reply packet.
- **Length.** This field defines the length of the whole LCP packet.
- **Information.** This field contains extra information needed for some LCP packets.

LCP Packets

Table 15.1 lists some LCP packets.

Table 15.1   *LCP packets and their codes*

Code	Packet Type	Description
01_{16}	Configure-request	Contains the list of proposed options and their values
02_{16}	Configure-ack	Accepts all options proposed
03_{16}	Configure-nak	Announces that some options are not acceptable
04_{16}	Configure-reject	Announces that some options are not recognized
05_{16}	Terminate-request	Requests to shut the line down
06_{16}	Terminate-ack	Accepts the shut-down request

Figure 15.6 *PAP*

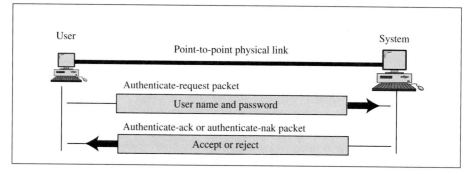

PAP Packets

PAP packets are encapsulated in a PPP frame. What distinguishes a PAP packet from other packets is the value of the protocol field, $C023_{16}$. There are three PAP packets: authenticate-request, authenticate-ack, and authenticate-nak. The first packet is used by the user to send the user name and password. The second is used by the system to allow access. The third is used by the system to deny access. Figure 15.7 shows the format of the three packets.

Figure 15.7 *PAP packets*

CHAP

The **Challenge Handshake Authentication Protocol (CHAP)** is a three-way hand-shaking authentication protocol that provides more security than PAP. In this method, the password is kept secret; it is never sent on-line.

- The system sends to the user a challenge packet containing a challenge value, usually a few bytes.
- The user applies a predefined function that takes the challenge value and the user's own password and creates a result. The user sends the result in the response packet to the system.
- The system does the same. It applies the same function to the password of the user (known to the system) and the challenge value to create a result. If the result created is the same as the result sent in the response packet, access is granted; otherwise, it is denied.

CHAP is more secure than PAP, especially if the system continuously changes the challenge value. Even if the intruder learns the challenge value and the result, the password is still secret. Figure 15.8 shows the idea.

Figure 15.8   *CHAP*

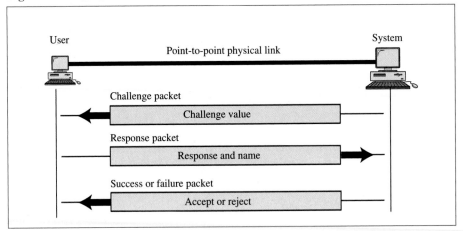

CHAP Packets

CHAP packets are encapsulated in the PPP frame. What distinguishes a CHAP packet from other packets is the value of the protocol field, $C223_{16}$. There are four CHAP packets: challenge, response, success, and failure. The first packet is used by the system to send the challenge value. The second is used by the user to return the result of the calculation. The third is used by the system to allow access to the system. The fourth is used by the system to deny access to the system. Figure 15.9 shows the format of the four packets.

15.5   NETWORK CONTROL PROTOCOL (NCP)

After the link has been established and authentication (if any) has been successful, the connection goes to the networking state. In this state, PPP uses another protocol called **Network Control Protocol (NCP).** NCP is a set of control protocols to allow the

Figure 15.9   *CHAP packets*

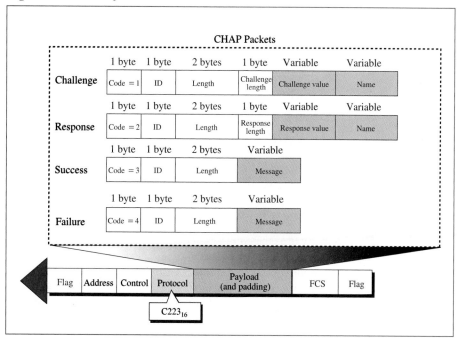
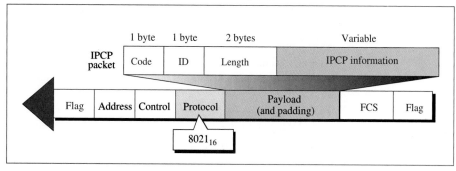

encapsulation of data coming from network layer protocols (such as IP, IPX, and AppleTalk) in the PPP frame.

IPCP

The set of packets that establish and terminate a network layer connection for IP packets is called **Internetwork Protocol Control Protocol (IPCP).** The format of an IPCP packet is shown in Figure 15.10. Note that the value of the protocol field, 8021_{16}, defines the packet encapsulated in the protocol as an IPCP packet.

Figure 15.10   *IPCP packet encapsulated in PPP frame*

Seven packets are defined for the IPCP protocol, distinguished by their code values as shown in Table 15.3.

Table 15.3   *Code value for IPCP packets*

Code	IPCP packet
01	Configure-request
02	Configure-ack
03	Configure-nak
04	Configure-reject
05	Terminate-request
06	Terminate-ack
07	Code-reject

A party uses the configure-request packet to negotiate options with the other party and to set the IP addresses, and so on.

After configuration, the link is ready to carry IP protocol data in the payload field of a PPP frame. This time, the value of the protocol field is 0021_{16} to show that the IP data packet, not the IPCP packet, is being carried across the link.

After IP has sent all of its packets the IPCP can take control and use the terminate-request and terminate-ack packets to end the network connection.

Other Protocols

Note that other protocols have their own sets of control packets defined by the value of the protocol field in the PPP frame.

15.6   AN EXAMPLE

Let us give an example of the states through which a PPP connection goes to deliver some network layer packets. Figure 15.11 shows the steps:

- **Establishing.** The user sends the configure-request packet to negotiate the options for establishing the link. The user requests PAP authentication. After the user receives the configure-ack packet, link establishing is done.

- **Authenticating.** The user sends the authenticate-request packet and includes the user name and password. After it receives the configure-ack packet, the authentication phase is over.

- **Networking.** Now the user sends the configure-request to negotiate the options for the network layer activity. After it receives the configure-ack, the user can send the network layer data, which may consume several frames. After all data are sent, the user sends the terminate-request to terminate the network layer activity. When the terminate-ack packet is received, the networking phase is complete. The connection goes to the terminating state.

Figure 15.11   *An example*

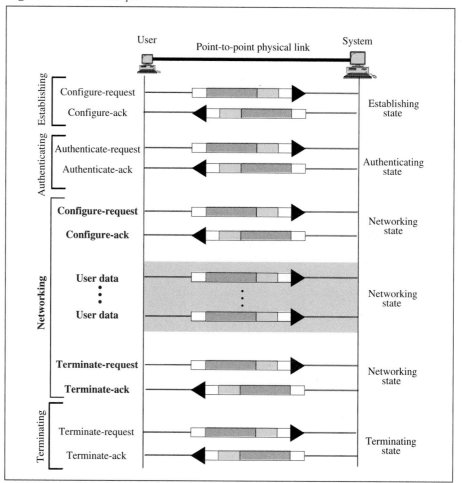

- **Terminating.** The user sends the terminate-request packet to terminate the link. With the receipt of the terminate-ack packet, the link is terminated.

15.7   KEY TERMS AND CONCEPTS

authenticating state	idle state
authentication	Internetwork Protocol Control Protocol (IPCP)
Challenge Handshake Authentication Protocol (CHAP)	Link Control Protocol (LCP)
establishing state	Network Control Protocol (NCP)

networking state   Serial Line Internet Protocol (SLIP)

Password Authentication Protocol (PAP)   terminating state

Point-to-Point Protocol (PPP)   transition state

15.8   SUMMARY

- The Point-to-Point Protocol (PPP) was designed for users who need to connect to a computer system through a telephone line.
- A PPP connection goes through various phases: idle, establishing, authenticating, networking, and terminating.
- PPP operates at the physical and data link layers of the OSI model.
- At the data link layer, PPP employs a version of HDLC.
- The Link Control Protocol (LCP) is responsible for establishing, maintaining, configuring, and terminating links.
- Password Authentication Protocol (PAP) and Challenge Handshake Authentication Protocol (CHAP) are two protocols used for authentication in PPP.
- PAP is a two-step process. The user sends authentication identification and a password. The system determines the validity of the information sent.
- CHAP is a three-step process. The system sends a value to the user. The user manipulates the value and sends its result. The system verifies the result.
- Network Control Protocol (NCP) is a set of protocols; each set is specific for a network layer protocol that requires the services of PPP.
- Internetwork Protocol Control Protocol (IPCP), an NCP protocol, establishes and terminates a network layer connection for IP packets.

15.9   PRACTICE SET

Review Questions

1. Which type of user needs PPP?
2. Describe each of the states of a PPP connection.
3. Discuss the physical layer of PPP.
4. Discuss the data link layer of PPP.
5. Discuss the control field of the PPP frame.
6. What is the purpose of the LCP?
7. Discuss the relationship between the LCP packet and the PPP frame.
8. What are the categories of LCP packets? What is the function of each category?
9. What two protocols are used for authentication in PPP?

10. How does PAP work? What is its primary deficiency?
11. How does CHAP work? Why is it superior to PAP?
12. How does the PPP frame carry authentication packets from PAP and CHAP?
13. What is the purpose of NCP?
14. What is the relationship between IPCP and NCP?

Multiple Choice Questions

15. A protocol to allow the telephone line connection of a computer to another computer is _____.
    a. PPP
    b. SLIP
    c. PLP
    d. a and b

16. According to the PPP transition state diagram, exchange of user control and data packets occurs in the _____ state.
    a. establishing
    b. authenticating
    c. networking
    d. terminating

17. According to the PPP transition state diagram, options are negotiated in the _____ state.
    a. establishing
    b. authenticating
    c. networking
    d. terminating

18. According to the PPP transition state diagram, verification of user identification occurs in the _____ state.
    a. establishing
    b. authenticating
    c. networking
    d. terminating

19. According to the PPP transition state diagram, the link is disconnected in the _____ state.
    a. establishing
    b. authenticating
    c. networking
    d. terminating

20. PPP is a _____ layer protocol.
    a. physical
    b. data link

    c. physical and data link

    d. seven

21. Which protocol(s) is (are) specified for the PPP physical layer?

    a. LCP

    b. SLIP

    c. CHAP and PAP

    d. no protocol is specified

22. In the PPP frame, the _____ field defines the contents of the data field.

    a. flag

    b. control

    c. protocol

    d. FCS

23. In the PPP frame, the _____ field is similar to that of the U-frame in HDLC.

    a. flag

    b. control

    c. protocol

    d. FCS

24. In the PPP frame, the _____ field has a value of 11111111 to indicate the broadcast address of HDLC.

    a. address

    b. control

    c. protocol

    d. FCS

25. In the PPP frame, the _____ field is for error control.

    a. flag

    b. control

    c. protocol

    d. FCS

26. What is the purpose of LCP packets?

    a. configuration

    b. termination

    c. option negotiation

    d. all of the above

27. _____ is a three-way handshake for user verification.

    a. PPP

    b. CHAP

    c. PAP

    d. b and c

28. A PAP packet and a CHAP packet can be distinguished by the value of the
    _____ field of the PPP frame.
    a. address
    b. control
    c. protocol
    d. FCS

29. PAP requires _____ and _____ from the user.
    a. a password; a calculated value
    b. authentication identification; a password
    c. a challenge value; a password
    d. authentication identification; a calculated value

30. For CHAP authentication, the user takes the system's _____ and its own
    _____ to create a result that is then sent to the system.
    a. authentication identification; password
    b. password; challenge value
    c. password; authentication identification
    d. challenge value; password

31. _____, an (a)_____ protocol, establishes and terminates a network layer con-
    nection for IP packets.
    a. NCP; IPCP
    b. CHAP; NCP
    c. IPCP; NCP
    d. SLIP; PPP

Exercises

32. What is the value of the flag, address, and control fields in hexadecimal?

33. Make a table to compare the PPP frame with the U-frame of HDLC. Which fields
    are the same? Which fields are different?

34. The value of the first few bytes of a frame is $7EFFC0C02105_{16}$. What is the proto-
    col of the encapsulated payload? What is the type of packet?

35. The value of the first few bytes of a frame is $7EFFC0C02109110014_{16}$. What is the
    protocol of the encapsulated payload? What type of packet is being carried? How
    many bytes of information are in the packet?

36. Show the contents of a configure-nak packet in the LCP protocol. Encapsulate the
    packet in a PPP frame.

37. Show the contents of a configure-nak packet in the NCP protocol. Encapsulate the
    packet in a PPP frame.

38. Compare the results of Exercises 36 and 37. What differences do you see?

39. Show the contents of an echo-request packet with the message "Hello." Write the whole packet in hexadecimal. Encapsulate the packet in a PPP frame and show the contents in hexadecimal.

40. Show the contents of an echo-reply in response to the packet in Exercise 39. Write the whole packet in hexadecimal. Encapsulate the packet in a PPP frame and show the contents in hexadecimal.

41. Show the contents of an authenticate-request packet using "Forouzan" as the user name and "797979" as the password. Encapsulate the packet in a PPP frame.

42. Show the contents of the authenticate-ack that is received in response to the packet in Exercise 41.

43. Show the contents of a challenge packet (CHAP) using $A4253616_{16}$ as the challenge value. Encapsulate the packet in a PPP frame.

44. Show the contents of a response packet (CHAP) using $6163524A_{16}$ as the response value. Encapsulate the packet in a PPP frame.

45. A system sends the challenge value $2A2B1425_{16}$. The password of the user is 22112211_{16}. The function to be used by the user adds the challenge value to the password; the result should be split into two and swapped to get the response. Show the response of the user.

46. If a user sends an LCP packet with code 02_{16}, what is the state of the connection after this event?

47. A connection is in the establishing state. If the user receives an LCP configure-nak packet, what is the new state?

48. A connection is in the networking state. If the user receives an NCP configure-nak packet, what is the new state?

49. Show the contents of all frames in Figure 15.11. What protocol (LCP, NCP, authentication, and so on) is involved in each transmission?

CHAPTER 16

Integrated Services Digital Network (ISDN)

Integrated Services Digital Network (ISDN) was developed by ITU-T in 1976. It is a set of protocols that combines digital telephony and data transport services. The whole idea is to digitize the telephone network to permit the transmission of audio, video, and text over existing telephone lines.

ISDN is an effort to standardize subscriber services, provide user/network interfaces, and facilitate the internetworking capabilities of existing voice and data networks.

The goal of ISDN is to form a wide area network that provides universal end-to-end connectivity over digital media. This can be done by integrating all of the separate transmission services into one without adding new links or subscriber lines.

16.1 SERVICES

The purpose of the ISDN is to provide fully integrated digital services to users. These services fall into three categories: bearer services, teleservices, and supplementary services (see Figure 16.1).

Bearer Services

Bearer services provide the means to transfer information (voice, data, and video) between users without the network manipulating the content of that information. The network does not need to process the information and therefore does not change the content. Bearer services belong to the first three layers of the OSI model and are well defined in the ISDN standard. They can be provided using circuit-switched, packet-switched, frame-switched, or cell-switched networks (discussed in Chapters 17, 18, and 19).

Teleservices

In teleservicing, the network may change or process the contents of the data. These services correspond to layers 4–7 of the OSI model. **Teleservices** rely on the facilities of

Figure 16.1   *ISDN services*

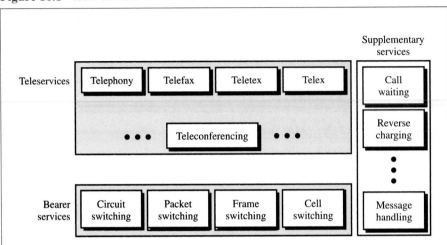

the bearer services and are designed to accommodate complex user needs without the user having to be aware of the details of the process. Teleservices include telephony, teletex, telefax, videotex, telex, and teleconferencing. Although the ISDN defines these services by name, they have not yet become standards.

Supplementary Services

Supplementary services are those services that provide additional functionality to the bearer services and teleservices. Examples of these services are reverse charging, call waiting, and message handling, all familiar from today's telephone company services.

16.2   HISTORY

The evolution of the ISDN reveals the concepts most critical to an understanding of it.

Voice Communication over Analog Networks

Initially, telecommunications networks were entirely **analog networks** and were used for the transmission of analog information in the form of voice. The local loops connecting the subscriber's handset to the telephone company's central office were also analog (see Figure 16.2).

Voice and Data Communication over Analog Networks

With the advent of digital processing, subscribers needed to exchange data as well as voice. Modems were developed to allow digital exchanges over existing analog lines (see Figure 16.3).

Figure 16.2 *Voice communication over an analog telephone network*

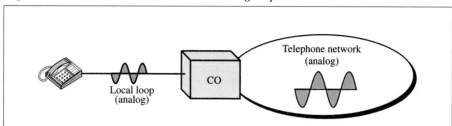

Figure 16.3 *Voice and data communication over an analog telephone network*

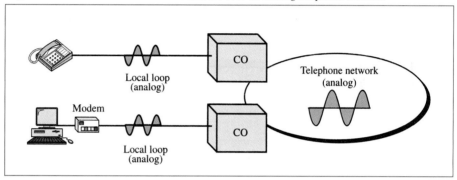

Analog and Digital Services to Subscribers

To reduce cost and improve performance, the telephone companies gradually began to add digital technologies while continuing their analog services to their customers (see Figure 16.4).

Three types of customers were identified at this time: traditional customers using their local loops only for analog purposes; customers using analog facilities to transmit digital information via modem; and customers using digital services to transmit digital information. Of these, the first group was still the most prominent and therefore most of the services offered remained analog.

Integrated Digital Network (IDN)

Next, customers began to require access to a variety of networks, such as packet-switched networks and circuit-switched networks. To meet these needs, the telephone companies created **Integrated Digital Networks (IDNs).** An IDN is a combination of networks available for different purposes (see Figure 16.5). Access to these networks is by **digital pipes,** which are time-multiplexed channels sharing very-high-speed paths. Customers can use their local loops to transmit both voice and data to their telephone company's central office. The office then directs these calls to the appropriate **digital networks** via the digital pipes. Notice that the majority of subscribers today continue to use analog local loops, although digital local loop services such as switched/56, DDS, and DS are available. (These services were discussed in Chapter 8.)

Figure 16.4   *Analog and digital services over the telephone network*

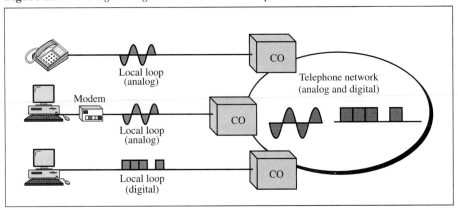

Figure 16.5   *IDN*

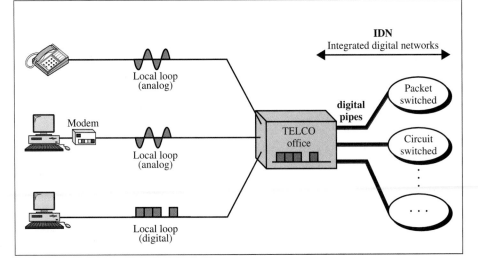

Integrated Services Digital Network (ISDN)

The ISDN integrates customer services with the IDN. As we saw in the discussion of packet-switched networks in Chapter 14, fully digital services are much more efficient and flexible than analog services. To receive the maximum benefit from the integrated digital networks, the next step is to replace the analog local loops with digital subscriber loops. Voice transmissions can be digitized at the source, thereby removing the final need for analog carriers. It then becomes possible to send data, voice, image, facsimile, and so on over any digital network. With ISDN all customer services will become digital rather than analog, and the flexibility offered by the new technology will allow customer services to be made available on demand. Most important, ISDN will allow all communication connections in a home or building to occur via a single interface.

> ISDN incorporates all communication connections in a home or building into a single interface.

Figure 16.6 gives a conceptual view of the connections between users and an ISDN central office. Each user is linked to the central office through a digital pipe. These pipes can be of different capacities to allow different rates of transmission and support different subscriber needs.

Figure 16.6 *ISDN*

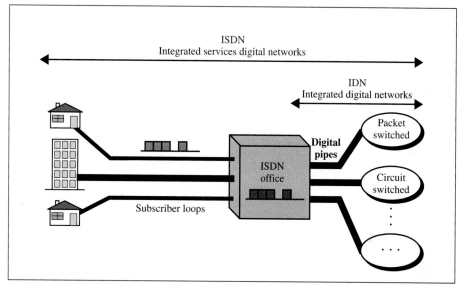

16.3   SUBSCRIBER ACCESS TO THE ISDN

To allow flexibility, digital pipes between customers and the ISDN office (the subscriber loops) are organized into multiple channels of different sizes. The ISDN standard defines three channel types, each with a different transmission rate: bearer channels, data channels, and hybrid channels (see Table 16.1).

Table 16.1 *Channel rates*

Channel	Data Rate (Kbps)
Bearer (B)	64
Data (D)	16, 64
Hybrid (H)	384, 1536, 1920

B Channels

A **bearer channel (B channel)** is defined at a rate of 64 Kbps. It is the basic user channel and can carry any type of digital information in full-duplex mode as long as the required transmission rate does not exceed 64 Kbps. For example, a B channel can be used to carry digital data, digitized voice, or other low data-rate information. Several transmissions can be accommodated at once if the signals are multiplexed first. Multiplexed transmissions of this sort, however, must be destined for a single recipient. A B channel carries transmissions end-to-end. It is not designed to demultiplex a stream midway in order to separate and divert transmissions to more than one recipient.

D Channels

A **data channel (D channel)** can be either 16 or 64 Kbps, depending on the needs of the user. Although the name says *data,* the primary function of a D channel is to carry control signaling for the B channels.

Up to this point, the transmission protocols we have examined all use in-channel **(in-band) signaling.** Control information (such as call establishment, ringing, call interrupt, or synchronization) is carried by the same channel that carries the message data. The ISDN separates control signals onto a channel of their own, the D channel. A D channel carries the control signaling for all of the channels in a given path, using a method called common-channel **(out-of-band) signaling.**

In this mechanism, a subscriber uses the D channel to connect to the network and secure a B channel connection. The subscriber then uses the B channel to send actual data to another user. All the devices attached to a given subscriber loop use the same D channel for signaling, but each sends data over a B channel dedicated to a single exchange for the duration of the exchange. Using the D channel is similar to having a telephone operator place a call for you. You pick up the phone and tell the operator what type of call you wish to place and the number you wish to contact. The operator finds an open line appropriate for your needs, rings your party, and connects you. The D channel acts like an operator between the user and the network at the network layer.

Less common uses for the D channel include low-rate data transfer and applications such as telemetry and alarm transmission.

H Channels

Hybrid channels (H channels) are available with data rates of 384 Kbps (H0), 1536 Kbps (H11), or 1920 Kbps (H12). These rates suit H channels for high data-rate applications such as video, teleconferencing, and so on.

User Interfaces

Digital subscriber loops are of two types: basic rate interface (BRI) and primary rate interface (PRI). Each type is suited to a different level of customer needs. Both include one D channel and some number of either B or H channels.

BRI

The **basic rate interface (BRI)** specifies a digital pipe consisting of two B channels and one 16 Kbps D channel (see Figure 16.7).

Figure 16.7   *BRI*

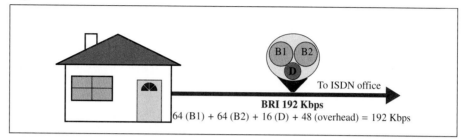

BRI 192 Kbps
64 (B1) + 64 (B2) + 16 (D) + 48 (overhead) = 192 Kbps

Two B channels of 64 Kbps each, plus one D channel of 16 Kbps, equals 144 Kbps. In addition, the BRI service itself requires 48 Kbps of operating overhead. BRI therefore requires a digital pipe of 192 Kbps. Conceptually, the BRI service is like a large pipe that contains three smaller pipes, two for the B channels and one for the D channel. The remainder of the space inside the large pipe carries the overhead bits required for its operation. In Figure 16.7, the overhead is shown by the shaded portion of the circle surrounding the B and D channels.

The BRI is designed to meet the needs of residential and small-office customers. In most cases, there is no need to replace the existing local-loop cable. The same twisted-pair local loop that delivers analog transmission can be used to handle digital transmission. Occasionally, however, some conditioning of the line is necessary.

PRI

The usual **primary rate interface (PRI)** specifies a digital pipe with 23 B channels and one 64 Kbps D channel (see Figure 16.8).

Figure 16.8   *PRI*

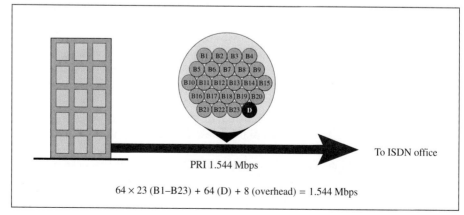

PRI 1.544 Mbps

64 × 23 (B1–B23) + 64 (D) + 8 (overhead) = 1.544 Mbps

Twenty-three B channels of 64 Kbps each, plus one D channel of 64 Kbps equals 1.536 Mbps. In addition, the PRI service itself uses 8 Kbps of overhead. PRI therefore requires a digital pipe of 1.544 Mbps. Conceptually, the PRI service is like a large pipe containing 24 smaller pipes, 23 for the B channels and 1 for the D channel. The rest of the pipe carries the overhead bits required for its operation. In Figure 16.8, the overhead is shown by the shaded portion of the circle surrounding the B and D channels.

The 23 B channels and 1 D channel indicate the maximum number of separate channels a PRI can contain. In other words, one PRI can provide full-duplex transmission between as many as 23 source and receiving nodes. The individual transmissions are collected from their sources and multiplexed onto a single path (digital subscriber line) for sending to the ISDN office.

The 1.544 Mbps of a PRI can be divided up in many other ways to meet the requirements of a number of users. For example, a LAN using a PRI to connect it to other LANs uses all 1.544 Mbps to send one 1.544 Mbps signal. Other applications can use other combinations of the 64 Kbps B channels. At 1.544 Mbps, the capacity of the PRI digital pipe is exactly the same as the capacity of the T-1 line used to support the North American DS-1 telephone service. This similarity is not a coincidence. PRI was designed to be compatible with existing T-1 lines. In Europe, the PRI includes 30 B channels and 2 D channels, giving it a capacity of 2.048 Mbps—the capacity of an E-1 line.

For more specialized transmission needs, other channel combinations are also supported by the PRI standard. They are 3H0 + D, 4H0 + D, and H12 + D.

Functional Grouping

In the ISDN standard, the devices that enable users to access the services of the BRI or PRI are described by their functional duties and collected in functional groupings. Subscribers choose the specific devices best suited to their needs from these groupings. Remember that the ISDN defines only the functional behavior of each group. The standard does not say anything about implementation. Each functional grouping is a model that can be implemented using devices or equipment chosen by the subscriber. Functional groupings used at the subscriber's premises include network terminations (types 1 and 2), terminal equipment (types 1 and 2), and terminal adapters.

Network Termination 1 (NT1)

A **network termination 1 (NT1)** device controls the physical and electrical termination of the ISDN at the user's premises and connects the user's internal system to the digital subscriber loop. These functions are comparable to those defined for the OSI physical layer (see Figure 16.9).

An NT1 organizes the data streams from a connected subscriber into frames that can be sent over the digital pipe, and translates the frames received from the network into a format usable by the subscriber's devices. To this end it performs the basic multiplexing functions of byte interleaving, but it is not a multiplexer. An NT1 synchronizes the data stream with the frame-building process in such a way that multiplexing occurs automatically.

The easiest way to visualize how frame building in an NT1 can result in an interleaved signal is by analogy. Imagine a manufacturing plant with two conveyor belts.

Figure 16.9   *Functional grouping*

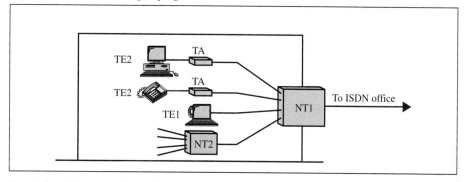

One belt collects a variety of completed products from several parts of the manufacturing department and carries them to the shipping department. At the shipping department, that belt meets a conveyor belt carrying boxes, each of which is designed to hold a specific product. The conveyer belt of products meets the conveyor belt of boxes at right angles. The two belts are synchronized so that as a given product reaches the end of its belt, it falls off into the appropriate box. The ordering of the boxes and products and the timing of the two belts must be controlled to keep the synchronization accurate. Discrepancies can result in a product's landing in the wrong box or missing the boxes altogether. With adequate synchronization, however, product packaging occurs accurately without switching or other manipulation. In the same way, an NT1 synchronizes the timing of the contributing data streams to the building of the outgoing frames so that bytes are interleaved without the need for multiplexing devices.

Network Termination 2 (NT2)

A **network termination 2 (NT2)** device performs functions at the physical, data link, and network layers of the OSI model (layers 1, 2, and 3). NT2s provide multiplexing (layer 1), flow control (layer 2), and packetizing (layer 3). An NT2 provides intermediate signal processing between the data-generating devices and an NT1. The NT1 is still required to provide a physical interface to the network. There must be a point-to-point connection between an NT2 and an NT1. NT2s are used primarily to interface between a multiuser system and an NT1 in a PRI (see Figure 16.9).

NT2s can be implemented by a variety of equipment types. For example, a **private branch exchange** (digital **PBX**) can be an NT2; it coordinates transmissions from a number of incoming links (user phone lines) and multiplexes them to make them transmittable by an NT1. A LAN also can function as an NT2.

If a PRI carries signals from multiple devices, those signals must be multiplexed in a separate process provided by the NT2 before the composite signal passes to the NT1 for transmission to the network. This multiplexing is explicit. A digital PBX is an example of an NT2 that contains explicit multiplexing functions.

Terminal Equipment 1 (TE1)

The term *terminal equipment* is used by the ISDN standard to mean the same thing as DTE in other protocols. It refers to digital subscriber equipment. **Terminal equipment 1 (TE1)** is any device that supports the ISDN standards. Examples of

TE1s are digital telephones, integrated voice/data terminals, and digital facsimiles (see Figure 16.9).

Terminal Equipment 2 (TE2)

To provide backward compatibility with a customer's existing equipment, the ISDN standard defines a second level of terminal equipment called **terminal equipment 2 (TE2)**. TE2 equipment is any non-ISDN device, such as a terminal, workstation, host computer, or regular telephone. TE2 devices are not immediately compatible with an ISDN network but can be used with the help of another device called a **terminal adapter (TA)**; see Figure 16.9.

Terminal Adapter (TA)

A terminal adapter (TA) converts information received in non-ISDN format from a TE2 into a format capable of being carried by the ISDN (see Figure 16.9).

Reference Points

Used here, the term *reference point* refers to the label used to identify individual interfaces between two elements of an ISDN installation. Just as the functional grouping defines the function of each type of equipment used in the ISDN, a reference point defines the functions of the connections between them. Specifically, a reference point defines how two network elements must be connected and the format of the traffic between them. We mention here only those reference points that define the interfaces between a subscriber's equipment and the network: reference points R, S, T, and U (see Figure 16.10). Other reference points define functions within the ISDN.

Figure 16.10 *Reference points*

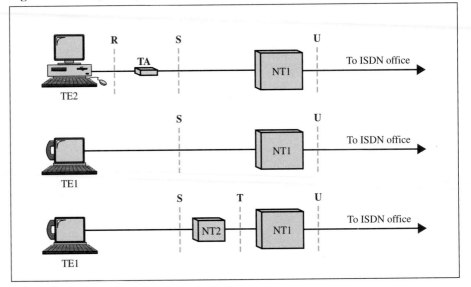

Reference point R defines the connection between a TE2 and a TA. **Reference point S** defines the connection between a TE1 or TA and an NT1 or NT2 (if present). **Reference point T** defines the interface between an NT2 and an NT1. Finally, **reference point U** defines the interface between an NT1 and the ISDN office. Figure 16.10 shows these reference points as they apply to three different scenarios. We will discuss the specifications for each reference point when we explore the different ISDN layers in the next section of this chapter.

16.4   THE ISDN LAYERS

It is difficult to apply the simple seven-layer architecture specified by the OSI to the ISDN. One reason is that the ISDN specifies two different channels (B and D) with different functionalities. As we saw earlier in this chapter, B channels are for user-to-user communication (information exchange). D channels are predominantly for user-to-network signaling. The subscriber uses the D channel to connect to the network, then the B channel to send information to another user. These two functions require different protocols from each other at many of the OSI layers. The ISDN also differs from the OSI standard in its management needs. A primary consideration of the ISDN is global integration. Maintaining the flexibility required to keep the network truly integrated using public services requires a great deal of management.

For these reasons, the ITU-T has devised an expanded model for the ISDN layers. Instead of a single seven-layer architecture like the OSI, the ISDN is defined in three separate planes: the **user plane,** the **control plane,** and the **management plane** (see Figure 16.11).

Figure 16.11   *ISDN layers*

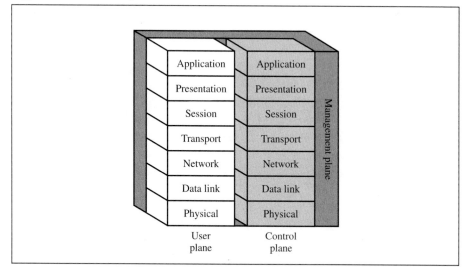

All three planes are divided into seven layers that correspond to the OSI model. The discussion of the management plane is beyond the scope of this book; the other two planes are discussed next.

Figure 16.12 shows a simplified version of the ISDN architecture for the user and control planes (B and D channels). At the physical layer, the B and D channels are alike. They use either the BRI or PRI interfaces and devices discussed earlier in this chapter. At the data link layer, the B channel uses LAPB or some version of it, discussed in Chapter 11. At the network layer, the B channel has many options. B channels (and D channels acting like B channels) can connect to circuit-switched networks, packet-switched networks (X.25), Frame Relay networks, and ATM networks, among others. The user-plane options for layers 4 through 7 are left to the user and are not defined specifically in the ISDN. In summary, we need only discuss the physical layer shared by the B and D channels and the second and third layers of the D channel standard.

Figure 16.12   *Simplified layers of ISDN*

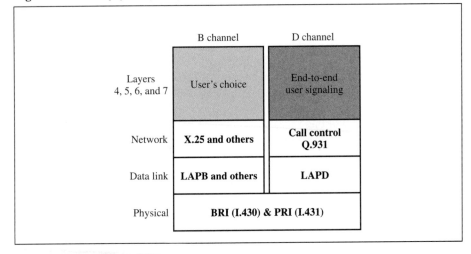

Physical Layer

The ISDN physical layer specifications are defined by two ITU-T standards: **I.430** for BRI access and **I.431** for PRI access. These standards define all aspects of the BRI and PRI. Of these aspects, four are of primary importance:

■ The mechanical and electrical specifications of interfaces R, S, T, and U.

■ Encoding.

■ Multiplexing channels to make them carriable by the BRI and PRI digital pipes.

■ Power supply.

Physical Layer Specifications for BRI

As you recall, a BRI consists of two B channels and one D channel. A subscriber connects to the BRI using the R, S, and U interfaces (reference points); see Figure 16.13.

R Interface   The R interface is not defined by the ISDN. A subscriber can use any of the EIA standards (such as EIA-232, EIA-499, or EIA-530) or any of the V or X series standards (such as X.21).

Figure 16.13   *BRI interfaces*

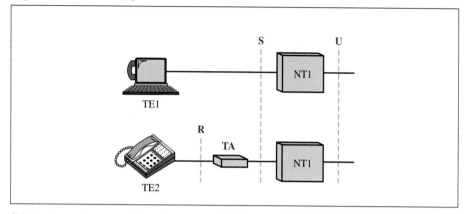

S Interface   For the S interface, the ITU-T specifies the ISO standard, ISO8887. This standard calls for four-, six-, or eight-wire connections. (At least four wires are necessary to support full-duplex communication over every B or D channel.) The jacks and plugs for these connections, along with the electrical specifications for each wire, are shown in Figure 16.14.

Figure 16.14   *S interface*

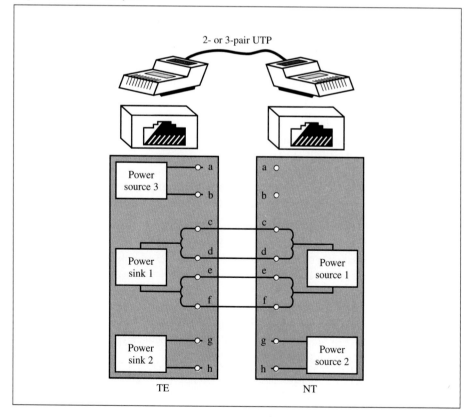

The individual wires in an S interface connection are organized according to Table 16.2. Only four of the wires are necessary for balanced transmission of data in full-duplex mode. (For a discussion of balanced transmission, see the section on the X.21 Interface in Chapter 6.) The others supply power to the NT1 and TE. The standard provides three methods for supplying power. In the first, the NT1 is the supplier. The power can come from a battery or power outlet, or it can come from the ISDN center to the NT1. In this case, only four connections are needed to connect the TE and NT1 (wires c, d, e, and f in Figure 16.14).

Table 16.2   *S interface pins*

Name	TE	NT
a	Power source 3	Power sink 3
b	Power source 3	Power sink 3
c	Transmit	Receive
d	Receive	Transmit
e	Receive	Transmit
f	Transmit	Receive
g	Power sink 2	Power source 2
h	Power sink 2	Power source 2

In the second case, the power again comes from the NT1, but two separate lines are used to relay it to the TE. In this case, six wires are used (c, d, e, f, g, and h in Figure 16.14). ISO8887 allows for another possibility: that the TE supplies the power itself and passes it to other TEs (using wires a and b). The ISDN, however, does not use this version. A two- or three-pair twisted cable is adequate to support all of the ISDN defined uses. The signal used in the S interface is **pseudoternary encoding,** as we saw in Chapter 5.

U Interface   For the U interface (digital subscriber or local loop), the ITU-T specifies a single-pair twisted-pair cable in each direction. Encoding for this interface uses a method called two binary, one quaternary (2B1Q). 2B1Q uses four voltage levels instead of two. Each level can therefore represent two bits rather than one, thereby lowering the baud rate and enabling more efficient use of the available bandwidth (see Figure 16.15). The four voltage levels represent the dibits 00, 01, 10, and 11.

BRI Frame   The format for a BRI frame is shown in Figure 16.16. Each B channel is sampled twice during each frame (eight bits per sample). The D channel is sampled four times during each frame (one bit per sample). The balance of the frame, shown in Figure 16.16 as black spaces, is reserved for overhead, the discussion of which is beyond the scope of this book. The entire frame consists of 48 bits: 32 bits for the B channels, 4 bits for the D channel, and 12 bits of overhead. (The reason that each B channel is sampled twice and the D channel four times is to create a longer frame. As we will see in Chapter 19, 48 bits makes the size of the BRI frame a precise match for the data portion of an ATM cell.)

Connection and Topology   BRI services can be supported by either a bus or star topology. The main restriction governing the choice of topology for a BRI is the

Figure 16.15   *2B1Q encoding*

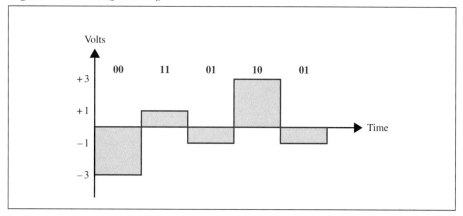

Figure 16.16   *BRI frame*

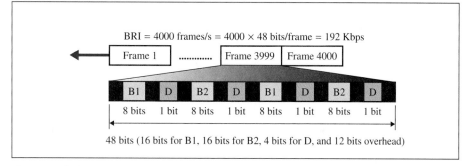

distance of the data devices from the NT1 (see Figure 16.17). In a point-to-point connection, each device can be as far as 1000 meters away from the NT1. In a multipoint connection, however, the maximum length of the line generally cannot be more than 200 meters. This restriction is necessary to ensure frame synchronization.

As we discussed earlier in this chapter, NT1s interleave the outputs of connected devices as part of the process of frame building. The results of this implicit multiplexing are evident in the structure of the frame. To make this implicit multiplexing possible, the frame-building functions of the NT1 must be timed to coordinate precisely with the data dumps of the connected devices. If the synchronization between the frame and the devices is off, data dumped by one device can end up in a part of the frame devoted to data from another device, or to another kind of information altogether. Unavoidable propagation delays over distance can result in a shifted frame. If the distance between the first and last device on a link is great enough, data collection timing can deteriorate the frame.

To ensure frame accuracy for multipoint links, we must limit the impact of timing shifts between the data units dumped by each device. We do so by limiting the link distance between the devices. In general, that means restricting the total length of the link to 200 meters, as noted above. However, if we cluster the devices at the end of the link farthest from the NT1, we can extend the length of the link to 500 meters. Clustering the devices means that propagation delays will impact the data from all devices almost

Figure 16.17 *BRI topology*

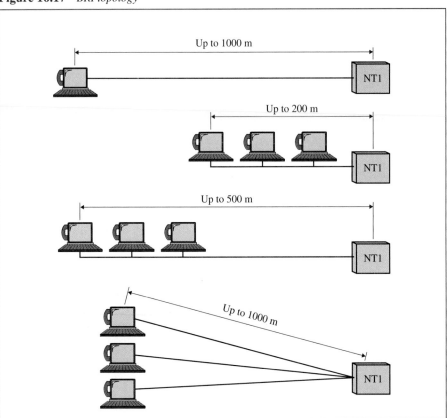

equally, allowing the relationships between the data units to remain predictable for 500 meters. If only one device is attached to a link, the NT1 does not need to distinguish between the data of different devices and greater timing distortions can be tolerated. Star topology links can be as long as 1000 meters (see Figure 16.17).

As many as eight devices can be connected to an NT1. Of these, only two can access the B channels at one time, one exchange per channel. Every device, however, can contend for access to the D channel. D channels use a mechanism like CSMA to control access. Once a device has access to the D channel, it can request a B channel. If a B channel is available, the connection is made by the D channel and the user may then send data.

Physical Layer Specifications for PRI

As you recall, the PRI consists of 23 B channels and 1 D channel. Interfaces associated with PRI usage include R, S, T, and U (see Figure 16.18).

The R and S standards are the same as those defined for the BRI. The T standard is identical to the S standard with the substitution of B8ZS encoding. The U interface is the same for both standards except that the PRI rate is 1.544 Mbps instead of 192 Kbps: 1.544 Mbps allows the PRI to be implemented using T-1 specifications (see Chapter 8).

Figure 16.18 *PRI interfaces*

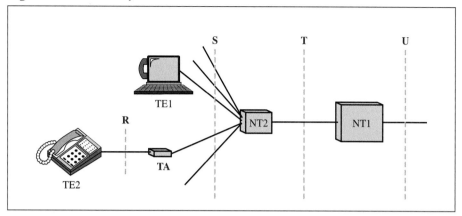

PRI Frame The B and D channels are multiplexed using synchronous TDM to create a PRI frame. The frame format is identical to that defined for T-1 lines. For convenience, we repeat the format here in Figure 16.19. Notice that the PRI frame samples each channel, including the D channel, only once per frame.

Figure 16.19 *PRI frame*

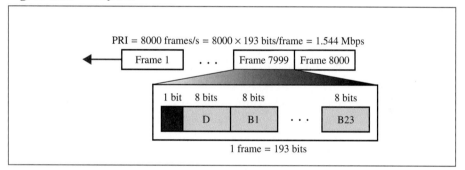

Connection and Topology Connection and topology considerations for linking data-generating devices to an NT2 can be the same as those described for the device-to-NT1 links in the BRI, or they can differ. Specific implementation depends on the application. If the NT2 is a LAN, its topology will be specified by the LAN being used; if the NT2 is a PBX, its topology will be specified by the PBX being used, and so on. The link from the NT2 to the NT1, however, must always be point-to-point.

Data Link Layer

B and D channels use different data link protocols. B channels use LAPB protocol. The D channel uses link access procedure for D channel (LAPD). LAPD is HDLC with a few modifications, two of which require explanation here. First, LAPD can be used in either unacknowledged (without sequence numbering) or acknowledged (with sequence numbering) formats. The unacknowledged format is used only seldomly, however, so in general practice LAPD and HDLC are alike. The second difference is addressing.

LAPD Addressing

The address field of the LAPD is two bytes long (see Figure 16.20). The first byte contains a six-bit field called a **service access point identifier (SAPI);** a one-bit command/response field set to 0 if the frame is a command and to 1 if the frame is a response; and a one-bit field set to 0 to indicate that the address is continued in the next byte (see HDLC, Chapter 11).

Figure 16.20 *LAPD address field*

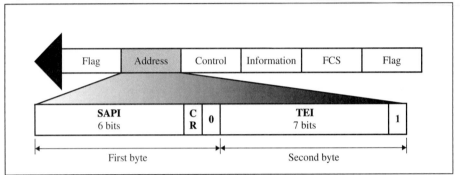

The second byte contains a seven-bit field called a **terminal equipment identifier (TEI)** and a one-bit field set to 1 to indicate that the address is complete.

SAPI Field   The SAPI field identifies the type of upper-layer service (network layer) using the frame. It indicates the intended use of the D channel. It is a six-bit field and can therefore define up to 64 different service access points. To date, however, only four of the possible bit combinations have been assigned:

■ **000000.** Call control for network layer (signaling use of D channel).
■ **000001.** Call control for upper layer (end-to-end signaling), not yet in use.
■ **010000.** Packet communication (data use of D channel).
■ **111111.** Management.

TEI Field   The TEI field is the unique address of the TE. It consists of seven bits and can therefore identify up to 128 different TEs.

Network Layer

Once a connection has been established by the D channel, the B channel sends data using circuit switching, X.25, or other similar protocols. The network layer functions of the D channel, however, must be discussed here. These functions are defined by the ITU-T **Q.931** standard.

The network layer packet is called a **message.** A message is encapsulated in the information field of an LAPD I-frame for transport across a link (see Figure 16.21).

The format of the message in this layer consists of a small but variable number of fields. These fields are of four types:

■ Protocol discriminator (a single one-byte field).
■ Call reference (two- or three-byte field).

Figure 16.21   *Network layer packet format*

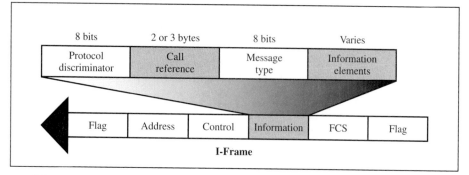

- Message type (a single one-byte field).
- Information elements (a variable number of variable-length fields).

Protocol Discriminator

The protocol discriminator field identifies the protocol in use. For Q.931, the value of this field is 00001000.

Call Reference

The call reference is the sequence number of the call. The format for this field is shown in Figure 16.22.

Figure 16.22   *Call reference field*

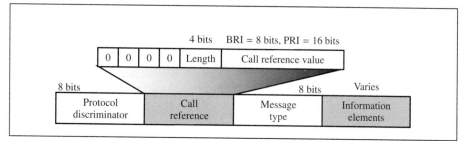

Message Type

The message type is a one-byte field that identifies the purpose of the message. There are four categories of message types: call establishment messages, call information messages, call clearing messages, and miscellaneous messages. The available messages are described below.

Call Establishment Messages   The following are call establishment messages:

- **Setup.** Sent by the calling user to the network or by the network to the called user to initiate a call.
- **Setup acknowledgment.** Sent by the called user to the network or by the network to the calling user to indicate that setup has been received. This message does not

mean that a connection is in place (more information may be required), merely that the desired process has begun.

■ **Connect.** Sent by the called user to the network or by the network to the calling user to indicate acceptance of the call.

■ **Connect acknowledgment.** Sent by the network to the called user to say that the desired connection has been awarded.

■ **Progress.** Sent by the network to the called user to indicate that call establishment is in progress. This message works as a "please stand by" request in case the call establishment process needs more time.

■ **Alerting.** Sent by the called user to the network or by the network to the calling user to indicate that the call user alert (ringing) has been initiated.

■ **Call processing.** Sent by the called user to the network or by the network to the calling user to indicate that the requested call establishment has been initiated and that no more information is needed.

Call Information Messages   The following are call information messages:

■ **Resume.** Sent by a user to the network to request that a suspended call be resumed.

■ **Resume acknowledgment.** Sent by the network to the user to acknowledge a request to resume the call.

■ **Suspend.** Sent by a user to request that the network suspend a call.

■ **Suspend acknowledgment.** Sent by the network to the user to acknowledge the requested suspension of the call.

■ **Suspend reject.** Sent by the network to the user to reject the requested suspension.

■ **User information.** Sent by a user to the network to be delivered to the remote user. This message allows the user to send information using out-of-band signaling.

Call Clearing Messages   The following are call clearing messages:

■ **Disconnect.** Sent by the calling user to the network or by the network to the called user to clear the end-to-end connection (termination).

■ **Release.** Sent by a user or network to indicate the intention to disconnect and release the channel.

■ **Release complete.** Sent by a user or network to show that the channel has been released.

Miscellaneous   Other messages carry information defined in the protocols of specific services. These messages are not used in routine communication and further discussion of them is beyond the scope of this book.

Information Elements

An information elements field carries specific details about the connection that are required for call establishment, for example, the addresses of the sender and receiver (discussed below), routing information, and the type of network that is desired for the B channel exchange (such as circuit-switched, X.25, ATM, or Frame Relay); see Figure 16.23. The details of the latter elements are complex and fall beyond the scope of this book.

Figure 16.23 *Information elements*

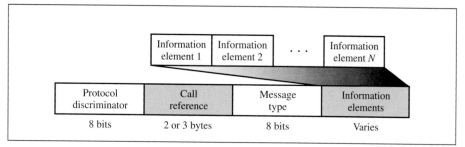

Information Element Types An **information element** consists of one or more bytes. A one-byte information element can be of type 1 or type 2. In type 1, the first bit is 0, the next three bits identify the information being sent, and the remaining four bits carry the specific content or attribute of the element. Type 2 elements start with a 1 bit. The remainder of the byte is reserved for the ID. In multibyte information elements, the first bit of the first byte is 0 and the remainder of the byte is the ID. The second byte defines the length of the content in bytes. The remaining bytes are content (see Figure 16.24).

Figure 16.24 *Information element types*

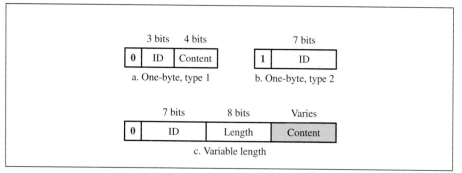

Addressing An important type of information element is addressing. The ISDN recommends an addressing system based on the format shown in Figure 16.25.

Figure 16.25 *Addressing in ISDN*

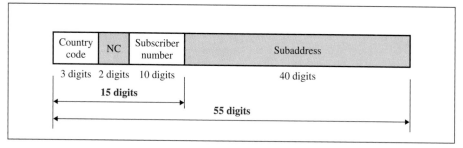

The country code consists of three digits. The NC field is the national code and consists of two digits. It identifies the specific network in countries with more than one ISDN network. The subscriber number is the 10-digit number familiar from national telephone numbers: a three-digit area code and a seven-digit phone number. Together these 15 digits define the access to a subscriber NT1. Often, however, a given NT1 may have multiple devices connected to it, either directly or indirectly through an NT2. In these situations, each device is identified by a subaddress. The ISDN allows up to 40 digits for a subaddress.

16.5   BROADBAND ISDN

When the ISDN was originally designed, data rates of 64 Kbps to 1.544 Mbps were sufficient to handle all existing transmission needs. As applications using the telecommunications networks advanced, however, these rates proved inadequate to support many applications. In addition, the original bandwidths proved too narrow to carry the large numbers of concurrent signals produced by a growing industry of digital service providers.

Figure 16.26 shows the bit rates required by a variety of applications. As you can see, several are beyond the capacities of both the BRI and PRI.

Figure 16.26   *Bit Rates for different applications*

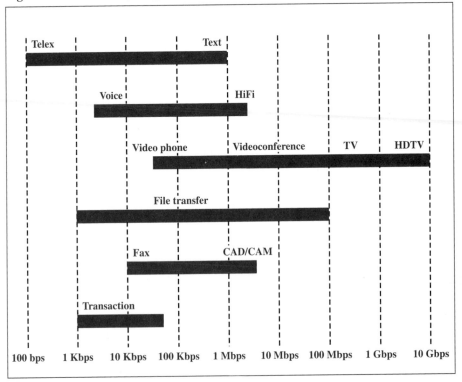

To provide for the needs of the next generation of technology, an extension of ISDN, called **broadband ISDN (B-ISDN),** is under study. The original ISDN is now known as narrowband ISDN (N-ISDN). B-ISDN provides subscribers to the network with data rates in the range of 600 Mbps, almost 400 times faster than the PRI rate. Technology exists to support higher rates but is not yet implemented or standardized.

As we saw earlier in this chapter, narrowband ISDN is an outcome of the logical evolution of the telephone system. Broadband ISDN, however, represents a revolution in thinking that radically alters entire aspects of communication. B-ISDN is based on a change from metal cable to fiber-optic cable at all levels of telecommunications. You have only to check the telephone wiring in your neighborhood to know that this revolution has not yet occurred on a wide basis. The majority of current research and development in the fields of telecommunications and networking, however, is devoted to bringing this revolution about.

Services

Broadband ISDN provides two types of services: interactive and distributive (see Figure 16.27).

Figure 16.27 *B-ISDN services*

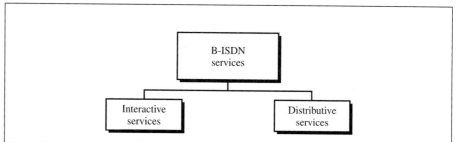

Interactive Services

Interactive services are those that require two-way exchanges between either two subscribers or between a subscriber and a service provider. These services are of three types: conversational, messaging, and retrieval.

Conversational Conversational services are those, such as telephone calls, that support real-time exchanges (as opposed to store and forward). These real-time services can be used for telephony, video telephony, video conferencing, data transfer, and so on.

Messaging Messaging services are store-and-forward exchanges. These services are bidirectional, meaning that all parties in an exchange can use them at the same time. The actual exchange, however, may not occur in real time. One subscriber asking another for information may have to wait for an answer, even though both parties are available at the same time. These services include voice mail, data mail, and video mail.

Retrieval Retrieval services are those used to retrieve information from a central source, called an information center. These services are like libraries; they must allow public access and allow users to retrieve information on demand. That is, information is not distributed unless asked for. An example of a retrieval service is a videotex that allows subscribers to select video data from an on-line library. The service is bidirectional because it requires action on the part of both the requester and the provider.

Distributive Services

Distributive services are unidirectional services sent from a provider to subscribers without the subscriber having to transmit a request each time a service is desired. These services can be without or with user control.

Without User Control   Distributive services without user control are broadcast to the user without the user's having requested them or having control over either broadcast times or content. User choice is limited to whether or not to receive the service at all. An example of this type of service is commercial TV. Programming content and times are decided by the provider alone. The user can turn on the television and change the channel but cannot request a specific program or a specific broadcast time.

With User Control   Distributive services with user control are broadcast to the user in a round-robin fashion. Services are repeated periodically to allow the user a choice of times during which to receive them. Which services are broadcast at which times, however, is the option of the provider alone. Examples of this type of service are educational broadcasting, teleadvertising, and pay TV. With pay TV, for example, a program is made available in a limited number of time slots. A user wishing to view the program must activate his or her television to receive it, but he or she has no other control.

Physical Specifications

The B-ISDN model is divided into layers that are different from those of N-ISDN. These layers are closely tied to the design of ATM (see Chapter 19).

Physical aspects of B-ISDN not related to ATM include access methods, functional equipment groupings, and reference points, described below.

Access Methods

B-ISDN defines three access methods designed to provide for three levels of user needs. They are symmetrical 155.520 Mbps, asymmetrical 155.520 Mbps/622.080 Mbps, and symmetrical 622.080 Mbps (see Figure 16.28).

■ **155.520 Mbps full-duplex.** This rate matches that of an OC-3 SONET link (see Chapter 20). It is high enough to support customers who need access to all narrowband ISDN services and to one or more regular video transmission services. This method is geared to fill the needs of most residential and many business subscribers.

■ **155.520 Mbps output/622.080 Mbps input.** This method provides asymmetrical full-duplex network access. The outgoing rate is 155.520 Mbps (the same as an OC-3 SONET link), but the incoming rate is 622.080 Mbps (the same as an OC-12 SONET link). It is designed to fill the needs of businesses that require the simultaneous receipt of multiple services and video conferencing but that are not service providers and do not broadcast distributive services. The input needs of these subscribers are far greater than their output needs. Providing only one rate would

Figure 16.28 *B-ISDN accesses*

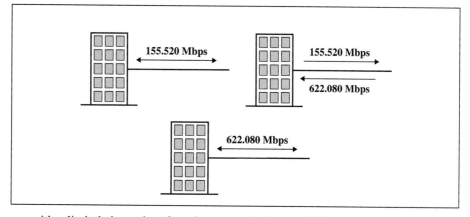

either limit their receipt of services or result in wasted link capacity. The asymmetrical configuration provides for a balanced use of resources.

- **622.080 Mbps full-duplex.** This final mechanism is designed for businesses that provide and receive distributive services.

Functional Grouping

The functional groupings of equipment in the B-ISDN model are the same as those for N-ISDN. Here, however, they are called B-NT1, B-NT2, B-TE1, B-TE2, and B-TA.

Reference Points

B-ISDN also uses the same reference points as N-ISDN (R, S, T, and U). Some of these, however, are currently under scrutiny and may be redefined.

16.6 FUTURE OF ISDN

The narrowband ISDN (N-ISDN) was designed to replace the analog telephone system with a digital one for both voice and data transmission. The design was based on the assumption that technological advances and mass production of N-ISDN equipment would make it affordable for the regular telephone subscriber.

In fact, N-ISDN has replaced the normal telephone line in some European countries in response to the demand of the users. In the United States, however, this replacement was delayed (it is available on demand) and new technologies (such as cable modem and ADSL) evolved that make the use of N-ISDN questionable. However, we believe that ISDN can still be considered a good solution for several reasons. First, ISDN can be brought to a subscriber premise with minimum cost and the services available can satisfy the needs of many users (not all users need video on demand). Second, new equipment has appeared on the market that allows a subscriber to use the entire bandwidth of an ISDN line (192 Kbps for BRI or 1.544 Mbps for PRI). This makes it competitive with some other technologies. Third, the protocol is flexible enough to be upgraded to higher data rates using new technology and new transmission media. Fourth, N-ISDN can be used as a forerunner for B-ISDN, the data rate of which is sufficient for several years to come.

16.7   KEY TERMS AND CONCEPTS

analog network	message
basic rate interface (BRI)	network termination 1 (NT1)
bearer channel (B channel)	network termination 2 (NT2)
bearer services	out-of-band signaling
broadband ISDN (B-ISDN)	primary rate interface (PRI)
control plane	private branch exchange (PBX)
data channel (D channel)	pseudoternary encoding
digital network	Q.931
digital pipe	R interface (R reference point)
distributive services	S interface (S reference point)
hybrid channel (H channel)	service access point identifier (SAPI)
I.430	supplementary services
I.431	T interface (T reference point)
in-band signaling	teleservice
information element	terminal adapter (TA)
integrated digital network (IDN)	terminal equipment 1 (TE1)
Integrated Services Digital Network (ISDN)	terminal equipment 2 (TE2)
interactive services	terminal equipment identifier (TEI)
management plane	U interface (U reference point)
	user plane

16.8   SUMMARY

- An ISDN provides digital services to users over integrated digital networks.
- Digital services fall into one of three classes:
  a. Bearer services—no network manipulation of the information contents.
  b. Teleservices—network may change or process information contents.
  c. Supplementary services—cannot stand alone; must be used with bearer or teleservices.
- A digital pipe is a high-speed path composed of time-multiplexed channels. There are three types of channels:
  a. Bearer (B)—basic user channel.
  b. Data (D)—for control of B channels, low-rate data transfer, and other applications.
  c. Hybrid (H)—high-data-rate applications.
- A BRI is a digital pipe composed of two B channels and one D channel.
- A PRI is a digital pipe composed of 23 B channels and one D channel.
- Three functional groupings of equipment enable users to access an ISDN: network terminations, terminal equipment, and terminal adapters.
- There are two types of network terminations:
  a. NT1—equipment that controls the physical and electrical termination of the ISDN at the user's premises.
  b. NT2—equipment that performs functions related to layers one through three of the OSI model.
- Terminal equipment (data sources similar to DTEs) can be classified as follows:
  a. TE1—subscriber equipment conforming to ISDN standards.
  b. TE2—subscriber equipment that does not conform to ISDN standards.
  c. TA—converts data from TE2s to ISDN format.
- A reference point defines ISDN interfaces. The reference points are:
  a. R—between a TE2 and a TA.
  b. S—between a TE or TA and an NT.
  c. T—between an NT1 and an NT2.
  d. U—between an NT1 and the ISDN office.
- ISDN architecture consists of three planes, each made up of the seven layers of the OSI model. The planes are:
  a. User plane—defines the functionality of the B and H channels.
  b. Control plane—defines the functionality of the D channel when used for signaling purposes.
  c. Management plane—encompasses the other two planes and is used for network management.
- The physical layer of the user and control planes is the same.

- BRI has a data rate of 192 Kbps (4000 frames/sec, 48 bits/frame).
- PRI has a data rate of 1.544 Mbps (8000 frames/sec, 193 bits/frame).
- The distance from a TE to an NT is dependent on connection, topology, and placement of multiple TEs.
- In the data link layer, the B channel (user) uses LAPB protocol. The D channel (control) uses LAPD protocol, which is also similar to HDLC.
- In the network layer, the D channel data packet is called a message. It has four fields:
  a. Protocol discriminator—identifies the protocol used.
  b. Call reference—identifies sequence number.
  c. Message type—identifies purpose of the message.
  d. Information elements (multifield)—information about the connection.
- Broadband ISDN (B-ISDN), using fiber-optic media, fulfills the needs of users who require a higher data rate than that offered by ISDN. B-ISDN has a data rate of 600 Mbps.
- B-ISDN offers two services:
  a. Interactive—two-way services (two subscribers or a subscriber–service provider pair).
  b. Distributive—one-way service from service provider to subscriber.
- Three access methods in B-ISDN are available:
  a. 155.520 Mbps, full-duplex.
  b. 155.520 Mbps outgoing and 622.080 Mbps incoming, asymmetric full-duplex.
  c. 622.080 Mbps, full-duplex.
- The functional grouping and reference points of B-ISDN are the same as for regular ISDN (also known as narrowband ISDN, N-ISDN).

16.9   PRACTICE SET

Review Questions

1. Explain each of the words in "Integrated Services Digital Network."
2. Contrast the three categories of services provided by ISDN.
3. Discuss briefly the evolution of ISDN.
4. How is an IDN different from ISDN?
5. What kind of information can a B channel transmit? What kind of information can a D channel transmit? What kind of information can an H channel transmit?
6. What is the difference between in-band signaling and out-of-band signaling?
7. Who are the subscribers to a BRI? Who are the subscribers to a PRI?
8. What is the data rate for a BRI? What is the data rate for a PRI?
9. What is an NT1?

    c. TE3

    d. TE4

36. _____ is a group of non-ISDN equipment.

    a. TE1

    b. TE2

    c. TEx

    d. T3

37. A _____ converts information from non-ISDN format to ISDN format.

    a. TE1

    b. TE2

    c. TEx

    d. TA

38. Reference point R is the specification for connecting TE2 and _____.

    a. TE1

    b. NT1

    c. NT2

    d. TA

39. Reference point U is the specification for connecting the ISDN office with

    _____.

    a. NT1

    b. NT2

    c. TE1

    d. TE2

40. Reference point _____ is the specification for connecting NT1 with NT2.

    a. R

    b. S

    c. T

    d. U

41. Which ISDN plane is associated with signaling and the D channel?

    a. user

    b. control

    c. management

    d. supervisory

42. Which ISDN plane is associated with the B channels and the transmission of user information?

    a. user

    b. control

    c. management

    d. supervisory

43. Each PRI frame lasts _____ microseconds.
    a. 1
    b. 1.544
    c. 125
    d. 193

44. In ISDN _____, the network can change or process the contents of the data.
    a. bearer services
    b. teleservices
    c. supplementary services
    d. none of the above

45. In ISDN _____, the network does not change or process the contents of the data.
    a. bearer services
    b. teleservices
    c. supplementary services
    d. none of the above

46. In B-ISDN, the general class of service between subscriber and service provider or between two subscribers is _____ services.
    a. interactive
    b. distributive
    c. conversational
    d. messaging

47. In B-ISDN, when you obtain information from a public center, you are using _____ services.
    a. conversational
    b. messaging
    c. retrieval
    d. distributive

48. In _____ services, all transmission is real-time between the two entities.
    a. conversational
    b. messaging
    c. retrieval
    d. distributive

49. When you store and forward messages in B-ISDN, you are using _____ services.
    a. conversational
    b. messaging
    c. retrieval
    d. distributive

50. Commercial TV is an example of _____.
    a. messaging services
    b. conversational services

    c. distributive services without user control

    d. distributive services with user control

51. Which B-ISDN access method is designed for customers who need to receive distributive services but do not provide distributive services to others?

    a. 155.520 Mbps full-duplex

    b. 155.520 and 622.080 Mbps asymmetrical full-duplex

    c. 622.080 Mbps full-duplex

    d. 400 Mbps full-duplex

Exercises

52. When a device uses a B channel, how many bits can it send per frame?

53. When a device uses a D channel, how many bits can it send per frame?

54. The contents of the address field of a D channel are 0100000000100101. What is the address of the TE?

55. The address of a TE is 104 and the D channel is used for signaling. Show the contents of the address field in the D frame.

56. Encode the bit pattern 011110111111 in 2B1Q.

57. Three devices are connected to an ISDN BRI service. The first device uses a B channel and sends the text "HI." The second device uses the other B channel and sends the text "BE." The third device uses the D channel and sends the bit pattern 1011. Show the contents of the BRI frame (ignore the overhead).

58. ISDN uses out-of-band signaling, in which the D channel is used for signaling. What happens if the D channel is used for data transfer? Is this still out-of-band signaling?

59. How many countries can be defined by the ISDN address field? How many networks can be defined for each country? How many subscribers per network (NT1 or NT2)? How many TEs per subscriber? How many TEs in total?

60. An NT1 with the address 445631411213121 wants to make a connection to another NT1 with the address 231131781211327. Is this connection intercountry or intracountry? What are the country codes of the source and destination? What are the network numbers?

61. Two TEs are connected through an ISDN network as shown in Figure 16.29. Show the sequence of D-channel packets exchanged between them (at the network layer) to establish the connection. Where are the ISDN addresses involved?

Figure 16.29   *Exercises 61 and 62*

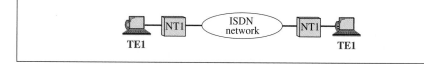

62. Repeat Exercise 61, but show the sequence of D-channel packets exchanged during connection termination.

CHAPTER 17

X.25

X.25 is a **packet-switching** wide area network developed by ITU-T in 1976; since then it has undergone several revisions. According to the formal definition given in the ITU-T standard, X.25 is an interface between data terminal equipment (DTE) and data circuit–terminating equipment (DCE) for terminal operation in the packet mode on public data networks.

Figure 17.1 gives a conceptual overview of X.25. Although X.25 is an end-to-end protocol, the actual movement of packets through the network is invisible to the user. The user sees the network as a cloud through which each packet passes on its way to the receiving DTE.

Figure 17.1 *X.25*

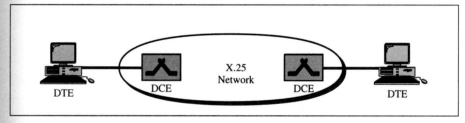

X.25 defines how a packet-mode terminal can be connected to a packet network for the exchange of data. It describes the procedures necessary for establishing, maintaining, and terminating connections. It also describes a set of services, called facilities, to provide functions such as reverse charge, call direct, and delay control.

X.25 is what is known as a subscriber network interface (SNI) protocol. It defines how the user's DTE communicates with the network and how packets are sent over that network using DCEs. It uses a virtual circuit approach to packet switching (SVC and PVC) and uses asynchronous (statistical) TDM to multiplex packets.

17.1   X.25 LAYERS

The X.25 protocol specifies three layers: the physical layer, the frame layer, and the packet layer. These layers define functions at the physical, data link, and network layers of the OSI model. Figure 17.2 shows the relationship between the X.25 layers and the OSI layers.

Figure 17.2   *X.25 layers in relation to the OSI layers*

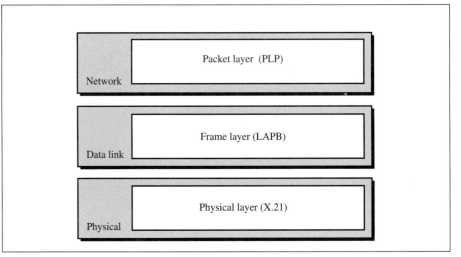

Physical Layer

At the physical layer, X.25 specifies a protocol called X.21 (or X.21bis), which has been specifically defined for X.25 by the ITU-T. X.21, however, is similar enough to other physical layer protocols, such as EIA-232, that X.25 is able to support them as well. (See Chapter 6 for a discussion of these interface protocols.)

Frame Layer

At the frame layer, X.25 provides data link controls using a bit-oriented protocol called **link access procedure, balanced (LAPB),** which is a subset of HDLC (see Chapter 11). Figure 17.3 shows the general format of the LAPB packet.

Figure 17.3   *Format of a frame*

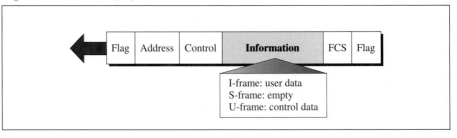

The flag, address, control, and FCS fields are exactly the same as we described in Chapter 11. However, because the communication here is point-to-point and in asynchronous balanced mode, the only two addresses are 00000001 (for a command issued by a DTE and the response to this command) and 00000011 (for a command issued by a DCE and the response to this command). Figure 17.4 shows how addresses are used in the frame (data link) layer.

Figure 17.4   *Addressing at the frame layer*

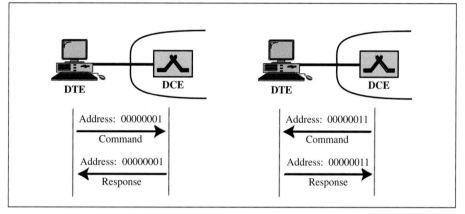

Three Categories of Frames

As discussed in Chapter 11, HDLC (and its derivation, LAPB) has three categories of frames: I-frames, S-frames, and U-frames.

I-Frames   I-frames are used to encapsulate PLP packets from the network layer.

S-Frames   S-frames are for flow and error control in the frame layer.

U-Frames   U-frames are used to set up and disconnect the links between a DTE and a DCE. The three packets most frequently used by LAPB in this category are SABM (or ESABM if the extended address mode is used), UA, and DISC (see Chapter 11 for a description of these packets).

Frame Layer Phases

In the frame layer, communication between a DTE and a DCE involves three phases: link setup, packet transfer, and link disconnect (see Figure 17.5).

Link Setup   The link between DTE and DCE must be set up before packets from the packet layer can be transferred. Either the DTE or the DCE can set up the link by sending an SABM (set asynchronous balanced mode) frame; the responding party sends a UA (unnumbered acknowledgment) frame to show that the link is actually set.

Transferring Data   After the link has been established, the two parties can send and receive network layer packets (data and control) using I-frames and S-frames.

Figure 17.5 *Three phases of the frame layer*

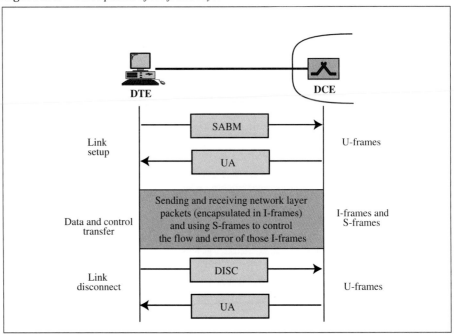

Link Disconnect When the network layer no longer needs the link, one of the parties can issue a disconnect (DISC) frame to request disconnection. The other party can answer with a UA frame.

Packet Layer

The network layer in X.25 is called the **packet layer protocol (PLP).** This layer is responsible for establishing the connection, transferring the data, and terminating the connection. In addition, it is responsible for creating the virtual circuits (discussed below) and negotiating network services between two DTEs. While the frame layer is responsible for making a connection between a DTE and a DCE, the packet layer is responsible for making a connection between two DTEs (end-to-end connection). Note that X.25 uses flow and error control at two levels (frame layer and packet layer). Flow and error control between a DTE and a DCE (link) are under the jurisdiction of the frame layer. End-to-end flow and error control between two DTEs (end-to-end) are under the jurisdiction of the packet layer. Figure 17.6 shows the difference between the frame layer and the packet layer domains of responsibility.

Virtual Circuits

The X.25 protocol is a **packet-switched** virtual circuit **network.** Note that the virtual circuits in X.25 are created at the network layer (not the data link layer as in some other wide area networks such as Frame Relay and ATM). This means that a physical

Figure 17.6   *Frame layer and packet layer domains*

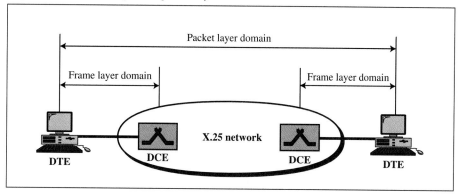

connection established between a DTE and DCE can carry several virtual circuits at the network layer with each circuit responsible for carrying either data or control information, a concept called in-band signaling. Figure 17.7 shows an X.25 network in which three virtual circuits have been created between DTE A and three other DTEs.

Figure 17.7   *Virtual circuits in X.25*

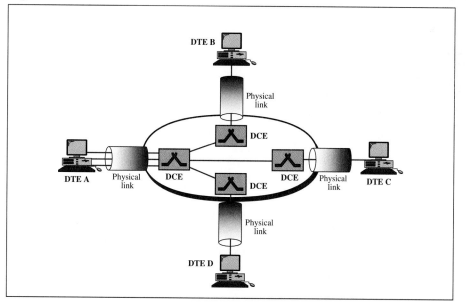

Virtual Circuit Identifiers

Each virtual circuit in X.25 should be identified for use by the packets. The **virtual circuit identifier** in X.25 is called the **logical channel number (LCN).** When a virtual circuit is established between two DTEs, there is always a pair of LCNs: one defining the virtual circuit between the local DTE and the local DCE and the other one between the remote DCE and the remote DTE. The reason for having two different LCNs is to make the LCN domain local. This allows the set of LCNs for each local connection to be small and consequently the LCN field to be short. A global LCN would require a larger set of LCNs and consequently a longer LCN field. The local LCN allows the same set of LCNs to be used by two different pairs of DTE–DCE links without confusion. Figure 17.8 shows the LCNs in an X.25 network.

Figure 17.8   *LCNs in X.25*

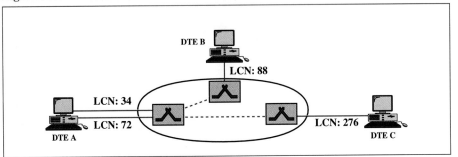

X.25 uses both permanent and switched virtual circuits (PVCs and SVCs). PVCs are established by the X.25 network providers. They are similar to the leased line in telephone networks. The LCNs are permanently assigned by the network provider.

SVCs are established at each session. The network layer uses a control packet to set up a connection. After the connection is established, both DTE–DCE links are assigned an LCN. After the data transfer, the virtual circuit is disconnected and the LCNs are no longer valid.

Note that the virtual circuit establishment and release at the network layer are different from link setup and disconnect at the frame layer. In a typical situation, the following five events occur:

■   A link is set up between the local DTE and DCE and also between the remote DTE and DCE.

■   A virtual circuit is established between the local DTE and the remote DTE.

■   Data are transferred between the two DTEs.

■   The virtual circuit is released.

■   The link is disconnected.

LCN Assignment

X.25 allows up to 4096 (2^{12}) LCNs. Figure 17.9 shows how these LCNs are assigned. The one-way LCNs are used for simplex communication; the two-way LCNs are used for duplex communication.

PLP Packets

The general format of a PLP packet, shown in Figure 17.10, has three or four bytes of header and an optional information field.

Figure 17.9   *LCN assignment*

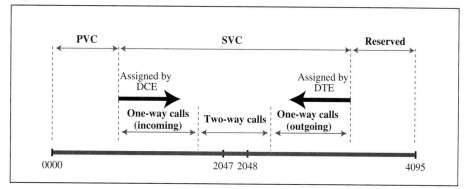

Figure 17.10   *PLP packet format*

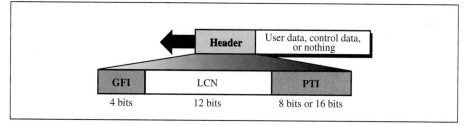

The fields in the header are as follows:

■ **General format identifier (GFI).** The **general format identifier (GFI)** is a four-bit field. The first bit, called the Q (qualifier) bit, defines the source of control information: 0 for PLP, 1 for other high-level protocols. The D (delivery) bit, defines which device should acknowledge the packet: 0 for the local DCE, 1 for the remote DTE. The last two bits of the GFI indicate the size of the sequence number fields. If these bits are 01, the sequence numbers are only 3 bits—modulo 8 (0 to 7). If these bits are 10, the sequence numbers are 7 bits—modulo 128 (0 to 127).

■ **Logical Channel Number (LCN).** The logical channel number (LCN) is a 12-bit field that identifies the virtual circuit chosen for a given transmission. The protocol originally defined a LGCN (logical group channel number) of 4 bits and an LCN (logical channel number) of 8 bits to give a sense of hierarchy to the virtual circuit identifier, but today, the combination is normally referred to as LCN.

■ **Packet Type Identifier (PTI).** The **packet type identifier (PTI)** defines the type of packet. The content of this field is different for each packet. We will discuss them in the next section.

Two Categories of Packets

Packets at the PLP level can be divided into two broad categories: data packets and control packets. The control packets, in addition, have two formats: one used for RR, RNR, and REJ packets and another for the remaining packets (see Figure 17.11).

Figure 17.11   *Categories of PLP packets*

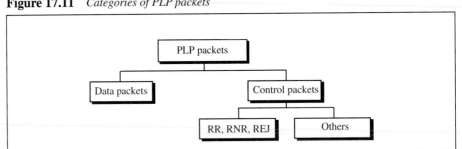

Data Packets   Data packets are used to transmit user data. Figure 17.12 shows the structure of a data packet. The general format is simple: a header and a user data field. The header, however, is complex and requires discussion here. There are two formats for information packets: short and long. The PTI field in the data packet consists of four sections. P(S) and P(R) carry the packet sequence numbers for flow and error control. P(S) stands for *packet send* and indicates the sequence number of the packet being sent. P(R) stands for *packet receive* and is the sequence number of the next packet expected by the receiver. This field is used to piggyback acknowledgments to data packets when both parties have data to send. In the short header, both the P(S) and P(R) fields are three bits long (sequence numbers from 0 to 7). In the long header, each field contains seven bits (sequence numbers from 0 to 127). The M (more) bit is used to define a set of packets belonging to the same unit. This bit is set to 1 if there are more packets in the unit (for example, a message); it is set to 0 if the packet is the last one. Data packets are differentiated from control packets by a 0 in the least significant bit in the third byte.

Figure 17.12   *Data packets in the PLP layer*

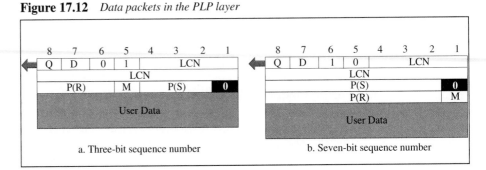

a. Three-bit sequence number   b. Seven-bit sequence number

RR, RNR, and REJ Packets   RR (receive ready), RNR (receive not ready), and REJ (reject) packets consists of just a header with the two least significant bits in the third byte set to 01. Figure 17.13 shows the general format of the packets. The header is essentially the same as the data packet's with only one difference; because these packets are used solely for flow and error control, they do not carry data and therefore do not have a P(S) field. Instead, they contain a new field, the packet type field, which carries a code that describes the purpose of the packet.

Figure 17.13 *RR, RNR, and REJ packets*

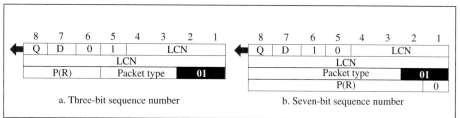

a. Three-bit sequence number   b. Seven-bit sequence number

These packets can be one of three types: receive ready (RR), receive not ready (RNR), and reject (REJ). They are described as follows:

- **RR (000).** Receive ready (RR) means that the device (DTE or DCE) is ready to receive more packets. It also acknowledges the receipt of a data packet by indicating the number of the next packet expected in the P(R) field.

- **RNR (001).** Receive not ready (RNR) means that the device cannot accept packets at this time. The other party must stop sending packets as soon as this packet is received.

- **REJ (010).** Reject (REJ) means that there was an error in the packet identified by the P(R) field. The other party must resend all packets including and following the packet indicated (go-back-*n* error recovery).

Other Control Packets   The other types of control packets may carry information in addition to the header. However, the information is only for control and does not contain user data. There is only one header size in this category because these packets do not carry sequence numbers. In these packets the two least significant bits in the third byte are set to 11. Figure 17.14 shows the general format of the header, which is essentially the same as the information packet, except that there are no P(R) or P(S) fields.

Figure 17.14 *Other control packets*

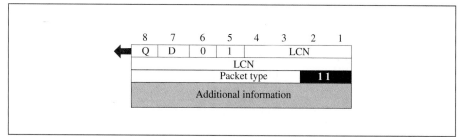

The packet type field in these control packets is six bits long and can be used to specify up to 64 different functions. As of this writing, however, only a handful of the possible codes have been assigned meanings. Table 17.1 shows some of these types. Packet formats for the various types are shown in Figure 17.15. The functions of each type are described next.

Table 17.1   *Control packet type*

DTE to DCE	DCE to DTE	Type
Call request	Incoming call	000010
Call accepted	Call connected	000011
Clear request	Clear indication	000100
Clear confirm	Clear confirm	000101
Interrupt	Interrupt	001000
Interrupt confirm	Interrupt confirm	001001
Reset request	Reset indication	000110
Reset confirm	Reset confirm	000111
Restart request	Restart indication	111110
Restart confirm	Restart confirm	111111
Registration request		111100
	Registration confirm	111101

Figure 17.15   *Control packet formats*

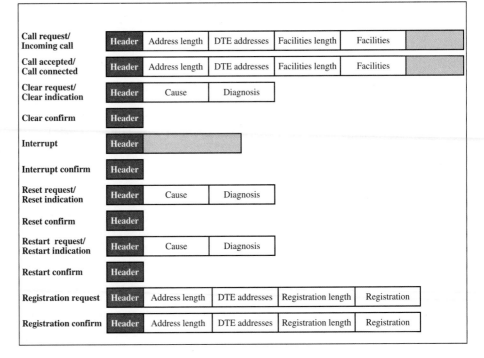

- **Call request/incoming call.** The call request and incoming call packets are used to request the establishment of a connection between two DTEs. Call request goes from the local DTE to the local DCE. Incoming call goes from the remote DCE to the remote DTE. In addition to the header, each of these packets includes fields specifying the length of the address, the addresses of the DTEs, the length of any facilities, and optional information such as log-on codes and database access information. Facilities are optional services that can be included on a contractual or per call basis. Facilities are made available by agreement between the users and network providers. Contractual options can include such services as incoming calls barred, outgoing calls barred, flow control parameter negotiation, fast select acceptance, and D-bit modification. Per call options can include flow control negotiation, fast select, and reverse charging.

- **Call accepted/call connected.** The call accepted and call connected packets indicate the acceptance of the requested connection by the called system. They are sent in response to the call request and incoming call packets. Call accepted is sent by the remote (called) DTE to the remote DCE. Call connected is sent by the local (calling) DCE to the local DTE.

- **Clear request/clear indication.** The clear request and clear indication packets are used at the end of an exchange to disconnect (clear) the connection. Either DTE or DCE can initiate the clearing. These packets also can be used by a remote DTE to respond negatively to an incoming call packet when it is unable to accept the requested connection.

- **Clear confirm.** The clear confirm packet is sent in response to the clear indication packet described above.

- **Interrupt.** The interrupt packet is used under unusual circumstances to break into an exchange and get attention. It can be sent by either of the DTEs or DCEs involved in the exchange and acts as an alert. For example, imagine that a local DTE waits a long time without receiving either a positive or negative acknowledgment from the remote DCE. Its window has reached the end. It cannot send more packets and it cannot quit. It sends an interrupt message to get attention.

- **Interrupt confirm.** The interrupt confirm packet confirms the receipt of the interrupt packet described above.

- **Reset request/reset indication.** The reset request and reset indication packets are used to reset the sequence numbers in an exchange over a particular virtual circuit. Reset packets are used when a connection has been damaged to the point where the virtual circuit must be reinitialized. The virtual circuit remains active, but the transmission begins again from a predetermined point; all packets from that point on are renumbered, starting from 0.

- **Reset confirm.** The reset confirm packet confirms the reset process.

- **Restart request/restart indication.** The restart request and restart indication packets restart all virtual circuits created by a DTE. This process is different from the reset process. Reset packets activate a new set of sequence numbers on an existing virtual circuit. Restart packets start up a new virtual circuit. Restart terminates and reestablishes a call by establishing a new virtual circuit for transmission. Any packets on the original pathway are lost and new packets are renumbered starting with 0. An analogy to this process is a phone call where the connection becomes so bad that you hang up and dial again.

- **Restart confirm.** The restart confirm packet confirms the restart request.
- **Registration request.** The registration request packet allows on-line registration of new users to the network.
- **Registration confirm.** The registration confirm packet confirms a registration.

17.2   OTHER PROTOCOLS RELATED TO X.25

There are other protocols in the X-series that are related to X.25. We discuss some of these protocols here.

X.121 Protocol

Since X.25 does not explicitly define what type of global addressing should be used during call setup to access a remote DTE (before the establishment of a virtual circuit), ITU-T has created **X.121** to globally address DTEs connected to a public or private network. Most X.25 networks today use the X.121 addressing scheme.

The address format as shown in Figure 17.16 is made of 14 digits. The first four digits, called the Data Network Identification Code (DNIC), define one specific network. Three digits define a country and one digit defines a network inside that country. The next 10 digits are the called the National Terminal Number (NTN) and define DTEs inside a particular network.

Figure 17.16   *X.121 address format*

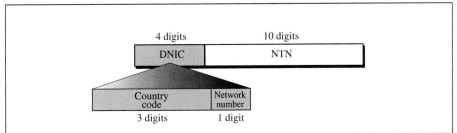

Triple-X Protocols

Three protocols, X.3, X.28, and X.29, collectively called **Triple-X protocols,** are used to connect a dumb terminal (instead of a DTE that can understand X.25 protocol) to an X.25 network (see Figure 17.17). We discuss each protocol briefly.

Figure 17.17 *Triple-X protocols*

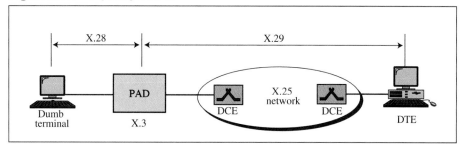

X.3

The **X.3** protocol defines a **packet assembler/disassembler (PAD).** A PAD is needed to connect a character-oriented (dumb) terminal to an X.25 network. On a terminal, we may use different character keys that are not necessarily sent over the network (such as arrow keys and delete keys). A PAD buffers all of these characters and assembles them into X.25 packets. When a packet arrives from the network, the PAD disassembles them so that they can be displayed on the screen or printed on the printer. X.3 defines 22 parameters that can be used by a PAD. For example, one parameter specifies that the PAD should echo characters sent from the terminal to the PAD.

X.28

The **X.28** protocol defines the rules for communication between a dumb terminal and a PAD. It defines different commands that can be used by the terminal or the PAD. For example, a command can be typed on the dumb terminal to request the establishment of a virtual connection between the PAD and the remote DTE.

X.29

The **X.29** protocol defines the relationship between a PAD and the remote terminal. Using this protocol, the remote terminal can set some of the parameters in the PAD. For example, the remote terminal can set the echo parameter in the PAD.

17.3   KEY TERMS AND CONCEPTS

general format identifier (GFI)

packet layer protocol (PLP)

link access procedure, balanced (LAPB)

packet-switched network

logical channel number (LCN)

packet switching

packet assembler/disassembler (PAD)

packet type identifier (PTI)

Triple-X protocols	X.28
virtual circuit identifier	
	X.29
X.3	
X.25	X.121

17.4 SUMMARY

- X.25 is a popular packet-switching wide area network.
- The X.25 protocol defines the procedures for data transmission between a DTE and a DCE for terminal operation in the packet mode on public data networks.
- The X.25 protocol specifies three layers: the physical layer, the frame layer, and the packet layer.
- The protocol at the physical layer can be X.21, X.21bis, EIA-232, or other similar protocols.
- LAPB is the protocol used by X.25 at the frame layer for data link control functions.
- The packet layer handles connection establishment, data transfer, connection termination, virtual circuit creation, and negotiation of network services between two DTEs.
- There are three types of X.25 packets: I-frames, S-frames, and U-frames. The first is a data packet; the latter two are control packets.
- There are flow and error control at both the frame layer and the packet layer.
- The virtual circuit identifier in X.25 is called a logical channel number (LCN).
- Both PVC and SVC connections are used by X.25.
- The X.121 protocol provides a method to globally address a DTE connected to a public or private network.
- The Triple-X protocols (X.3, X.28, and X.29) define the connection of a dumb terminal to an X.25 network.

17.5 PRACTICE SET

Review Questions

1. What are the X.25 layers? How does each relate to the OSI model?
2. How does the frame layer address field differ from the HDLC address field?
3. Name the X.25 frame types and their primary functions.
4. What are the frame layer phases involved in the communication between a DTE and a DCE? Which frame types are associated with each phase?

5. How are flow and error control handled by X.25? Are all the layers involved?
6. What is in-band signaling?
7. How are packets associated with the virtual circuit on which they travel?
8. What is the purpose of an LCN?
9. What kind of virtual circuits does X.25 use?
10. List the fields of a PLP packet header.
11. What are the two general PLP packet types?
12. Do all control packets consist of just a header field? Give an example of a control packet with a nonheader-type field. Give an example of a control packet with just a header field.
13. What is the purpose of the X.121 protocol?
14. What is the purpose of the Triple-X protocols?

Multiple Choice Questions

15. X.25 protocol uses _____ for end-to-end transmission.
    a. message switching
    b. circuit switching
    c. the datagram approach to packet switching
    d. the virtual circuit approach to packet switching
16. The X.25 protocol operates in the _____ of the OSI model.
    a. physical layer
    b. data link layer
    c. network layer
    d. all of the above
17. The physical layer protocol directly specified for the X.25 protocol is _____.
    a. RS-232
    b. X.21
    c. DB-15
    d. DB-37
18. The PLP packet is a product of the _____ layer in the X.25 standard.
    a. physical
    b. frame
    c. packet
    d. transport
19. The PLP _____ is used to transport data from the upper layers in the X.25 standard.
    a. S-packet
    b. data packet
    c. C-packet
    d. P-packet

20. When no data need to be sent but an acknowledgment is necessary, the PLP _____ is used.
    a. S-packet
    b. data packet
    c. control packet
    d. P-packet

21. In the X.25 standard, the PLP _____ is used for connection establishment, connection release, and other control purposes.
    a. S-packet
    b. data packet
    c. control packet
    d. P-packet

22. In the X.25 standard, if the _____ bit is set to 1, the remote DTE should acknowledge the packet.
    a. Q
    b. D
    c. M
    d. P

23. If the _____ bit in the X.25 standard is set to 1, it means that there is more than one packet.
    a. Q
    b. D
    c. M
    d. P

24. The _____ bit in the X.25 standard allows the user to define the source of control information.
    a. Q
    b. D
    c. M
    d. P

25. X.25 protocol requires error checking at the _____ layer.
    a. physical
    b. frame
    c. packet
    d. b and c

26. X.25 is _____ protocol.
    a. a UNI
    b. an SNI
    c. an NNI
    d. an SSN

27. LAPB is a subset of _____.
    a. HDLC
    b. ITU-T
    c. X.25
    d. DTE

28. Flow and error control between a DTE–DCE link are under the jurisdiction of the _____.
    a. physical layer
    b. frame layer
    c. packet layer
    d. b and c

29. Flow and error control between a DTE–DTE link are under the jurisdiction of the _____.
    a. physical layer
    b. frame layer
    c. packet layer
    d. b and c

30. The LCN identifies the link between the _____ DTE and the local DCE and between the _____ DTE and the remote DCE.
    a. remote; local
    b. local; local
    c. remote; remote
    d. local; remote

31. The _____ field contains a qualifier bit, a delivery bit, and two sequence bits.
    a. GFI
    b. LCN
    c. PTI
    d. PTA

32. The _____ field indicates the PLP packet type.
    a. GFI
    b. LCN
    c. PTI
    d. PTA

33. The difference between a long packet and a short packet is due to the length of the _____ field.
    a. LCN
    b. P(S)
    c. P(R)
    d. b and c

34. A PLP packet need not contain a _____ field.
    a. P(S)
    b. P(R)
    c. LCN
    d. a or b

Exercises

35. In the X.121 protocol, how many countries can the address field define? How many networks can be defined for each country? How many terminals (DTEs) for each network? How many terminals (DTEs) in total?

36. Repeat Exercise 35 if the first digit of the country code cannot be 1 or 8 (reserved).

37. In the X.121 protocol, what will happen if a country like the United States has more than 10 X.25 networks? What do you suggest?

38. Show the contents of a SABM frame sent from a DTE to a DCE (see Chapter 11). Ignore the information field.

39. Show the contents of a UA frame sent in response to Exercise 38.

40. What do you think will happen if a DTE sends an SABM frame to a DCE and then does not receive a UA frame in response?

41. Show the contents of a DISC frame sent from a DTE to a DCE (see Chapter 11). Ignore the information field.

42. Show the contents of the UA frame sent in response to Exercise 41.

43. Show the contents of an I-frame carrying a data packet sent from a DTE to a DCE.

44. Show the contents of an S-frame sent in response to the I-frame in Exercise 43. The S-frame acknowledges the receipt of the I-frame and announces that it is ready to receive more frames.

45. Repeat Exercise 44 if the DCE accepts the I-frame, but cannot accept more.

46. Repeat Exercise 44 if the DCE discards the I-frame due to an error.

47. A DTE with an X.121 address of 44563141121312 wants to make a connection to another DTE with an X.121 address of 23113178121132. Is this connection inter-country or intracountry? What are the country codes of the source and destination? What are the network numbers? What are the terminal numbers?

48. A DTE sends a call request to its local DCE. Which device chooses the LCN for the connection between the local DTE and the local DCE? What is the range of this LCN? Which device chooses the LCN for the connection between the remote DCE and the remote DTE? What is the range of this LCN?

49. Can a DTE send a data packet and control packet belonging to the same virtual connection using two different LCNs? How is this interpreted in relation to the claim that X.25 uses *in-band* signaling at the network layer?

50. Does the fact that multiplexing in X.25 is done at the network layer mean two different packets belonging to two different connections can be carried in one frame? Explain your answer.

51. Can an RR packet (at the network layer) be encapsulated in an RR frame (at the data link layer)?

52. Can an RR packet (at the network layer) be encapsulated in an I-frame (at the data link layer)?

53. In Figure 17.18 show the type of packets and frames exchanged. The inner boxes represent packets; the outer boxes represent frames.

Figure 17.18   *Exercise 53*

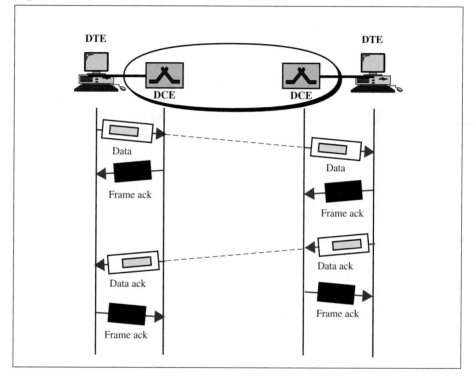

CHAPTER 18

Frame Relay

18.1 INTRODUCTION

Recently, the nature of the demands on WANs has changed dramatically. Previous WAN technologies, such as T-lines or X.25, were not responding to the needs of the user. Users were looking for higher data rates, lower cost, efficient handling of bursty data transmissions, and less overhead. **Frame Relay** is a virtual-circuit technology that provides low-level (physical and data link layers) service in response to the following demands:

■ **Higher Data Rate at Lower Cost.** In the past, many organizations used a WAN technology such as a leased line or X.25 to connect single computers. The data rate was relatively low. Today, most organizations use high-speed LANs and want to use WANs to connect these LANs. One solution is to use T-lines, but these lines provide only point-to-point connections, not many-to-many. Creating a mesh network out of T-lines is very expensive. For example, to connect six LANs, we need 15 T-lines. On the other hand, we need only six T-lines to connect the same six LANs to a Frame Relay network. Frame Relay provides the same type of service at lower cost. Figure 18.1 shows the difference.

Although Frame Relay originally was designed to provide a 1.544-Mbps data rate (equivalent to a T-1 line), today most implementations can handle up to 44.376 Mbps (equivalent to a T-3 line).

■ **Bursty Data.** Some services offered by wide area network providers assume that the user has a fixed-rate need. For example, a T-1 line is designed for a user who wants to use the line at a consistent 1.544 Mbps. This type of service is not suitable for the many users today that need to send **bursty data.** For example, a user may want to send data at 6 Mbps for 2 seconds, 0 Mbps (nothing) for 7 seconds, and 3.44 Mbps for 1 second for a total of 15.44 Megabits during a period of 10 seconds. Although, the average data rate is still 1.544 Mbps, the T-1 line cannot accept this type of demand because it is designed for fixed-rate data, not bursty data. Bursty data requires what is called **bandwidth on demand.** The user needs different bandwidth allocations at different times. Figure 18.2 shows the difference between fixed-rate data and bursty data.

Figure 18.1   *Frame Relay versus pure mesh T-line network*

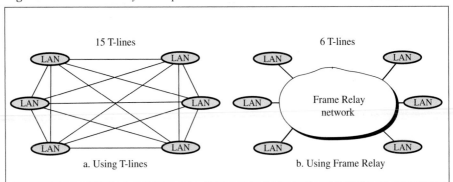

a. Using T-lines   b. Using Frame Relay

Figure 18.2   *Fixed-rate versus bursty data*

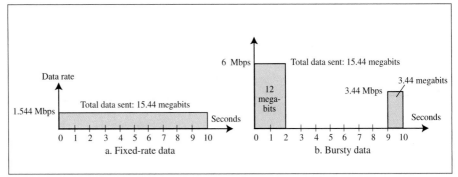

a. Fixed-rate data   b. Bursty data

Frame Relay accepts bursty data. A user is granted an average data rate that can be exceeded during bursty periods.

- **Less Overhead Due to Improved Transmission Media.** The quality of transmission media has improved tremendously since the last decade. They are more reliable and less error prone. There is no need to have a WAN that spends time and resources checking and double-checking potential errors. X.25 provides extensive error checking and flow control. Frames are checked for accuracy at each station (node) to which they are routed. Each station keeps a copy of the original frame until it receives confirmation from the next station that the frame has arrived intact. Such station-to-station checking is implemented at the data link layer of the OSI model. But X.25 does not stop there. It also checks for errors from source to receiver at the network layer. The source keeps a copy of the original frame until it receives confirmation from the final destination. Much of the traffic on an X.25 network is devoted to error checking to ensure complete reliability of service. Figure 18.3 shows the traffic required to transmit one frame from source to receiver. The white boxes show the data and data link acknowledgments. The colored boxes show the network layer confirmation and acknowledgments. Only one-fourth of this traffic is message data; the rest is reliability. Such extensive traffic was necessary at the time X.25 was introduced because transmission media were more error prone then than they are today.

Figure 18.3 *X.25 traffic*

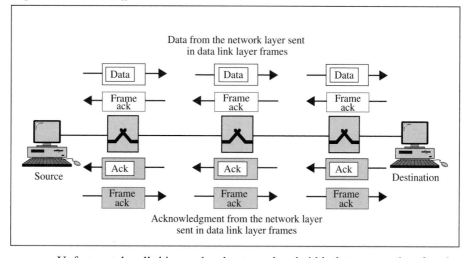

Unfortunately, all this overhead eats up bandwidth that cannot therefore be used for message data. If bandwidth is limited, the data rate of the transmission, which is proportional to the available channel width, is severely reduced. In addition, the requirement that each station keep a copy of the frame in its storage while it waits for acknowledgment results in another traffic bottleneck and further reductions in speed.

Improvements in traditional transmission media and a greater use of fiber-optic cable, which is far less susceptible to noise than metallic cable, have decreased the probability of transmission error to a point where this level of caution is not only unnecessary but counterproductive as well.

Frame Relay does not provide error checking or require acknowledgment in the data link layer. Instead, all error checking is left to the protocols at the network and transport layers, which use the services of Frame Relay. (Frame Relay operates at only the physical and data link layers.) Many data link layer operations are eliminated while others are combined. Instead of the complex situation shown in Figure 18.3, we now have the simplified transmission shown in Figure 18.4.

Figure 18.4 *Frame Relay traffic*

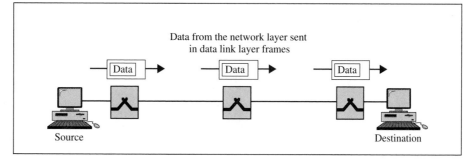

We summarize the differences between X.25 and Frame Relay in Table 18.1.

Table 18.1   *Comparison between X.25 and Frame Relay*

Feature	X.25	Frame Relay
Connection establishment	At the network layer	None
Hop-by-hop flow control and error control	At the data link layer	None
End-to-end flow control and error control	At the network layer	None
Data rate	Fixed	Bursty
Multiplexing	At the network layer	At the data link layer
Congestion control	Not necessary	Necessary

Advantages

Frame Relay has several advantages over comparable wide area networks such as X.25 and T-lines:

■ Frame Relay operates at a higher speed (1.544 Mbps and recently 44.376 Mbps). This means that it can easily be used instead of a mesh of T-1 or T-3 lines.

■ Frame Relay operates in just the physical and data link layers. This means it easily can be used as a backbone network to provide services to protocols that already have a network layer protocol. For example, the TCP/IP protocol (see Chapter 24) already has a network layer protocol (IP). If TCP/IP wants to use the services of X.25, there is a duplication in the network layer functions: X.25 has its own network layer and TCP/IP has its own. There is no duplication in the case of Frame Relay: TCP/IP uses its own network layer and Frame Relay provides services at the physical and the data link layers.

■ Frame Relay allows bursty data. Users do not have to adhere to a fixed data rate as in the case of X.25 or T-lines.

■ Frame Relay allows a frame size of 9000 bytes, which can accommodate all local area network frames.

■ Frame Relay is less expensive than other traditional WANs.

Disadvantages

Frame Relay is not perfect. Despite its low cost, there are some disadvantages:

■ Although some Frame Relay networks operate at 44.376 Mbps, this is still not high enough for protocols with even higher data rates (such as B-ISDN).

■ Frame Relay allows variable-length frames. This may create varying delays for different users. A Frame Relay switch handles a large frame from one user and a small frame from another user the same way. They are stored in the same queue if they are going out the same interface. The delay of a small frame following a large frame may be different than the delay of a small frame following another small frame; users of small frames are punished.

■ Because of the varying delays, which are not under user control, Frame Relay is not suitable for sending delay sensitive data such as real-time voice or video. For example, Frame Relay is not suitable for teleconferencing.

Role of Frame Relay

To summarize, Frame Relay can be used as a low-cost, high-speed backbone wide area network to connect local area networks that do not need real-time communication but may have bursty data to send. In addition, today, Frame Relay provides both permanent and switched connections. A user who needs a permanent connection pays on a leased basis. A user who needs a switched connection pays on a used basis.

18.2   FRAME RELAY OPERATION

Frame Relay provides permanent virtual and switched virtual connections. The devices that connect users to the network are DTEs. The switches that route the frames through the network are DCEs (see Figure 18.5). Frame Relay is normally used as a WAN to connect LANs or mainframe computers. In the first case, a router or a bridge can serve as the DTE and connects, through a leased line, the LAN to the Frame Relay switch, which is considered a DCE. In the second case, the mainframe itself can be used as a DTE with the installation of appropriate software.

Figure 18.5   *Frame Relay network*

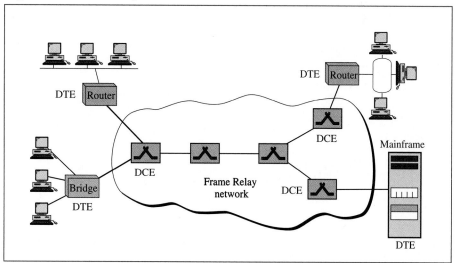

Virtual Circuits

Frame Relay is a virtual circuit network. It therefore does not use physical addresses to define the DTEs connected to the network. Like any other virtual circuit network, it uses a virtual circuit identifier. However, virtual circuit identifiers in Frame Relay operate at the data link layer, in contrast with X.25, where they operate at the network layer.

A virtual circuit in Frame Relay is identified by a number called a **data link connection identifier (DLCI).** When a virtual circuit is established by the network, a DTE is given a DLCI number that it can use to access the remote DTE. The local DTE uses this DLCI to send frames to the remote DTE. Figure 18.6 shows several virtual circuits and their DLCIs. Note that there are two DLCIs of 33; both are valid because they define different virtual circuits originating from different DTEs.

Figure 18.6   *DLCIs*

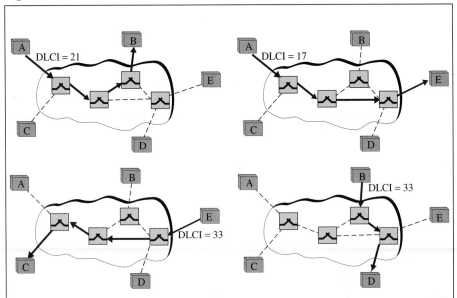

To understand how DLCIs are assigned to a virtual connection, let us first discuss the two types of connections in Frame Relay: PVC and SVC.

PVC

A permanent virtual circuit (PVC) connection is established between two DTEs by the network provider. The two DTEs are connected permanently through a virtual connection. Two DLCIs are assigned to the UNI interfaces at both ends of the connection, as seen in Figure 18.7.

When DTE A wants to send a frame to DTE B, it uses DLCI 122. When DTE B wants to send a frame to DTE A, it uses DLCI 077. Note that the DLCIs have local jurisdiction and it is possible that two DTEs have (accidentally) the same DLCI, but this is not usually the case.

Figure 18.7   *PVC DLCIs*

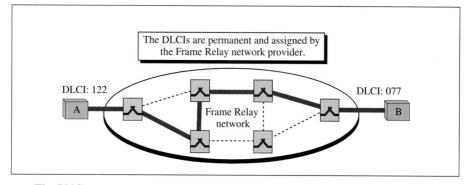

The DLCIs are permanent and assigned by the Frame Relay network provider.

DLCI: 122

DLCI: 077

A

B

Frame Relay network

The PVC connection was the only type possible in the early days of Frame Relay, but today DTEs can also communicate with each other using switched virtual circuits.

SVC

In a switched virtual circuit (SVC) connection, each time a DTE wants to make a connection with another DTE, a new virtual circuit connection should be established. How can this be done? In this case, Frame Relay cannot do the job by itself, but needs the services of another protocol that has a network layer and network layer addresses (such as ISDN or IP). The signaling mechanism of this other protocol makes a connection request using the network layer addresses of DTE A and DTE B. The exact mechanism depends on the network layer protocol, but the general idea is shown in Figure 18.8.

Figure 18.8   *SVC setup and release*

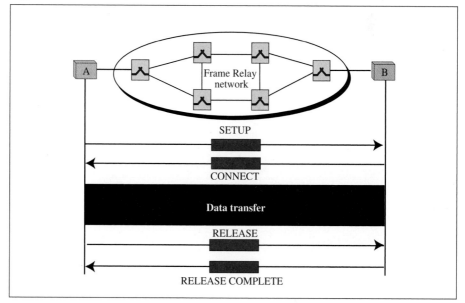

A

B

Frame Relay network

SETUP

CONNECT

Data transfer

RELEASE

RELEASE COMPLETE

The local DTE sends a SETUP message to the remote DTE, which responds with a CONNECT message. After the connection phase, the virtual circuit is established so the two DTEs can exchange data. Either DTE can issue a RELEASE message to terminate the connection. Figure 18.9 shows the DLCIs in an SVC connection.

Figure 18.9 *SVC DLCIs*

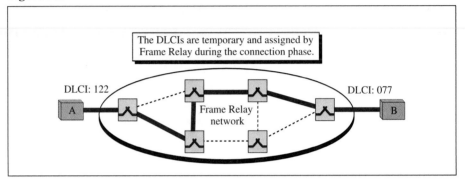

DLCI: 122

The DLCIs are temporary and assigned by Frame Relay during the connection phase.

DLCI: 077

A

Frame Relay network

B

DLCIs Inside the Network

DLCIs are assigned not only to define the virtual circuit between a DTE and DCE, but also to define the virtual circuit between two DCEs (switches) inside the network. A switch assigns a DLCI to each virtual connection in an interface. This means that two different connections belonging to two different interfaces may have the same DLCIs. In other words, DLCIs are unique only for a particular interface. Figure 18.10 shows the DLCIs inside a network.

Figure 18.10 *DLCIs inside a network*

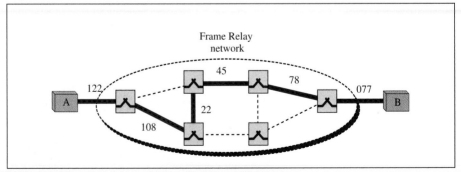

Frame Relay network

A

122

45

78

077

B

22

108

Switches

Each switch in a Frame Relay network has a table to route frames. The table matches an incoming interface–DLCI combination with an outgoing interface–DLCI combination. For example, Figure 18.11 shows two frames arriving at the switch on interface 1, one with DLCI = 121 and the other with DLCI = 124. The first one leaves the switch on interface 2, with the new DLCI = 041 (see line 1 of the table) and the second one leaves the switch on interface 3 with DLCI = 112 (see line 2 of the table).

Figure 18.11   *Frame Relay switch*

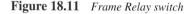
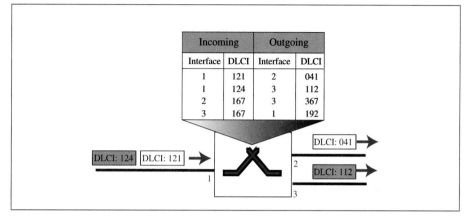

Incoming		Outgoing	
Interface	DLCI	Interface	DLCI
1	121	2	041
1	124	3	112
2	167	3	367
3	167	1	192

18.3   FRAME RELAY LAYERS

Figure 18.12 shows the Frame Relay layers. Frame Relay has only physical and data link layers.

Figure 18.12   *Frame Relay layers*

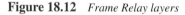
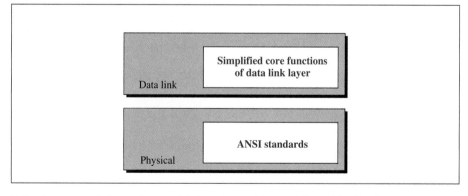

Data link	Simplified core functions of data link layer
Physical	ANSI standards

> Frame Relay operates only at the physical and data link layers.

Figure 18.13 compares Frame Relay layers to the conventional layers of a packet-switching network such as X.25. Frame Relay has only 1.5 layers whereas X.25 has 3 layers. Frame Relay eliminates all of the network layer functions and a portion of the conventional data link layer functions.

Figure 18.13 *Comparing layers in Frame Relay and X.25*

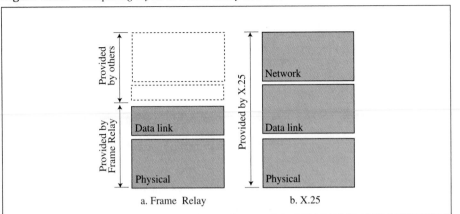

a. Frame Relay   b. X.25

Physical Layer

No specific protocol is defined for the physical layer in Frame Relay. Instead, it is left to the implementer to use whatever is available. Frame Relay supports any of the protocols recognized by ANSI.

Data Link Layer

At the data link layer, Frame Relay employs a simplified version of HDLC called core LAPF. The simpler version is used because HDLC provides extensive error and flow control fields that are not needed in Frame Relay.

Figure 18.14 shows the format of a Frame Relay frame. The frame is similar to that of HDLC. In fact, the flag, FCS, and information fields are the same. However, the control field is missing. The address field defines the DLCI as well as some bits used to control congestion and traffic.

Figure 18.14 *Frame Relay frame*

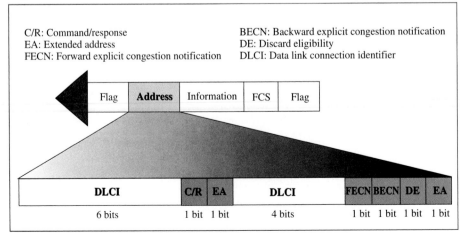

C/R: Command/response
EA: Extended address
FECN: Forward explicit congestion notification
BECN: Backward explicit congestion notification
DE: Discard eligibility
DLCI: Data link connection identifier

The detailed descriptions of the fields are as follows:

- **Address (DLCI) field.** The first six bits of the first byte make up part 1 of the DLCI. The second part of the DLCI uses the first four bits of the second byte. These bits are part of the 10-bit data link connection identifier defined by the standard. The function of the DLCI was discussed previously. We will discuss extended addressing at the end of the chapter.

- **Command/Response (C/R).** The command/response (C/R) bit is provided to allow upper layers to identify a frame as either a command or a response. It is not used by the Frame Relay protocol.

- **Extended address (EA).** The extended address (EA) bit indicates whether or not the current byte is the final byte of the address. An EA of 0 means that another address byte is to follow. An EA of 1 means that the current byte is the final one.

- **Forward explicit congestion notification (FECN).** The **forward explicit congestion notification (FECN)** bit can be set by any switch to indicate that traffic is congested in the direction in which the frame is traveling. This bit informs the destination that congestion has occurred. We will discuss the use of this bit when we discuss congestion control.

- **Backward explicit congestion notification (BECN).** The **backward explicit congestion notification (BECN)** bit is set to indicate a congestion problem in the direction opposite to the one in which the frame is traveling. This bit informs the sender that congestion has occurred. We will discuss the use of this bit when we discuss congestion control.

- **Discard eligibility (DE).** The **discard eligibility (DE)** bit indicates the priority level of the frame. In emergency situations, switches may have to discard frames to relieve bottlenecks and keep the network from collapsing due to overload. When set (DE 1), this bit tells the network not to discard this frame as long as there are other frames in the stream with priorities of 0. This bit can be set either by the sender of the frames (user) or by any switch in the network.

18.4   CONGESTION CONTROL

Congestion in a network may occur if users send data into the network at a rate greater than that allowed by network resources. For example, congestion may occur because the switches in a network have a limited buffer size to store arrived packets before processing.

Congestion in a Frame Relay network is a problem that must be avoided because it decreases throughput and increases delay. A high throughput and low delay are the main goals of the Frame Relay protocol.

A packet-switched network such as X.25 uses flow control at both the data link layer and the network layer. Flow control at the network layer is end-to-end. Flow control at the data link layer is node-to-node. Both mechanisms prevent users from sending excessive traffic into the network.

:

Frame Relay protocol does not have a network layer. Even at the data link layer, Frame Relay does not use flow control. In addition, Frame Relay allows the user to transmit bursty data. This means that a Frame Relay network has the potential to be really congested with traffic, thus requiring **congestion control.**

Congestion Avoidance

For **congestion avoidance,** the Frame Relay protocol uses two bits in the frame to explicitly warn the source and the destination of the presence of congestion.

BECN

The backward explicit congestion notification (BECN) bit warns the sender of congestion in the network. One might ask how this is accomplished since the frames are traveling away from the sender. In fact, there are two methods: the switch can use response frames from the receiver (full-duplex mode) or else the switch can use a predefined connection (DLCI = 1023) to send special frames for this specific purpose. The sender can respond to this warning by simply reducing the data rate. Figure 18.15 shows the use of BECN.

Figure 18.15 *BECN*

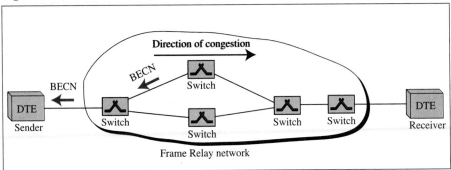

FECN

The forward explicit congestion notification (FECN) bit is used to warn the receiver of congestion in the network. It might appear that the receiver cannot do anything to relieve the congestion. However, the Frame Relay protocol assumes that the sender and receiver are communicating with each other and are using some type of flow control at a higher level. For example, if there is an acknowledgment mechanism at this higher level, the receiver can delay the acknowledgment, thus forcing the sender to slow down. Figure 18.16 shows the use of FECN.

Four Situations

When two DTEs are communicating using a Frame Relay network, four situations may occur with regard to congestion. Figure 18.17 shows these four situations and the values of FECN and BECN.

Figure 18.16   *FECN*

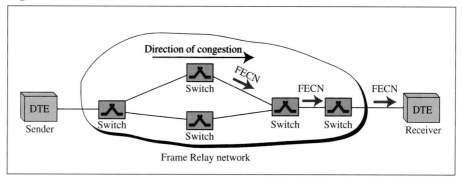

Figure 18.17   *Four cases of congestion*

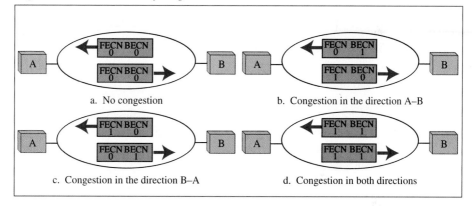

Discarding

If users do not respond to the congestion notices, the Frame Relay network has to discard frames. Which frames are discarded is the subject of the section called **traffic control.**

The users are notified of the congestion implicitly when the upper-layer protocols (such as the transport layer) find that some frames have not reached the destination. It is the responsibility of the sender to stop and allow the network to recover from the congestion and resend the discarded frames.

18.5   LEAKY BUCKET ALGORITHM

The behavior of a switch in a Frame Relay network can be simulated by a leaky bucket. If a bucket has a small hole at the bottom, the water leaks from the bucket at a constant rate as long as there is water in the bucket. The rate at which the water leaks does not depend on the rate at which the water is input to the bucket. The input rate can vary, but the output rate remains constant (see Figure 18.18).

Figure 18.18 *Leaky bucket*

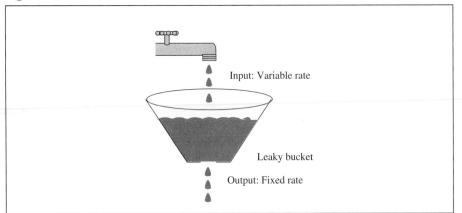

Input: Variable rate

Leaky bucket

Output: Fixed rate

It is obvious that if more water enters the bucket than is leaked, the time will come when the bucket overflows. The same situation occurs in a packet-switched network such as Frame Relay that does not use flow control. Each switch can send data out at a certain rate. If data are received faster than transmitted, the switch can be congested and discard some frames.

How can the leaky bucket control bursty input? Imagine water is leaking at the rate of 2 gallons per minute. If we have an input burst with a rate of 10 gallons per minute for a duration of 12 seconds and then nothing during the next 48 seconds, what should be the capacity of the bucket to avoid overflow? We can find the capacity using the following calculation:

$$\text{Total water during the burst duration} = 10 \times (12/60) = 2 \text{ gallons}$$

If the capacity of the bucket is two gallons, it can hold the water for the duration of the burst and let it leak continuously for a period of one minute. Note that the capacity can be slightly less than two gallons because some of the water is leaking out during the burst interval. It is customary to use the upper limit.

We can apply the idea to each output interface of each switch in Frame Relay. The output is a fixed rate (1.544 Mbps for example), while the input can be bursty. The switch can use a queue (buffer) to serve as the bucket. The bursty data can be stored in the queue and then sent at the fixed rate.

For example, imagine a switch with only one input and one output interface. If the data rate at the output interface is 1.544 Mbps and the input data are bursty with a rate of 40 Mbps for the duration of 100 milliseconds (and nothing else until the next second), what should be the size of the queue?

$$40 \text{ Mbps} \times (100/1000) = 4 \text{ megabits}$$

The output interface should have a queue (buffer) of 4 million bits or half a million bytes. Figure 18.19 shows the design.

But how can we control the output data rate to be always less than a fixed rate (for example, 1.544 Mbps) in a packet-switched network where the size of each packet can be different? We can use a counter and clock. At the tick of the clock (the beginning of the second, for example), the counter is set to the amount of data that can be output in

Figure 18.19 *A switch controlling the output rate*

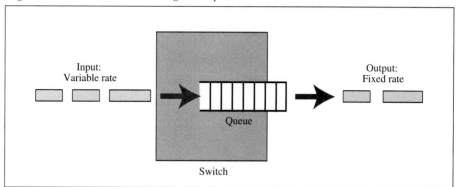

one tick (usually in bytes). The algorithm then checks the size of the frame at the front of the queue. If the size is less than or equal to the value of the counter, the packet is sent; if the size is greater than the value of the counter, the packet is left in the queue and waits for the next tick of the clock. Figure 18.20 shows the flowchart of the **leaky bucket algorithm.**

Figure 18.20 *Flowchart for leaky bucket algorithm*

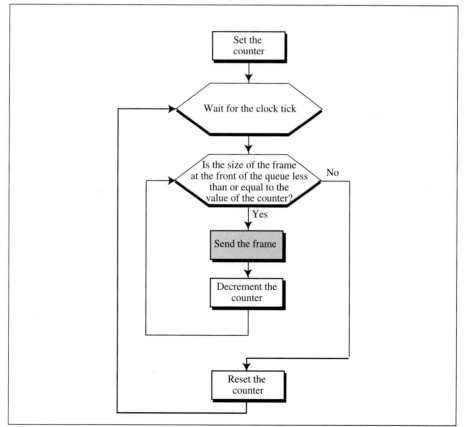

Note that for this algorithm to work, the size of the frame should be smaller than the maximum counter value.

Figure 18.21 shows an example. Assume that the output rate is 80 Kbps. This means 80,000 bits per second or 10,000 bytes per second. The counter is originally set to 10,000; after sending three frames, the value of the counter is 600, which is less than the size of the next frames. The next three frames cannot be sent. They need to wait for the next tick of the clock.

Figure 18.21   *Example of leaky bucket algorithm*

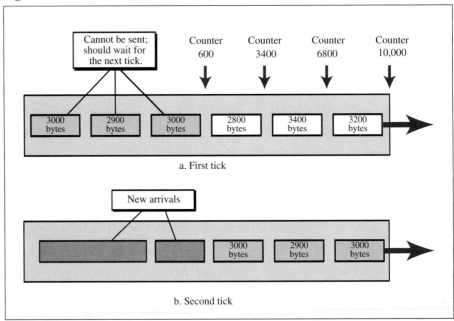

18.6   TRAFFIC CONTROL

Congestion strategies require Frame Relay to take traffic control measurements to determine when BECN or FECN bits should be set, when the DE bit should be set, and also when a frame should be discarded.

Four different attributes to control traffic have been devised: access rate, committed burst size, committed information rate, and excess burst size. These are set during the negotiation between the user and the network. For PVC connections, they are negotiated once; for SVC connections, they are negotiated for each connection during connection setup. Figure 18.22 shows the relationships between these four measurements.

Figure 18.22   *Relationship between traffic control attributes*

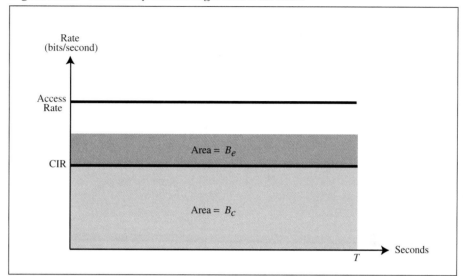

Access Rate

For every connection, an **access rate** (in bits/second) is defined. The access rate actually depends on the bandwidth of the channel connecting the user to the network. The user can never exceed this rate. For example, if the user is connected to a Frame Relay network by a T-1 line, the access rate is 1.544 Mbps and can never be exceeded.

Committed Burst Size

For every connection, Frame Relay defines a **committed burst size (B_c).** This is the maximum number of bits in a predefined period of time that the network is committed to transfer without discarding any frame or setting the DE bit. For example, if a B_c of 400 kilobits for a period of four seconds is granted, the user can send up to 400 kilobits during a four-second interval without worrying about any frame loss. Note that this is not a rate defined for each second. It is a cumulative measurement. The user can send 300 kilobits during the first second, no data during the second and the third seconds, and finally 100 kilobits during the fourth second.

Committed Information Rate

The **committed information rate (CIR)** is similar in concept to committed burst size except that it defines an average rate in bits per second. If the user follows this rate continuously, the network is committed to deliver the frames. However, because it is an average measurement, a user may send data higher than the CIR at times or lower at other times. As long as the average for the predefined period is met, the frames will be delivered.

The cumulative number of bits sent during the predefined period should not exceed B_c. Note that the CIR is not an independent measurement; it can be calculated using the following formula:

$$\text{CIR} = B_c/T \qquad \text{bps}$$

For example, if the B_c is five kilobits in a period of five seconds, the CIR is 5000/5, or 1 Kbps.

Excess Burst Size

For every connection, Frame Relay defines an **excess burst size (B_e)**. This is the maximum number of bits in excess of B_c that a user can send during a predefined period of time. The network is committed to transfer these bits if there is no congestion. Note that there is less commitment here than in the case of B_c. The network is committing itself conditionally.

User Rate

Figure 18.23 shows how a user can send bursty data. If the user never exceeds B_c, the network is committed to transmit the frames without discarding any. If the user exceeds B_c by less than B_e (that is, the total bits are less than $B_c + B_e$), the network is committed to transfer all of the frames if there is no congestion. If there is congestion, some frames will be discarded. The first switch that receives the frames from the user has a counter and sets the DE bit for the frames that exceed the B_c. The rest of the switches will discard these frames if there is congestion. Note that a user who needs to send data faster may exceed the B_c level. As long as the level is not above $B_c + B_e$, there is a chance that the frames will reach the destination without being discarded. Remember, however, that the moment the user exceeds the $B_c + B_e$ level, all of the frames sent after that are discarded by the first switch.

Figure 18.23 *User rate in relation to* B_c *and* $B_c + B_e$

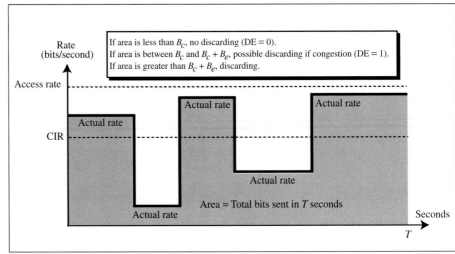

18.7   OTHER FEATURES

Some other features of Frame Relay are briefly discussed here.

Extended Address

To increase the range of DLCIs, the Frame Relay address has been extended from the original two-byte address to three- or four-byte addresses. Figure 18.24 shows the different addresses. Note that the EA field defines the number of bytes; it is 1 in the last byte of the address and it is 0 in the other bytes. Note that in the three- and four-byte formats, the bit before the last bit is set to 0.

Figure 18.24   *Three address formats*

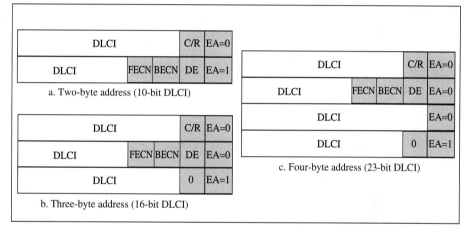

a. Two-byte address (10-bit DLCI)

b. Three-byte address (16-bit DLCI)

c. Four-byte address (23-bit DLCI)

FRADs

To handle frames arriving from other protocols, Frame Relay uses a device called a **Frame Relay assembler/disassembler (FRAD).** A FRAD assembles and disassembles frames coming from other protocols to allow them to be carried by Frame Relay frames. A FRAD can be implemented as a separate device or as part of a switch. Figure 18.25 shows two FRADs connected to a Frame Relay network.

Figure 18.25   *FRAD*

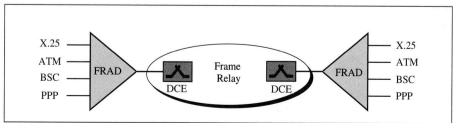

VOFR

Frame Relay networks offer an option called **Voice Over Frame Relay (VOFR)** that sends voice through the network. Voice is digitized using PCM and then compressed. The result is sent as data frames over the network. This feature allows the inexpensive sending of voice over long distances. However, note that the quality of voice is not as good compared to voice over a circuit-switching network such as the telephone network. Also, the varying delay mentioned earlier sometimes corrupts real-time voice.

LMI

Frame Relay was originally designed to provide PVC connections. There was not, therefore, a provision for controlling or managing interfaces. **Local management information (LMI)** is a protocol added recently to the Frame Relay protocol to provide more management features. In particular, LMI can provide:

■ A keepalive mechanism to check if data are flowing.

■ A multicast mechanism to allow a local DTE to send frames to more than one remote DTE.

■ A mechanism to allow a DTE to check the status of a DCE (e.g., to see if the DCE is congested).

18.8   KEY TERMS AND CONCEPTS

access rate

backward explicit congestion notification (BECN)

bandwidth on demand

bursty data

committed burst size (B_c)

committed information rate (CIR)

congestion

congestion avoidance

congestion control

data link connection identifier (DLCI)

discard eligibility (DE)

excess burst size (B_e)

forward explicit congestion notification (FECN)

Frame Relay

Frame Relay assembler/disassembler (FRAD)

leaky bucket algorithm

local management information (LMI)

traffic control

Voice Over Frame Relay (VOFR)

18.9   SUMMARY

- Frame Relay is a cost-effective technology that connects LANs.
- Frame Relay can handle bursty data.
- Frame Relay eliminates the extensive error checking necessary in X.25 protocol.
- Both PVC and SVC connections are used in Frame Relay.
- The data link connection identifier (DLCI) identifies a virtual circuit in Frame Relay.
- Frame Relay operates in the physical and data link layers of the OSI model.
- In the data link layer, Frame Relay uses a simplified version of HDLC protocol.
- In Frame Relay, routing and switching are functions of the data link layer. Frames, not packets, are switched.
- Flow control is handled through the backward explicit congestion notification (BECN) bit and/or the forward explicit congestion notification (FECN) bit of the address field of the frame.
- The leaky bucket algorithm is a model for frame transmission at a switch. The queue outputs bits at a fixed rate while the bits enter the queue at a variable rate.
- Frame Relay traffic is dependent on four factors: access rate, committed burst size, committed information rate, and excess burst size.

18.10   PRACTICE SET

Review Questions

1. How is flow control handled in Frame Relay?
2. How are Frame Relay assemblers/dissemblers (FRADs) used in a Frame Relay backbone?
3. Name some advantages of Frame Relay over X.25.
4. How does a frame get retransmitted in Frame Relay?
5. Compare the format of an HDLC protocol frame with a Frame Relay protocol frame. Which fields are missing in the Frame Relay protocol frame? Which fields are added in the Frame Relay protocol frame?
6. Why is the control field from HDLC totally dropped from Frame Relay?
7. HDLC has three types of frames (I-frame, S-frame, and U-frame). Which one corresponds to the Frame Relay frame?
8. Is there a need for a sliding window in Frame Relay protocol?
9. There are no sequence numbers in Frame Relay. Why?
10. Can two devices connected to the same Frame Relay network use the same DLCIs?
11. Why is Frame Relay a better solution for connecting LANs than T-1 lines?

12. What is the definition of bursty data?

13. Why is Frame Relay unsuitable for real-time communication such as teleconferencing?

14. Compare an SVC with a PVC.

15. Discuss the Frame Relay physical layer.

16. What does the DE bit have to do with congestion?

17. How can the BECN bit inform the sender of congestion in the network?

18. How can the FECN bit inform the receiver of congestion in the network?

19. Is the output rate at a Frame Relay switch really a fixed rate? Why or why not?

20. How is the committed burst size related to the committed information rate?

21. What is the function of the EA bit in the address field?

Multiple Choice Questions

22. Frame Relay requires error checking at the _____ layer.
    a. physical
    b. data link
    c. network
    d. none of the above

23. Frame Relay operates in the _____.
    a. physical layer
    b. data link layer
    c. physical and data link layers
    d. physical, data link, and network layers

24. In the data link layer, Frame Relay uses _____.
    a. BSC protocol
    b. a simplified HDLC protocol
    c. LAPB
    d. any ANSI standard protocol

25. Which bit in the address field in Frame Relay is set to one to signify the last address byte?
    a. discard eligibility (DE)
    b. extended address (EA)
    c. command/response (C/R)
    d. forward explicit congestion notification (FECN)

26. Which bit in the address field in Frame Relay determines whether or not a frame may be eliminated in emergency cases?
    a. discard eligibility (DE)
    b. extended address (EA)
    c. command/response (C/R)

    d. forward explicit congestion notification (FECN)

27. Routing and switching in Frame Relay are performed by the _____ layer.

    a. physical

    b. data link

    c. network

    d. b and c

28. Which field contains the permanent virtual circuit address in Frame Relay?

    a. EA

    b. FECN/BECN

    c. DE

    d. DLCI

29. The data rate for a Frame Relay network can be as much as _____ Mbps.

    a. 1.544

    b. 3.88

    c. 44.376

    d. 60

30. What is a factor contributing to the decreased overhead in Frame Relay compared to X.25?

    a. higher data rate

    b. full-duplex mode

    c. packet-switched network

    d. no acknowledgments

31. Bursty data are allowed on a _____.

    a. Frame Relay network

    b. X.25 network

    c. T-line

    d. all of the above

32. Frame Relay is unsuitable for _____ due to possible delays in transmission resulting from variable frame sizes.

    a. real-time video

    b. file transfers

    c. fixed-rate data communication

    d. all of the above

33. In a Frame Relay network used as a WAN, the Frame Relay switch can be considered a _____ and the router that connects the LAN to the Frame Relay switch can be considered a _____.

    a. DTE; DCE

    b. DTE; DTE

    c. DCE; DTE

    d. DCE; DCE

34. Frame Relay provides _____ connections.

    a. PVC

    b. SVC

    c. DLCI

    d. a and b

35. In X.25 the virtual circuit identifier operates at the _____ layer; in Frame Relay the virtual circuit identifier operates at the _____ layer.

    a. data link; physical

    b. network; data link

    c. network; physical

    d. data link; network

36. The FECN informs the _____ of congestion while the BECN informs the _____ of congestion.

    a. destination; interface

    b. destination; sender

    c. sender; destination

    d. interface; sender

37. In a Frame Relay network connecting DTE A with DTE Z, there is congestion in the A to Z direction. A frame traveling from A to Z would have the FECN bit _____ and the BECN bit _____.

    a. set; set

    b. set; not set

    c. not set; set

    d. not set; not set

38. B_c, when added to B_e, should be less than the _____.

    a. CIR

    b. access rate

    c. committed burst size

    d. a and b

39. What is the relationship between the access rate and the CIR?

    a. CIR is always equal to the access rate.

    b. CIR is greater than the access rate.

    c. CIR is less than the access rate.

    d. CIR plus B_e is equal to the access rate.

40. A Frame Relay network is committed to transfer _____ bits per second without discarding any frames.

    a. B_c

    b. B_e

    c. CIR

   d. a and b

41. B_c is _____ than B_e for a specified time period.

   a. always greater than

   b. always less than

   c. always equal to

   d. none of the above

42. In Frame Relay the transmission rate can never exceed _____.

   a. B_c

   b. B_e

   c. the CIR

   d. the access rate

43. A Frame Relay network is committed to transfer a maximum of _____ bits in a specified time period if there is no congestion.

   a. B_c

   b. B_e

   c. $B_c + B_e$

   d. none of the above

44. The Frame Relay address field is _____ in length.

   a. four bytes

   b. two bytes

   c. three bytes

   d. any of the above

45. A device called a _____ allows packets from an ATM network to be transmitted across a Frame Relay network.

   a. LMI

   b. VOFR

   c. FRAD

   d. DLCI

46. _____ is a protocol to control and manage interfaces in Frame Relay networks.

   a. LMI

   b. VOFR

   c. FRAD

   d. DLCI

47. _____ is a Frame Relay option that transmits voice through the network.

   a. LMI

   b. VOFR

   c. FRAD

   d. DLCI

Exercises

48. The address field of a Frame Relay frame is 1011000100010110. What is the DLCI (in decimal)?

49. The address field of a Frame Relay frame is 1011000100010110. Is there any congestion in the forward direction? Is there any congestion in the backward direction?

50. The address field of a Frame Relay frame is 1011001000101110. Will this frame be discarded if there is congestion?

51. The address field of a Frame Relay frame is 101100000101001. Is this valid?

52. Find the DLCI value if the first three bytes received are 7C 74 E1 in hexadecimal.

53. Find the value of the two-byte address field in hexadecimal if the DLCI is 178. Assume no congestion.

54. A frame goes from DTE A to DTE B. There is congestion in the A to B direction. Is the FECN bit set? Is the BECN bit set?

55. A frame goes from DTE B to DTE A. There is congestion in the A to B direction. Is the FECN bit set? Is the BECN bit set?

56. A frame goes from DTE A to DTE B. There is congestion in both directions. Is the FECN bit set? Is the BECN bit set?

57. In a leaky bucket, what should be the capacity of the bucket if the output rate is 5 gallons per minute, and there is an input burst of 100 gallons per minute for 12 seconds and there is no input for 48 seconds?

58. An output interface in a switch is designed using the leaky bucket algorithm to send 8000 bytes per second (tick). If the following frames are received in sequence, show the frame(s) that are sent during each second.

    Frames 1, 2, 3, 4: 4000 bytes each
    Frames 5, 6, 7: 3200 bytes each
    Frames 8, 9: 400 bytes each
    Frames 10, 11, 12: 2000 bytes each

59. A user is connected to a Frame Relay network through a T-1 line. The granted CIR is 1 Mbps with a B_c of 5 million bits per 5 seconds and B_e of 1 million bits per 5 seconds. Answer the following questions:

    a. What is the access rate?

    b. Can the user send data at 1.6 Mbps?

    c. Can the user send data at 1 Mbps all the time? Is it guaranteed that frames are never discarded in this case?

    d. Can the user send data at 1.2 Mbps all the time? Is it guaranteed that frames are never discarded in this case? If the answer is no, is it guaranteed that frames are discarded only if there is congestion?

    e. Repeat the question in part d for a constant rate of 1.4 Mbps.

    f. What is the maximum data rate the user can use all of the time without worrying about the frames being discarded?

    g. If the user wants to take a risk, what is the maximum data rate that can be used with no chance of discarding if there is no congestion.

60. In Exercise 59 the user sends data at 1.4 Mbps for two seconds and nothing for the next three seconds. Is there a danger of discarding if there is no congestion? Is there a danger of discarding if there is congestion?

61. In Figure 18.26 a virtual connection is established between DTE A and DTE B. Show the DLCI for each link.

Figure 18.26   *Exercise 61*

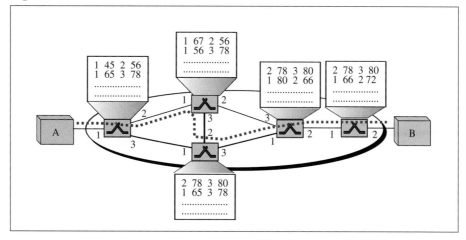

62. In Figure 18.27 a virtual connection is established between DTE A and DTE B. Show the corresponding entries in the tables of each switch.

Figure 18.27   *Exercise 62*

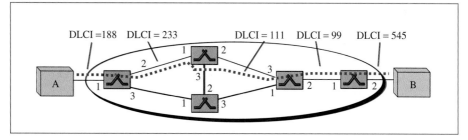

CHAPTER 19

ATM

Asynchronous Transfer Mode (ATM) is the **cell relay** protocol designed by the ATM Forum and adopted by the ITU-T. The combination of ATM and B-ISDN will allow high-speed interconnection of all the world's networks. In fact, ATM can be thought of as the "highway" of the information superhighway.

19.1 DESIGN GOALS

Among the challenges faced by the designers of ATM, six stand out. First and foremost is the need for a transmission system to optimize the use of high-data-rate transmission media, in particular optical fiber. In addition to offering large bandwidths, newer transmission media and equipment are dramatically less susceptible to noise degradation. A technology is needed to take advantage of both factors and thereby maximize data rates.

Second is the need for a system that can interface with existing systems, such as the various packet networks, and to provide wide area interconnectivity between them without lowering their effectiveness or requiring their replacement. ATM is potentially as effective a LAN and short-haul mechanism as it is a WAN mechanism. Its proponents hope that it will eventually replace the existing systems. Until that happens, however, the protocol provides mechanisms for mapping the packets and frames of other systems onto ATM cells.

Third is the need for a design that can be implemented inexpensively so that cost would not be a barrier to adoption. If ATM is to become the backbone of international communications, as intended, it must be available at low cost to every user who wants it.

Fourth, the new system must be able to work with and support the existing telecommunications hierarchies (local loops, local providers, long-distance carriers, and so on).

Fifth, the new system must be connection-oriented to ensure accurate and predictable delivery.

And last but not least, one objective is to move as many of the functions to hardware as possible (for speed) and eliminate as many software functions as possible (again for speed).

Before discussing the solutions to these design requirements, it is useful to examine some of the problems associated with existing systems.

In ATM, some software functions have moved to hardware; this can increase the data rate.

Packet Networks

Data communications today are based on packet switching and packet networks. As explained in Chapter 14, a packet is a combination of data and overhead bits that can be passed through the network as a self-contained unit. The overhead bits, in the form of a header and trailer, act as an envelope that provides identification and addressing information as well as the data required for routing, flow control, error control, and so on.

Different protocols use packets of varying size and intricacy. As networks become more complex, the information that must be carried in the header becomes more extensive. The result is larger and larger headers relative to the size of the data unit. In response, some protocols have enlarged the size of the data unit to make header use more efficient (sending more data with the same size header). Unfortunately, large data fields create waste. If there is not much information to transmit, much of the field goes unused. To improve utilization, some protocols provide variable packet sizes to users. We now have packets that can be as long as 65,545 bytes sharing long-haul links with packets of fewer than 200 bytes.

Mixed Network Traffic

As you can imagine, the variety of packet sizes makes traffic unpredictable. Switches, multiplexers, and routers must incorporate elaborate software systems to manage the various sizes of packets. A great deal of header information must be read, and each bit counted and evaluated to ensure the integrity of every packet. Internetworking among the different packet networks is slow and expensive at best, and impossible at worst.

Another problem is that of providing consistent data-rate delivery when packet sizes are unpredictable and can vary so dramatically. To get the most out of broadband technology, traffic must be time-division multiplexed onto shared paths. Imagine the results of multiplexing packets from two networks with different requirements (and packet designs) onto one link (see Figure 19.1). What happens when line 1 uses large packets (usually data packets) while line 2 uses very small packets (the norm for audio and video information)?

If line 1's gigantic packet X arrives at the multiplexer even a moment earlier than line 2's packets, the multiplexer puts packet X onto the new path first. After all, even if line 2's packets have priority, the multiplexer has no way of knowing to wait for them and processes the packet that has arrived. Packet A must therefore wait for the entire X bit stream to move into place before it can follow. The sheer size of X creates an unfair delay for packet A. The same imbalance can affect all of the packets from line 2. As an analogy, imagine yourself in a car arriving at a crossroad just after

Figure 19.1 *Multiplexing using different packet sizes*

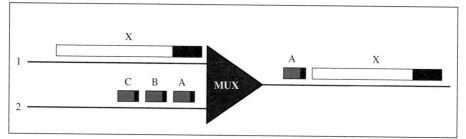

a parade has arrived from the opposite direction. The parade takes the same outbound road that you need to take but, because it arrived just before you did, it is already beginning its turn when you get there. You have to wait for the entire parade to turn onto the road before you can follow. Now imagine that you had been following another car that made the turn before the parade. You will now arrive at your shared destination separated by a huge gap of time.

Because audio and video packets ordinarily are small, mixing them with conventional data traffic often creates unacceptable delays of this type and makes shared packet links unusable for audio and video information. Traffic must travel over different paths, much the same way that automobile and train traffic do. But to fully utilize broad bandwidth links, we need to be able to send all kinds of traffic over the same links.

Cell Networks

Many of the problems associated with packet internetworking are solved by adopting a concept called cell networking. A cell is a small data unit of fixed size. In a **cell network,** which uses the **cell** as the basic unit of data exchange, all data are loaded into identical cells that can be transmitted with complete predictability and uniformity. As packets of different sizes and formats reach the cell network from a tributary network, they are split into multiple small data units of equal length and loaded into cells. The cells are then multiplexed with other cells and routed through the cell network. Because each cell is the same size and all are small, the problems associated with multiplexing different-sized packets are avoided.

> A cell network uses the cell as the basic unit of data exchange. A cell is defined as a small, fixed-sized block of information.

Advantages of Cells

Figure 19.2 shows the multiplexer from Figure 19.1 with the two lines sending cells instead of packets. Packet X has been segmented into three cells: X, Y, and Z. Only the first cell from line 1 gets put on the link before the first cell from line 2. The cells from the two lines are interleaved so that none suffers a long delay.

A second advantage of this same scenario is that the high speed of the links coupled with the small size of the cells means that, despite interleaving, cells from each line arrive at their respective destinations in an approximation of a continuous stream (much as a movie appears to your brain to be continuous action when in fact it is really

Figure 19.2   *Multiplexing using cells*

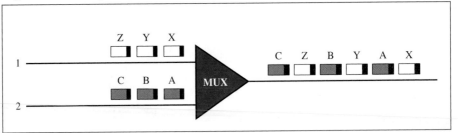

a series of separate still photos). In this way, a cell network can handle real-time transmissions, such as a phone call, without the parties being aware of the segmentation or multiplexing at all.

In addition, the predictability conferred by a fixed cell size allows switches and terminals to treat each cell as a unit rather than as a bit stream. In other words, to a cell network the smallest unit is a cell, not a bit. This distinction makes network operation not only more efficient but also cheaper. Switching and multiplexing can be implemented in hardware rather than software, resulting in devices that are less expensive both to produce and to maintain.

Asynchronous TDM

ATM uses asynchronous time-division multiplexing (see Chapter 8)—that is why it is called Asynchronous Transfer Mode—to multiplex cells coming from different channels. It uses fixed-size slots (size of a cell). ATM multiplexers fill a slot with a cell from any input channel that has a cell; the slot is empty if none of the channels has a cell to send.

Figure 19.3 shows how cells from three inputs are multiplexed. At the first tick of the clock, channel 2 has no cell (empty input slot), so the multiplexer fills the slot with a cell from the third channel. When all the cells from all the channels are multiplexed, the output slots are empty.

Figure 19.3   *ATM multiplexing*

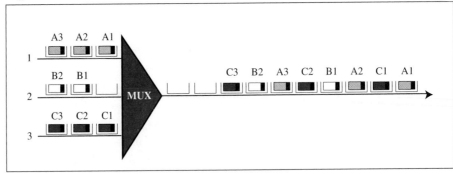

19.2   ATM ARCHITECTURE

ATM is a cell-switched network. The user access devices, called the end points, are connected through a **user-to-network interface (UNI)** to the switches inside the network. The switches are connected through **network-to-network interfaces (NNIs).** Figure 19.4 shows an example of an ATM network.

Figure 19.4   *Architecture of an ATM network*

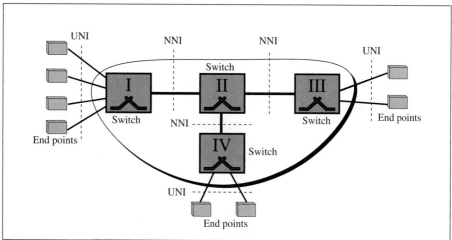

Virtual Connection

Connection between two end points is accomplished through transmission paths (TPs), virtual paths (VPs), and virtual circuits (VCs). A **transmission path (TP)** is the physical connection (wire, cable, satellite, and so on) between an end point and a switch or between two switches. Think of two switches as two cities. A transmission path is the set of all highways that directly connects the two cities.

A transmission path is divided into several virtual paths. A **virtual path (VP)** provides a connection or a set of connections between two switches. Think of a virtual path as a highway that connects two cities. Each highway is a virtual path; the set of all highways is the transmission path.

Cell networks are based on **virtual circuits (VCs).** All cells belonging to a single message follow the same virtual circuit and remain in their original order until they reach their destination. Think of a virtual circuit as the lanes of a highway (virtual path). Figure 19.5 shows the relationship between a transmission path (a physical connection), virtual paths (a combination of virtual circuits that are bundled together because parts of their paths are the same), and virtual circuits that logically connect two points together.

To better understand the concept of VPs and VCs, look at Figure 19.6. In this figure, eight end points are communicating using four VCs. However, the first two VCs seem to share the same virtual path from switch I to switch III, so it is reasonable to bundle these two VCs together to form one VP. On the other hand, it is clear that the

Figure 19.5 *TP, VPs, and VCs*

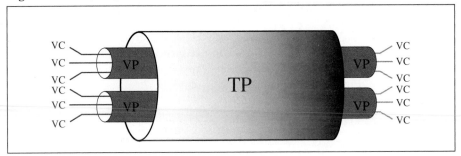

Figure 19.6 *Example of VPs and VCs*

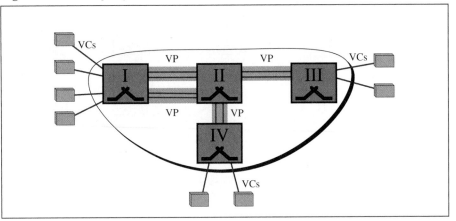

other two VCs share the same path from switch I to switch IV, so it is also reasonable to combine them to form one VP.

Identifiers

In a virtual circuit network, to route data from one end point to another, the virtual connections need to be identified. For this purpose, the designers of ATM created a hierarchical identifier with two levels: a **virtual path identifier (VPI)** and a **virtual circuit identifier (VCI)**. The VPI defines the specific VP and the VCI defines a particular VC inside the VP. The VPI is the same for all virtual connections that are bundled (logically) into one VP.

> Note that a virtual connection is defined by a pair of numbers: the VPI and the VCI.

Figure 19.7 shows the VPIs and VCIs for a transmission path (TP). The rationale for dividing an identifier into two parts will become clear when we discuss routing in an ATM network.

The lengths of the VPIs for UNI and NNI interfaces are different. In a UNI interface, the VPI is 8 bits, whereas in an NNI, the VPI is 12 bits. The length of the VCI is the same

Figure 19.7   *Connection identifiers*

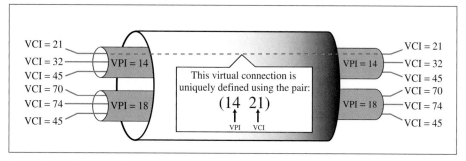

in both interfaces (16 bits). We therefore can say that a virtual connection is identified by 24 bits in a UNI interface and by 28 bits in an NNI interface (see Figure 19.8).

Figure 19.8   *Virtual connection identifiers in UNIs and NNIs*

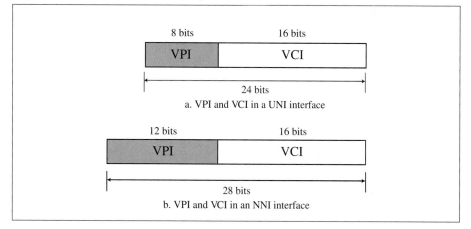

Cells

The basic data unit in an ATM network is called a cell. A cell is only 53 bytes long with 5 bytes allocated to header and 48 bytes carrying payload (user data may be less than 48 bytes). We will study in detail the fields of a cell, but for the moment it suffices to say that most of the header is occupied by the VPI and VCI that define the virtual connection through which a cell should travel from an end point to a switch or from a switch to another switch. Figure 19.9 shows the cell structure.

Connection Establishment and Release

Like X.25 and Frame Relay, ATM uses two types of connections: PVC and SVC.

PVC

A permanent virtual circuit (PVC) connection is established between two end points by the network provider. The VPIs and VCIs are defined for the permanent connections and the values are entered for the tables of each switch.

Figure 19.9 *An ATM cell*

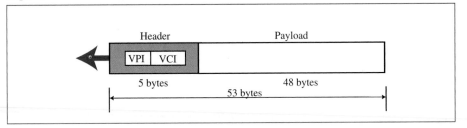

SVC

In a switched virtual circuit (SVC) connection, each time an end point wants to make a connection with another end point, a new virtual circuit should be established. ATM cannot do the job by itself, but needs network layer addresses and the services of another protocol (such as B-ISDN or IP). The signaling mechanism of this other protocol makes a connection request using the network layer addresses of the two end points. The actual mechanism depends on the network layer protocol. The general idea is shown in Figure 19.10.

Figure 19.10 *SVC setup*

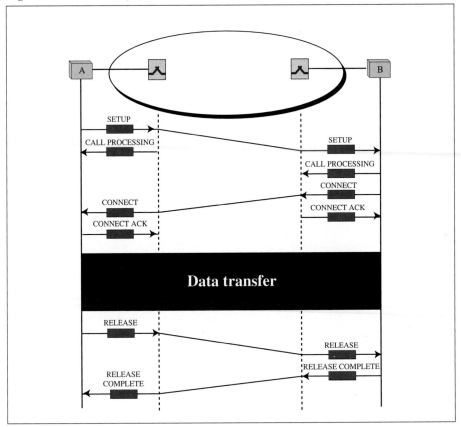

19.3   SWITCHING

ATM uses switches to route the cell from a source end point to the destination end point. However, to make switching more efficient, it normally uses two types of switches: VP and VPC.

VP Switch

A VP switch routes the cell using only the VPI. Figure 19.11 shows how a VP switch routes the cell. A cell with a VPI of 153 arrives at switch interface 1. The switch checks its switching table, which stores four pieces of information per row: arrival interface number, incoming VPI, corresponding outgoing interface number, and the new VPI. The switch finds the entry with interface 1 and VPI 153 and discovers that the combination corresponds to output interface 3 with VPI 140. It changes the VPI in the header to 140 and sends the cell out through interface 3.

Figure 19.11   *Routing with a VP switch*

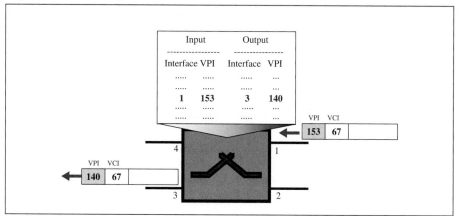

Figure 19.12 shows a conceptual view of a VP switch. The VPIs change, but the VCIs will remain the same.

Figure 19.12   *A conceptual view of a VP switch*

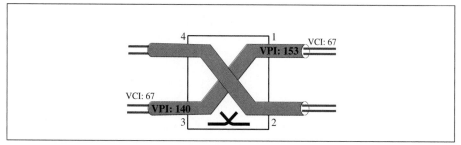

VPC Switch

A VPC switch routes the cell using both the VPIs and the VCIs. The routing requires the whole identifier. Figure 19.13 shows how a VPC switch routes the cell. A cell with a VPI of 153 and VCI of 67 arrives at switch interface 1. The switch checks its switching table, which stores six pieces of information per row: arrival interface number, incoming VPI, incoming VCI, corresponding outgoing interface number, the new VPI, and the new VCI. The switch finds the entry with the interface 1, VPI 153, and VCI 67 and discovers that the combination corresponds to output interface 3, VPI 140, and VCI 92. It changes the VPI and VCI in the header to 140 and 92, respectively, and sends the cell out through interface 3.

Figure 19.13   *Routing with a VPC switch*

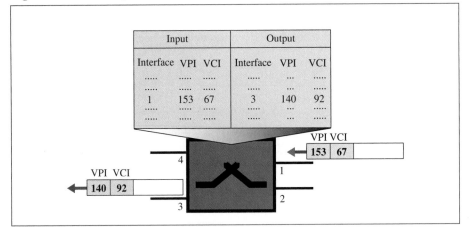

Figure 19.14 shows a conceptual view of a VPC switch. We can think of a VPC switch as a combination of a VP switch and a VC switch.

Figure 19.14   *A conceptual view of a VPC switch*

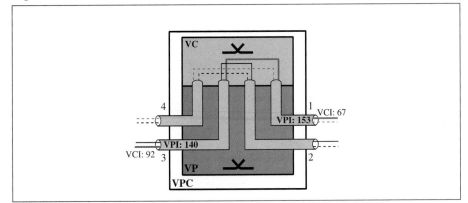

The whole idea behind dividing a virtual connection identifier into two parts is to allow hierarchical routing. Most of the switches in a typical ATM network are

VP switches; they only route using VPIs. The switches at the boundaries of the network, those that interact directly with the end point devices, use both VPIs and VCIs.

19.4   SWITCH FABRICS

The whole idea of ATM is to transfer cells through the network very quickly. For an ATM network that operates at 155 Mbps, over 350,000 cells per second may be arriving at each interface of a switch. It is clear that there is a need for switches that can receive and route cells as fast as possible. In addition, the switches in ATM must be synchronized, although there may be no cells in some slots. The switch has a clock and delivers one cell to the output at each tick.

We discuss several approaches that have been devised to accommodate these requirements.

Crossbar Switch

The simplest type of switch for ATM is the crossbar switch discussed in Chapter 14 and repeated in Figure 19.15.

Figure 19.15   *Crossbar switch*

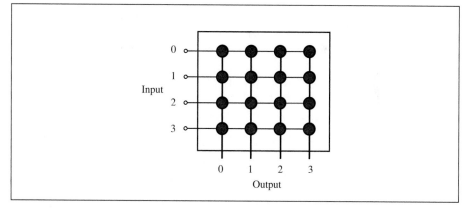

Knockout Switch

The problem with the crossbar switch is the collision that results when two cells arriving at different inputs need to go out the same output. The **knockout switch** uses distributors and queues to direct the cells to different queues at the output. However, the knockout switch is still inefficient. With n inputs and n outputs, we still need n^2 crosspoints. Figure 19.16 shows a knockout switch.

Banyan Switch

A more realistic approach is a switch called a **banyan switch** (named after the banyan tree). A banyan switch is a multistage switch with microswitches at each stage that

Figure 19.16 *Knockout switch*

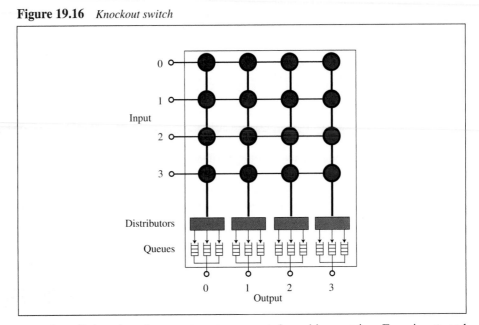

route the cells based on the output port represented as a binary string. For n inputs and n outputs, we will have $\log_2(n)$ stages with $n/2$ microswitches at each stage. The first stage routes the cell based on the high order bit of the binary string. The second stage routes the cells based on the second high order bit, and so on. Figure 19.17 shows a banyan switch with eight inputs and eight outputs. The number of stages is $\log_2(8) = 3$.

Figure 19.17 *A banyan switch*

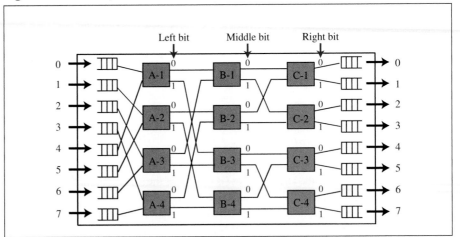

Figure 19.18 shows the operation. In part a, a cell has arrived at input port 1 and should go to output port 6 (110 in binary). The first microswitch (A-2) routes the cell based on the first bit (1), the second microswitch (B-4) routes the cell based on the second bit (1), and the third microswitch (C-4) routes the cell based on the third bit (0). In

Figure 19.18   *Examples of routing in a banyan switch*

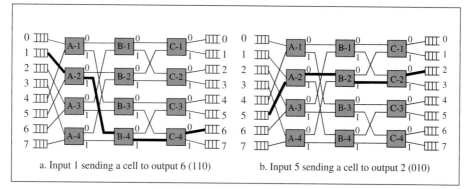

a. Input 1 sending a cell to output 6 (110)   b. Input 5 sending a cell to output 2 (010)

part b, a cell has arrived at input port 5 and should go to output port 2 (010 in binary). The first microswitch (A-2) routes the cell based on the first bit (0), the second microswitch (B-2) routes the cell based on the second bit (1), and the third microswitch (C-2) routes the cell based on the third bit (0).

Batcher-Banyan Switch

The problem with the banyan switch is the possibility of internal collision even when two cells are not heading for the same output port. We can solve this problem by sorting the arriving cells based on their destination port.

K. E. Batcher designed a switch that comes before the banyan switch and sorts the incoming cells according to their final destination. The combination is called the **Batcher-banyan switch.** The sorting switch uses hardware merging techniques, but we will not discuss the details here. Normally, another hardware module called the trap is added between the Batcher switch and the banyan switch. (See Figure 19.19.) The trap module prevents duplicate cells (cells with the same output destination) from passing to the banyan switch simultaneously. Only one cell for each destination is allowed at each tick; if there are more than one, they should wait for the next tick.

Figure 19.19   *Batcher-banyan switch*

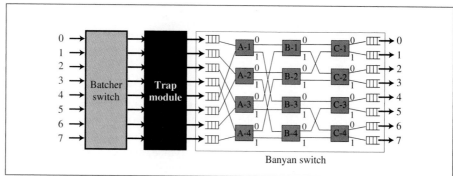

Banyan switch

19.5 ATM LAYERS

The ATM standard defines three layers. They are, from top to bottom, the application adaptation layer, the ATM layer, and the physical layer (see Figure 19.20).

Figure 19.20 *ATM layers*

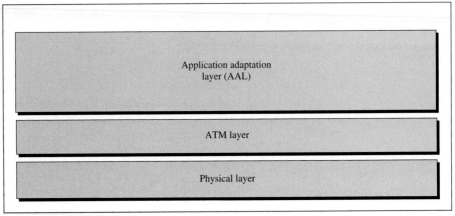

The end points use all three layers while the switches use only the two bottom layers (see Figure 19.21).

Figure 19.21 *ATM layers in end-point devices and switches*

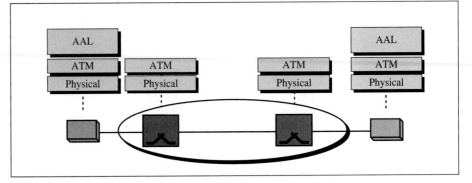

Application Adaptation Layer (AAL)

The **application adaptation layer (AAL)** allows existing networks (such as packet networks) to connect to ATM facilities. AAL protocols accept transmissions from upper-layer services (e.g., packet data) and map them into fixed-sized ATM cells. These transmissions can be of any type (voice, data, audio, video) and can be of variable or fixed rates. At the receiver, this process is reversed—segments are reassembled into their original formats and passed to the receiving service.

Data Types

Instead of one protocol for all types of data, the ATM standard divides the AAL layer into categories, each supporting the requirements of a different type of application. In defining these categories, the ATM designers identified four types of data streams: constant-bit-rate data, variable-bit-rate data, connection-oriented packet data, and connectionless packet data.

■ **Constant-bit-rate (CBR)** data refers to applications that generate and consume bits at a constant rate. In this type of application, transmission delays must be minimal and transmission must simulate real time. Examples of constant-bit-rate applications include real-time voice (telephone calls) and real-time video (television).

■ **Variable-bit-rate (VBR)** data refers to applications that generate and consume bits at variable rates. In this type of application, the bit rate varies from section to section of the transmission, but within established parameters. Examples of variable-bit-rate applications include compressed voice, data, and video.

■ Connection-oriented packet data refers to conventional packet applications (such as X.25 and the TCP protocol of TCP/IP) that use virtual circuits.

■ Connectionless packet data refers to applications that use a datagram approach to routing (such as the IP protocol in TCP/IP).

The ITU-T recognized the need for an additional category, one that cuts across all of the above data types but is adapted for point-to-point rather than multipoint or internetwork transmissions. The sublayer designed to meet the needs of this type of transmission is called the simple and efficient adaptation layer (SEAL).

The AAL categories designed to support each of these types of data have been called AAL1, AAL2, AAL3, AAL4, and AAL5, respectively. More recently however, it has been decided that there is too much overlap between AAL3 and AAL4 to justify their remaining separate, so they have been combined into a single category, AAL3/4. AAL2, though still a part of the ATM design, may also be dropped and its functions combined with those of another category.

Convergence and Segmentation

In addition to dividing the AAL by category, the ITU-T also divides it by function. As a result, each of the AAL categories is actually two layers: the **convergence sublayer (CS)** and the **segmentation and reassembly (SAR)** sublayer; see Figure 19.22. The duties of these two sublayers vary and will be described as we describe each AAL category.

AAL1

AAL1 supports applications that transfer information at constant bit rates, such as video and voice, and allows ATM to connect existing digital telephone networks such as DS-3 or E-1.

Convergence Sublayer   The convergence sublayer divides the bit stream into 47-byte segments and passes them to the SAR sublayer below.

Figure 19.22 *AAL types*

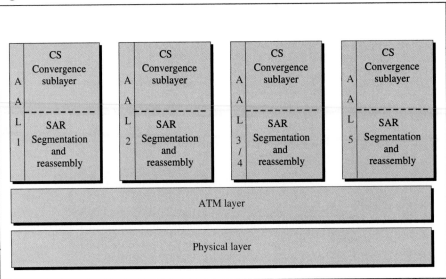

Segmentation and Reassembly Figure 19.23 shows the format of an AAL1 data unit at the SAR layer. As you can see, this layer accepts a 47-byte payload from the CS and adds a one-byte header. The result is a 48-byte data unit that is then passed to the ATM layer, where it is encapsulated in a cell.

Figure 19.23 *AAL1*

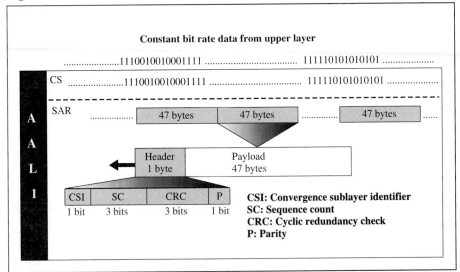

The header at this layer consists of four fields:

■ **Convergence sublayer identifier (CSI).** The one-bit CSI field will be used for signaling purposes that are not yet clearly defined.

- **Sequence count (SC).** The three-bit SC field is a modulo 8 sequence number to be used for ordering and identifying the cells for end-to-end error and flow control.

- **Cyclic redundancy check (CRC).** The three-bit CRC field is calculated over the first four bits using the four-bit divisor $x^3 + x + 1$. Three bits may seem like too much redundancy. However, they are intended not only to detect a single- or multiple-bit error, but also to correct single-bit errors. In non-real-time applications, an error in a cell is inconsequential (the cell can be retransmitted). In real-time applications, however, retransmission is not an option. With no retransmission, the quality of the received data deteriorates. With one missing cell, you might hear a click during a telephone call or see a black dot on your video monitor; large numbers of missing cells can destroy intelligibility. Automatic correction of single-bit header errors dramatically reduces the number of cells that are missing and is therefore a boon to quality of service.

- **Parity (P).** The one-bit P field is a standard parity bit calculated over the first seven bits of the header. A parity bit can detect an odd number of errors but not an even number of errors. This feature can be used for error correction of the first four bits. If one single bit is in error, both the CRC and the P bit will detect it. In this case, the CRC corrects the bit and the cell is accepted. However, if there are two bits in error, the CRC will detect them and the P bit will not. In this case, the CRC correction is invalid and the cell is discarded.

AAL2

AAL2 is intended to support variable bit-rate applications. For example, in a news broadcast, when the news anchor's face is on the screen, there is a minimum amount of change. Compare this to news footage of a basketball game where there is a huge amount of change. In the first case, the data can be sent at a lower data rate, while in the second case the data can be transferred at a higher data rate. How AAL2 will do so has not yet been explicitly defined.

Convergence Sublayer   The format for reordering the received bit stream and adding overhead is not defined here. Different applications may use different formats.

Segmentation and Reassembly   Figure 19.24 shows the format of an AAL2 data unit at the SAR layer. Functions at this layer accept a 45-byte payload from the CS and add a one-byte header and two-byte trailer. The result is a 48-byte data unit that is then passed to the ATM layer, where it is encapsulated in a cell.

The overhead at this layer consists of three fields in the header and two fields in the trailer:

- **Convergence sublayer identifier (CSI).** The one-bit CSI field will be used for signaling purposes that are not yet clearly defined.

- **Sequence count (SC).** The three-bit SC field is a modulo 8 sequence number to be used for ordering and identifying the cells for end-to-end error and flow control.

- **Information type (IT).** The IT bits identify the data segment as falling at the beginning, middle, or end of the message.

- **Length indicator (LI).** The first six bits of the trailer are used with the final segment of a message (when the IT in the header indicates the end of the message) to

Figure 19.24   *AAL2*

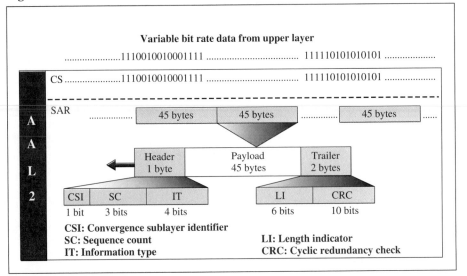

indicate how much of the final cell is data and how much is padding. If the original bit stream is not evenly divisible by 45, dummy bits are added to the last segment to make up the difference. This field indicates where in the segment those bits start.

- **CRC.** The last 10 bits of the trailer are a CRC for the entire data unit. This can also be used to correct single-bit errors in the data unit.

AAL3/4

Initially, AAL3 was intended to support connection-oriented data services and AAL4 to support connectionless services. As they evolved, however, it became evident that the fundamental issues of the two protocols were the same. They have therefore been combined into a single format called **AAL3/4.**

Convergence Sublayer   The convergence sublayer accepts a data packet of no more than 65,535 ($2^{16} - 1$) bytes from an upper layer service (such as SMDS or Frame Relay) and adds a header and trailer (see Figure 19.25). The header and trailer indicate the beginning and end of the message (for reassembly purposes), as well as how much of the final frame is data and how much is padding. Because packets vary in length, padding may be required to ensure that segments are of the same size and that the final control fields fall where the receiver expects to find them. Once the header, trailer, and padding are in place, the CS passes the message in 44-byte segments to the SAR layer.

It is important to note that the CS header and trailer are added to the beginning and end of the original packet, not to every segment. The middle segments are passed to the SAR layer without added overhead. In this way, ATM retains the integrity of the original packets and keeps the ratio of overhead to data bytes low. The AAL3/4 CS header and trailer fields are as follows:

- **Type (T).** The one-byte T field is a holdover from the previous version of AAL3 and is set to 0 in this format.

Figure 19.25 *AAL3/4*

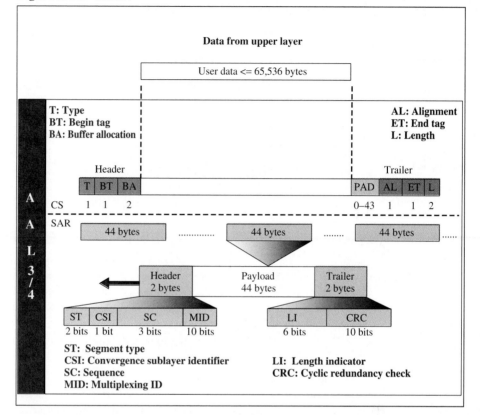

- **Begin tag (BT).** The one-byte BT field serves as a beginning flag. It identifies the first cell of a segmented packet and provides synchronization for the receiving clock.
- **Buffer allocation (BA).** The two-byte BA field tells the receiver what size buffer is needed for the coming data.
- **Pad (PAD).** As mentioned above, padding is added when necessary to fill out the final cell(s) in a segmented packet. Total padding for a packet can be between 0 and 43 bytes and is added to the last or the last two segments. There are three possible padding scenarios:
    a. When the number of data bytes in the final segment is exactly 40, no padding is required (the 4-byte trailer is added to the 40-byte segment to make it 44 bytes).
    b. When the number of data bytes in the final segment is less than 40 (0 to 39), we add padding bytes (40 to 1) to bring the total to 40.
    c. When the number of data bytes available for the final segment is between 41 and 44, we add padding bytes (43 to 40) to bring the total to 84. The first 44 bytes make a complete segment. The next 40 bytes and the trailer make the last segment.
- **Alignment (AL).** The one-byte AL field is included to make the rest of the trailer four bytes long.

- **Ending Tag (ET).** The one-byte ET field serves as an ending flag for synchronization.
- **Length (L).** The two-byte L field indicates the length of the data unit.

Segment and Reassembly   Figure 19.25 shows the format of an AAL3/4 data unit. Functions at this layer accept a 44-byte payload from the CS and add a 2-byte header and a 2-byte trailer. The result is a 48-byte data unit that is passed to the ATM layer for inclusion in a cell.

The header and the trailer at this sublayer consist of six fields:

- **Segment type (ST).** The two-bit ST identifier tells whether the segment belongs to the beginning, middle, or end of a message, or is a single-segment message.
- **Convergence sublayer identifier (CSI).** The one-bit CSI field will be used for signaling purposes that are not yet clearly defined.
- **Sequence count (SC).** The three-bit SC field is a modulo 8 sequence number to be used for ordering and identifying the cells for end-to-end error and flow control.
- **Multiplexing identification (MID).** The 10-bit MID field identifies cells coming from different data flows and multiplexed on the same virtual connection.
- **Length indicator (LI).** The first six bits of the trailer are used in conjunction with the ST to indicate how much of the last segment is message and how much is padding. The LI field is used only in frames identified by the ST as being the last in the message (end of packet).
- **CRC.** The last 10 bits of the trailer are a CRC for the entire data unit.

AAL5

AAL3/4 provides comprehensive sequencing and error control mechanisms that are not necessary to every application. When transmissions are not routed through multiple nodes or multiplexed with other transmissions, sequencing and elaborate error correction mechanisms are an unnecessary overhead. ATM backbones and LANs that use point-to-point links are examples of applications that are more efficient without them. For these applications, the designers of ATM have provided a fifth AAL sublayer called the simple and efficient adaptation layer (SEAL). **AAL5** assumes that all cells belonging to a single message travel sequentially and that the rest of the functions usually provided by the CS and SAR headers are already included in the upper layers of the sending application. AAL5 therefore provides no addressing, sequencing, or other header information either at the CS or SAR. Instead, only padding and a four-field trailer are added at the CS.

Convergence Sublayer   The convergence sublayer accepts a data packet of no more than 65,535 bytes from an upper-layer service and adds an 8-byte trailer as well as any padding required to ensure that the position of the trailer falls where the receiving equipment expects it (at the last 8 bytes of the last data unit); see Figure 19.26. Once the padding and trailer are in place, the CS passes the message in 48-byte segments to the SAR layer.

Figure 19.26   *AAL5*

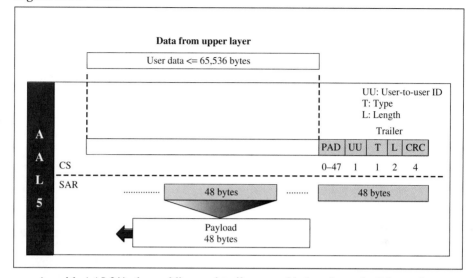

As with AAL3/4, the padding and trailer are added to the end of the entire message, not to each segment. Segments therefore consist of 48 bytes of data or, in the case of the last segment, 40 bytes of data and 8 of overhead (trailer). Fields added at the end of the message include the following:

■ **Pad (PAD).** The total padding for a packet can be between 0 and 47 bytes. The rules for padding are the same as those described above for AAL3/4, with the difference that body segments must equal 48 bytes rather than 44.

■ **User-to-user ID (UU).** Use of the one-byte UU field is left to the discretion of the user.

■ **Type (T).** The one-byte T field is reserved but not yet defined.

■ **Length (L).** The two-byte L field indicates how much of the message is data and how much is padding.

■ **CRC.** The last four bytes are an error check for the entire data unit.

Segmentation and Reassembly   No header or trailer is defined for the SAR level. Instead it passes the message in 48-byte segments directly to the ATM layer.

ATM Layer

The ATM layer provides routing, traffic management, switching, and multiplexing services. It processes outgoing traffic by accepting 48-byte segments from the AAL sublayers and transforming them into 53-byte cells by the addition of a 5-byte header (see Figure 19.27).

Figure 19.27 *ATM layer*

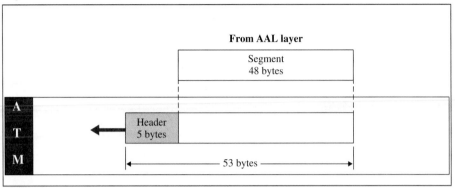

Header Format

ATM uses two formats for this header, one for user-to-network interface (UNI) cells and another for network-to-network interface (NNI) cells. Figure 19.28 shows these headers in the byte-by-byte format preferred by the ITU-T (each row represents a byte).

Figure 19.28 *ATM headers*

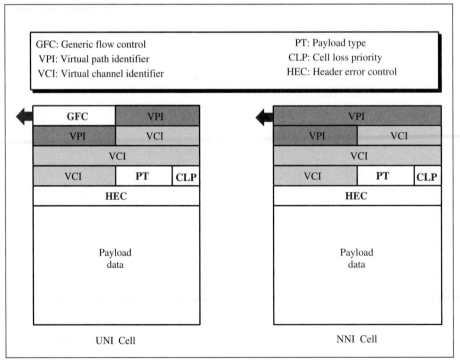

- **Generic flow control (GFC).** The four-bit GFC field provides flow control at the UNI level. The ITU-T has determined that this level of flow control is not necessary at the NNI level. In the NNI header, therefore, these bits are added to the VPI.

The longer VPI allows more virtual paths to be defined at the NNI level. The format for this additional VPI has not yet been determined.

■ **Virtual path identifier (VPI).** The VPI is an 8-bit field in a UNI cell and a 12-bit field in an NNI cell (see above).

■ **Virtual channel identifier (VCI).** The VCI is a 16-bit field in both frames.

■ **Payload type (PT).** In the three-bit PT field, the first bit defines the payload as user data or managerial information. The interpretation of the last two bits depends on the first bit (see Figure 19.29).

Figure 19.29 *PT fields*

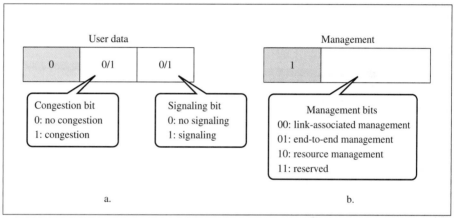

■ **Cell loss priority (CLP).** The one-bit CLP field is provided for congestion control. When links become congested, low-priority cells may be discarded to protect the quality of service for higher priority cells. This bit indicates to a switch which cells may be dropped and which must be retained. A cell with its CLP bit set to 1 must be retained as long as there are cells with a CLP of 0. This ability to distinguish priority is useful in many circumstances. For example, suppose a user is assigned a bit rate of x bits per second but is unable to create data that fast. He or she can insert dummy cells into the data stream to raise the bit rate artificially. These dummy cells will show a priority of 0 to indicate that they can be discarded without consequence to the actual data. A second scenario is that of a user who has been assigned one data rate but decides to transmit at a higher one. In this case, the network can set this field to 0 in some cells to indicate that they must be dropped if the link becomes overloaded.

■ **Header error correction (HEC).** The HEC is a code computed for the first four bytes of the header. It is a CRC using the divisor $x^8 + x^2 + x + 1$ that is used to correct single-bit errors and a large class of multiple-bit errors.

Physical Layer

The physical layer defines the transmission medium, bit transmission, encoding, and electrical to optical transformation. It provides convergence with physical transport protocols, such as SONET (described in Chapter 20) and T-3, as well as the mechanisms for transforming the flow of cells into a flow of bits.

The ATM Forum has left most of the specifications for this level to the implementor. For example, the transport medium can be twisted-pair, coaxial, or fiber-optic cable (although the speed necessary to support B-ISDN is unlikely to be achieved with twisted-pair cable).

19.6   SERVICE CLASSES

The ATM Forum defines four service classes: CBR, VBR, ABR, and UBR. VBR is divided into two subclasses VBR-RT and VBR-NRT (see Figure 19.30).

Figure 19.30   *Service classes*

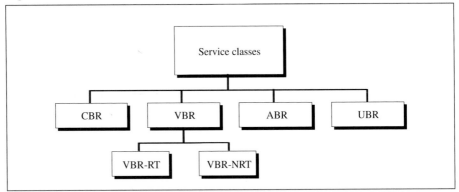

- ■   **CBR.** The **constant bit rate (CBR)** class is designed for customers that need real-time audio or video services. The service is similar to that provided by a dedicated line such as a T-line.

- ■   **VBR.** The variable bit rate (VBR) class is divided into two subclasses: **real time (VBR-RT)** and **nonreal time (VBR-NRT).** VBR-RT is designed for those users that need real-time services (such as voice and video transmission) and use compression techniques to create a variable bit rate. VBR-NRT is designed for those users that do not need real-time services but use compression techniques to create a variable bit rate.

- ■   **ABR.** The **available bit rate (ABR)** class delivers cells at a minimum rate. If more network capacity is available, this minimum rate can be exceeded. ABR is particularly suitable for applications that are bursty in nature.

- ■   **UBR.** The **unspecified bit rate (UBR)** class is a best-effort delivery service that does not guarantee anything.

Figure 19.31 shows the relationship of different classes to the total capacity of the network.

Figure 19.31 *Relationship of service classes to the total capacity of the network*

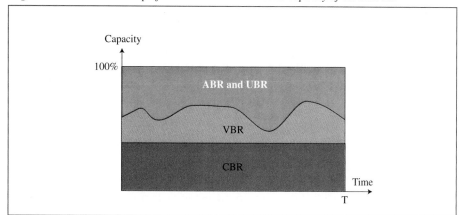

Quality of Service (QoS)

The **quality of service (QoS)** defines a set of attributes related to the performance of the connection. For each connection, the user can request a particular attribute. Each service class is associated with a set of the attributes. We can categorize the attributes into those related to the user and those related to the network. Figure 19.32 shows the two categories and some important attributes in each category.

Figure 19.32 *QoS*

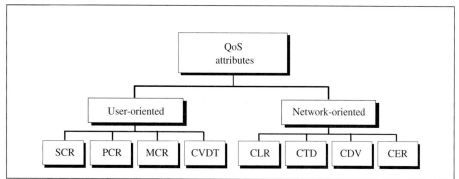

User-Related Attributes

User-related attributes are those attributes that define how fast the user wants to send data. These are negotiated at the time of contract between a user and a network. The following are some user-related attributes:

■ **SCR.** The **sustained cell rate (SCR)** is the average cell rate over a long time interval. The actual cell rate may be lower or higher than this value, but the average should be equal to or less than the SCR.

■ **PCR.** The **peak cell rate (PCR)** defines the sender's maximum cell rate. The user's cell rate can sometimes reach this peak, as long as the SCR is maintained.

- **MCR.** The **minimum cell rate (MCR)** defines the minimum cell rate acceptable to the sender. For example, if the MCR is 50,000, the network must guarantee that the sender can send at least 50,000 cells per second.
- **CVDT.** The **cell variation delay tolerance (CVDT)** is a measure of the variation in cell transmission times. For example, if the CVDT is 5 ns, this means that the difference between the minimum and the maximum delays in delivering the cells should not exceed 5 ns.

Network-Related Attributes

The network-related attributes are those that define characteristics of the network. The following are some network-related attributes:

- **CLR.** The **cell loss ratio (CLR)** defines the fraction of cells lost (or delivered so late that they are considered lost) during transmission. For example, if the sender sends 100 cells and one of them is lost, the CLR is

$$CLR = 1/100 = 10^{-2}$$

- **CTD.** The **cell transfer delay (CTD)** is the average time needed for a cell to travel from source to destination. The maximum CTD and the minimum CTD are also considered attributes.
- **CDV.** The **cell delay variation (CDV)** is the difference between the CTD maximum and the CTD minimum.
- **CER.** The **cell error ratio (CER)** defines the fraction of the cells delivered in error.

Traffic Descriptors

The mechanisms by which the service classes and QoS attributes are implemented are called the traffic descriptors. A traffic descriptor defines how the system enforces and polices traffic. The algorithm to implement traffic descriptors is called the generalized cell rate algorithm (GCRA). It uses variations of the leaky bucket algorithm (defined in Chapter 18) for each type of service class. A discussion of this algorithm is beyond the scope of this book.

19.7 ATM APPLICATIONS

ATM is used in both LANs and WANs. We give an overview of both applications here.

ATM WANs

ATM is basically a WAN technology that delivers cells over a long distance. In this type of application, ATM is mainly used to connect LANs or other WANs together. A router between the ATM network and the other network serves as an end point. The router has two stacks of protocols: one belonging to the ATM and the other belonging to the other protocol. Figure 19.33 shows the situation.

Figure 19.33   *ATM WAN*

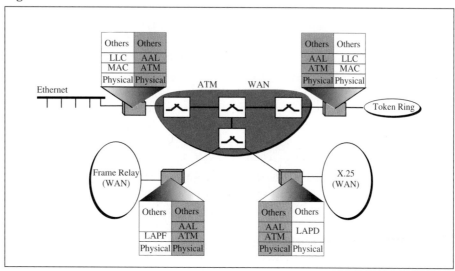

ATM LANs

ATM was originally designed as a WAN technology. However, the high data rate of the technology (155 and 622 Mbps) has attracted the attention of designers who are looking for more and more speed in LANs. At the surface level, the use of ATM technology in LANs seems very natural. For example, compare part *a* and part *b* of Figure 19.34. Part *a* shows a switched Ethernet; part *b* shows an ATM LAN. Both use a switch to route packets or cells between computers. However, the similarity is only at the surface level; a lot of issues need to be resolved. Some of them are summarized below:

Figure 19.34   *Ethernet switch and ATM switch*

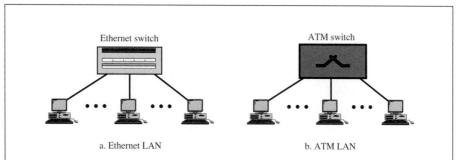

■ **Connectionless versus connection-oriented.** Traditional LANs such as Ethernet are connectionless protocols. A station sends data packets to another station whenever the packets are ready. There is no connection establishment or connection termination phase. On the other hand, ATM is a connection-oriented protocol; a station that wishes to send cells to another station should first establish a connection and, after all of the cells are sent, terminate the connection.

■ **Physical addresses versus virtual connection identifiers.** Closely related to the first issue is the difference in addressing. A connectionless protocol such as Ethernet defines the route of a packet through source and destination addresses. However, a connection-oriented protocol such as ATM defines the route of a cell through virtual connection identifiers (VPIs and VCIs).

■ **Multicasting and broadcasting delivery.** Traditional LANs such as Ethernet can both multicast and broadcast packets; a station can send packets to a group of stations or to all stations. There is no easy way to multicast or broadcast on an ATM network although point-to-multipoint connections are available.

LANE

An approach called **local area network emulation (LANE)** enables an ATM switch to behave like a LAN switch: it provides connectionless service, lets the stations use their traditional addresses instead of connection identifiers (VPI/VCI), and allows broadcast delivery. It is based on a client/server approach; all stations use **LANE client (LEC)** software and two servers use two different LANE server software called LES and BUS. Figure 19.35 shows the idea.

Figure 19.35 *LANE approach*

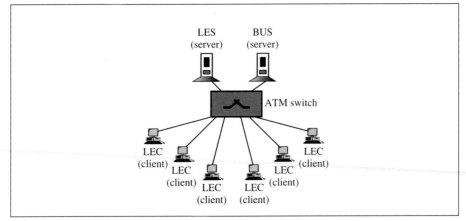

LEC software is installed on each station on top of the three ATM protocols. The upper-layer protocols are unaware of the existence of the ATM technology. These protocols send their requests to LEC for a LAN service such as connectionless delivery using MAC unicast, multicast, or broadcast addresses. The LEC, however, just interprets the request and uses the services of either LES or BUS to do the job.

The **LANE server (LES)** software is installed on the LES server. When a station receives a frame to be sent to another station using a physical address, LEC sends a special frame to the LES server. The server creates a virtual circuit between the source and the destination station. The source station can now use this virtual circuit (and the corresponding identifier) to send the frame or frames to the destination.

Multicasting and broadcasting require the use of another server called the **broadcast/unknown server** or **BUS.** If a station needs to send a frame to a group of stations or to every station, the frame first goes to the BUS server; this server has permanent virtual connections to every station. The server creates copies of the received frame and sends a copy to a group of stations or to all stations, simulating a multicasting or broadcasting process. The server can also deliver a unicast frame by sending the frame to every station. In this case the destination address is unknown. This is sometimes more efficient than getting the connection identifier from the LES server.

Figure 19.36 shows the layers in each station, the LES server, and the BUS server.

Figure 19.36   *LEC, LES, and BUS*

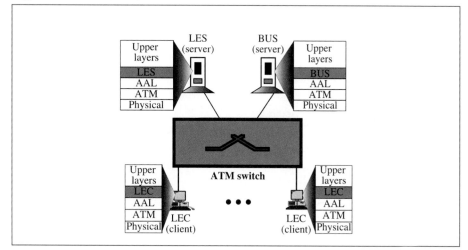

19.8   KEY TERMS AND CONCEPTS

AAL1	cell
AAL2	cell delay variation (CDV)
AAL3/4	cell error ratio (CER)
AAL5	cell loss ratio (CLR)
application adaptation layer (AAL)	cell network
asynchronous transfer mode (ATM)	cell relay
available bit rate (ABR)	cell transfer delay (CTD)
banyan switch	cell variation delay tolerance (CVDT)
Batcher-banyan switch	constant bit rate (CBR)
broadcast/unknown server (BUS)	convergence sublayer (CS)

knockout switch

LANE client (LEC)

LANE server (LES)

local area network emulation (LANE)

minimum cell rate (MCR)

network-to-network interface (NNI)

peak cell rate (PCR)

quality of service (QoS)

segmentation and reassembly (SAR)

sustained cell rate (SCR)

transmission path (TP)

unspecified bit rate (UBR)

user-to-network interface (UNI)

variable bit rate (VBR)

variable bit rate nonreal time
   (VBR-NRT)

variable bit rate real time (VBR-RT)

virtual circuit (VC)

virtual circuit identifier (VCI)

virtual path (VP)

virtual path identifier (VPI)

19.9   SUMMARY

■ Asynchronous Transfer Mode (ATM) is a cell relay protocol that, in combination with B-ISDN, will allow high-speed interconnection of all the world's networks.

■ A cell is a small fixed-size block of information.

■ The ATM data packet is a cell composed of 53 bytes (5 bytes of header and 48 bytes of payload).

■ ATM eliminates the varying delay times associated with different-sized packets.

■ ATM can handle real-time transmission.

■ Switching and multiplexing functions in ATM can be implemented in hardware.

■ ATM uses asynchronous time-division multiplexing and is based on permanent virtual circuits.

■ A user-to-network interface (UNI) is the interface between a user and an ATM switch.

■ A network-to-network interface (NNI) is the interface between two ATM switches.

■ Connection between two end points is accomplished through transmission paths (TPs), virtual paths (VPs), and virtual circuits (VCs).

■ A combination of a virtual path identifier (VPI) and a virtual circuit identifier (VCI) identify a virtual connection.

■ ATM can use a permanent virtual circuit (PVC) or a switched virtual circuit (SVC).

- An ATM switch is categorized as either a VP switch or a VPC switch. The former routes the cell using only the VPI; the latter routes the cell using both the VPI and the VCI.
- A crossbar switch, a knockout switch, a banyan switch, and a Batcher-banyan switch can all serve as an ATM switch.
- The ATM standard defines three layers:
  a. Application adaptation layer (AAL)—accepts transmissions from upper-layer services and maps them into ATM cells.
  b. ATM layer—provides routing, traffic management, switching, and multiplexing services.
  c. Physical layer—defines the transmission medium, bit transmission, encoding, and electrical-to-optical transformation.
- The AAL is divided into two sublayers:
  a. Convergence sublayer (CS)—adds overhead and manipulates the data stream at the sending station; performs the opposite function at the receiving station.
  b. Segmentation and reassembly (SAR)—at the sending station, segments the bit stream into same-sized packets; adds headers and trailers; performs the opposite function at the receiving station.
- There are four different AALs, each for a specific data type:
  a. AAL1—constant bit-rate stream.
  b. AAL2—variable bit-rate stream.
  c. AAL3/4—conventional packet switching (virtual circuit approach or datagram approach).
  d. AAL5—packets requiring no information from the SAR layer.
- In the ATM layer, a 5-byte header is added to each 48-byte segment.
- Switches in ATM provide both switching and multiplexing.
- An ATM service class is defined by the bit rate attribute a user requires.
- Quality of service (QoS) attributes are related to the performance of the connection and can be classified as those that are user-related and those that are network-related.
- Traffic descriptors implement service classes and QoS attributes.
- ATM, though originally a WAN technology, is also used in LANs.
- Local area network emulation (LANE) enables an ATM switch to behave like a LAN switch.

19.10   PRACTICE SET

Review Questions

1. What six requirements must the infrastructure of an information superhighway have?
2. Why is multiplexing more efficient if all the data units are the same size?

3. Discuss the relationship between delay length, data unit size, and real-time audio and video transmission.

4. How does an NNI differ from a UNI?

5. What is the relationship between TPs, VPs, and VCs?

6. How is an ATM virtual connection identified?

7. How are ATM cells multiplexed?

8. Describe the format of an ATM cell.

9. Compare and contrast a VP switch and a VPC switch.

10. Why is the Batcher-banyan switch superior to the plain banyan switch?

11. Discuss the different methods of error detection in each of the AAL types.

12. Which AAL type has no header added to its SAR layer?

13. Why is padding necessary for ATM cells?

14. What is the purpose of service classes?

15. What is the difference between the PCR and the MCR?

16. What is the purpose of the CLP bit in the ATM layer header?

17. Why are the VPI 12 bits for an NNI connection and 8 bits for a UNI connection?

18. Name the ATM layers and their functions.

19. Name the four ATM service classes and the type of customer each serves.

20. How is ATM used in a WAN?

21. Discuss the issues involved when ATM is used in LANs.

22. What is the purpose of LES client/server software?

23. What is the purpose of BUS client/server software?

Multiple Choice Questions

24. ATM can use _____ as a transmission medium.
    a. twisted-pair cable
    b. coaxial cable
    c. fiber-optic cable
    d. all of the above

25. In data communications, ATM is an acronym for _____.
    a. Automated Teller Machine
    b. Automatic Transmission Model
    c. Asynchronous Telecommunication Method
    d. Asynchronous Transfer Mode

26. Because ATM _____, which means that cells follow the same path, the cells do not usually arrive out of order.
    a. is asynchronous
    b. is multiplexed
    c. is a network
    d. uses virtual circuit routing

27. Which layer in ATM protocol reformats the data received from other networks?
    a. physical
    b. ATM
    c. application adaptation
    d. data adaptation

28. Which layer in ATM protocol has a 53-byte cell as an end product?
    a. physical
    b. ATM
    c. application adaptation
    d. cell transformation

29. Which AAL type can best process a data stream having a nonconstant bit rate?
    a. AAL1
    b. AAL2
    c. AAL3/4
    d. AAL5

30. Which AAL type is designed to support a data stream that has a constant bit rate?
    a. AAL1
    b. AAL2
    c. AAL3/4
    d. AAL5

31. Which AAL type is designed to support conventional packet switching that uses the virtual circuit approach?
    a. AAL1
    b. AAL2
    c. AAL3/4
    d. AAL5

32. Which AAL type is designed to support SEAL?
    a. AAL1
    b. AAL2
    c. AAL3/4
    d. AAL5

33. The end product of the SAR is a data packet that is _____.
    a. variable in length
    b. 48 bytes long
    c. 44 to 48 bytes long
    d. greater than 48 bytes long

34. In the SAR sublayer of _____, 1 byte of header is added to 47 bytes of data.
    a. AAL1

b. AAL2

c. AAL3/4

d. AAL5

35. In the SAR sublayer of _____, 1 byte of header and 2 bytes of trailer are added to a 45-byte payload.

a. AAL1

b. AAL2

c. AAL3/4

d. AAL5

36. In the SAR sublayer of _____, the payload is 48 bytes and there is no added header or trailer.

a. AAL1

b. AAL2

c. AAL3/4

d. AAL5

37. A _____ field on a UNI cell header is used for connection purposes.

a. VPI (virtual path identifier)

b. VCI (virtual circuit identifier)

c. CLP (cell loss priority)

d. GFC (generic flow constant)

38. A _____ field on a cell header in the ATM layer determines whether a cell can be dropped.

a. VPI (virtual path identifier)

b. VCI (virtual circuit identifier)

c. CLP (cell loss priority)

d. GFC (generic flow constant)

39. ATM multiplexes cells using _____.

a. asynchronous FDM

b. synchronous FDM

c. asynchronous TDM

d. synchronous TDM

40. In an ATM network, all cells belonging to a single message follow the same _____ and remain in their original order until they reach their destination.

a. transmission path

b. virtual path

c. virtual circuit

d. none of the above

41. A _____ provides a connection or a set of connections between switches.

a. transmission path

b. virtual path

c. virtual circuit

d. none of the above

42. A _____ is the physical connection between an end point and a switch or between two switches.

a. transmission path

b. virtual path

c. virtual circuit

d. none of the above

43. The VPI of a UNI is _____ bits in length.

a. 8

b. 12

c. 16

d. 24

44. The VPI of an NNI is _____ bits in length.

a. 8

b. 12

c. 16

d. 24

45. In a VP switch the _____ does not change while the _____ can change.

a. VPI; VCI

b. VCI; VPI

c. VP; VPC

d. VPC; VP

46. In a _____ switch, both the VPI and the VCI can change.

a. VP

b. VPC

c. VPI

d. VCI

47. The _____ switch is a multistage switch with microswitches at each stage that route the cells based on the output port.

a. crossbar

b. knockout

c. banyan

d. Batcher-banyan

48. The _____ switch uses a distributor and a queue to direct cells to queues at the output.

a. crossbar

b. knockout

c. banyan

d. Batcher-banyan

49. The _____ switch has $n \times m$ crosspoints for n inputs and m outputs and no provision for collision.
    a. crossbar
    b. knockout
    c. banyan
    d. Batcher-banyan

50. The _____ switch eliminates the possibility of internal collision in a switch.
    a. crossbar
    b. knockout
    c. banyan
    d. Batcher-banyan

51. The cell _____ is the difference between the CTD maximum and minimum.
    a. loss ratio
    b. transfer delay
    c. delay variation
    d. error ratio

52. The cell _____ is the ratio of lost cells to cells sent.
    a. loss ratio
    b. transfer delay
    c. delay variation
    d. error ratio

53. The _____ service class is particularly suitable for applications with bursty data.
    a. CBR
    b. VBR
    c. ABR
    d. UBR

54. The _____ service class is suitable for customers who need real-time video transmission.
    a. CBR
    b. VBR
    c. ABR
    d. UBR

55. The _____ is greater than the SCR.
    a. PCR
    b. MCR
    c. CVDT
    d. all of the above

56. _____ measures the variation in cell transmission time.
    a. SCR

    b. PCR

    c. MCR

    d. CVDT

57. If the SCR is 60,000, the PCR is 70,000, and the MCR is 55,000, what is the minimum number of cells that can be sent per second?

    a. 55,000

    b. 60,000

    c. 70,000

    d. 5000

58. The _____ is the fraction of the cells delivered in error.

    a. CLR

    b. CTD

    c. CDV

    d. CER

59. If the maximum CTD is 10 microseconds and the minimum CTD is 1 microsecond, the _____ is 9 microseconds.

    a. CLR

    b. CTD

    c. CDV

    d. CER

60. _____ is software that allows an ATM switch to emulate a LAN switch.

    a. LEC

    b. BUS

    c. BES

    d. LANE

61. The _____ server software allows multicasting and broadcasting on an ATM LAN.

    a. LEC

    b. BUS

    c. BVD

    d. BES

Exercises

62. An AAL1 layer receives data at 2 Mbps. How many cells are created per second by the ATM layer?

63. What is the total efficiency of ATM using AAL1 (the ratio of received bits to the sent bits)?

64. An AAL2 layer receives data at 2 Mbps. How many cells are created per second by the ATM layer?

65. What is the total efficiency of ATM using AAL2 (the ratio of received bits to the sent bits)?

66. If an application uses AAL3/4 and there are 47,787 bytes of data coming into the CS sublayer, how many padding bytes are necessary? How many data units get passed from the SAR to the ATM layer? How many cells are produced?

67. Does the efficiency of ATM using AAL3/4 depend on the size of the packet? Explain your answer.

68. What is the minimum number of cells resulting from an input packet in the AAL3/4 layer? What is the maximum number of cells resulting from an input packet?

69. What is the minimum number of cells resulting from an input packet in the AAL5 layer? What is the maximum number of cells resulting from an input packet?

70. Explain why padding is unnecessary in AAL1 and AAL2, but necessary in AAL3/4 and AAL5.

71. Using AAL3/4, show the situation where we need _____ of padding.
    a. zero bytes (no padding)
    b. 40 bytes
    c. 43 bytes

72. Using AAL5, show the situation where we need _____ of padding.
    a. zero bytes (no padding)
    b. 40 bytes
    c. 47 bytes

73. In a 53-byte cell, how many bytes belong to the user in (assume no padding):
    a. AAL1
    b. AAL2
    c. AAL3/4 (not the first or last cell)
    d. AAL5 (not the first or last cell)

74. Using Exercise 73, what is the efficiency of each AAL?

75. Compare AAL1 and AAL2. If both receive at the same bit rate, which produces more cells?

76. Complete Table 19.1 to show which sublayer is active in the different AALs.

Table 19.1 *Exercise 76*

Sublayer	AAL1	AAL2	AAL3/4	AAL5
CS				
SAR				

77. Complete Table 19.2 by entering the size of the data unit at the SAR sublayer for all AALs.

Table 19.2 *Exercise 77*

Sublayer	AAL1	AAL2	AAL3/4	AAL5
SAR				

78. Put an "X" in the appropriate column in Table 19.3 for the fields used by the CS sublayer in each AAL.

Table 19.3   *Exercise 78*

Sublayer	AAL1	AAL2	AAL3/4	AAL5
T				
BT				
BA				
AL				
ET				
L				
UU				

79. Put an "X" in the appropriate column in Table 19.4 for the fields used by the SAR sublayer in each AAL.

Table 19.4   *Exercise 79*

Sublayer	AAL1	AAL2	AAL3/4	AAL5
CSI				
SC				
CRC				
P				
IT				
LI				
ST				
MID				

80. Show the output of the ATM multiplexer in Figure 19.37.

81. How many virtual connections can be defined in a UNI interface? How many virtual connections can be defined in an NNI interface?

82. A user wants to send an average of one cell every microsecond with the possibility of sending one cell every nanosecond at the peak time. The user, however, needs a guarantee of being able to send one cell every millisecond. Answer the following questions:

a. What is the MCR?

b. What is the PCR?

c. What is the SCR?

Figure 19.37   *Exercise 80*

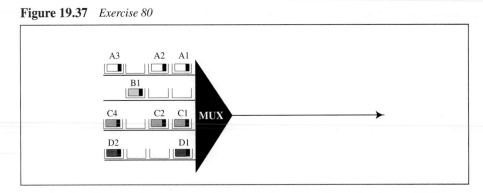

83. If each cell takes 10 microseconds to reach the destination, what is the CTD?

84. A network has lost 5 cells out of 10,000 and 2 are in error. What is the CLR? What is the CER?

CHAPTER 20

SONET/SDH

The high bandwidths of fiber-optic cable are suitable for today's highest data-rate technologies (such as video conferencing) and for carrying large numbers of lower-rate technologies at the same time. For this reason, the importance of fiber optics grows in conjunction with the development of technologies requiring high data rates or wide bandwidths for transmission. With their prominence came a need for standardization. Without standards, internetworking among the existing proprietary systems is impossible. The United States (ANSI) and Europe (ITU-T) have responded by defining standards that, though independent, are fundamentally similar and ultimately compatible. The ANSI standard is called the **Synchronous Optical Network (SONET).** The ITU-T standard is called the **Synchronous Digital Hierarchy (SDH).** These two standards are nearly identical.

> SONET was developed by ANSI. SDH was developed by ITU-T.

Among the concerns addressed by the designers of SONET and SDH, three are of particular interest to us. First, SONET/SDH is a synchronous network. A single clock is used to handle the timing of transmissions and equipment across the entire network. Networkwide synchronization adds a level of predictability to the system. This predictability, coupled with a powerful frame design, enables individual channels to be multiplexed, thereby improving speed and reducing cost.

Second, SONET/SDH contains recommendations for the standardization of fiber-optic transmission system (FOTS) equipment sold by different manufacturers. Third, the SONET/SDH physical specifications and frame design include mechanisms that allow it to carry signals from incompatible tributary systems (particularly asynchronous services such as DS-0 and DS-1). It is this flexibility that gives SONET a reputation for universal connectivity.

It is important to emphasize that SONET is a multiplexed transport mechanism and as such can be the carrier for broadband services, particularly ATM and B-ISDN.

20.1   SYNCHRONOUS TRANSPORT SIGNALS

As the first step in its flexibility, SONET defines a hierarchy of signaling levels called **synchronous transport signals (STSs).** Each STS level (STS-1 to STS-192) supports a certain data rate, specified in megabits per second (see Table 20.1). The physical links defined to carry each level of STS are called **optical carriers (OCs).** OC levels describe the conceptual and physical specifications of the links required to support each level of signaling. Actual implementation of those specifications is left up to the manufacturers. Currently, the most popular implementations are OC-1, OC-3, OC-12, and OC-48.

Table 20.1   *SONET/SDH rates*

STS	OC	Rate (Mbps)	STM
STS-1	OC-1	51.840	
STS-3	OC-3	155.520	STM-1
STS-9	OC-9	466.560	STM-3
STS-12	OC-12	622.080	STM-4
STS-18	OC-18	933.120	STM-6
STS-24	OC-24	1244.160	STM-8
STS-36	OC-36	1866.230	STM-12
STS-48	OC-48	2488.320	STM-16
STS-96	OC-96	4976.640	STM-32
STS-192	OC-192	9953.280	STM-64

A glance through Table 20.1 reveals some interesting points. First, the lowest level in this hierarchy has a data rate of 51.840 Mbps, which is greater than that of the DS-3 service and T-3 line (44.736 Mbps). That means that the lowest SONET level supports greater bit rates than the highest T level. (T-3 is the highest common electrical line commercially available today, although T-4 is defined.) In fact, the STS-1 is designed to accommodate data rates equivalent to those of the DS-3. The difference in capacity is provided to handle the overhead needs of the optical system.

Second, the STS-3 rate is exactly three times the STS-1 rate; and the STS-9 rate is exactly half the STS-18 rate. These relationships mean that 18 STS-1 channels can be multiplexed into one STS-18, six STS-3 channels can be multiplexed into one STS-18, and so on. As you can see, the concept of hierarchy here is similar to that for DS signals and T lines (see Chapter 8).

SDH specifies a similar system called **synchronous transport module (STM).** STM is intended to be compatible with existing European hierarchies, such as E lines, and with STS levels. To this end, the lowest STM level, STM-1, is defined at 155.520 Mbps, which is exactly equal to STS-3.

20.2 PHYSICAL CONFIGURATION

Figure 20.1 shows the devices used in a SONET transmission system and some possible ways of arranging and linking those devices.

Figure 20.1 *A SONET system*

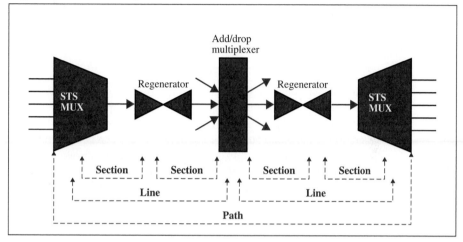

SONET Devices

SONET transmission relies on three basic devices: STS multiplexers, regenerators, and add/drop multiplexers. STS multiplexers mark the beginning and end points of a SONET link. They provide the interface between a tributary network and the SONET. The devices between them can be of any number and configuration required by the system. Regenerators extend the length of the links possible between generator and receiver. Add/drop multiplexers allow insertion and extraction of SONET paths.

- **STS Multiplexer/Demultiplexer.** An STS multiplexer/demultiplexer either multiplexes signals from multiple sources into an STS signal or demultiplexes an STS signal into different destination signals.

- **Regenerator.** An STS **regenerator** is a repeater (see Chapter 21) that takes a received optical signal and regenerates it. Regenerators in this system, however, add a function to those of physical layer repeaters. A SONET regenerator replaces some of the existing overhead information (header information) with new information. These devices function at the data link layer.

- **Add/drop multiplexer.** An **add/drop multiplexer** can add signals coming from different sources into a given path or remove a desired signal from a path and redirect it without demultiplexing the entire signal. Instead of relying on timing and bit positions, add/drop multiplexers use header information such as addresses and pointers (described later in this section) to identify individual streams.

In the simple configuration shown by Figure 20.1, a number of incoming electronic signals are fed into an STS multiplexer, where they are combined into a single optical signal. The optical signal is transmitted to a regenerator, where it is recreated without noise it has picked up in transit. The regenerated signals from a number of sources are then fed into an add/drop multiplexer. The add/drop multiplexer reorganizes these signals, if necessary, and sends them out as directed by information in the data frames. These remultiplexed signals are sent to another regenerator and from there to the receiving STS multiplexer, where they are returned to a format usable by the receiving links.

Sections, Lines, and Paths

As you can see from Figure 20.1, the various levels of SONET connections are called sections, lines, and paths. A section is the optical link connecting two neighbor devices: multiplexer to multiplexer, multiplexer to regenerator, or regenerator to regenerator. A line is the portion of the network between two multiplexers: STS multiplexer to add/drop multiplexer, two add/drop multiplexers, or two STS multiplexers. A path is the end-to-end portion of the network between two STS multiplexers. In a simple SONET of two STS multiplexers linked directly to each other, the section, line, and path are the same.

Figure 20.2 shows a typical SONET network with five STS multiplexer/demultiplexers, two add/drop multiplexers, and six regenerators.

Figure 20.2 *An example of a SONET network*

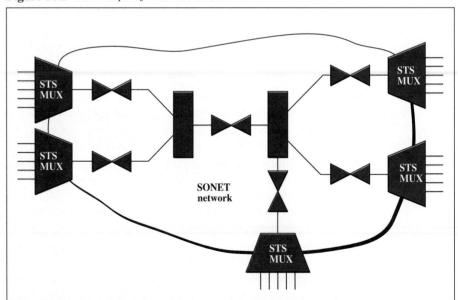

20.3   SONET LAYERS

The SONET standard includes four functional layers: the photonic layer, the section layer, the line layer, and the path layer. These layers are usually thought to correspond only to the first layer (physical) of the OSI model. In fact, they correspond to both the physical and the data link layers (see Figure 20.3). The headers added to the frame at the various layers are discussed later in this chapter.

> SONET defines four layers. The photonic layer is the lowest and performs physical layer activities. The section, line, and path layers correspond to the OSI model's data link layer.

Figure 20.3   *SONET layers*

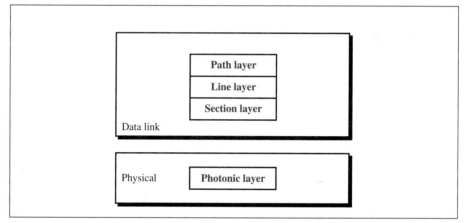

Photonic Layer

The **photonic layer** corresponds to the physical layer of the OSI model. It includes physical specifications for the optical fiber channel, the sensitivity of the receiver, multiplexing functions, and so on. SONET uses NRZ encoding with the presence of light representing 1 and the absence of light representing 0.

Section Layer

The **section layer** is responsible for the movement of a signal across a physical section. It handles framing, scrambling, and error control. Section layer overhead is added to the frame at this layer.

Line Layer

The **line layer** is responsible for the movement of a signal across a physical line. Line layer overhead is added to the frame at this layer. STS multiplexers and add/drop multiplexers provide line layer functions.

Path Layer

The **path layer** is responsible for the movement of a signal from its optical source to its optical destination. At the optical source, the signal is changed from an electronic form into an optical form, multiplexed with other signals, and encapsulated in a frame. At the optical destination, the received frame is demultiplexed, and the individual optical signals are changed back into their electronic forms. Path layer overhead is added at this layer. STS multiplexers provide path layer functions.

Device–Layer Relationships

Figure 20.4 shows the relationship between the devices used in SONET transmission and the four layers of the standard. As you can see, an STS multiplexer is a four-layer device. An add/drop multiplexer is a three-layer device. A regenerator is a two-layer device.

Figure 20.4   *Device-layer relationship in SONET*

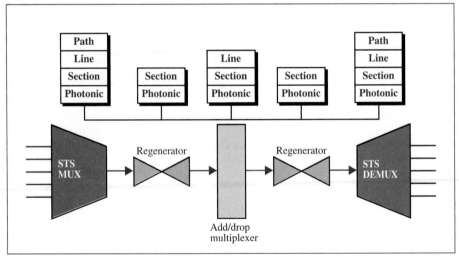

20.4   SONET FRAME

Data received from an electronic interface, such as a T-1 line, is encapsulated in a frame at the path layer and overhead is added. Additional overhead is added, first at the line layer and then at the section layer. Finally, the frame is passed to the photonic layer, where it is transformed into an optical signal (see Figure 20.5).

Note, however, that SONET overhead is not added as headers and trailers as we have seen in other protocols. Instead, SONET inserts overhead at a variety of locations in the middle of the frame. The locations and meanings of these insertions are discussed next.

Figure 20.5   *Data encapsulation in SONET*

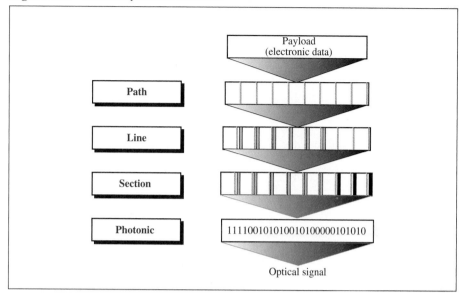

Frame Format

The basic format of an STS-1 frame at the photonic layer is shown in Figure 20.6. Each frame contains 6480 bits (810 octets). STS-1 transmits at a rate of 51.840 Mbps.

Figure 20.6   *STS-1 frame*

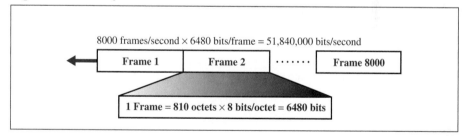

A SONET frame is a matrix of nine rows of 90 octets each, for a total of 810 octets (see Figure 20.7).

The first three columns of the frame are used for section and line overhead. The upper three rows of the first three columns are used for **section overhead.** The lower six are **line overhead.** The rest of the frame is called the synchronous payload envelope (SPE). It contains user data and details about charges and payment required for transmission (if any). One column of the SPE, however, is used for **path overhead** (usually the first). Path overhead includes end-to-end tracking information.

Figure 20.7 *STS-1 frame overheads*

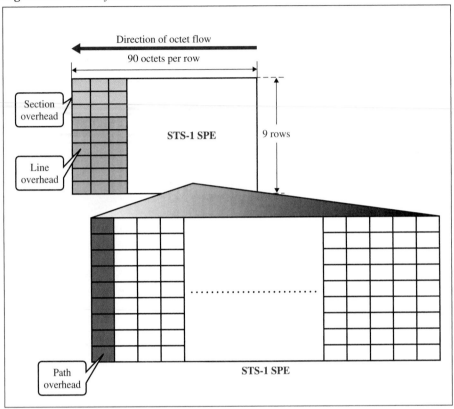

Section Overhead

Section overhead consists of nine octets. The labels, functions, and organization of these octets are shown in Figure 20.8.

Figure 20.8 *STS-1 frame: section overhead*

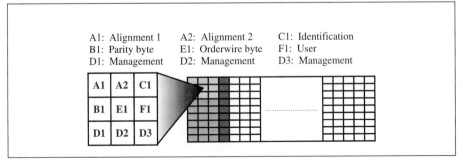

- **Alignment bytes (A1 and A2).** Bytes A1 and A2 are used for framing and synchronization and are called alignment bytes. These bytes alert a receiver that a frame is arriving and give the receiver a predetermined bit pattern on which to synchronize. The bit patterns for these two bytes in both hexadecimal and binary form are as follows:

  A1 ⇨ F6 ⇨ 11110110
  A2 ⇨ 28 ⇨ 00101000

- **Identification byte (C1).** Byte C1 carries a unique identifier for the STS-1 frame. This byte is necessary when multiple STS-1s are multiplexed to create a higher rate STS (STS-3, STS-9, STS-12, etc.). Information in this byte allows the various signals to be recognized easily upon demultiplexing.

- **Parity byte (B1).** Byte B1 is for bit interleaved parity (BIP-8). Its value is based on the section header of the previous STS-1, and it is inserted in the current STS-1. It functions as a longitudinal redundancy check.

- **Orderwire byte (E1).** Byte E1 is the orderwire byte. Orderwire bytes in consecutive frames form a channel of 64 Kbps (8000 frames per second times 8 bits per frame). This channel is used for communication between regenerators, or between terminals and regenerators.

- **User's byte (F1).** The F1 bytes in consecutive frames form a 64-Kbps channel that is reserved for user needs at the section level.

- **Management bytes (D1, D2, and D3).** Bytes D1, D2, and D3 together form a 192-Kbps channel ($3 \times 8000 \times 8$) called the data communication channel. This channel is required for operation, administration, and maintenance (OAM) signaling.

Line Overhead

Line overhead consists of 18 bytes. The labels, functions, and arrangement of these bytes are shown in Figure 20.9.

Figure 20.9 *STS-1 frame: line overhead*

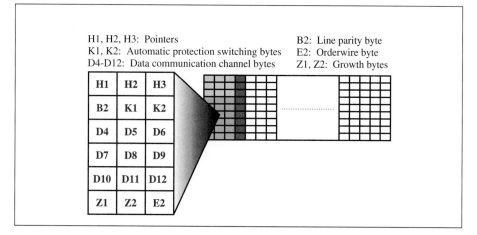

■ **Pointer bytes (H1, H2, and H3).** Bytes H1, H2, and H3 are pointers. They identify the location of the payload in the frame when the payload starts somewhere
other than at the beginning of the STS envelope (see Figure 20.10). Pointers are
essential in several situations. SONET is a synchronous protocol. Frames are built
by matching the timing of the data input to the network frame functions. For this
reason, data collected from asynchronous network inputs may not be synchronized
with the SPE and may end up occupying two frames. Pointers enable SONET to
accommodate such framing discrepancies. In these cases, bytes H1, H2, and H3
together form a pointer to the beginning byte of the payload. Other, more complex
uses for pointers also exist; a discussion of them is beyond the scope of this book.

Figure 20.10 *Payload pointers*

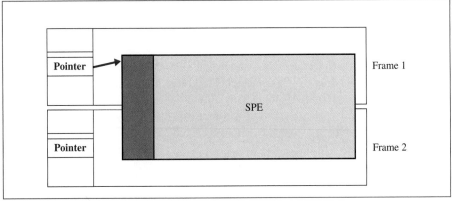

■ **Line parity byte (B2).** Byte B2 is for bit interleaved parity, like byte B1, but calculated for the line header.
■ **Automatic protection switching bytes (K1 and K2).** The K1 and K2 bytes in
consecutive frames form a 128-Kbps channel used for automatic detection of problems in line-terminating equipment (e.g., multiplexers).
■ **Data communication channel bytes (D4 to D12).** The line-overhead D bytes (D4
to D12) in consecutive frames form a 576-Kbps channel that provides the same
service as the D1–D3 bytes (OAM), but at the line rather than the section level.
■ **Growth bytes (Z1 and Z2).** The Z1 and Z2 bytes are reserved for future use.
■ **Orderwire byte (E2).** The E2 bytes in consecutive frames form a 64-Kbps channel that provides the same functions as the E1 orderwire byte, but at the line level.

Path Overhead

Path overhead consists of nine bytes. The labels, functions, and arrangement of these
bytes are shown in Figure 20.11.

■ **Path trace byte (J1).** The J1 bytes in consecutive frames form a 64-Kbps channel
used for tracking the path. The J1 byte sends a continuous 64-bit string to verify
the connection. The choice of the string is left to the application program.

Figure 20.11   *STS-1 frame: path overhead*

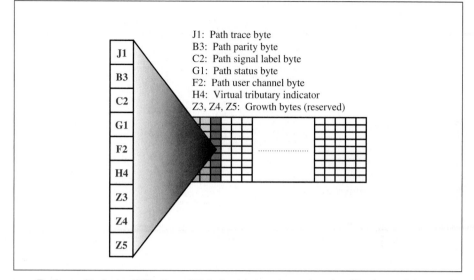

■ **Path parity byte (B3).** Byte B3 is for bit interleaved parity, like bytes B1 and B2, but calculated for the path header.

■ **Path signal label byte (C2).** Byte C2 is the path identification byte. It is used to identify different protocols used at higher levels (such as FDDI or SMDS).

■ **Path status byte (G1).** Byte G1 is sent by the receiver to communicate its status to the sender.

■ **Path user channel byte (F2).** The F2 bytes in consecutive frames, like the F1 bytes, form a 64-Kbps channel that is reserved for user needs, but at the path level.

■ **Virtual tributary indicator (H4).** Byte H4 is the multiframe indicator. It indicates payloads that cannot fit into a single frame. Virtual tributaries are discussed in the next section.

■ **Growth bytes (Z3, Z4, and Z5).** Bytes Z3, Z4, and Z5 are reserved for future use.

Virtual Tributaries

SONET is designed to carry broadband payloads. Current digital hierarchy data rates (DS-1 to DS-3), however, are lower than STS-1. To make SONET backward compatible with the current hierarchy, its frame design includes a system of **virtual tributaries** (**VTs**) (see Figure 20.12). A virtual tributary is a partial payload that can be inserted into an STS-1 and combined with other partial payloads to fill out the frame. Instead of using all 86 payload columns of an STS-1 frame for data from one source, we can subdivide the SPE and call each component a VT.

Types of VTs

Four types of VTs have been defined to accommodate existing digital hierarchies (see Figure 20.13). Notice that the number of columns allowed for each type of VT can be

Figure 20.12   *Virtual tributaries*

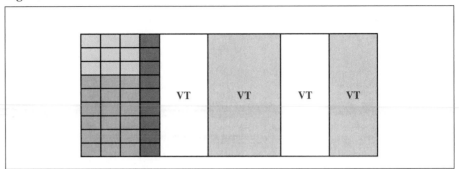

Figure 20.13   *VT types*

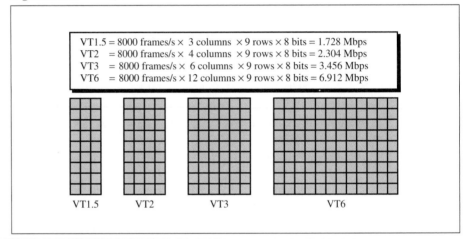

determined by doubling the type identification number (VT1.5 gets three columns, VT2 gets four columns, etc.).

■   **VT1.5.** VT1.5 accommodates the U.S. DS-1 service (1.544 Mbps).

■   **VT2.** VT2 accommodates the European CEPT-1 service (2.048 Mbps).

■   **VT3.** VT3 accommodates the DS-1C service (fractional DS-1, 3.152 Mbps).

■   **VT6.** VT6 accommodates the DS-2 service (6.312 Mbps).

When two or more tributaries are inserted into a single STS-1 frame, they are interleaved column by column. SONET provides mechanisms for identifying each VT and separating them without demultiplexing the entire stream. Discussion of these mechanisms and the control issues behind them are beyond the scope of this book.

20.5   MULTIPLEXING STS FRAMES

Lower-rate STSs can be multiplexed to make them compatible with higher-rate systems. For example, three STS-1s can be combined into one STS-3, four STS-3s can be multiplexed into one STS-12, and so on. The general format for an STS-*n* made up of lower-rate STSs is shown in Figure 20.14.

Figure 20.14   *STS*-n

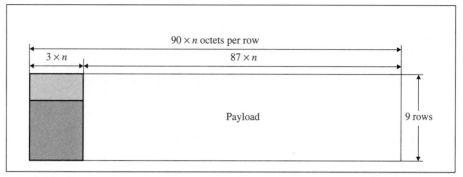

Figure 20.15 shows how three STS-1s are multiplexed into a single STS-3. To create an STS-12 out of lower-rate services, we could multiplex either 12 STS-1s or 4 STS-3s.

Figure 20.15   *STS multiplexing*

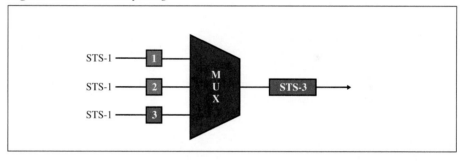

ATM Convergence to SONET/SDH

The most important physical carrier for ATM is projected to be SONET's STS-3 service (STM-1 in Europe's SDH). Because ATM provides multiplexing, the entire payload of the STS-3 can be used for cell transport without the additional overhead required by other systems. One possible mapping of ATM to an STS-3 envelope is shown in Figure 20.16.

Each row of the frame (envelope) consists of 270 octets (3×90). Of these, nine octets are used for section and line overhead, and one octet is used for path overhead. The remaining 260 octets can carry close to five cells ($5 \times 53 = 265$). The fifth frame in the first row must be split between the first and second rows. Other rows may have partial cells at both ends.

Figure 20.16 *ATM in an STS-3 envelope*

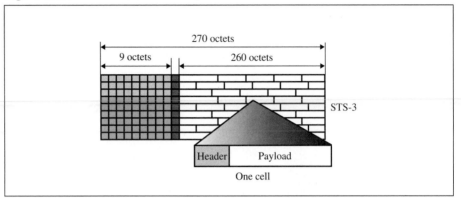

20.6 APPLICATIONS

SONET is designed to provide a backbone network for WANs. With a data rate of more than three gigabits per second, it can find applications in many areas. Some of these applications can be summarized as follows:

- SONET can replace existing T-1 or T-3 lines. A T-1 load can easily be carried in a VT1.5 tributary and a T-3 load can easily be carried in a full SPE of an STS-1 frame.
- A lot of fiber-optic cables have already been laid without a common protocol. These can be combined into a network (or networks) using the SONET protocol. Most of these cables are not being used to their full capacity because of the lack of a protocol.
- SONET can be the carrier for ISDN and B-ISDN.
- SONET can be the carrier for ATM cells (as shown in the text).
- SONET can support bandwidth on demand.
- SONET can replace the fiber-optic cables used in cable TV networks.
- SONET can be used as the backbone or totally replace other networking protocols such as SMDS or FDDI.

20.7 KEY TERMS AND CONCEPTS

add/drop multiplexer	path layer
line layer	path overhead
line overhead	photonic layer
optical carrier (OC)	regenerator

section layer

synchronous transport module (STM)

section overhead

Synchronous Digital Hierarchy (SDH)

synchronous transport signal (STS)

Synchronous Optical Network
(SONET)

virtual tributary (VT)

20.8 SUMMARY

- Synchronous Optical Network (SONET) is a standard developed by ANSI for fiber-optic networks.
- SONET has defined a hierarchy of signals (similar to the DS hierarchy) called synchronous transport signals (STS).
- Optical carrier (OC) levels are the implementation of STSs.
- SONET defines four layers. The photonic layer is the lowest and performs physical layer activities.
- SONET's section, line, and path layers correspond to the OSI model's data link layer. Each of these layers is responsible for signal transfer across a specific portion of the transmission path.
- A SONET system can use the following equipment:
  a. STS multiplexer—combines several optical signals to make an STS signal.
  b. Regenerator—removes noise from an optical signal.
  c. Add/drop multiplexer—adds STS signals from different paths and removes STS signals from a path.
- A frame at the photonic layer for STS-1 consists of 6480 bits. There are 8000 frames/second.
- Overhead and data (payload) in an STS-1 are arranged in a matrix configuration (nine rows of 90 octets).
- SONET is backward compatible with the current DS hierarchy through the virtual tributary (VT) concept. VTs are a partial payload consisting of an m by n block of octets. An STS payload can be a combination of several VTs.
- STSs can be multiplexed to get a new STS with a higher data rate.

20.9 PRACTICE SET

Review Questions

1. How is an STS multiplexer different from an add/drop multiplexer since both can add signals together?
2. What is the relationship between STS levels and OC levels?

3. What is the purpose of the pointer in the line overhead?
4. Compare the STS hierarchy with the DS hierarchy.
5. Discuss the SONET configuration as a physical carrier for ATM.
6. What is the relationship between SONET and Synchronous Digital Hierarchy (SDH)?
7. Why is SONET called a synchronous network?
8. What is the relationship between STS and STM?
9. What is the function of a SONET regenerator?
10. What are the four SONET layers?
11. Discuss the functions of each SONET layer.
12. What kind of encoding is used by SONET?
13. Compare the SONET layers to the layers of the OSI model.
14. Discuss the location of overhead information for each SONET layer.
15. How is an STS-1 frame organized?
16. What is a virtual tributary?
17. How does SONET carry data from a DS-1 service?
18. How can lower-data-rate STSs be made compatible with higher-data-rate STSs?

Multiple Choice Questions

19. SONET is a standard for _____ networks.
    a. twisted-pair cable
    b. coaxial cable
    c. Ethernet
    d. fiber-optic cable
20. SONET is an acronym for _____ Network.
    a. Synchronous Optical
    b. Standard Optical
    c. Symmetrical Open
    d. Standard Open
21. In a SONET system, _____ removes noise from a signal and can also add or remove headers.
    a. an STS multiplier
    b. a regenerator
    c. an add/drop multiplexer
    d. a repeater
22. In a SONET system, _____ can remove signals from a path.
    a. an STS multiplier
    b. a regenerator
    c. an add/drop multiplexer
    d. a repeater

23. The optical link between any two SONET devices is called _____.
    a. a section
    b. a line
    c. a path
    d. none of the above

24. The optical link between an STS multiplexer and a regenerator is called _____.
    a. a section
    b. a line
    c. a path
    d. none of the above

25. The optical link between an STS multiplexer and an add/drop multiplexer is called _____.
    a. a section
    b. a line
    c. a path
    d. none of the above

26. SONET's _____ layer corresponds to the OSI model's physical layer.
    a. path
    b. line
    c. section
    d. photonic

27. SONET's _____ layer performs framing, scrambling, and error handling.
    a. path
    b. line
    c. section
    d. photonic

28. SONET's _____ layer transfers a signal across a physical line.
    a. path
    b. line
    c. section
    d. photonic

29. SONET's _____ layer transfers data from its optical source to its optical destination.
    a. path
    b. line
    c. section
    d. photonic

30. Which of the following SONET layers corresponds to the OSI's data link layer?
    a. path
    b. line

   c. section

   d. all of the above

31. An STS multiplexer operates in _____ layers: _____.

   a. four; path, line, section, and photonic

   b. two; section and photonic

   c. three; line, section, and photonic

   d. two; photonic and path

32. An add/drop multiplexer operates in _____ layers: _____.

   a. four; path, line, section, and photonic

   b. two; section and photonic

   c. three; line, section, and photonic

   d. two; photonic and path

33. A regenerator operates in _____ layers: _____.

   a. four; path, line, section, and photonic

   b. two; section and photonic

   c. three; line, section, and photonic

   d. two; photonic and path

34. In an STS-1 frame, the first three columns contain _____.

   a. section and line overhead

   b. user data

   c. section, line, and path overhead

   d. path overhead

35. The synchronous payload envelope (SPE) of an STS-1 frame contains _____.

   a. pointers

   b. user data

   c. path overhead

   d. b and c

36. A parity byte exists for an STS-1 frame's _____.

   a. section overhead

   b. line overhead

   c. path overhead

   d. all of the above

37. Which overhead contains the pointers to the payload?

   a. section

   b. line

   c. path

   d. a and b

38. What is the maximum number of VT1.5s that STS-1 can accommodate?

   a. 3

   b. 9

c. 28

d. 29

39. What is the maximum number of VT2s that STS-1 can accommodate?

   a. 4

   b. 21

   c. 22

   d. 23

Exercises

40. Using Figure 20.14 prove that the data rate of STS-3 is 155.520 Mbps.

41. Repeat Exercise 40 for STS-9, STS-12, ..., STS-192. See Table 20.1 for data rates.

42. Prove that the data rate for SPE in STS-1 is only 50.112 Mbps (hint: subtract the bits used for section and line overhead).

43. Prove that the user data rate for STS-1 is only 49.536 Mbps (hint: subtract the bits used for section, line, and path overhead).

44. Repeat Exercise 42 for STS-3, STS-9, ..., STS-192.

45. Repeat Exercise 43 for STS-3, STS-9, ..., STS-192.

46. Show how STS-9s can be multiplexed to create an STS-36. Is there any extra overhead involved in this type of multiplexing? Why or why not?

47. What is the duration of a frame in STS-1?

48. What is the duration of a frame in STS-3, STS-9, ..., STS-192?

49. How many VT1.5s can be carried in an STS-1 frame?

50. How many VT2s can be carried in an STS-1 frame?

51. How many VT3s can be carried in an STS-1 frame?

52. How many VT6s can be carried in an STS-1 frame?

53. A user needs to send data at 3 Mbps. Which VT (or combination of VTs) can be used?

54. A user needs to send data at 7 Mbps. Which VT (or combination of VTs) can be used?

55. A user needs to send data at 12 Mbps. Which VT (or combination of VTs) can be used?

56. Which VT transmits at almost the same data rate as a T-1 line?

57. Which VT or STS transmits at almost the same data rate as a T-3 line?

58. A company wants to use SONET to multiplex up to 100 digitized voices. Which VT (or combination of VTs) is suitable for this company?

59. Draw a SONET network using all of the following devices. Label all lines, sections, and paths.

   a. Three STS multiplexers (two as input and one as output).

   b. Four add/drop multiplexers.

   c. Five regenerators.

CHAPTER 21

Networking and Internetworking Devices

Two or more devices connected for the purpose of sharing data or resources can form a network. Putting together a network is often more complicated than simply plugging cable into a hub. A local area network (LAN) may need to cover more distance than its media can handle effectively. Or the number of stations may be too great for efficient frame delivery or management of the network, and the network may need to be subdivided. In the first case, a device called a repeater or regenerator is inserted into the network to increase the coverable distance. In the second, a device called a bridge is inserted for traffic management.

When two or more separate networks are connected for exchanging data or resources, they become an internetwork (or internet). Linking a number of LANs into an internet requires additional **internetworking devices** called routers and gateways. These devices are designed to overcome obstacles to interconnection without disrupting the independent functioning of the networks.

> An internet is an interconnection of individual networks. To create an internet, we need internetworking devices called routers and gateways.

Note: Do not confuse the term *internet* (lowercase *i*) with *the Internet* (uppercase *I*). The first is a generic term used to mean an interconnection of networks. The second is the name of a specific worldwide network.

> An internet is different from the Internet.

As mentioned above, networking and internetworking devices are divided into four categories: repeaters, bridges, routers, and gateways (see Figure 21.1).

Each of these four device types interacts with protocols at different layers of the OSI model. Repeaters act only upon the electrical components of a signal and are therefore active only at the physical layer. Bridges utilize addressing protocols and can affect the flow control of a single LAN; they are most active at the data link layer. Routers provide links between two separate but same-type LANs and are most active at the

Figure 21.1 *Connecting devices*

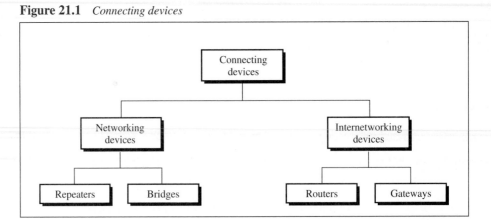

network layer. Finally, gateways provide translation services between incompatible LANs or applications and are active in all of the layers. Each of these internetworking devices also operates in all of the layers below the one in which it is most active (see Figure 21.2).

Figure 21.2 *Connecting devices and the OSI model*

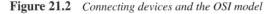
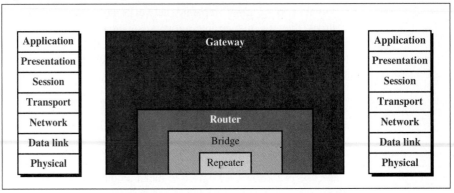

21.1   REPEATERS

A **repeater** (or regenerator) is an electronic device that operates on only the physical layer of the OSI model (see Figure 21.3). Signals that carry information within a network can travel a fixed distance before attenuation endangers the integrity of the data. A repeater installed on a link receives the signal before it becomes too weak or corrupted, regenerates the original bit pattern, and puts the refreshed copy back onto the link.

A repeater allows us to extend only the physical length of a network. The repeater does not change the functionality of the network in any way (see Figure 21.4). The two sections connected by the repeater in Figure 21.4 are, in reality, one network. If station A sends a frame to station B, all stations (including C and D) will receive the frame, just as

Figure 21.3   *A repeater in the OSI model*

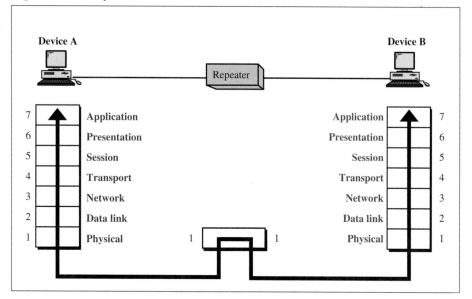

they would without the repeater. The repeater does not have the intelligence to keep the frame from passing to the right side when it is meant for a station on the left. The difference is that, with the repeater, stations C and D receive a truer copy of the frame than would otherwise have been possible.

Figure 21.4   *A repeater*

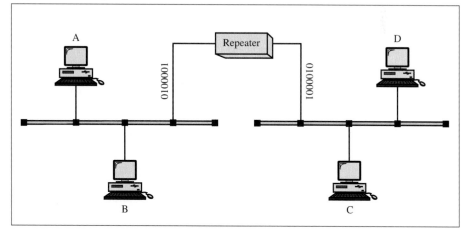

Not an Amplifier

It is tempting to compare a repeater to an amplifier, but the comparison is inaccurate. An amplifier cannot discriminate between the intended signal and noise; it amplifies equally everything fed into it. A repeater does not amplify the signal; it regenerates it.

When it receives a weakened or corrupted signal, it creates a copy bit for bit, at the original strength.

> A repeater is a regenerator, not an amplifier.

The location of a repeater on a link is vital. A repeater must be placed so that a signal reaches it before any noise changes the meaning of any of its bits. A little noise can alter the precision of a bit's voltage without destroying its identity (see Figure 21.5). If the corrupted bit travels much farther, however, accumulated noise can change its meaning completely. At that point, the original voltage becomes unrecoverable and the error can be corrected only by retransmission. A repeater placed on the line before the legibility of the signal becomes lost can still read the signal well enough to determine the intended voltages and replicate them in their original form.

Figure 21.5 *Function of a repeater*

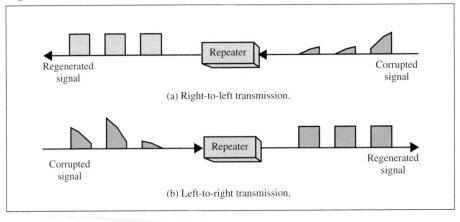

(a) Right-to-left transmission.

(b) Left-to-right transmission.

21.2 BRIDGES

Bridges operate in both the physical and the data link layers of the OSI model (see Figure 21.6). Bridges can divide a large network into smaller segments (see Figure 21.7). They can also relay frames between two originally separate LANs. Unlike repeaters, however, bridges contain logic that allows them to keep the traffic for each segment separate. In this way, they filter traffic, a fact that makes them useful for controlling congestion and isolating problem links. Bridges can also provide security through this partitioning of traffic.

A bridge operates at the data link layer, giving it access to the physical addresses of all stations connected to it. When a frame enters a bridge, the bridge not only regenerates the signal but checks the address of the destination and forwards the new copy only to the segment to which the address belongs. As a bridge encounters a packet, it reads the address contained in the frame and compares that address with a table of all the stations on both segments. When it finds a match, it discovers to which segment the station belongs and relays the packet only to that segment.

Figure 21.6 *A bridge in the OSI model*

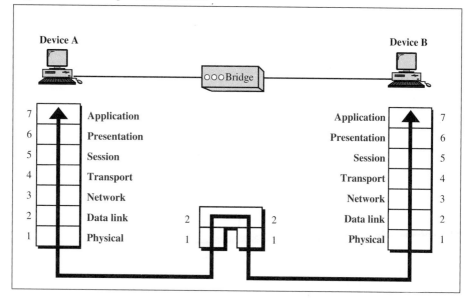

Figure 21.7 *A bridge*

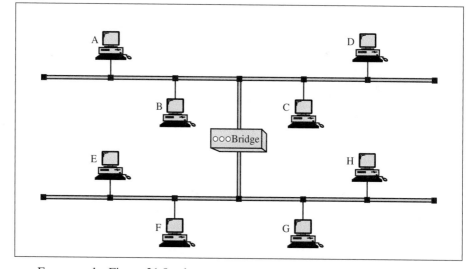

For example, Figure 21.8*a* shows two segments joined by a bridge. A packet from station A addressed to station D arrives at the bridge. Station A is on the same segment as station D; therefore, the packet is blocked from crossing into the lower segment. Instead the packet is relayed to the entire upper segment and received by station D.

In Figure 21.8*b*, a packet generated by station A is intended for station G. The bridge allows the packet to cross and relays it to the entire lower segment, where it is received by station G.

Figure 21.8 *Function of a bridge*

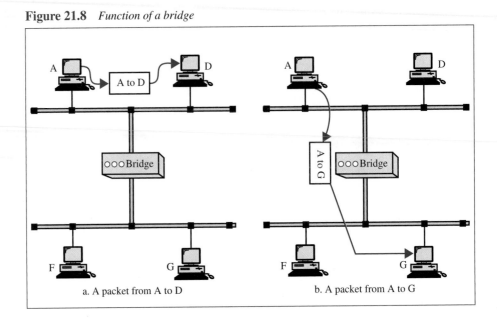

a. A packet from A to D   b. A packet from A to G

Types of Bridges

To select between segments, a bridge must have a look-up table that contains the physical addresses of every station connected to it. The table indicates to which segment each station belongs.

Simple Bridge

Simple bridges are the most primitive and least expensive type of bridge. A simple bridge links two segments and contains a table that lists the addresses of all the stations included in each of them. What makes it primitive is that these addresses must be entered manually. Before a simple bridge can be used, an operator must sit down and enter the addresses of every station. Whenever a new station is added, the table must be modified. If a station is removed, the newly invalid address must be deleted. The logic included in a simple bridge, therefore, is of the pass/no pass variety, a configuration that makes a simple bridge straightforward and inexpensive to manufacture. Installation and maintenance of simple bridges are time-consuming and potentially more trouble than the cost savings are worth.

Multiport Bridge

A **multiport bridge** can be used to connect more than two LANs (see Figure 21.9). In this figure, the bridge has three tables, each one holding the physical addresses of stations reachable through the corresponding port.

Transparent Bridge

A **transparent,** or learning, **bridge** builds its table of station addresses on its own as it performs its bridge functions. When the transparent bridge is first installed, its table is

Figure 21.9 *Multiport bridge*

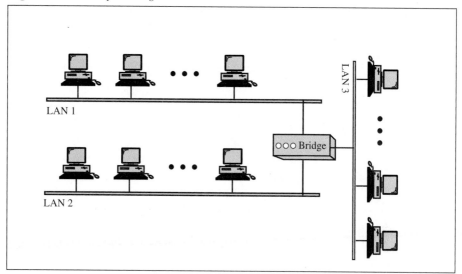

empty. As it encounters each packet, it looks at both the destination and the source addresses. It checks the destination to decide where to send the packet. If it does not yet recognize the destination address, it relays the packet to all of the stations on both segments. It uses the source address to build its table. As it reads the source address, it notes which side the packet came from and associates that address with the segment to which it belongs. For example, if the bridge in Figure 21.8 is a transparent bridge, then when station A sends its packet to station G, the bridge learns that packets coming from A are coming from the upper segment, and that station A must be located in the upper segment. Now, whenever the bridge encounters packets addressed to A, it knows to relay them only to the upper segment.

With the first packet transmitted by each station, the bridge learns the segment associated with that station. Eventually it has a complete table of station addresses and their respective segment stored in its memory.

By continuing this process even after the table is complete, a transparent bridge is also self-updating. Suppose the person at station A trades offices with the person at station G, and they both take their computers (including their NICs) with them. All of a sudden, the stored segment locations for both stations are wrong. But because the bridge is constantly checking the source address of received packets, it notices that packets from station A are now coming from the lower segment and that packets from station G are coming from the upper segment and updates its table accordingly.

Spanning Tree Algorithm   Bridges are normally installed redundantly, which means that two LANs may be connected by more than one bridge. In this case, if the bridges are transparent bridges, they may create a loop, which means a packet may be going round and round, from one LAN to another and back again to the first LAN. To avoid this situation, bridges today use what is called the **spanning tree algorithm.** See Appendix I for a discussion of this situation and the spanning tree algorithm.

Source Routing Another solution to prevent loops in the LANs connected by bridges is **source routing.** In this method, the source of the packet defines the bridges and the LANs through which the packet should go before reaching the destination.

Bridges Connecting Different LANs

Theoretically a bridge should be able to connect LANs using different protocols at the data link layer, such as an Ethernet LAN to a Token Ring LAN. However, there are many issues to be considered, some of which are mentioned below:

- **Frame format.** Frames sent by different LANs have different formats (compare an Ethernet frame with a Token Ring frame).

- **Payload size.** The size of the data that can be encapsulated in a frame varies from protocol to protocol (compare the maximum payload size of an Ethernet frame with that of a Token Ring).

- **Data rate.** Different protocols use different data rates (compare the 10-Mbps data rate of an Ethernet with the 16-Mbps data rate of a Token Ring); the bridge should buffer the frame to compensate for this difference.

- **Address bit order.** The bit order of addresses in different LAN protocols is not the same; for example, a bridge should reverse an address if it is connecting an Ethernet LAN to a Token Ring LAN.

- **Other issues.** There are other issues that should be resolved, such as acknowledgment, collision, and priority, which may be part of one LAN protocol but not the other.

However, there are bridges today that can handle all of these problems and can connect one type of LAN to another.

21.3 ROUTERS

Repeaters and bridges are simple hardware devices capable of executing specific tasks. **Routers** are more sophisticated. They have access to network layer addresses and contain software that enables them to determine which of several possible paths between those addresses is the best for a particular transmission. Routers operate in the physical, data link, and network layers of the OSI model (see Figure 21.10).

Routers relay packets among multiple interconnected networks. They route packets from one network to any of a number of potential destination networks on an internet. Figure 21.11 shows a possible internetwork of five networks. A packet sent from a station on one network to a station on a neighboring network goes first to the jointly held router, which switches it over to the destination network. If there is no one router connected to both the sending and receiving networks, the sending router transfers the packet across one of its connected networks to the next router in the direction of the ultimate destination. That router forwards the packet to the next router on the path, and so on, until the destination is reached.

Routers act like stations on a network. But unlike most stations, which are members of only one network, routers have addresses on, and links to, two or more networks

Figure 21.10   *A router in the OSI model*

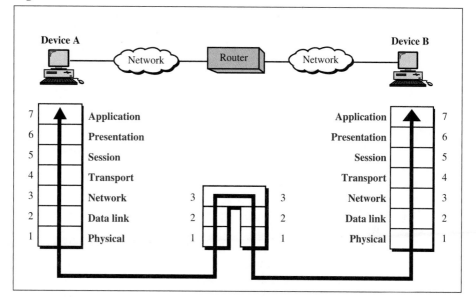

Figure 21.11   *Routers in an internet*

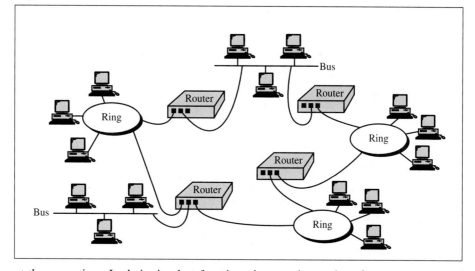

at the same time. In their simplest function, they receive packets from one connected network and pass them to a second connected network. However, if a received packet is addressed to a node on a network of which the router is not a member, the router is capable of determining which of its connected networks is the best next relay point for the packet. Once a router has identified the best route for a packet to travel, it passes the packet along the appropriate network to another router. That router checks the destination address, finds what it considers the best route for the packet, and passes it to the destination network (if that network is a neighbor) or across a neighboring network to the next router on the chosen path.

Routing Concepts

As we have seen, the job of routers is to forward packets through a set of networks. Imagine, for example, that we want to move a packet from network A to network C via router (network) B. Often, however, more than one pathway exists between the point of origin and the point of destination. For example, the packet could reach network C by going through router D instead of router B, or possibly even going directly from A to C. Whenever there are multiple options, the router chooses the pathway.

Least-Cost Routing

But which path does it choose? The decision of the **least-cost routing** is based on efficiency: which of the available pathways is the cheapest or, in networking terminology, the shortest? A value is assigned to each link; the length of a particular route is equal to the total of the values of the component links. The term *shortest,* in this context, can mean either of two things depending on the protocol. In some cases, shortest means the route requiring the smallest number of relays, or hops; for example, a direct link from A to D would be considered shorter than the route A-B-C-D even if the actual distance covered by the latter is the same or less. In other cases, shortest means fastest, cheapest, most reliable, most secure, or best of any other quality that can make one particular link (or combination of links) more attractive than another. Usually, shortest means a combination of all of these.

> In routing the term *shortest* can mean the combination of many factors including shortest, cheapest, fastest, most reliable, and so on.

When shortest means the pathway requiring the smallest number of relays, it is called **hop-count** routing, in which every link is considered to be of equal length and given the value one. Equal link values make hop-count routing simple: one-hop routes are always equal to one, two-hop routes are always equal to two, and so on. Routes need updating only when a link becomes unavailable. In that case, the value of the link becomes infinite and an alternate is found. Hop-count algorithms usually limit the routes known by a single router to those within 15 hops. For transmissions with special requirements (e.g., military transmissions that require highly secure lines), a particular hop-count algorithm may be customized. In such cases, some links will be given a value of one, while others will have higher values and will be avoided. Novell, AppleTalk, OSI, and TCP/IP protocols all use hop count as the basis for their routing algorithms.

Other protocols factor a number of qualities relevant to the functioning of a link before assigning a value to a link. These qualities can include speed, traffic congestion, and link medium (telephone line, satellite transmission, etc.). When all relevant factors for a particular link are combined, a number that represents the value or length of the link is issued. This number represents an assessment of efficiency, not a physical distance; thus, it is called the symbolic length of the link.

> We can combine all of the factors affecting a link into one number and call that number the symbolic length of the link.

In some protocols, each link in a network is assigned a length based on whatever qualities are considered important to that network. If the link between two routers is half-duplex or full-duplex (has two-way traffic), the length of the link in one direction might be different from the length of the link in the other direction. The physical distance that the signal has to travel is not changed, but other factors, such as traffic load or quality of the cable, may differ. As with hop-count routing, the decision of which route is best is based on shortest distance, calculated by totaling the lengths of every link used by a given path. In hop-count routing, all three-hop paths have a total length of three and are considered longer than two-hop paths. When different links are assigned different lengths, however, the total length of a three-hop link may turn out to be shorter than that of a two-hop link.

Nonadaptive versus Adaptive Routing

Routing is classified as nonadaptive or adaptive.

Nonadaptive Routing   In some routing protocols, once a pathway to a destination has been selected, the router sends all packets for that destination along that one route. In other words, the routing decisions are not made based on the condition or topology of the networks.

Adaptive Routing   Other routing protocols employ a technique called adaptive routing, by which a router may select a new route for each packet (even packets belonging to the same transmission) in response to changes in condition and topology of the networks. Given a transmission from network A to network D, a router may send the first packet by way of network B, the second packet by way of network C, and the third packet by way of network Q, depending on which route is most efficient at the moment.

Packet Lifetime

Once a router has decided on a pathway, it passes the packet to the next router on that path and forgets about it. The next router, however, may choose the same pathway or may decide that a different pathway is shorter and relay the packet to the next router in that direction. This handing-off of responsibility allows each router to contain minimal logic, keeps the amount of control information that must be contained in the frame to a minimum, and allows for route adjustment based on up-to-the-minute appraisals of each link. It also creates the potential for a packet's getting stuck in a never-ending loop or bounce in which a packet is passed around from router to router without ever actually reaching its destination.

Loops and bouncing can occur when a router updates its routing table, then relays a packet based on new pathways before the receiving router has updated its own vector. For example, A believes that the shortest route to C is through B and relays a packet accordingly. Before B receives the packet, it learns that its link to C has been disabled. B updates its vector and finds that the current shortest route from itself to C is through A. The packet is sent back to A. A has not yet received the information about the B–C link and still believes the best route to C to be through B. The packet is relayed back to B. B relays it back to A, and so on. Problems of this sort are more likely on systems using distance vector algorithms than on those using link state algorithms. (The former send update packages more frequently than the latter; see Section 21.6 "Routing Algorithms.")

The problem created by looping and bouncing is not primarily one of lost packets—the data link functions of the transmission's originator and receiver report lost frames and replace them with new copies. The problem is that processing eternally looping packets uses network resources and increases congestion. Looping packets must be identified and destroyed to free the links for legitimate traffic.

The solution is an added packet field called **packet lifetime,** or **time to live (TTL).** As it is generated, each packet is marked with a lifetime, usually the number of hops that are allowed before a packet is considered lost and, accordingly, destroyed. Each router to encounter the packet subtracts 1 from the total before passing it on. When the lifetime total reaches 0, the packet is destroyed.

21.4 GATEWAYS

Gateways potentially operate in all seven layers of the OSI model (see Figure 21.12). A gateway is a **protocol converter.** A router by itself transfers, accepts, and relays packets only across networks using similar protocols. A gateway, on the other hand, can accept a packet formatted for one protocol (e.g., AppleTalk) and convert it to a packet formatted for another protocol (e.g., TCP/IP) before forwarding it.

Figure 21.12 *A gateway in the OSI model*

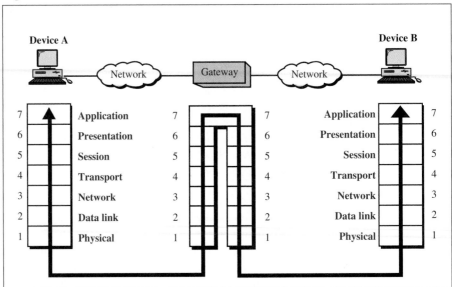

A gateway is generally software installed within a router. The gateway understands the protocols used by each network linked into the router and is therefore able to translate from one to another. In some cases, the only modifications necessary are the header and trailer of the packet. In other cases, the gateway must adjust the data rate, size, and format as well. Figure 21.13 shows a gateway connecting an SNA network (IBM) to a NetWare network (Novell).

Figure 21.13 *A gateway*

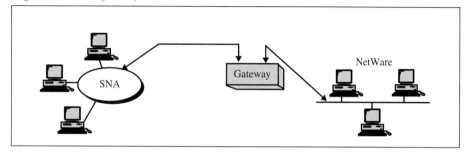

21.5 OTHER DEVICES

In this section, we briefly define other devices used for connecting networks.

Multiprotocol Routers

At the network layer, a router by default is a single-protocol device. In other words, if two LANs are to be connected through a router, they should use the same protocol at the network layer. For example, both should use IP (the network layer protocol of the Internet) or IPX (the network layer protocol for Novell). The reason behind this is that the routing table should use one single addressing format.

However, **multiprotocol routers** have been designed to route packets belonging to two or more protocols. For example, a two-protocol router (for example, IP and IPX) can handle packets belonging to either of the two protocols. It can receive, process, and send a packet using the IP protocol or it can receive, process, and send a packet using the IPX protocol. In this case, the router has two routing tables: one for IP and one for IPX. Of course, the router cannot route a packet based on other protocols. Figure 21.14 shows the idea of a multiprotocol router.

Brouters

A **brouter (bridge/router)** is a single-protocol or multiprotocol router that sometimes acts as a router and sometimes as a bridge.

When a single-protocol brouter receives a packet belonging to the protocol for which it is designed, it routes the packet based on the network layer address; otherwise, it acts as a bridge and passes the packet using the data link layer address.

When a multiprotocol brouter receives a packet belonging to one of the protocols for which it is designed, it routes the packet based on the network layer address; otherwise, it acts as a bridge and passes the packet using the data link layer address. Figure 21.15 shows the concept of a brouter.

Figure 21.14 *Single-protocol versus multiprotocol router*

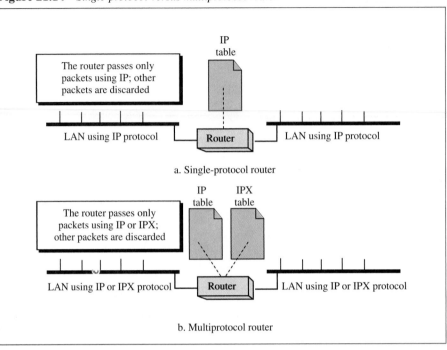

Figure 21.15 *Brouter*

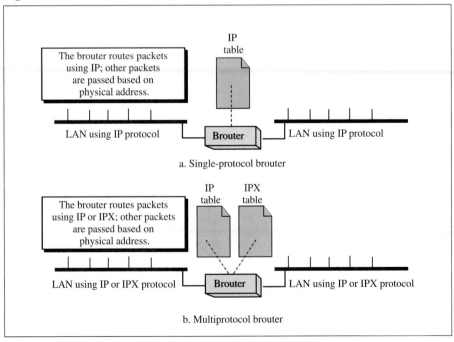

Switches

Traditionally, a switch is a device that provides bridging functionality with greater efficiency. As we saw in a previous section, a switch may act as a multiport bridge to connect devices or segments in a LAN. The switch normally has a buffer for each link (network) to which it is connected. When it receives a packet, it stores the packet in the buffer of the receiving link and checks the address (and sometimes CRC) to find the outgoing link. If the outgoing link is free (no chance of collision), the switch sends the frame to that particular link.

Switches are made based on two different strategies (called fabrics): *store-and-forward* and *cut-through*. A **store-and-forward switch** stores the frame in the input buffer until the whole packet has arrived. A **cut-through switch,** on the other hand, forwards the packet to the output buffer as soon as the destination address is received. Figure 21.16 shows the concept of a switch. A frame arrives at port 2 and is stored in the buffer. The CPU and the control unit, using the information in the frame, consult the switching table to find the output port. The frame is then sent to port 5 for transmission.

Figure 21.16 *Switch*

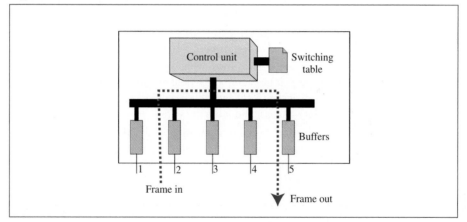

Routing Switches

A new generation of switches that are a combination of a router and a bridge has recently appeared on the market. These **routing switches** use the network layer destination address to find the output link to which the packet should be forwarded. The process is faster because the network layer software in a regular router finds only the network address of the next station and then passes this information to the data link layer software to find the output link.

21.6 ROUTING ALGORITHMS

As explained earlier, in routing the pathway with the lowest cost is considered the best. As long as the cost of each link is known, a router can find the optimal combination for any transmission. Several **routing algorithms** exist for making these calculations. The most popular are distance vector routing and link state routing.

> Two common methods are used to calculate the shortest path between two routers: distance vector routing and link state routing.

21.7 DISTANCE VECTOR ROUTING

In **distance vector routing,** each router periodically shares its knowledge about the entire network with its neighbors. The three keys to understanding how this algorithm works are as follows:

1. **Knowledge about the whole network.** Each router shares its knowledge about the entire network. It sends all of its collected knowledge about the network to its neighbors. At the outset, a router's knowledge of the network may be sparse. How much it knows, however, is unimportant: it sends whatever it has.

2. **Routing only to neighbors.** Each router periodically sends its knowledge about the network only to those routers to which it has direct links. It sends whatever knowledge it has about the whole network through all of its ports. This information is received and kept by each neighboring router and used to update that router's own information about the network.

3. **Information sharing at regular intervals.** For example, every 30 seconds, each router sends its information about the whole network to its neighbors. This sharing occurs whether or not the network has changed since the last time information was exchanged.

> In distance vector routing, each router periodically shares its knowledge about the entire network with its neighbors.

Sharing Information

To understand how distance vector routing works, examine the internet shown in Figure 21.17. In this example, the clouds represent local area networks (LANs). The number inside each cloud is that LAN's network ID. These LANs can be of any type (Ethernet, Token Ring, FDDI, etc.). The LANs are connected by routers (or gateways), represented by the boxes labeled A, B, C, D, E, and F.

Distance vector routing simplifies the routing process by assuming a cost of one unit for every link. In this way, the efficiency of transmission is a function only of the

Figure 21.17   *Example of an internet*

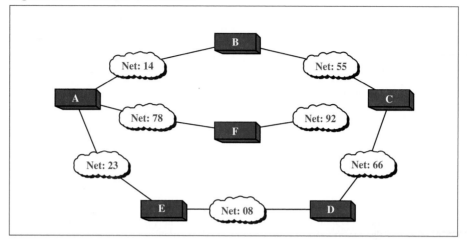

number of links required to reach a destination. In distance vector routing, the cost is based on hop count.

Figure 21.18 shows the first step in the algorithm. The text boxes indicate the relationships of the routers in Figure 21.17 to their neighbors. As you can see, each router sends its information about the internetwork only to its immediate neighbors. How, then, do nonneighboring routers learn about each other and share knowledge?

Figure 21.18   *The concept of distance vector routing*

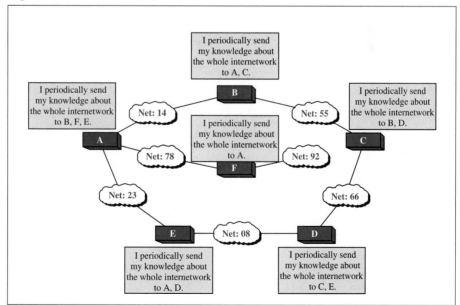

A router sends its knowledge to its neighbors. The neighbors add this knowledge to their own knowledge and send the whole table to their own neighbors. In this way, the first router gets its own information back plus new information about its neighbor's other neighbors. Each of these neighbors adds its knowledge and sends the updated table on to its own neighbors (to neighbors of neighbors of neighbors of the original router), and so on. Eventually, every router knows about every other router in the internetwork.

Routing Table

Now let's examine how each router gets its initial knowledge about the internetwork and how it uses shared information to update that knowledge.

Creating the Table

At start-up, a router's knowledge of the internetwork is sparse. All it knows is that it is connected to some number of LANs (two or more). Because a router is a station on each of those LANs, it also knows the ID of each station. In most systems, a station port ID and a network ID share the same prefix. So a router can discover to which networks it is connected by examining its own logical addresses (remember, a router has as many logical addresses as it has connected ports). This information is enough for it to construct its original **routing table** (see Figure 21.19).

Figure 21.19 *Distance vector routing table*

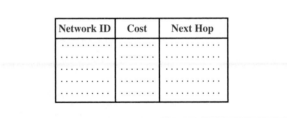

A routing table has columns for at least three types of information (some protocols require more): the network ID, the cost, and the ID of the next router (next hop). The network ID is the final destination of the packet. The cost is the number of hops a packet must make to get there. And the next router is the router to which a packet must be delivered on its way to a particular destination. The table tells a router that it costs *x* to reach network Y via router Z.

The original routing tables for our sample internetwork are shown in Figure 21.20. At this point, the third column is empty because the only destination networks identified are those attached to the current router. No multiple-hop destinations and therefore no next routers have been identified. These basic tables are sent out to neighbors (as shown in the figure by arrows). For example, A sends its routing table to routers B, F, and E; B sends its routing table to routers C and A; and so on.

Figure 21.20 *Routing table distribution in distance vector routing*

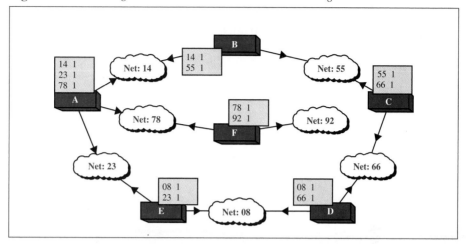

Updating the Table

When A receives a routing table from B, it uses the information to update its own table (see Figure 21.21). It says to itself: "B has sent me a table that shows how its packets can get to networks 55 and 14. I know that B is my neighbor, so my packets can reach B in one hop. So, if I add one hop to all of the costs shown in B's table, the sum will be my cost for reaching those other networks." Therefore, A adjusts the information shown in B's table by adding one to each listed cost. It then combines this table with its own to create a new, more comprehensive table.

Figure 21.21 *Updating routing table for router A*

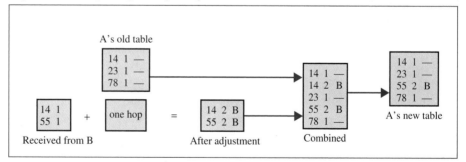

This combined table may contain duplicate data for some network destinations. Router A therefore finds and purges any duplications and keeps whichever version shows the lowest cost. For example, as Figure 21.21 shows, router A can send a packet to network 14 in two ways. The first, which uses no next router, costs one hop. The second, via router B, requires two hops (A to B, then B to 14). The first option has the lower cost; it is kept and the second entry is dropped. This selection process is the reason for the cost column: the cost allows the router to differentiate between various routes to the same destination.

This process continues for all routers. Every router receives information from neighbors and updates its routing table. If there are no more changes, the final tables may look like those shown in Figure 21.22.

Figure 21.22   *Final routing tables*

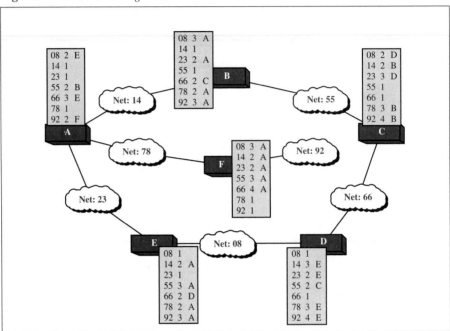

Updating Algorithm

The updating algorithm requires that the router first add one hop to the hop count field for each advertised route. The router should then apply the following rules to each advertised route:

1. If the advertised destination is not in the routing table, the router should add the advertised information to the table.

2. If the advertised destination is in the routing table,

   a. If the next-hop field is the same, the router should replace the entry in the table with the advertised one. Note that even if the advertised hop count is larger, the advertised entry should replace the entry in the table because the new information invalidates the old.

   b. If the next-hop field is not the same,

      i. If the advertised hop count is smaller than the one in the table, the router should replace the entry in the table with the new one.

      ii. If the advertised hop count is not smaller (same or larger), the router should do nothing.

Example 21.1

Figure 21.23 shows an example of updating the routing table.

Figure 21.23   *Example 21.1*

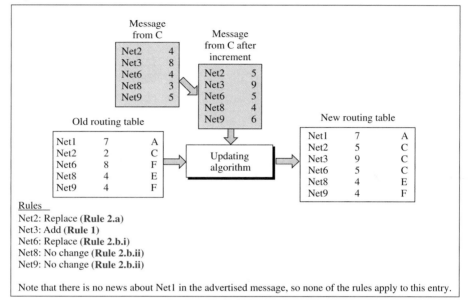

Rules
Net2: Replace (**Rule 2.a**)
Net3: Add (**Rule 1**)
Net6: Replace (**Rule 2.b.i**)
Net8: No change (**Rule 2.b.ii**)
Net9: No change (**Rule 2.b.ii**)

Note that there is no news about Net1 in the advertised message, so none of the rules apply to this entry.

21.8   LINK STATE ROUTING

The keys to understanding **link state routing** are different from those in distance vector routing. In link state routing, each router shares its knowledge of its neighborhood with every other router in the internetwork. The following are true of link state routing:

1. **Knowledge about the neighborhood.** Instead of sending its entire routing table, a router sends information about its neighborhood only.

2. **To all routers.** Each router sends this information to every other router on the internetwork, not just to its neighbors. It does so by a process called **flooding.** Flooding means that a router sends its information to all of its neighbors (through all of its output ports). Each neighbor sends the packet to all of its neighbors, and so on. Every router that receives the packet sends copies to all of its neighbors. Finally, every router (without exception) receives a copy of the same information.

3. **Information sharing when there is a change.** Each router sends out information about the neighbors when there is a change.

> In link state routing, each router shares its knowledge of its neighborhood with all routers in the internetwork.

Information Sharing

Let's examine the link state routing process using the same internetwork we used for distance vector routing (see Figure 21.17).

The first step in link state routing is information sharing (see Figure 21.24). Each router sends its knowledge about its neighborhood to every other router in the internetwork.

Figure 21.24 *Concept of link state routing*

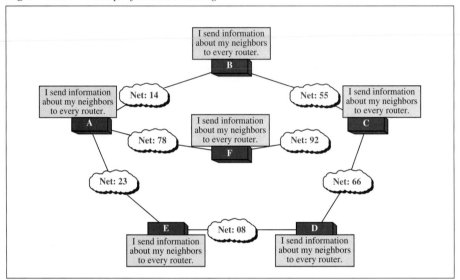

Packet Cost

Both distance vector and link state routing are lowest-cost algorithms. In distance vector routing, cost refers to hop count. In link state routing, cost is a weighted value based on a variety of factors such as security levels, traffic, or the state of the link. The cost from router A to network 14, therefore, might be different from the cost from A to 23.

In determining a route, the cost of a hop is applied to each packet as it leaves a router and enters a network. (Remember, cost is just a weighting and should not be confused with the transmission fees paid by the sender or receiver.) This cost is an outbound cost, meaning that it is applied when a packet leaves the router. Two factors govern how cost is applied to packets in determining a route:

■ Cost is applied only by routers and not by any other stations on a network. Remember, the link from one router to the next is a network, not a point-to-point cable. In many topologies (such as ring and bus), every station on the network examines the header of every packet that passes. If cost was added by every station, instead of by routers alone, it would accumulate unpredictably (the number of stations in a network can change for a variety of reasons, many of them unpredictable).

■ Cost is applied as a packet leaves the router rather than as it enters. Most networks are broadcast networks. When a packet is in the network, every station, including the router, can pick it up. Therefore, we cannot assign any cost to a packet when it goes from a network to a router.

Figure 21.25 shows our sample internet as it appears to the link state routing algorithm. The costs shown are arbitrary; in actual practice they would reflect attributes of each network.

Figure 21.25 *Cost in link state routing*

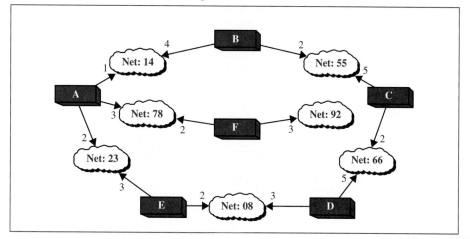

Link State Packet

When a router floods the network with information about its neighborhood, it is said to be advertising. The basis of this advertising is a short packet called a **link state packet (LSP);** see Figure 21.26. An LSP usually contains four fields: the ID of the advertiser, the ID of the destination network, the cost, and the ID of the neighbor router.

Figure 21.26 *Link state packet*

Advertiser	Network	Cost	Neighbor
. . . .	. . . . . .	. . . .	. . . .
. . . .	. . . . . .	. . . .	. . . .
. . . .	. . . . . .	. . . .	. . . .

Getting Information about Neighbors

A router gets its information about its neighbors by periodically sending them a short greeting packet. If the neighbor responds to the greeting as expected, it is assumed to be alive and functioning. If it does not, a change is assumed to have occurred and the sending router then alerts the rest of the network in its next LSP. These greeting packets are small enough that they do not use network resources to any significant degree (unlike the routing tables used by distance vector routing).

Initialization

Imagine that all routers in our sample internetwork come up at the same time. Each router sends a greeting packet to its neighbors to find out the state of each link. It then prepares an LSP based on the results of these greetings and floods the network with it. Figure 21.27 shows this process for router A. The same steps are performed by every router in the network as each comes up.

Figure 21.27   *Flooding of A's LSP*

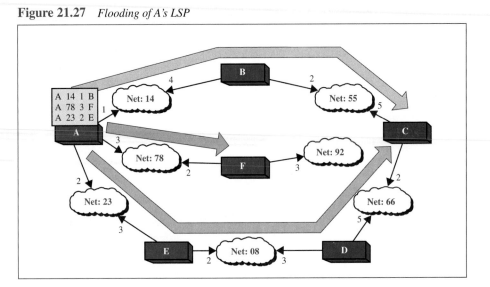

Link State Database

Every router receives every LSP and puts the information into a **link state database.**
Figure 21.28 shows the database for our sample internetwork.

Figure 21.28   *Link state database*

Advertiser	Network	Cost	Neighbor
A	14	1	B
A	78	3	F
A	23	2	E
B	14	4	A
B	55	2	C
C	55	5	B
C	66	2	D
D	66	5	C
D	08	3	E
E	23	3	A
E	08	2	D
F	78	2	A
F	92	3	—

Because every router receives the same LSPs, every router builds the same database. It stores this database on its disk and uses it to calculate its routing table. If a router is added to or deleted from the system, the whole database must be shared for fast updating.

> In link state routing, every router has exactly the same link state database.

The Dijkstra Algorithm

To calculate its routing table, each router applies an algorithm called the **Dijkstra algorithm** to its link state database. The Dijkstra algorithm calculates the shortest path between two points on a network using a graph made up of nodes and arcs. Nodes are of two types: networks and routers. Arcs are the connections between a router and a network (router to network and network to router). Cost is applied only to the arc from router to network. The cost of the arc from network to router is always zero (see Figure 21.29).

Figure 21.29   *Costs in the Dijkstra algorithm*

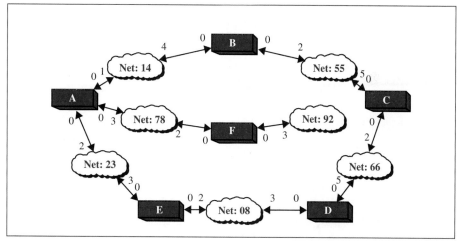

Shortest Path Tree

The Dijkstra algorithm follows four steps to discover what is called the **shortest path tree** (routing table) for each router:

■ The algorithm begins to build the tree by identifying its root. The root of each router's tree is the router itself. The algorithm then attaches all nodes that can be reached from that root—in other words, all of the other neighbor nodes. Nodes and arcs are temporary at this step.

■ The algorithm compares the tree's temporary arcs and identifies the arc with the lowest cumulative cost. This arc and the node to which it connects are now a permanent part of the shortest path tree.

■ The algorithm examines the database and identifies every node that can be reached from its chosen node. These nodes and their arcs are added temporarily to the tree.

■ The last two steps are repeated until every node in the network has become a permanent part of the tree. The only permanent arcs are those that represent the shortest (lowest-cost) route to every node.

Figure 21.30 shows the steps of the Dijkstra algorithm applied by node A of our sample internet. The cost number next to each node represents the cumulative cost from the root node, not the cost of the individual arc. The second and third steps are repeated until four more nodes have become permanent.

Figure 21.30 *Shortest path calculation, part 1*

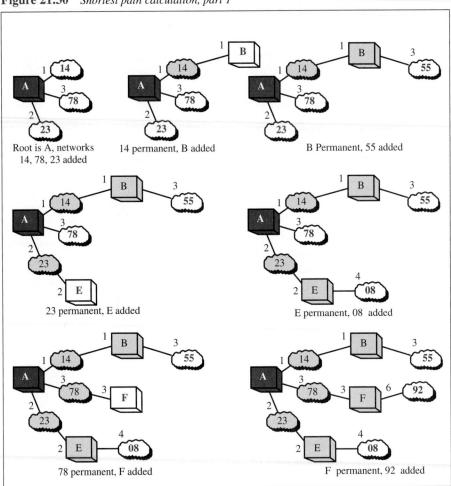

Figure 21.31 shows the completion of the shortest path tree for router A.

Routing Table

Each router now uses the shortest path tree to construct its routing table. Each router uses the same algorithm and the same link state database to calculate its own shortest path tree and routing table: these are different for each router. Figure 21.32 shows the table developed by router A.

> In link state routing, the link state database is the same for all routers, but the shortest path trees and the routing tables are different for each router.

Figure 21.31 *Shortest path calculation, part 2*

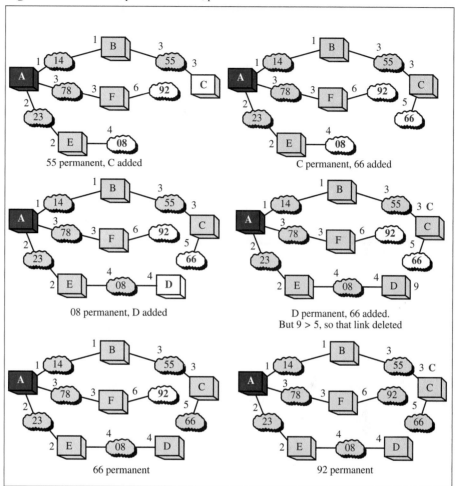

55 permanent, C added

C permanent, 66 added

08 permanent, D added

D permanent, 66 added.
But 9 > 5, so that link deleted

66 permanent

92 permanent

Figure 21.32 *Link state routing table for router A*

Net	Cost	Next router
08	4	E
14	1	
23	2	
55	3	B
66	5	B
78	3	
92	6	F

21.9   KEY TERMS AND CONCEPTS

bridge	packet lifetime
brouter (bridge/router)	protocol converter
cut-through switch	repeater
Dijkstra algorithm	router
distance vector routing	routing
flooding	routing algorithm
gateway	routing switch
hop count	routing table
internetworking devices	shortest path tree
least-cost routing	simple bridge
link state database	source routing
link state packet (LSP)	spanning tree algorithm
link state routing	store-and-forward switch
multiport bridge	time to live (TTL)
multiprotocol router	transparent bridge

21.10   SUMMARY

- Internetworking devices connect networks to create an internet.
- Networking and internetworking devices are divided into four categories: repeaters, bridges, routers, and gateways.
- A repeater is a device that operates in the physical layer of the OSI model. Its purpose is regeneration of the signal.
- Bridges operate in the physical and data link layers of the OSI model. They have access to station addresses and can forward or filter a packet in a network.
- Routers operate in the physical, data link, and network layers of the OSI model. They decide the path a packet should take.

- Gateways operate in all seven layers of the OSI model. They convert one protocol to another and can therefore connect two dissimilar networks.
- There are two methods to calculate the shortest path between two routers: distance vector routing and link state routing.
- In distance vector routing, each router periodically shares its own knowledge about the network with its immediate neighbor routers.
- In distance vector routing, each router has a table with information about networks (ID, cost, and the router to access the particular network).
- In link state routing, each router creates its own link state packet (LSP). Every other router receives this LSP through the flooding process. All routers therefore have the same information; this is compiled into the link state database. From this common database, each router finds its own shortest paths to the other routers by using the Dijkstra algorithm.
- A cost is assigned to a packet when it leaves the router in link state routing.
- In link state routing, every router has its own unique routing table.

21.11   PRACTICE SET

Review Questions

1. How is a repeater different from an amplifier?
2. Describe the functions of the four connecting devices mentioned in this chapter.
3. Rank the connecting and interconnecting devices according to their complexity and give the OSI layers in which they operate.
4. What is the LSP database, and how is it created?
5. Describe some of the factors that need to be considered in connecting networks.
6. Contrast and compare distance vector routing with link state routing.
7. What is a network?
8. What is an internetwork?
9. What do we mean when we say that a bridge can filter traffic? Why is filtering important?
10. What is the difference between a simple bridge and a transparent (learning) bridge?
11. What is the function of a router?
12. How does a router differ from a bridge?
13. In routing, what does the term *shortest* mean?
14. Why is adaptive routing superior to nonadaptive routing?
15. What is the router's role in controlling the packet lifetime?
16. What is the function of a gateway?
17. How does a multiprotocol router differ from a traditional single-protocol router?
18. How does a brouter decide where an incoming packet should go?

19. How does a data-link-layer switch increase the efficiency of a network?
20. What are the two most popular routing algorithms?
21. What are the three main elements of distance vector routing?
22. Describe an initial routing table for a distance vector router.
23. What are the three main elements of link state routing?
24. What algorithm does link state routing use to calculate the routing tables?

Multiple Choice Questions

25. Which of the following is not an internetworking device?
    a. bridge
    b. gateway
    c. router
    d. all of them are
26. Which of the following uses the greatest number of layers in the OSI model?
    a. bridge
    b. repeater
    c. router
    d. gateway
27. A bridge forwards or filters a packet by comparing the information in its address table to the packet's _____.
    a. layer 2 source address
    b. source node's physical address
    c. layer 2 destination address
    d. layer 3 destination address
28. A simple bridge does which of the following?
    a. filters a data packet
    b. forwards a data packet
    c. extends LANs
    d. all of the above
29. Which of the following are bridge types?
    a. simple, complex, transparent
    b. simple, transparent, multiport
    c. simple, complex, multiport
    d. spanning, contract, suspension
30. The shortest path in routing can refer to _____.
    a. the least expensive path
    b. the least distant path
    c. the path with the smallest number of hops
    d. any or a combination of the above

31. Which routing algorithm requires more traffic between routers for setup and updating?
    a. distance vector
    b. link state
    c. Dijkstra
    d. vector link

32. In distance vector routing, each router receives vectors from _____.
    a. every router in the network
    b. every router less than two units away
    c. a table stored by the software
    d. its neighbors only

33. If there are five routers and six networks in an internetwork using link state routing, how many routing tables are there?
    a. 1
    b. 5
    c. 6
    d. 11

34. If there are five routers and six networks in an internetwork, how many link state databases are there?
    a. 1
    b. 5
    c. 6
    d. 11

35. In link state routing, flooding allows changes to be recorded by _____.
    a. all routers
    b. neighbor routers only
    c. some routers
    d. all networks

36. In an LSP, the advertiser is _____.
    a. a router
    b. a network
    c. a data packet
    d. none of the above

37. Which of the following can be handled by a gateway?
    a. protocol conversion
    b. packet resizing
    c. data encapsulation
    d. a and b

38. Gateways function in which OSI layers?
    a. the lower three

    b. the upper four

    c. all seven

    d. all but the physical layer

39. Repeaters function in the _____ layer(s).

    a. physical

    b. data link

    c. network

    d. a and b

40. Bridges function in the _____ layer(s).

    a. physical

    b. data link

    c. network

    d. a and b

41. A repeater takes a weakened or corrupted signal and _____ it.

    a. amplifies

    b. regenerates

    c. resamples

    d. reroutes

42. A bridge has access to the _____ address of a station on the same network.

    a. physical

    b. network

    c. service access point

    d. all of the above

43. What type of bridge must have its address table entered manually?

    a. simple

    b. transparent

    c. multiport

    d. b and c

44. Which type of bridge builds and updates its tables from address information on packets?

    a. simple

    b. transparent

    c. a and b

    d. none of the above

45. Routers function in the _____ layers.

    a. physical and data link

    b. physical, data link, and network

    c. data link and network

    d. network and transport

46. In which routing method do all the routers have a common database?
    a. distance vector
    b. link state
    c. link vector
    d. none of the above
47. A packet traveling from one Token Ring network to another Token Ring network uses the services of a _____. (Each network is an independent network.)
    a. simple bridge
    b. repeater
    c. router
    d. transparent bridge

Exercises

48. Suppose a bridge connects two 802.5 (Token Ring) LANs as shown in Figure 21.33. A station on the left network sends a frame to a station on the right network. The bridge acts as one station in the left network and as another in the right network. Should the bridge, after forwarding a copy to the right network, pretend that it has received the frame by setting the address-recognized and frame-copied bits and then sending the frame to the next station in the left network or should the bridge ignore this issue and behave as though the frame is lost?

Figure 21.33 *Exercise 48*

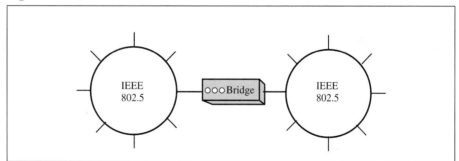

49. If we connect two 802.3 (Ethernet) LANs, do we have the problem mentioned in Exercise 48?
50. If we connect an 802.3 (Ethernet) LAN to an 802.5 (Token Ring) LAN, do we have the problem mentioned in Exercise 48?
51. Suppose a bridge connects an 802.3 (Ethernet) LAN to an 802.5 (Token Ring) LAN as shown in Figure 21.34.

    If the bridge forwards a frame from the Ethernet to the Token Ring, answer the following questions:
    a. Does the bridge have to reformat the frame?
    b. Does the bridge need to recalculate the value of the CRC field?

Figure 21.34 *Exercise 51*

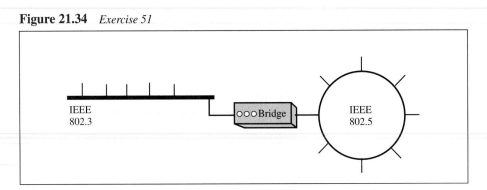

   c. Does the bit order need to be reversed?

   d. How is the priority bit for the Token Ring set?

52. Repeat Exercise 51 for a frame going from the Token Ring to the Ethernet.

53. In Exercise 52, suppose the Token Ring transmits at 16 Mbps and the Ethernet receives at 10 Mbps. The bridge needs a buffer to store information so that it can send at a slower pace. What happens if the buffer overflows?

54. If a bridge sends data from an Ethernet network to a Token Ring network, how is a collision handled by the bridge?

55. If a bridge sends data from a Token Ring network to an Ethernet network how is a collision handled by the bridge?

56. A router using distance vector routing has the following routing table:

        Net2   6   A
        Net3   4   E
        Net4   3   A
        Net6   2   D
        Net7   1   B

The router receives the following packet from router C:

        Net2   4
        Net3   5
        Net4   2
        Net6   3
        Net7   2

Show the updated routing table for the router.

57. A router using distance vector routing has the following routing table:

        Net2   6   A
        Net3   4   E
        Net4   3   A
        Net6   2   C
        Net7   8   B

The router receives the following packet from router C:

        Net2   4
        Net4   3
        Net7   3

Show the updated routing table for the router.

58. A router using distance vector routing has the following routing table:

Net2	6	A
Net3	4	C
Net4	3	A
Net6	2	C
Net7	3	B

    The router receives the following packet from router C:

Net2	4
Net3	5
Net4	4
Net6	3
Net7	2

    Show the updated routing table for the router.

59. Using Figure 21.29, find the shortest path tree and the routing table for router B.

60. Using Figure 21.29, find the shortest path tree and the routing table for router C.

61. Using Figure 21.29, find the shortest path tree and the routing table for router D.

62. Using Figure 21.29, find the shortest path tree and the routing table for router E.

63. Using Figure 21.29, find the shortest path tree and the routing table for router F.

CHAPTER 22

Transport Layer

The **transport layer** is the core of the OSI model. Protocols at this layer oversee the delivery of data from an application program on one device to an application program on another device. More important, they act as a liaison between the upper-layer protocols (session, presentation, and application) and the services provided by the lower layers (network, data link, and physical). The upper layers can use the services of the transport layer to interact with the network without ever having to interact directly with or even be aware of the existence of the lower layers. To make this separation possible, the transport layer itself is independent of the physical network.

To better understand the role of the transport layer, it is helpful to visualize an internet made up of a variety of different physical networks such as the LANs, MANs, and WANs shown in Figure 22.1. These networks are connected to enable the transport of data from a computer on one network to a computer on another network. As a transmission moves from network to network, the data may be encapsulated in different types and lengths of packets. One network's network or data link functions may chop it into smaller segments to fit a more restricted packet or frame size, while another network's peer functions may link several segments together in a single large packet. The data may even share a frame with other, nonrelated data segments. No matter what transformations they must go through on the way, however, the data must arrive at their destination in their original form.

Figure 22.1 *An internetwork*

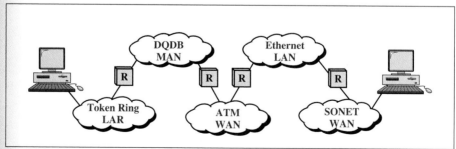

The upper-layer protocols are kept unaware of the intricacy of the physical networks, so that only one set of upper-layer software has to be developed. To the upper layers, the individual physical networks are a simple homogeneous cloud that somehow takes data and delivers it to its destination safe and sound. For example, even if an Ethernet in the internet is replaced by a Token Ring, the upper layers remain unaware of it. To them, the internet is a single and essentially unchanging network. The transport layer provides this transparency.

Examples of transport layer protocols are Ttransmission Control Protocol (TCP) and User Datagram Protocol (UDP), both of which will be discussed in Chapter 24.

22.1   DUTIES OF THE TRANSPORT LAYER

Transport layer services are implemented by a transport protocol used between two transport entities (see Figure 22.2).

Figure 22.2   *Transport layer concept*

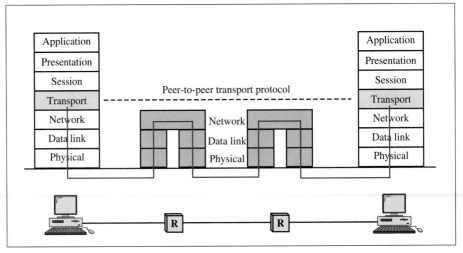

The services provided are similar to those of the data link layer. The data link layer, however, is designed to provide its services within a single network, while the transport layer provides these services across an internetwork made of many networks. The data link layer controls the physical layer, while the transport layer controls all three of the lower layers (see Figure 22.3).

The services provided by transport layer protocols can be divided into five broad categories: end-to-end delivery, addressing, reliable delivery, flow control, and multiplexing (see Figure 22.4).

End-to-End Delivery

The network layer oversees the end-to-end delivery of individual packets but does not see any relationship between those packets, even those belonging to a single message.

Figure 22.3   *Transport layer compared with data link layer*

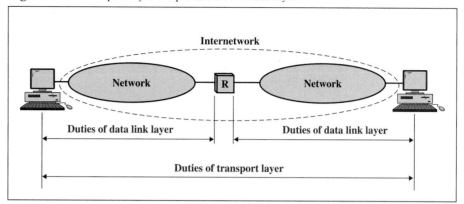

Figure 22.4   *Transport layer duties*

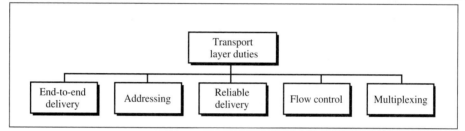

It treats each as an independent entity. The transport layer, on the other hand, makes sure that the entire message (not just a single packet) arrives intact. Thus, it oversees the **end-to-end (source-to-destination) delivery** of an entire **message.**

Addressing

The transport layer interacts with the functions of the session layer. However, many protocols (or protocol stacks, meaning groups of protocols that interact at different levels) combine session, presentation, and application level protocols into a single package, called an application. In these cases, delivery to the session layer functions is, in effect, delivery to the application. So communication occurs not just from end machine to end machine but from end application to end application. Data generated by an application on one machine must be received not just by the other machine but by the correct application on that other machine.

In most cases, therefore, we end up with communication between many-to-many entities, called **service access points** (see Figure 22.5). But how does the network identify which service access point on one host is communicating with which service access point on the other host?

To ensure accurate delivery from service access point to service access point, we need another level of addressing in addition to those at the data link and network levels. Data link level protocols need to know which two computers within a network are communicating. Network level protocols need to know which two computers within an

Figure 22.5 *Service access points*

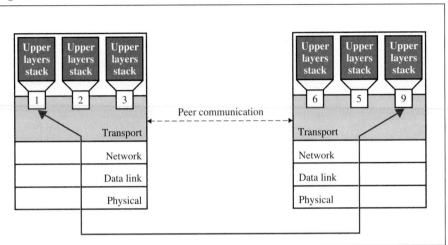

internet are communicating. But at the transport level, the protocol needs to know which upper-layer protocols are communicating.

Reliable Delivery

At the transport layer, **reliable delivery** has four aspects: error control, sequence control, loss control, and duplication control (see Figure 22.6).

Figure 22.6 *Aspects of reliable delivery*

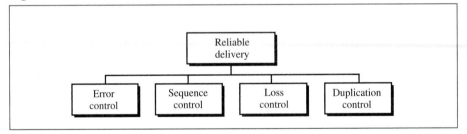

Error Control

When transferring data, the primary goal of reliability is **error control.** As we said earlier, data must be delivered to their destination exactly as they originated from the source. The realities of physical data transport are that, while 100 percent error-free delivery is probably impossible, transport layer protocols are designed to come as close as possible.

Mechanisms for error handling at this layer are based on error detection and retransmission with the error handling usually performed using algorithms implemented in software, such as checksum (see Chapter 9, "Error Detection and Correction").

But if we already have error handling at the data link layer, why do we need it at the transport layer? Data link layer functions guarantee error-free delivery node-to-node for each link. However, node-to-node reliability does not ensure end-to-end reliability. Figure 22.7 shows a situation where an error is introduced that cannot be caught by data link layer error controls.

Figure 22.7 *Transport and data link error control*

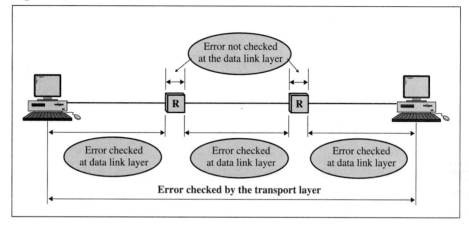

In Figure 22.7, the data link layer ensures that packets passing between each network are error free. But an error is introduced as the packet is processed inside one of the routers. This error will not be caught by the data link functions of the next link because those functions just check to see that no errors have been introduced between the beginning and end of that link. The transport layer must therefore do its own checking end-to-end to make sure that the packet has arrived as intended by the source.

Sequence Control

The second aspect of reliability implemented at the transport layer is **sequence control.** On the sending end, the transport layer is responsible for ensuring that data units received from the upper layers are usable by the lower layers. On the receiving end, it is responsible for ensuring that the various pieces of a transmission are correctly reassembled.

Segmentation and Concatenation   When the size of the data unit received from the upper layer is too long for the network layer datagram or data link layer frame to handle, the transport protocol divides it into smaller, usable blocks. The dividing process is called **segmentation.** When, on the other hand, the size of the data units belonging to a single session are so small that several can fit together into a single datagram or frame, the transport protocol combines them into a single data unit. The combining process is called **concatenation.**

Sequence Numbers   Most transport layer services add a **sequence number** at the end of each segment. If a longer data unit has been segmented, the numbers indicate the order for reassembly. If several shorter units have been concatenated, the numbers indicate the end of each subunit and allow them to be separated accurately at the destination. In addition, each segment carries a field that indicates whether it is the final segment of a transmission or a middle segment with more still to come.

Imagine a situation in which a bank customer sends a message to the bank instructing it to first transfer $5000 from a checking account to a savings account and then to transfer the balance of the checking account to the checking account of another customer. Imagine what would happen if the two parts of the message were received out of order (see Figure 22.8).

Figure 22.8   *Sequence control*

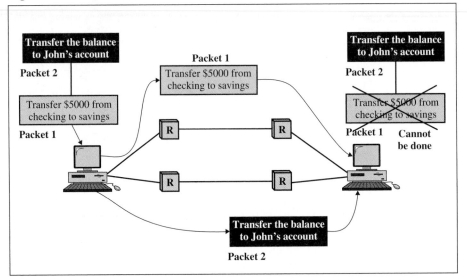

From the sender's and receiver's points of view, it is not important in what order pieces of a transmission travel. What is important is that they are properly reassembled at the destination—just as, for example, you don't care how the pieces of your car got to the assembly plant but you do want them put together properly by the time the car is delivered to you.

Loss Control

The third aspect of reliability covered by the transport layer is **loss control.** The transport layer ensures that all pieces of a transmission arrive at the destination, not just some of them. When data have been segmented for delivery, some segments may be lost in transit (see Figure 22.9). Sequence numbers allow the receiver's transport layer protocol to identify any missing segments and request redelivery.

Duplication Control

The fourth aspect of reliability covered by the transport layer is **duplication control.** Transport layer functions must guarantee that no pieces of data arrive at the receiving system duplicated. Just as they allow identification of lost packets, sequence numbers allow the receiver to identify and discard duplicate segments.

Duplication may seem like a trivial problem, but it can have major consequences. Imagine that a bank customer sends a message instructing the bank to

Figure 22.9   *Loss control*

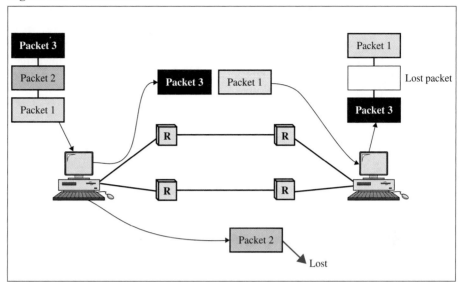

transfer $5000 from his account to John's account. What happens if this message is duplicated? See Figure 22.10.

Figure 22.10   *Duplication control*

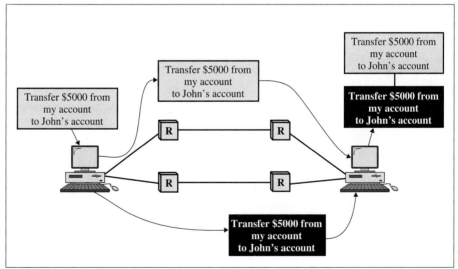

Flow Control

Like the data link layer, the transport layer is responsible for flow control. However, flow control at this layer is performed end-to-end rather than across a single link. Transport layer flow control also uses a sliding window protocol. However, the window at the transport layer can vary in size to accommodate buffer occupancy.

With a varying-size window, the actual amount of data the window can hold is negotiable. In most cases, control of window size is the province of the receiver. The receiver, in its acknowledgment packet, can specify that the size of the window be increased (or decreased, but most protocols do not allow decreases in size). In most cases, sliding windows at the transport layer are based on the number of bytes that the receiver can accommodate rather than the number of frames. A pair of communicating entities will use a buffer of *x* bytes that may accommodate *y* frames.

> A sliding window is used to make data transmission more efficient as well as to control the flow of data so that the receiver does not become overwhelmed. Sliding windows used at the transport layer are usually byte oriented rather than frame oriented.

Some points about sliding windows at the transport layer are as follows:

- The sender does not have to send a full window's worth of data.
- An acknowledgment can expand the size of the window based on the sequence number of the acknowledged data segment.
- The size of the window can be increased or decreased by the receiver.
- The receiver can send an acknowledgment at anytime.

To accommodate the variability in size, transport layer sliding windows use three pointers (which act as virtual walls) to identify the buffer (see Figure 22.11). The left wall moves to the right when acknowledgments are received. The middle wall moves to the right as data are sent. The right wall moves to the right or left to fix the size of the window. If acknowledgments are received and the size of the window is not changed, this third wall moves to the right to keep the size of the window constant (because the left wall has moved to the right). For example, if five bytes are acknowledged and the size of the window is not changed, then the left wall has moved to the right five bytes,

Figure 22.11   *Sliding window*

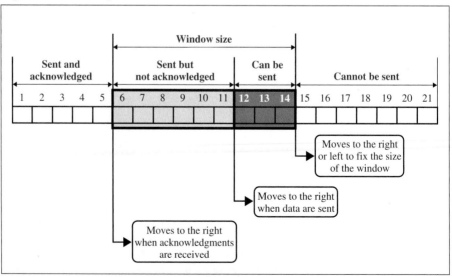

shrinking the window, so the right wall must move to the right five bytes for the size of the window to remain constant. If 5 bytes are acknowledged but the receiver also increases the size of the window by 10 bytes, the right wall must move 15 bytes to the right to accommodate the new size.

Multiplexing

To improve transmission efficiency, the transport layer has the option of multiplexing. Multiplexing at this layer occurs two ways: upward, meaning that multiple transport-layer connections use the same network connection, or downward, meaning that one transport-layer connection uses multiple network connections (see Figure 22.12).

Figure 22.12   *Multiplexing*

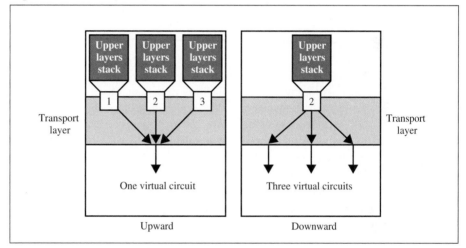

Upward

The transport layer uses virtual circuits based on the services of the lower three layers. Normally, the underlying networks charge for each virtual circuit connection. To make more cost-effective use of an established circuit, the transport layer can send several transmissions bound for the same destination along the same path by **upward multiplexing.** This means if the underlying network protocol has a high throughput, for example in the range of 1 Gbps, and the user can create data only in the range of Mbps, then several users can share one network connection.

Downward

Downward multiplexing allows the transport layer to split a single connection among several different paths to improve throughput (speed of delivery). This option is useful when the underlying networks have low or slow capacity. For example, some network layer protocols have restrictions on the sequence numbers that can be handled. X.25 uses a three-bit numbering code, so sequence numbers are restricted to the range of 0 to 7 (only eight packets may be sent before acknowledgment is required). In this case, throughput can be unacceptably low. To counteract this problem, the transport layer can opt to use more than one virtual circuit at the network layer to improve throughput. By sending several data segments at once, delivery is faster (see Figure 22.12).

22.2 CONNECTION

End-to-end delivery can be accomplished in either of two modes: connection-oriented or connectionless. Of these two, the connection-oriented mode is the more commonly used. A connection-oriented protocol establishes a virtual circuit or pathway through the internet between the sender and receiver. All of the packets belonging to a message are then sent over this same path. Using a single pathway for the entire message facilitates the acknowledgment process and retransmission of damaged or lost frames. **Connection-oriented services,** therefore, are generally considered reliable.

Connection-oriented transmission has three stages: connection establishment, data transfer, and connection termination.

Connection Establishment

Before either communicating device can send data to the other, the initiating device must first determine the availability of the other to exchange data and a pathway must be found through the network by which the data can be sent. This step is called **connection establishment** (see Figure 22.13). Connection establishment requires three actions in what is called a **three-way handshake:**

■ The computer requesting the connection sends a **connection request** packet to the intended receiver.

■ The responding computer returns a confirmation packet to the requesting computer.

■ The requesting computer returns a packet acknowledging the confirmation.

Figure 22.13 *Connection establishment*

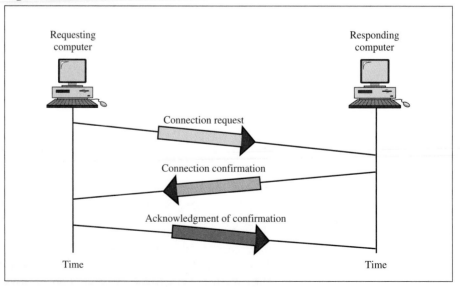

Connection Termination

Once all of the data have been transferred, the connection must be terminated (see Figure 22.14).

Figure 22.14   *Connection termination*

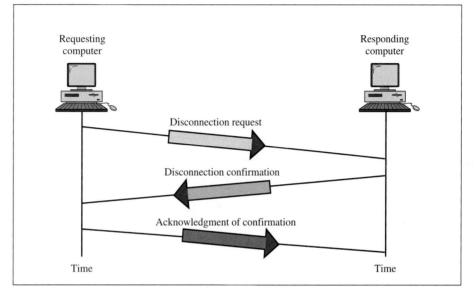

Connection termination also requires a three-way handshake:

■ The requesting computer sends a disconnection request packet.

■ The responding computer confirms the disconnection request.

■ The requesting computer acknowledges the confirmation.

22.3   THE OSI TRANSPORT PROTOCOL

As an example, let's examine the transport layer in the OSI model.

Transport Classes

To avoid redundant services, the OSI model defines five types of **transport classes:**

■ **TP0.** Simple class.

■ **TP1.** Basic error recovery class.

■ **TP2.** Multiplexing class.

■ **TP3.** Error recovery and multiplexing class.

■ **TP4.** Error detection and recovery class.

Which class is used depends on the type of service required by the upper layers. The transport layer tries to match these requests to the available networking services:

■ TP0 and TP2 are used with perfect network layers. A perfect network layer is one in which the number of packets that are lost or damaged is almost zero.

■ TP1 and TP3 are used with residual-error network layers. A residual-error network layer is one in which some percentage of errors are never corrected.

■ TP4 is used with unreliable network layers. TP4 provides fully reliable, full-duplex, connection-oriented services similar to TCP in the TCP/IP protocol suite.

Transport Protocol Data Unit (TPDU)

The format of a **transport protocol data unit (TPDU)** is shown in Figure 22.15. Each TPDU consists of four general fields: length, fixed parameters, variable parameters, and data.

Figure 22.15 *TPDU*

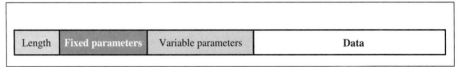

| Length | Fixed parameters | Variable parameters | Data |

Length   The length field occupies the first byte and indicates the total number of bytes (excluding the length field itself) in the TPDU.

Fixed Parameters   The fixed parameters field contains parameters, or control fields, that are commonly present in all transport layer packets. It consists of five parts: code, source reference, destination reference, sequence number, and credit allocation.

■ **Code.** The code identifies the type of the data unit; for example, CR for connection request or DT for data. The following codes are recognized by the ISO and ITU-T:

> CR: Connection request
> CC: Connection confirm
> DR: Disconnect request
> DC: Disconnect confirm
> DT: Data
> ED: Expedited data
> AK: Data acknowledge
> EA: Expedited data acknowledge
> RJ: Reject
> ER: Error

■ **Source and destination reference.** The source and destination reference fields contain the addresses of the original sender and the ultimate destination of the packet.

■ **Sequence number.** As a transmission is divided into smaller packets for transport, each segment is given a number that identifies its place in the sequence. Sequence numbers are used for acknowledgment, flow control, and reordering of packets at the destination.

■ **Credit allocation. Credit allocation** enables a receiving station to tell the sender how many more data units may be sent before the sender must wait for an acknowledgment. It allows the receiver to supersede existing sliding window or flow control restrictions and to change the allocation at any time based on its processing needs. Credit allocation separates flow control from acknowledgments and means that the sender and receiver need not have the same sliding window size. For example, a remote station may return an AK 3 and a credit 7. This combination tells the sender that all units up to 2 have been received successfully, that the next unit expected is number 3, and that seven more units may be sent before the sender must wait for another acknowledgment.

Variable Parameters   The variable parameters section of a TPDU contains parameters that occur infrequently. These control codes are used mostly for management (e.g., testing the reliability of a router).

Data   The data section of a TPDU may contain regular data or expedited data coming from the upper layers. Expedited data consist of a high-priority message that must be handled out of sequence. An urgent request (such as an interrupt command to a remote log-in) can supersede the incoming queue of the receiver and be processed ahead of packets that have been received before it.

Connection-Oriented and Connectionless Services

The OSI model supports both connection-oriented and connectionless transport services. Of these two, the connection-oriented mode is the more commonly used.

Connection-Oriented Transport Services

Connection-oriented transport services (COTS) first create a virtual circuit between two remote entities. To this end, COTS makes four different kinds of services available to the upper layers: T-CONNECT, T-DATA, T-EXPEDITED-DATA, and T-DISCONNECT (T stands for transfer). The relationship of these services to the upper and lower layers of the OSI model is illustrated in Figure 22.16.

Figure 22.16   *Transport layer protocols in the OSI model*

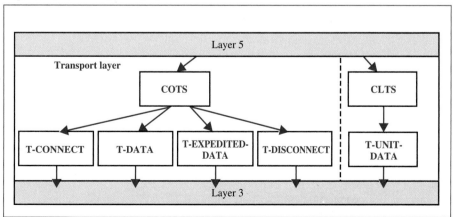

The upper-layer user of COTS first uses the T-CONNECT service to set up a full-duplex transport connection with a peer function on a remote device. During the establishment of the transport connection, the users can negotiate the **quality of services (QoS)** desired and decide between normal and expedited data transfer modes.

Once the connection has been established, the two peers can transfer data using the services of either T-DATA or T-EXPEDITED-DATA. T-DATA provides nonconfirmed service but is still reliable. Successfully delivered packets are not acknowledged. If a failure occurs, however, the transport service provider notifies the sender of the failure so that corrections can be made. The amount of user data that can be carried by a T-DATA TPDU is restricted to a size negotiated by the two parties making the exchange.

If the T-EXPEDITED-DATA service is used, the amount of expedited data that can be carried is limited (by common agreement) to 16 octets (bytes).

Either the user or the transport service provider may employ the T-DISCONNECT service to terminate a transport connection at any time during the data transfer. The T-DISCONNECT is destructive. Any data still in transit when it is invoked may be lost. T-DISCONNECT can also be used by the transport service provider or the called user to reject a connection request.

Connectionless Transport Services

Connectionless transport services (CLTS) provide only one kind of service to the upper layers: T-UNIT-DATA.

T-UNIT-DATA provides a single freestanding data unit for all transmissions. Each unit contains all of the protocol control information necessary for delivery but contains no provision for sequencing or flow control.

22.4   KEY TERMS AND CONCEPTS

concatenation	credit allocation
connection establishment	downward multiplexing
connection-oriented service	duplication control
connection-oriented transmission	end-to-end message delivery
connection-oriented transport service (COTS)	error control
connection request	loss control
connection termination	quality of service (QoS)
connectionless transport service (CLTS)	reliable delivery

segmentation   three-way handshake

sequence control   transport class

sequence number   transport layer

service access point   transport protocol data unit (TPDU)

source-to-destination delivery   upward multiplexing

22.5   SUMMARY

- The transport layer, by hiding all of the manipulations necessary to move a message from source to destination, makes data transmission transparent to the upper layers.
- The data link and transport layers perform many of the same duties. The data link layer functions in a single network, while the transport layer operates across an internet.
- The transport layer needs ports or service access points.
- Reliable delivery requires error control, sequence control, loss control, and duplication control.
- Flow control at the transport level is handled by a three-walled sliding window.
- Multiplexing can be downward or upward in the transport layer.
- Connection establishment and termination are both accomplished through three-way handshakes.
- The transport layer is responsible for end-to-end delivery, segmentation, and concatenation.
- The transport layer supports two service types:
  a. Connection-oriented transport services (COTS).
  b. Connectionless transport services (CLTS).
- The transport protocol data unit (TPDU) format consists of four fields:
  a. Length.
  b. Fixed parameters.
  c. Variable parameters.
  d. Data.
- The five types of transport classes are based on the reliability of the lower layers. Class TP4 is similar to TCP in the TCP/IP suite.

22.6   PRACTICE SET

Review Questions

1. Many of the duties of the transport layer (e.g., flow control and reliable delivery) are also handled by the data link layer. Is this a duplication of effort? Why or why not?
2. Compare the sliding window protocol in the data link layer versus that in the transport layer.
3. What are the three phases a connection-oriented transport service goes through?
4. What are the two transport services defined by the OSI model?
5. Discuss the relationship between the transport layer and the upper OSI layers.
6. Discuss the relationship between the transport layer and the lower OSI layers.
7. What are the five main categories of transport layer services?
8. What is the difference between end-to-end delivery in the transport layer and end-to-end delivery in the network layer?
9. Why is a service access point necessary?
10. What factors determine the reliability of a delivery?
11. Why is there a need for sequence control?
12. When is upward multiplexing used?
13. When is downward multiplexing used?
14. What are the five transport classes defined by the OSI model?
15. What are the fields in the TPDU?
16. Define the concept of credit allocation in the TPDU.

Multiple Choice Questions

17. The transport layer performs the same types of functions as the _____ layer.
    a. session
    b. network
    c. data link
    d. physical
18. End-to-end delivery is the movement of a message from _____.
    a. one station to the next station
    b. one network to the next network
    c. source to destination
    d. none of the above
19. What type of addressing is specifically used by the transport layer?
    a. station addresses
    b. network addresses

    c. application program port addresses

    d. dialog addresses

20. Error control is needed at the transport layer because of potential errors occurring
    _____.

    a. from transmission line noise

    b. in routers

    c. from out-of-sequence delivery

    d. from packet losses

21. Making sure that data segments arrive in the correct order is _____ control.

    a. error

    b. sequence

    c. loss

    d. duplication

22. Making sure that all the data packets of a message are delivered to the destination
    is _____ control.

    a. error

    b. sequence

    c. loss

    d. duplication

23. If two identical data packets arrive at a destination, then _____ control is not
    functioning.

    a. error

    b. sequence

    c. loss

    d. duplication

24. Which transport class should be used with a perfect network layer?

    a. TP0 and TP2

    b. TP1 and TP3

    c. TP0, TP1, and TP3

    d. TP0, TP1, TP2, TP3, and TP4

25. Which transport class should be used with a residual-error network layer?

    a. TP0 and TP2

    b. TP1 and TP3

    c. TP1, TP3, and TP4

    d. TP0, TP1, TP2, TP3, and TP4

26. In _____ services, connections must be established and terminated.

    a. connectionless

    b. connection-oriented

   c. segmentation

   d. none of the above

27. In _____ services, no connection establishment is needed.

   a. connectionless

   b. connection-oriented

   c. segmentation

   d. none of the above

28. In the transport layer, _____ is a connectionless service.

   a. CONS

   b. CLNS

   c. COTS

   d. CLTS

29. A virtual circuit is associated with a _____ service.

   a. connectionless

   b. connection-oriented

   c. segmentation

   d. none of the above

30. In _____ services, packets of a single transmission travel from source to destination via different paths.

   a. connectionless

   b. connection-oriented

   c. segmentation

   d. none of the above

Exercises

31. The left edge of a sliding window is at the beginning of byte 1201. The size of the window is 2000 bytes. If 800 bytes have been sent and no acknowledgment received, show the positions of the three walls (see Figure 22.17)

Figure 22.17 *Exercises 31–37*

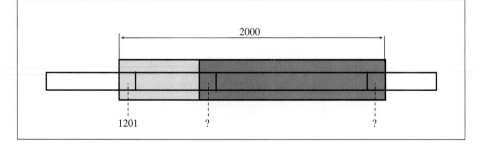

32. In Figure 22.17, if 800 bytes are sent, byte 1701 is acknowledged, and the size of the window is increased to 2200, what would be the position of the walls?

33. In Figure 22.17, if 700 bytes are sent, byte 1601 is acknowledged, and the size of the window is decreased to 800, what would be the position of the walls?
34. In Figure 22.17, if 2000 bytes are sent and nothing acknowledged, what would be the position of the walls?
35. In Figure 22.17, when will the left and the middle walls overlap?
36. In Figure 22.17, when will the right and the middle walls overlap?
37. In Figure 22.17, when will the three walls overlap?

CHAPTER 23

Upper
OSI Layers

The upper layers of the OSI model—the session layer, the presentation layer, and the application layer—are considered the user layers. They are implemented primarily in software. In most protocols (such as TCP/IP and Novell), the services of these layers are implemented by a single layer called the **application layer.** For this reason, we cover them together in one chapter.

23.1 SESSION LAYER

The fifth layer of the OSI model is the session layer. The session layer establishes, maintains, and synchronizes **dialogs** between communicating upper layers (communication may be between either users or applications). The session layer also handles upper-level problems such as inadequate disk space or lack of paper for the printer. Although the session layer is described as a user layer, it is often implemented within the operating system as system software.

The concept behind the session layer is illustrated in Figure 23.1. The session layer manages the back-and-forth nature of the exchange. Imagine that we need a system to

Figure 23.1 *Session layer dialog*

Hello Hilda? I need a favor. Over.
Hi Enrique. What can I do for you? Over.
I need a copy of the last project. Over.
Sure. Over.

manage interactions between application programs. Within this system, user application programs must be able to communicate and exchange files or transactions with each other. How do we coordinate the activities of each user application program? Do we allow each application program to transfer a file or transaction at any time? Do we provide periodic checkpoints to allow the application programs to back up their work and recover from processing? Should the process be full- or half-duplex? If half-duplex, how do we control the direction of flow? These and other issues are the responsibilities of the session layer.

Services of the session layer:

■   To coordinate connection and disconnection of dialogs between applications.
■   To provide synchronization points for data exchange.
■   To coordinate who sends when.
■   To ensure that the data exchange is complete before the session closes (a graceful close).

Session and Transport Interaction

The concept of a graceful close illustrates an important difference between the behavior of the transport layer and that of the session layer. The transport layer can make an abrupt disconnection. The session layer, on the other hand, has an obligation to the user and cannot disconnect until the session can be brought to a graceful conclusion.

Imagine you are trying to get cash from the automated teller machine (ATM) at your bank. You are involved in a session made up of many different half-duplex information exchanges. First, you insert your ATM card into the machine and, in response to prompts, enter your PIN, type of the transaction, and the amount of cash that you want. Then you wait while the computer checks the validity of your card, PIN, and balance. Once all of these factors have been verified, the computer updates your balance by the amount you are withdrawing and sends a command to the ATM to give you your cash.

But assume that, just then, something goes wrong with the network and the message to give you your money does not reach the machine. Your account has been debited by the amount of your intended withdrawal, but you do not receive any cash. Fortunately, the session layer is handling the problem behind the scenes. First of all, it does not allow the transaction to close until all of the steps have been completed. It must update the account, but it leaves the update pending until it receives a confirmation from the ATM that the money has been delivered. The transport layer quits after the delivery of the message to the machine to give you your money. The session layer cannot finish until it receives confirmation that the transaction has actually been completed. It can continue the session with another transport layer connection.

The transport layer is allowed to do "some" of the job; but the session layer must do "all or none."

Session-to-Transport Communication

For any of these services to work, the session layer must communicate with the transport layer. This communication can be of three types: one-to-one, many-to-one, and one-to-many. Figure 23.2 illustrates each type.

Figure 23.2   *Session-to-transport layer communication*

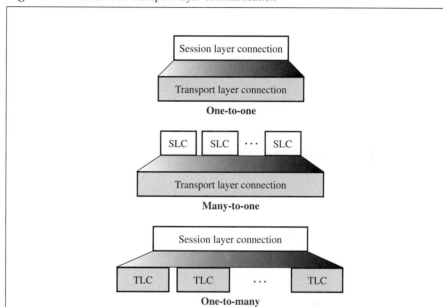

In a one-to-one communication, there is one session layer connection for each transport layer connection. In a many-to-one communication, multiple session layer connections share the services of one transport layer connection. In a one-to-many communication, one session layer connection needs many transport layer connections to handle the task.

Synchronization Points

As we have seen, the transport layer is responsible for delivering a transmission with complete reliability. But what if an error is introduced after the transmission has been delivered to the destination process but before it can be used (due, perhaps, to a bug in the processing software)? The session layer provides a mechanism, called **synchronization points,** for recovering data that have been delivered but mishandled.

To control the flow of information and allow recovery from software or operator errors, the session layer allows reference points to be introduced into the data. Depending on the type of service being used, these points may call for user acknowledgment or just may provide a go-back facility for data recovery.

Two types of synchronization points may be used: major and minor. **Major synchronization points** divide an exchange into a series of dialogs. Generally, each major synchronization point must be acknowledged before the session can continue. If an error occurs, data can be recovered only up to the last major point. A session layer activity can be a single dialog or several dialogs separated by major synchronization points.

Minor synchronization points are inserted into the middle of dialogs and may or may not require confirmation, depending on the application. They are primarily security blankets. If an error occurs, the control can go back one or more minor synchronization points within a dialog to recover the data. The two types of synchronization points are shown in Figure 23.3.

> The major synchronization points must be confirmed. If there is an error, the control can go back only to the last major synchronization point. The minor synchronization points do not need to be confirmed; they are only security blankets. If there is an error, the control can go back one or more minor synchronization points and resend the data.

Figure 23.3 *Synchronization points*

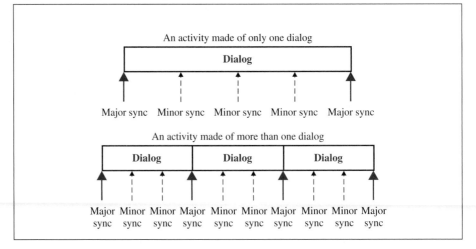

Imagine that a consumer database is being transferred from one location to another. The transfer takes three hours. Assume that after one hour and 20 minutes, a failure occurs and communication is interrupted. When communication resumes, the system can go back to the last major synchronization point and resend the data from that point.

Session Protocol Data Unit

The session layer supports 36 different types of **session protocol data units (SPDUs).** Fortunately, all of them follow the same general format (see Figure 23.4). The fields are as follows:

- **SPDU identifier (SI).** The SPDU identifier indicates the type of the data unit.
- **Length indicator (LI).** The length indicator gives the length of the SPDU parameter field.

■ **Parameter group information/parameter information (PGI/PI).** The parameter group information/parameter information field includes control information and quality of service specifications.

Figure 23.4 *SPDU*

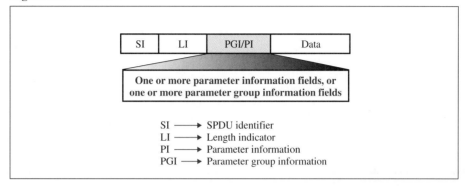

| SI | LI | PGI/PI | Data |

One or more parameter information fields, or one or more parameter group information fields

SI ⟶ SPDU identifier
LI ⟶ Length indicator
PI ⟶ Parameter information
PGI ⟶ Parameter group information

23.2 PRESENTATION LAYER

The sixth layer in the OSI model is the presentation layer. The functions performed in this layer include translation, encryption/decryption, authentication, and **compression** (see Figure 23.5).

Figure 23.5 *Presentation layer functions*

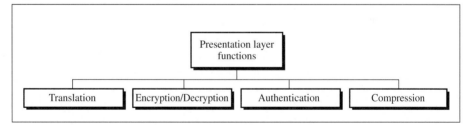

Translation

The internal representation of a piece of information might vary enormously from one machine to the other. For example, one computer may store a character string in the form of ASCII code (see Appendix A), while another may store the same character string in the form of EBCDIC code. If a piece of information is sent by one computer in ASCII format and is interpreted by the other computer in EBCDIC, the result will be gibberish. The presentation layer is responsible for solving this problem.

The problem can be solved either directly or indirectly. In the direct **translation** method (we assume simplex transmission; the half-duplex and full-duplex cases are almost the same), ASCII code is translated into EBCDIC code at the receiver. In the indirect method, ASCII code is translated to a standard format at the sender and translated into EBCDIC at the receiver (see Figure 23.6).

Figure 23.6 *Direct and indirect methods of translation*

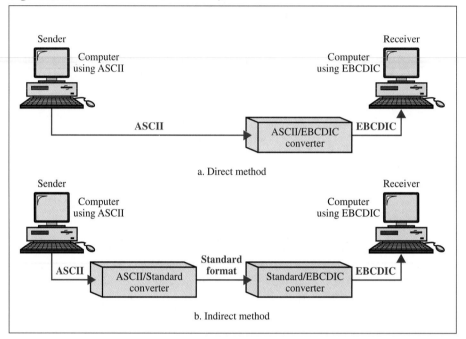

The direct method is not acceptable in most cases. If a computer is communicating with several other computers, it may need several conversion tables.

The indirect method is recommended by the OSI. The recommended model is called **abstract syntax notation 1 (ASN.1).** This model not only takes care of the translation problem but also handles other formatting problems such as the diverse nature of data (text, program, etc.) and the diversity in data storage (one computer may store data in one format, another computer in another format).

ASN.1 provides a mechanism for defining data types (such as integer, real, bits, strings, etc.) in an implementation-independent format. ASN.1 uses the concept of objects. An object is defined as an information entity with type and value that can be easily translated from one representation to another.

As an analogy, imagine that you want to order a glass of club soda in a country whose language has no word for club soda. Instead of continuing to order club soda and getting no response, you identify the physical elements of club soda and look up the words *carbonated* and *water* in your dictionary. Club soda is a culturally specific concept. Carbonated water, however, is an abstract description that can be translated into any number of languages. ASN.1 is the OSI equivalent to defining club soda by its component elements, carbonation and water.

Encryption/Decryption

To carry sensitive information, such as military or financial data, a system must be able to assure privacy. Microwave, satellite, and other wireless media, however, cannot be protected from the unauthorized reception (or interception) of transmissions. Even cable systems cannot always prevent unauthorized access. Cables pass through out-of-the-way areas (such as basements) that provide opportunities for malicious access to the cable and illegal reception of information.

It is unlikely that any system can completely prevent unauthorized access to transmission media. A more practical way to protect information is to alter it so that only an authorized receiver can understand it. Data tampering is not a new issue, nor is it unique to the computer era. In fact, efforts to make information unreadable by unauthorized receivers date from Julius Caesar (100–44 B.C.). The method used today is called the encryption and decryption of information. **Encryption** means that the sender transforms the original information to another form and sends the resulting unintelligible message out over the network. **Decryption** reverses the encryption process in order to transform the message back to its original form.

Figure 23.7 shows the basic encryption/decryption process. The sender uses an encryption algorithm and a key to transform the **plaintext** (as the original message is called) into a **ciphertext** (as the encrypted message is called). The receiver uses a decryption algorithm and a key to transform the ciphertext back to the original plaintext.

Figure 23.7 *Concept of encryption and decryption*

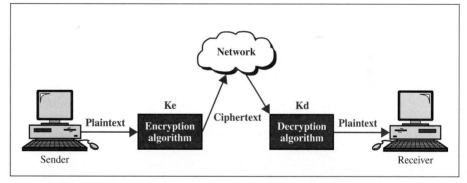

Encryption and decryption methods fall into two categories: conventional and public key (see Figure 23.8).

Figure 23.8 *Encryption/decryption methods*

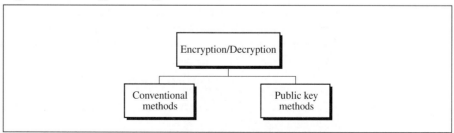

Conventional Methods

In **conventional encryption** methods, the encryption key (Ke) and the decryption key (Kd) are the same and secret. We can roughly divide conventional methods into two categories: character-level encryption and bit-level encryption.

Character-Level Encryption   In this method, encryption is done at the character level. There are two general methods for **character-level encryption:** *substitutional* and *transpositional*.

■ **Substitutional.** The simplest form of character-level encryption is substitutional ciphering. In *monoalphabetic substitution,* sometimes called the Caesar Cipher, each character is replaced by another character in the set. The **monoalphabetic encryption** algorithm simply adds a number to the ASCII code of the character; the decryption algorithm simply subtracts the same number from the ASCII code. Ke and Kd are the same and define the added or subtracted value. Figure 23.9 shows the idea. The value of the key is 3, which means each character will be replaced by another character that is located three ahead (D is replaced by G, E is replaced by K, and so on). To make it simple, we do not encode the space character. If the substituted character is beyond the last character (Z), we wrap it around.

Figure 23.9   *Monoalphabetic substitution*

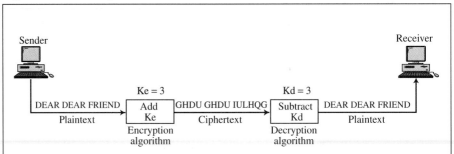

Monoalphabetic substitution is very simple, but the code can be broken easily by snoopers. The reason is that the method cannot hide the natural frequencies of characters in the language being used. For example, in English, the most frequently used characters are E, T, O, and A. A snooper can easily break the code by finding which character is used the most and replace that one with the letter E. It can then find the next most frequent and replace it with T, and so on.

In *polyalphabetic substitution,* each occurrence of a character can have a different substitute. One **polyalphabetic encryption** technique is to find the position of the character in the text and use that value as the key. Figure 23.10 shows an example of polyalphabetic substitution using the same plaintext as in Figure 23.9. Here the two occurrences of the word "DEAR" are encrypted differently. In this way, the frequencies of the characters are not preserved and it is more difficult to break the code. However, polyalphabetic substitution is not very secure either. The reason is that although "DEAR DEAR" is replaced by "EGDV JLIA", the order of characters in "EGDV" and "JLIA" is still the same; the code can easily be broken by a more experienced snooper.

Figure 23.10 *Polyalphabetic substitution*

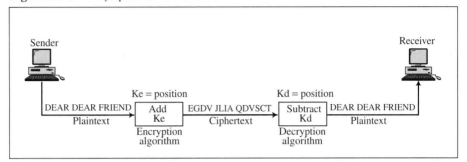

An example of polyalphabetic substitution is the **Vignere cipher.** In this scheme, the key is a two-dimensional table (26 × 26), in which each row is a permutation of 26 characters (A to Z). To replace a character, the algorithm finds the position of the character in the text, which it uses as the row number, and the position of the character in the alphabet (A as 1, B as 2, and so on), which it uses as the column number. The algorithm then replaces the character with the character in the table that corresponds to the column and row number.

- **Transpositional.** An even more secure method is **transpositional encryption,** in which the characters retain their plaintext form but change their positions to create the ciphertext. The text is organized into a two-dimensional table, and the columns are interchanged according to a key. For example, we can organize the plaintext into an eleven-column table and then reorganize the columns according to a key that indicates the interchange rule. Figure 23.11 shows an example of transpositional encryption. The key defines which columns should be swapped. As you have guessed, transpositional encryption is not very secure either. The character frequencies are preserved and the snooper can find the plaintext through trial and error.

Figure 23.11 *Transpositional encryption*

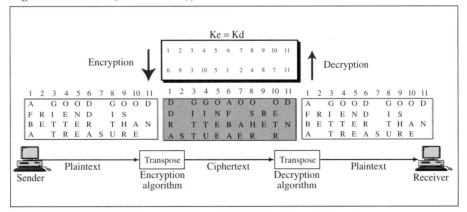

Bit-Level Encryption   In **bit-level encryption** techniques, data as text, graphics, audio, or video are first divided into blocks of bits, then altered by encoding/decoding, permutation, substitution, exclusive OR, rotation, and so on.

■ **Encoding/decoding.** In **encoding** and **decoding** a decoder changes an input of n bits into an output of 2^n bits. The output should have only one single 1, located at the position determined by the input. An encoder, on the other hand, has 2^n inputs and only n outputs. The input should have only one single 1. Figure 23.12 shows the 2-bit decoder and encoder.

Figure 23.12   *Encoding/decoding*

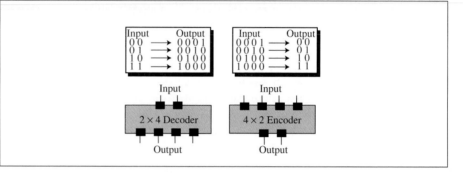

■ **Permutation.** Permutation is in fact transposition at the bit level. In *straight permutation*, the number of bits in the input and output are preserved; only the positions are changed. In **compressed permutation,** the number of bits is reduced (some of the bits are dropped). In **expanded permutation,** the number of bits is increased (some bits are repeated). A permutation unit can easily be made as a hardware circuit with internal wiring so that operations can be performed very quickly. These units are referred to as **P-boxes.** Figure 23.13 shows the three types of permutation using P-boxes.

Figure 23.13   *Permutation*

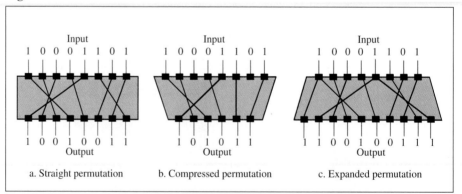

■ **Substitution. Substitution** of n bits by another n bits can be achieved using a combination of P-boxes, encoders, and decoders. Figure 23.14 shows a two-bit **S-box** that replaces every 00 by 01, 01 by 00, 10 by 11, and 11 by 10. The decoder changes the two bits into four bits. The P-box changes the position of the 1. The encoder then changes the four bits into a two-bit pattern.

Figure 23.14   *Substitution*

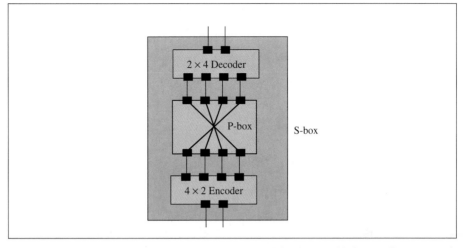

■   **Product.** The P-boxes and S-boxes can be combined and called a **product.** A product unit is made of several stages of P-boxes and S-boxes, as shown in Figure 23.15.

Figure 23.15   *Product*

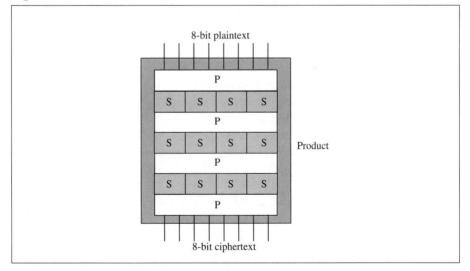

■   **Exclusive OR.** A very interesting operation on data at the bit level is the **exclusive OR.** The result of the exclusive-OR operation on two bits is 0 if the two bits are the same and 1 if the two bits are different. The input and the key are exclusive ORed together to create the output. Figure 23.16 shows an example. As the figure shows, the exclusive-OR operation is reciprocal, which means that the same key can be used with the ciphertext at the receiver to recreate the original plaintext.

■   **Rotation.** Another way to encrypt a bit pattern is to rotate bits to the right or to the left. The key is the number of bits to be rotated. Figure 23.17 shows plaintext rotated to create ciphertext.

Figure 23.16   *Exclusive OR*

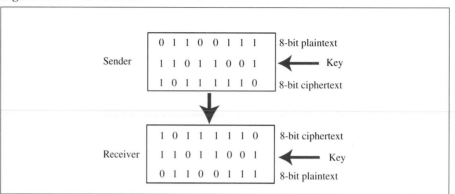

Figure 23.17   *Rotation*

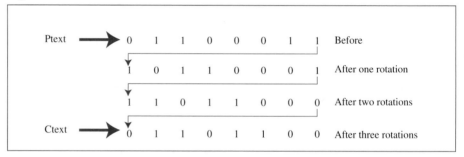

Data Encryption Standard (DES)

One example of bit-level encryption is the **data encryption standard (DES). DES** was designed by IBM and adopted by the U.S. government as the standard encryption method for nonmilitary and nonclassified use. The algorithm encrypts a 64-bit plaintext using a 56-bit key. The text is put through 19 different and very complex procedures to create a 64-bit ciphertext.

Figure 23.18 shows a schematic diagram of DES. The first and the last two steps are relatively simple. However, steps 2 through 17 are complex, each requiring substeps that are combinations of transposition, substitution, swapping, exclusive OR, and rotation. Although steps 2 through 17 are the same, each uses a different key derived from the original key. Additional complexity is achieved by having each step use the output of the previous step as input.

Figure 23.19 shows how a 56-bit key generates 16 different subkeys, each of 48 bits. Figure 23.20 illustrates the operations involved in each of the 16 complex steps.

Public Key Methods

In conventional encryption/decryption methods, the decryption algorithm is always the inverse of the encryption algorithm and uses the same key. Anyone who knows the encryption algorithm and key can deduce the decryption algorithm. For this reason, security can be assured only if the entire process is kept secret. In cases where there are many senders and one receiver, however, this level of secrecy can be inconvenient. For

Figure 23.18 *DES*

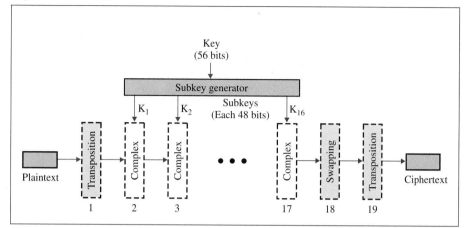

Figure 23.19 *Subkey generation in DES*

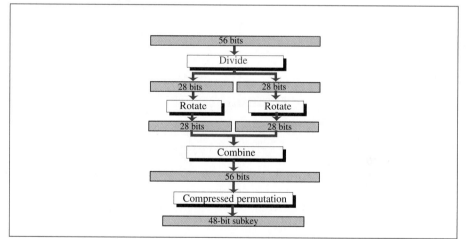

example, imagine that a bank wants to give customers remote access to their accounts. To limit each customer's access to only his or her own account using conventional encryption, the bank would have to create millions of encryption algorithms and keys. This solution is impractical, particularly with old customers leaving and new customers joining the bank all the time. On the other hand, if the bank were to give the same encryption algorithm and key to every customer, it could not guarantee the privacy of any customer.

The solution is **public key encryption.** In this method, every user has the same encryption algorithm and key. The decryption algorithm and key, however, are kept secret. Anyone can encrypt information, but only an authorized receiver can decrypt it. The decryption algorithm is designed in such a way that it is not the inverse of the encryption algorithm. The encryption and decryption algorithms use completely different functions, and knowing one does not enable a user to know the other. In addition,

Figure 23.20 *One of the 16 steps in DES*

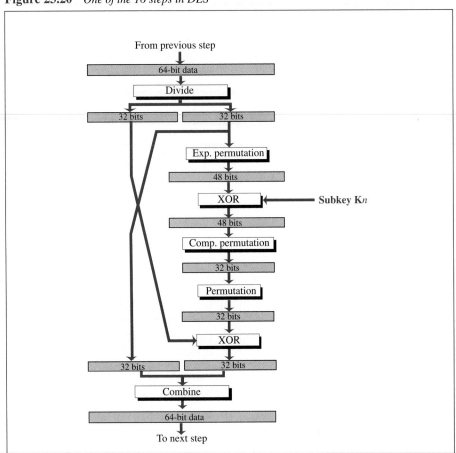

the keys are different. Even with the encryption algorithm and encryption key, an intruder still will be unable to decipher the code (at least not easily).

Figure 23.21 illustrates the idea of using **public keys** for customer access to bank services. The encryption algorithm and key are publicly announced. Every customer can use them. The decryption algorithm and key are kept secret and used only by the bank.

RSA Encryption

One public key encryption technique is called **Rivest, Shamir, Adleman (RSA) encryption.** In this method, one party (a bank customer, for example) uses a public key, K_p. The other party uses a secret **(private) key,** K_s. Both use a number, N. Figure 23.22 shows the encryption and decryption.

The encryption algorithm follows these steps:

■ Encode the data to be encrypted as a number to create the plaintext P.

■ Calculate the ciphertext C as $C = P^{K_p}$ modulo N (modulo means divide P^{K_p} by N and keep only the remainder).

■ Send C as the ciphertext.

Figure 23.21   *Public key encryption*

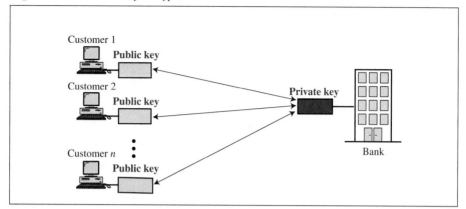

Figure 23.22   *RSA*

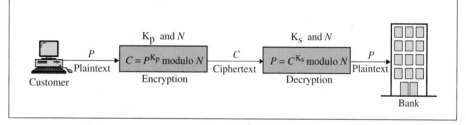

The decryption algorithm follows these steps:

■ Receive *C*, the ciphertext.

■ Calculate plaintext $P = C^{K_s}$ modulo *N*.

■ Decode *P* to the original data.

Before discussing the selection of K_p, K_s, and *N*, we give an example. In Figure 23.23, we choose $K_p = 5$, $K_s = 77$, and *N* = 119.

In this example, character F is encoded as 6 (F is the sixth character in the alphabet). We calculate 6^{K_p} modulo 119, which is 41. At the receiver, we calculate 41^{K_s} modulo 119, which is 6, and then decode 6 as F.

Choosing K_p, K_s, and *N*   The whole idea behind RSA is the way in which K_p, K_s, and *N* are chosen. This is done using number theory:

■ First, choose two prime numbers (a prime number is divisible only by 1 and itself), *p* and *q*. (We chose 7 and 17.)

■ Calculate $N = p \times q$. (In our example, *N* = 7 × 17 = 119.)

■ Select K_p such that it is not a factor of $(p - 1) \times (q - 1) = 96$. The factors of 96 are 2, 2, 2, 2, 2, and 3. We chose 5, which is not a factor of 96.

■ Select K_s such that $(K_p \times K_s)$ modulo $(p - 1) \times (q - 1) = 1$. We chose 77. If you check, you will see that in our example, 5 × 77 = 385 and 385 = 4 × 96 + 1.

Figure 23.23   *RSA encryption and decryption*

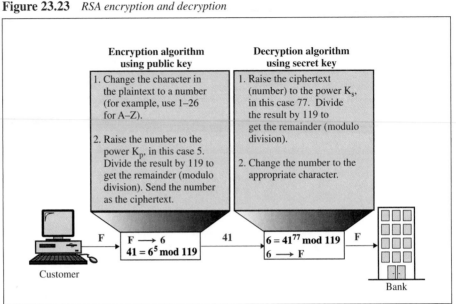

Security of RSA   In the bank example, the pair of numbers K_p and N is given to customers publicly. The bank keeps K_s as the secret key. The question is, if the bank can calculate K_s, why can't a snooper? The answer lies in the complexity of the process. The bank starts with two prime numbers p and q to calculate N, K_p, and K_s. The snooper does not know p or q. He needs to use N to first find p and q and then guess K_s. If p and q are chosen such that N is a few hundred digits long, it is extremely difficult to find its prime factors (p and q). Figure 23.24 illustrates this situation.

Figure 23.24   *Security of RSA*

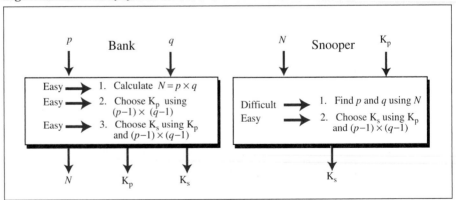

Mathematicians have calculated that, for example, it would take more than 70 years to find the prime factors (p and q) of a number with 100 digits (N).

Reciprocity of RSA   The RSA algorithm is reciprocal. This means that the bank can use the same secret key, K_s, to send a reply to the customer and the customer can decrypt the message using his own private key.

Authentication

Authentication means verifying the identity of a sender. In other words, an authentication technique tries to verify that a message is coming from an authentic sender and not from an imposter. Although many methods have been developed for authentication, we will discuss only a method called **digital signature,** which is based on public key encryption/decryption.

The concept of a digital signature is similar to that of signing transaction documents when you do business with a bank. To withdraw large amounts of money from your bank, you go to the bank and fill out a withdrawal form. The bank requires that you sign the form and keeps the signed form on record. The signature is required in case there is any question later about authorization for the withdrawal. If, for example, you say later that you never withdrew money in that amount, the bank can show you your signature (or show it to a judge in court), proving that you did.

In network transactions, you cannot personally sign the request for withdrawal. You however, can, create the equivalent of an electronic or digital signature by the way you send data.

One implementation uses the reciprocity of RSA. As we said before, K_p and K_s are reciprocal. Digital signatures add another level of encryption and decryption to the process discussed above. This time, however, a secret key encryption key is kept by the customer while the corresponding public key is used by the bank. In this case, the customer uses one public and one secret key and the bank uses one secret key and one public key.

Figure 23.25 shows how a digital signature works. The customer encrypts the plaintext (P) using a secret key, K_s-1, and creates the first level of ciphertext (C1). The first ciphertext is encrypted again using the public key, K_p-1, to create the second ciphertext (C2). C2 is sent through the network and received by the bank. The bank uses the secret key (K_s-2) to decipher C2 into C1. It then uses the public key (K_p-2) to

Figure 23.25 *Signature authentication*

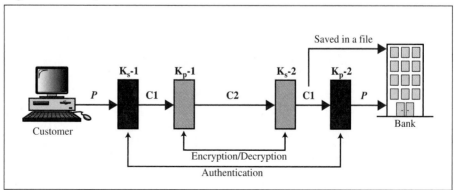

decipher C1 into the original plaintext. Before it does so, however, it copies C1 and stores it in a separate file.

If one day the customer claims never to have made such a transaction, the bank can take C1 out of its file and apply K_p-2 to it to show that it creates P. This decryption would not be possible unless the customer had originally applied K_s-1 to P to create C1. Unless the customer, in fact, had sent the transaction, the C1 could not exist. The customer cannot claim that the bank created C1 because the bank does not have the K_s-1 required to do so. The customer may claim, of course, that an unauthorized user obtained access to the K_s-1. In that case, however, the court can point out that it was the customer's responsibility to keep the K_s-1 secret, thereby absolving the bank of liability.

Data Compression

Even with a very fast transmission media, there is always a need to send data in a short amount of time. **Data compression** reduces the number of bits sent. Data compression becomes particularly important when we send data that are not pure text such as audio and video.

The methods used to compress data are generally divided into two broad categories: lossless and lossy (see Figure 23.26).

Figure 23.26   *Data compression methods*

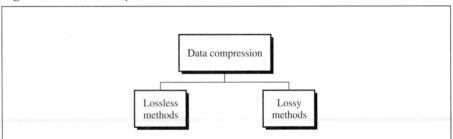

Lossless Compression

In **lossless data compression,** the compressing and decompressing algorithms are usually the inverse of each other. In other words, after decompressing, we will get the exact data as they were before compressing. Nothing is lost. The following are some of the techniques used in lossless compression.

Run-Length Encoding   When data contain strings of repeated symbols (such as bits or characters), the strings can be replaced by a special marker, followed by the repeated symbol, followed by the number of occurrences. For example, in Figure 23.27, the symbol # is the marker. The symbol being repeated (the run symbol) follows the marker. After the run symbol, the number of occurrences (length) is shown by a two-digit number. This run-length encoding method can be used in audio (silence is a run of 0s) and video (run of a picture element having the same brightness and color).

Statistical Compression   Another method of lossless compression is **statistical compression.** This method uses short codes for frequent symbols and long codes for

Figure 23.27   *Run-length encoding*

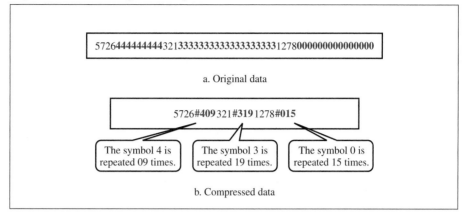

infrequent symbols. In this way, the length of the total data is reduced tremendously. The three common encoding systems using this principle are Morse code, Huffman encoding, and Lempel-Ziv-Welch encoding.

- **Morse code. Morse code** uses variable-length combinations of mark (dash) and space (dot) to encode data. One-symbol codes represent the most frequent characters and five-symbol codes represent the least frequent characters. For example, a dot (.) represents the character E and four dashes and a dot (--.--) represent the character Q.

- **Huffman encoding. Huffman encoding** (see Appendix F) uses variable-length codes (a string of 0s and 1s) to encode a set of symbols.

- **Lempel-Ziv-Welch encoding. Lempel-Ziv-Welch (LZW) encoding** (see Appendix G) looks for repeated strings or words and stores them in variables. It then replaces occurrences of that string with a pointer to that variable. For example, the words *the*, *then*, *and*, and even some strings such as *-in* and *-tion* are often repeated many times. Each of these words or strings can be stored in separate variables and then pointers can point to them. A pointer (address) requires only a few bits, while a word may need tens of bits. This method is used in UNIX.

Relative Compression   Another way of reducing the number of bits is a method called **relative compression** or differential encoding. This is extremely useful if we are sending, for example, video. Commercial TVs send 30 frames of 0s and 1s every second. However, usually there is little difference between consecutive frames. So, instead of sending an entire frame, we send only the difference between consecutive frames. The small differences can be encoded into small streams of bits.

Lossy Compression

If the decompressed information need not be an exact replica of the original information but something very close, we can use a **lossy data compression** method. For example, in video transmission, if an image does not have sharp discontinuities, after transformation to a mathematical expression, most of the information is contained in the first few terms. Sending only these terms may allow us to reproduce the frame with enough accuracy. These methods are called lossy compression methods because we will lose some of the original data in the process.

Several methods have been developed using lossy compression techniques. **Joint photographic experts group (JPEG)** is used to compress pictures and graphics. **Motion picture experts group (MPEG)** is used to compress video.

23.3   APPLICATION LAYER

The seventh layer of the OSI model is the application layer. The application layer contains whatever functions are required by the user—for example, **electronic mail**—and as such, no standardization in general is possible. However, the ITU-T has recognized that there are several common applications for which standardization is possible. We will examine five of them here: the message handling system (MHS); file transfer, access, and management (FTAM); virtual terminal (VT); directory system (DS); and common management information protocol (CMIP).

Message Handling System (MHS)

Message handling system (MHS) is the OSI protocol that underlies electronic mail and store-and-forward handling. It is derived from the ITU-T **X.400** series. MHS is the system used to send any message (including copies of data or files) that can be delivered in a store-and-forward manner. Store-and-forward delivery means that, instead of opening an active channel between the sender and receiver, the protocol provides a delivery service that forwards the message when a link becomes available. In most information-sharing protocols, both the sender and the receiver must be able to participate in the exchange concurrently. In a store-and-forward system, the sender passes the message to a delivery system. The delivery system may not be able to transmit the message immediately, in which case it stores the message until conditions change. When the message is delivered, it is stored in the recipient's mailbox until called for.

The regular postal system provides a good analogy to the OSI model's message handling system: A sender composes and addresses a letter and deposits it in a mailbox for collection. The postal carrier collects the letter and passes it to a postal office. The postal service routes the letter through the necessary intervening post offices to the office that serves the address of the recipient. Another postal carrier delivers the letter to the mailbox of the recipient. Finally, the recipient checks his or her mailbox and finds the letter.

Similarly, in an electronic mail system, the user deposits an electronic message with an electronic mail delivery system. The delivery system cooperates with other systems to transfer the message to the mailbox of the intended receiver.

The Structure of the MHS

The structure of the OSI message handling system is shown in Figure 23.28. Each user communicates with a program or process called a user agent (UA). The UA is unique for each user (each user receives a copy of the program or process). An example of a UA is the electronic mail program associated with a specific operating system that allows a user to type and edit messages.

Figure 23.28   *MHS*

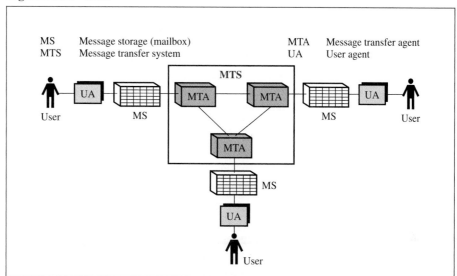

Each user has message storage (MS), which consists of disk space in a mail storage system and is usually referred to as a mailbox. Message storage can be used for storing, sending, or receiving messages.

The message storage communicates with a series of processes called **message transfer agents (MTAs).** MTAs are like the different departments of a post office. The combined MTAs make up the **message transfer system (MTS).**

Message Format

The MHS standard defines the format of a message (see Figure 23.29). The body of the message corresponds to the material (like a letter) that goes inside the envelope of a conventional mailing. Every message can include the address (name) of the sender, the

Figure 23.29   *Message format in MHS*

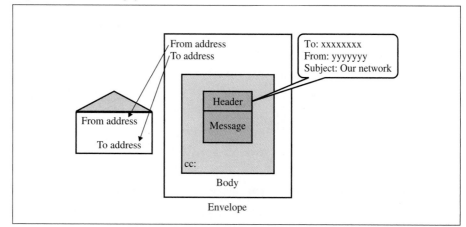

address (name) of the recipient, the subject of the message, and a list of anyone other than the primary recipient who is to receive a copy.

File Transfer, Access, and Management (FTAM)

The **file transfer, access, and management (FTAM)** protocol is used to transfer (copy); access (read, write, or modify); and manage (control) files.

Files are stored differently in different systems. In a UNIX environment, a file is a sequence of characters (bytes). In an IBM VMS environment, on the other hand, a file is a collection of records. The organization of a file depends on the operating system of the host.

Virtual Files and Filestores

To allow the interaction of different file systems, FTAM uses the concept of virtual files and virtual filestores. A **virtual filestore** is a nonimplementation-specific model for files and databases that can be used as an intermediary for file transfer, access, and management. The concept of filestore for files is similar to that of ASN.1 (described earlier in this chapter as part of the presentation layer) for data.

FTAM is based on asymmetrical access of a **virtual file.** By asymmetrical, we mean that each transaction requires an initiator and a responder. The initiator requests the transfer of, access to, or management of a file from the responder. The responder creates a virtual file model of its actual file and allows the initiator to use the virtual model rather than the real file (see Figure 23.30). Because the model is software, it can be designed to be independent of hardware and operating system constraints. The model also creates a secure separation between the file to which the initiator is allowed access and others in the same real storage.

Figure 23.30   *Virtual file storage*

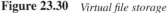

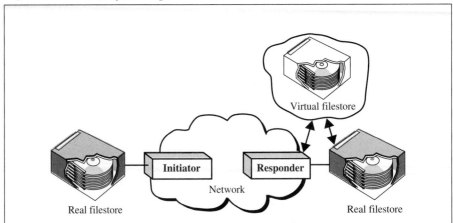

Attribute and Content

The creation of a virtual filestore is based on two aspects of the file in question: attributes and content. The attributes of a file are a set of properties or security measures used to control either the contents or access. FTAM distinguishes between two different types of attributes: per-content and per-access. Per-content attributes are those related to the contents of the file. Per-access attributes are security measures that control access to the file.

Virtual Terminal (VT)

One of the most important applications defined in the OSI model is the virtual terminal (VT).

Remote Access

Ordinarily, access to a host (such as a minicomputer, workstation, or mainframe) is gained through a terminal. Terminals are physically linked to the host. This physical connection is referred to as **local access** (see Figure 23.31). Each host contains software (called a terminal driver) designed to provide an interface with the specific terminal types usually attached to it. For example, an IBM computer is designed to communicate with IBM terminals, DEC computers are designed to communicate with DEC terminals, and so on.

Figure 23.31   *Local access*

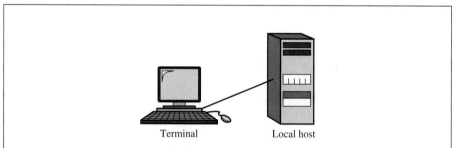

One of the attractions of networks, however, is the ability to log on to a host to which your terminal is not directly linked. The user's terminal is connected to a local host, which is connected in turn through a network to a remote host (see Figure 23.32).

Figure 23.32   *Remote access*

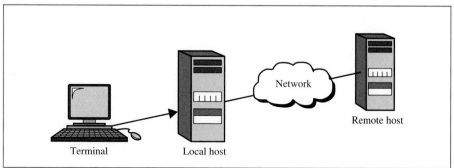

If the terminal and remote host are of the same type (both IBM, for example), then the network merely acts as an extra-long local link. Problems arise, however, when a terminal of one type wishes to be connected (remotely or locally) to a host of another type. A machine designed to communicate with every type of terminal in the world would require hundreds of terminal drivers. The challenge to the designers of the OSI model was to create a mechanism that would allow any terminal to have access to any computer despite hardware incompatibility.

Virtual Terminal

The problem is solved by a construct called a **virtual terminal (VT).** A virtual terminal is an imaginary terminal (a software model of a terminal) with a set of standard characteristics that every host understands. It is a software version of a physical terminal.

A terminal that wishes to communicate with a remote host communicates to its local host. The local host contains VT software that translates the request or data received from the actual terminal into the intermediary format used by the virtual terminal. The reformatted data travel over the network to the remote host. The remote host passes the transmission to its own VT software, which transforms it from its VT format into the format used by the remote host's own terminals. The remote host, therefore, receives the input as if from a local host (the virtual terminal). After processing the request, the remote host can return a response following the same procedure in reverse (see Figure 23.33).

Figure 23.33   *Virtual terminal*

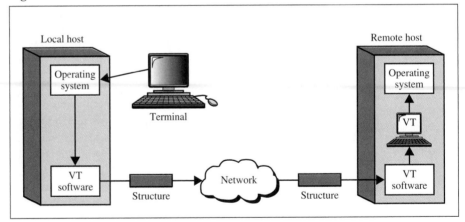

Directory Services (DS)

The OSI **directory service (DS)** is designed according to the ITU-T **X.500** standard. A directory is a global source of information about many different objects. An OSI directory service is an application program used to represent and locate objects (such as people, organizations, logical groups, programs, and files) contained in an OSI directory. The type of information that a directory holds varies according to the type of the object.

To the user of a directory service, all of this information appears to be stored in a single database, located in a single host. In fact, such an arrangement would be supremely impractical. A directory is a distributed database, with each host holding only a part. The access mechanism, however, is structured so that users know of only one entry port from which all information may be retrieved. (Note that the user of a directory service can be either a person or an application.)

DIB

The information contained in the directory is called the **directory information base (DIB).** It is stored as a set of entries, each describing one object. An entry may consist of several parts, each of which describes a different attribute of the object. For example, an entry about the ISO might include a short description of the purpose of the organization, a mailing address, phone number, and so on.

The entire structure is organized as a tree with different levels of generality at each branch.

DUAs and DSAs

Users gain access to the DS through a mechanism called a **directory user agent (DUA).** The DUA communicates with one or more entities called **directory system agents (DSAs)** contained within the directory system itself.

The DUA passes a request for information to a DSA. If the DSA knows the whereabouts of the information sought, it either fills the request or passes it on to another DSA with the necessary access, and so on. The requested information is retrieved and passed back through the successive DSAs to the DUA.

If a DSA does not know how to fill a request, it has three options: it can forward the request to a DSA with access to a different level of the tree; it can broadcast the request and wait for a response; or it can return a report of failure to the DUA.

Common Management Information Protocol (CMIP)

The ISO and the ITU-T, working together, have developed a series of services for the management of an OSI system. The most important OSI management services are called the **common management information services (CMIS).** The protocol for implementing those services is called the **common management information protocol (CMIP).**

All CMIP management occurs by monitoring and manipulating communication between OSI entities called *managed objects.* A managed object is a network resource such as a workstation, a switch, routing hardware or software, queuing programs, and so on. CMIP allows users to perform actions on managed objects (including changing their status for efficiency or testing purposes) and to collect data about the status of those objects. By keeping logs of collected data (e.g., the number of bytes of data processed by a router over specified periods of time) and by changing the settings of a managed object and monitoring the response, a user can evaluate the performance of a system and identify problems as they arise.

CMIS

The common management information services (CMIS) have been designed to fulfill five objectives:

- **Fault management.** Services are included to detect, isolate, and correct any abnormal operation of the OSI environment. Specific tasks include diagnostic testing, fault tracing, and, when possible, fault correction.
- **Accounting management.** Services are included to track user costs and charges and, if necessary, to place limits on the use of managed objects.
- **Configuration and name management.** Services are included for initializing and closing down managed objects, for reconfiguring an open system, and for associating names with objects or sets of objects. CMIS allows a user to ensure the continuous operation of communications services in a changing environment.
- **Performance management.** Services are provided to allow users to evaluate the behavior of managed objects and the effectiveness of networking functions.
- **Security management.** Services are provided to evaluate the effectiveness and operability of network security measures.

CMISE

The specific services provided by CMIS are called **common management information service elements (CMISEs).** These service elements fall into three categories: management association services, management notification services, and management operation services.

Management Association Services

Management association services establish application associations to allow CMIS users to communicate. CMIS includes three association service elements. M-INITIAL-IZE is used to establish an association with a peer CMISE service. M-TERMINATE is used to obtain normal termination of an association. M-ABORT is used to obtain an abrupt release from an association.

Management Notification Services

Management notification services are used to convey notifications of managed object events. M-EVENT-REPORT is used to report managed object events to a service user. A report can be about any event the CMISE user chooses to collect and includes a time stamp of the occurrence.

Management Operation Services

Management operation services include six services used to convey management information about system operations to a CMISE user:

- **M-GET.** M-GET requests the retrieval of management information from a peer CMISE user.
- **M-CANCEL-GET.** M-CANCEL-GET requests cancellation of a previous M-GET request.

- **M-SET.** M-SET requests the modification of specific attribute values of a managed object.
- **M-ACTION.** M-ACTION requests another user to perform an action on a managed object.
- **M-CREATE.** M-CREATE requests another user to create a representation of an instance of a managed object and the associated management information values.
- **M-DELETE.** M-DELETE requests a peer user to delete an instance of a managed object (the opposite of M-CREATE).

23.4   KEY TERMS AND CONCEPTS

abstract syntax notation 1 (ASN.1)

application layer

authentication

bit-level encryption

character-level encryption

ciphertext

common management information protocol (CMIP)

common management information service (CMIS)

common management information service element (CMISE)

compressed permutation

compression

conventional encryption

data compression

data encryption standard (DES)

decoding

decryption

dialog

digital signature

directory information base (DIB)

directory service (DS)

directory system agent (DSA)

directory user agent (DUA)

electronic mail

encoding

encryption

exclusive OR

expanded permutation

file transfer, access, and management (FTAM)

Huffman encoding

joint photographic experts group (JPEG)

Lempel-Ziv-Welch (LZW) encoding

local access

lossless data compression

lossy data compression

major synchronization point

message handling system (MHS)

message transfer agent (MTA)

message transfer system (MTS)

minor synchronization point

monoalphabetic encryption

Morse code

motion picture experts group (MPEG)

P-box

plaintext

polyalphabetic encryption

private key

product

public key

public key encryption

relative compression

Rivest, Shamir, Adleman (RSA) encryption

run-length encoding

S-box

session protocol data unit (SPDU)

statistical compression

substitution

synchronization points

translation

transpositional encryption

Vignere cipher

virtual file

virtual filestore

virtual terminal (VT)

X.400

X.500

23.5   SUMMARY

- The session layer establishes, maintains, and synchronizes dialogs between nodes.
- Flow and error control in the session layer use synchronization points, which are reference points introduced into the data.
- The presentation layer handles translation, encryption, authentication, and compression.
- Encryption renders a message (plaintext) unintelligible to unauthorized personnel.
- Decryption transforms an intentionally unintelligible message (ciphertext) into meaningful information.

- Encryption/decryption methods can be broadly classified into the conventional methods and the public key methods.

- Substitution and transpositional encryption are character-level encryption methods.

- Bit-level encryption methods include encoding/decoding, permutation, substitution, product, exclusive OR, and rotation.

- DES is a bit-level encryption method adopted by the U.S. government.

- In conventional encryption, the encrypting algorithm is known by everyone but the key is secret except to the sender and receiver.

- In public key encryption, both the encrypting algorithm and the encryption key are known to everyone but the decryption key is known only to the receiver.

- One of the commonly used public key encryption methods is the RSA algorithm.

- Digital signature is one of the authentication methods used today.

- The goal of data compression is to reduce the number of transmitted bits.

- Data compression methods are either lossless (all information is recoverable) or lossy (some information is lost).

- Five standard application protocols are the following:

  - Mail handling system (MHS)—the protocol for electronic mail and store-and-forward handling.

  - File transfer, access, and management (FTAM)—transfers, accesses, and manages files. FTAM uses virtual files.

  - Virtual terminal (VT)—allows dissimilar terminals or machines to communicate with one another.

  - Directory service (DS)—an application program that allows users access to databases.

  - Common management information protocol (CMIP)—implements an OSI management service.

- Changing the internal representation of data from one form to another is called translation.

23.6   PRACTICE SET

Review Questions

1. Discuss the functions of the session layer.
2. Define the term *graceful close*.
3. In what situation would synchronization points be largely unnecessary?
4. In what situation would synchronization points be important?
5. What is the difference between minor synchronization points and major synchronization points?
6. Discuss the functions of the presentation layer.

7. What is the translation method recommended by the OSI model? What is the role of ASN.1?

8. What is the relationship between plaintext and ciphertext?

9. What are the two categories of encryption/decryption methods? What is the main difference between the categories?

10. What is the concept behind substitutional character-level encryption?

11. Why is polyalphabetic substitution superior to monoalphabetic substitution?

12. What is the concept behind transpositional character-level encryption?

13. What sort of operations can be performed on bits in bit-level encryption?

14. Contrast straight, compressed, and expanded permutation.

15. What does the U.S. government use as its standard encryption method for nonmilitary and nonclassified information?

16. Why are conventional encryption/decryption methods not suitable for a bank?

17. For private key encryption, discuss the keys and their ownership.

18. For public key encryption, discuss the keys and their ownership.

19. Discuss the term *reciprocity* in relation to the RSA algorithm.

20. Why is authentication necessary in Internet communication?

21. What are the two categories of data compression methods? What is the main difference between the categories?

22. What is run-length encoding?

23. What is statistical compression?

24. How does Morse code reduce the amount of bits transmitted?

25. How does Lempel-Ziv-Welch encoding reduce the amount of bits transmitted?

26. What is relative compression?

27. Name the components and functions of the message handling system.

28. What is a virtual filestore and why is it needed?

29. What is a virtual terminal and how is it used in remote access?

30. Discuss the relationships between the DIB, DUA, and DSA in the OSI model's directory services.

31. How do CMIP, CMIS, and CMISE interrelate?

32. Why is the concept of the virtual terminal needed?

Multiple Choice Questions

33. Encryption and decryption are functions of the _____ layer.
    a. transport
    b. session
    c. presentation
    d. application

34. Which of the following describes a user agent?
    a. a process with which a user communicates

    b. the person that is sending the message

    c. the storage facility for a spooled message

    d. the operating system used by MHS

35. Which of the following is true about FTAM?

    a. The filestore is a collection of files.

    b. Attributes and contents define a file.

    c. It was developed as a method to handle different file mechanisms on different operating systems.

    d. All of the above.

36. The _____ layer is responsible for dialog establishment, maintenance, synchronization, and termination.

    a. transport

    b. session

    c. presentation

    d. application

37. The _____ layer can disconnect a session abruptly, while the _____ layer provides for graceful closure.

    a. session; presentation

    b. session; application

    c. session; transport

    d. transport; session

38. _____ points provide a method to recover data that have been delivered but not yet used.

    a. Segmentation

    b. Concatenation

    c. Translation

    d. Synchronization

39. Which of the following is/are presentation layer functions?

    a. encryption of data

    b. compression of data

    c. translation of data

    d. all of the above

40. A _____ is an application program that can represent and locate objects in a directory.

    a. MHS

    b. FTAM

    c. DS

    d. CMIP

41. The _____ uses a store-and-forward method for mail delivery.

    a. MHS

    b. FTAM

    c. DS

    d. CMIP

42. The protocol to define services that manage a system based on the OSI model is called _____.

    a. MHS

    b. FTAM

    c. DS

    d. CMIP

43. A protocol that is concerned with file transfer, management, and access is _____.

    a. MHS

    b. FTAM

    c. DS

    d. CMIP

44. In MHS, the UA is _____.

    a. the user

    b. a program

    c. disk space for storage

    d. the transmission media

45. In the conventional method of encryption and decryption, which key is publicly known?

    a. Ke only

    b. Kd only

    c. Ke and Kd

    d. none

46. In the public key method of encryption and decryption, which key is publicly known?

    a. Ke only

    b. Kd only

    c. Ke and Kd

    d. none

47. In the public key method of encryption and decryption, only the receiver has possession of the _____.

    a. Ke

    b. Kd

    c. Ke and Kd

    d. none of the above

48. We use an encryption method in which both plaintext and ciphertext have the same number of As, Bs, Cs, and so on. This is probably _____ substitution.

    a. monoalphabetic

   b. polyalphabetic

   c. transpositional

   d. rotational

49. We use an encryption method in which the character Z always substitutes for the character G. This is probably _____ substitution.

   a. monoalphabetic

   b. polyalphabetic

   c. transpositional

   d. rotational

50. We use an encryption method in which the plaintext AAAAAA becomes the ciphertext BCDEFG. This is probably _____ substitution.

   a. monoalphabetic

   b. polyalphabetic

   c. transpositional

   d. DES

51. An encryption method used by the U.S. government for nonmilitary and nonclassified use is _____.

   a. monoalphabetic substitution

   b. polyalphabetic substitution

   c. transpositional substitution

   d. the data encryption standard

52. In _____ permutation, the number of outputs is greater than the number of inputs.

   a. a straight

   b. a compressed

   c. an expanded

   d. a rotational

53. The RSA algorithm is the basis of a _____ encryption method.

   a. public key

   b. private key

   c. conventional

   d. denominational

54. The success of the RSA encryption method lies in the difficulty of _____.

   a. finding K_p

   b. finding the prime factors of K_p

   c. finding N

   d. finding the prime factors of N

55. Data are compressed using pointers to frequently used strings. This is _____.

   a. differential encoding

   b. Lempel-Ziv-Welch encoding

    c. Morse coding

    d. lossy coding

56. Data are compressed by sending just the differences between video frames. This is
    _____.

    a. differential encoding

    b. Lempel-Ziv-Welch encoding

    c. Morse coding

    d. lossy coding

57. A string of 100 0s is replaced by a marker, a 0, and the number 100. This is
    _____.

    a. run-length encoding

    b. Morse code

    c. differential encoding

    d. Lempel-Ziv-Welch encoding

58. An example of lossy compression is _____.

    a. differential encoding

    b. Lempel-Ziv-Welch encoding

    c. run-length encoding

    d. JPEG

Exercises

59. Encrypt the following message using monoalphabetic substitution with key = 4.

                       THIS IS A GOOD EXAMPLE

60. Decrypt the following message using monoalphabetic substitution with key = 4.

                       IRGVCTXMSR MW JYR

61. Decrypt the following message using monoalphabetic substitution without knowing the key.

    KTIXEVZOUT OY ROQK KTIRUYOTM G YKIXKZ OT GT KTBKRUVK

62. Encrypt the following message using polyalphabetic substitution. Use the position
of each character as the key.

        One plus one is two, one plus two is three, one plus three is four.

63. Encrypt the following bit pattern using the exclusive-OR operator and the given
key.

                  Plaintext: 1001111111100001
                  Key: 1000111110001111

64. Use the ciphertext of Exercise 63 to get the original plaintext.

65. Use the following encrypting algorithm to encrypt the message "GOOD DAY":
    a. Replace each character with its ASCII code.
    b. Add a 0 bit at the left to make each character 8 bits long.
    c. Swap the first four bits with the last four bits.
    d. Replace every four bits with its hexadecimal equivalent.
    What is the key in this method?

66. Use the following encrypting algorithm to encrypt the message "ABCADEFGH" (assume that the message is always made of uppercase letters).
    a. Treat each character as a decimal number using ASCII code (between 65 and 90).
    b. Subtract 65 from each coded character.
    c. Change each number into a five-bit pattern.

67. In traditional encryption/decryption algorithms, one way to create and exchange a secret key is known as the Diffie-Hellman method. In this method, two parties use the following steps to establish a secret key between themselves:
    a. They exchange two numbers, b and n. These two numbers are not secret. They are available to everyone.
    b. The first party chooses a number, x_1, and calculates $y_1 = (b^{x_1} \% n)$ and sends y_1 to the second party.
    c. The second party chooses a number, x_2, and calculates $y_2 = (b^{x_2} \% n)$ and sends y_2 to the first party.
    d. The first party chooses $k = (y_2^{x_1} \% n)$ as the secret key.
    e. The second party chooses $k = (y_1^{x_2} \% n)$ as the secret key.
    Using number theory, it can be proven that the secret key is the same for both parties. Use $b = 3$, $n = 10$, $x_1 = 5$, and $x_2 = 11$ to find the secret key for both parties and prove that they are the same.

68. Encrypt and decrypt the message "BE" using the RSA algorithm with key pairs $K_p = 3$ and $K_s = 11$. Use $N = 15$.

69. Given the two prime numbers $p = 19$ and $q = 23$, try to find N, K_p, and K_s.

70. To understand the security of the RSA algorithm, find K_s if you know that $K_p = 17$ and $N = 187$.

71. In the RSA algorithm, we use $(C = P^{K_p} \% N)$ to encrypt a number. If K_p and N are large numbers (each hundreds of digits), the calculation is impossible and creates an overflow error even in a supercomputer. One solution (not the best one) using number theory involves several steps, where each step uses the result of the previous step:
    a. $C = 1$
    b. Repeat K_p times
    $$C = (C \times P) \% N$$

In this way, a computer program can be written that calculates C using a loop. For example 6^5 % 119, which is 41, can be calculated as follows:

a. (1×6) % 119 = 6

b. (6×6) % 119 = 36

c. (36×6) % 119 = 97

d. (97×6) % 119 = 106

e. (106×6) % 119 = 41

Use this method to calculate 227^{16} % 100.

CHAPTER 24

TCP/IP Protocol Suite: Part 1

The **Transmission Control Protocol/Internetworking Protocol (TCP/IP)** is a set of protocols, or a protocol suite, that defines how all transmissions are exchanged across the Internet. Named after its two most popular protocols, TCP/IP has been in active use for many years and has demonstrated its effectiveness on a worldwide scale.

24.1 OVERVIEW OF TCP/IP

In 1969, a project was funded by the **Advanced Research Project Agency (ARPA),** an arm of the U.S. Department of Defense. ARPA established a packet-switching network of computers linked by point-to-point leased lines called **Advanced Research Project Agency Network (ARPANET)** that provided a basis for early research into networking. The conventions developed by ARPA to specify how individual computers could communicate across that network became TCP/IP.

As networking possibilities grew to include other types of links and devices, ARPA adapted TCP/IP to the demands of the new technology. As involvement in TCP/IP grew, the scope of ARPANET expanded until it became the backbone of an internetwork today referred to as the Internet.

TCP/IP and the Internet

TCP/IP and the concept of internetworking developed together, each shaping the growth of the other. Before moving more deeply into the protocols, however, we need to understand how TCP/IP relates to the physical entity of any internet it serves.

An internet under TCP/IP operates like a single network connecting many computers of any size and type. Internally, an internet (or, more specifically, the Internet) is an interconnection of independent physical networks (such as LANs) linked together by internetworking devices. Figure 24.1 shows the topology of a possible internet. In this example, the letters A, B, C, and so on represent hosts. A **host** in TCP/IP is a computer. The solid circles in the figure, numbered 1, 2, 3, and so on, are routers or gateways. The larger ovals containing roman numerals (I, II, III, etc.) represent separate physical networks.

Figure 24.1 *An internet according to TCP/IP*

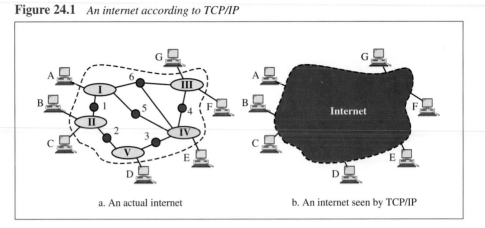

a. An actual internet   b. An internet seen by TCP/IP

To TCP/IP, the same internet appears quite differently (see again Figure 24.1). TCP/IP considers all interconnected physical networks to be one huge network. It considers all of the hosts to be connected to this larger logical network rather than to their individual physical networks.

TCP/IP and OSI

Transmission Control Protocol (TCP) was developed before the OSI model. Therefore, the layers in the TCP/IP protocol do not match exactly with those in the OSI model. The TCP/IP protocol is made of five layers: physical, data link, network, transport, and application. The application layer in TCP/IP can be equated with the combination of session, presentation, and application layers of the OSI model.

At the transport layer, TCP/IP defines two protocols: TCP and **User Datagram Protocol (UDP).** At the network layer, the main protocol defined by TCP/IP is **Internetworking Protocol (IP),** although there are some other protocols that support data movement in this layer.

At the physical and data link layers, TCP/IP does not define any specific protocol. It supports all of the standard and proprietary protocols discussed earlier in this book. A network in a TCP/IP internetwork can be a local area network (LAN), a metropolitan area network (MAN), or a wide area network (WAN).

Encapsulation

Figure 24.2 shows the encapsulation of data units at different layers of the TCP/IP protocol suite. The data unit created at the application layer is called a *message*. TCP or UDP creates a data unit that is called either a **segment** or a **user datagram.** The IP layer in turn will create a data unit called a **datagram.** The movement of the datagram across the Internet is the responsibility of the TCP/IP protocol. However, to be able to move physically from one network to another, the datagram must be encapsulated in a frame in the data link layer of the underlying network and finally transmitted as signals along the transmission media.

Figure 24.2 *TCP/IP and OSI model*

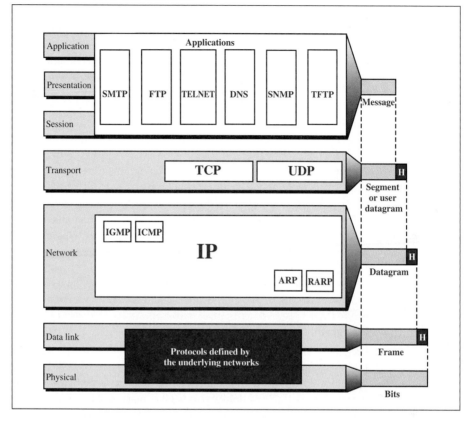

24.2 NETWORK LAYER

At the network layer (or, more accurately, the internetwork layer), TCP/IP supports the internetwork protocol (IP). IP, in turn, contains four supporting protocols: ARP, RARP, ICMP, and IGMP. Each of these protocols is described in detail later in this chapter.

Internetwork Protocol (IP)

IP is the transmission mechanism used by the TCP/IP protocols. It is an unreliable and connectionless datagram protocol—a best-effort delivery service. The term *best-effort* means that IP provides no error checking or tracking. IP assumes the unreliability of the underlying layers and does its best to get a transmission through to its destination, but with no guarantees. As we have seen in previous chapters, transmissions along physical networks can be destroyed for a number of reasons. Noise can cause bit errors during transmission across a medium; a congested router may discard a datagram if it is unable to relay it before a time limit runs out; routing quirks can end in looping and the ultimate destruction of a datagram; and disabled links may leave no usable path to the destination.

If reliability is important, IP must be paired with a reliable protocol such as TCP. An example of a more commonly understood best-effort delivery service is the post office. The post office does its best to deliver the mail but does not always succeed. If an unregistered letter is lost, it is up to the sender or would-be recipient to discover the loss and rectify the problem. The post office itself does not keep track of every letter and cannot notify a sender of loss or damage. An example of a situation similar to pairing IP with a protocol that contains reliability functions is a self-addressed, stamped postcard included in a letter mailed through the post office. When the letter is delivered, the receiver mails the postcard back to the sender to indicate success. If the sender never receives the postcard, he or she assumes the letter was lost and sends out another copy.

IP transports data in packets called datagrams (described below), each of which is transported separately. Datagrams may travel along different routes and may arrive out of sequence or duplicated. IP does not keep track of the routes and has no facility for reordering datagrams once they arrive. Because it is a connectionless service, IP does not create virtual circuits for delivery. There is no call setup to alert the receiver to an incoming transmission.

The limited functionality of IP should not be considered a weakness, however. IP provides bare-bones transmission functions that free the user to add only those facilities necessary for a given application and thereby allows for maximum efficiency.

Datagram

Packets in the IP layer are called datagrams. Figure 24.3 shows the **IP datagram** format. A datagram is a variable-length packet (up to 65,536 bytes) consisting of two parts: header and data. The header can be from 20 to 60 bytes and contains information essential to routing and delivery. It is customary in TCP/IP to show the header in four-byte sections. A brief description of each field is in order.

- **Version.** The first field defines the version number of the IP. The current version is 4 (**IPv4**), with a binary value of 0100.
- **Header length (HLEN).** The HLEN field defines the length of the header in multiples of four bytes. The four bits can represent a number between 0 and 15, which, when multiplied by 4, gives a maximum of 60 bytes.
- **Service type.** The service type field defines how the datagram should be handled. It includes bits that define the priority of the datagram. It also contains bits that specify the type of service the sender desires such as the level of throughput, reliability, and delay.
- **Total length.** The total length field defines the total length of the IP datagram. It is a two-byte field (16 bits) and can define up to 65,535 bytes.
- **Identification.** The identification field is used in **fragmentation.** A datagram, when passing through different networks, may be divided into fragments to match the network frame size. When this happens, each fragment is identified with a sequence number in this field.

Figure 24.3 *IP datagram*

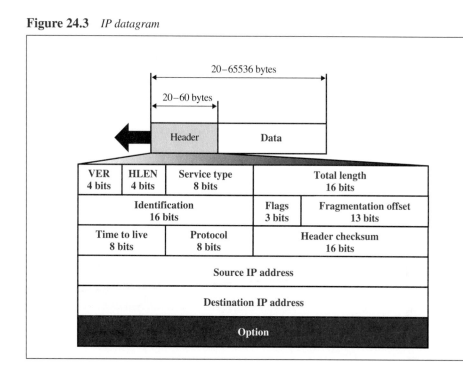

- **Flags.** The bits in the flags field deal with fragmentation (the datagram can or cannot be fragmented; can be the first, middle, or last fragment; etc.).

- **Fragmentation offset.** The fragmentation offset is a pointer that shows the offset of the data in the original datagram (if it is fragmented).

- **Time to live.** The time-to-live field defines the number of hops a datagram can travel before it is discarded. The source host, when it creates the datagram, sets this field to an initial value. Then, as the datagram travels through the Internet, router by router, each router decrements this value by 1. If this value becomes 0 before the datagram reaches its final destination, the datagram is discarded. This prevents a datagram from going back and forth forever between routers.

- **Protocol.** The protocol field defines which upper-layer protocol data are encapsulated in the datagram (TCP, UDP, ICMP, etc.).

- **Header checksum.** This is a 16-bit field used to check the integrity of the header, not the rest of the packet.

- **Source address.** The source address field is a four-byte (32-bit) Internet address. It identifies the original source of the datagram.

- **Destination address.** The destination address field is a four-byte (32-bit) Internet address. It identifies the final destination of the datagram.

- **Options.** The options field gives more functionality to the IP datagram. It can carry fields that control routing, timing, management, and alignment.

24.3   ADDRESSING

In addition to the physical addresses (contained on NICs) that identify individual devices, the Internet requires an additional addressing convention: an address that identifies the connection of a host to its network.

Each **Internet address** consists of four bytes (32 bits), defining three fields: class type, netid, and hostid. These parts are of varying lengths, depending on the class of the address (see Figure 24.4).

Figure 24.4   *Internet address*

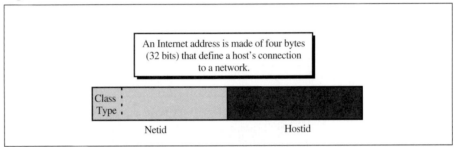

An Internet address is made of four bytes (32 bits) that define a host's connection to a network.

Class Type

Netid   Hostid

Classes

There are currently five different field-length patterns in use, each defining a **class of address.** The different classes are designed to cover the needs of different types of organizations. For example, class A addresses are numerically the lowest. They use only one byte to identify class type and netid, and leave three bytes available for hostid numbers. This division means that class A networks can accommodate far more hosts than can class B or class C networks, which provide two- and one-byte hostid fields, respectively. Currently both class A and class B are full. Addresses are available in class C only.

Class D is reserved for **multicast addresses. Multicasting** allows copies of a datagram to be passed to a select group of hosts rather than to an individual host. It is similar to **broadcasting,** but, where broadcasting requires that a packet be passed to all possible destinations, multicasting allows transmission to a selected subset. Class E addresses are reserved for future use. Figure 24.5 shows the structure of each **IP address class.**

Example 24.1

What is the class of each of the following addresses?
   a. 10011101 10001111 11111100 11001111
   b. 11011101 10001111 11111100 11001111
   c. 01111011 10001111 11111100 11001111
   d. 11101011 10001111 11111100 11001111
   e. 11110101 10001111 11111100 11001111

Solution

The first bits define the class:

    a. Class B

    b. Class C

    c. Class A

    d. Class D

    e. Class E

Figure 24.5 *Internet classes*

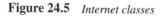

Dotted-Decimal Notation

To make the 32-bit form shorter and easier to read, Internet addresses are usually written in decimal form with decimal points separating the bytes—**dotted-decimal notation.** Figure 24.6 shows the bit pattern and decimal format of a possible address.

Figure 24.6 *IP addresses in decimal notation*

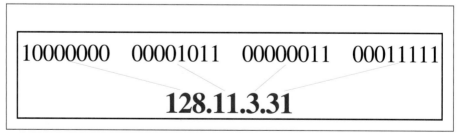

    Looking at the first byte of an address in decimal form allows us to determine at a glance to which class a particular address belongs (see Figure 24.7).

Example 24.2

Write each of following in dotted-decimal notation:

    a. 10011101 10001111 11111100 11001111

    b. 11011101 10001111 11111101 00001111

Figure 24.7   *Class ranges of Internet addresses*

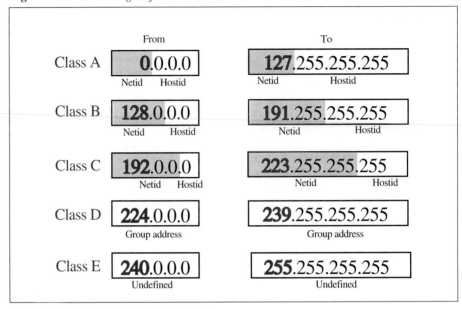

c. 01011101 00011111 00000001 11110101

d. 11111101 10001010 00001111 00111111

e. 11111110 10000001 01111110 00000001

Solution

Each byte is converted to a decimal number between 0 and 255.

    a. 157.143.252.207

    b. 221.143.253.15

    c. 93.31.1.245

    d. 253.138.15.63

    e. 254.129.126.1

Example 24.3

Find the class of each address:

    a. 4.23.145.90

    b. 227.34.78.7

    c. 246.7.3.8

    d. 29.6.8.4

    e. 198.76.9.23

Solution

The first byte defines the class.

    a. Class A

    b. Class D

    c. Class E

d. Class B

e. Class C

Example 24.4

Find the netid and the hostid for each address:

a. 4.23.145.90

b. 227.34.78.7

c. 246.7.3.8

d. 129.6.8.4

e. 198.76.9.23

Solution

First find the class and then find the netid and hostid.

a. Class A,   netid: 4   hostid: 23.145.90

b. Class D,   no hostid or netid

c. Class E,   no hostid or netid

d. Class B,   netid: 129.6   hostid:8.4

e. Class C,   netid: 198.76.9   hostid: 23

Example 24.5

Find the network address for each address:

a. 4.23.145.90

b. 227.34.78.7

c. 246.7.3.8

d. 129.6.8.4

e. 198.76.9.23

Solution

First find the class and then find the network address.

a. Class A,   network address: 4.0.0.0

b. Class D,   no network address

c. Class E,   no network address

d. Class B,   network address: 129.6.0.0

e. Class C,   network address: 198.76.9.0

Nodes with More Than One Address

As we have said, an internet address defines the node's connection to its network. It follows, therefore, that any device connected to more than one network (e.g., any router) must have more than one internet address. In fact, a device has a different address for each network connected to it.

A Sample Internet

An internet address specifies both the network to which a host belongs **(netid)** and the host itself **(hostid).** Figure 24.8 shows a portion of the Internet made up of LANs (three Ethernets and a Token Ring). Routers are indicated by circles containing Rs. Gateways are indicated by boxes containing Gs. Each has a separate address for each of its connected networks. The figure also shows the network addresses in color. A network address is the netid with the hostid part set to 0s. The network addresses in the figure are 129.8.0.0 (class B), 124.0.0.0 (class A), 134.18.0.0 (class B), and 220.3.6.0 (class C).

Figure 24.8 *Network and host addresses*

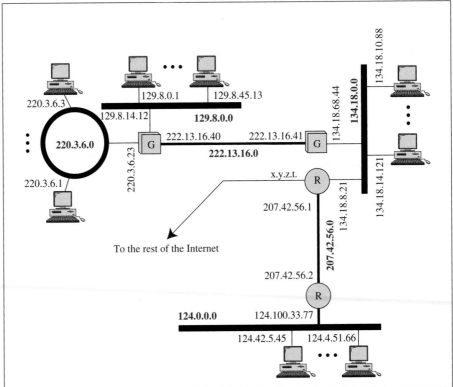

24.4   SUBNETTING

As we previously discussed, an **IP address** is 32 bits long. One portion of the address indicates a network (netid), and the other portion indicates the host (or router) on the network (hostid). This means that there is a sense of hierarchy in IP addressing. To reach a host on the Internet, we must first reach the network using the first portion of the address (netid). Then we must reach the host itself using the second portion (hostid). In other words, classes A, B, and C in IP addressing are designed with two levels of hierarchy.

However, in many cases, these two levels of hierarchy are not enough. For example, imagine an organization with a class B address. The organization has two-level hierarchical addressing, but it cannot have more than one physical network (see Figure 24.9).

Figure 24.9 *A network with two levels of hierarchy (not subnetted)*

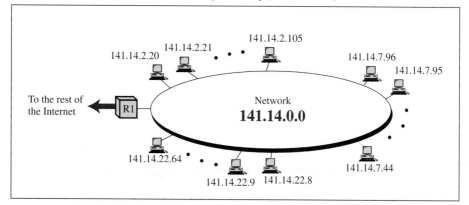

With this scheme, the organization is limited to two levels of hierarchy. The hosts cannot be organized into groups, and all of the hosts are at the same level. The organization has one network with many hosts.

One solution to this problem is **subnetting,** the further division of a network into smaller networks called **subnetworks.** For example, Figure 24.10 shows the network in Figure 24.9 divided into three subnetworks.

Figure 24.10 *A network with three levels of hierarchy (subnetted)*

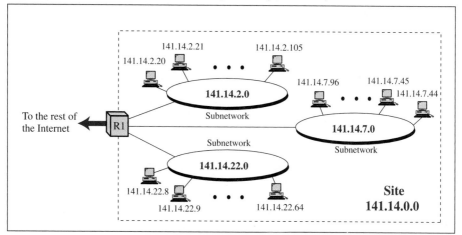

In this example, the rest of the Internet is not aware that the network is divided into three physical subnetworks: the three subnetworks still appear as a single network to the rest of the Internet. A packet destined for host 141.14.2.21 still reaches router R1. The destination address of the IP datagram is still a class B address where 141.14 defines the netid and 2.21 defines the hostid.

However, when the packet arrives at router R1, the interpretation of the IP address changes. Router R1 knows that the network 141.14 is physically divided into three subnetworks. It knows that the last two octets define two things: subnetid and hostid. Therefore, 2.21 must be interpreted as subnetid 2 and hostid 21. The router R1 uses the first two octets (141.14) as the netid, the third octet (2) as the subnetid, and the fourth octet (21) as the hostid.

Three Levels of Hierarchy

Adding subnetworks creates an intermediate level of hierarchy in the IP addressing system. Now we have three levels: netid, subnetid, and hostid. The netid is the first level; it defines the site. The second level is the *subnetid;* it defines the physical subnetwork. The hostid is the third level; it defines the connection of the host to the subnetwork. See Figure 24.11.

Figure 24.11   *Addresses in a network with and without subnetting*

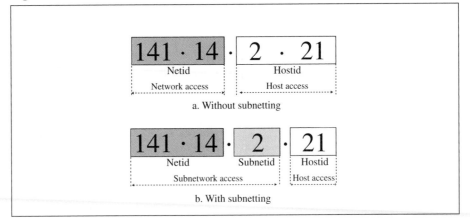

The routing of an IP datagram now involves three steps: delivery to the site, delivery to the subnetwork, and delivery to the host.

Masking

Masking is a process that extracts the address of the physical network from an IP address. Masking can be done whether we have subnetting or not. If we have not subnetted the network, masking extracts the network address from an IP address. If we have subnetted, masking extracts the **subnetwork address** from an IP address (see Figure 24.12).

Masks without Subnetting

To be compatible, routers use a mask even if there is no subnetting. The masks for networks that are not subnetted can be defined in Table 24.1.

Figure 24.12 *Masking*

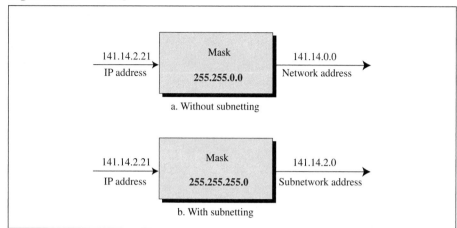

a. Without subnetting

b. With subnetting

Table 24.1 *Mask for unsubnetted networks*

Class	Mask	Address (Example)	Network Address (Example)
A	255.0.0.0	15.32.56.7	15.0.0.0
B	255.255.0.0	135.67.13.9	135.67.0.0
C	255.255.255.0	201.34.12.72	201.34.12.0
D	N/A	N/A	N/A
E	N/A	N/A	N/A

Masks with Subnetting

When there is subnetting, the mask can vary. Table 24.2 shows some examples of masks used for subnetting.

Table 24.2 *Masks for subnetted networks*

Class	Mask	Address (Example)	Network Address (Example)
A	255.255.0.0	15.32.56.7	15.32.0.0
B	255.255.255.0	135.67.13.9	135.67.13.0
C	255.255.255.192	201.34.12.72	201.34.12.64
D	N/A	N/A	N/A
E	N/A	N/A	N/A

Finding the Subnetwork Address

To find the subnetwork address, apply the mask to the IP address.

Boundary-Level Masking

If the masking is at the boundary level (the mask numbers are either 255 or 0), finding the subnetwork address is very easy. Follow these two rules:

1. The bytes in the IP address that correspond to 255 in the mask will be repeated in the subnetwork address.
2. The bytes in the IP address that correspond to 0 in the mask will change to 0 in the subnetwork address.

Example 24.6

The following shows how to get the subnetwork address from an IP address:

IP address	45	23	21	8
Mask	255	255	0	0
Subnetwork address	45	23	0	0

Example 24.7

The following shows how to get the subnetwork address from an IP address:

IP address	173	23	21	8
Mask	255	255	255	0
Subnetwork address	173	23	21	0

Nonboundary-Level Masking

If the masking is not at the boundary level (the mask numbers are not just 255 or 0), finding the subnetwork address involves using the bit-wise AND operator. Follow these three rules:

1. The bytes in the IP address that correspond to 255 in the mask will be repeated in the subnetwork address.
2. The bytes in the IP address that correspond to 0 in the mask will change to 0 in the subnetwork address.
3. For other bytes, use the bit-wise AND operator.

Example 24.8

The following shows how to get the network address from an IP address:

IP address	45	123	21	8
Mask	255	192	0	0
Subnetwork address	45	64	0	0

As you can see, three bytes are easy to determine. However, the second byte needs the *bit-wise AND* operation. The bit-wise AND operation is very simple. If two bits are both 1s, the result is 1; otherwise, the result is 0.

```
123                        0 1 1 1 1 0 1 1
192                        1 1 0 0 0 0 0 0
----------------------------------------------------------------
64                         0 1 0 0 0 0 0 0
```

Example 24.9

The following shows how to get the subnetwork address from an IP address:

IP address	213	.	23	.	47	.	37
Mask	255	.	255	.	255	.	240
Subnetwork address	213	.	23	.	47	.	32

As you can see, three bytes are easy to determine. However, the fourth byte needs the bit-wise AND operation.

```
37                         0 0 1 0 0 1 0 1
240                        1 1 1 1 0 0 0 0
----------------------------------------------------------------
32                         0 0 1 0 0 0 0 0
```

24.5   OTHER PROTOCOLS IN THE NETWORK LAYER

TCP/IP supports four other protocols in the network layer: ARP, RARP, ICMP, and IGMP.

Address Resolution Protocol (ARP)

The **address resolution protocol (ARP)** associates an IP address with the physical address. On a typical physical network, such as a LAN, each device on a link is identified by a physical or station address usually imprinted on the network interface card (NIC).

Physical addresses have local jurisdiction and can be changed easily. For example, if the NIC on a particular machine fails, the physical address changes. The IP addresses, on the other hand, have universal jurisdiction and cannot be changed. ARP is used to find the physical address of the node when its Internet address is known.

Anytime a host, or a router, needs to find the physical address of another host on its network, it formats an ARP query packet that includes the IP address and broadcasts it over the network (see Figure 24.13). Every host on the network receives and processes the ARP packet, but only the intended recipient recognizes its internet address and sends back its physical address. The host holding the datagram adds the address of the target host both to its cache memory and to the datagram header, then sends the datagram on its way.

Figure 24.13 *ARP*

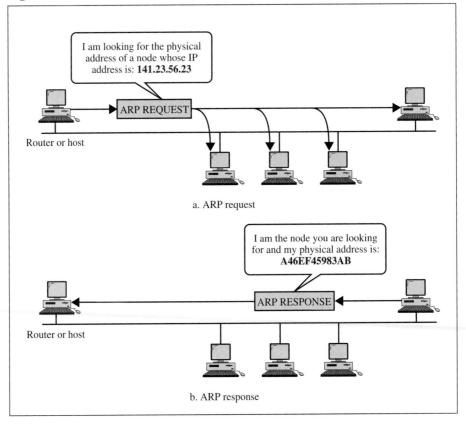

a. ARP request

b. ARP response

Reverse Address Resolution Protocol (RARP)

The **reverse address resolution protocol (RARP)** allows a host to discover its internet address when it knows only its physical address. The question here is, Why do we need RARP? A host is supposed to have its internet address stored on its hard disk!

Answer: True, true. But what if the host is a diskless computer? Or what if the computer is being connected to the network for the first time (when it is being booted)? Or what if you get a new computer but decide to keep the old NIC?

RARP works much like ARP. The host wishing to retrieve its internet address broadcasts an RARP query packet that contains its physical address to every host on its physical network. A server on the network recognizes the RARP packet and returns the host's internet address.

Internet Control Message Protocol (ICMP)

The **internet control message protocol (ICMP)** is a mechanism used by hosts and routers to send notification of datagram problems back to the sender.

As we saw above, IP is essentially an unreliable and connectionless protocol. ICMP, however, allows IP to inform a sender if a datagram is undeliverable. A datagram travels from router to router until it reaches one that can deliver it to its final destination. If a router is unable to route or deliver the datagram because of unusual conditions (disabled links, or the device is on fire) or because of network congestion, ICMP allows it to inform the original source.

ICMP uses echo test/reply to test whether a destination is reachable and responding. It also handles both control and error messages, but its sole function is to report problems, not correct them. Responsibility for correction lies with the sender.

Note that a datagram carries only the addresses of the original sender and the final destination. It does not know the addresses of the previous router(s) that passed it along. For this reason, ICMP can send messages only to the source, not to an intermediate router.

Internet Group Message Protocol (IGMP)

The IP protocol can be involved in two types of communication: unicasting and multicasting. Unicasting is the communication between one sender and one receiver. It is a one-to-one communication. However, some processes sometimes need to send the same message to a large number of receivers simultaneously. This is called *multicasting,* which is a one-to-many communication. Multicasting has many applications. For example, multiple stockbrokers can simultaneously be informed of changes in a stock price, or travel agents can be informed of a trip cancellation. Some other applications include distance learning and video-on-demand.

IP addressing supports multicasting. All 32-bit IP addresses that start with 1110 (class D) are multicast addresses. With 28 bits remaining for the group address, more than 250 million addresses are available for assignment. Some of these addresses are permanently assigned.

The **internet group message protocol (IGMP)** has been designed to help a multicast router identify the hosts in a LAN that are members of a multicast group. It is a companion to the IP protocol.

24.6   TRANSPORT LAYER

The transport layer is represented in TCP/IP by two protocols: TCP and UDP. Of these, UDP is the simpler; it provides nonsequenced transport functionality when reliability and security are less important than size and speed. Most applications, however, require reliable end-to-end delivery and so make use of TCP.

The IP delivers a datagram from a source host to a destination host, making it a host-to-host protocol. Today's operating systems, however, support multiuser and multiprocessing environments. An executing program is called a process. A host receiving a datagram may be running several different concurrent processes, any one of which is a possible destination for the transmission. In fact, although we have been talking about hosts sending messages to other hosts over a network, it is actually a source process that is sending a message to a destination process.

The transport protocols of the TCP/IP suite define a set of conceptual connections to individual processes called protocol ports or, more simply, ports. A protocol port is a destination point (usually a buffer) for storing data for use by a particular process. The interface between processes and their corresponding ports is provided by the operating system of the host.

The IP is a host-to-host protocol, meaning that it can deliver a packet from one physical device to another. TCP/IP's transport level protocols are port-to-port protocols that work on top of the IP protocols to deliver the packet from the originating port to the IP services at the start of a transmission, and from the IP services to the destination port at the end (see Figure 24.14).

Figure 24.14   *Port addresses*

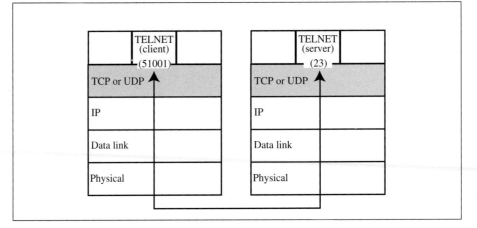

Each port is defined by a positive integer address carried in the header of a transport layer packet. An IP datagram uses the host's 32-bit internet address. A frame at the transport level uses the process **port address** of 16 bits, enough to allow the support of up to 65,536 (0 to 65535) ports.

User Datagram Protocol (UDP)

The user datagram protocol (UDP) is the simpler of the two standard TCP/IP transport protocols. It is an end-to-end transport level protocol that adds only port addresses, checksum error control, and length information to the data from the upper layer. The packet produced by the UDP is called a user datagram (see Figure 24.15). A brief description of its fields is in order.

- **Source port address.** The source port address is the address of the application program that has created the message.
- **Destination port address.** The destination port address is the address of the application program that will receive the message.
- **Total length.** The total length field defines the total length of the user datagram in bytes.
- **Checksum.** The checksum is a 16-bit field used in error detection.

Figure 24.15   *UDP datagram format*

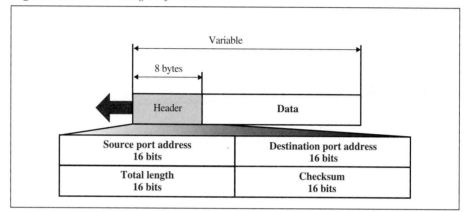

UDP provides only the basic functions needed for end-to-end delivery of a transmission. It does not provide any sequencing or reordering functions and cannot specify the damaged packet when reporting an error (for which it must be paired with ICMP). UDP can discover that an error has occurred; ICMP can then inform the sender that a user datagram has been damaged and discarded. Neither, however, has the ability to specify which packet has been lost. UDP contains only a checksum; it does not contain an ID or sequencing number for a particular data segment.

Transmission Control Protocol (TCP)

The Transmission Control Protocol (TCP) provides full transport layer services to applications. TCP is a reliable stream transport port-to-port protocol. The term *stream,* in this context, means connection-oriented: a connection must be established between both ends of a transmission before either may transmit data. By creating this connection, TCP generates a virtual circuit between sender and receiver that is active for the duration of a transmission. (Connections for the duration of an entire exchange are different, and are handled by session functions in individual applications.) TCP begins each transmission by alerting the receiver that datagrams are on their way (connection establishment) and ends each transmission with a connection termination. In this way, the receiver knows to expect the entire transmission rather than a single packet.

IP and UDP treat multiple datagrams belonging to a single transmission as entirely separate units, unrelated to each other. The arrival of each datagram at the destination is therefore a separate event, unexpected by the receiver. TCP, on the other hand, as a connection-oriented service, is responsible for the reliable delivery of the entire stream of bits contained in the message originally generated by the sending application. Reliability is ensured by provision for error detection and retransmission of damaged frames; all segments must be received and acknowledged before the transmission is considered complete and the virtual circuit is discarded.

At the sending end of each transmission, TCP divides long transmissions into smaller data units and packages each into a frame called a segment. Each segment includes a sequencing number for reordering after receipt, together with an acknowledgment ID number and a window-size field for sliding window ARQ. Segments are carried across network links inside of IP datagrams. At the receiving end, TCP collects each datagram as it comes in and reorders the transmission based on sequence numbers.

The TCP Segment

The scope of the services provided by TCP requires that the segment header be extensive (see Figure 24.16). A comparison of the TCP segment format with that of a UDP user datagram shows the differences between the two protocols. TCP provides a comprehensive range of reliability functions but sacrifices speed (connections must be established, acknowledgments waited for, etc.). Because of its smaller frame size, UDP is much faster than TCP, but at the expense of reliability. A brief description of each field is in order.

Figure 24.16   *TCP segment format*

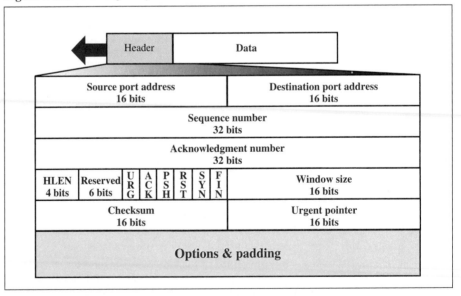

- **Source port address.** The source port address defines the application program in the source computer.
- **Destination port address.** The destination port address defines the application program in the destination computer.

■ **Sequence number.** A stream of data from the application program may be divided into two or more TCP segments. The sequence number field shows the position of the data in the original data stream.

■ **Acknowledgment number.** The 32-bit acknowledgment number is used to acknowledge the receipt of data from the other communicating device. This number is valid only if the ACK bit in the control field (explained later) is set. In this case, it defines the byte sequence number that is next expected.

■ **Header length (HLEN).** The four-bit HLEN field indicates the number of 32-bit (four-byte) words in the TCP header. The four bits can define a number up to 15. This is multiplied by 4 to give the total number of bytes in the header. Therefore, the size of the header can be a maximum of 60 bytes (4 × 15). Since the minimum required size of the header is 20 bytes, 40 bytes are thus available for the options section.

■ **Reserved.** A six-bit field is reserved for future use.

■ **Control.** Each bit of the six-bit control field functions individually and independently. A bit can either define the use of a segment or serve as a validity check for other fields. The urgent bit, when set, validates the urgent pointer field. Both this bit and the pointer indicate that the data in the segment are urgent. The ACK bit, when set, validates the acknowledgment number field. Both are used together and have different functions, depending on the segment type. The PSH bit is used to inform the sender that a higher throughput is needed. If possible, data must be pushed through paths with higher throughput. The reset bit is used to reset the connection when there is confusion in the sequence numbers. The SYN bit is used for sequence number synchronization in three types of segments: connection request, connection confirmation (with the ACK bit set), and confirmation acknowledgment (with the ACK bit set). The FIN bit is used in connection termination in three types of segments: termination request, termination confirmation (with the ACK bit set), and acknowledgment of termination confirmation (with the ACK bit set).

■ **Window size.** The window is a 16-bit field that defines the size of the sliding window.

■ **Checksum.** The checksum is a 16-bit field used in error detection.

■ **Urgent pointer.** This is the last required field in the header. Its value is valid only if the URG bit in the control field is set. In this case, the sender is informing the receiver that there are **urgent data** in the data portion of the segment. This pointer defines the end of urgent data and the start of normal data.

■ **Options and padding.** The remainder of the TCP header defines the optional fields. They are used to convey additional information to the receiver or for alignment purposes.

24.7   KEY TERMS AND CONCEPTS

address resolution protocol (ARP)

Advanced Research Project Agency (ARPA)

Advanced Research Project Agency Network (ARPANET)

broadcasting

class of address	multicast address
datagram	multicasting
dotted-decimal notation	netid
fragmentation	port address
host	reverse address resolution protocol (RARP)
hostid	
Internet address	segment
internet control message protocol (ICMP)	subnetting
	subnetwork
internet group message protocol (IGMP)	subnetwork address
Internetworking Protocol (IP)	Transmission Control Protocol (TCP)
IP address	Transmission Control Protocol /Internetworking Protocol (TCP/IP)
IP address class	
IP datagram	urgent data
IPv4	user datagram
masking	User Datagram Protocol (UDP)

24.8   SUMMARY

- Transmission Control Protocol/Internetworking Protocol (TCP/IP) is a set of rules and procedures that govern the exchange of messages in an internetwork.
- TCP/IP was originally developed as a protocol for networks that wanted to be connected to ARPANET, a U.S. Department of Defense project. ARPANET is now known as the Internet.
- TCP/IP is a five-layer protocol suite whose bottom four layers match the OSI model fairly closely. The highest level, the application layer, corresponds to OSI's top three layers.

■ The Internetwork Protocol (IP) is defined at the network layer. IP is unreliable and connectionless.

■ The IP packet, called the datagram, consists of a variable header and a variable data field.

■ An internet address (better known as the IP address) uniquely defines the connection of a host to its network.

■ The four-byte IP address is usually written n1.n2.n3.n4, n*x* being the decimal equivalent of each byte. The IP address contains three pieces of information:

a. Class type—A, B, C, D, or E.

b. Netid—network identification number.

c. Hostid—host address.

■ If the hostid is 0, we are referring to the whole physical network.

■ Subnetting allows an additional level of hierarchy in IP addressing.

■ The address resolution protocol (ARP) finds the physical address of a device if its IP address is known.

■ The reverse address resolution protocol (RARP) will find a host's IP address from its physical address.

■ The internet control message protocol (ICMP) handles control and error messages in the IP layer.

■ There are two protocols at the transport level:

a. User Datagram Protocol (UDP).

b. Transmission Control Protocol (TCP).

■ A protocol port is a source or destination point of an executing program in the application layer.

■ UDP is unreliable and connectionless. UDP communication is port-to-port. The UDP packet is called a user datagram.

■ TCP is reliable and connection-oriented. TCP communication is also port-to-port. The packet is called a segment.

24.9   PRACTICE SET

Review Questions

1. What is the difference between a physical address and a logical address?
2. What are the advantages of using UDP over TCP?
3. What is the connection between the TCP/IP protocol suite and ARPA?
4. What is the definition of an internet? What is the definition of the Internet?
5. Relate the TCP/IP application layer to its OSI model equivalent.
6. What are the physical and data link layer protocols of the TCP/IP protocol suite?
7. What are the data packets at each TCP/IP protocol suite layer called?

8. Name the protocols at the network layer of the TCP/IP protocol suite.
9. What is a best-effort delivery service?
10. What is the purpose of the time-to-live field in the IP datagram header?
11. Given an IP address in decimal-dotted notation, how can its class be determined?
12. How can a device have more than one IP address?
13. Discuss the relationship between the class of the network and the number of hosts allowed.
14. What is a hostid and what is a netid?
15. How does a netid differ from a network address?
16. What is the purpose of subnetting?
17. How is masking related to subnetting?
18. What is the difference between boundary-level masking and nonboundary-level masking?
19. What is the purpose of ARP?
20. What is the purpose of RARP?
21. What is the purpose of ICMP?
22. What is the purpose of IGMP?
23. Compare a host-to-host protocol such as IP to a port-to-port protocol such as TCP.
24. What is the difference between a logical address and a port address?
25. Describe the steps required for data communication for a connection-oriented protocol.

Multiple Choice Questions

26. Which OSI layer corresponds to the TCP-UDP layer?
    a. physical
    b. data link
    c. network
    d. transport
27. Which OSI layer corresponds to the IP layer?
    a. physical
    b. data link
    c. network
    d. transport
28. Which OSI layer(s) correspond to TCP/IP's application layer?
    a. application
    b. presentation
    c. session
    d. all of the above

29. Which of the following is true about the IP address?
    a. It's divided into exactly two classes.
    b. It contains a fixed-length hostid.
    c. It was established as a user-friendly interface.
    d. It is 32 bits long.
30. Which IP address class has few hosts per network?
    a. A
    b. B
    c. C
    d. D
31. For what does the data link layer look for as it sends a frame from one link to another?
    a. hostid
    b. IP address
    c. domain name
    d. station address
32. The purpose of ARP on a network is to find the _____ given the _____.
    a. Internet address, domain name
    b. Internet address, netid
    c. Internet address, station address
    d. station address, Internet address
33. Which of the following apply to UDP?
    a. is unreliable and connectionless
    b. contains destination and source port addresses
    c. reports certain errors
    d. all of the above
34. Which of the following applies(y) to both UDP and TCP?
    a. transport layer protocols
    b. port-to-port communication
    c. services of IP layer used
    d. all of the above
35. Which of the following is a class A host address?
    a. 128.4.5.6
    b. 117.4.5.1
    c. 117.0.0.0
    d. 117.8.0.0
36. Which of the following is a class B host address?
    a. 230.0.0.0
    b. 130.4.5.6
    c. 230.0.0.0

d. 30.4.5.6

37. Which of the following is a class C host address?

    a. 230.0.0.0
    b. 130.4.5.6
    c. 200.1.2.3
    d. 30.4.5.6

38. The data unit in the TCP/IP application layer is called a _____.

    a. message
    b. segment
    c. datagram
    d. frame

39. The data unit in the TCP/IP data link layer is called a _____.

    a. message
    b. segment
    c. datagram
    d. frame

40. The data unit in the TCP/IP IP layer is called a _____.

    a. message
    b. segment
    c. datagram
    d. frame

41. The data unit from the transport layer that uses UDP is called a _____.

    a. user datagram
    b. message
    c. segment
    d. frame

42. TCP/IP's _____ layer corresponds to the OSI model's top three layers.

    a. application
    b. presentation
    c. session
    d. transport

43. When a host knows its physical address but not its IP address, it can use _____.

    a. ICMP
    b. IGMP
    c. ARP
    d. RARP

44. This transport layer protocol is connectionless.

    a. UDP
    b. TCP
    c. FTP

  d. NVT

45. This transport layer protocol requires acknowledgment.

    a. UDP

    b. TCP

    c. FTP

    d. NVT

46. Which of the following is the default mask for the address 198.0.46.201?

    a. 255.0.0.0

    b. 255.255.0.0

    c. 255.255.255.0

    d. 255.255.255.255

47. Which of the following is the default mask for the address 98.0.46.201?

    a. 255.0.0.0

    b. 255.255.0.0

    c. 255.255.255.0

    d. 255.255.255.255

48. Which of the following is the default mask for the address 190.0.46.201?

    a. 255.0.0.0

    b. 255.255.0.0

    c. 255.255.255.0

    d. 255.255.255.255

Exercises

49. Show by calculation how many networks (not hosts) each IP address class (A, B, and C only) can have.

50. Show by calculation how many hosts per network each IP address class (A, B, and C only) can have.

51. Change the following IP addresses from dotted-decimal notation to binary notation:

    a. 114.34.2.8

    b. 129.14.6.8

    c. 208.34.54.12

    d. 238.34.2.1

    e. 241.34.2.8

52. Change the following IP addresses from binary notation to dotted-decimal notation:

    a. 01111111 11110000 01100111 01111101

    b. 10101111 11000000 11110000 00011101

    c. 11011111 10110000 00011111 01011101

    d. 11101111 11110111 11000111 00011101

    e. 11110111 11110011 10000111 11011101

53. Find the class of the following IP addresses:

    a. 208.34.54.12

    b. 238.34.2.1

    c. 114.34.2.8

    d. 129.14.6.8

    e. 241.34.2.8

54. Find the class of the following IP addresses:

    a. 11110111 11110011 10000111 11011101

    b. 10101111 11000000 11110000 00011101

    c. 11011111 10110000 00011111 01011101

    d. 11101111 11110111 11000111 00011101

    e. 01111111 11110000 01100111 01111101

55. Find the netid and the hostid of the following IP addresses:

    a. 114.34.2.8

    b. 19.34.21.5

    c. 23.67.12.1

    d. 126.23.4.0

56. Find the netid and the hostid of the following IP addresses:

    a. 129.14.6.8

    b. 132.56.8.6

    c. 171.34.14.8

    d. 190.12.67.9

57. Find the netid and the hostid of the following IP addresses:

    a. 192.8.56.2

    b. 220.34.8.9

    c. 208.34.54.12

    d. 205.23.67.8

58. Find the network address of the following IP addresses:

    a. 114.34.2.8

    b. 171.34.14.8

    c. 192.8.56.2

    d. 205.23.67.8

    e. 226.7.34.5

    f. 225.23.6.7

    g. 245.34.21.5

59. Find the network address of the following IP addresses:

    a. 23.67.12.1

    b. 126.23.4.0

    c. 190.12.67.9

    d. 220.34.8.9

    e. 237.34.8.2

    f. 240.34.2.8

    g. 247.23.4.78

60. Write the following masks in binary notation:

    a. 255.255.255.0

    b. 255.255.0.0

    c. 255.0.0.0

61. Write the following masks in binary notation:

    a. 255.255.192.0

    b. 255.255.224.0

    c. 255.255.255.240

62. Write the following masks in dotted-decimal notation:

    a. 11111111111111111111111111111000

    b. 11111111111111111111111111100000

    c. 11111111111111111111100000000000

63. Show the bit pattern for each of the following masks used in class B networks.

    a. 255.255.192.0

    b. 255.255.0.0

    c. 255.255.224.0

    d. 255.255. 255.0

64. Show the bit pattern for each of the following masks used in class C networks.

    a. 255.255.255.192

    b. 255.255.255.224

    c. 255.255.255.240

    d. 255.255. 255.0

65. What is the maximum number of subnets in class A networks using the following masks?

    a. 255.255.192.0

    b. 255.192.0.0

    c. 255.255.224.0

    d. 255.255.255.0

66. What is the maximum number of subnets in class B networks using the following masks?

    a. 255.255.192.0

    b. 255.255.0.0

    c. 255.255.224.0

    d. 255.255.255.0

67. What is the maximum number of subnets in class C networks using the following masks?

   a. 255.255.255.192

   b. 255.255.255.224

   c. 255.255.255.240

   d. 255.255.255.0

68. Find the subnetwork address for the following:

     IP address: 125.34.12.56   Mask: 255.255.0.0

69. Find the subnetwork address for the following:

     IP address: 120.14.22.16   Mask: 255.255.128.0

70. Find the subnetwork address for the following:

     IP address: 140.11.36.22   Mask: 255.255.255.0

71. Find the subnetwork address for the following:

     IP address: 141.181.14.16   Mask: 255.255.224.0

72. Find the subnetwork address and host address for the following:

     IP address: 200.34.22.156   Mask: 255.255.255.240

73. Figure 24.17 shows a site with a given network address and mask. The administration has divided the site into several subnetworks. Choose appropriate subnetwork addresses, host addresses, and router addresses.

Figure 24.17 *Site for Exercise 73*

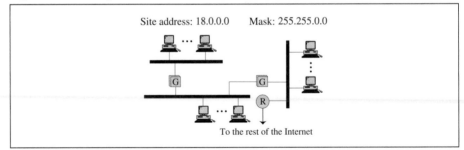

74. Figure 24.18 shows a site with a given network address and mask. The administration has divided the site into several subnetworks. Choose appropriate subnetwork addresses, host addresses, and router addresses.

75. Figure 24.19 shows a site with a given network address and mask. The administration has divided the site into several subnetworks. Choose appropriate subnetwork addresses, host addresses, and router addresses.

Figure 24.18   *Site for Exercise 74*

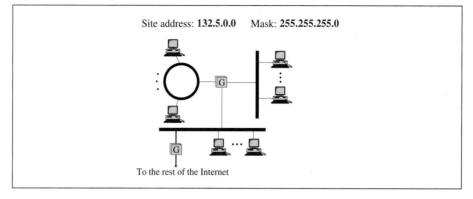

Site address: **132.5.0.0**   Mask: **255.255.255.0**

To the rest of the Internet

Figure 24.19   *Site for Exercise 75*

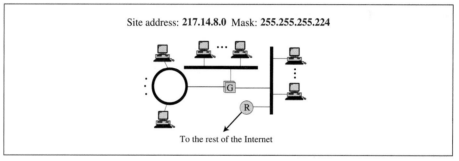

Site address: **217.14.8.0** Mask: **255.255.255.224**

To the rest of the Internet

CHAPTER 25

TCP/IP Protocol Suite: Part 2, Application Layer

Because the TCP/IP protocol suite was designed before the OSI model, the layers in TCP/IP do not correspond exactly to the OSI layers. TCP/IP has five layers: the lower four correspond to the lower four OSI layers. The TCP/IP application layer, however, is equivalent to the combined session, presentation, and application layers of the OSI model. This means that all of the functionalities associated with those three layers are handled in one single layer, the application layer (see Figure 25.1).

Figure 25.1 *Comparison between OSI and TCP/IP*

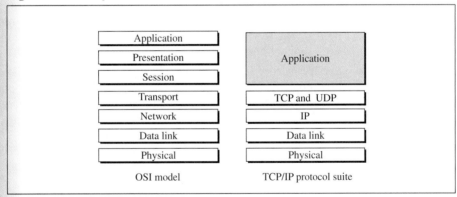

25.1 CLIENT–SERVER MODEL

To use the services available on an internet, application programs, running at two end computers and communicating with each other, are needed. In other words, in an internet, the application programs are the entities that communicate with each other, not the computers or users.

The application programs using the Internet follow these **client–server model** strategies:

- An application program, called the **client,** running on the local machine, requests a service from another application program, called the **server,** running on the remote machine. Figure 25.2 illustrates this.

Figure 25.2 *Client-server model*

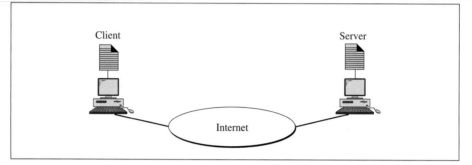

- A server can provide a service for any client, not just a particular client. In other words, the client–server relationship is many-to-one. Many clients can use the services of one server.
- Generally, a client program, which requests a service, should run only when it is needed. The server program, which provides a service, should run all of the time because it does not know when its service is needed.
- Services needed frequently and by many users have specific client–server application programs. For example, we should have client–server application programs that allow users to access files, send e-mail, and so on. For services that are more customized, we should have one generic application program that allows users to access the services available on a remote computer.

Client

A client is a program running on the local machine requesting service from a server. A client program is finite, which means it is started by the user (or another application program) and terminates when the service is complete.

Server

A server is a program running on the remote machine providing service to the clients. When it starts, it opens the door for incoming requests from clients, but it never initiates a service until it is requested to do so.

A server program is an infinite program. When it starts, it runs infinitely unless a problem arises. It waits for incoming requests from clients. When a request arrives, it responds to the request.

25.2   BOOTSTRAP PROTOCOL (BOOTP) AND DYNAMIC HOST CONFIGURATION PROTOCOL (DHCP)

Each computer that is attached to a TCP/IP internet must know the following information:

■   Its IP address.

■   Its subnet mask.

■   The IP address of a router.

■   The IP address of a name server.

This information is usually stored in a configuration file and accessed by the computer during the bootstrap process. But what about a diskless workstation or a computer with a disk that is booted for the first time?

In the case of a diskless computer, the operating system and the networking software could be stored in read-only memory (ROM). However, the above information is not known to the manufacturer and thus cannot be stored in ROM. The information is dependent on the individual configuration of the machine and relates to the network to which the machine is connected.

BOOTP

Bootstrap protocol (BOOTP) is a client–server protocol designed to provide the four previously mentioned pieces of information for a diskless computer or a computer that is booted for the first time. We have already studied one protocol, RARP, that provides the IP address for a diskless computer. Why do we need yet another protocol? The answer is that RARP provides only the IP address and not the other information. If we use BOOTP, we do not need RARP.

DHCP

BOOTP is not a dynamic configuration protocol. When a client requests its IP address, the BOOTP server searches a table that matches the physical address of the client with its IP address. This implies that the binding between the physical address and the IP address of the client should already exist. The binding is predetermined.

However, what if a host moves from one physical network to another? What if a host wants a temporary IP address? BOOTP cannot handle these problems because the binding between the physical and IP addresses is static and fixed in a table until changed by the administrator. BOOTP is a static configuration protocol.

The **dynamic host configuration protocol (DHCP)** has been devised to provide dynamic configuration. DHCP is an extension to BOOTP. It enhances BOOTP and is backward compatible with BOOTP. This means a host running the BOOTP client can request a static configuration from a DHCP server.

DHCP is also needed when a host moves from network to network or is connected and disconnected from a network (like a subscriber to a service provider). DHCP provides temporary IP addresses for a limited period of time.

25.3   DOMAIN NAME SYSTEM (DNS)

To identify an entity, TCP/IP protocols use the IP address, which uniquely identifies the connection of a host to the Internet. However, people prefer to use names instead of addresses. Therefore, we need a system that can map a name to an address and conversely an address to a name. In TCP/IP, this is the **Domain Name System (DNS).**

DNS in the Internet

DNS is a protocol that can be used in different platforms. In the Internet, the domain name space (tree) is divided into three different sections: generic domains, country domains, and inverse domain (see Figure 25.3).

Figure 25.3   *DNS in the Internet*

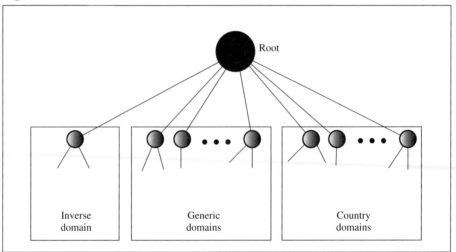

Generic Domains

The **generic domains** define registered hosts according to their generic behavior. Each node in the tree defines a domain, which is an index to the domain name space database (see Figure 25.4).

Looking at the tree, we see that the first level in the generic domain section allows seven possible three-character labels. These labels describe the organization types as listed in Table 25.1.

Recently a few more first-level labels have been proposed; these are shown in Table 25.2.

Figure 25.4   *Generic domains*

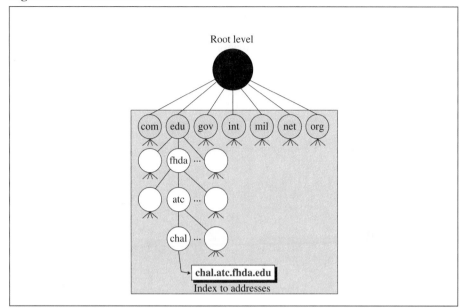

Table 25.1   *Generic domain labels*

Label	Description
com	Commercial organizations
edu	Educational institutions
gov	Government institutions
int	International organizations
mil	Military groups
net	Network support centers
org	Nonprofit organizations

Table 25.2   *Proposed generic domain labels*

Label	Description
arts	Cultural organizations
firm	Businesses or firms
info	Information service providers
nom	Personal nomenclatures
rec	Recreation/entertainment organizations
store	Businesses offering goods to purchase
web	Web-related organizations

Country Domains

The **country domain** section follows the same format as the generic domains but uses two-character country abbreviations (e.g., "us" for United States) in place of the three-character organizational abbreviations at the first level. Second-level labels can be organizational, or they can be more specific, national designations. The United States, for example, uses state abbreviations as a subdivision of "us" (e.g., ca.us.).

Figure 25.5 shows the country domain section. The address *anza.cup.ca.us* can be translated to De Anza College in Cupertino in California in the United States.

Figure 25.5 *Country domains*

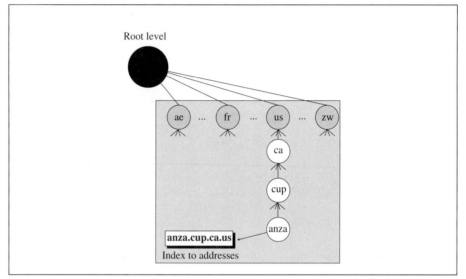

Inverse Domain

The **inverse domain** is used to map an address to a name. This may happen, for example, when a server has received a request from a client to do a task. Whereas the server has a file that contains a list of authorized clients, the server lists only the IP address of the client (extracted from the received IP packet). To determine if the client is on the authorized list, it can send a query to the DNS server and ask for a mapping of address to name. See Figure 25.6.

25.4 TELNET

The main task of the Internet and its TCP/IP protocol suite is to provide services for users. For example, users want to be able to run different application programs at a remote site and create results that can be transferred to their local site. One way to satisfy these demands is to create different client–server application programs for each desired service. Programs such as file transfer programs (FTP and TFTP), e-mail

Figure 25.6 *Inverse domain*

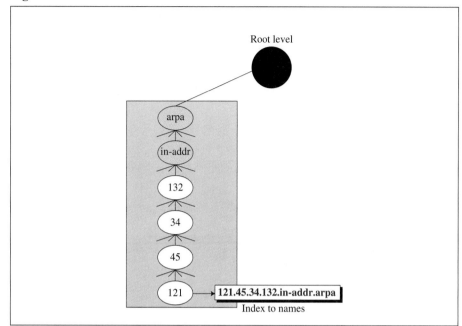

(SMTP), and so on are already available. But it would be impossible to write a specific client–server program for each demand.

The better solution is a general-purpose client–server program that lets a user access any application program on a remote computer; in other words, allow the user to log on to a remote computer. After logging on, a user can use the services available on the remote computer and transfer the results back to the local computer.

In this section, we discuss a popular client–server application program called TELNET. **TELNET** is an abbreviation for **TErminaL NETwork.** TELNET enables the establishment of a connection to a remote system in such a way that the local terminal appears to be a terminal at the remote system.

> TELNET is a general-purpose client–server application program.

Local Login   When a user logs into a local time-sharing system, it is called **local login.** As a user types at a terminal or at a workstation running a terminal emulator, the keystrokes are accepted by the terminal driver. The terminal driver passes the characters to the operating system. The operating system, in turn, interprets the combination of characters and invokes the desired application program or utility (see Figure 25.7).

The mechanism, however, is not as simple as it seems because the operating system may assign special meanings to special characters. For example, in UNIX some combinations of characters have special meanings, such as the combination of the control character with the character "z", which means suspend; the combination of the control character with the character "c", which means abort; and so on. Whereas these special situations do not create any problem in local login because the terminal

Figure 25.7 *Local login*

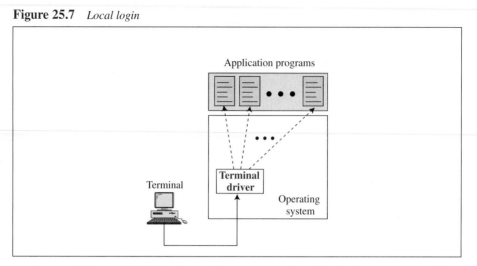

emulator and the terminal driver know the exact meaning of each character or combination of characters, they may create problems in remote login. Which process should interpret special characters? The client or the server? We will clarify this situation later in this section.

Remote Login When a user wants to access an application program or utility located on a remote machine, he or she performs **remote login.** Here the TELNET client and server programs come into use. The user sends the keystrokes to the terminal driver where the local operating system accepts the characters but does not interpret them. The characters are sent to the TELNET client, which transforms the characters to a universal character set called *network virtual terminal characters* and delivers them to the local TCP/IP stack (see Figure 25.8).

Figure 25.8 *Remote login*

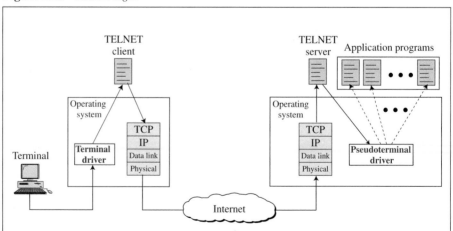

The commands or text, in NVT form, travel through the Internet and arrive at the TCP/IP stack at the remote machine. Here the characters are delivered to the operating system and passed to the TELNET server, which changes the characters to the corresponding characters understandable by the remote computer. However, the characters cannot be passed directly to the operating system because the remote operating system is not designed to receive characters from a TELNET server: it is designed to receive characters from a terminal driver. The solution is to add a piece of software called a *pseudoterminal driver,* which pretends that the characters are coming from a terminal. The operating system then passes the characters to the appropriate application program.

Network Virtual Terminal (NVT)

The mechanism to access a remote computer is complex. This is because every computer and its operating system accepts a special combination of characters as tokens. For example, the end-of-file token in a computer running the DOS operating system is Ctrl+z, while the **UNIX** operating system recognizes Ctrl+d.

We are dealing with heterogeneous systems. If we want to access any remote computer in the world, we first must know to what type of computer we will be connected, and we also must install the specific terminal emulator used by that computer. TELNET solves this problem by defining a universal interface called the **network virtual terminal (NVT)** character set. Via this interface, the client TELNET translates characters (data or commands) that come from the local terminal into NVT form and delivers them to the network. The server TELNET, on the other hand, translates data and commands from NVT form into the form acceptable by the remote computer. For an illustration of this concept, see Figure 25.9.

Figure 25.9   *Concept of NVT*

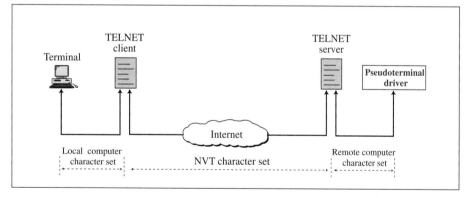

25.5   FILE TRANSFER PROTOCOL (FTP)

File transfer protocol (FTP) is the standard mechanism provided by TCP/IP for copying a file from one host to another. Transferring files from one computer to another is one of the most common tasks expected from a networking or internetworking environment.

Although transferring files from one system to another seems simple and straight-forward, some problems must be dealt with first. For example, two systems may use different file name conventions. Two systems may have different ways to represent text and data. Two systems may have different directory structures. All of these problems have been solved by FTP in a very simple and elegant approach.

FTP differs from other client–server applications in that it establishes two connections between the hosts. One connection is used for **data transfer,** the other for control information (commands and responses). Separation of commands and data transfer makes FTP more efficient. The control connection uses very simple rules of communication. We need to transfer only a line of command or a line of response at a time. The data connection, on the other hand, needs more complex rules due to the variety of data types transferred.

Figure 25.10 shows the basic model of FTP. The client has three components: the user interface, the client control process, and the client data transfer process. The server has two components: the server control process and the server data transfer process. The control connection is made between the control processes. The data connection is made between the data transfer processes.

Figure 25.10   *FTP*

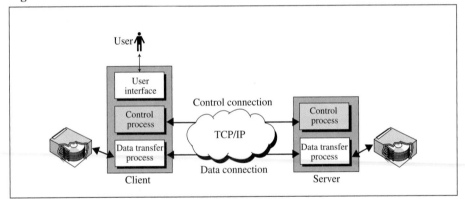

The control connection remains connected during the entire interactive FTP session. The data connection is opened and then closed for each file transferred. It opens each time commands that involve transferring files are used, and it closes when the file is transferred. The two FTP connections, control and data, use different strategies and different port numbers.

25.6   TRIVIAL FILE TRANSFER PROTOCOL (TFTP)

There are occasions when we need to simply copy a file without the need for all of the functionalities of the FTP protocol. For example, when a diskless workstation or a router is booted, we need to download the bootstrap and configuration files. Here we do not need all of the sophistication provided in FTP. We just need a protocol that quickly copies the files.

Trivial File Transfer Protocol (TFTP) is designed for these types of file transfer. It is so simple that the software package can fit into the read-only memory of a diskless workstation. It can be used at bootstrap time. TFTP can read or write a file for the client. *Reading* means copying a file from the server site to the client site. *Writing* means copying a file from the client site to the server site.

25.7   SIMPLE MAIL TRANSFER PROTOCOL (SMTP)

One of the most popular network services is **electronic mail (e-mail).** The TCP/IP protocol that supports electronic mail on the Internet is called **Simple Mail Transfer Protocol (SMTP).** It is a system for sending messages to other computer users based on e-mail addresses. SMTP provides for mail exchange between users on the same or different computers and supports:

- Sending a single message to one or more recipients.
- Sending messages that include text, voice, video, or graphics.
- Sending messages to users on networks outside the Internet.

Figure 25.11 shows the basic idea.

Figure 25.11   *SMTP concept*

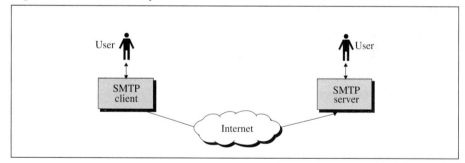

Starting with this simple figure, we will examine the components of the SMTP system, gradually adding complexity. Let us begin by breaking down both the SMTP client and server into two components: **user agent (UA)** and **mail transfer agent (MTA).**

The UA prepares the message, creates the envelope, and puts the message in the envelope. The MTA transfers the mail across the Internet. Figure 25.12 shows the previous figure with the addition of these two components.

SMTP protocol allows a more complex system than the one shown. Relaying could be involved. Instead of just one MTA at the sender site and one at the receiving site, other MTAs, acting either as client or server, can relay the mail (see Figure 25.13).

The relaying system allows sites that do not use the TCP/IP protocol suite to send e-mail to users on other sites that may or may not use the TCP/IP protocol suite. This is accomplished through the use of a **mail gateway,** which is a relay MTA that can

Figure 25.12 *UAs and MTAs*

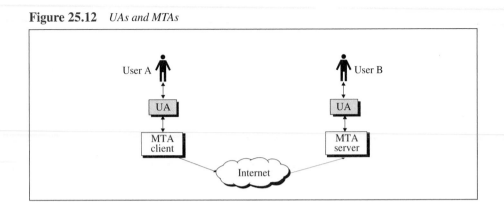

Figure 25.13 *Relay MTAs*

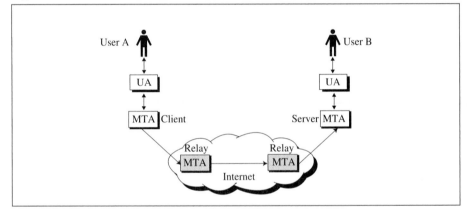

receive mail prepared by a protocol other than SMTP and transform it to SMTP format before sending it. It can also receive mail in SMTP format and change it to another format before sending it (see Figure 25.14).

Figure 25.14 *Mail gateway*

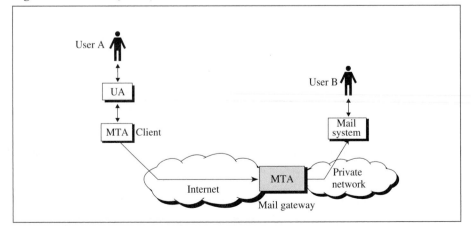

User Agent (UA)

A user agent is defined in SMTP, but the implementation details are not. The UA is normally a program used to send and receive mail. Popular user agent programs are MH, Berkeley Mail, Elm, Zmail, and Mush.

Some user agents have an extra user interface that allows window-type interactions with the system.

Addresses

To deliver mail, a mail handling system must use a unique addressing system. The addressing system used by SMTP consists of two parts: a *local part* and a *domain name,* separated by an @ sign (see Figure 25.15).

Figure 25.15 *E-mail address*

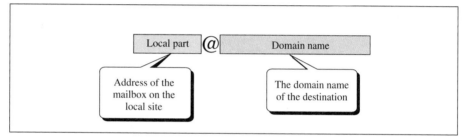

Local Part

The local part defines the name of a special file, called the user mailbox, where all of the mail received for a user is stored for retrieval by the user agent.

Domain Name

The second part of the address is the domain name. An organization usually selects one or more hosts to receive and send e-mail; they are sometimes called *mail exchangers.* The domain name assigned to each mail exchanger either comes from the DNS database or is a logical name (for example, the name of the organization).

Mail Transfer Agent (MTA)

The actual mail transfer is done through mail transfer agents (MTAs). To send mail, a system must have a client MTA, and to receive mail, a system must have a server MTA. Although SMTP does not define a specific MTA, Sendmail is a commonly used UNIX system MTA.

SMTP simply defines how commands and responses must be sent back and forth. Each network is free to choose a software package for implementation. Figure 25.16 illustrates the process of sending and receiving e-mail as described above. For a computer to be able to send and receive mail using SMTP, it must have most of the entities (the user interface is not necessary) defined in the figure. The user interface is a component that creates a user-friendly environment.

Figure 25.16   *The entire e-mail system*

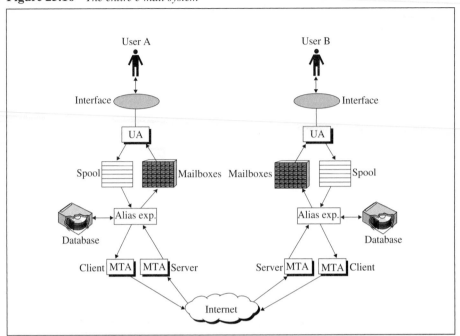

Multipurpose Internet Mail Extensions (MIME)

SMTP is a simple mail transfer protocol. Its simplicity, however, comes with a price. SMTP can send messages only in NVT seven-bit ASCII format. In other words, it has some limitations. For example, it cannot be used for languages that are not supported by seven-bit ASCII characters (such as French, German, Hebrew, Russian, Chinese, and Japanese). Also, it cannot be used to send binary files or to send video or audio data.

Multipurpose Internet Mail Extension (MIME) is a supplementary protocol that allows non-ASCII data to be sent through SMTP. MIME is not a mail protocol and cannot replace SMTP; it is only an extension to SMTP.

MIME transforms non-ASCII data at the sender site to NVT ASCII data and delivers it to the client SMTP to be sent through the Internet. The server SMTP at the receiving side receives the NVT ASCII data and delivers it to MIME to be transformed back to the original data.

We can think of MIME as a set of software functions that transform non-ASCII data to ASCII data and vice versa (see Figure 25.17).

Post Office Protocol (POP)

SMTP expects the destination host, the mail server receiving the mail, to be on-line all the time; otherwise, a TCP connection cannot be established. For this reason, it is not practical to establish an SMTP session with a desktop computer because desktop computers are usually powered down at the end of the day.

Figure 25.17   *MIME*

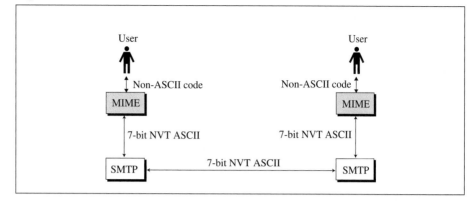

In many organizations, mail is received by an SMTP server that is always on-line. This SMTP server provides a mail-drop service. The server receives the mail on behalf of every host in the organization. Workstations interact with the SMTP host to retrieve messages by using a client–server protocol such as **Post Office Protocol (POP),** version 3 (POP3).

Although POP3 is used to download messages from the server, the SMTP client is still needed on the desktop to forward messages from the workstation user to its SMTP mail server (see Figure 25.18).

Figure 25.18   *POP3 and SMTP*

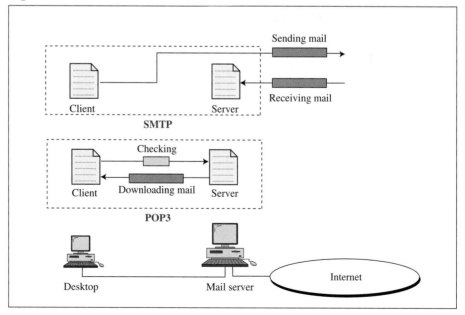

25.8 SIMPLE NETWORK MANAGEMENT PROTOCOL (SNMP)

The **Simple Network Management Protocol (SNMP)** is a framework for managing devices in an internet using the TCP/IP protocol suite. It provides a set of fundamental operations for monitoring and maintaining an internet.

Concept

SNMP uses the concept of manager and agent. That is, a manager, usually a host, controls and monitors a set of agents, usually routers (see Figure 25.19).

Figure 25.19 *SNMP concept*

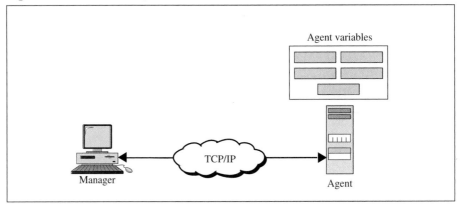

SNMP is an application-level protocol in which a few manager stations control a set of agents. The protocol is designed at the application level so that it can monitor devices made by different manufacturers and installed on different physical networks. In other words, SNMP frees management tasks from both the physical characteristics of the managed devices and the underlying networking technology. It can be used in a heterogeneous internet made of different LANs and WANs connected by routers or gateways made by different manufacturers.

Managers and Agents

A management station, called a **manager,** is a host that runs the SNMP client program. A managed station, called an **agent,** is a router (or a host) that runs the SNMP server program. Management is achieved through simple interaction between a manager and an agent.

The agent keeps performance information in a database. The manager has access to the values in the database. For example, a router can store in appropriate variables the number of packets received and forwarded. The manager can fetch and compare the values of these two variables to see if the router is congested or not.

The manager can also make the router perform certain actions. For example, a router periodically checks the value of a reboot counter to see when it should reboot itself. It reboots itself, for example, if the value of the counter is 0. The manager can use this feature to reboot the agent remotely at any time. It simply sends a packet to force a 0 value in the counter.

Agents can also contribute to the management process. The server program running on the agent can check the environment and, if it notices something unusual, it can send a warning message (called a *trap*) to the manager.

In other words, management with SNMP is based on three basic ideas:

1. A manager checks an agent by requesting information that reflects the behavior of the agent.
2. A manager forces an agent to perform a task by resetting values in the agent database.
3. An agent contributes to the management process by warning the manager of an unusual situation.

Components

Management in the Internet is achieved not only through the SNMP protocol but also by using other protocols that cooperate with SNMP. At the top level, management is accomplished with two other protocols: **structure of management information (SMI)** and **management information base (MIB).** SNMP uses the services provided by these two protocols to do its job. In other words, management is a team effort by SMI, MIB, and SNMP. All three use other protocols such as abstract syntax notation 1 (ASN.1) and **basic encoding rules (BER).** We discuss SMI, MIB, and SNMP in the next three sections (see Figure 25.20).

Figure 25.20   *Internet management components*

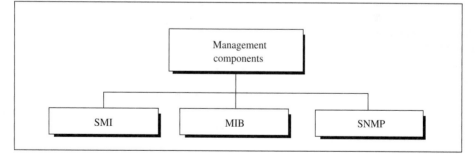

SMI

The SMI is a component used in network management. Its functions are to name objects; to define the type of data that can be stored in an object, and to show how to encode data for transmission over the network.

MIB

The **management information base (MIB)** is the second component used in network management. Each agent has its own MIB, which is a collection of all the objects that the manager can manage. The objects in the MIB are categorized under eight different groups: system, interface, address translation, ip, icmp, tcp, udp, and egp. These groups are under the mib object in the object identifier tree (see Figure 25.21). Each group has defined variables and/or tables.

Figure 25.21 *MIB*

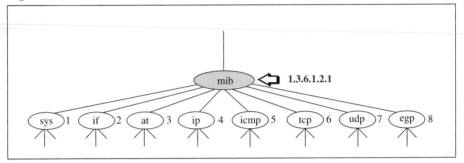

SNMP

SNMP defines five messages: GetRequest, GetNextRequest, SetRequest, GetResponse, and Trap (see Figure 25.22).

Figure 25.22 *SNMP messages*

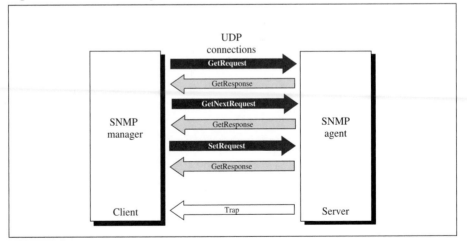

GetRequest The GetRequest message is sent from the manager (client) to the agent (server) to retrieve the value of a variable.

GetNextRequest The GetNextRequest message is sent from the manager to the agent to retrieve the value of a variable. The retrieved value is the value of the object following the defined object in the message. It is mostly used to retrieve the values of the entries in a table. If the manager does not know the indexes of the entries, it cannot retrieve the values. However, it can use GetNextRequest and define the object.

GetResponse The GetResponse message is sent from an agent to a manager in response to GetRequest and GetNextRequest. It contains the value of the variable(s) requested by the manager.

SetRequest The SetRequest message is sent from the manager to the agent to set (store) a value in a variable.

Trap The Trap message is sent from the agent to the manager to report an event. For example, if the agent is rebooted, it informs the manager and reports the time of rebooting.

25.9 HYPERTEXT TRANSFER PROTOCOL (HTTP)

The **Hypertext Transfer Protocol (HTTP)** is a protocol used mainly to access data on the World Wide Web (see next section). The protocol transfers data in the form of plain text, hypertext, audio, video, and so on. However, it is called the hypertext transfer protocol because its efficiency allows its use in a hypertext environment where there are rapid jumps from one document to another.

HTTP functions like a combination of FTP and SMTP. It is similar to FTP because it transfers files and uses the services of TCP. However, it is much simpler than FTP because it uses only one TCP connection. There is not a separate control connection; only data are transferred between the client and the server.

HTTP is like SMTP because the data transferred between the client and the server look like SMTP messages. In addition, the format of the messages is controlled by MIME-like headers. However, HTTP differs from SMTP in the way the messages are sent from the client to the server and from the server to the client. Unlike SMTP, the HTTP messages are not destined to be read by humans; they are read and interpreted by the HTTP server and HTTP client **(browser).** SMTP messages are stored and forwarded, but HTTP messages are delivered immediately.

The idea of HTTP is very simple. A client sends a request, which looks like mail, to the server. The server sends the response, which looks like a mail reply, to the client. The request and response messages carry data in the form of a letter with MIME-like format.

The commands from the client to the server are embedded in a letterlike request message. The contents of the requested file or other information are embedded in a letterlike response message.

HTTP Transaction

Figure 25.23 illustrates the HTTP transaction between the client and server. The client initializes the transaction by sending a request message. The server replies by sending a response.

Figure 25.23 *HTTP transaction*

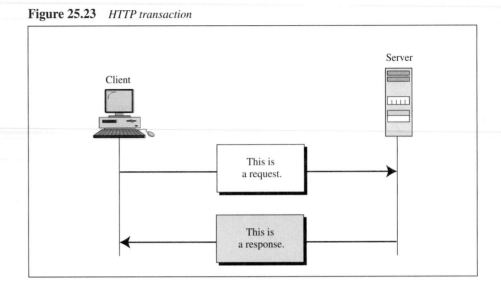

Messages

There are two general types of HTTP messages, shown in Figure 25.24: request and response. Both message types follow almost the same format.

Figure 25.24 *Message categories*

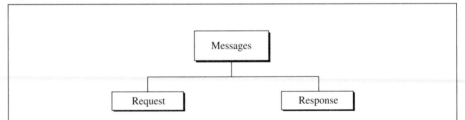

Request Messages

A request message consists of a request line, headers, and sometimes a body. See Figure 25.25.

Response Message

A response message consists of a status line, headers, and sometimes a body. See Figure 25.26.

Uniform Resource Locator (URL)

A client that wants to access a document needs an address. To facilitate the access of documents distributed throughout the world, HTTP uses the concept of locators. The **uniform resource locator (URL)** is a standard for specifying any kind of information

Figure 25.25 *Request message*

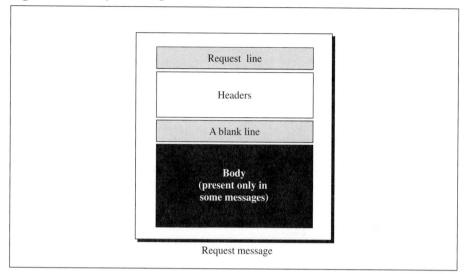

Request message

Figure 25.26 *Response message*

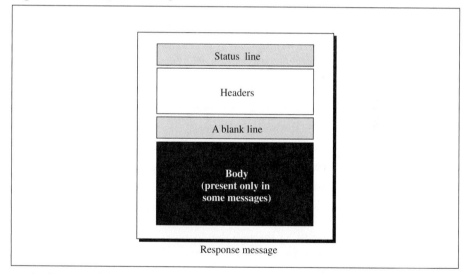

Response message

on the Internet. The URL defines four things: method, host computer, port, and path (see Figure 25.27).

The *method* is the protocol used to retrieve the document, for example HTTP. The *host* is the computer where the information is located, although the name of the computer can be an alias. Web pages are usually stored in computers, and computers are given alias names that usually begin with the characters "www." This is not mandatory, however, as the host can be any name given to the computer that hosts the web page.

The URL optionally can contain the port number of the server. If the *port* is included, it should be inserted between the host and the path, and it should be separated from the host by a colon.

Figure 25.27 *URL*

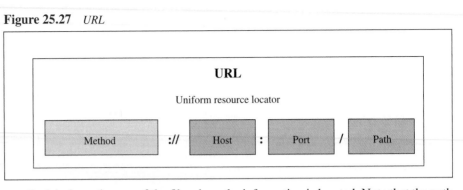

Path is the pathname of the file where the information is located. Note that the path can itself contain slashes that, in the UNIX operating system, separate the directories from the subdirectories and files.

25.10   WORLD WIDE WEB (WWW)

The **World Wide Web (WWW),** or the **web,** is a repository of information spread all over the world and linked together. The WWW has a unique combination of flexibility, portability, and user-friendly features that distinguish it from other services provided by the Internet.

The WWW project was initiated by CERN (European Laboratory for Particle Physics) to create a system to handle distributed resources necessary for scientific research.

The WWW today is a distributed client–server service, in which a client using a browser can access a service using a server. However, the service provided is distributed over many locations called *web sites* (see Figure 25.28).

Hypertext and Hypermedia

The WWW uses the concept of hypertext and hypermedia. In a hypertext environment, information is stored in a set of documents that are linked together using the concept of pointers. An item can be associated with another document using a pointer. The reader who is browsing through the document can move to other documents by choosing (clicking) the items that are linked to other documents. Figure 25.29 shows the concept of hypertext.

Whereas hypertext documents contain only text, hypermedia documents can contain pictures, graphics, and sound.

A unit of hypertext or hypermedia available on the Web is called a *page*. The main page for an organization or an individual is known as a **homepage.**

Browser Architecture

A variety of vendors offer commercial browsers that interpret and display a web document, and all of them use nearly the same architecture. Each browser usually consists

Figure 25.28 *Distributed services*

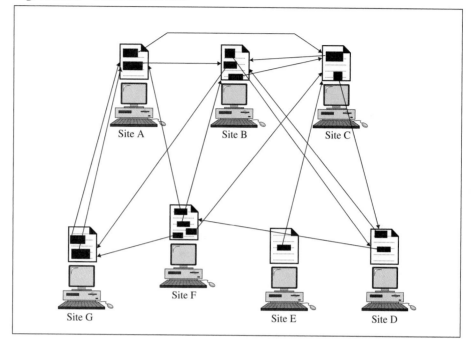

Figure 25.29 *Hypertext*

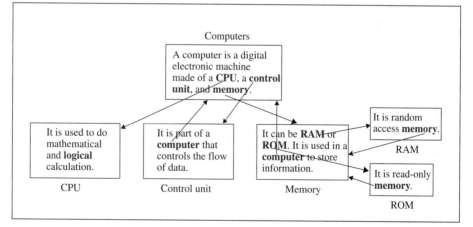

of three parts: a controller, client programs, and interpreters. The controller receives input from the keyboard or the mouse and uses the client programs to access the document. After the document has been accessed, the controller uses one of the interpreters to display the document on the screen. The client programs can be one of the methods (protocols) described previously such as HTTP, FTP, or TELNET. The interpreter can be HTML or Java, depending on the type of document (see Figure 25.30).

Figure 25.30 *Browser architecture*

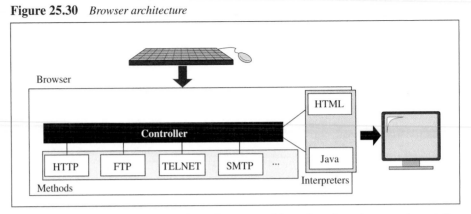

The documents in the WWW can be grouped into three broad categories: static, dynamic, and active (see Figure 25.31). The category is based on the time when the contents of the document are determined.

Figure 25.31 *Categories of Web documents*

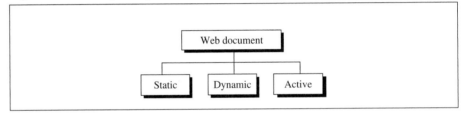

Static Documents

Static documents are fixed-content documents that are created and stored in a server. The client can get only a copy of the document. In other words, the contents of the file are determined when the file is created, not when it is used. Of course, the contents in the server can be changed, but the user cannot change it. When a client accesses the document, a copy of the document is sent. The user can then use a browsing program to display the document (see Figure 25.32).

HTML

HyperText Markup Language (HTML) is a language for creating **web pages.** The term *markup language* comes from the book publishing industry. Before a book is typeset and printed, a copy editor reads the manuscript and puts a lot of marks on it. These marks tell the designer how to format the text. For example, if the copy editor wants part of a line to be printed in boldface, he or she draws a wavy line under that part. In the same way, data for a web page are formatted for interpretation by a browser.

Let us explain the idea with an example. To make part of a text displayed in bold-face with HTML, we must include the beginning and ending boldface tags (marks) in the text, as shown in Figure 25.33.

Figure 25.32 *Static document*

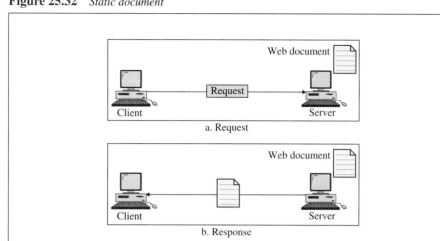

a. Request

b. Response

Figure 25.33 *Boldface tags*

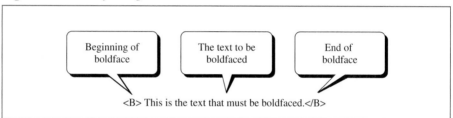

The two tags <B> and </B> are instructions for the browser. When the browser sees these two marks, it knows that the text must be boldfaced (see Figure 25.34).

Figure 25.34 *Effect of boldface tags*

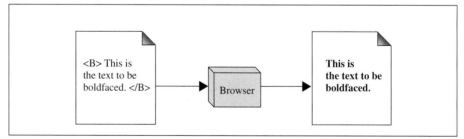

HTML lets us use only ASCII characters for both the main text and formatting instructions. In this way, every computer can receive the whole document as an ASCII document. The main text is the data, and the formatting instructions can be used by the browser to format the data.

Structure of a Web Page

A web page is made up of two parts: the head and the body.

Head   The head is the first part of a web page. The head contains the title of the page and other parameters that the browser will use.

Body   The actual contents of a page are in the body, which includes the text and the tags. Whereas the text is the actual information contained in a page, the tags define the appearance of the document. Every HTML tag is a name followed by an optional list of attributes, all enclosed between less than and greater than brackets (< and >).

An attribute, if present, is followed by an equal sign and the value of the attribute. Some tags can be used alone; some must be used in pairs. Those that are used in pairs are called *starting* and *ending* tags. The starting tag can have attributes and values. The ending tag cannot have attributes or values but must have a slash before the name.

Tags

The browser makes a decision about the structure of the text based on the tags, which are marks that are embedded into the text. A tag is enclosed in two brackets (< and >) and usually comes in pairs. The beginning tag starts with the name of the tag, and the ending tag starts with a slash followed by the name of the tag.

A tag can have a list of attributes, each of which can be followed by an equal sign and a value associated with the attribute. Figure 25.35 shows the format of a tag.

Figure 25.35   *Beginning and ending tags*

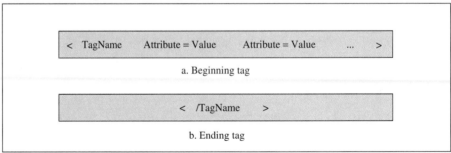

Dynamic Documents

Dynamic documents do not exist in a predefined format. Instead, a dynamic document is created by a web server whenever a browser requests the document. When a request arrives, the web server runs an application program that creates the dynamic document. The server returns the output of the program as a response to the browser that requested the document. Because a fresh document is created for each request, the contents of a dynamic document can vary from one request to another. A very simple example of a dynamic document is getting the time and date from the server. Time and date are kinds of information that are dynamic in that they change from moment to moment. The client can request that the server run a program such as the date program in UNIX and send the result of the program to the client. Figure 25.36 illustrates the steps in sending and responding to a dynamic document.

Figure 25.36 *Dynamic document*

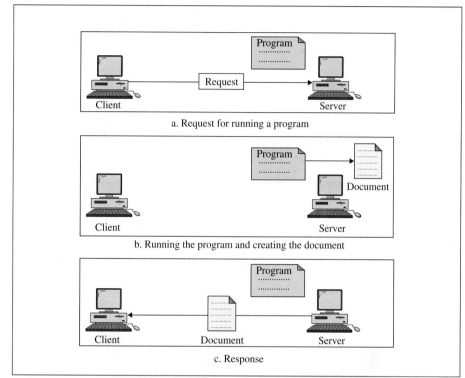

a. Request for running a program

b. Running the program and creating the document

c. Response

A server that handles dynamic documents follows these steps:

1. The server examines the URL to find if it defines a dynamic document.
2. If the URL defines a dynamic document, the server executes the program.
3. The server sends the output of the program to the client (browser).

Common Gateway Interface (CGI)

Common gateway interface (CGI) is a technology that creates and handles dynamic documents. CGI is a set of standards that defines how a dynamic document should be written, how input data should be supplied to the program, and how the output result should be used.

CGI is not a new language; instead, it allows programmers to use any of several languages such as C, C++, Bourne Shell, Korn Shell, C Shell, Tcl, or Perl. The only thing that CGI defines is a set of rules and terms that the programmer should follow.

The use of *common* in CGI indicates that the standard defines a set of rules that are common to any language or platform. The term *gateway* here means that a CGI program is a gateway that can be used to access other resources such as databases, graphic packages, and so on. The term *interface* here means that there is a set of predefined terms, variables, calls, and so on that can be used in any CGI program.

CGI Program

A CGI program in its simplest form is code written in one of the languages supporting the CGI. Any programmer that can encode a sequence of thoughts in a program and knows the syntax of one of the above-mentioned languages can write a simple CGI program.

Active Documents

For many applications, we need a program to be run at the client site. These are called **active documents.** For example, imagine we want to run a program that creates animated graphics on the screen or interacts with the user. The program definitely needs to be run at the client site where the animation or interaction takes place. When a browser requests an active document, the server sends a copy of the document in the form of bytecode. The document is then run at the client (browser) site (see Figure 25.37).

Figure 25.37 *Active document*

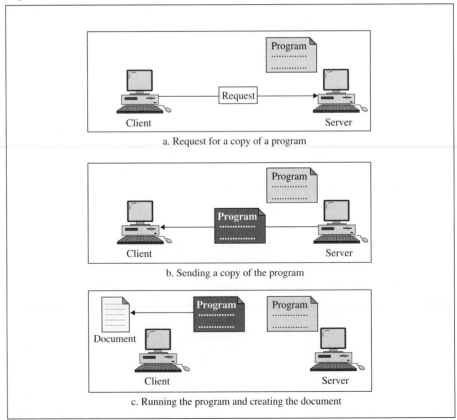

a. Request for a copy of a program

b. Sending a copy of the program

c. Running the program and creating the document

An active document in the server is stored in the form of binary code. However, it does not create overhead for the server in the same way that a dynamic document does. Although an active document is not run on the server, it is stored as a binary document that is retrieved by a client. When a client receives the document, it can also store it in its own storage area. In this way, the client can run the document again without making another request.

An active document is transported from the server to the client in binary form. This means that it can be compressed at the server site and decompressed at the client site, saving both bandwidth and transmission time.

Java

Java is a combination of a high-level programming language, a run-time environment, and a class library that allows a programmer to write an active document and a browser to run it. It can also be used as a stand-alone program without using a browser. However, Java is mostly used to create an **applet** (a small application program).

Java is an object-oriented language that is, syntactically and semantically, very similar to C++. However, it does not have some of the complexities of C++ such as operator overloading or multiple inheritance. Java is also hardware independent and does not use pointers. In Java, like any other object-oriented language, a programmer defines a set of objects and a set of operations (methods) to operate on those objects. It is a *typed* language, which means that the programmer must declare the type of any piece of data before using it.

25.11 KEY TERMS AND CONCEPTS

active document

agent

applet

basic encoding rule (BER)

bootstrap protocol (BOOTP)

browser

client

client–server model

common gateway interface (CGI)

country domain

data transfer

Domain Name System (DNS)

dynamic document

dynamic host configuration protocol (DHCP)

electronic mail (e-mail)

file transfer protocol (FTP)

generic domain

homepage

HyperText Markup Language (HTML)

Hypertext Transfer Protocol (HTTP)	Simple Mail Transfer Protocol (SMTP)
inverse domain	Simple Network Management Protocol (SNMP)
Java	static document
local login	
mail gateway	structure of management information (SMI)
mail transfer agent (MTA)	Terminal Network (TELNET)
management information base (MIB)	Trivial File Transfer Protocol (TFTP)
manager	uniform resource locator (URL)
Multipurpose Internet Mail Extension (MIME)	user agent (UA)
network virtual terminal (NVT)	UNIX
Post Office Protocol (POP)	web
remote login	web page
server	World Wide Web (WWW)

25.12   SUMMARY

■ The TCP/IP application layer corresponds to the combined session, presentation, and application layers of the OSI model.

■ In the client–server model, the client runs a program to request a service and the server runs a program to provide the service. These two programs communicate with each other.

■ One server program can provide services for many client programs.

■ The server program is on at all times while the client program is run only when needed.

■ Services needed frequently and by many users have specific client–server programs.

■ A client is a finite program running on the local machine requesting service from a server.

■ A server is an infinite program running on the remote machine providing service to the clients.

■ Domain Name System (DNS) is a client–server application that identifies each host on the Internet with a unique user-friendly name.

■ The domain name space is divided into three sections: generic domains, country domains, and inverse domain.

■ There are seven generic domains, each specifying an organization type.

■ Each country domain specifies a country.

■ The inverse domain finds a domain name for a given IP address. This is called address-to-name resolution.

■ TELNET is a client–server application that allows a user to log on to a remote machine, giving the user access to the remote system.

■ TELNET uses the network virtual terminal (NVT) system to encode characters on the local system. On the server machine, NVT decodes the characters to a form acceptable to the remote machine.

■ File transfer protocol (FTP) is a TCP/IP client–server application for copying files from one host to another.

■ FTP requires two connections for data transfer: a control connection and a data connection.

■ Trivial file transfer protocol (TFTP) is a simple file transfer protocol without the complexities and sophistication of FTP.

■ The TCP/IP protocol that supports e-mail on the Internet is called Simple Mail Transfer Protocol (SMTP).

■ Both SMTP client and server require a user agent (UA) and a mail transfer agent (MTA).

■ The UA prepares the message, creates the envelope, and puts the message in the envelope.

■ The mail address consists of two parts: a local address (user mailbox) and a domain name. The form is localname@domainname.

■ A mail gateway translates mail formats.

■ Multipurpose Internet Mail Extension (MIME) is an extension of SMTP that allows the transfer of multimedia messages.

■ Post Office Protocol (POP) is a protocol used by a mail server in conjunction with SMTP to receive and hold mail for hosts.

■ Simple Network Management Protocol (SNMP) is a framework for managing devices in an internet using the TCP/IP protocol suite.

■ A manager, usually a host, controls and monitors a set of agents, usually routers.

■ The manager is a host that runs the SNMP client program.

■ The agent is a router or host that runs the SNMP server program.

■ SNMP uses the services of two other protocols: structure of management information (SMI) and management information base (MIB).

■ MIB is a collection of groups of objects that can be managed by SNMP.

- SNMP defines five messages: GetRequest, GetNextRequest, SetRequest, GetResponse, and Trap.
- The Hypertext Transfer Protocol (HTTP) is the main protocol used to access data on the World Wide Web (WWW).
- The uniform resource locator (URL) is a standard for specifying any kind of information on the World Wide Web.
- The World Wide Web (WWW) is a repository of information spread all over the world and linked together.
- Hypertext and hypermedia are documents linked to one another through the concept of pointers.
- Browsers interpret and display a web document.
- A browser consists of a controller, client programs, and interpreters.
- A web document can be classified as static, dynamic, or active.
- A static document is one in which the contents are fixed and stored in a server. The client can make no changes in the server document.
- HyperText Markup Language (HTML) is a language used to create static web pages.
- A web page has a head and a body.
- Tags provide structure to a document, define titles and headers, format text, control the data flow, insert figures, link different documents together, and define executable code.
- A dynamic web document is created by a server only at a browser request.
- The common gateway interface (CGI) is a standard for creating and handling dynamic web documents.
- An active document is a copy of a program retrieved by the client and run at the client site.
- Java is a combination of a high-level programming language, a run-time environment, and a class library that allows a programmer to write an active document and a browser to run it.

25.13 PRACTICE SET

Review Questions

1. Compare the layers of the TCP/IP protocol suite with the layers of the OSI model.
2. In the client–server model, what is the role of the client program? What is the role of the server program?
3. Why is the client program finite and the server program infinite?
4. What kind of configuration information should a computer on the Internet have?
5. What are the two methods available for a diskless computer to obtain configuration information?

6. How is BOOTP different from DHCP?

7. What is the purpose of the Domain Name System?

8. Discuss the three main divisions of the domain name space.

9. What application program allows connection to a remote system in such a way that the local terminal appears to be a terminal at the remote system?

10. Why is NVT needed in remote login?

11. Discuss the TCP connections needed in FTP.

12. How is TFTP different from FTP?

13. What is the function of SMTP?

14. What is the difference between a user agent (UA) and a mail transfer agent (MTA)?

15. How does MIME enhance SMTP?

16. Why is an application such as POP needed for electronic messaging?

17. What three functions can SNMP perform to manage network devices?

18. What are the three protocols that interact to manage a network?

19. How are HTTP and the WWW related to the Internet?

20. Compare and contrast the three types of WWW documents.

21. What is the purpose of HTML?

22. What is the relationship between CGI and dynamic documents?

23. What is Java?

Multiple Choice Questions

24. _____ can request a service.
    a. A socket interface
    b. A port
    c. A client
    d. A server

25. The client program is _____ because it terminates after it has been served.
    a. active
    b. passive
    c. finite
    d. infinite

26. The server program is _____ because it is always available, waiting for a client request.
    a. active
    b. passive
    c. finite
    d. infinite

27. The TCP/IP application layer corresponds to the OSI model's _____ layers.
    a. physical, data link, and network
    b. transport and network
    c. session and transport
    d. session, presentation, and application

28. To find the IP address of a host when the domain name is known, the _____ can be used.
    a. inverse domain
    b. generic domains
    c. country domains
    d. b or c

29. Remote login can involve _____.
    a. NVT
    b. TELNET
    c. TCP/IP
    d. all of the above

30. The _____ at the remote site sends received characters to the operating system.
    a. terminal driver
    b. pseudoterminal driver
    c. TELNET client
    d. TELNET server

31. The _____ translates local characters into NVT form.
    a. terminal driver
    b. pseudoterminal driver
    c. TELNET client
    d. TELNET server

32. The _____ translates NVT characters into a form acceptable by the operating system.
    a. terminal driver
    b. pseudoterminal driver
    c. TELNET client
    d. TELNET server

33. Which of the following is true?
    a. FTP allows systems with different directory structures to transfer files.
    b. FTP allows a system using ASCII and a system using EBCDIC to transfer files.
    c. FTP allows a PC and a SUN workstation to transfer files.
    d. all of the above

34. During an FTP session, the control connection is opened _____.
    a. exactly once

    b. exactly twice

    c. as many times as necessary

    d. all of the above

35. During an FTP session, the data connection is opened _____.

    a. exactly once

    b. exactly twice

    c. as many times as necessary

    d. all of the above

36. The purpose of the UA is _____.

    a. message preparation

    b. envelope creation

    c. transferal of messages across the Internet

    d. a and b

37. The purpose of the MTA is _____.

    a. message preparation

    b. envelope creation

    c. transferal of messages across the Internet

    d. a and b

38. When a message is sent using SMTP, _____ UA(s) are involved.

    a. only one

    b. only two

    c. only three

    d. at least two

39. E-mail cannot be sent _____.

    a. if the sending site does not use TCP/IP

    b. if the receiving site does not use TCP/IP

    c. through private networks

    d. none of the above

40. A _____ can transform non-SMTP mail to SMTP format and vice versa.

    a. mail spool

    b. mail gateway

    c. mail file

    d. mail exchanger

41. In the mail address mackenzie@pit.arc.nasa.gov, what is the domain name?

    a. mackenzie

    b. pit.arc.nasa.gov

    c. mackenzie@pit.arc.nasa.gov

    d. a and b

42. MIME allows _____ data to be sent through SMTP.

    a. audio

    b. non-ASCII data

    c. image

    d. all of the above

43. Which of the following is associated with SNMP?

    a. MIB

    b. SMI

    c. BER

    d. all of the above

44. _____ runs the SNMP client program; _____ runs the SNMP server program.

    a. A manager; a manager

    b. An agent; an agent

    c. A manager; an agent

    d. An agent; a manager

45. _____ names objects, defines the type of data that can be stored in an object, and encodes data for network transmission.

    a. MIB

    b. SMI

    c. SNMP

    d. ASN.1

46. Which of the following is a collection of objects to be managed?

    a. MIB

    b. SMI

    c. SNMP

    d. ASN.1

47. Which is a manager duty?

    a. Retrieve the value of an object defined in an agent.

    b. Store the value of an object defined in an agent.

    c. Send an alarm message to the agent.

    d. a and b

48. _____ specifies which data types are available for the MIB.

    a. BER

    b. SNMP

    c. ASN.1

    d. SMI

49. An SNMP agent can send _____ messages.

    a. GetRequest

    b. SetRequest

    c. GetNextRequest

    d. Trap

50. An SNMP manager can send _____ messages.
    a. GetRequest
    b. SetRequest
    c. GetNextRequest
    d. all of the above

51. An SNMP agent can send _____ messages.
    a. GetResponse
    b. GetRequest
    c. SetRequest
    d. GetNextRequest

52. HTTP has similarities to both _____ and _____.
    a. FTP; SNMP
    b. FTP; SMTP
    c. FTP; MTV
    d. FTP; URL

53. A request message always contains _____.
    a. a header and a body
    b. a request line and a header
    c. a status line, a header, and a body
    d. a status line and a header

54. What does the URL need to access a document?
    a. pathname
    b. host computer
    c. retrieval method
    d. all of the above

55. Which of the following is a retrieval method?
    a. HTTP
    b. FTP
    c. TELNET
    d. all of the above

56. Hypertext documents are linked through _____.
    a. DNS
    b. TELNET
    c. pointers
    d. homepages

57. Which of the following is not an interpreter?
    a. HTTP
    b. HTML
    c. CGI
    d. Java

58. What are the components of a browser?
   a. retrieval method, host computer, pathname
   b. controller, client program, interpreter
   c. hypertext, hypermedia, HTML
   d. all of the above

59. Which type of web document is run at the client site?
   a. static
   b. dynamic
   c. active
   d. all of the above

60. Which type of web document is created at the server site only when requested by a client?
   a. static
   b. dynamic
   c. active
   d. all of the above

61. Which type of web document is fixed-content and is created and stored at the server site?
   a. static
   b. dynamic
   c. active
   d. all of the above

62. A program can use _____ to write a CGI program.
   a. Bourne shell script
   b. Perl
   c. C
   d. any of the above

63. Which type of web document is transported from the server to the client in binary form?
   a. static
   b. dynamic
   c. active
   d. all of the above

64. _____ is used to enable the use of active documents.
   a. HTML
   b. CGI
   c. Java
   d. all of the above

65. Java is _____.
    a. a programming language
    b. a run-time environment
    c. a class library
    d. all of the above
66. An applet is _____ document application program.
    a. a static
    b. an active
    c. a passive
    d. a dynamic

Exercises

67. Which type of domain is used by your company or school (generic or country)?
68. Most companies prefer generic domains to country domains. Why?
69. What is the most common generic domain you have used in your e-mails?
70. Break your e-mail address into the domain name and the local name.
71. Do you know anyone using a country domain?
72. Have you ever used an inverse domain?
73. Have you ever used a TELNET command? Which one?
74. Can a TELNET command use an IP address?
75. When you want to send an e-mail, what happens if your computer cannot find a DNS server?
76. What user agent program does your system use?
77. Does your e-mail program use MIME?
78. Does your e-mail program use POP?
79. Use the get command in FTP and report the result.
80. Use the put command in FTP and report the result.
81. Find the list of user commands in FTP.
82. Do some research on anonymous FTP and discuss its function.
83. Have you ever created an e-mail list?
84. Do some research and find at least five different tags used in HTML.

APPENDIX A

ASCII Code

The **American Standard Code for Information Interchange (ASCII)** is the most commonly used code for encoding printable and nonprintable (control) characters.

ASCII uses seven bits to encode each character. It can therefore represent up to 128 characters. Table A.1 lists the ASCII characters and their codes in both binary and hexadecimal form.

Table A.1   *ASCII table*

Decimal	Hexadecimal	Binary	Character	Description
0	00	0000000	NUL	Null
1	01	0000001	SOH	Start of header
2	02	0000010	STX	Start of text
3	03	0000011	ETX	End of text
4	04	0000100	EOT	End of transmission
5	05	0000101	ENQ	Enquiry
6	06	0000110	ACK	Acknowledgment
7	07	0000111	BEL	Bell
8	08	0001000	BS	Backspace
9	09	0001001	HT	Horizontal tab
10	0A	0001010	LF	Line feed
11	0B	0001011	VT	Vertical tab
12	0C	0001100	FF	Form feed
13	0D	0001101	CR	Carriage return
14	0E	0001110	SO	Shift out
15	0F	0001111	SI	Shift in
16	10	0010000	DLE	Data link escape
17	11	0010001	DC1	Device control 1

Table A.1 (*Continued*)   *ASCII table*

Decimal	Hexadecimal	Binary	Character	Description
18	12	0010010	DC2	Device control 2
19	13	0010011	DC3	Device control 3
20	14	0010100	DC4	Device control 4
21	15	0010101	NAK	Negative acknowledgment
22	16	0010110	SYN	Synchronous idle
23	17	0010111	ETB	End of transmission block
24	18	0011000	CAN	Cancel
25	19	0011001	EM	End of medium
26	1A	0011010	SUB	Substitute
27	1B	0011011	ESC	Escape
28	1C	0011100	FS	File separator
29	1D	0011101	GS	Group separator
30	1E	0011110	RS	Record separator
31	1F	0011111	US	Unit separator
32	20	0100000	SP	Space
33	21	0100001	!	Exclamation mark
34	22	0100010	"	Double quote
35	23	0100011	#	Pound sign
36	24	0100100	$	Dollar sign
37	25	0100101	%	Percent sign
38	26	0100110	&	Ampersand
39	27	0100111	'	Apostrophe
40	28	0101000	(	Open parenthesis
41	29	0101001	)	Close parenthesis
42	2A	0101010	*	Asterisk
43	2B	0101011	+	Plus sign
44	2C	0101100	,	Comma
45	2D	0101101	-	Hyphen
46	2E	0101110	.	Period
47	2F	0101111	/	Slash
48	30	0110000	0	
49	31	0110001	1	
50	32	0110010	2	
51	33	0110011	3	
52	34	0110100	4	

Table A.1 (*Continued*)   *ASCII table*

Decimal	Hexadecimal	Binary	Character	Description
53	35	0110101	5	
54	36	0110110	6	
55	37	0110111	7	
56	38	0111000	8	
57	39	0111001	9	
58	3A	0111010	:	Colon
59	3B	0111011	;	Semicolon
60	3C	0111100	<	Less than sign
61	3D	0111101	=	Equal sign
62	3E	0111110	>	Greater than sign
63	3F	0111111	?	Question mark
64	40	1000000	@	At sign
65	41	1000001	A	
66	42	1000010	B	
67	43	1000011	C	
68	44	1000100	D	
69	45	1000101	E	
70	46	1000110	F	
71	47	1000111	G	
72	48	1001000	H	
73	49	1001001	I	
74	4A	1001010	J	
75	4B	1001011	K	
76	4C	1001100	L	
77	4D	1001101	M	
78	4E	1001110	N	
79	4F	1001111	O	
80	50	1010000	P	
81	51	1010001	Q	
82	52	1010010	R	
83	53	1010011	S	
84	54	1010100	T	
85	55	1010101	U	
86	56	1010110	V	
87	57	1010111	W	

Table A.1 (*Continued*) *ASCII table*

Decimal	Hexadecimal	Binary	Character	Description
88	58	1011000	X	
89	59	1011001	Y	
90	5A	1011010	Z	
91	5B	1011011	[	Open bracket
92	5C	1011100	\	Backslash
93	5D	1011101	]	Close bracket
94	5E	1011110	^	Caret
95	5F	1011111	_	Underscore
96	60	1100000	`	Grave accent
97	61	1100001	a	
98	62	1100010	b	
99	63	1100011	c	
100	64	1100100	d	
101	65	1100101	e	
102	66	1100110	f	
103	67	1100111	g	
104	68	1101000	h	
105	69	1101001	i	
106	6A	1101010	j	
107	6B	1101011	k	
108	6C	1101100	l	
109	6D	1101101	m	
110	6E	1101110	n	
111	6F	1101111	o	
112	70	1110000	p	
113	71	1110001	q	
114	72	1110010	r	
115	73	1110011	s	
116	74	1110100	t	
117	75	1110101	u	
118	76	1110110	v	
119	77	1110111	w	
120	78	1111000	x	
121	79	1111001	y	
122	7A	1111010	z	

Table A.1 (*Concluded*)   *ASCII table*

Decimal	Hexadecimal	Binary	Character	Description
123	7B	1111011	{	Open brace
124	7C	1111100	|	Bar
125	7D	1111101	}	Close brace
126	7E	1111110	~	Tilde
127	7F	1111111	DEL	Delete

APPENDIX B

Numbering Systems and Transformation

Today's computers make use of four numbering systems: decimal, binary, octal, and hexadecimal. Each has advantages for different levels of digital processing. In the first section of this appendix, we describe each of the four systems. In the second section, we show how a number in one system can be transformed into a number in another system.

B.1 NUMBERING SYSTEMS

All of the numbering systems examined here are positional, meaning that the position of a symbol in relation to other symbols determines its value. Within a number, each symbol is called a digit (decimal digit, binary digit, octal digit, or hexadecimal digit). For example, the decimal number 798 has three decimal digits. Digits are arranged in order of ascending value, moving from the lowest value on the right to the highest on the left. For this reason, the leftmost digit is referred to as the most significant and the rightmost as the least significant digit (see Figure B.1). For example, in the decimal number 1234, the most significant digit is the 1 and the least significant is the 4.

Figure B.1 *Digit positions and their significance*

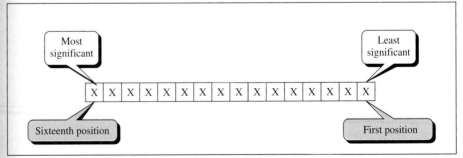

Decimal Numbers

The **decimal number system** is the one most familiar to us in everyday life. All of our terms for indicating countable quantities are based on it, and, in fact, when we speak of other numbering systems, we tend to refer to their quantities by their decimal equivalents. Also called base 10, the name *decimal* is derived from the Latin stem *deci,* meaning 10. The decimal system uses 10 symbols to represent quantitative values: 0, 1, 2, 3, 4, 5, 6, 7, 8, and 9.

Decimal numbers use 10 symbols: 0, 1, 2, 3, 4, 5, 6, 7, 8, and 9.

Weight and Value

In the decimal system, each weight equals 10 raised to the power of its position. The weight of the first position, therefore, is 10^0, which equals 1. So the value of a digit in the first position is equal to the value of the digit times 1. The weight of the second position is 10^1, which equals 10. The value of a digit in the second position, therefore, is equal to the value of the digit times 10. The weight of the third position is 10^2. The value of a digit in the third position is equal to the value of the digit times 100 (see Table B.1).

Table B.1   *Decimal weights*

Position	Fifth	Fourth	Third	Second	First
Weight	10^4	10^3	10^2	10^1	10^0
	(10,000)	(1000)	(100)	(10)	(1)

The value of the number as a whole is the sum of each digit times its weight. Figure B.2 shows the weightings of the decimal number 4567.

Figure B.2   *Example of a decimal number*

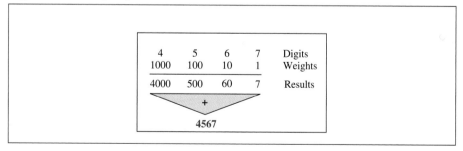

Binary Numbers

The **binary number system** provides the basis for all computer operations. Computers work by manipulating electrical current on and off. The binary system uses two symbols, *0* and *1*, so it corresponds naturally to a two-state device, such as a switch, with 0 to represent the off state and 1 to represent the on state. Also called base 2, the word *binary* derives from the Latin stem *bi,* meaning two.

Binary numbers use two symbols: 0 and 1.

Weight and Value

The binary system is also a weighted system. Each digit has a weight based on its position in the number. Weight in the binary system is two raised to the power represented by a position, as shown in Table B.2. Note that the value of the weightings is shown in decimal terms next to the weight itself. The value of a specific digit is equal to its face value times the weight of its position.

Table B.2   *Binary weights*

Position	Fifth	Fourth	Third	Second	First
Weight	2^4	2^3	2^2	2^1	2^0
	(16)	(8)	(4)	(2)	(1)

    To calculate the value of a number, multiply each digit by the weight of its position and then add together the results. Figure B.3 demonstrates the weightings of the binary number 1101. As you can see, 1101 is the binary equivalent of decimal 13.

Figure B.3   *Example of a binary number*

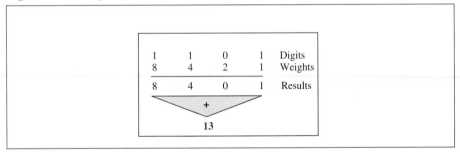

Octal Numbers

The **octal number system** is used by computer programmers to represent binary numbers in a compact form. Also called base 8, the term *octal* derives from the Greek stem *octa,* meaning eight. Eight is a power of two (2^3) and therefore can be used to model binary concepts. The octal system uses eight symbols to represent quantitative values: 0, 1, 2, 3, 4, 5, 6, and 7.

Octal numbers use eight symbols: 0, 1, 2, 3, 4, 5, 6, and 7.

Weight and Value

The octal system is also a weighted system. Each digit has a weight based on its position in the number. Weight in octal is eight raised to the power represented by a position, as shown in Table B.3. Once again, the value represented by each weighting is given in decimal terms next to the weight itself. The value of a specific digit is equal to its face value times the weight of its position. For example, a 4 in the third position has the equivalent decimal value 4×64, or 256.

Table B.3   *Octal weights*

Position	Fifth	Fourth	Third	Second	First
Weight	8^4	8^3	8^2	8^1	8^0
	(4096)	(512)	(64)	(8)	(1)

To calculate the value of an octal number, multiply the value of each digit by the weight of its position, then add together the results. Figure B.4 shows the weightings for the octal number 3471. As you can see, 3471 is the octal equivalent of decimal 1849.

Figure B.4   *Example of an octal number*

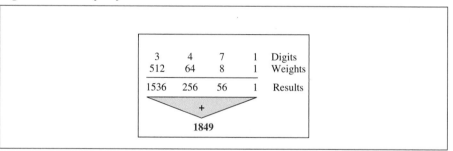

Hexadecimal Numbers

The term *hexadecimal* is derived from the Greek stem *hexadeca,* meaning 16 (*hex* means 6 and *deca* means 10). So the **hexadecimal number system** is base 16. Sixteen is also a power of 2 (2^4). Like octal, therefore, the hexadecimal system is used by programmers to represent binary numbers in a compact form. Hexadecimal uses 16 symbols to represent data: 0, 1, 2, 3, 4, 5, 6, 7, 8, 9, A, B, C, D, E, and F.

> Hexadecimal numbers use 16 symbols: 0, 1, 2, 3, 4, 5, 6, 7, 8, 9, A, B, C, D, E, and F.

Weight and Value

Like the others, the hexadecimal system is a weighted system. Each digit has a weight based on its position in the number. The weight is used to calculate the value represented by the digit. Weight in hexadecimal is 16 raised to the power represented by a position, as shown in Table B.4. Once again, the value represented by each weighting is given in decimal terms next to the weight itself. The value of a specific digit is equal to its face value times the weight of its position. For example, a 4 in the third position has the equivalent decimal value 4×256, or 1024. To calculate the value of a hexadecimal number, multiply the value of each digit by the weight of its position, then add together the results. Figure B.5 shows the weightings for the hexadecimal number 3471. As you can see, 3471 is the hexadecimal equivalent of decimal 13,425.

Table B.4   *Hexadecimal weights*

Position	Fifth	Fourth	Third	Second	First
Weight	16^4	16^3	16^2	16^1	16^0
	(65,536)	(4096)	(256)	(16)	(1)

Figure B.5   *Example of a hexadecimal number*

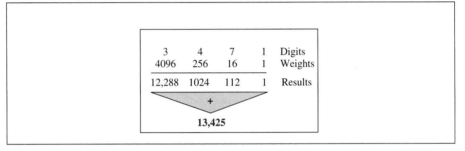

B.2   TRANSFORMATION

The different numbering systems provide different ways of thinking about a common subject: quantities of single units. A number from any given system can be transformed into its equivalent in any other system. For example, a binary number can be converted to a decimal number, and vice versa, without altering its value. Table B.5 shows how each system represents the decimal numbers 0 through 15. As you can see, decimal 13 is equivalent to binary 1101, which is equivalent to octal 15, which is equivalent to hexadecimal D.

Table B.5   *Comparison of four systems*

Decimal	*Binary*	*Octal*	*Hexadecimal*
0	0	0	0
1	1	1	1
2	10	2	2
3	11	3	3
4	100	4	4
5	101	5	5

Table B.5 (*Continued*)   *Comparison of four systems*

Decimal	Binary	Octal	Hexadecimal
6	110	6	6
7	111	7	7
8	1000	10	8
9	1001	11	9
10	1010	12	A
11	1011	13	B
12	1100	14	C
13	1101	15	D
14	1110	16	E
15	1111	17	F

From Other Systems to Decimal

As we saw in the discussions above, binary, octal, and hexadecimal numbers can be transformed easily to their decimal equivalents by using the weights of the digits. Figure B.6 shows the decimal value 78 represented in each of the other three systems.

Figure B.6   *Transformation from other systems to decimal*

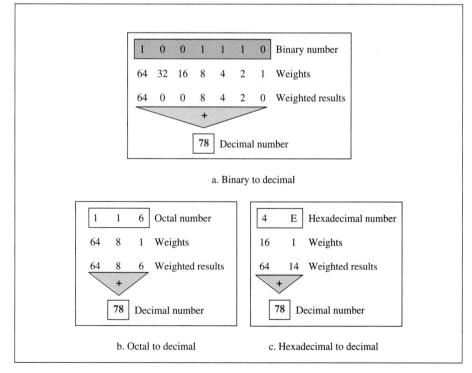

a. Binary to decimal

b. Octal to decimal   c. Hexadecimal to decimal

From Decimal to Other Systems

A simple division trick gives us a convenient way to convert a decimal number to its binary, octal, or hexadecimal equivalent (see Figure B.7).

Figure B.7   *Transformation from decimal to other systems*

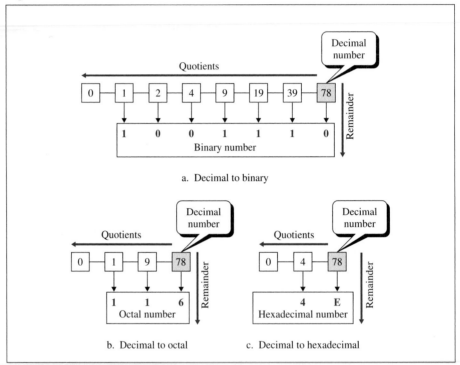

a. Decimal to binary

b. Decimal to octal   c. Decimal to hexadecimal

To convert a number from decimal to binary, divide the number by 2 and write down the resulting remainder (1 or 0). That remainder is the least significant binary digit. Now, divide the result of that division by 2 and write down the new remainder in the second position. Repeat this process until the quotient becomes zero.

In Figure B.7, we convert the decimal number 78 to its binary equivalent. To check the validity of this method, we convert 1001110 to decimal using the weights of each position. From left to right:

$$2^6 + 2^3 + 2^2 + 2^1 \quad \Rightarrow \quad 64 + 8 + 4 + 2 \quad \Rightarrow \quad 78$$

To convert a number from decimal to octal, the procedure is the same but the divisor is 8 instead of 2. To convert from decimal to hexadecimal, the divisor is 16.

From Binary to Octal or Hexadecimal

To change a number from binary to octal, we first group the binary digits from right to left by threes. Then we convert each tribit to its octal equivalent and write the result under the tribit. These equivalents, taken in order (not added), are the octal equivalent of the original number. In Figure B.8, we convert binary 1001110.

Figure B.8 *Transformation from binary to octal or hexadecimal*

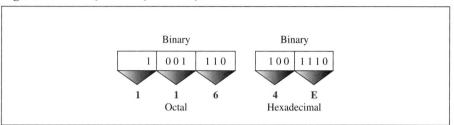

To change a number from binary to hexadecimal, we follow the same procedure but group the digits from right to left by fours. This time we convert each quadbit to its hexadecimal equivalent (use Table B.5). In Figure B.8, we convert binary 1001110 to hexadecimal.

From Octal or Hexadecimal to Binary

To convert from octal to binary, we reverse the procedure above. Starting with the least significant digit, we convert each octal digit into its equivalent three binary digits. In Figure B.9, we convert octal 116 to binary.

Figure B.9 *Transformation from octal or hexadecimal to binary*

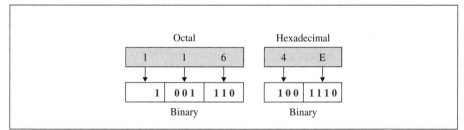

To convert a number from hexadecimal to binary, we convert each hexadecimal digit to its equivalent four binary digits, again starting with the least significant digit. In Figure B.9, we convert hexadecimal 4E to binary.

APPENDIX C

Representation of Binary Numbers

Binary numbers can be used and stored in either of two formats: unsigned or signed. **Unsigned numbers** mean without a + or − sign, and refers to positive values only. **Signed numbers** can be either positive or negative. Unsigned numbers are represented in only one format. However, computers use three different formats for representing signed numbers: sign-and-magnitude, one's complement, and two's complement (see Figure C.1).

Figure C.1 *Binary representation*

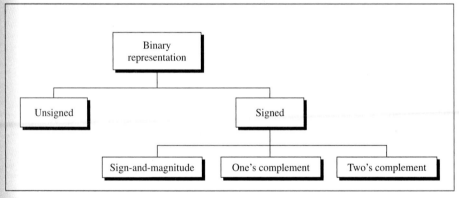

C.1 UNSIGNED NUMBERS

The buffer size limits the amount of space we have in which to store and represent information about a number. All essential information about a given value must be contained within this space, including whether a value is positive or negative. If a number is unsigned, however, it is assumed to be positive. With no need to indicate the sign, all bits become available to represent digits. In a 16-bit buffer, we can represent any whole number between 0 (0000000000000000) and 65,535 (1111111111111111); see Figure C.2.

Figure C.2   *Unsigned*

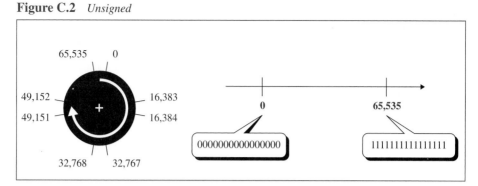

Another way to visualize the limitations of a 16-bit range is with a circle (see Figure C.2). As you can see, with 16 available bits, we can count from 0 to 65,535. When we add 1 to our maximum value of 65,535, we find ourselves back at 0. The process is called modular arithmetic. The most common example of modular arithmetic in everyday life is the 12-hour clock: when you add 1 to 12 you get 1, not 13.

From Decimal to Unsigned

To change a decimal value to its unsigned binary form, follow these steps:

    a. Change the number to its binary form.

    b. Fill in all empty cells on the left with 0s. (If you are using a 16-bit register, you need to fill all 16 cells; with an 8-bit register, you need to fill 8 cells; etc.)

Example C.1

Change 76 to its unsigned representation.

Solution

    a. 76 in binary is 1001100.

    b. Adding 0s to make the number 16 bits long gives us 0000000001001100.

C.2   SIGNED NUMBERS

Representation of signed binary numbers presents more challenges than does representation of unsigned numbers. Given the same bit limitations, how do we include the sign (+ or −) in the number? Three methods are commonly used: sign-and-magnitude, one's complement, and two's complement.

Sign-and-Magnitude

In sign-and-magnitude representation, the most significant bit is reserved to indicate the sign. If the bit is 0, the number is positive. If it is 1, the number is negative. Notice that application of this method gives us two 0 values: +0 (0000000000000000) and −0 (1000000000000000). Reserving one bit to show sign also limits the range of values that can be represented in a given number of bits. Given a 16-bit buffer, one cell is now consumed by the sign, leaving only 15 to represent the absolute value of a number. This changes the possible range of numbers that can be represented, as shown in Figure C.3. As you can see, with only 15 possible digits, the range of representable numbers becomes −32,767 to +32,767.

Figure C.3   *Sign-and-magnitude representation*

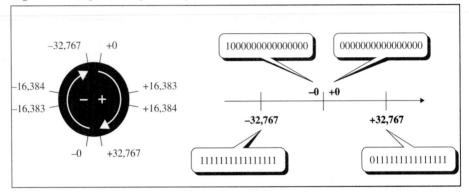

Once again, the circle provides a useful way to visualize a number range. Starting from +0 (0000000000000000), we add 1s, increasing the value until we reach +32,767 (0111111111111111). The next added 1 changes the value to −0 (0111111111111111 + 1 = 1000000000000000). Continuing to advance by 1s, we move around the circle to −32,767 (1111111111111111). The next added 1 changes the available bits to 0000000000000000 (+0), and the cycle begins again (see Figure C.3).

From Decimal to Sign-and-Magnitude

To change a decimal value to its sign-and-magnitude binary form, follow these steps:

    a. Ignore the sign.

    b. Change the absolute value of the number to its binary form.

    c. Fill in all empty cells, except the last one on the left, with 0s (if you are using a 16-bit register, you need to fill 15 cells; with an 8-bit register, you need to fill 7 cells; etc.).

    d. Now check the sign: if the number is positive, fill the last cell with 0. If the number is negative, fill the cell with 1.

Example C.2

Change −77 to its sign-and-magnitude representation.

Solution

    a.   The absolute value is 77.

    b.   77 in binary is 1001101.

    c.   Adding 0s to make the number 15 bits long gives us 000000001001101.

    d.   The sign was negative, so we add a 1 as the last bit: **1**000000001001101.

One's Complement

In the one's complement method, all the bits, not just the most significant, take part in the representation of sign. One's complement is a symmetrical system: numbers are paired with their complements. Adding a number to its complement equals 0. To find the complement of a number, invert all of its digits. For example, inverting the digits of the number 0000000000000001 (+1), gives us 1111111111111110 (−1). This symmetry extends to zero: 0000000000000000 = +0, and 1111111111111111 = −0 (see Figure C.4).

Figure C.4 *One's complement*

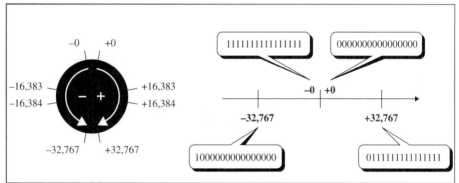

As you can see from Figure C.4, positive numbers in this method use the same digits as those in sign-and-magnitude (and the same digits as the unsigned numbers 0 to 32,767). In this method, also, the sign of a number is immediately apparent from its most significant digit. (Positive numbers always start with 0, and negative numbers always start with 1.) However, the numerical representation of negative numbers is very different in one's complement from that in sign-and-magnitude.

One's complement is used in data communications to check the accuracy of a received transmission.

From Decimal to One's Complement

To change a decimal value to its one's complement binary form, follow these steps:

a. Ignore the sign.

b. Change the absolute value of the number to its binary form.

c. Fill in all empty cells on the left with 0s. (If you are using a 16-bit register, you need to fill all 16 cells; with an 8-bit register, you need to fill 8 cells; etc.)

d. Now check the sign: if the number is positive, stop here. If the number is negative, complement the digits (invert each 0 to 1 and each 1 to 0).

Example C.3

Change −77 to its one's complement form.

Solution

    a. The absolute value is 77.

    b. 77 in binary is 1001101.

    c. Adding 0s to make the number 16 bits long gives us 0000000001001101.

    d. The sign was negative, so we complement the number obtained in step c by inverting its digits, giving us 1111111110110010.

Two's Complement

In the **two's complement** method, as in one's complement, all the bits change when the sign of the number changes. The entire number, not just the most significant bit, takes part in the negation process. This time, however, we add a step, resulting in an asymmetrical system with only one representation of 0.

As Figure C.5 shows, having only a single representation of 0 results in the availability of an extra negative number: −32,768. In this way, a 16-bit integer variable can store numbers from −32,768 through +32,767.

Figure C.5   *Two's complement*

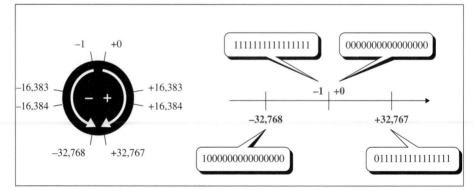

An examination of Figure C.5 reveals another interesting fact: in two's complement 0 and −1 are bitwise inverses of each other. They are not complements of each other—adding them together does not yield 0. In fact, 0000000000000000 (0) + 1111111111111111 (−1) = 1111111111111111 (−1). In the same way, +32,767 and −32,768 are inverses of each other. These patterns allow two's complement to replicate decimal arithmetic on the machine level, as we shall see below.

From Decimal to Two's Complement

To change a decimal number to its two's complement form, follow these steps:

    a. Ignore the sign.

    b. Change the absolute value of the number to its binary form.

c. Fill in all empty cells on the left with 0s. (If you are using a 16-bit register, you need to fill all 16 cells; with an 8-bit register, you need to fill 8 cells; etc.)

d. Now check the sign: if the number is positive, stop here. If the number is negative, complement the digits (invert each 0 to 1 and each 1 to 0) and then add 1 to the resulting number. If adding 1 results in a carry from the most significant digit, that carry is dropped.

Example C.4

Change −77 to its two's complement form.

Solution

a. The absolute value is 77.

b. 77 in binary is 1001101.

c. Adding 0s to make the number 16 bits long gives us 0000000001001101.

d. The sign was negative, so we complement the number, giving us 1111111110110010. Now we add 1 to 1111111110110010, giving us the two's complement: 1111111110110011.

C.3   MORE ABOUT ONE'S COMPLEMENT

Because one's complement arithmetic is used in checksum calculation, we discuss some features of one's complement arithmetic in more detail here.

Finding the Complement

The one's complement of any number is another number, such that the sum of the two is equal to 0. For example, the one's complement of A is −A. To complement a binary number, invert every 1 to 0 and 0 to 1 (see Figure C.6).

Figure C.6   *One's complement*

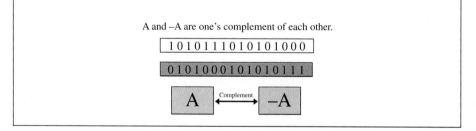

As we mentioned before, we have two 0s in this arithmetic: +0 and −0. The positive zero in a 16-bit buffer is 0000000000000000, and the negative zero in a 16-bit buffer is 1111111111111111.

We have two 0s in one's complement arithmetic:	
+0 ➪ 0000000000000000	−0 ➪ 1111111111111111

Adding Two Numbers

To add two digits in one's complement arithmetic, we use the same steps as in base 10 addition, but in base 2. We add the two values in one column together. The box below expresses this process as a series of four simple rules.

Four simple rules of adding one column:

1. If there are no 1s, the result is 0.
2. If there is only one 1, the result is 1.
3. If there are two 1s, the result is 0 and 1 is carried to the next column.
4. If there are three 1s, the result is 1 and 1 is carried to the next column.

To add two multibit numbers, we extend this process.

Two simple rules for adding two numbers made of two or more columns:

1. Add the bits in each column.
2. If the last column generates a carry, add 1 to the result.

Figure C.7 shows an example of adding two numbers in one's complement where no carry is produced from the last column.

Figure C.7   *Adding in one's complement*

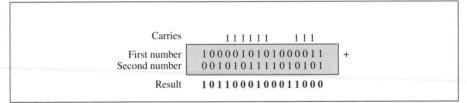

Figure C.8 shows an example of adding two numbers in one's complement where the last column generates a carry. The carry is then added to the result.

Figure C.8   *Adding in one's complement with carry from the last column*

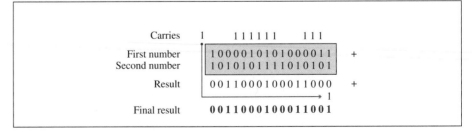

Following the previous logic, if we add a number to its complement A, the result will be all 1s, which, as we have seen, is equal to −0 (see Figure C.9).

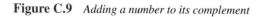

If we add a number to its complement, we get −0, which means all 1s.

Figure C.9   *Adding a number to its complement*

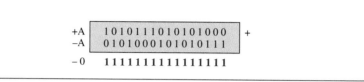

APPENDIX D

Fourier Analysis

A sine wave can be mathematically defined as:

$$x(t) = A\sin(2\pi ft + \theta)$$

where
$x(t)$ is the signal at time t
A is the maximum amplitude of the signal
f is the number of cycles per second
θ is the phase of the signal

If the phase shift is 90 degrees ($\pi/2$ radians), the same signal can be expressed as a cosine wave instead of a sine wave:

$$x(t) = A\cos(2\pi ft)$$

Example D.1

The electricity that comes into a house is a good example of a simple sine wave. The maximum amplitude is approximately 155 volts and the frequency is 60 Hz. Write the mathematical equation.

Solution

$$2\pi f = 2 \times 3.14 \times 60 = 377 \text{ radians/second}$$

$$x(t) = A\sin(2\pi ft + \theta) = 155\sin(377t + \theta)$$

The phase shift is usually zero.

Example D.2

The electricity produced by a six-volt battery is direct current (DC) with frequency zero. It can be described by the following equation, where θ is $-\pi/2$ because the voltage starts at +6 volts instead of zero.

Solution

$$x(t) = A\sin(2\pi ft - \pi/2) = A\cos(2\pi ft) = A\cos(0) = A = 6$$

Example D.3

Your voice is a summation of sine waves, each sine wave having its own frequency, phase, and amplitude. The bandwidth is normally between 300 Hz and 3300 Hz. Give a general equation.

Solution

$$x(t) = A_1 \sin (2\pi f_1 t + \theta_1) + A_2 \sin (2\pi f_2 t + \theta_2) + \cdots + A_n \sin (2\pi f_n t + \theta_n)$$

with f_1 as the fundamental frequency and $f_2, f_3, \ldots, f_n$ the harmonics.

D.1   FOURIER SERIES

The **Fourier series** allows us to decompose a composite periodic signal into a possibly infinite series of sine waves, each having a different frequency and phase. A periodic signal $x(t)$ can be decomposed as follows:

$$x(t) = c_0 + c_1 \sin (2\pi f_1 t + \phi_1) + c_2 \sin (2\pi f_2 t + \phi_2) + \cdots + c_n \sin (2\pi f_n t + \phi_n) + \cdots$$

The coefficients $c_0, c_1, c_2, c_3, \ldots, c_n$ are the amplitudes of the simple signals. Coefficient c_0 is the amplitude of the signal with frequency 0 (the DC component). Coefficient c_1 is the amplitude of the signal with the same frequency as the original signal. Coefficient c_2 is the amplitude of the signal with a frequency two times that of the original signal, and so on. ϕ_0 is the phase of the signal with frequency 0 (the DC component). ϕ_1 is the phase of the signal with the same frequency as the original signal. ϕ_2 is the phase of the signal with a frequency two times that of the original signal, and so on.

Amplitude and phase are calculated using the Fourier series formulas. We will not give the proof of the Fourier series here; we will mention only how to calculate amplitude and phase. Interested readers can check the proof in any book on advanced mathematics.

To simplify the calculations, we use the geometric fact that

$$c_n \sin (2\pi f_n t + \phi_n) = a_n \sin (2\pi f_n t) + b_n \cos (2\pi f_n t)$$

which means that any signal can be decomposed into sine and cosine components. Now, calculating a_n and b_n becomes simpler:

$$a_0 = 1/T \int x(t) \, dt$$

$$a_n = 2/T \int x(t) \, \cos (2\pi f t) \, dt$$

$$b_n = 2/T \int x(t) \, \sin (2\pi f t) \, dt$$

where T is the period of the signal and $f = 1/T$.

Example D.4

Find the coefficients of the Fourier series for the signal in Figure D.1.

Solution

Using the formulas shown above, we get

$$a_0 = 0$$

$$a_1 = 4A/\pi \qquad a_2 = 0 \qquad a_3 = -4A/3\pi \qquad a_4 = 0 \qquad \ldots$$

Figure D.1   *Example D.4*

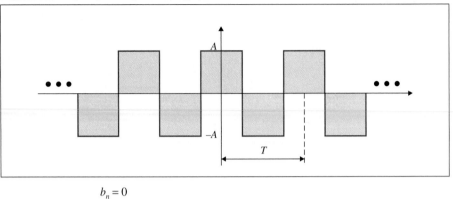

$$b_n = 0$$

Example D.5

Find the coefficients of the Fourier series for the signal in Figure D.2.

Figure D.2   *Example D.5*

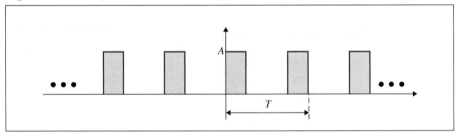

Solution

Using the formulas shown above, we get

$$a_0 = 0.33A$$

$a_1 = 0.28A$	$a_2 = -0.14A$	$a_3 = 0$	$a_4 = 0.07A$ . . .
$b_1 = 3A/2\pi$	$b_2 = 3A/4\pi$	$b_3 = 0$	$b_4 = 3A/8\pi$ . . .

Example D.6

Find the coefficients of the Fourier series for the signal in Figure D.3.

Solution

Using the formulas shown above, we get

$$a_0 = 0 \qquad a_n = 0$$

$$b_1 = 2A/\pi \qquad b_2 = -A/\pi \qquad b_3 = 2A/3\pi \qquad b_4 = -A/2\pi \quad . . .$$

Figure D.3   *Example D.6*

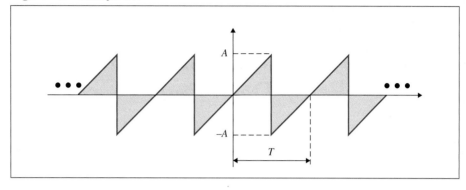

D.2   FOURIER TRANSFORM

The Fourier transform allows us to decompose a composite aperiodic signal into an infinite series of simple sine waves, each having a different frequency and phase. In this case, however, the frequencies are not discrete but rather a continuous spectrum. Transformation changes the time domain to frequency domain and vice versa. Because the spectrum is continuous, the result is an envelope of the frequency-domain components rather than a plot of the components themselves.

To calculate the envelope, the following integrals are used:

$$X(f) = \int X(t)\, e^{-j2\pi ft}\, dt$$

$$X(t) = \int X(f)\, e^{j2\pi ft}\, dt$$

Example D.7

Find the Fourier transform for the signal in Figure D.4.

Figure D.4   *Example D.7*

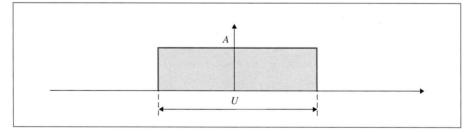

Solution

Using the integral shown above, we get

$$V(f) = 2A/2\pi f_0 \, \sin\,(2\pi fU/2)$$

APPENDIX E

Hardware Equipment for Error Detection

In this appendix, we discuss the equipment used for error detection. First, three electronic devices are introduced. Then we show how these devices are used to make VRC, LRC, and CRC generators and checkers.

E.1 ELECTRONIC DEVICES

Three electronic devices are used for the generation and analysis of redundancy checks: XOR gates, NOT gates, and shift registers.

XOR Gate

An exclusive OR (XOR) gate is an electronic device with two inputs and one output. XOR gates compare two bits of data. If the input bits are equal (both 1s or both 0s), the output of the XOR gate is a 0. If the bits are unequal (one 0 and the other 1), the output of the XOR gate is a 1. Figure E.1 shows the results of passing each of the four possible two-bit combinations through an XOR.

Figure E.1 *XOR gate*

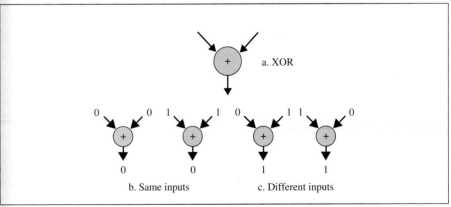

NOT Gate

The NOT gate is an electronic device with one input and one output. The name *NOT* is not an acronym—it means what it says. Any bit input will be output as what it is not. NOT gates invert input by changing 0 to 1 and 1 to 0. They are used in odd-parity generators where a result is generated and then inverted. Figure E.2 shows the output of a NOT gate.

Figure E.2   *NOT gate*

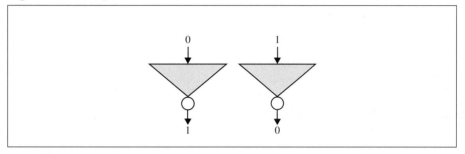

Shift Register

A register is a group of binary storage cells, each of which holds one bit. A register that can move its contents one place to the right or to the left is called a shift register (see Figure E.3).

Figure E.3   *Shift registers*

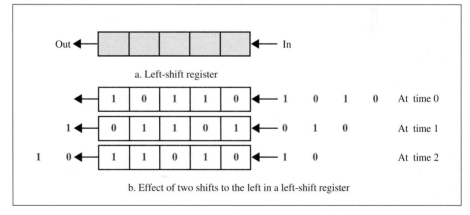

A shift register is connected to a timing pulse. With each pulse, the contents of the register shift one cell to the left (or to the right if it is a right-shift register). Each unit (binary 1 or 0) advances one position. The contents of the last cell get pushed out of the register, and a new unit moves from the waiting stream (if there is one) into the first cell of the register. Figure E.3 shows a left-shift register. A right-shift register behaves the same way but in the opposite direction.

E.2   VERTICAL REDUNDANCY CHECK (VRC)

As we learned in Chapter 9, the vertical redundancy check (VRC) is used for odd and even parity checking. In this section, we show how we can use electronic devices to make a VRC generator or checker.

VRC Generator

A VRC generator is a series of XOR gates. The number of gates in the generator is one less than the number of bits in the data unit. The final result is the even-parity bit. Figure E.4 shows how this process works. To generate an odd-parity bit, the output of the last XOR gate is passed through a NOT gate.

Figure E.4   *VRC generator, even parity*

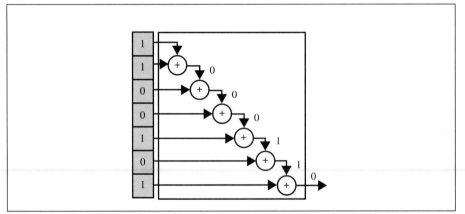

VRC Checker

The VRC checker at the receiving end has one extra XOR gate to accommodate the parity bit. The process is also the same: the output of each XOR gate is passed to the next XOR gate, where it is added to the next bit in the data unit. As with parity generation, an odd-parity checker is identical to an even-parity checker except for the addition of a NOT gate after the last XOR gate.

   If the final output is 0, the transmission is assumed to be intact, the parity bit is dropped, and the data are accepted. If the output is 1, the data are rejected. Figure E.5 shows an even-parity VRC checker.

Figure E.5   *VRC checker, even parity*

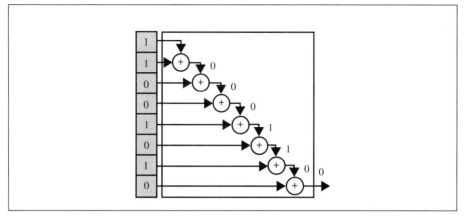

E.3   LONGITUDINAL REDUNDANCY CHECK (LRC)

As we learned in Chapter 9, the longitudinal redundancy check (LRC) is used for more efficient error checking. In this section, we show how to make an LRC generator and checker.

LRC Generator

Figure E.6 shows how the LRC is calculated. The least significant bits are added together and their parity found; then the second bits are added and their parity found, and so on. The final bit of the LRC is both the parity bit for the LRC data unit itself and the parity bit for all the VRC parity bits in the block.

Figure E.6   *LRC generator*

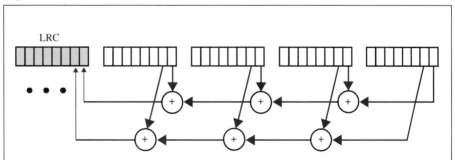

LRC Checker

An LRC checker works like an LRC generator, but we need extra XOR gates. Figure E.7 shows an LRC checker.

Figure E.7   *LRC checker*

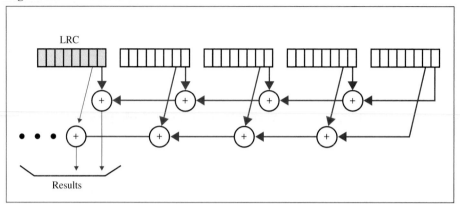

E.4   CYCLIC REDUNDANCY CHECK (CRC)

As we learned in Chapter 9, the cyclic redundancy check (CRC) is more efficient than VRC or LRC. In this section, we show how to make a CRC generator and checker.

The CRC Generator

Designing a CRC generator from a given polynomial is easily done following these steps:

■   Change the polynomial to a divisor of size $N + 1$. (N is the order of the polynomial.)

■   Make a shift register of size N.

■   Align the shift register cells with the divisor so that the cells are located between the bits.

■   Put an XOR where there is a 1 in the divisor except for the leftmost bit.

■   Make a feedback connection from the leftmost bit to the XORs.

■   Add a switch to direct the data and the generated CRC output.

Figure E.8 shows the CRC generator derived from the ITU-T polynomial.

One set of bits moves through the CRC generator to the switch; the other is sent directly to the switch. The switch uses a counter to send the data first and then the remainder (CRC). Figure E.9 shows the generation of the CRC remainder. In each line, the XOR gates add two bits together. After this operation, all bits are then shifted one position to the left. The last line shows the CRC remainder in the shift register.

The CRC Checker

The CRC hardware at the receiving end of the transmission works in precisely the same way except that it tests the whole package, including the data and the CRC, to determine the accuracy of the received data (see Figure E.10).

Figure E.8   *From polynomial to CRC generator*

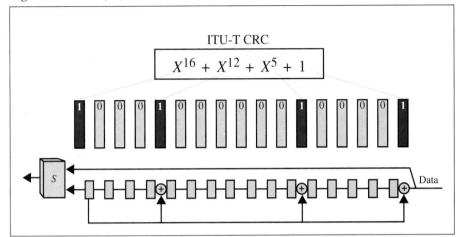

Figure E.9   *An example of a CRC generator*

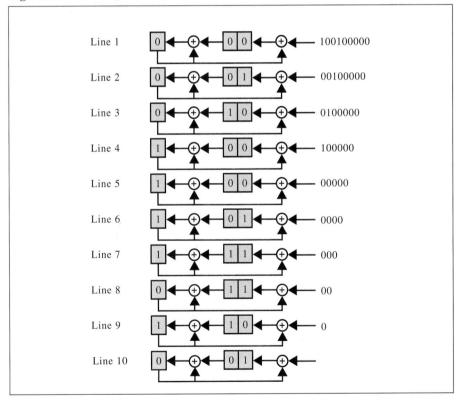

Figure E.10 *CRC checker*

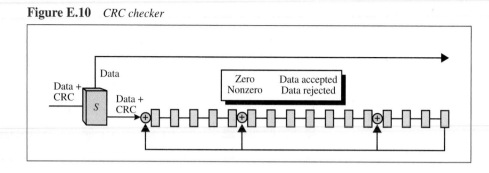

APPENDIX F

Huffman Encoding

ASCII is a fixed-length code. Each ASCII character consists of seven bits. Character length does not vary. Although the character E occurs more frequently than the character Z, both are assigned the same number of bits in a given code. This consistency means that every character uses the maximum number of bits, resulting in lengthy encoded messages.

Huffman coding, however, makes coding more efficient. In this mechanism, we assign shorter codes to characters that occur more frequently and longer codes to those that occur less frequently. For example, E and T, the two characters that occur most frequently in the English language, are assigned one bit each. A, I, M, and N, which also occur frequently but less frequently than E and T, are assigned two bits each. C, G, K, R, S, U, and W are the next most frequent and are assigned three bits each, and so on. In a given piece of text, only some of the characters will require the maximum bit length. The overall length of the transmission, therefore, is shorter than that resulting from fixed-length encoding.

Difficulty arises, however, if the bit patterns associated with each character are assigned randomly. Consider the example in Figure F.1. Note that we have purposely limited the number of characters in the example to only a few from the complete alphanumeric and special character set in order to make the demonstration easier to follow.

Figure F.1 *Bit assignments based on frequency of the character*

E:0	T:1						
A:00	I:01	M:10	N:11				
C:000	D:001	G:010	K:011	O:100	R:101	S:110	U:111

As you can see, each character is represented by a unique bit pattern and is easily distinguishable when presented separately. But what happens when these characters are formed into a data stream? Figure F.2 shows the possible results. Without a predictable character bit length, the receiver may misinterpret the code.

Figure F.2   *Multiple interpretations of transmitted data*

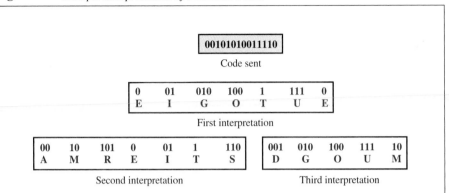

Huffman coding is designed to counter this ambiguity while retaining the bit count advantages of a compression code. Not only does it vary the length of the code based on the frequency of the character represented, but each character code is chosen in such a way that no code is the prefix of another code. For example, no three-bit code has the same pattern as the first three bits of a four- or five-bit code (prefix property code).

F.1   CHARACTER TREE

Using the character set from the example above, let's examine how a Huffman code is built.

Before we can assign bit patterns to each character, we assign each character a weight based on its frequency of use. In our example, we assume that the frequency of the character E in a text is 15 percent, the frequency of the character T is 12 percent, and so on (see Figure F.3).

Figure F.3   *Character weights*

E = 15	T = 12	A = 10	I = 08	M = 07	N = 06	C = 05
D = 05	G = 04	K = 04	O = 03	R = 03	S = 02	U = 02

Once we have established the weight of each character, we build a tree based on those values. The process for building this tree is shown in Figure F.4. It follows two basic steps:

1. First we organize the entire character set into a row, ordered according to frequency from highest to lowest (or vice versa). Each character is now a node at the leaf level of a tree.

2. Next, we find the two nodes with the smallest combined frequency weightings and join them to form a third node, resulting in a simple two-level tree. The weight of

Figure F.4   *Huffman tree, part 1*

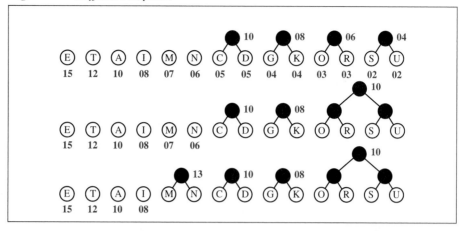

the new node is the combined weights of the original two nodes. This node, one level up from the leaves, is eligible to be combined with other nodes. Remember, the sum of the weights of the two nodes chosen must be smaller than the combination of any other possible choices.

3. We repeat step 2 until all of the nodes, on every level, are combined into a single tree.

Figure F.4 shows part of this process. The first row of the figure shows the leaf-level nodes representing the original characters arranged in descending order of value. We locate the two nodes with the smallest values and combine them. As you can see, this process results in the creation of a new node (represented by a solid circle). The frequency value (weight) of this new node is the sum of the weights of the two nodes. The first row shows four combined nodes.

In the second row, the nodes with the lowest values are found one level up from the characters rather than among the characters themselves. We combine them into a node two levels up from the leaves. In the third row, the lowest value node has a value of 8 (I) and the second lowest value is 10. But there are three 10s—one at the leaf level (A), one a level up from the leaves (C-D), and one two levels up from the leaves (O-R-S-U). Which should we choose? We choose whichever of the 10s is adjacent to the 8. This decision keeps the branch lines from crossing and allows us to preserve the legibility of the tree.

If none of the higher values are adjacent to the lower value, we can rearrange the nodes for clarity (see Figure F.5). In the figure (third row), we have moved the character T from the left side of the tree to the right in order to combine it with a node on that side. We move the character E for the same reason.

Figure F.6 shows the rest of the process. As you can see, the completed tree results in a single node at the root level (with a value of 86).

Figure F.5   *Huffman tree, part 2*

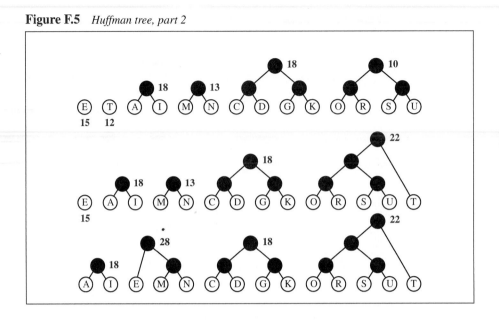

Figure F.6   *Huffman tree, part 3*

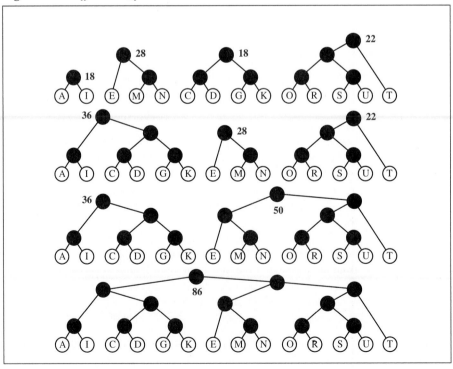

F.2   ASSIGNING THE CODES

Once the tree is complete, we use it to assign codes to each character. First, we assign a bit value to each branch (see Figure F.7). Starting from the root (top node), we assign 0 to the left branch and 1 to the right branch and repeat this pattern at each node. Which branch becomes 0 and which becomes 1 is left to the designer—as long as the assignments are consistent throughout the tree.

Figure F.7   *Code assignment*

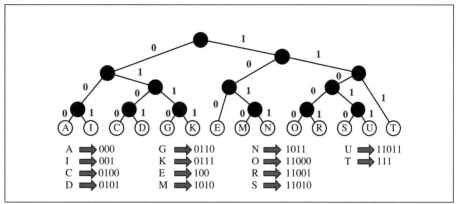

A character's code is found by starting at the root and following the branches that lead to that character. The code itself is the bit value of each branch on the path taken in sequence. In our example, for instance, A = 000, G = 0110, and so on. The code for each character and the frequency of the character are shown in Table F.1. As you can see, no code is the prefix of any other code because each has been obtained by following a different path from the root. The three-bit codes representing the characters E, T, A, and I do not match the first three bits of any four- or five-bit code, and the four-bit codes do not match the first three bits of any five-bit code.

Table F.1   *Code assignment table*

Character	Frequency	Code	Character	Frequency	Code
E	15	100	D	5	0101
T	12	111	G	4	0110
A	10	000	K	4	0111
I	8	001	O	3	11000
M	7	1010	R	3	11001
N	6	1011	S	2	11010
C	5	0100	U	2	11011

F.3   DECODING

A message encoded in this fashion can be interpreted without ambiguity, using the following process:

1. The receiver stores the first three bits received in memory and attempts to match them with one of the three-bit codes. If a match is found, that character is selected and the three bits are discarded. The receiver then repeats this step with the next three bits.

2. If a match is not found, the receiver reads the next bit from the stream and adds it to the first three. It then attempts to find a match among the four-bit codes. If a match is found, the corresponding character is selected and the bits are discarded.

3. If a match is not found, the receiver reads the next bit from the stream and tries to match all five bits to one of the five-bit codes. If a match is found, the character is assigned and the bits are discarded. If not, an error is issued.

Figure F.8 shows a series of bits and their interpretation by the receiver. The receiver reads the first three bits (110) and looks for a match among the three-bit codes. Not finding a match, it adds the next bit (1). It now tries to match the sequence 1101 with a four-bit code. Again finding no match, it adds the next bit (0) and compares 11010 to the five-bit codes. 11010 is found to represent S. S is selected, those five bits are discarded, and the process starts again with the next three bits (101).

Figure F.8   *Unambiguous transmission*

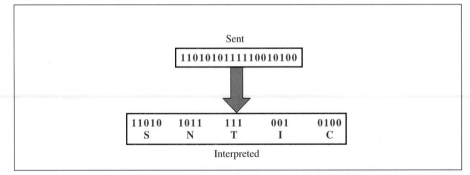

APPENDIX G

LZW (Lempel-Ziv-Welch) Compression Method

The LZW method to compress data is an evolution of the method originally created by Abraham Lempel and Jacob Ziv (Lempel-Ziv method). Later the algorithm was improved by the two originators (called LZ77 and LZ78). Terry Welch further modified the algorithm and it is now called the LZW (Lempel-Ziv-Welch) method.

We present here a very simplified version as an introduction for students and readers encountering it for the first time. We have deliberately omitted a lot of details and error-checking subtleties.

The beauty of the method is that it is a lossless compression method, in which the whole text can be totally recovered. The method is sometimes preferable to Huffman encoding because prior knowledge of the symbol frequencies is not required.

G.1 COMPRESSION

The compression, which takes place at the sender site, has the following components: a dictionary, a buffer, and an algorithm.

Dictionary

To compress and decompress, LZW uses a dictionary made of two rows (or columns). The first row defines the code; the second row defines the string corresponding to that code.

Before compression begins, the dictionary is initialized with only the set of alphabet characters in the text. For example, if the text consists of only three symbols, A, B, and C, the dictionary originally has only 3 columns, but it becomes larger and larger as the text is being compressed or decompressed (see Table G.1).

Table G.1 *Original dictionary for a three-symbol text*

1	*2*	*3*				
A	B	C				

Buffer

LZW uses a buffer. The symbols enter the buffer from one side one by one. The strings are transferred to the dictionary and the corresponding code is sent out according to the algorithm discussed below. Figure G.1 shows the buffer.

Figure G.1 *Buffer at the compression site*

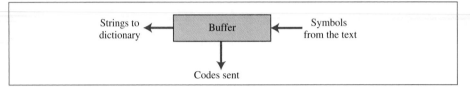

Compression Algorithm

Figure G.2 shows the flowchart for the compression algorithm.

Figure G.2 *Compression algorithm*

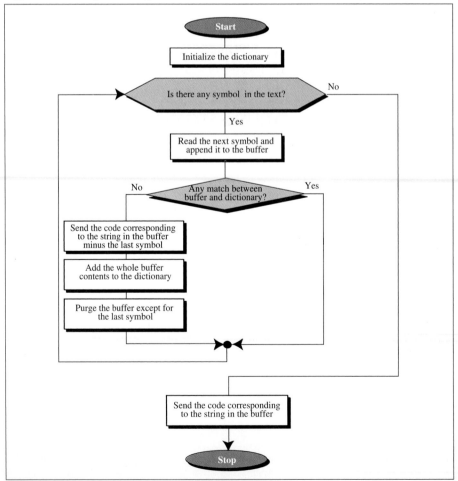

The algorithm, which is a very simplified version of the one in the literature, tries to match the input to the longest string in the dictionary. To accomplish this, it reads symbols, one by one, from the input string and stores them in the buffer. For each reading, it checks to see if the matching string can be found in the dictionary. If found, it tries to read more symbols. If after reading one more symbol there is no match, the process sends the code corresponding to the string without the last symbol (it is guaranteed that it can be found in the dictionary). It then adds the whole string to the dictionary (for later use). It purges the buffer except for the last symbol because the last symbol is not sent out yet. The last character remains in the buffer to become part of the next string.

Example of Compression

Figure G.3 shows an example of compression using the LZW method. The input text, BABACABABA, is compressed to 214358 as follows:

- The dictionary is initialized to the three symbols (A, B, and C in this example). The buffer is empty.
- The first symbol of the text (B) enters the buffer. This symbol is already in the dictionary, so the algorithm continues with the next iteration.
- The second symbol (A) enters the buffer. The string BA is not found in the dictionary, so string B (the whole string without the last) is encoded as 2 and is sent. String (BA) is added to the dictionary and the buffer is purged of B (only A remains in the buffer).
- The third symbol (B) now enters the buffer. The string AB is not found in the dictionary, so string A is encoded as 1 and is sent. String AB is added to the dictionary and the buffer is purged of A (only B remains in the buffer).
- The fourth symbol (A) now enters the buffer. The string BA is already in the dictionary, so the algorithm continues with the next iteration.
- The fifth symbol (C) now enters. String BAC is not found in the dictionary, so BA is encoded as 4 and is sent. String BAC is added to the dictionary. The buffer is purged of what has been encoded and sent (BA). The only symbol left in the buffer is C.
- The sixth symbol (A) now enters. String CA is not in the dictionary, so C is encoded as 3 and is sent. String CA is added to the dictionary. The buffer is purged of what has been encoded and sent (C). The only symbol left in the buffer is A.
- The seventh symbol (B) now enters. String AB is in the dictionary.
- The eighth symbol (A) now enters. String ABA is not found in the dictionary, so AB is encoded as 5 and is sent. String ABA, is added to the dictionary. The buffer is purged of what has been encoded and sent (AB). The only symbol left in the buffer is A.
- The ninth symbol (B) now enters. String AB is in the dictionary.
- The tenth symbol (A) now enters. String ABA is in the dictionary, so the algorithm wants to start the next iteration but there are no more symbols. The algorithm terminates the loop and sends the code corresponding to the string ABA (code 8).

Figure G.3   *Compression example*

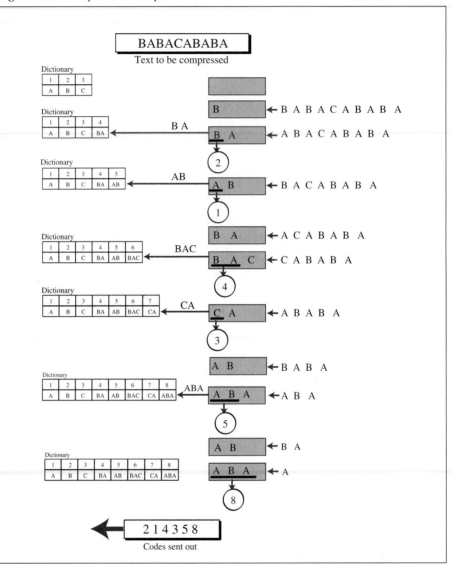

G.2   DECOMPRESSION

The decompression process, which takes place at the receiver site, uses the same components as the compression process.

Dictionary

A very interesting point is that the sender does not send the dictionary created by the compression process; instead, the dictionary will be created at the receiver site and, surprisingly, it is the exact replica of the dictionary created at the sender site. In other words, the information in the dictionary is somehow embedded in the codes transmitted.

Buffers

The decompression process uses two buffers. The arriving codes are decoded and the resulting symbols are kept in a temporary buffer before entering, one symbol at a time, the main buffer. Since each code may represent more than one symbol, the temporary buffer is needed to hold symbols before individual consumption by the main buffer (see Figure G.4).

Figure G.4 *Buffers at the decompression site*

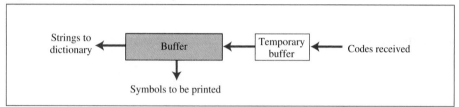

Decompression Algorithm

Figure G.5 shows the flowchart for the decompression algorithm. Our algorithm, which again is a very simplified version of the one in the literature, has two loops. The first loop, in each iteration, decodes each code received and sends the resulting symbols to the temporary buffer. The second loop reads the symbols one by one from the temporary buffer and eventually does the same thing as the compression algorithm. In this way, the temporary buffer simulates the input string in the compression algorithm. The algorithm gradually builds the dictionary that allows the incoming codes to be decoded. The interesting point about the algorithm is that, before any code is received, the entry in the dictionary needed for decoding that particular code is already there. In other words, the previous codes always prepare the dictionary for the next code.

Decompression Example

Figure G.6 shows an example of decompression. We use the same code sent by the sender in the compression example and see if we can get the original text without loss. The process is almost the same as compression.

■　The dictionary is initialized with the three symbols that we are using in this example. The buffer and the temporary buffer are empty.

■　The first code (2) is decoded and the corresponding symbol (B) enters the temporary buffer. The buffer reads this symbol. The string is in the dictionary.

■　The second code (1) is decoded and the corresponding symbol (A) enters the temporary buffer. The buffer reads it. Now the string BA is in the buffer; the symbol B

Figure G.5   *Decompression algorithm*

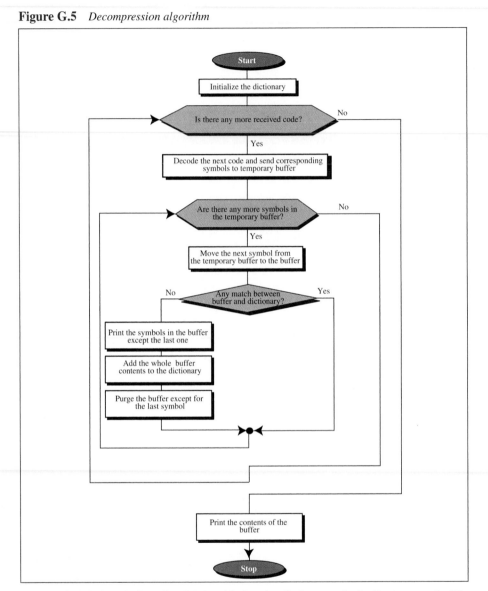

is printed; the whole string BA is added to the dictionary; the buffer is purged of B; the only symbol left is A.

■   The temporary buffer is empty, so the next code should be decoded. The next code is 4 (note that the corresponding entry for 4 is already in the dictionary as it was entered by the previous iteration) which is decoded as BA. The string enters the temporary buffer. The buffer reads only the first character and appends this to the buffer contents. The result is AB. The code is not in the dictionary, so A is printed and AB is added to the dictionary and the buffer is purged of A; the only symbol left over is B.

■   The rest of the process is similar. We leave it to the reader to follow through.

Figure G.6   *Decompression example*

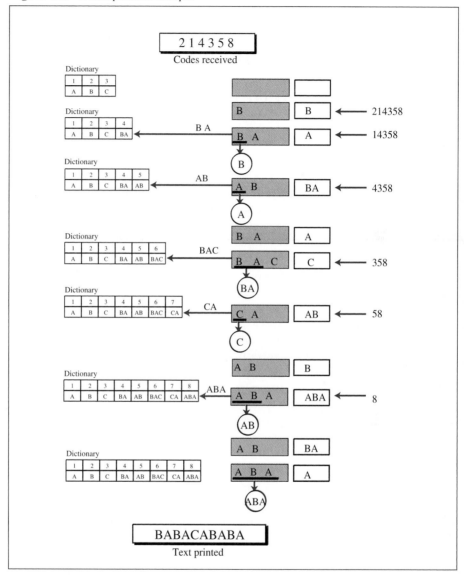

APPENDIX H

Next Generation of TCP/IP Protocol Suite: IPv6 and ICMPv6

The network layer protocol in the TCP/IP protocol suite is currently IPv4 (Internet-working Protocol, version 4). IPv4 provides the host-to-host communication between systems in the Internet. Although IPv4 is well designed, data communication has evolved since the inception of IPv4 in the 1970s. IPv4 has some deficiencies that make it unsuitable for the fast-growing Internet, including the following:

- IPv4 has a two-level address structure (netid and hostid) categorized into five classes (A, B, C, D, and E). The use of address space is inefficient. For instance, when an organization is granted a class A address, 16 million addresses from the address space are assigned for the organization's exclusive use. If an organization is granted a class C address, on the other hand, only 256 addresses are assigned to this organization, which may not be a sufficient number. Also, millions of addresses are wasted in classes D and E. This method of addressing has depleted the address space of IPv4, and soon there will not be any addresses left to assign to any new system that wants to be connected to the Internet. Although the subnetting and supernetting strategies have alleviated some of the addressing problems, sub-netting and supernetting make routing more complicated, as we have seen in the previous chapters.

- The Internet must accommodate real-time audio and video transmission. This type of transmission requires minimum delay strategies and reservation of resources not provided in the IPv4 design.

- The Internet must accommodate encryption and authentication of data for some applications. No encryption or authentication is provided by IPv4.

To overcome these deficiencies, **IPv6** (Internetworking Protocol, version 6), also known as **IPng (Internetworking Protocol, next generation)** was proposed and is now a standard. In IPv6, the Internet protocol was extensively modified to accommo-date the unforeseen growth of the Internet. The format and the length of the IP addresses were changed along with the packet format. Related protocols, such as ICMP, were also modified. Other protocols in the network layer, such as ARP, RARP, and IGMP, were either deleted or included in the ICMP protocol. Routing protocols, such as RIP and OSPF, were also slightly modified to accommodate these changes.

Communication experts predict that IPv6 and its related protocols will soon replace the current IP version. In this chapter we talk first about IPv6. Then we discuss ICMPv6.

H.1   IPv6

The next-generation IP, or IPv6, has some advantages over IPv4 that can be summarized as follows:

- **Larger address space.** An IPv6 address is 128 bits long. Compared with the 32-bit address of IPv4, this is a four fold increase in the address space.
- **Better header format.** IPv6 uses a new header format in which options are separated from the base header and inserted, when needed, between the base header and the upper-layer data. This simplifies and speeds up the routing process because most of the options do not need to be checked by routers.
- **New options.** IPv6 has new options to allow for additional functionalities.
- **Allowance for extension.** IPv6 is designed to allow the extension of the protocol if required by new technologies or applications.
- **Support for resource allocation.** In IPv6, the type-of-service field has been removed, but a mechanism (called *flow label*) has been added to enable the source to request special handling of the packet. This mechanism can be used to support traffic such as real-time audio and video.
- **Support for more security.** The encryption and authentication options in IPv6 provide confidentiality and integrity of the packet.

IPv6 Addresses

An IPv6 address consists of 16 bytes (octets), making it 128 bits long (see Figure H.1).

Figure H.1   *IPv6 address*

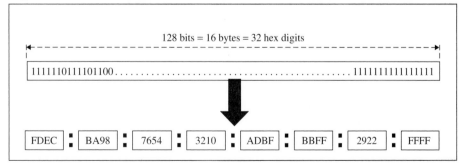

Hexadecimal Colon Notation

To make addresses more readable, IPv6 address protocol specifies **hexadecimal colon notation.** In this notation, 128 bits are divided into eight sections, each two bytes in length. Two bytes in hexadecimal notation require four hexadecimal digits. Therefore, the address consists of 32 hexadecimal digits, with every four digits separated by a colon.

Abbreviation Although the IP address, even in hexadecimal format, is very long, many of the digits are zeros. In this case, we can abbreviate the address. The leading zeros of a section (four digits between two colons) can be omitted. Only the leading zeros can be dropped, not the trailing zeros. For an example, see Figure H.2.

Figure H.2 *Abbreviated address*

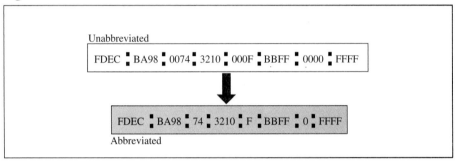

Using this form of abbreviation, 0074 can be written as 74, 000F as F, and 0000 as 0. Note that 3210 cannot be abbreviated. Further abbreviations are possible if there are consecutive sections consisting of zeros only. We can remove the zeros altogether and replace them with a double semicolon. Figure H.3 shows the concept.

Figure H.3 *Abbreviated address with consecutive zeros*

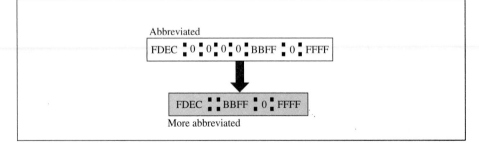

Note that this type of abbreviation is allowed only once per address. If there are two runs of zero sections, only one of them can be abbreviated. Reexpansion of the abbreviated address is very simple: align the unabbreviated portions and insert zeros to get the original expanded address.

Sometimes we need to refer to only part of the address, not all of it. To do so, place a slash after the digits you wish to keep, and follow it with the number of digits kept. For example, Figure H.4 shows how the first six sections can be written in a shortened form.

Figure H.4 *Partial address*

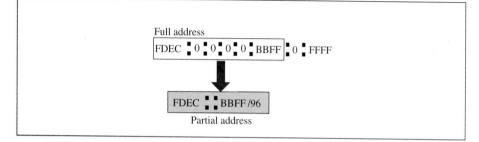

Full address

Partial address

Categories of Addresses

IPv6 defines three types of addresses: unicast, anycast, and multicast.

Unicast Addresses A **unicast** address defines a single computer. The packet sent to a unicast address should be delivered to that specific computer.

Anycast Addresses An anycast address defines a group of computers whose addresses have the same prefix. For example, all computers connected to the same physical network share the same prefix address. A packet sent to an anycast address should be delivered to exactly one of the members of the group—the closest or most easily accessible.

Multicast Addresses A multicast address defines a group of computers that may or may not share the same prefix and may or may not be connected to the same physical network. A packet sent to a multicast address should be delivered to each member of the set.

Address Space Assignment

The address space has many different purposes. The designers of the IP addresses divided the address space into two parts, with the first part called the *type prefix*. This variable-length prefix defines the purpose of the address. The codes are designed such that no code is identical to the first part of any other code. In this way, there is no ambiguity; when an address is given, the type prefix can easily be determined. Figure H.5 shows the IPv6 address format.

Figure H.5 *Address structure*

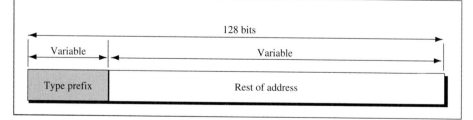

Table H.1 shows the prefix for each type of address. The third column shows the fraction of each type of address relative to the whole address space.

Table H.1   *Type prefixes for IPv6 addresses*

Type Prefix	Type	Fraction
0000 0000	Reserved	1/256
0000 0001	Reserved	1/256
0000 001	NSAP (Network Service Access Point)	1/128
0000 010	IPX (Novell)	1/128
0000 011	Reserved	1/128
0000 100	Reserved	1/128
0000 101	Reserved	1/128
0000 110	Reserved	1/128
0000 111	Reserved	1/128
0001	Reserved	1/16
001	Reserved	1/8
010	**Provider-based unicast addresses**	**1/8**
011	Reserved	1/8
100	Geographic unicast addresses	1/8
101	Reserved	1/8
110	Reserved	1/8
1110	Reserved	1/16
1111 0	Reserved	1/32
1111 10	Reserved	1/64
1111 110	Reserved	1/128
1111 1110 0	Reserved	1/512
1111 1110 10	Link local addresses	1/1024
1111 1110 11	Site local addresses	1/1024
1111 1111	Multicast addresses	1/256

Provider-Based Unicast Addresses   The provider-based address is generally used by a normal host as a unicast address. The address format is shown in Figure H.6.

Fields for the provider-based addresses are as follows:

- **Type identifier.** This three-bit field defines the address as a provider-based address.
- **Registry identifier.** This five-bit field indicates the agency that has registered the address. Currently three registry centers have been defined: INTERNIC (code

Figure H.6 *Provider-based address*

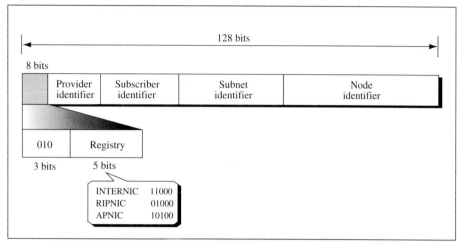

11000) is the center for North America; RIPNIC (code 01000) is the center for
European registration; and APNIC (code 10100) is for Asian and Pacific countries.

■ **Provider identifier.** This variable-length field identifies the provider for Internet
access. A 16-bit length is recommended for this field.

■ **Subscriber identifier.** When an organization subscribes to the Internet through a
provider, it is assigned a subscriber identification. A 24-bit length is recommended
for this field.

■ **Subnet identifier.** Each subscriber can have many different subnetworks and each
network can have different identifiers. The subnet identifier defines a specific network under the territory of the subscriber. A 32-bit length is recommended for this
field.

■ **Node identifier.** The last field defines the identity of the node connected to a subnet. A length of 48 bits is recommended for this field to make it compatible with
the 48-bit link (physical) address used by Ethernet. In the future, this link address
will probably be the same as the node physical address.

We can think of a provider-based address as a hierarchical identity having several prefixes. As shown in Figure H.7, each prefix defines a level of hierarchy. The type prefix

Figure H.7 *Address hierarchy*

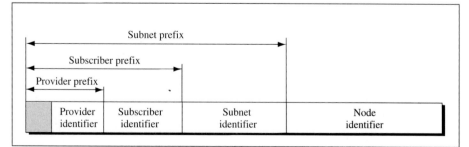

defines the type, the registry prefix uniquely defines the registry level, the provider prefix uniquely defines a provider, the subscriber prefix uniquely defines a subscriber, and the subnet prefix uniquely defines a subnet.

Other Addresses   Other address types are used for purposes that are beyond the scope of this book. For further information, see *TCP/IP Protocol Suite* by Behrouz Forouzan.

IPv6 Packet Format

The IPv6 packet is shown in Figure H.8. Each packet is composed of a mandatory **base header** followed by the payload. The payload consists of two parts: optional **extension headers** and data from an upper layer. The base header occupies 40 bytes, whereas the extension headers and data from the upper layer usually contain up to 65,535 bytes of information.

Figure H.8   *IPv6 datagram*

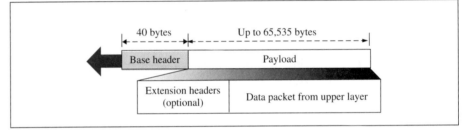

Base Header

Figure H.9 shows the base header with its eight fields. These fields are as follows:

- **Version.** This four-bit field defines the version number of the IP. For IPv6, the value is 6.

Figure H.9   *Format of an IPv6 datagram*

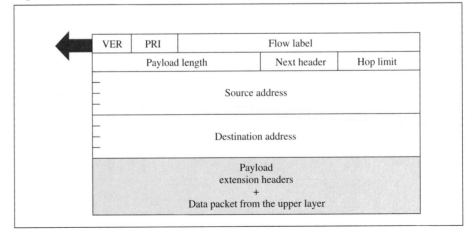

- **Priority.** The four-bit priority field defines the priority of the packet with respect to traffic congestion. We will discuss this field later.

- **Flow label.** The flow label is a three-byte (24-bit) field that is designed to provide special handling for a particular flow of data. We will discuss this field later.

- **Payload length.** This two-byte payload length field defines the total length of the IP datagram excluding the base header.

- **Next header.** The next header is an eight-bit field defining the header that follows the base header in the datagram. The next header is either one of the optional extension headers used by IP or the header for an upper-layer protocol such as UDP or TCP. Each extension header also contains this field. Table H.2 shows the values of next headers. Note that this field in version 4 is called the *protocol*.

Table H.2 *Next header codes*

Code	Next Header
0	Hop-by-hop option
2	ICMP
6	TCP
17	UDP
43	Source routing
44	Fragmentation
50	Encrypted security payload
51	Authentication
59	Null (no next header)
60	Destination option

- **Hop limit.** This eight-bit hop limit field serves the same purpose as the TTL field in IPv4.

- **Source address.** The source address field is a 16-byte (128-bit) Internet address that identifies the original source of the datagram.

- **Destination address.** The destination address field is a 16-byte (128-bit) Internet address that usually identifies the final destination of the datagram. However, if source routing is used, this field contains the address of the next router.

Priority

The priority field of the IPv6 packet defines the priority of each packet with respect to other packets from the same source. For example, if one of two consecutive datagrams must be discarded due to congestion, the datagram with the lower priority will be discarded. IPv6 divides traffic into two broad categories: congestion-controlled and noncongestion-controlled.

Congestion-Controlled Traffic   If a source adapts itself to traffic slowdown when there is congestion, the traffic is referred to as *congestion-controlled traffic*. For example, the TCP protocol, which uses the sliding window protocol, can easily respond to the traffic. In congestion-controlled traffic, it is understood that packets may arrive delayed or even be lost or received out of order. Congestion-controlled data are assigned priorities from 0 to 7, as listed in Table H.3. A priority of 0 is the lowest; a priority of 7 is the highest.

Table H.3   *Priorities for congestion-controlled traffic*

Priority	Meaning
0	No specific traffic
1	Background data
2	Unattended data traffic
3	Reserved
4	Attended bulk data traffic
5	Reserved
6	Interactive traffic
7	Control traffic

The priority descriptions are as follows:

- **No specific traffic.** The priority 0 is assigned to a packet when the process does not define a priority.
- **Background data.** This group (priority 1) defines data that are usually delivered in the background. Delivery of the news is a good example.
- **Unattended data traffic.** If the user is not waiting (attending) for the data to be received, the packet will be given priority 2. E-mail belongs to this group. A user initiates an e-mail message to another user, but the receiver does not know that an e-mail will arrive soon. In addition, an e-mail is usually stored before it is forwarded. A little bit of delay is of little consequence.
- **Attended bulk data traffic.** The protocol that transfers the bulk of data while the user is waiting (attending) to receive the data (possibly with delay) is given priority 4. FTP and HTTP belong to this group.
- **Interactive traffic.** Protocols such as TELNET that need interaction with the user are assigned the second highest priority (6) in this group.
- **Control traffic.** Control traffic has been given the highest priority (7) in this category. Routing protocols such as OSPF and RIP and management protocols such as SNMP use this priority.

Noncongestion-Controlled Traffic   This refers to a type of traffic that expects minimum delay. Discarding of packets is not desirable. Retransmission in most cases is impossible. In other words, the source does not adapt itself to congestion. Real-time audio and video are good examples of this type of traffic.

Priority numbers from 8 to 15 are assigned to noncongestion-controlled traffic. Although there are not yet any particular standard assignments for this type of data, the priorities are usually assigned based on how much the quality of received data can be affected by discarding some packets. Data containing less redundancy (such as low-fidelity audio or video) can be given a higher priority (15). Data containing more redundancy (such as high-fidelity audio or video) should be given lower priority (8). See Table H.4

Table H.4   *Priorities for noncongestion-controlled traffic*

Priority	Meaning
8	Data with most redundancy
.	.
.	.
.	.
15	Data with least redundancy

Flow Label

A sequence of packets, sent from a particular source to a particular destination, that needs special handling by routers is called a *flow* of packets. The combination of the source address and the value of the *flow label* uniquely defines a flow of packets.

To a router, a flow is a sequence of packets that share the same characteristics, such as traveling the same path, using the same resources, having the same kind of security, and so on. A router that supports the handling of flow labels has a flow label table. The table has an entry for each active flow label; each entry defines the services required by the corresponding flow label. When the router receives a packet, it consults its flow label table to find the corresponding entry for the flow label value defined in the packet. It then provides the packet with the services mentioned in the entry. However, note that the flow label itself does not provide the information for the entries of the flow label table; that information is provided by other means such as the hop-by-hop options or other protocols.

In its simplest form, a flow label can be used to speed up the processing of a packet by a router. When a router receives a packet, instead of consulting the routing table and going through a routing algorithm to define the address of the next hop, it can easily look in a flow label table for the next hop.

In its more sophisticated form, a flow label can be used to support the transmission of real-time audio and video. Real-time audio or video, particularly in digital form, requires resources such as high bandwidth, large buffers, long processing time, and so on. A process can make a reservation for these resources beforehand to guarantee that real-time data will not be delayed due to a lack of resources. The use of real-time data and the reservation of these resources requires other protocols such as Real Time Protocol (RTP) and Resource Reservation Protocol (RSVP) in addition to IPv6.

To allow the effective use of flow labels, three rules have been defined:

1. The flow label is assigned to a packet by the source host. The label is a random number between 1 and $2^{24} - 1$. A source must not reuse a flow label for a new flow while the existing flow is still alive.

2. If a host does not support the flow label, it sets this field to zero. If a router does not support the flow label, it simply ignores it.

3. All packets belonging to the same flow should have the same source, same destination, same priority, and same options.

Comparison between IPv4 and IPv6 Headers

Table H.5 compares IPv4 and IPv6 headers.

Table H.5 *Comparison between IPv4 and IPv6 packet header*

Comparison
1. The header length field is eliminated in IPv6 because the length of the header is fixed in this version.
2. The service type field is eliminated in IPv6. The priority and flow label fields together take over the function of the service type field.
3. The total length field is eliminated in IPv6 and replaced by the payload length field.
4. The identification, flag, and offset fields are eliminated from the base header in IPv6. They are included in the fragmentation extension header.
5. The TTL field is called hop limit in IPv6.
6. The protocol field is replaced by the next header field.
7. The header checksum is eliminated because the checksum is provided by upper layer protocols; it is therefore not needed at this level.
8. The option fields in IPv4 are implemented as extension headers in IPv6.

Extension Headers

The length of the base header is fixed at 40 bytes. However, to give more functionality to the IP datagram, the base header can be followed by up to six extension headers. Many of these headers are options in IPv4. Figure H.10 shows the extension header format.

Six types of extension headers have been defined: hop-by-hop option, source routing, fragmentation, authentication, encrypted security payload, and destination option (see Figure H.11).

Figure H.10   *Extension header format*

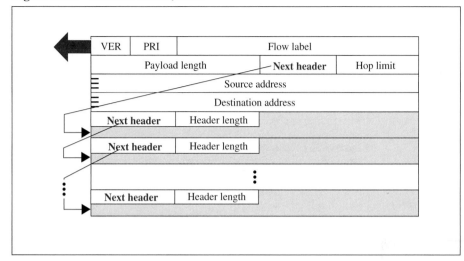

Figure H.11   *Extension header types*

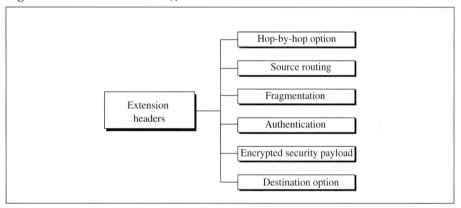

H.2   ICMPv6

Another protocol that has been modified in version 6 of the TCP/IP protocol suite is ICMP (ICMPv6). This new version follows the same strategy and purposes of version 4, but ICMPv4 has been modified to make it more suitable for IPv6. In addition, some protocols that were independent in version 4 are now part of ICMPv6. Figure H.12 compares the network layers of version 4 and version 6.

The ARP and IGMP protocols in version 4 are combined in ICMPv6. The RARP protocol is dropped from the suite because it is not used often.

Figure H.13 shows two broad categories of ICMP messages: error-reporting and query.

Figure H.14 shows the five different error-reporting messages: destination unreachable, packet too big, time exceeded, parameter problems, and redirection.

Figure H.12   *Comparison of network layers in version 4 and version 6*

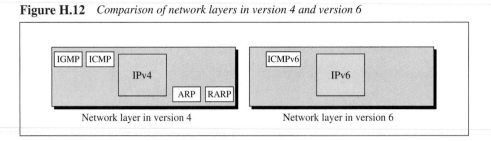

Figure H.13   *Categories of ICMP messages*

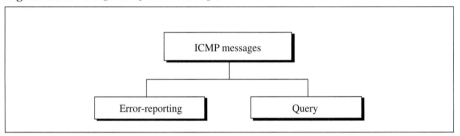

Figure H.14   *Types of error-reporting messages*

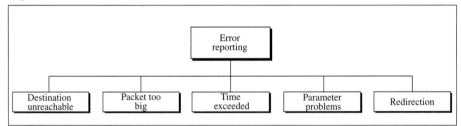

Figure H.15 shows the four different query messages: echo request and reply, router solicitation and advertisement, neighbor solicitation and advertisement, and group membership.

Figure H.15   *Types of query messages*

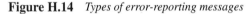

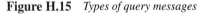

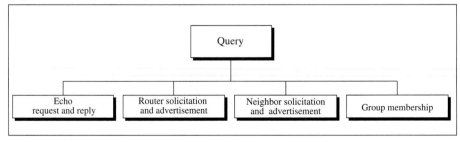

APPENDIX I

Spanning Tree

The spanning tree algorithm is used in data structures to create a tree out of a graph. The tree should include all the vertices (nodes), with a minimum number of edges (lines) connecting the vertices. Any vertex can be selected as the root of the spanning tree. Even after selecting one specific root, we can have several spanning trees based on which subsets of branches are selected to connect each vertex to the root. However, after selecting the root, we are normally interested in one specific spanning tree, the one in which each vertex has the shortest path to the root. The shortest path is defined as the sum of the weights from a specific vertex to the root. If the graph is not weighted, each edge is assigned a weight of 1.

Figure I.1 shows a weighted graph and its spanning tree. Vertex A was chosen as the root.

Figure I.1 *A graph and its spanning tree*

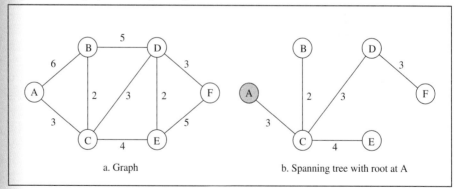

a. Graph   b. Spanning tree with root at A

I.1   SPANNING TREES AND BRIDGES

In Chapter 3, we discussed bridges and mentioned that learning bridges can determine to which LAN segment a host is connected. To create redundancy in case a bridge fails, LAN segments are normally connected by more than one bridge. However, redundancy creates loops in which a packet or several copies of a packet go from one bridge to another for ever. Let us give a very simple example. In Figure I.2, two LAN segments are connected by two bridges (Br1 and Br2).

Figure I.2   *Two LANs connected by two bridges*

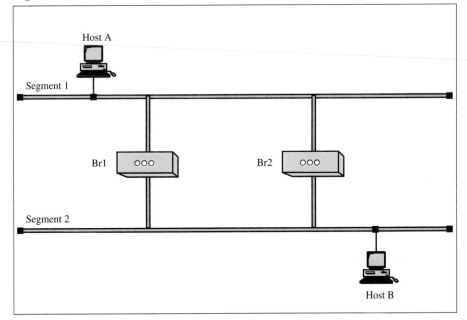

Imagine host B has not sent out any packet, so neither bridge knows to which segment host B is connected. Now consider this sequence of events:

1. Host A sends a packet to host B.
2. One of the bridges, we will say Br1, receives the packet first and, not knowing where host B is, forwards the packet to segment 2.
3. The packet goes to its destination (host B), but, at the same time, Br2 receives the packet via segment 2.
4. The packet source address is host A; its destination address is host B. Br2 erroneously assumes that host A is connected to segment 2 and updates its table accordingly. Because it does not have any information about host B, Br2 forwards the packet to segment 1.
5. The packet is then received for the second time by Br1. Br1 thinks it is a new packet from host A and, because it has no information about host B, Br1 forwards the packet to segment 2.
6. Now Br2 receives the packet once again, and the cycle will repeat endlessly.

This situation occurs due to three factors:

■   We are using learning bridges that do not have information about the location of hosts until they receive at least one packet from them.

■   The bridges are not aware of the existence of other bridges.

■   We have created a graph instead of a tree.

The situation can be corrected if we create a spanning tree out of the graph.

Algorithm

Although most data structures books give the algorithm to form a spanning tree out of a graph, they assume that the topology of the graph is already known. However, when a learning bridge is installed, it does not know the location of other bridges. The spanning tree, therefore, must be formed dynamically.

An ID number is assigned to each bridge. The ID can be any arbitrary number determined by the network manager or the address of one of the ports, normally the smallest one.

Each port is assigned a cost. Normally the cost is determined by the bit rate supported by the port. The higher the bit rate, the lower the cost. If bit rate is irrelevant, then the path cost for each port is set to 1 (hop count).

The process of finding the spanning tree can be summarized in three steps:

1. The bridges choose a bridge to be the *root* of the tree. This is done by assigning an ID to the bridge and then finding the bridge with the smallest ID.

2. Each bridge determines its *root port,* the port that has the least *root path cost* to the root. The root path cost is the accumulated cost of the path from the port to the root.

3. One *designated bridge* is chosen for each segment.

All the bridges regularly exchange a special frame called the *bridge protocol data unit* (BPDU). Each BPDU contains the bridge ID of the source, the accumulated root path cost, and some other information. When a BPDU is initiated from a bridge, the accumulated root path cost is zero.

Finding the Root Bridge

When a bridge receives a BPDU, it compares the source's bridge ID with its own ID.

■   If its own ID is larger than the source's bridge ID, it increments the root path cost by the cost of the receiving port and forwards the frame. It also stops sending its own BPDU because it knows that it will not be chosen as the root bridge (another bridge has a lower ID).

■   If its own ID is smaller than the source's bridge ID, the bridge discards the BPDU.

It is obvious that after a while, the only BPDU that is being circulated is the one with the smallest source bridge ID, the root bridge. In this way, every bridge knows which is the root bridge.

Finding the Root Port

After the root bridge has been established, the bridge records the accumulated root cost of every BPDU received for each port. The root port is the port whose BPDU has the minimum accumulated root cost. Note that the root bridge does not have a root port.

Choosing the Designated Bridge

After the root port is determined for each bridge, all bridges connected to the same segment send BPDUs to each other. The bridge that can carry a frame from the segment to the root with the cheapest root cost is selected as the designated bridge and the particular port that connects the bridge to that segment is called the *designated port*. Note that the root port cannot be chosen as a designated port. Also, note that although a bridge can have only one root port (except the root bridge, which has no root port), it can have more than one designated port.

Forming the Spanning Tree

After the root bridge, the root port for each bridge, and the designated ports for each bridge are determined, the ports of a bridge are divided into two separate groups. The *forwarding ports* are the root port and all of the designated ports. The rest of the ports are considered to be *blocking ports*. When a bridge receives a data frame, it forwards it through its *forwarding ports*. It does not forward the frame through the blocking ports.

Example

Figure I.3 shows an example of five LAN segments connected together by five bridges. Each bridge has an ID number (shown inside the box). The cost of handling a packet from a bridge to the LAN segment is shown next to the connecting line.

Figure I.3   *A LAN before using the spanning-tree algorithm*

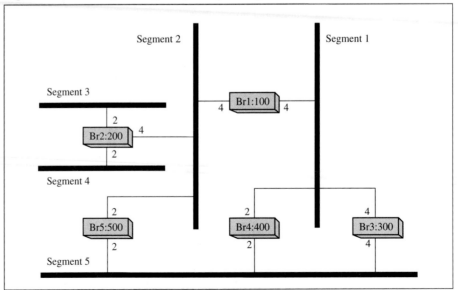

Figure I.4 shows the topology after applying the spanning tree algorithm. The bridge with the lowest ID (Br1) is chosen as the root bridge. Each bridge has one root port (shown by an arrow). Because there are five LAN segments, we have five designated ports (marked as Des.). All the ports of bridges Br1, Br2, and Br4 are forwarding ports. Bridges Br3 and Br5 each has one blocking port.

Figure I.4   *The LAN after using the spanning-tree algorithm*

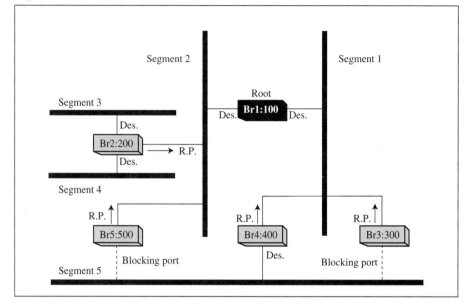

We claim that with this configuration each LAN segment will receive one and only one copy of a frame sent by any host on any other segment; this guarantees loop-free operation.

■ A frame sent by a host on segment 1 will reach segment 2 through Br1, will reach segment 3 and segment 4 through Br1-Br2, and will reach segment 5 through Br4.

■ A frame sent by a host on segment 2 will reach segment 1 through Br1, will reach segment 3 and segment 4 through Br2, and will reach segment 5 through Br1-Br4.

■ A frame sent by a host on segment 3 will reach segment 4 and segment 2 through Br2, will reach segment 1 through Br2-Br1, and will reach segment 5 through Br2-Br1-Br4.

■ A frame sent by a host on segment 4 will reach segment 3 and segment 2 through Br2, will reach segment 1 through Br2-Br1, and will reach segment 5 through Br2-Br1-Br4.

■ A frame sent by a host on segment 5 will reach segment 1 through Br4, will reach segment 2 through Br4-Br1, and will reach segment 3 and segment 4 through Br4-Br1-Br2.

I.2   SPANNING TREES AND MULTICAST ROUTING

The spanning tree concept is also used in multicast routing to produce a loop-free forwarding path for datagrams in the IP layer. The idea is essentially the same as that for bridges. Here, bridges are replaced by routers, and LAN segments are replaced by LANs or WANs. The routers choose a root router among themselves. Each router then finds its root port and finally each LAN or WAN is assigned a designated router. The ports of a router are divided into forwarding and blocking ports. When a router receives a multicast datagram, it forwards only through its forwarding ports.

References

Bates, Bud, and Donald Gregory. *Voice and Data Communications Handbook.* Burr Ridge, IL: McGraw-Hill, 1996.

Beyda, William J. *Data Communications*, 2nd ed. Upper Saddle River, NJ: Prentice-Hall, 1996.

Black, Uyless. *Data Link Protocols.* Upper Saddle River, NJ: Prentice-Hall, 1993.

Black, Uyless. *Emerging Communications Technologies.* Upper Saddle River, NJ: Prentice-Hall, 1994.

Comer, Douglas E. *Internetworking with TCP/IP*, vol. 1. Upper Saddle River, NJ: Prentice-Hall, 1995.

———. *Internetworking with TCP/IP*, vol. 2. Upper Saddle River, NJ: Prentice-Hall, 1996.

———. *Internetworking with TCP/IP*, vol. 3. Upper Saddle River, NJ: Prentice-Hall, 1999.

———. *The Internet Book.* Upper Saddle River, NJ: Prentice-Hall, 1995.

Dickie, Mark. *Routing in Today's Internetworks.* New York, NY: Van Nostrand Reinhold, 1994.

Forouzan, Behrouz. *Introduction to Data Communications and Networking.* Burr Ridge, IL: McGraw-Hill, 1998.

Halsall, Fred. *Data Communications, Computer Networks and Open Systems,* 4th ed. Reading, MA: Addison-Wesley, 1995.

Hardy, James K. *Inside Networks.* Upper Saddle River, NJ: Prentice-Hall, 1995.

Herrick, Clyde N., and C. Lee McKim. *Telecommunication Wiring.* Upper Saddle River, NJ: Prentice-Hall, 1992.

Hioki, Warren. *Telecommunications*, 2nd ed. Upper Saddle River, NJ: Prentice-Hall, 1995.

Huitema, Christian. *Routing in the Internet.* Upper Saddle River, NJ: Prentice-Hall, 1995.

Johnson, Howard W. *Fast Ethernet.* Upper Saddle River, NJ: Prentice-Hall, 1996.

McClimans, Fred J. *Communications Wiring and Interconnections.* Burr Ridge, IL: McGraw-Hill, 1992.

Miller, Philip. *TCP/IP Explained.* Newton, MA: Digital Press, 1997.

Morley, John, and Stan Gelber. *The Emerging Digital Future.* Danver, MA: Boyd & Fraser, 1996.

Moy, John. *OSPF.* Reading, MA: Addison-Wesley, 1998.

Naugle, Matthew G. *Network Protocol Handbook.* Burr Ridge, IL: McGraw-Hill, 1994.

Partridge, Craig. *Gigabit Networking.* Reading, MA: Addison-Wesley, 1994.

Pearson, John E. *Basic Communication Theory.* Upper Saddle River, NJ: Prentice-Hall, 1992.

Perlman, Radia. *Interconnections: Bridges and Routers.* Reading, MA: Addison-Wesley, 1992.

Shay, William A. *Understanding Data Communications and Networks.* Boston, MA: PWS, 1994.

Siyan, Karanjit S. *Inside TCP/IP,* 3rd ed. Indianapolis, IN: New Riders, 1997.

Smith, Philip. *Frame Relay.* Reading, MA: Addison-Wesley, 1993.

Stallings, William. *Data and Computer Communications,* 5th ed. Upper Saddle River, NJ: Prentice-Hall, 1997.

Stevens, W. Richard. *TCP/IP Illustrated,* vol. 1. Reading, MA: Addison-Wesley, 1994.

———. *TCP/IP Illustrated,* vol. 3. Reading, MA: Addison-Wesley, 1996.

Tanenbaum, Andrew S. *Computer Networks,* 3rd ed. Upper Saddle River, NJ: Prentice-Hall, 1996.

Thomas, Stephen A. *IPng and the TCP/IP Protocols.* New York, NY: Wiley, 1996.

Washburn, Kevin, and Jim Evans. *TCP/IP: Running a Successful Network,* 2nd ed. Reading, MA: Addison-Wesley, 1996.

Wright, Gary R., and W. Richard Stevens. *TCP/IP Illustrated,* vol. 2. Reading, MA: Addison-Wesley, 1995.

Glossary

1Base5 The IEEE 802.3 standard for low-data-rate Ethernet using twisted-pair cable and daisy-chained connections.

10Base-T The IEEE 802.3 standard for twisted-pair Ethernet.

10Base2 The IEEE 802.3 standard for Ethernet using thin coaxial cable.

10Base5 The IEEE 802.3 standard for Ethernet using thick coaxial cable.

100Base-FX A version of the IEEE 802.3 standard for Fast Ethernet using 2 optical fibers.

100Base-T A version of the IEEE 802.3 standard for Fast Ethernet using twisted-pair cable.

100Base-T4 A version of the IEEE 802.3 standard for Fast Ethernet using four UTP pairs.

100Base-TX A version of the IEEE 802.3 standard for Fast Ethernet using two UTP or STP pairs.

56K modem A modem technology using two different data rates: one for uploading and one for downloading from the Internet.

802 See *IEEE Project 802*, See also *Project 802*.

802.1 See *IEEE 802.1.*

802.2 See *IEEE 802.2.*

802.3 See *IEEE 802.3.*

802.4 See *IEEE 802.4.*

802.5 See *IEEE 802.5.*

A

AAL1 An AAL layer in the ATM protocol that processes constant-bit-rate data.

AAL2 An AAL layer in the ATM protocol that processes variable-bit-rate data.

AAL3/4 An AAL layer in the ATM protocol that processes connectionless or connection-oriented packet data.

AAL5 An AAL layer in the ATM protocol that processes data with extensive header information from upper layer protocols; also called the simple and efficient adaptation layer (SEAL).

abort To terminate a process abruptly.

abstract syntax notation 1 (ASN.1)   A formal language using abstract syntax for defining the structure of a protocol data unit (PDU).

access control (AC) field   A field in a Token Ring frame containing priority, token, monitor, and reservation bits.

access rate   In Frame Relay, the data rate that can never be exceeded.

acknowledgment (ACK)   A response sent by the receiver to indicate the successful receipt and acceptance of data.

active document   In the World Wide Web, a document executed at the local site using Java.

active hub   A hub that repeats or regenerates a signal. It functions as a repeater.

add/drop multiplexer   A SONET device that multiplexes signals from different sources or demultiplexes a signal to multiple destinations.

address field   A field containing the address of a sender or receiver.

address resolution protocol (ARP)   In TCP/IP, a protocol for obtaining the physical address of a node when the Internet address is known.

Advanced Research Project Agency (ARPA)   The government agency that funded ARPANET.

Advanced Research Project Agency Network (ARPANET)   The packet-switching network that was funded by ARPA.

agent   A router or a host that runs the SNMP server program.

alternate mark inversion (AMI)   A digital-to-digital bipolar encoding method in which the amplitude representing 1 alternates between positive and negative voltages.

American National Standards Institute (ANSI)   A national standards organization that defines standards in the United States.

American Standard Code for Information Interchange (ASCII)   A character code developed by ANSI and used extensively for data communication.

amplitude   The strength of a signal, usually measured in volts, amperes, or watts.

amplitude modulation (AM)   An analog-to-analog conversion method in which the carrier signal's amplitude varies with the amplitude of the modulating signal.

amplitude shift keying (ASK)   A modulation method in which the amplitude of the carrier signal is varied to represent binary 0 or 1.

analog   A continuously varying entity.

analog data   Data that are continuous and smooth and not limited to a specific number of values.

analog hierarchy   A telephone company system in which multiplexed signals are combined into successively larger groups for more efficient transmission.

analog leased service   A service featuring a dedicated line between two users.

analog network   A network that uses analog signals.

analog service   A telephone service using analog transmission.

analog signal   A continuous waveform that changes smoothly over time.

analog switched service   A temporary analog connection between two users.

analog-to-analog modulation   The representation of analog information by an analog signal.

analog-to-digital conversion   The representation of analog information by a digital signal.

angle of incidence   In optics, the angle formed by a light ray approaching the interface between two media and the line perpendicular to the interface.

angle of reflection   In optics, the angle formed by a reflected light ray at the interface between two media and the line perpendicular to the interface.

angle of refraction   In optics, the angle formed by a refracted light ray at the interface between two media and the line perpendicular to the interface.

aperiodic signal   A signal that does not exhibit a pattern or repeating cycle.

applet   A computer program for creating an active web document. It is usually written in Java.

application adaptation layer (AAL)   A layer in ATM protocol that breaks user data into 48-byte payloads.

application layer   The seventh layer in the OSI model; provides access to network resources.

asymmetric digital subscriber line (ADSL)   A communication technology in which the downstream data rate is higher than the upstream rate.

asynchronous balanced mode (ABM)   In HDLC, a communication mode in which all stations are equal.

asynchronous protocol   A set of rules for asynchronous transmission.

asynchronous response mode (ARM)   A communication mode between a primary and a secondary device in which the secondary is allowed to initiate a transmission.

asynchronous time-division multiplexing   Time-division multiplexing in which link time is allocated dynamically according to the activity of the links.

Asynchronous Transfer Mode (ATM)   A wide area network protocol featuring high data rates and equal-sized packets (cells); ATM is suitable for transferring text, audio, and video data.

asynchronous transmission   Transfer of data with start and stop bit(s) and a variable time interval between data units.

attachment unit interface (AUI)   A 10Base5 cable that performs the physical interface functions between the station and the transceiver.

attenuation   The loss of a signal's energy due to the resistance of the medium.

authenticating state   In PPP, an optional state that verifies the identity of the receiver.

authentication   Verification of the sender of a message.

automatic repeat request (ARQ)   An error-control method in which correction is made by retransmission of data.

available bit rate (ABR)   The minimum data rate in ATM at which cells can be delivered.

B

B channel   An ISDN channel type with a 64-Kbps data rate; the basic user channel; also known as the bearer channel.

backbone   The major transmission path in a network.

backward explicit congestion notification (BECN)   A bit in the Frame Relay packet that notifies the sender of congestion.

balanced configuration   In HDLC protocol, a configuration in which two stations are of the combined type.

bandwidth   The difference between the highest and the lowest frequencies of a composite signal. It also measures the information-carrying capacity of a line or a network.

bandwidth on demand   A digital service that allows subscribers higher speeds through the use of multiple lines.

banyan switch   A multistage switch with microswitches at each stage that route the cells based on the output port.

base header   In IPv6, the main header of the datagram.

baseband   Referring to a technology in which a signal is transmitted directly onto a channel without modulating a carrier.

basic encoding rule (BER)   A standard that encodes data to be transferred through a network.

basic rate interface (BRI)   In ISDN, an electrical interface providing two B channels (64 Kbps) and one D channel (16 Kbps). The total data rate is 192 Kbps, which includes some overhead.

Batcher-banyan switch   An enhanced banyan switch in which a switch (before the banyan switch) sorts the cells according to destination.

baud rate   The number of signal elements transmitted per second. A signal element consists of one or more bits.

bearer channel   An ISDN channel type with the 64 Kbps data rate; the basic user channel. See *B channel.*

bearer services   In ISDN, a service that does not manipulate the content of the transmission.

Bell modems   Modems produced by the Bell Telephone Company.

Bellcore   Bell Communication Research. See *Telcordia.*

Bellman-Ford algorithm   An algorithm used to calculate routing tables in the distance vector routing method.

binary number system   A method of representing information using only two symbols (0 and 1).

binary synchronous communication (BSC)   A popular character-oriented data link protocol.

bipolar 8-zero substitution (B8ZS)   A digital-to-digital bipolar encoding method used in North America to provide synchronization of long strings of 0s.

bipolar encoding   A digital-to-digital encoding method in which 0 amplitude represents binary 0 and positive and negative amplitudes represent alternate 1s.

bit   A binary digit; the smallest unit of information; 1 or 0.

bit interval   The time required to send one bit.

bit-level encryption   A conventional encryption method in which the data are first divided into blocks of bits prior to encryption.

bit-oriented protocol   A protocol in which a frame is seen as a bit stream.

bit rate   The number of bits transmitted per second.

bit stuffing   In HDLC, the addition of an extra 0 to prevent the receiver from mistaking the data for a flag. In synchronous TDM, a technique that adds bits for synchronization purposes.

bits per second (bps)   A measurement of data speed; bits transmitted per second.

block check count (BCC)   One or two characters used for error detection at the end of a BSC frame.

blocked asynchronous transmission (BLAST)   A more powerful version of XMODEM, featuring full-duplex transmission and sliding window flow control.

blocking   An event that occurs when a switching network is working at its full capacity and cannot accept more input.

bootstrap protocol (BOOTP)   The protocol that provides configuration information from a table (file).

bridge   A network device operating at the first two layers of the OSI model with filtering and forwarding capabilities.

broadband   Referring to a technology in which a signal shares the bandwidth of a medium.

broadband ISDN (B-ISDN)   ISDN with a high data rate based upon cell-relay delivery.

broadcast/unknown server (BUS)   A server connected to an ATM switch that can multicast and broadcast frames.

broadcasting   Transmission of a message to all nodes in a network.

brouter (bridge/router)   A device that functions as both a bridge and a router.

browser   An application program that displays a WWW document. A browser usually uses other Internet services to access the document.

buffer   Memory set aside for temporary storage.

burst error   Error in a data unit in which two or more bits have been altered.

bursty data   Data with varying instantaneous transmission rates.

bus topology   A network topology in which all computers are attached to a shared medium (often a single cable).

byte   A group of eight bits.

byte-oriented protocol   See *character-oriented protocol*.

C

cable modem   A technology in which the TV cable provides Internet access.

carrier sense multiple access (CSMA)   A contention access method in which each station listens to the line before transmitting data.

carrier sense multiple access with collision detection (CSMA/CD)   CSMA with retransmission when collision is detected.

carrier signal   A high frequency signal used for digital-to-analog or analog-to-analog modulation. One of the characteristics of the carrier signal (amplitude, frequency, or phase) is changed according to the modulating data.

carrierless amplitude/phase (CAP)   A modulation technique similar to QAM, but without a carrier signal.

cell   A small, fixed-size data unit; also, in cellular telephony, a geographical area served by a cell office.

cell delay variation (CDV)   In ATM, the difference between the CTD maximum and the CTD minimum.

cell error ratio (CER)   In ATM, the fraction of cells delivered in error.

cell loss ratio (CLR)   In ATM, the fraction of cells lost during transmission.

cell network   A network using the cell as its basic data unit.

cell relay   A communication technology using a fixed-size data unit as the packet; used by ATM.

cell transfer delay (CTD)   In ATM, the average time needed for a cell to travel from source to destination.

cell variation delay tolerance (CVDT)   In ATM, a measure of the variation in cell transmission times.

cellular telephony   A wireless communication technique in which an area is divided into cells. A cell is served by a transmitter.

Challenge Handshake Authentication Protocol (CHAP)   In PPP, a three-way handshaking protocol used for authentication.

channel   A communications pathway.

character-level encryption   A conventional encryption method in which the character is the unit of encryption.

character-oriented protocol   A protocol in which the frame or packet is interpreted as a series of characters.

cheapernet   See *10Base2*.

cheapnet   See *10Base2*.

checksum   A field used for error detection. It is formed by adding bit streams using one's complement arithmetic and then complementing the result.

ciphertext   The encrypted data.

circuit switching   A switching technology that establishes an electrical connection between stations using a dedicated path.

cladding   Glass or plastic surrounding the core of an optical fiber; the optical density of the cladding must be less than that of the core.

class of address   The category of an IPv4 address.

client   A program that initiates communication with another program called the server.

client–server model   The model of interaction between two application programs in which a program at one end (client) requests a service from a program at the other end (server).

coaxial cable   A transmission medium consisting of a conducting core, insulating material, and a second conducting sheath.

code   An arrangement of symbols to stand for a word or an action.

collision   The event that occurs when two transmitters send at the same time on a channel designed for only one transmission at a time; data will be destroyed.

combined station   In HDLC protocol, a station that can function as a primary or secondary station at the same time.

committed burst size (B_c)   The maximum number of bits in a specific time period that a Frame Relay network must transfer without discarding any frames.

committed information rate (CIR)   The committed burst size divided by time.

common carrier   A transmission facility available to the public and subject to public utility regulation.

common gateway interface (CGI)   A standard for communication between HTTP servers and executable programs. CGI is used in creating dynamic documents.

common management information protocol (CMIP)   A protocol to implement OSI management services.

common management information service (CMIS)   An OSI management service.

common management information service element (CMISE)   A specific service provided by CMIS.

composite signal   A signal composed of more than one sine wave.

compressed permutation   A bit-level encryption technique in which bit positions are changed and bits are dropped.

compression   The reduction of a message without significant loss of information.

concatenation   Combining two or more data units coming from the session layer to form one segment in the transport layer.

conditioning   Improving the quality of a line by lessening the attenuation and distortion.

congestion   Excessive network or internetwork traffic causing a general degradation of service.

congestion avoidance   In Frame Relay, a method using two bits that explicitly notify the source and destination of congestion.

congestion control   A method to manage network and internetwork traffic to improve throughput.

connection establishment   The preliminary setup necessary for a logical connection prior to actual data transfer.

connection-oriented network service (CONS)   A network-level data protocol with formal rules for establishment and termination of a connection.

connection-oriented service   A service for data transfer involving establishment and termination of a connection.

connection-oriented transmission   Data transfer involving establishment and termination of a connection.

connection-oriented transport service (COTS)   A transport-level protocol with formal establishment and termination of a connection.

connection request   A message sent to establish a connection.

connection termination   A message sent to end a connection.

connectionless network service (CLNS)   A network-level protocol without formal rules for connection establishment or termination.

connectionless service   A service for data transfer without connection establishment or termination.

connectionless transmission   Data transfer without connection establishment or termination.

connectionless transport service (CLTS)   A transport-level data transfer protocol without formal connection establishment or termination.

constant bit rate (CBR)   The data rate of an ATM service class that is designed for customers requiring real-time audio or video services.

constellation   A graphical representation of the phase and amplitude of different bit combinations in digital-to-analog modulation.

contention   An access method in which two or more devices try to transmit at the same time on the same channel.

control character   A character in BSC used to convey information about the transmission.

control plane   In ISDN, a set of layers that define the functionality of the D channel.

conventional encryption   A method of encryption in which the encryption and decryption algorithms use the same key, which is kept secret.

convergence sublayer (CS)   In ATM protocol, the upper AAL sublayer that adds a header or a trailer to the user data.

country domain   A subdomain in the domain name system that uses two characters to identify a country as the last suffix.

credit allocation   Part of the fixed parameter field in the TPDU; the number of data units that can be sent before the sender must wait for an acknowledgment.

critical angle   In refraction, the value of the angle of incidence that produces a 90-degree angle of refraction.

crossbar switch   A switch consisting of a lattice of horizontal and vertical paths. At the intersection of each horizontal and vertical path, there is a crosspoint that can connect the input to the output.

crosspoint   The junction of an input and an output on a crossbar switch.

crosstalk   The noise on a line caused by signals traveling along another line.

cut-through switch   A switch that forwards a packet to an output buffer as soon as the destination address is received.

cycle   The repetitive unit of a periodic signal.

cyclic redundancy check (CRC)   A highly accurate error-detection method based on interpreting a pattern of bits as a polynomial.

D

Data channel (D channel)   An ISDN channel used primarily to carry control signals. It can also be used for low-rate data transfer.

data circuit–terminating equipment (DCE)   A device used as an interface between a DTE and a network.

data communication   The interchange of information between two or more entities.

data compression   The reduction of the amount of data to be transmitted without significant loss of information.

data encryption standard (DES)   The U.S. government standard encryption method for nonmilitary and nonclassified use.

data link connection identifier (DLCI)   A number that identifies the virtual circuit in Frame Relay.

data link layer   The second layer in the OSI model. It is responsible for node-to-node delivery.

data terminal equipment (DTE)   A device that is an information source or an information sink. It is connected to a network through a DCE.

data transfer   The movement of data from one location to another.

datagram   In packet-switching, an independent data unit.

datagram approach to packet switching   A data transmission method in which each data unit is independent of others.

DB-9   An EIA-232 implementation or an EIA-449 implementation, each specifying a 9-pin connector.

DB-15   An X.21 implementation specifying a 15-pin connector.

DB-25   An EIA-232 implementation specifying a 25-pin connector.

DB-37   An EIA-449 implementation specifying a 37-pin connector.

DC component   See *direct current*.

de facto standard A standard that has not been approved by an organized body but has been adopted as a standard through widespread use.

de jure standard A standard that has been legislated by an officially recognized body.

decibel (dB) A measure of the relative strength of two signal points.

decimal number system A method of representing information using 10 symbols (0, 1, 2, 3, 4, 5, 6, 7, 8, and 9).

decoding Process of restoring an encoded message to its pre-encoded form.

decryption Recovery of the original message from the encrypted data.

demodulation The process of separating the carrier signal from the information-bearing signal.

demodulator A device that performs demodulation.

demultiplexer (DEMUX) A device that separates a multiplexed signal into its original components.

destination address (DA) The address of the receiver of the data unit.

dialog The exchange between two communicating devices.

dibit A unit of data consisting of two bits.

differential Manchester encoding A digital-to-digital polar encoding method that features a transition at the middle of the bit interval as well as an inversion at the beginning of each 1 bit.

differential phase shift keying (DPSK) A digital-to-analog encoding method in which the bit pattern defines the phase change instead of the current phase.

digital A discontinuous or discrete entity.

digital data Data represented by discrete values or conditions.

digital data service (DDS) A digital version of an analog leased line with a rate of 64 Kbps.

digital network A network that transmits digital signals.

digital pipe A high-speed path composed of time-multiplexed channels.

digital service unit (DSU) A device that allows the connection of a user's device to a digital line.

digital service unit/channel service unit (DSU/CSU) A device that allows multiple users of a single T line by dividing the capacity of the line into interleaved channels.

digital signal A discrete signal with a limited number of values.

digital signature A method to authenticate the sender of a message.

digital subscriber line (DSL) A technology using existing telecommunications networks to accomplish high-speed delivery of data, voice, video, and multimedia.

digital-to-analog modulation The representation of digital information by an analog signal.

digital-to-digital encoding The representation of digital information by a digital signal.

Dijkstra algorithm In link state routing, an algorithm that finds the shortest path to other routers.

direct current (DC) A zero-frequency signal with a constant amplitude.

directory information base (DIB) The set of entries that make up the database of the OSI directory service.

directory service (DS)   A service that can provide the e-mail address of an individual.

directory system agent (DSA)   A part of DS that handles DUA requests.

directory user agent (DUA)   A part of DS that communicates with the user and passes user requests to the DSA.

discard eligibility (DE)   A bit that defines that a packet can be discarded if there is congestion in the network.

discrete multitone technique (DMT)   A modulation method combining elements of QAM and FDM.

distance vector routing   A routing method in which each router sends its neighbors a list of networks it can reach and the distance to that network.

distortion   Any change in a signal due to noise, attenuation, or other influences.

distributed processing   A strategy in which services provided for the network reside at multiple sites.

distributed queue dual bus (DQDB)   A protocol (IEEE 802.6) used by SMDS.

distributive services   In B-ISDN, unidirectional services sent from a provider to subscribers automatically.

Domain Name System (DNS)   A TCP/IP application service that converts user-friendly names to IP addresses.

dotted-decimal notation   A notation devised to make the IP address easier to read; each byte is converted to its decimal equivalent and then set off from its neighbor by a period.

downlink   Transmission from a satellite to an earth station.

downloading   Retrieving a file or data from a remote site.

downward multiplexing   A transport layer technique that splits a single connection into several different paths to improve throughput.

dual attachment concentrator (DAC)   In FDDI, a device that connects a combination of SASs or DASs to the dual ring. It makes the combination look like a single SAS unit.

dual attachment station (DAS)   In FDDI, a station that can be connected to two rings.

dual bus   Two buses; in DQDB, one bus is used for upstream, the other for downstream transmission.

duplex mode   See *full-duplex mode*.

duplication control   A transport layer function that ensures that there are no duplicate data units at the receiver.

dynamic document   A web document created by running a CGI program at the server site.

dynamic host configuration protocol (DHCP)   An extension to BOOTP that dynamically assigns configuration information.

E

E lines   The European equivalent of T lines.

e-mail   See *electronic mail*.

EIA-232   A common 25-pin interface standard developed by the EIA.

EIA-449   An interface standard specifying a 37-pin connector and a 9-pin connector developed by the EIA.

EIA-530   An interface standard based on EIA-449 that uses DB-25 pins.

electromagnetic interference (EMI)   A noise on the data transmission line that can corrupt the data. It can be created by motors, generators, and so on.

electromagnetic spectrum   The frequency range occupied by electromagnetic energy.

electronic mail (e-mail)   A method of sending messages electronically based on mailbox addresses rather than a direct host-to-host exchange.

Electronics Industries Association (EIA)   An organization that promotes electronics manufacturing concerns. It has developed interface standards such as EIA-232, EIA-449, and EIA-530.

encapsulation   The technique in which a data unit from one protocol is placed within the data field portion of the data unit of another protocol.

encoding   Transforming information into signals.

encryption   Converting a message into an unintelligible form that is unreadable unless decrypted.

end of transmission (EOT)   A frame sent to end the communication between two devices.

end-to-end message delivery   Delivery of all parts of a message from the sender to the receiver.

enquiry/acknowledgment (ENQ/ACK)   A line discipline method used in point-to-point connections. An ENQ frame is transmitted by a station wishing to send data; an ACK is returned if the station is ready to receive the data.

error   A mistake in data transmission.

error control   The detection and handling of errors in data transmission.

error correction   The process of correcting bits that have been changed during transmission.

error detection   The process of determining whether or not some bits have been changed during transmission.

error handling   The methods used to detect or correct errors.

error recovery   The ability of a system to resume normal activity after errors are detected.

establishing state   In PPP, a state in which communication begins and options are negotiated.

Ethernet   A local area network using CSMA/CD access method. See *IEEE 802.3*.

even parity   An error-detection method in which an extra bit is added to the data unit so that the total number of 1s becomes even.

excess burst size (B_e)   In Frame Relay, the maximum number of bits in excess of B_c that the user can send during a predefined period of time.

exclusive OR   A bit-level encryption technique using the exclusive-OR operation.

expanded permutation   A bit-level permutation in which the output bits are more than the input bits.

extension header   Extra headers in the IPv6 datagram that provide additional functionality.

extremely high frequency (EHF)   Radio waves in the 30-GHz to 300-GHz range using space propagation.

F

Fast Ethernet   See *100Base-T.*

Federal Communications Commission (FCC)   A government agency that regulates radio, television, and telecommunications.

fiber distributed data interface (FDDI)   A high-speed (100-Mbps) LAN, defined by ANSI, using fiber optics, dual ring topology, and the token-passing access method. Today an FDDI network is also used as a MAN.

fiber-optic cable   A high-bandwidth transmission medium that carries data signals in the form of pulses of light. It consists of a thin cylinder of glass or plastic, called the core, surrounded by a concentric layer of glass or plastic called the cladding.

fiber to the curb (FTTC)   A cost-cutting data delivery method in which the optical fiber stops at the subscriber's curb.

file transfer, access, and management (FTAM)   In the OSI model, an application layer service for remote file handling.

file transfer protocol (FTP)   In TCP/IP, an application layer protocol that transfers files between two sites.

final bit (F bit)   An HDLC control bit sent by the secondary station to indicate whether or not more frames are coming. See *P/F bit*.

flag   In HDLC, a field that alerts the receiver to the beginning or ending of a frame.

flooding   Saturation of a network with a message.

flow control   A technique to control the rate of flow of frames (packets or messages).

forum   An organization that tests, evaluates, and standardizes a specific new technology.

forward explicit congestion notification (FECN)   A bit in the Frame Relay packet that notifies the destination of congestion.

Fourier analysis   The mathematical technique used to obtain the frequency spectrum of an aperiodic signal if the time-domain representation is given.

Fourier series   A mathematical technique that reduces a composite periodic signal to a series of simple sine waves.

Fourier transform   A mathematical technique that reduces an aperiodic signal to a series of simple sine waves.

fractional T line   A T line shared by multiple users.

fragmentation   The division of a packet into smaller units to accommodate a protocol's MTU.

frame   A group of bits representing a block of data.

frame check sequence (FCS)   The HDLC error-detection field containing either a two- or four-byte CRC.

Frame Relay   A packet-switching specification defined for the first two layers of the OSI model. There is no network layer. Error checking is done on end-to-end basis instead of on each link.

Frame Relay assembler/disassembler (FRAD)   A device used in Frame Relay to handle frames coming from other protocols.

framing bit   A bit used for synchronization purposes in synchronous TDM.

frequency   The number of cycles per second of a periodic signal.

frequency-division multiplexing (FDM)   The combining of analog signals into a single signal.

frequency-domain plot   A graphical representation of a signal's frequency components.

frequency modulation (FM)   An analog-to-analog modulation method in which the carrier signal's frequency varies with the amplitude of the modulating signal.

frequency shift keying (FSK)   A digital-to-analog encoding method in which the frequency of the carrier signal is varied to represent binary 0 or 1.

full-duplex mode   A transmission mode in which communication can be two way simultaneously.

G

gateway   A device used to connect two separate networks that use different communication protocols.

general format identifier (GFI)   A PLP packet field that defines the source of control information, the acknowledging device, and the size of the sequence number bits.

generic domain   A subdomain in the domain name system (DNS) that uses generic suffixes.

geosynchronous orbit   An orbit that allows a satellite to remain fixed above a certain spot on earth.

Gigabit Ethernet   An Ethernet technology using a data rate of 1 Gbps.

gigahertz (GHz) 10^9 hertz

go-back-*n* ARQ   An error-control method in which the frame in error and all following frames must be retransmitted.

group   An analog signal created by 12 voice channels multiplexed together.

guard band   A bandwidth separating two signals.

guided media   Transmission media with a physical boundary.

H

hybrid channel (H channel)   In ISDN, a hybrid channel available in a variety of data rates; suitable for high-data-rate applications.

half-duplex mode   A transmission mode in which communication can be two way but not at the same time.

Hamming code   A method that adds redundant bits to a data unit to detect and correct bit errors.

handshaking   A process to establish or terminate a connection.

harmonics   Components of a digital signal, each having a different amplitude, frequency, and phase.

Hayes-compatible modem   An intelligent modem capable of more than just modulation and demodulation.

header   Control information added to the beginning of a data packet.

hertz (Hz)   Unit of measurement for frequency.

hexadecimal colon notation   In IPv6, an address notation consisting of 32 hexadecimal digits, with every four digits separated by a colon.

hexadecimal number system   A method of representing information using 16 symbols (0, 1, . . . , 9, A, B, C, D, E, and F).

high bit rate digital subscriber line (HDSL)   A DSL-based technology that uses 2B1Q encoding to lessen the effects of attenuation.

high-density bipolar 3 (HDB3)   A digital-to-digital encoding method used in Europe that provides synchronization of long strings of 0s.

high frequency (HF)   Radio waves in the 3-MHz to 30-MHz range using line-of-sight propagation.

high-level data link control (HDLC)   A bit-oriented data link protocol defined by the ISO. It is used in X.25 protocol. A subset, called link access procedure (LAP), is used in other protocols. It is also a base for many data link protocols used in LANs.

homepage   A hypertext document that is the main page for an organization or individual.

hop count   The number of nodes along a route. It is a measurement of distance in routing algorithms.

horn antenna   A scoop-shaped antenna used in terrestrial microwave communication.

host   A station or node on a network.

hostid   The part of an IP address that identifies a host.

hub   A central device in a star topology that provides a common connection among the nodes.

Huffman encoding   A statistical compression method using variable-length codes to encode a set of symbols.

hybrid topology   A topology composed of more than one basic topology.

HyperText Markup Language (HTML)   The computer language for specifying the contents and format of a web document. It allows additional text to include codes that define fonts, layouts, embedded graphics, and hypertext links.

HyperText Transfer Protocol (HTTP)   An application service for retrieving a web document.

I

I.430   An ITU-T standard for BRI physical layer specifications.

I.431   An ITU-T standard for PRI physical layer specifications.

I-frame   In HDLC, an information frame that carries user data and control information.

idle state   In PPP, a state in which the link is inactive.

IEEE project 802   A project by IEEE to define LAN standards for the physical and data link layers of OSI model. It divides the data link layer into two sublayers called logical link control and medium access control.

IEEE 802.1   The standard developed by IEEE Project 802 for local area networks. It covers the internetworking aspect of LANs.

IEEE 802.2   The standard developed by IEEE Project 802 for local area networks. It covers the LLC sublayer.

IEEE 802.3   The standard developed by IEEE Project 802 for local area networks. It covers the MAC sublayer for networks using the CSMA/CD access method and provides a formal definition for Ethernet.

IEEE 802.4   The standard developed by IEEE Project 802 for local area networks. It covers the MAC sublayer for networks using a bus topology and token-passing access method and provides a formal definition for token bus.

IEEE 802.5   The standard developed by IEEE Project 802 for local area networks. It covers the MAC sublayer for networks using a ring topology and token-passing access method and provides a formal definition for Token Ring.

IEEE 802.6   The standard developed by IEEE Project 802 for distributed queue dual bus.

in-band signaling   A method of signaling in which both control and user data share the same channel.

information element   A field in an ISDN packet with specific details about the connection.

information frame   See *I-frame*.

infrared light   Electromagnetic waves with frequencies just below the visible spectrum.

Institute of Electrical and Electronics Engineers (IEEE)   A group consisting of professional engineers that has specialized societies whose committees prepare standards in members' areas of specialty.

integrated digital network (IDN)   The integration of communication functions using digital technology in a telecommunication network.

Integrated Services Digital Network (ISDN)   An ITU-T standard for an end-to-end global digital communication system providing fully integrated digital services.

intelligent modem   A modem that has extra functions such as automatic answering and dialing.

interactive services   In B-ISDN, services that require two-way exchanges.

interface   The boundary between two pieces of equipment. It also refers to mechanical, electrical, and functional characteristics of the connection.

interleaving   Taking a specific amount of data from each device in a regular order.

International Standards Organization (ISO)   A worldwide organization that defines and develops standards on a variety of topics.

International Telecommunications Union–Telecommunication Standardization Sector (ITU–T)   A telecommunication standards organization formerly known as the CCITT.

internet   A collection of networks connected by internetworking devices such as routers or gateways.

Internet   A global internet that uses the TCP/IP protocol suite.

Internet address   A 32-bit or 128-bit network-layer address used to uniquely define a host on an internet using the TCP/IP protocol.

internet control message protocol (ICMP)   A protocol in the TCP/IP protocol suite that handles error and control messages.

internet group message protocol (IGMP)   A protocol in the TCP/IP protocol suite that handles multicasting.

Internet Protocol   See *Internetworking Protocol.*

Internet Society (ISOC)   The nonprofit organization established to publicize the Internet.

internetwork   Another term for internet.

Internetwork Protocol Control Protocol (IPCP)   In PPP, the set of protocols that establish and terminate a network layer connection for IP packets.

internetworking   Connecting several networks together using internetworking devices such as routers and gateways.

internetworking devices   Electronic devices such as routers and gateways that connect networks together to form an internet.

Internetworking Protocol (IP)   The network-layer protocol in the TCP/IP protocol suite governing connectionless transmission across packet-switching networks.

inverse domain   A subdomain in the DNS that finds the domain name given the IP address.

inverse multiplexing   Taking data from one source and breaking it into portions that can be sent across lower-speed lines.

ionosphere   The layer of atmosphere above the troposphere but below space.

ionospheric propagation   Transmission in which radio waves radiate up into the ionosphere and then reflect back to earth.

IP address   See *Internet address.*

IP address class   In IPv4, one of the five groups of addresses; classes A, B, and C consist of a netid, hostid, and class ID; class D holds multicast addresses; class E is reserved for future use.

IP datagram   The Internetworking Protocol data unit.

IPng (IP next generation)   See *IPv6.*

IPv4   The Internetworking Protocol, version 4. It is the current version.

IPv6   The Internetworking Protocol, version 6. A proposed internetworking protocol that features major IP addressing changes.

J

Java   A programming language used to create active web documents.

joint photographic experts group (JPEG)   A standard for compressing continuous-tone picture.

jumbo group   An analog signal created by six multiplexed master groups.

K

Kbps   Kilobits per second.

Kermit   A widely used asynchronous protocol.

kilohertz (KHz)   1000 hertz.

knockout switch   An enhanced crossbar switch in which distributors and queues direct the cells at the output to avoid collision.

L

LANE client (LEC)   Client software that receives requests for a LAN service; part of a LANE.

LANE server (LES)   Server software that creates a virtual circuit between the source and destination; part of a LANE.

laser   Acronym for Light Amplification by Stimulated Emissions of Radiation. A pure and narrow light beam that can be used as the light source in fiber-optic transmission.

layer   One of the seven levels involved in data transmission in the OSI model; each level is a functional grouping of related activities.

leaky bucket algorithm   An algorithm to shape bursty traffic.

learning bridge   A bridge that builds its table of station addresses on its own.

least-cost routing   A routing strategy based on some minimum characteristic.

Lempel-Ziv-Welch (LZW) encoding   A string-based compression method using pointers to repeated strings.

light-emitting diode (LED)   A light source for optical fiber; usually limited to shorter distances.

line configuration   The relationship between communication devices and their pathway.

line discipline   A data link layer procedure that defines which device has the right to send data; also referred to as access control.

line layer   A SONET layer responsible for the movement of a signal across a physical line.

line-of-sight propagation   The transmission of very high frequency signals in straight lines directly from antenna to antenna.

line overhead   Control information used by the line layer in SONET.

link   The physical communication pathway that transfers data from one device to another.

link access procedure (LAP)   A bit-oriented data link protocol derived from HDLC.

link access procedure, balanced (LAPB)   A LAP protocol in which stations can function only in the balanced mode.

link access procedure for B channel (LAPB)   A LAP protocol defined for the B channel in ISDN.

link access procedure for D channel (LAPD)   A LAP protocol defined for the D channel in ISDN.

link access procedure for modems (LAPM)   A LAP protocol defined for modems.

Link Control Protocol (LCP)   A PPP protocol responsible for establishing, maintaining, configuring, and terminating links.

link state database   In link state routing, a database common to all routers and created from LSP packets.

link state packet (LSP)   In link state routing, a small packet containing routing information sent by a router to all other routers.

link state routing   A routing method in which each router shares its knowledge of changes in its neighborhood with all other routers.

local access   Using a terminal directly connected to the computer.

local area network (LAN)   A network connecting devices inside a single building or inside buildings close to each other.

local area network emulation (LANE)   Software that enables an ATM switch to behave like a LAN switch.

local login   See *local access.*

local loop   The link that connects a subscriber to the telephone central office.

local management information (LMI)   A protocol used in Frame Relay to provide management features.

logical address   An address defined in the network layer.

logical channel number (LCN)   The virtual circuit identifier in X.25.

logical link control (LLC)   The upper sublayer of the data link layer as defined by IEEE Project 802.2.

longitudinal redundancy check (LRC)   An error-detection method dividing a data unit into rows and columns and performing parity checks on corresponding bits of each column.

loss control   A transport layer function that ensures that all data units of a transmission arrive at the destination.

lossless data compression   Data compression in which no data are lost.

lossy data compression   Data compression in which some original data are lost.

low frequency (LF)   Radio waves in the 30-KHz to 300-KHz range.

M

MAC address   See *physical address*.

mail gateway   A relay MTA that can receive both SMTP mail and non-SMTP mail.

mail transfer agent (MTA)   An MHS component that accepts a message, examines it, and routes it.

major synchronization point   A synchronization point that must be confirmed before continuation of the session.

management information base (MIB)   The database used by SNMP that holds the information necessary for management of a network.

management plane   In ISDN, a set of layers that encompass both the user and control plane and is used for managing the whole network.

manager   The host that runs the SNMP client program.

Manchester encoding   A digital-to-digital polar encoding method in which a transition occurs at the middle of each bit interval for the purpose of synchronization.

masking   A process that extracts the address of the physical network from an IP address.

master group   An analog signal created by 10 multiplexed supergroups.

maximum transfer unit (MTU)   The largest size data unit a specific network can handle.

Mbps   Megabits per second.

media interface connector (MIC)   A type of interface card used in FDDI.

medium   The physical path by which data travel.

medium access control (MAC)   The lower sublayer in the data link layer defined by the IEEE 802 project. It defines the access method and access control in different local area network protocols.

medium attachment unit (MAU)   See *transceiver*.

medium bandwidth   The difference between the highest and lowest frequencies a medium can support.

megahertz (MHz)   One million hertz.

mesh topology   A network configuration in which each device has a dedicated point-to-point link to every other device.

message   Data sent from source to destination.

message handling system (MHS)   An OSI protocol that underlies electronic mail.

message switching   A switching method in which the whole message is stored in a switch and forwarded when a route is available.

message transfer agent (MTA)   An MHS component that accepts a message, examines it, and routes it.

message transfer system (MTS)   A group of message transfer agents (MTAs).

metropolitan area network (MAN)   A network that can span a geographical area the size of a city.

microsecond (μs)   One-millionth (10^{-6}) of a second.

microwave   Electromagnetic waves ranging from 2 GHz to 40 GHz.

microwave transmission   Communication using microwaves.

middle frequency (MF)   Radio waves in the 300-KHz to 3-MHz range.

millisecond (ms)   One-thousandth (10^{-3}) of a second.

minimum cell rate (MCR)   In ATM, the minimum data rate acceptable to the sender.

minor synchronization point   A synchronization point that may or may not be confirmed before continuation of the session.

mobile telephone switching office (MTSO)   An office that controls and coordinates communication between all of the cell offices and the telephone control office.

modem   A device consisting of a modulator and a demodulator. It converts a digital signal into an analog signal (modulation) and vice versa (demodulation).

modulation   Modification of one or more characteristics of a carrier wave by an information-bearing signal.

modulator   A device that converts a digital signal to an analog signal suitable for transmission across a telephone line.

monitor station   In the Token Ring protocol, a station that is responsible for generating and controlling the token.

monoalphabetic encryption   A substitutional encryption method in which each occurrence of a character is replaced by another character in the set.

Morse code   A statistical compression method using different length combinations of mark and space to encode data.

motion picture experts group (MPEG)   A method to compress videos.

multicast address   An address used for multicasting.

multicasting   A transmission method that allows copies of a single packet to be sent to a selected group of receivers.

multidrop line configuration   An alternative name for multipoint line configuration.

multimode graded-index fiber   An optical fiber with a core having a graded index of refraction.

multimode step-index fiber   An optical fiber with a core having a uniform index of refraction. The index of refraction changes suddenly at the core/cladding boundary.

multiple access (MA)   A line access method in which every station can access the line freely.

multiplexer (MUX)   A device used for multiplexing.

multiplexing   The process of combining signals from multiple sources for transmission across a single data link.

multipoint line configuration   A line configuration in which three or more devices share a common transmission line.

multiport bridge   A bridge that connects more than two LANs.

multiprotocol router   A router that can handle packets from different protocols.

Multipurpose Internet Mail Extension (MIME)   A supplement to SMTP that allows non-ASCII data to be sent through SMTP.

multistage switch   An array of switches designed to reduce the number of crosspoints.

multistation access unit (MAU)   In Token Ring, a device that houses individual automatic switches.

N

nanosecond (ns) 10^{-9} second.

negative acknowledgment (NAK)   A message sent to indicate the rejection of received data.

netid   The part of an IP address that identifies the network.

network   A system consisting of connected nodes made to share data, hardware, and software.

Network Control Protocol (NCP)   In PPP, a set of control protocols that allows the encapsulation of data coming from network layer protocols.

network interface card (NIC)   An electronic device, internal or external to a station, that contains circuitry to enable the station to be connected to the network.

network layer   The third layer in the OSI model, responsible for the delivery of a packet to the final destination.

network termination 1 (NT1)   In ISDN, devices between a user site and the central office that perform functions related to the first layer of the OSI model.

network termination 2 (NT2)   In ISDN, devices that perform functions related to the first three layers of the OSI model.

network-to-network interface (NNI)   An interface between two wide area networks or between two switches inside a wide area network.

network virtual terminal (NVT)   A TCP/IP application protocol that allows remote login.

networking state   A PPP state in which packets of user data and packets for control are transmitted.

node   An addressable communication device (e.g., a computer or router) on a network.

node-to-node delivery   Transfer of a data unit from one node to the next.

noise   Random electrical signals that can be picked up by the transmission medium and result in degradation or distortion of the data.

nonreturn to zero (NRZ)   A digital-to-digital polar encoding method in which the signal level is always either positive or negative.

nonreturn to zero, invert (NRZ-I)   An NRZ encoding method in which the signal level is inverted each time a 1 is encountered.

nonreturn to zero, level (NRZ-L)   An NRZ encoding method in which the signal level is directly related to the bit value.

normal response mode (NRM)   In HDLC, a communication mode in which the secondary station must have permission from the primary station before transmission can proceed.

null modem   An interface specification for transferring data between two close, compatible DTEs.

Nyquist theorem   A theorem which states that the number of samples needed to adequately represent an analog signal is equal to twice the highest frequency of the original signal.

O

octal number system   A method of representing information using eight symbols (0, 1, 2, 3, 4, 5, 6, and 7).

octet   An eight-bit unit.

odd parity   An error-detection method in which an extra bit is added to the data unit such that the sum of all 1-bits becomes odd.

one's complement   A representation of binary numbers in which the complement of a number is found by complementing all bits.

open system   A model that allows two different systems to communicate regardless of their underlying architecture.

Open Systems Interconnection (OSI)   A seven-layer model for data communication defined by ISO.

optical carrier (OC)   The hierarchy of fiber-optic carriers defined in SONET. The hierarchy defines up to 10 different carriers (OC-1, OC-3, OC-12, . . . , OC-192), each with a different data rate.

optical fiber   See *fiber-optic cable*.

out-of-band signaling   A method of signaling in which control data and user data travel on different channels.

overhead   Extra bits added to the data unit for control purposes.

P

P-box   A hardware circuit used in encryption that connects input to output.

packet   Synonym for data unit; mostly used in the network layer.

packet assembler/dissembler (PAD)   A device that connects a character-oriented (dumb) terminal to an X.25 network.

packet layer protocol (PLP)   The network layer in X.25 protocol.

packet lifetime   The number of stations a packet can visit before being discarded.

packet-switched network   A network in which data are transmitted in independent units called packets.

packet switching   Data transmission using a packet-switched network.

packet type identifier (PTI)   A PLP packet field that defines the type of packet.

parabolic dish antenna   An antenna shaped like a parabola used for terrestrial microwave communication.

parallel transmission   Transmission in which bits in a group are sent simultaneously, each using a separate link.

parity bit   A redundant bit added to a data unit (usually a character) for error checking.

parity check   An error-detection method using a parity bit.

passive hub   A hub used only for connection; it does not regenerate the signal.

Password Authentication Protocol (PAP)   A simple two-step authentication protocol used in PPP.

path   The channel through which a signal travels.

path layer   A SONET layer responsible for the movement of a signal from its optical source to its optical destination.

path overhead   Control information used by the SONET path layer.

peak cell rate (PCR)   In ATM, the sender's maximum cell rate.

peer-to-peer protocol   A protocol defining the rule of communication between two equal layers in the OSI model.

period   The amount of time required to complete one full cycle.

periodic signal   A signal that exhibits a repeating pattern.

permanent virtual circuit (PVC)   A virtual circuit transmission method in which the same virtual circuit is used between source and destination on a continual basis.

phase   The relative position of a signal in time.

phase modulation (PM)   An analog-to-analog modulation method in which the carrier signal's phase varies with the amplitude of the modulating signal.

phase shift   The phase change of a signal.

phase shift keying (PSK)   A digital-to-analog modulation method in which the phase of the carrier signal is varied to represent a specific bit pattern.

photonic layer   The SONET layer that corresponds to the OSI model's physical layer.

physical address   The address of a device used at the data link layer (MAC address).

physical layer   The first layer of the OSI model, responsible for the mechanical and electrical specifications of the medium.

picosecond 10^{-12} second.

piggybacking   The inclusion of acknowledgment on a data frame.

plaintext   In encryption/decryption, the original message.

point-to-point connection   A dedicated transmission link between two devices.

Point-to-Point Protocol (PPP)   A protocol for data transfer across a serial line.

polar encoding   A digital-to-analog encoding method that uses two levels (positive and negative) of amplitude.

poll   In the primary/secondary access method, a procedure in which the primary station asks a secondary station if it has any data to transmit.

poll/final (P/F) bit   A bit in the control field of HDLC; if the primary is sending, it can be a poll bit; if the secondary is sending, it can be a final bit.

poll/select   An access method protocol using poll and select procedures. See *poll*. See *select*.

polyalphabetic encryption   A substitutional encryption method in which each occurrence of a character can have a different substitute.

port address   In TCP/IP protocol an integer identifying a process.

Post Office Protocol (POP)   A client-server protocol that is used between a user work station and a mail server.

preamble   The seven-byte field of an IEEE 802.3 frame consisting of alternating 1s and 0s that alert and synchronize the receiver.

presentation layer   The sixth layer of the OSI model, responsible for translation, encryption, authentication, and data compression.

primary rate interface (PRI)   An ISDN electrical interface providing 23 B channels (64 Kbps) and one D channel (64 Kbps). The total data rate is 1.544 Mbps, which includes some overhead.

primary–secondary protocol   A protocol defining the rule of communication where one device controls traffic and the others must transmit through it.

primary station   In primary/secondary access method, a station that issues commands to the secondary stations.

private branch exchange (PBX)   A switching system for telephones on extension lines that allow access to the public telephone network.

private key   In conventional encryption, a key shared by only one pair of devices, a sender and a receiver. In public key encryption, the private key is known only to the receiver.

product   A bit-level encryption method using a combination of P-boxes and S-boxes.

Project 802   The project undertaken by the IEEE in an attempt to solve LAN incompatibility. See also *IEEE Project 802*.

propagation speed   The rate at which a signal or bit travels; measured by distance/second.

propagation time   The time required for a signal to travel from one point to another.

protocol   Rules for communication.

protocol converter   A device such as a gateway that changes one protocol to another.

protocol data unit (PDU)   A data unit defined in each layer of the OSI model. In particular, a data unit specified by IEEE 802.2 in the LLC sublayer.

pseudoternary encoding   A variation of bipolar AMI, in which binary 0 alternates between positive and negative voltages.

public key   In public key encryption, a key known to everyone.

public key encryption   A method of encryption based on a nonreversible encryption algorithm. The method uses two types of keys: The public key is known to the public; the private key (secret key) is known only to the receiver.

Public Switched Telephone Network (PSTN)   A circuit-switched telephone network in use today.

pulse amplitude modulation (PAM)   A technique in which an analog signal is sampled; the result is a series of pulses based on the sampled data.

pulse code modulation (PCM)   A technique that modifies PAM pulses to create a digital signal.

Q

Q.931   The ITU-T standard that defines network layer functions of the ISDN related to the D channel.

quadbit   A unit of data consisting of four bits.

quadrature amplitude modulation (QAM)   A digital-to-analog modulation method in which the phase and amplitude of the carrier signal vary with the modulating signal.

quality of service (QoS)   In ATM, a set of attributes related to the performance of the connection.

queue   A waiting list.

R

R interface   See *R reference point*.

R reference point   In ISDN, the interface between a TE2 and a TA.

radio wave   Electromagnetic energy in the 3-KHz to 300-GHz range.

rate adaptive asymmetrical digital subscriber line (RADSL)   A DSL-based technology that features different data rates depending on the type of communication.

receiver   The target point of a transmission.

redirection   An ICMP message type that informs the sender of a preferred route.

redundancy   The addition of bits to a message for error control.

reflection   The phenomenon related to the bouncing back of light at the boundary of two media.

refraction   The phenomenon related to the bending of light when it passes from one medium to another.

regenerator   A device that regenerates the original signal from a corrupted signal. See also *repeater.*

regulatory agency   A government agency that protects the public interest.

relative compression   A compression method that sends only the difference between frames.

reliable delivery   Receipt of a message without duplication, loss, or out-of-sequence packets.

remote access   Using a terminal that is not directly connected to a computer.

remote login   The process of logging on to a remote computer from a terminal connected to a local computer.

repeater   A device that extends the distance a signal can travel by regenerating the signal.

return to zero (RZ)   A digital-to-digital encoding technique in which the voltage of the signal is zero for the second half of the bit interval.

reverse address resolution protocol (RARP)   A TCP/IP protocol that allows a host to find its Internet address given its physical address.

ring topology   A topology in which the devices are connected in a ring. Each device on the ring receives the data unit from the previous device, regenerates it, and forwards it to the next device.

Rivest, Shamir, Adleman (RSA) encryption   See *RSA encryption.*

route   A path traveled by a packet.

route discovery   The task of finding the optimum route a data unit must take.

router   An internetworking device operating at the first three OSI layers. A router is attached to two or more networks and forwards packets from one network to another.

routing   The process performed by a router.

routing algorithm   The algorithm used by a router to determine the optimum path for a packet.

routing information protocol (RIP)   A routing protocol based on the distance vector routing algorithm.

routing switch   A switch that combines the functions of a bridge and a router using the network layer destination address.

routing table   A table containing information a router needs to route packets. The information may include the network address, the cost, the address of the next hop, and so on.

RS-232   See *EIA-232.*

RS-422 standard   A balanced circuit specification used by EIA-449 to define electrical parameters.

RS-423 standard   An unbalanced circuit specification used by EIA-449 to define electrical parameters.

RSA encryption   A popular public key encryption method developed by Rivest, Shamir, and Adleman.

run-length encoding   A compression method in which a run of symbols is replaced by the symbol and the number of symbols.

S

S-box   An encryption device made of decoders, P-boxes, and encoders.

S-frame An HDLC frame used for supervisory functions such as acknowledgment, flow control, and error control; it contains no user data.

S interface See *S reference point*.

S reference point In ISDN, the interface between a TE1 or a TA and an NT.

sampling The process of obtaining amplitudes of a signal at regular intervals.

sampling rate The number of samples obtained per second in the sampling process.

secondary station In poll/select access method, a station that sends a response in answer to a command from a primary station.

section layer A SONET layer responsible for the movement of a signal across a physical section.

section overhead Control information used by the SONET section layer.

security The protection of a network from unauthorized access, viruses, and catastrophe.

segment The packet at the TCP layer.

segmentation The splitting of a message into multiple packets; usually performed at the transport layer.

segmentation and reassembly (SAR) The lower AAL sublayer in the ATM protocol in which a header and/or trailer may be added to produce a 48-byte element.

select In poll/select access method, a procedure in which the primary station asks a secondary station if it is ready to receive data.

selective-reject ARQ An error-control method in which only the frame in error is resent.

self-synchronizing coding A coding method that provides for the synchronization of long strings of 1s or 0s.

semantics The meaning or interpretation of a set of bits.

sender The originator of a message.

sequence control A transport layer function that ensures the correct assembly of the data units of a message.

sequence number The number that denotes the location of a frame or packet in a message.

Serial Line Internet Protocol (SLIP) A protocol that prepares IP datagrams for serial line transmission.

serial transmission Transmission of data one bit at a time using only one single link.

server A program that can provide services to other programs, called clients.

service access point (SAP) A type of address that identifies the user of a protocol.

service access point identifier (SAPI) In ISDN, a type of address that identifies the user of a protocol.

session layer The fifth layer of the OSI model, responsible for the establishment, management, and termination of logical connections between two end users.

session protocol data unit (SPDU) The data unit defined in the session layer of the OSI model.

Shannon capacity The theoretical highest data rate for a channel.

shielded twisted-pair (STP) Twisted-pair cable enclosed in a foil or mesh shield that protects against electromagnetic interference.

shortest path tree A routing table formed by using the Dijkstra algorithm.

signal Electromagnetic waves propagated along a transmission medium.

signed number   A representation of binary numbers including the sign (plus or minus). Signed numbers can be represented using three different formats: sign-and-magnitude, one's complement, and two's complement.

simple bridge   A networking device that links two segments; requires manual maintenance and updating.

Simple Mail Transfer Protocol (SMTP)   The TCP/IP protocol defining electronic mail service on the Internet.

Simple Network Management Protocol (SNMP)   The TCP/IP protocol that specifies the process of management in the Internet.

simplex mode   A transmission mode in which communication is one way.

sine wave   An amplitude-versus-time representation of a rotating vector.

single attachment station (SAS)   In FDDI, a station that can be connected only to one ring.

single-bit error   Error in a data unit in which only one single bit has been altered.

single-mode fiber   An optical fiber with an extremely small diameter that limits beams to a few angles, resulting in an almost horizontal beam.

sliding window   A protocol that allows several data units to be in transition before receiving an acknowledgment.

sliding window ARQ   An error-control protocol using sliding window concept.

slot   A space for data.

SMDS interface protocol (SIP)   A three-level protocol that governs access to SMDS.

source address (SA)   The address of the sender of the message.

source routing   Explicitly defining the route of a packet by the sender of the packet.

source-to-destination delivery   The transmission of a message from the original sender to the intended recipient.

space-division switching   Switching in which the paths are separated from each other spatially.

space propagation   A type of propagation that can penetrate the ionosphere.

spanning tree algorithm   An algorithm that prevents looping when two LANs are connected by more than one bridge.

spectrum   The range of frequencies of a signal.

standard   A basis or model to which everyone has agreed.

standards creation committee   A group that produces a basis or model to which everyone has agreed.

star topology   A topology in which all stations are attached to a central device (hub).

starLAN   A LAN using star topology with a 1-Mbps data rate in which the stations can be daisy chained.

start bit   In asynchronous transmission, a bit to indicate the beginning of transmission.

start frame delimiter (SFD)   A one-byte field in the IEEE 802.3 frame that signals the beginning of the readable (nonpreamble) bit stream.

static document   On the World Wide Web, a fixed-content document that is created and stored in a server.

static routing   A type of routing in which the routing table remains unchanged.

statistical compression A lossless compression method that uses short codes for frequent symbols and long codes for infrequent symbols.

statistical time-division multiplexing See *asynchronous TDM*.

stop-and-wait A flow-control method in which each data unit must be acknowledged before the next one can be sent.

stop-and-wait ARQ An error-control protocol using stop-and-wait flow control.

stop bit In asynchronous transmission, one or more bits to indicate the end of transmission.

store and forward Another name for message switching.

store-and-forward switch A switch that stores the frame in an input buffer until the whole packet has arrived.

structure of management information (SMI) In SNMP, a component used in network management.

subnet See *subnetwork*.

subnetting The further division of a network into smaller networks.

subnetwork A part of a network.

subnetwork address The network address of a subnet.

substitution A bit-level encryption method in which n bits substitute for another n bits as defined by P-boxes, encoders, and decoders.

supergroup A signal composed of five multiplexed groups.

superhigh frequency (SHF) Radio waves in the 3-GHz to 30-GHz range using line-of-sight and space propagation.

supervisory frame See *S-frame*.

supplementary services ISDN services that provide additional functionality to bearer services and teleservices.

sustained cell rate (SCR) In ATM, the average cell rate.

switch A device connecting multiple communication lines together.

switched/56 A temporary 56-Kbps digital connection between two users.

Switched Ethernet An Ethernet in which a switch, replacing the hub, can direct a transmission to the destination.

switched multimegabit data service (SMDS) A protocol for handling high-speed communications for MANs.

switched virtual circuit (SVC) A virtual circuit transmission method in which a virtual circuit is created and in existence only for the duration of the exchange.

symmetric digital subscriber line (SDSL) A DSL-based technology similar to HDSL, but using only one single twisted-pair cable.

symmetrical configuration A configuration in which each physical station on the link consists of two logical stations, one primary and one secondary.

synchronization points Reference points introduced into the data by the session layer for the purpose of flow and error control.

synchronous data link control (SDLC) A precursor of HDLC pioneered by IBM.

Synchronous Digital Hierarchy (SDH) The ITU-T equivalent of SONET.

Synchronous Optical Network (SONET) A standard developed by ANSI for fiber-optic technology that can transmit high-speed data. It can be used to deliver text, audio, and video.

synchronous time-division multiplexing   A multiplexing technique in which each frame contains at least one time slot for each device.

synchronous transmission   A transmission method that requires a constant timing relationship between the sender and the receiver.

synchronous transport module (STM)   A signal in the SDH hierarchy.

synchronous transport signal (STS)   A signal in the SONET hierarchy.

syntax   The structure or format of data.

T

T interface   See *T reference point*.

T lines   A hierarchy of digital lines designed to carry speech and other signals in digital forms. The hierarchy defines T-1, T-2, T-3, and T-4 lines.

T-1 line   A 1.544-Mbps digital transmission line.

T-2 line   A 6.312-Mbps digital transmission line.

T-3 line   A 44.736-Mbps digital transmission line.

T-4 line   A 274.176-Mbps digital transmission line.

T reference point   In ISDN, the interface between an NT1 and an NT2.

TCP/IP protocol suite   A group of hierarchical protocols used in an internet.

TDM bus   A time-division switch in which the input and output lines are connected to a high-speed bus through microswitches.

Telcordia   A company (formerly Bellcore) involved in the research and development of telecommunications technology.

telecommunication   Exchange of information over distance using electronic equipment.

teleservices   In ISDN, services in which the network may change or process the contents of the data.

terahertz (THz) 10^{12} hertz.

terminal adapter (TA)   A device that converts information from non-ISDN terminals into a format capable of being carried by an ISDN network.

terminal equipment 1 (TE1)   An ISDN standard terminal.

terminal equipment 2 (TE2)   A non-ISDN terminal.

terminal equipment identifier (TEI)   An LAPD field that identifies terminal equipment.

Terminal Network (TELNET)   A general purpose client–server program that allows remote login.

terminating state   A PPP state in which several packets are exchanged between the two ends for house cleaning and closing the link.

terminator   An electronic device that prevents signal reflections at the end of a cable.

terrestrial microwave   Microwave transmission between antennas.

thick Ethernet   See *10Base5*.

Thicknet   See *10Base5*.

thin Ethernet   See *10Base2*.

Thinnet   See *10Base2*.

three-way handshake   A sequence of events for connection establishment or termination consisting of the request, then the acknowledgment of the request, and then confirmation of the acknowledgment.

throughput   The number of bits that can pass through a point in one second.

time-division multiplexing (TDM)   The technique of combining signals coming from low-speed channels to share time on a high-speed path.

time-division switching   A circuit-switching technique in which time-division multiplexing is used to achieve switching.

time-domain plot   A graphical representation of a signal's amplitude versus time.

time-slot interchange (TSI)   A time-division switch consisting of RAM and a control unit.

time to live (TTL)   See *packet lifetime.*

timing   A protocol factor referring to when data should be sent and the speed of transmission.

token   A small packet used in token-passing access method.

Token Bus   A LAN using a bus topology and token-passing access method.

token passing   An access method in which a token is circulated in the network. The station that captures the token can send data.

Token Ring   A LAN using a ring topology and token-passing access method.

topology   The structure of a network including physical arrangement of devices.

Touch-Tone dialing   A telephone dialing method in which each key is represented by two small bursts of analog signals.

traffic control   A method for shaping and controlling traffic in a wide area network.

trailer   Control information appended to a data unit.

transceiver   A device that both transmits and receives.

transceiver cable   In Ethernet, the cable that connects the station to the transceiver. Also called the attachment unit interface.

transition state   The different phases through which a PPP connection goes.

translation   Changing from one code or protocol to another.

Transmission Control Protocol (TCP)   A transport protocol in the TCP/IP protocol suite.

Transmission Control Protocol/Internetworking Protocol (TCP/IP)   A five-layer protocol suite that defines the exchange of transmissions across the Internet.

transmission medium   The physical path linking two communication devices.

transmission path (TP)   In ATM, the physical connection between two switches.

transmission rate   The number of bits sent per second.

transparency   The ability to send any bit pattern as data without it being mistaken for control bits.

transparent bridge   Another name for a learning bridge.

transparent data   Data that can contain control bit patterns without being interpreted as control.

transport class   One of five transport categories used by the upper layers; class selection is dependent on the type of service required.

transport layer   The fourth layer in the OSI model; responsible for reliable end-to-end delivery and error recovery.

transport protocol data unit (TPDU)   The data unit defined in the transport layer of the OSI model.

transpositional encryption   A character-level encryption method in which the position of the character changes.

tree topology   A topology in which stations are attached to a hierarchy of hubs. Tree topology is an extension of star topology with more than one level.

trellis-coded modulation   A modulation technique that includes error correction.

tribit   A unit of data consisting of three bits.

Triple-X protocols   Protocols X.3, X.28, and X.29 that are used to connect a dumb terminal to an X.25 network.

Trivial File Transfer Protocol (TFTP)   An unreliable TCP/IP protocol for file transfer that does not require complex interaction between client and server.

troposphere   The layer of atmosphere surrounding the earth.

tropospheric propagation   Line-of-sight transmission from antenna to antenna or earth to troposphere to earth.

twisted-pair cable   A transmission medium consisting of two insulated conductors in a twisted configuration.

twisted-pair Ethernet   An Ethernet using twisted-pair cable; 10Base-T.

two's complement   A representation of binary numbers in which the complement of a number is found by complementing all bits and adding a 1 after that.

U

U-frame   An HDLC unnumbered frame carrying link management information.

U interface   See *U reference point.*

U reference point   In ISDN, the interface between an NT1 and the rest of the network.

ultrahigh frequency (UHF)   Radio waves in the 300-MHz to 3-GHz range using line-of-sight propagation.

unbalanced configuration   An HDLC configuration in which one device is primary and the others secondary.

unguided medium   A transmission medium with no physical boundaries.

unicast   The sending of a packet to just one destination.

uniform resource locator (URL)   A string of characters (address) that identifies a page on the World Wide Web.

unipolar encoding   A digital-to-digital encoding method in which one nonzero value represents either 1 or 0; the other bit is represented by a zero value.

universal time   A standard time reference formerly known as Greenwich Mean Time.

UNIX   The operating system used in the Internet.

unnumbered frame   See *U-frame.*

unshielded twisted-pair (UTP)   A cable with wires that are twisted together to reduce noise and crosstalk. See also *twisted-pair cable* and *shielded twisted-pair.*

unsigned number   A representation of binary numbers without sign (plus or minus).

unspecified bit rate (UBR)   The data rate of an ATM service class specifying only best-effort delivery.

uplink   Transmission from an earth station to a satellite.

uploading   Sending a local file or data to a remote site.

upward multiplexing   A transport layer function in which several transmissions bound for the same destination are sent along the same path by multiplexing.

urgent data   In TCP/IP, data that must be delivered to the application program as quickly as possible.

user agent (UA)   An SMTP component that prepares the message, creates the envelope, and puts the message in the envelope.

user datagram   The name of the packet in the UDP protocol.

User Datagram Protocol (UDP)   A connectionless TCP/IP transport layer protocol.

user plane   In ISDN, a set of layers that define the functionality of the B channel.

user-to-network interface (UNI)   In ATM, the interface between an end point (user) and an ATM switch.

V

V series   ITU-T standards that define data transmission over telephone lines.

V.21   An ITU-T 300-baud modem using FSK modulation.

V.22   An ITU-T 600-baud modem using 4-PSK modulation.

V.22bis   An ITU-T two-speed modem based on V.22.

V.29   An ITU-T 2400-baud modem using 16-QAM modulation.

V.32   An ITU-T modem that is an enhanced version of V.29; uses trellis-coded modulation.

V.32bis   An ITU-T modem that is an enhanced version of V.32; features an automatic fall-back and fall-forward mechanism.

V.33   An ITU-T 2400-baud modem that is an enhanced version of V.32; uses trellis-coded modulation based on 128-QAM.

V.34   An ITU-T 2400-baud modem that provides data compression.

V.42   An ITU-T modem that uses LAPM and Error Correction Procedure for DCEs.

V.42bis   An ITU-T modem that is an enhanced version of V.42; uses Lempel-Ziv-Welch compression.

vampire tap   An Ethernet transceiver used in thick Ethernet (10Base5). The transceiver is housed in a clamplike device with a sharp metal prong that "bites" Thicknet cable.

variable bit rate (VBR)   The data rate of an ATM service class for users needing a varying bit rate.

variable bit rate nonreal time (VBR-NRT)   A VBR subclass for users who do not need real-time services.

variable bit rate real time (VBR-RT)   A VBR subclass for users needing real-time services.

vertical redundancy check (VRC)   An error-detection method based on per-character parity check.

very high bit rate digital subscriber line (VDSL)   A DSL-based technology for short distances.

very high frequency (VHF)   Radio waves in the 30-MHz to 300-MHz range using line-of-sight propagation.

very low frequency (VLF)   Radio waves in the 3-KHz to 30-KHz range using surface propagation.

videoconferencing   A service that allows a group of users to exchange information over a network.

Vignere cipher   A polyalphabetic substitution scheme that uses the position of a character in the plaintext and the character's position in the alphabet.

virtual circuit (VC)   A logical circuit made between the sending and receiving computer. The connection is made after both computers do handshaking. After the connection, all packets follow the same route and arrive in sequence.

virtual circuit approach to packet switching   A packet switching method in which all packets of a message or session follow the exact same route.

virtual circuit identifier (VCI)   A field in an ATM cell header that defines a channel.

virtual file   A model of an actual file created by a responder.

virtual filestore   A nonimplementation-specific model for files and databases that can be used as an intermediary for file handling.

virtual path (VP)   In ATM, a connection or set of connections between two switches.

virtual path identifier (VPI)   A field in an ATM cell header that identifies a path.

virtual path identifier/virtual channel identifier (VPI/VCI)   Two fields used together to route an ATM cell.

virtual terminal (VT)   The OSI remote login protocol.

virtual tributary (VT)   A partial payload that can be inserted into a SONET frame and combined with other partial payloads to fill out the frame.

voice grade channel   A communication path suitable for voice transmission.

Voice Over Frame Relay (VOFR)   A Frame Relay option that can handle voice data.

W

wave-division multiplexing (WDM)   The combining of modulated light signals into one signal.

wavelength   The propagation speed of a signal divided by its frequency.

web   Synonym for World Wide Web (WWW).

web page   A unit of hypertext or hypermedia available on the Web.

wide area network (WAN)   A network that uses a technology that can span a large geographical distance.

wireless communication   Data transmission using unguided media.

World Wide Web (WWW)   A multimedia Internet service that allows users to traverse the Internet by moving from one document to another via links that connect them together.

X

X.3   A Triple-X protocol that defines a PAD.

X.21   An ITU-T standard defining the interface between a DTE and a DCE.

X.25   An ITU-T standard that defines the interface between a data terminal device and a packet-switching network.

X.28   A Triple-X protocol that defines the rules for communication between a dumb terminal and a PAD.

X.29   A Triple-X protocol that defines the relationship between a PAD and the remote terminal.

X.121 A protocol used by most X.25 networks that globally addresses DTEs connected to a public or private network.

X.400 An ITU-T standard for electronic mail and message handling.

X.500 An ITU-T standard for directory service.

XMODEM An asynchronous protocol for telephone-line communication between PCs.

Y

YMODEM An asynchronous protocol differing from XMODEM in the data unit size, transmission abort method, error checking, and file transfer.

Z

ZMODEM An asynchronous protocol combining features of both XMODEM and YMODEM.

Index